These People Have Always Been a Republic

THE DAVID J. WEBER SERIES IN THE NEW BORDERLANDS HISTORY

Andrew R. Graybill and Benjamin H. Johnson, *editors*

Editorial Board
Juliana Barr
Sarah Carter
Kelly Lytle Hernández
Cynthia Radding
Samuel Truett

The study of borderlands—places where different peoples meet and no one polity reigns supreme—is undergoing a renaissance. The David J. Weber Series in the New Borderlands History publishes works from both established and emerging scholars that examine borderlands from the precontact era to the present. The series explores contested boundaries and the intercultural dynamics surrounding them and includes projects covering a wide range of time and space within North America and beyond, including both Atlantic and Pacific worlds.

Published with support provided by the William P. Clements Center for Southwest Studies at Southern Methodist University in Dallas, Texas.

MAURICE CRANDALL

These People Have Always Been a Republic

Indigenous Electorates in the U.S.-Mexico Borderlands, 1598–1912

The University of North Carolina Press *Chapel Hill*

© 2019 The University of North Carolina Press
All rights reserved
Set in Arno by Westchester Publishing Services
Manufactured in the United States of America

The University of North Carolina Press has been a member of the
Green Press Initiative since 2003.

Library of Congress Cataloging-in-Publication Data
Names: Crandall, Maurice, author.
Title: These people have always been a republic : indigenous electorates in the
 U.S.-Mexico borderlands, 1598–1912 / Maurice Crandall.
Other titles: David J. Weber series in the new borderlands history.
Description: Chapel Hill : University of North Carolina Press, [2019] | Series:
 The David J. Weber series in the new borderlands history | Includes
 bibliographical references and index.
Identifiers: LCCN 2019008154 | ISBN 9781469652658 (cloth : alk. paper) |
 ISBN 9781469652665 (pbk : alk. paper) | ISBN 9781469652672 (ebook)
Subjects: LCSH: Indians of North America—Political activity. | Indians of Mexico—
 Political activity. | Indians of North America—Government relations. |
 Indians of Mexico—Government relations. | Indians of North America—
 Legal status, laws, etc. | Indians of Mexico—Legal status, laws, etc. |
 Mexican-American Border Region—History.
Classification: LCC E91 .C73 2019 | DDC 323.1197—dc23 LC record
 available at https://lccn.loc.gov/2019008154

Cover illustrations: Top, Hopi landscape (photo by author); bottom, Underwood &
Underwood, *Pueblos Bring First Protest since Lincoln*, ca. 1923 (courtesy of Library of Congress
Prints and Photographs Division, LC-DIG-ppmsca-05081).

Contents

Acknowledgments ix

Introduction 1

CHAPTER ONE
Repúblicas de Indios in Spanish New Mexico 13

CHAPTER TWO
Hopis, Yaquis, and O'odhams in the Spanish Arizona-Sonora Borderlands: Political Incorporation by Degrees 55

CHAPTER THREE
Pueblo Contestations of Power in the Mexican Period 106

CHAPTER FOUR
The Politics of Inclusion/Exclusion in the Arizona-Sonora Borderlands during the Mexican Period 139

CHAPTER FIVE
Refusing Citizenship: Pueblo Indians and Voting during the United States Territorial Period 177

CHAPTER SIX
Disparate Designs: Indian Voting in Territorial Arizona 226

Conclusion 283

Notes 291

Bibliography 339

Index 361

Illustrations and Maps

ILLUSTRATIONS

Laguna Pueblo inauguration, 1887 31

Hopis and burros on the road 59

Río Yaqui 73

Baboquivari Peak 93

Portrait of Jesus Antonia Moya 123

Plaza in Oraibi 143

Bells at Tórim 150

O'odham chapel in San Ignacio 169

Reenactment of Pueblo officers with General Kearny 180

Hopi children eating melon 236

Yaqui deer dancer 256

Jose Lopez, O'odham teacher 269

MAPS

New Mexico Pueblo Indian Territory 22

Hopi Territory 57

Yaqui Territory along the Río Yaqui 71

Tohono O'odham Territory 92

Southern Arizona Yaqui communities 251

Acknowledgments

This book would not have been possible without the unwavering support of my wonderful wife and best friend, Connie, and our amazing children, Avery, Ira, Perry, and Ada. The process of researching and writing a book of this scope involved years of work, travel, and late nights, plus several relocations to destinations far from "home." I am deeply indebted to all of them for their sacrifice and love; I would not have survived this process without them. At the University of New Mexico, where this project began, I am grateful to Margaret Connell-Szasz, Durwood Ball, Sam Truett, and Barbara Reyes for their guidance and assistance. The "Review Crew" at the *New Mexico Historical Review* were fantastic colleagues and a great support system. I am fortunate to work with brilliant colleagues in Native American Studies at Dartmouth who have supported me as I've completed my manuscript; warm thanks to Colin Calloway, Bruce Duthu, Nick Reo, Dale Turner, Melanie Taylor, Vera Palmer, Sergei Kan, and Sheila Laplante. I am extremely grateful to Ruth Ann Elmore, Andrew Graybil, and Neil Foley at the Clements Center for Southwest Studies, and to my fellow fellows Eric Meeks, Uzma Quraishi, and Farina King, for the critiques, suggestions, and encouragement I received while a fellow there. I appreciate the kindness of Andrés Reséndez and John Kessell, who carefully read my manuscript and made valuable suggestions in a workshop organized by the Clements Center, as well as the contributions of workshop participants Edward Countryman, Sunday Eiselt, Matt Babcock, and Celeste Menchaca, who also offered helpful insights. I also thank Steve Denson and Alexis McCrossen of Southern Methodist University for their support and encouragement.

Numerous individuals assisted in my research at various locations. I am grateful to Nancy Brown-Martinez, Samuel Cisneros, and Christopher Geherin at the Center for Southwest Research at the University of New Mexico for their assistance in locating and deciphering materials. Christina Antipa at the Arizona State Museum provided valuable research assistance, especially at a time when the museum holdings were being recatalogued and my visit was no small inconvenience. Staff at the University of Arizona Special Collections and the Fray Angélico Chávez History Library at the Palace of the Governors in Santa Fe, New Mexico, were very helpful, as was Gregory Pass at the

Knights of Columbus Vatican Film Library at Saint Louis University. I am grateful to Sean Armstrong for securing copies of documents for me at the Archives of the Archdiocese of Santa Fe, and to both Adam Tafoya and Shawn Austin for assistance with translation at an early stage of my research.

I am grateful to my tribal nation, the Yavapai-Apache Nation, for its continued support over the years, and particularly to Lisa Sandoval in the Higher Education Program. I was fortunate to work with outstanding colleagues at the Indian Pueblo Cultural Center, and I offer heartfelt thanks to Monique Fragua, Amy Cisneros, Deborah Jojola, and Travis Suazo for all that they taught me. A special thanks goes to Carlos Valencia of the Pascua Yaqui Tribe for organizing a trip to the Río Yaqui; to our Yaqui hosts, Juan Silverio Jaime León, Mariaotilia "Machita" Salazar of Loma de Bácum, and Armando Sanchez Madueño of Vícam Switch; and to my Yaqui travel companions, Maria Gonzales, Selina Martinez, and Ray Martinez. I also offer my thanks to the many Indigenous scholars and allies who have both influenced my work and provided feedback, encouragement, and support throughout the years; they include K. Tsianina Lomawaima, Matthew Sakiestewa Gilbert, Cathleen Cahill, Coll Thrush, Jean O'Brien, Kent Blansett, Jeffrey Shepherd, Brenden Rensink, Ari Kelman, and Joseph Henry Suina.

I am appreciative of my series editors, Andrew Graybill and Benjamin Johnson, for their support of this project. I am also grateful to my editor at the University of North Carolina Press, Chuck Grench, and his editorial assistant, Dylan White, for their patience and assistance through this process. Finally, like all book projects, this one spanned several years, with numerous people aiding in its production. With so many individuals involved, I am bound to forget someone, and I offer my sincere apologies to anyone I have failed to thank.

These People Have Always Been a Republic

Introduction

There is power in stories. I recognized this from a young age. Like many Native Americans, I was reared on—and delighted in—stories from my grandparents about when they were young. From my grandma, Bonnie Moore Russell, I learned that her relatives were Okies, at least sort of. They had made their way to the Southwest in the early part of the twentieth century. My great-grandfather Perry Moore was of mixed Pawnee and Anglo-American heritage. He secured a good job as a bookkeeper, was married to a non-Indian, and settled into a relatively comfortable middle-class life.[1] While he was Pawnee, and, judging by family photos, clearly Indian (at least to my eyes), he somehow "passed" as non-Indian and avoided the prejudice of the era. I learned from my grandpa Ned Russell that his parents, Daisy Quesada (Dilzhe'e Apache) and Henry Russell (Yavapai), had met and married on the San Carlos Indian Reservation in southeastern Arizona. This was at a time when the U.S. Army had rounded up Yavapais, Dilzhe'e Apaches, Pinal Apaches, Aravaipa Apaches, White Mountain Apaches, Chiricahua Apaches, Cibecue Apaches, and Warm Springs Apaches, concentrating the eight groups on a single reservation.[2] My great-grandparents' relationship, which paired an Apache and a Yavapai, was born of this congregative federal Indian policy. My grandparents met in the sleepy, mining company town of Clarkdale, Arizona, where two of my great-grandfathers—one Yavapai, one Pawnee—found work.[3]

Like my family history, Indigenous history is an extraordinary confluence of stories. And it was a particular family story that inspired my interest in the history of Indian voting in New Mexico and Arizona. On two separate occasions during his adolescence, my grandfather Ned was arrested and punished in the Arizona justice system without a formal trial. In the first instance, he and a group of non-Indian friends broke into the local general store and helped themselves to several items. My grandfather, who lived in destitute conditions in the Clarkdale Yavapai-Apache community, took a pair of boots, some dungarees, and a wallet. When the local sheriff noticed a poor Indian boy with new boots and jeans, he immediately nabbed him. Ned refused to implicate his friends, some of whom were the sons of prominent members of the local white community, and was sent to the "Boys' Ranch," as it was called, a juvenile detention center at Fort Grant in Wilcox, Arizona. He was incarcerated for "three months, three weeks, and three days."[4]

Fort Grant was remarkably similar to Ned's previous Indian boarding school experience at Truxton Canyon Indian School, and he did not find his incarceration terribly trying. But from that point on Ned was labeled a "troublemaker," a situation only compounded by the fact that he was Indian and rather headstrong. As Ned later recalled, about a year after his first incarceration, he was falsely accused of a "burglary or whatever." Law enforcement officers returned him to Fort Grant, intending to keep him there for one year. But a remarkable thing happened after his arrival there for the second time. One of the prison guards knew an elderly rancher couple who lived in the foothills of the nearby Galiuro Mountains. Ned was sent to live with the family, where his situation resembled that of an indentured servant. He recalled being expected to "milk cows, slop the hogs, feed all the livestock.... I also plowed the fields." Somewhat surprisingly, Ned grew to like the elderly couple, and looked favorably upon his year on their ranch.[5]

On both occasions, which took place during the 1930s, my grandfather had no civil rights. In the rural and racially divided Arizona of that day, there was no presumption of innocence for a Native American young man accused of a crime, and he received neither representation nor a trial in juvenile court. Even though the U.S. Congress had passed the Indian Citizenship Act in 1924, through which, in the words of historian John R. Wunder, "the citizenship odyssey for American Indians was concluded,"[6] and which granted all Indians birthright citizenship, the reality was that Native people had virtually none of the rights of white citizens throughout much of the United States during the first half of the twentieth century, as suggested by my grandfather's experiences. How could he and others like him have secured their civil rights under such circumstances? Wunder commented, "Colonial power over Indian peoples and their lands constituted a direct destruction of individual rights and collective entitlements," and asked, "Might a bill of rights have prevented the loss of rights for Native Americans?"[7] Felix S. Cohen, "the father of federal Indian law," who worked to secure the legal rights of Native Americans in the United States during the first half of the twentieth century and authored a seminal work on the subject, wrote, "In a democracy suffrage is the most basic civil right, since its exercise is the chief means whereby other rights may be safeguarded. The enfranchisement of the Indians has been ... slow and is still an incomplete process."[8]

In many ways, the 2018 U.S. midterm elections represented important victories for Native American voters and politicians in this slow and incomplete process. Deb Haaland of Laguna Pueblo was elected from New Mexico's 1st Congressional District, while Sharice Davids of the Ho-Chunk Nation was victorious in Kansas' 3rd Congressional District. The two became the first Native American women elected to Congress.[9] For both women, their status as Indigenous persons, together with historical struggles by fellow Native Americans to vote in the United States, were strong motivators. Haaland, for example, became particularly active during John Kerry's presidential campaign in 2004. She recalled, "I would go into the campaign office, ask for a list of Native voters around the country, and call them." During Barack Obama's 2008 campaign, she took "a carload of people and we'd go canvass in a Native American community every evening." Her main motivation in this work was to "get out [the vote in] underrepresented communities—which, in New Mexico, are Native American communities."[10] Davids represented several firsts for Kansas as the state's first Native American woman and openly gay individual elected to Congress. The victories of Haaland and Davids were seen as important milestones in Native American voting and political participation, and as another hurdle surmounted by Indigenous peoples who have long struggled to break barriers in American politics. As one journalist reported, "The wins for Haaland and Davids ... highlight the long road to full participation and representation for Native Americans in politics. The United States government only granted citizenship to all Native Americans in 1924 [through the Indian Citizenship Act]; Haaland's home state of New Mexico was the last state to grant them the right to vote" in 1948.[11]

From this perspective, which finds iterations, if not outright support, in various sources, Indian voting is seen as a long but ultimately successful political process. Having won the franchise, Native Americans could then secure and safeguard their other civil rights. While undertaking to research and write an expansive history of Indian voting in the U.S.-Mexico Borderlands that covered all three colonial regimes—Spain, Mexico, and the United States—I uncovered a narrative that is neither facile nor triumphalist, which came as no surprise to me. Some tellings of the history of Native American voting can read this way: Indians suffered under Spain and Mexico, but eventually "won" their long struggle for the right to vote in U.S. courts. Such a narrative, even if nuanced and well written, only serves to reinforce a dominant Anglo-American historical trope: namely, that what came before the U.S. seizure of much of the American Southwest from Mexico only set the stage for the more important events that would follow. Spain and Mexico were the introductory acts in this epic play, while the United States offered the dramatic conclusion. Indians "finally" won their civil rights thanks to the U.S. legal system. Such an argument is simply not borne out by my research.

The reality, and my argument in this book, is that during all three colonial periods Indians absorbed and adapted colonially imposed forms of electoral politics and exercised political sovereignty based on localized political, economic, and social needs. Community sovereignty and internal control were important to Native Americans above all else. Thus, Indians in New Mexico and Arizona-Sonora created hybridized forms of colonial civil government and electoral processes—many of which are still in practice today—that were (and are) distinctly Indigenous, and always sought to protect the interests of their communities. The story of Indian voting in New Mexico and Arizona-Sonora must be seen as a long struggle to *continue* to secure the franchise—to use the vote to protect internal citizenship and the sovereignty of independent Native communities and thereby to challenge and subvert colonial power. This is the story that I found, one that counters prevailing progressive narratives of a long struggle with a positive ending in the post–World War II civil rights era and after.

Recent works on the history of Indian voting in the United States have largely centered on events from the second half of the nineteenth century through the 2010s. Historians have focused on the Voting Rights Act of 1965 (VRA) and subsequent amendments to it, showing the undeniable importance of the VRA and how Native Americans have struggled to secure equal voting rights in the decades after its passage.[12] Other works have framed the "fight" for Indian suffrage within a specific geographical and chronological setting, such as in New Mexico and Arizona, tracing Indian suffrage mainly as a phenomenon following the Treaty of Guadalupe Hidalgo in 1848.[13] Other scholars writing on the history of U.S. federal Indian law and policy have also dedicated significant attention to Indian voting, covering such important topics as Indian citizenship, the relationship between Native Americans and the U.S. Supreme Court, assimilation policies aimed at political incorporation, and the overall place of Native peoples within the political landscape.[14]

While these works effectively cover the history of Indian voting in many ways, they have frequently focused more attention on forms of voting and democracy within the U.S. system. The colonial era under Spain and the brief period of Mexican independence in today's U.S. Southwest are not commonly characterized as times of Indian voting. This is not to suggest that previous scholarship neglected to point to Spanish-Mexican legal precedents in the history of Indian voting in the U.S.-Mexico Borderlands, for it certainly does. For example, when Mexico became an independent nation in 1821, it declared Indians citizens. Thus, Indians living in the territory conquered during the

U.S.-Mexico War (1846–48), which included New Mexico and Arizona, technically possessed the right to vote.[15] But Indian enfranchisement in this region took several forms before the nineteenth and twentieth centuries. In some ways, the Anglo-American tendency to look from east to west, against which Herbert Eugene Bolton battled so long, persists to the present day.

A larger, hemispheric historiography has stressed the importance of colonial Indigenous leaders and political institutions, particularly in Latin American history. Scholars have examined the important changes to Indigenous town government under Spanish rule, as well as the prominent roles that Indigenous leaders played within that system. Through every period of Latin American history, from the political reordering of societies such as the Aztec and Inca empires in the immediate aftermath of the Spanish conquest to the Mexican Revolution, Indigenous leaders were central to political developments and governed their communities through a combination of traditional Indigenous practice and colonial imposition. The Catholic mission system, in which Spanish political forms and town democracy were forced upon Indigenous peoples, is also a key part of this historiography, and in that system Indigenous peoples struggled against clerics for control of village governance.[16]

My primary approach in this work is to center on Indigenous electorates. I consider Indian citizenship and civil rights prior to the so-called full enfranchisement of Indians, which, as previously mentioned, was not granted in Arizona and New Mexico until 1948. I explore the adoption and incorporation of voting and civil government on the village level by assessing four major groups of New Mexico and Arizona-Sonora Indians: Pueblos, Hopis, Yaquis, and Tohono O'odhams. All four groups share the experience (although their responses have differed widely) of Spanish, Mexican, and U.S. colonial administrations, and for all of them, the local community was and has remained, by far, the most important political entity. As Regis Pecos of Cochiti Pueblo pointed out in a statement that could also apply to all Indigenous peoples, "As Pueblo Indians, we value our people, traditions, and culture as vital to the continuation of our communities. It is the community that has survived the loss of land and near extinction of portions of our culture. The emphasis on our communities and our ceremonies ensures the continuity of our culture and traditions."[17]

As I wove together the stories of these communities, what I already knew became clearer to me: they already had democratic forms of government from time immemorial. My title pays homage to this fact. When Fray Alonso de Benavides famously surveyed New Mexico's Pueblo Indians in 1630, he articulated the operational principle of my work: *"These people have always had a government and been a republic.* The elders customarily meet with the primary captain to confer with each other and discuss matters of common interest. After they have reached a conclusion on some issue, the primary captain goes out to proclaim the new orders about the town. To the present day, the announcement of what course of action a pueblo will take is seen as an act of great authority on the part of the primary captains."[18] While the colonizers brought their own forms of democratic town government, and attempted to incorporate Indigenous peoples into the political mainstream and to reorder political life, they neither destroyed nor replaced Indigenous forms of democracy traditionally rooted in concepts of consensus, dialogue, persuasion, and the power of words.

My ambitious project has required extensive research and the critical and creative use of a variety of sources, such as oral histories; Spanish, Mexican, and U.S. archival documents; period travel accounts; anthropological works; church records; letters and reports of federal Indian agents and military officers; conversations with Indigenous peoples; and many other materials. Interpreting the colonizers' documents is always a tricky endeavor. The principal goal of any careful reading of such sources should always be to uncover the Native voice, and thereby bring to light the stories that lie at the center of Indigenous existence. Stories have the power to help us, as Indigenous peoples, make sense of our existence. They also counter, subvert, and contradict prevailing hegemonic colonial narratives. The individual and collective voices in the chapters that follow demonstrate inventiveness, adaptability, and a certain cleverness, even a coyote-like ability to lead hearers to unexpected places.

With that said, an important alternate narrative must be kept in mind. What James C. Scott referred to as the "hidden transcript" pervades Indigenous history, and governs the stories we tell among ourselves and to others. Scott's hidden transcript applies to the Native peoples and communities in this study: "That hidden transcript could be recovered only in the clubs, homes, and small gatherings" of colonized peoples.[19] In most cases, I have used public transcripts, not hidden ones, in this work. While I have had access to the hidden transcript through interviews and conversations with members of the specific groups, I believe that much of the hidden transcript, especially when it looks at sensitive issues such as internal governance or ceremonialism, is the property of the community and ought to remain private. In the words of Pueblo scholar Joseph "Woody" Aguilar (San Ildefonso Pueblo), there is a dialogue about the Pueblo Revolt that exists only within the Pueblos—it is a hidden transcript consisting of the stories Pueblo people share with one another about this transformative moment in their history, a moment in which they successfully expelled the Spanish colonizers.[20] Such stories told only within Indigenous communities must be respected.

Indian Republics in the U.S.-Mexico Borderlands

Structurally, this work is divided into three main sections. The first centers on Spanish imperatives regarding Indigenous town governance, and on the responses of Indigenous peoples in communities under Spanish colonialism, while the other two focus on the Mexican and U.S. territorial periods, respectively. While Spain perpetrated innumerable acts of violence toward the Indigenous peoples of the Western Hemisphere from the earliest days of colonization, it was equally clear that the original inhabitants of these conquered lands had a place in the new political order. Spain was in the business of empire for the "three G's"—gold, God, and glory—but gold took precedence over the other two. While waves of disease, warfare, and enslavement decimated Indigenous populations, Spain turned to administering the survivors. The ultimate goal was to "Hispanicize" Indians, turning them into taxpaying citizens, but this would be done in stages. Missionization would last ten years and would transition Indians to "civilization" and eventual citizenship. Political administration would be placed in the hands of Native officers, elected to yearly terms. These officers could include a governor, a lieutenant governor, sheriffs, ditch captains,[21] church officers, and others, who comprised a local village council, or *ayuntamiento*, modeled after the Iberian model of town governance.

Such missionized Indian communities, commonly referred to as *repúblicas de indios*, were to be transitional political arrangements. But as is often the case with the best-laid plans, things sometimes went awry. Among the Pueblo Indians of New Mexico, *caciques* (the principal leaders in many of New Mexico's Pueblo communities), society leaders, and moiety chiefs selected the annual officers.[22] To them were delegated purely civil-secular responsibilities, and these officers shielded the traditional Pueblo leadership structures from outside interference, largely shouldering the burdensome and time-consuming work of dealing with Spanish civil leaders and Franciscan clerics. At the Hopi Pueblo, missionization came later than it did for their eastern Rio Grande Pueblo neighbors, but it came all the same. The historical record does not indicate how Hopis handled the electoral process mandated by Spanish law. Perhaps Franciscan missionaries simply chose Hopi officers. It also could have resembled a true election with votes cast, or it might have been a selective process. What is known for certain is that the Hopi-Spanish system of village government did not survive the year 1700. That December, Hopis from surrounding villages converged on Awat'ovi, which seemed poised to welcome the Franciscans after some twenty years of absence in the wake of the Pueblo Revolt. In the ensuing massacre, the Hopi perpetrators not only destroyed the village most sympathetic to Spanish colonial aims, they also destroyed whatever Hopi-Spanish electoral model had existed.[23]

Far to the south, Yaquis initially offered fierce resistance to Spanish Jesuit incursions, thereby engendering the "savage" and "bloodthirsty" Yaqui trope. Yaquis eventually negotiated a peace with the Spaniards, and completed the near-full implementation of the Spanish town electoral model in the eight villages along the Río Yaqui. After Jesuits repeatedly infringed upon Yaqui sovereignty—including elections—the Yaquis violently revolted in 1740. Although the revolt failed, it demonstrated Yaqui resolve to protect town electoral institutions, a trend that would repeat itself over the following centuries. The electoral experiences of O'odhams of Pimería Alta, the region that straddles today's U.S.-Mexico border, lacked the community control of both Pueblos and Yaquis. The Jesuits who missionized O'odhams at villages such as San Xavier del Bac and Tumacácori showed far more interest in overseeing sham elections that propped up their own candidates. Jesuit chroniclers who labored among the O'odhams—familiar names such as Ignaz Pfefferkorn, Jacobo Sedelmayr, Joseph Och, and Juan Nentvig—repeatedly described an anemic O'odham-Spanish electoral system in the accounts they left behind. Even so, O'odham officers advocated on behalf of their people in confronting Spanish civil, military, and ecclesiastical authority. As the subjects of chapter 2, these three groups—Hopis, Yaquis, and O'odhams—provide a useful comparison in the varying implementation of a system of Indian voting under Spanish control.

Mexico and the Indian Citizenship Project

Although the Mexican period was relatively brief (1821–46), the Indigenous peoples of New Mexico, northern Sonora, and what would become Arizona participated in electoral activities outside their communities in unprecedented ways, which is the focus of chapters 3 and 4. When Mexico declared all Indians citizens of the republic, Pueblo Indians and their Hispano neighbors seemed headed, more than ever, for a greater degree of cultural convergence. Mexican law, which brought about a municipal system that combined both groups into the same electorate for ayuntamientos, resulted in mixed governing bodies with both Pueblo Indian and Hispano council members. Even in town councils on which Pueblos did not serve, they still made their political voice heard. In the most significant show of Pueblo electoral power up to that point, Pueblo Indians took an active role in the Rio Arriba Rebellion of 1837 that toppled the government of New Mexico and briefly placed an Indian in the governor's seat. This stands in stark contrast to Hopis, whose traditional governing structures remained untouched during the Mexican period. Some of the only political contacts between New Mexico and Hopis came in the form of isolated Hopi visits to Santa Fe for assistance against Apache raiders, emboldened by weak Mexican control of the Arizona-Sonora Borderlands, or Mexican raiders in search of Hopi captives for the lucrative slave trade.

Yaquis similarly struggled against outside forces, and these came mainly in the form of the Mexican military. A subsequent Yaqui revolt resisted Mexican aspirations to control their territory. Much of the trouble stemmed from Mexican administrative changes that aimed to bring Yaqui towns under the control of Mexican municipalities. Yaquis, with a weaker tradition of coexistence with their Mexican neighbors, actively resisted any diminution of town autonomy, while Mexican officials proved unwilling to leave Yaquis to fully govern their own communities. The Yaqui town electoral system survived the failed revolt, but was stretched to the breaking point in the decades that followed. O'odhams in Pimería Alta also faced dire circumstances during the Mexican period. The missions of northern Sonora had sharply declined after the expulsion of Jesuits in 1767. By the 1830s, many of the missions of Pimería Alta had been completely abandoned. Those missions that survived did so mostly because O'odhams from the desert, the Tohono O'odhams, replaced dying mission populations. Epitomizing the challenges of this era, the Tohono O'odhams of San Xavier del Bac, whom Mexico had abandoned in the face of increasing Apache raids and Mexican encroachments, maintained the mission edifices, if not the mission electoral institutions.

An Act of Refusal

Article VIII of the Treaty of Guadalupe Hidalgo stipulated that Mexican citizens living in the conquered territory could become United States citizens if they so chose. This would inspire a decades-long dilemma for Pueblo Indians. On one side, many Hispanos and Anglo-Americans favored full Pueblo citizenship. Citizenship would open up Pueblo lands to alienation and the eventual demise of Pueblo communities, as neither old Spanish protections to Indian land nor U.S. legal measures forbidding outsiders from settling on Indians lands would apply to Pueblo Indians if they were citizens. On the other side, the U.S. Office of Indian Affairs employees favored a plan whereby the Pueblos would be made wards of the federal government and their lands protected from outside encroachments. This plan would require Pueblo Indians to forego voting in elections outside their communities. For their part, the Pueblos favored federal wardship, even if it resulted in several decades of Pueblo disenfranchisement. Such a course, they believed, provided the best protection for Pueblo community sovereignty.

Hopis had found themselves under the greatest degree of outside influence since the seventeenth century. The Office of Indian Affairs undertook various measures during the territorial period (1848–1912)—including assimilationist education, allotment in severalty, and physical force—in its attempt to bring Hopis to "civilization" and citizenship. But Hopi citizenship, never mind a Hopi electorate, failed to develop. Citizenship and voting offered no tangible benefits for Hopis, who principally aimed to protect their villages from outside forces. Yaquis, who fled en masse to southern Arizona to escape extermination and mass deportation, rejected citizenship and the franchise for other reasons. Fearful for their lives in the United States, or at the very least wary of deportation, Yaquis did not seek to vote, because they lacked a homeland or even a reservation, and also had none of the protections offered to other Arizona tribal nations. These nations included the Tohono O'odhams of San Xavier del Bac. Just as Pueblos, Hopis, and Yaquis had shown little enthusiasm for the franchise, Tohono O'odhams did not seek to vote during the Arizona territorial period. Although they had a long history of colonial interaction and participated in the regional economy, which was highly transnational, political involvement in issues outside their communities only opened up their villages to further incursions by forces they preferred to keep out. Although Pueblos, Hopis, Yaquis, and Tohono O'odhams rejected the vote for differing reasons, as chapters 5 and 6 point out, they all did so in order to protect village sovereignty and because they had, in Benavides's words, "always had a government and been a republic."

TAKEN IN ITS TOTALITY, the history of Indian voting in New Mexico and the Arizona-Sonora Borderlands presents an intriguing story of colonial relations, contested power, and Indigenous sovereignty. In New Mexico, an effort that began as a Spanish attempt to more easily control and govern Pueblo communities—the governor system—eventually became a deeply ingrained element of Pueblo culture. Pueblo people initially embraced this system out of compulsion, but over the decades and centuries that followed, they came to rely on its resilience in safeguarding Pueblo land, culture, and rights. Thus, when U.S. officials proposed political changes that would shift power away from Pueblo officers and place the Pueblos within the political mainstream, the Pueblos labored to reinforce the governor system, even though it was a colonially imposed form of electoral politics. The Pueblos embraced voting when they came to understand that it would reinforce their ability to function as sovereign Pueblo nations, and on occasion they even went outside their communities in their voting and political participation. But during the U.S. territorial period, the Pueblos preferred to continue under the political system imposed by Spain in the early seventeenth century, a system that looked inward and protected internal Pueblo autonomy.

In Arizona-Sonora, Hopis, Yaquis, and O'odhams confronted colonial power and electoral institutions in vastly differing ways. While Hopis repeatedly resisted colonial domination and succeeded in remaining outside the political mainstream well into the U.S. period, Yaquis readily incorporated Spanish concepts of village government and electoral politics. Hopis found sovereignty in isolation and resistance; by contrast, Yaquis used colonial structures to maintain an evolving, complex religious/social/political culture. But under both Spain and Mexico, Yaqui political power proved too much of a good thing. While Spain and Mexico sought politically self-sufficient communities, they did not want them to be *too* self-sufficient. Yaquis made voting a bulwark in their defense against colonial aggression. Mexico eventually broke the Yaquis' power, forcing them to flee for their lives across the border with the United States. In southern Arizona's Yaqui communities, survival depended on political anonymity. O'odhams' choices lay in between Hopis and Yaquis, both geographically and politically. A weak town electoral model was in place at the missions of Pimería Alta during the Spanish period, but it eventually reverted to traditional methods of leadership selection. O'odham governors still performed many of the functions of their Yaqui and Pueblo counterparts, but mission decay, depopulation, Hispano encroachments, and Apache raids in the late Spanish period and throughout the Mexican era eventually led to the complete erosion of the tenuous O'odham-Spanish electoral system. The United States believed it had found ideal potential Indian citizens in the Tohono O'odhams of San Xavier del Bac. But Tohono O'odham citizenship and voting proved as elusive as they had been in the Pueblos. Tohono O'odhams, who had been subjected to forced schooling, allotment, and assimilation by the federal government, mainly ignored pleas by their Indian agent to go to the polls. Once again, an Indigenous group under U.S. colonial domination could see no material benefits to embracing U.S. citizenship and the franchise.

With a few exceptions, such as Pueblo political forays during the Mexican era, voting as a colonial imposition only succeeded on the village level from the Spanish period through U.S. statehood in New Mexico and Arizona. When colonizers attempted to bring New Mexico and Arizona-Sonora Indians into elections outside their towns, they remained largely unresponsive. For Pueblo Indians, Hopis, Yaquis, and Tohono O'odhams alike, voting in larger municipalities beyond Indigenous boundaries meant further opening up their communities to outside forces. Voting and civil government in Indian towns worked within the colonial sphere because they could be used to deflect, and sometimes stymie, colonial power. At some point all these groups embraced voting as a concept of internal governance. For those who succeeded in indigenizing the vote and harnessing its potential, it became a powerful tool in maintaining citizenship in the Indigenous nation and protecting both sovereignty and nationhood.

CHAPTER ONE

Repúblicas de Indios in Spanish New Mexico

In his groundbreaking work, *The Tewa World: Space, Time, Being, and Becoming in a Pueblo Society*, published in 1969, the anthropologist Alfonso Ortiz deftly delineated the Tewa Pueblo worldview as no previous scholar had. Born and raised at Ohkay Owingeh Pueblo, Ortiz sought to "fill a serious gap in the ethnographic literature on the Pueblos of the American Southwest."[1] Among the rich descriptions contained in *The Tewa World* was that of a Tewa annual election of civil officers. While many travelers, ethnographers, and historians had previously outlined Pueblo elections, Ortiz's work remains the most vivid narration of the Pueblo electoral process. Drawing on his fieldwork while a graduate student at the University of Chicago in the 1960s, as well as his own traditional knowledge as a citizen of the Pueblo, Ortiz described a tripartite political organization consisting of fourteen officials. The *Kwaku tsonin*, or Spanish officials, were first among the three groups, and included a governor, two lieutenants, and an *alguacil*, or sheriff. Next were the *Towa é*, which included a War Chief, Assistant War Chief, and four other officers, all of whom were charged with guarding the Pueblo's traditional ways. Third were the *Fiscales* (*Pika* in Tewa),[2] or church officers, who were four in number. Together, these fourteen men constituted the civil arm of government in the middle of the twentieth century.[3]

Ortiz's description of the process for electing these officers is as follows: as the year drew to a close, the Summer and Winter moiety chiefs[4] began to "draw up a mental list of those whom they wish to appoint to the various offices for the following year."[5] The two chiefs alternated years as head of the Pueblo. If it was the Winter chief's year as head, he would go to the home of the Summer chief on 29 December. After being seated and smoking together, the Winter chief named his candidate for governor. "Usually, the Summer chief will have no objections, so he in turn offers his nomination for '*Santu tenente*' (holy lieutenant)."[6] They continued alternating with the nominations for a second lieutenant and alguacil, thus completing the nominating process for the four Spanish officers. All of this was done with scripted, ceremonial language, and then the Winter chief proceeded with the nomination of the *Towa é sehn*, "to head those of our *Towa puxu* (traditional ways)."[7] They alternated nominating the rest of the six Towa é, and proceeded with nominations for the Fiscales.

The Winter chief first nominated the *Santu Pika mayo*, or holy Fiscal major, and then the pair alternated in selecting the other three Fiscales.[8]

The next step in the election process was the inclusion of the heads of five of the six Made People's societies, who arrived at the Summer chief's home. The women's society, *Apienu*, does not take part in the electoral process.[9] After some "smoking and small talk," the Summer and Winter chiefs presented their candidates to the society leaders. The society leaders "usually concur, but any one of them protesting vigorously can negate one of the nominations." Such protests were rare, and occurred only when "the Made person can show proof that the nominee is unworthy, or that he would be placed under an intolerable burden if given the office." When the group had achieved unanimity, they dispersed for the day.[10] The following day, 30 December, the moiety chiefs went to the sitting governor's home, where he and all of the *punan* (previous governors) had gathered. At this point the election was closed, and the names of the new officers were presented to the assembled group, but this was "merely to notify the governor and *punan*."[11] On 31 December the governor brought all outgoing officers to his home and informed them of their replacements for the next year. He told them, "These . . . are the ones you will bring in tomorrow. But do not say anything, for they may hide or run away."[12] The governor and his first lieutenant then went to the Summer Chief's house (the leader who had appointed them the previous year) and delivered a speech to the chief that their authority had returned to the chief, the spirits, and the sacred mountains, whence it had derived. "This retires the governor and his lieutenant."[13] The chief thanked them, and then they returned to the governor's home and notified them of their release. They were told, "Each one of you will bring your counterpart [replacement]."[14]

On the morning of 1 January, the "still unsuspecting" new officers were "accosted in their homes" by those whom they would replace. They were told to come to the governor's house, the meaning of which was clear. Most offered only "mild protest." At the outgoing governor's house, they were met by the retiring officers, Made People's society heads, and the previous governors. Incoming officers could protest their elections, and many "vigorously" did so. But "All protest is futile; in the end, often late in the afternoon [after protest and discussion], each official kneels before the Winter chief and is sworn in with a prayer."[15] As each officer was sworn in, "the Winter chief gives him the metal-tipped cane symbolic of his office." This completed the first part of the installation process.[16] The following day all fourteen new officers gathered at the new governor's house. They held a ceremony that invoked the blessings of the spirits, thereby legitimizing their authority. They then went to the Catholic priest's home "to buy a mass for the new officials, so that the priest may invoke the blessings of God and the saints." On 6 January, Three Kings' Day, the priest celebrated the mass. "Then and only then is their authority completely official; this double spiritual sanction assures the new officials obedience from the people."[17]

As a historical document, Ortiz's account deftly details the inner workings of a Pueblo election in the 1960s. But his account has far greater value as one of the only thorough accounts of such an election—in any era—written by a Pueblo citizen. Its value also lies in the fact that this process has repeated itself on an annual basis, in some form, in all of New Mexico's Pueblo Indian nations for more than four hundred years. While the electoral process certainly had evolved between Spain's invasion of the Pueblo homelands in the sixteenth century and Ortiz's time, many of the hallmarks of the Spanish-Indian town electoral model had persisted: nomination of candidates by traditional religious leaders; approval of candidates by society leaders; absence of campaigning for office; elections taking place at the New Year; a clearly defined, typically limited, electorate; unanimity as a guiding principle; use of scripted, ceremonial language throughout the process; swearing in of officers by both traditional Pueblo and Spanish Catholic officials; and distribution of ceremonial canes to elected officers as insignias of power.[18] First mandated by Spanish royal Indian policy, the town electoral model became so entrenched at the Pueblos during the colonial era that Spanish and Pueblo customs are disentangled only with great difficulty.[19] This commingling of traditional Pueblo practice and Spanish institutions of town government resulted in the Pueblo-Spanish *repúblicas de indios* of the colonial era.[20]

Indigenous Electoral Foundations in Spanish Colonial America

By the time Spain violated the territorial sovereignty of the Pueblos in the sixteenth century, it had a well-established conception of the legality of conquering and subjugating other peoples, especially those it considered heathens. After decades of Crusades and warfare to expel Muslims from Iberia, the pope, as the supreme Christian head of both temporal and spiritual matters, sanctioned the invasion and colonization of all lands "discovered" by the Spanish and Portuguese, the conversion of their infidel inhabitants, and their eventual incorporation into the political-economic sphere.[21] As Spain entered the Western Hemisphere and encountered diverse Indigenous nations, it developed a relatively nuanced system of othering, whereby not all Indians were simply lumped into a single group. *Indios bárbaros* (savage Indians), such as Comanches,

Navajos, and Apaches, often fell outside of Spanish political and religious institutions, and did not experience the same degree of colonization and incorporation, the exception being the *genízaros*, or detribalized Indians, who often came from Comanche and Apache nations. By contrast, Spaniards referred to Indians who lived under Spanish rule as *Indios naturales*, or simply *naturales*.[22] A logical, natural step in the progression of Indios naturales was their organization into bodies politic. Pueblo Indians fell into this category, and Spain would attempt such organization beginning in the sixteenth century.

The foundations of Indian civil government are clearly discernible in Spanish colonial law and policy. One need only follow El Camino Real—the "Royal Road" connecting Santa Fe and Mexico City—deep into Mexico, then to the first Spanish island settlements in the Caribbean, and back to Iberia to elucidate these foundations. In the decades following its first encounters with the Indigenous peoples of the Western Hemisphere, imperial Spain dictated Indian policy through a series of lengthy, often clunky, councils and legal codes. The ultimate goal of these legal measures was to transform Indians into "tax-paying and God-fearing Christians."[23] The *Leyes de Burgos* (Laws of Burgos), established in Burgos, Castile, in 1512 and amended in 1513 was the first comprehensive Spanish code designed specifically for administering Indians. Among other things, the Leyes de Burgos bolstered the encomienda system,[24] highlighted the importance of placing Indians in a town setting, and stated, "It is our determination to remove the said Indians and have them dwell near the Spaniards,"[25] so that they could be more easily converted, surveiled, and controlled, thereby avoiding the backsliding that occurred when Indians lived in remote areas, far from Spanish eyes. Once Indians were converted and sufficiently instructed, they would be ready to govern themselves. Amendment IV (1513) stated, "in the course of time, what with their indoctrination and association with Christians," Indians would become so "ready to become Christians, and so civilized and educated, that they will be capable of governing themselves." It further stipulated that Indians "competent to live by themselves and govern themselves" would do so "under the direction and control of [their own] judges," under an obligation "to serve [only] in those things in which our vassals in Spain are accustomed to serve, so that they may serve and pay the tribute which they [our vassals] are accustomed to pay to their princes."[26] Spanish authorities repeatedly underscored this concept, as in a 1570 royal order that the Indians of Nueva Galicia (in present-day north-central Mexico) be gathered into towns and live under organized civil government: "[Where] Indian inhabitants of the province are not gathered into towns where they may have political government, much harm is done and many difficulties arise." For their salvation and welfare, the Crown ordered that Indians should be congregated "into towns where they may live in a civilized manner and have their organized government, that they may better communicate with each other, have order and system in their living."[27]

With an eye towards eventual Indian citizenship and tax collection, Spaniards thus attempted to reduce Indians and instruct them in government and religion. The bureaucratic arm of Indian policy that followed the Leyes de Burgos, the Council of the Indies, was formally established 4 August 1524. The Council developed the *Leyes de Indias* (Laws of the Indies), the legal code by which Spain governed its new colonies, and this code was in a process of evolution until 1680. In 1681, these laws were compiled and codified as the *Recopilación de Leyes de los Reinos de las Indias*. The *Recopilación* was a "heterogeneous mass of laws, pragmatics, ordinances, provisions, cédulas, resolutions, and decisions which attempted to regulate the procedure, duties, and guarantees of the various governing agencies and the peoples governed."[28] Taken collectively, the Indian ordinances in the *Recopilación* worked to organize Indigenous peoples into what came to be termed *repúblicas de indios*, or Indian republics. Based on St. Augustine's *City of God*, Indians did not fit neatly into the ordered republic that was the ideal of Spanish colonial society. Inhabiting a space outside of conquistadors, *encomenderos*, and *vecinos* (settlers), Indians had their own physical and ideological space in the republic of Indians.[29]

Within the Indian republic, each community formed its own town government and council. The Spanish town council, or *cabildo* (variously referred to as a cabildo, ayuntamiento, or even república), served as the model for the Indian town council.[30] Dating back to at least Roman times, cabildos grew in number in the Castilian towns of the Christian Reconquest of Spain, and were then exported to Spanish colonial America.[31] The cabildo was, in fact, the only political institution of self-government in Spanish North America for both Spaniards and colonized Indigenous peoples.[32] The *Recopilación* mandated that each new settlement in Spain's American colonies have a cabildo. Title 7, Law 18 of Book IV of the *Recolpilación* stated that a "Justicia and governing body shall be chosen from among the settlers" of each town, while Title 10 clarified that "Citizens of the village must be elected as officials."[33] Indian town officers were to be chosen through elections held on or near the first of the calendar year. Officers included a *gobernador* (governor), *alcaldes* (mayors), *alcaldes mayores* (local chief magistrates), *principales* (headmen or nobles), *regidores* (aldermen or town councilmen), and *corregidores* (local magistrates, similar to alcaldes mayores). Hernán Cortés is often credited with instituting Spanish-style Indian town government in 1525, when he conferred the titles of gobernador, alcalde, regidor, *escribano* (notary), and *oficial* on Indigenous elites in Milpa Alta, Oaxaca.[34] But Spanish and Indian cabildo offices and election processes evolved over time, and included a number of options: selection by Spanish officials; selection through restricted suffrage; appointment by an Indigenous council; inherited office; and even outright purchase.[35]

Spanish colonial Indigenous communities are best described as semisovereign. Indian officers had jurisdiction over their towns, but were answerable to local and provincial clerics, officials, and courts, all of which intervened in Indigenous governance on numerous occasions, thus limiting the sovereignty of Indian towns. The *Juzgado General de Indios* (General Indian Court) in Mexico City heard a wide variety of cases involving Indian litigation, including electoral disputes.[36] By law, towns elected officers at intervals of one or two years, with elections on the first of January.[37] Electoral processes varied, sometimes widely, from one Indian town to another. In Cuernavaca (in the present-day Mexican state of Morelos), for example, the vote was restricted to males in the upper echelons of local society, while in the Franciscan missions of California, missionaries retained tight control of Indian elections, even restricting which Indians could stand as candidates for office, thereby guaranteeing the election of men favorable to missionary aims.[38] In the sophisticated colonial *altepetl* (Nahua ethnic state) of central Mexico, a corporate body of senior noblemen elected officers from among their own group, with voting generally being unanimous.[39] Across all colonial Indian towns, elections were a major event in the annual calendar, with voters often called to the community house by town criers, trumpets, and/or drums. In most instances the elections maintained some precontact traditions. For example, it was common for voters to deliberate all day and only elect officers through consensus.[40]

Juan Solórzano Pereyra (1575–1655), the preeminent scholar of Indian law of the seventeenth century, wrote extensively on the legal framework governing Spain's Indian communities in the Western Hemisphere. His three-volume *Política Indiana* treats nearly every aspect of Spanish legal tradition concerning Indians. Pereyra served as *oidor*, or judge, in the Real Audiencia de Lima, and as a council member of the Royal and Supreme Council of the Indies.[41] Pereyra opined that, in general, man is "'sociable,' 'political' [and] 'civil,'" and his ideal state is to live in towns and places where he can communicate well, help others, and defend himself. He wrote categorically that Indians must be congregated in towns, with every community possessing a church, Catholic ministers, Indian instructors of doctrine, Indians trained as singers to lead mission church services, a *sacristán* (an Indian charged with the care of the sacristy and church possessions), and a *fiscal* (the church officer who made sure town residents attended Mass and generally obeyed doctrine). Each Spanish Indian community of forty households or more was to elect an alcalde annually. Towns with more than eighty households would elect an alcalde and a regidor. Very large villages could not have more than two alcaldes and four regidores, with these officials "being elected as is customary in towns of Spaniards and in the presence of the curates." Furthermore, "because Indians are fond of wandering," Pereyra stressed that Indians from one town should not be allowed to live in another Indian town, and that Indians be barred from relocating to other Indian villages. Pereyra also underscored the policy, which would be a point of contention in New Mexico throughout the colonial era, that "Spaniards, blacks, mestizos, and mulattos not live in [Indian] pueblos, unless they are mestizos born of Indians of the same pueblo."[42] Taken as a whole, Pereyra's work summarized the goal of Spanish Indian policy: reduction, conversion, and self-government.

Inevitably, election disputes emerged in Indian towns in central Mexico after the establishment of Spanish-Indian electoral systems in the first half of the sixteenth century. These disputes demonstrate the seriousness with which both Indians and Spaniards approached these institutions. For example, a series of letters relating to elections in the Indian town of Otumba, some thirty-seven miles northeast of Mexico City, narrate ongoing electoral disputes and irregularities. In a 29 December 1589 letter, the viceroy notified the local Spanish official of complaints he had received from the Indian headmen of Otumba and others that the same four men had been holding and controlling the office of alcalde for over ten years, "soliciting and gaining votes from their important friends by extraordinary means [connotes extralegal means]," and that the people of the town "receive notable vexations from the abovementioned men." In response, the viceroy set term limits to the office of alcalde. A man could serve only a single term, and two years must lapse before he could be elected again.[43]

Spaniards were concerned not only with who was elected and how but also with the part non-Indians played in elections. Initial policy dictated that elections take place in the presence of a local curate, but persistent Indian complaints of outsider interference led the Crown to do away with this requirement in 1622.[44] The presence of Spanish clerics and civil officials clearly put undue pressure on Indians to elect officers favorable to Spanish interests. For instance, the Spanish magistrate of Otumba received another letter in 1590, which read, "The Alcaldes and Rejidores and headmen of the town have made known to me that in order for them to freely hold the elections of the República that are to be held in the coming year 1591, as is customary, that religious officials or people who are not citizens of the town must not disturb the voting process."⁴⁵ Spanish officials in the Indian town of Otzolotepec, a mere ten miles west of Mexico City, received the same rebuke the following year. Viceroy Luís de Velasco wrote to the local Spanish magistrate that the Indian officials of the town had made known to him that while attempting to "hold their cabildos and ayuntamientos to elect officials of the Republic," the Religious and other Spaniards who resided nearby would "enter into the cabildos to obstruct them so that they do not elect sufficient and worthy people to the said positions." The viceroy ordered that "no Spanish enter into their councils," except with his "express permission."⁴⁶ Missionaries and Spanish alcaldes were the most frequent meddlers in Indian elections—they lived in or near Indian communities—but in theory, at least, Indian elections were to be free and open to Indians only.⁴⁷ By the time Spaniards permanently settled in New Mexico, the Spanish-Indian electoral tradition was already nearly eighty years old.

Sweeping statements about the powers and responsibilities of elected Indian officers in New Spain are tricky; they were adapted to suit the needs of the individual village. In colonial Cuernavaca, for example, Indian officers collected and delivered tribute to Spanish officials, managed the municipal treasury used for community expenses and emergencies, supported the local Catholic church, and oversaw cases involving petty crime and community land issues, among other things.⁴⁸ Generally speaking, Indigenous officers in the repúblicas de indios participated in some or all of the following activities: traveling to the capital of the jurisdiction to receive ceremonial staffs (Santa Fe in the case of New Mexico); overseeing the Mass and communal meal for the newly elected officials each year; judging minor crimes; directing the planting and harvesting of crops on communal lands, and the necessary labor for this work; paying for and coordinating the repairs of the church, village meeting house, and community roads; funding and presiding over the fiesta of the Pueblo's patron saint; paying for and consulting with attorneys regarding village litigation; and carrying out the annual elections for the new government.⁴⁹ While all these responsibilities point to limits on Indigenous sovereignty under the Spanish system, the melding of Spanish and Indigenous institutions, coupled with at times relatively weak imperial control over village life, resulted in Indigenous towns that saw themselves as distinctive, separate communities. Even with the Catholic, civil, and military presence at Indian towns, a thinly spread state machinery, especially in borderlands such as New Mexico and northern Sonora (as we will see), allowed Indian communities to make many of their own decisions in local matters.⁵⁰ In this respect they truly were Indian republics.

Pueblo Elections, Civil Government, and Officers in New Mexico

The ancestral Puebloan homelands once extended over a vast area, covering portions of what are today New Mexico, Arizona, Colorado, and Utah. Although numbering only nineteen today, New Mexico's Pueblos were far more numerous at the time of the Spanish entrada in the sixteenth century. The area around Jemez, for example, had as many as eleven villages. Spaniards found the Pueblos at or near the sites they now occupy, but there were numerous other villages along the Rio Grande and in the foothills of the mountains near El Paso to the south to Taos Pueblo to the north.[51] Generally speaking, they are grouped into three language groups: Tewa (Nambé, Ohkay Owingeh, Pojoaque, San Ildefonso, Santa Clara, Tesuque), Tiwa (Isleta, Picuris, Sandia, Taos), and Towa (Jemez, Pecos), which comprise the Tanoan language group; Keresan (Acoma, Cochiti, Laguna, San Felipe, Santa Ana, Santo Domingo, Zia); and Zunian. They further break down into geographic groupings. As the Jemez Pueblo scholar Joe Sando pointed out, each Pueblo is an independent entity with a unique identity, but they collectively share a "common traditional native religion ... a similar lifestyle and philosophy; and a common economy based on the same geographical region occupied by them for thousands of years."[52]

A veritable mountain of scholarly work—anthropological, ethnographic, and historical—exists on the Pueblos and their culture. Generally speaking, the Pueblos trace their origins to a place in the north, sometimes called *Shibapu*, where they emerged from the underworld by way of a lake. They journeyed south, settling eventually in their present locations. Supernatural beings guided them on their journey south, teaching them the necessity of planting and harvesting crops for food, showing them the plants and herbs that sustain life, and demonstrating how to hunt the animals necessary for survival. Pueblo culture developed around corn in particular, and corn cultivation shaped Pueblo religion, with prayers and rituals designed to bring the rain and other conditions favorable to its cultivation. Prayers and dances followed a seasonal cycle, bringing the harmony and bounty necessary for life in an arid, mountainous, desert environment.[53]

The ancient spiritual guides also taught the Pueblo people to organize their communities. The cacique is the titular head of the community, "from the time of emergence from the underworld," as Pueblo oral tradition relates. The cacique's mandate is to guide the people spiritually, and in him the Spirits vested the authority to legislate laws for the community. Under the cacique are the

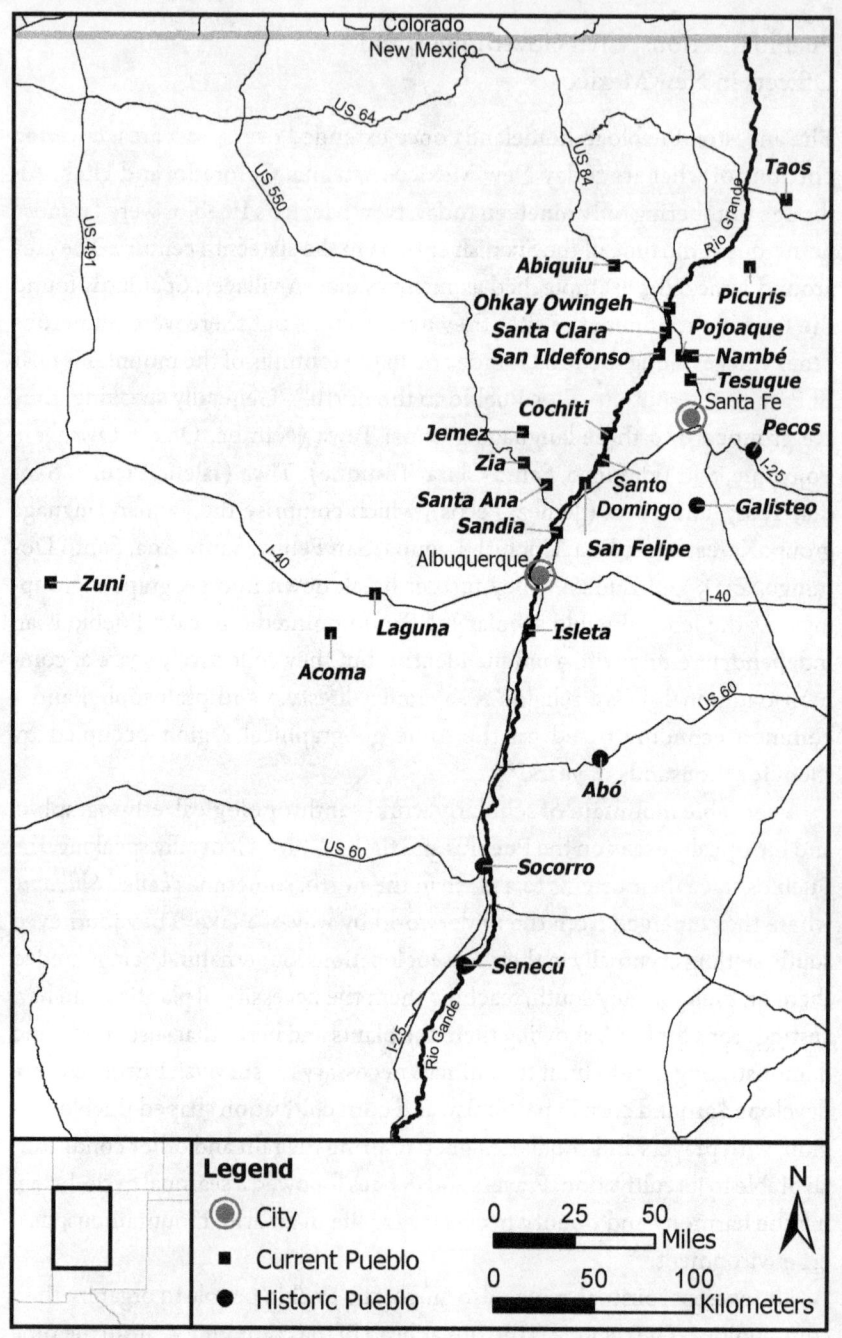

New Mexico Pueblo Indian Territory. Map by Alex Ochoa.

war chief and his assistants, who are the "functioning arm of the leadership that enforces the rules, regulations, and ordinances of the theocratic system." Under the war chief are the war captains and their aides, who are responsible for policing the community and supervising traditional social activities. The people further divide into moieties for ceremonial and social purposes such as Turquoise and Squash, Summer and Winter, North and South, and the like.[54]

The earliest Spanish accounts often described Pueblo Indians in positive terms, depicting them as tractable communities and ideal candidates for conversion and self-government. In reality, Spaniards had little idea of the complexity of the world into which they had entered. They saw sedentary, stable communities of farmers who lived in fixed abodes, sometimes three or four stories high (hence the Spanish name "pueblo"), who would presumably require little by way of reduction when compared to other Indigenous nations they had encountered. They were quickly convinced that the Pueblos possessed a favorable, docile disposition. Hernando de Alvarado, a member of Coronado's 1540–42 expedition, who spent time among the Tiwas of the middle Rio Grande Valley, related, "The people seem excellent, more like farmers than warriors. . . . [Pueblo peoples from surrounding areas] came to this place to offer me their friendship." Alvarado further commended the Tiwas, who had erected crosses, and described showing them how to "venerate them." He recorded that the Tiwas "offer their powders and feathers [to the crosses], and some leave the *mantas*[55] they are wearing. . . . Others brought ladders [and] climbed up to tie on yarn in order to attach roses and feathers."[56] He clearly failed to see that leaving feathers and offering prayers at shrines were traditional Pueblo religious activities, but Alvarado's characterization of Pueblos followed a common trope.

Hernán Gallegos, notary of the Chamuscado-Rodríguez expedition of 1581–82, commented on Pueblo housing in the Tigua Province, and seemed surprised to find that the inhabitants wore clothing. He described it as "for barbarians . . . the best that has been found." He also described them as "handsome and fair-skinned," "very industrious," and "very clean people." Best of all, the men tended to the cornfields while the women prepared food and made and painted pottery, thus closely conforming to Spanish gender roles. He concluded that if his party had brought interpreters, they would easily have converted some of the Indians they encountered, as a result of their intelligence and servility.[57] But not all of the early Spanish descriptions were so positive. Antonio de Espejo, who went to New Mexico in 1582–83, described the Piro Pueblos' religion as satanic. Still, at Zia he walked around the village and admired the cotton blankets, corn, turkeys, and cornbread. The Zians possessed a "form of government," and he characterized them as intelligent and orderly. They had attractive plazas and well-arranged houses. He believed this indicated that they would "learn quickly any matter dealing with good government."[58]

To the Spaniards, the Pueblos were well-mannered, well-dressed, industrious people ready for the benefits of "good government." Under such ostensibly favorable circumstances, Spaniards hoped to quickly pacify, convert, and then incorporate Pueblo Indians into civil society. And yet the reality that the Iberians encountered was quite different from what they had hoped for. Coronado, for example, met with fierce resistance along the middle Rio Grande during the brutal Tiquex War of 1540–41, and horrific violence perpetrated by Spaniards at Acoma in 1599 threatened to derail Oñate's nascent colony. In spite of these violent early encounters, Spaniards intended to bring Pueblo Indians into the sphere of Spanish institutions, including citizenship and access to the Spanish legal system.[59] Soldiers would accomplish the goal of pacification, while Franciscans would tackle conversion. Most important of all, in order for peace and order to be established so that the civilizing program could proceed, the Pueblos would have to be politically reorganized into Indian republics.

Gaspar Castaño de Sosa illegally attempted to colonize New Mexico in 1590, but was arrested at Santo Domingo Pueblo by Spanish soldiers sent after him the following year. In the winter of 1590–1591, his party attacked Pecos Pueblo, and traveled to other Pueblos, where they met Indians who "swore obedience in the name of the king our sovereign." An officer in de Sosa's party reported accepting the allegiance of Pueblo Indians they encountered, and appointing governors, alcaldes, and alguaciles in the name of the king.[60] This was the first mention of Spanish civil government at the Pueblos.

Juan de Oñate, who led the first successful colonization effort to New Mexico in 1598, mentioned the coming of civil government at initial meetings with the Pueblos, but did not immediately appoint officers. When Oñate met with a large delegation of Pueblo leaders at Santo Domingo,[61] he told them that he had come in the name of King Philip for the salvation of their souls, and "to have them as his subjects and to protect and bring justice to them." Oñate noted "how the government and republics of these lands, as far as could be ascertained, were all free and independent heads without subjection to any monarch or ruler." But he stressed the importance of their submission "of their own free will and in their own names and in those of their pueblos and republics," promising that "by doing so they would live in peace, justice, and orderliness, protected from their enemies, and benefited in their arts and trades and in their crops and cattle." He also warned of severe punishment for disobedience.[62] He received similar submissions at other Pueblos, intimating the future political organization. At Ohkay Owingeh, Oñate told those assembled that they must obey and respect the king "in those [matters] relating to the government of their republics."⁶³ At Acolocu, he told the Indians that becoming vassals of King Philip "would benefit them in many ways in matters pertaining to administrative and economic relations, as would be explained to them more extensively later."⁶⁴ At Acoma, he promised that the king would "employ them in positions and occupations in political and economic affairs," but that this would be explained in detail at a later date.⁶⁵

Pueblo oral histories record these encounters quite differently. Dr. Joseph Henry Suina, who served two separate terms as governor of Cochiti Pueblo in 1998 and 2014, recounted the oral tradition of the meeting between Oñate and Pueblo leaders at Santo Domingo, contending that the submission of Pueblo leaders to Spanish civil and Catholic religious authorities likely made no sense.⁶⁶ Santa Ana Pueblo oral tradition recalls that, "compared to demands for all of a pueblo's food and clothing in the harshest part of winter, this request [to kneel and kiss the ring of the priest and Spanish governor] may have seemed insignificant." The Pueblo inhabitants could not have known that Spaniards considered this simple act a renunciation of their Indigenous government, religion, and rights.⁶⁷ But they had submitted, and significant political change soon followed.

When precisely it happened remains unclear. Alfonso Ortiz asserted it was not known when Spanish-style government was imposed at the Pueblos, due to the burning of most church and administrative records in New Mexico during the Pueblo Revolt of 1680.⁶⁸ While Spaniards recognized and acknowledged the status of the Pueblos as *repúblicas*, or semiautonomous communities with some inherent rights to self-government, they felt wary of dealing with large cadres of traditional religious leaders and elders. Therefore, whittling down the governing officers at each Pueblo to a manageable number for easier dealings with Santa Fe was a priority.⁶⁹ It is likely that for approximately the first twenty years of the seventeenth century, Spanish governors and Catholic missionaries appointed Pueblo governors, bypassing participation by Pueblo peoples themselves.⁷⁰

Yet Spaniards soon feuded over the appointment of Indian officers. In fact, the selection of Pueblo officers played a significant part in the heated conflicts between church and state in seventeenth-century New Mexico. A famed New Mexico historian, France Scholes, described Juan de Eulate, who served as governor of New Mexico from 1618 to 1625, as a "petulant, tactless, irreverent soldier whose actions were inspired by open contempt for the Church and its ministers and by an exaggerated conception of his own authority as the representative of the Crown." Franciscans accused Eulate of telling Pueblo Indians that they did not have to obey or serve the friars in any manner; they only needed to attend Mass when called by their missionaries. They portrayed Eulate as lax on the enforcement of strict prohibitions against traditional Pueblo practices in an effort to win Pueblo affections so that they could more easily be exploited for state labor and tribute. To the Franciscans, his actions amounted to grievous interference in mission administration. They also accused Eulate of using his power to influence the elections of Indian officers at the Pueblos.[71]

For his part, Eulate asserted that the Father Custodian of New Mexico and other missionaries had told the Pueblos that their authority was superior to the governor's and that the Indians need not obey him.[72] Each side accused the other of preventing Pueblo Indians from providing the essential manpower for their various work projects.[73] The issue came to a head in 1620, when the viceroy of New Spain, Diego Fernandez de Cordova, wrote to Governor Eulate, alarmed at "certain differences and disputes which there have been between you and the Father Custodian of the Religious of Sr. St. Francisco and the Religious themselves . . . in matters of jurisdiction."[74] Jockeying for control of Pueblo elections by civil officials and clerics undermined Spanish power in New Mexico and hamstrung the Pueblos as self-governing Indian republics.

In the subheading of the viceroy's letter titled "Elections," he clearly outlined procedures for Pueblo elections. It reads:

> And Because of the part of the said custodian and [other] Religious some complaints have been presented to me to the effect that Ye interfere in the matters under their care even to naming the *fiscales* of the church and in other lesser things, Ye shall give order how each of the pueblos of those provinces, on the first day of January of each year, may hold its elections of governor, *alcaldes, topiles, fiscales,* and the others who serve the Republic, without You or any other Judiciary, the custodian of other Religious being present at the said elections, so that in them the said Indians may have the liberty which is fitting. And the [elections] which in this manner they may hold, they shall report them to You that ye may confirm them if they have been effected by the majority and with the liberty Stated, that everything is in accord with what is customary in this New Spain.[75]

Mirroring events in central Mexico, where Spaniards unduly influenced or obstructed Indian elections, Pueblo officers were to be elected by a majority vote of their own people, absent the presence of outsiders, and to be confirmed by the governor. What eventually resulted was not what Spaniards envisioned for a Pueblo town democracy; rather, this 1620 letter opened the door to the "Pueblofication" of the Spanish town electoral system.

The Evolution of Pueblo Elections

The decree of 1620 notwithstanding, Spaniards continued to appoint Pueblo men to various offices. Sometimes Spaniards appointed Pueblo Indians to offices for life as a reward for service to the Crown. For example, on 9 February 1665 Mateo Pacheco of Jemez Pueblo was appointed governor "por todos los días de su vida" (for all the days of his life). Pacheco had fought valiantly against Apaches, and was instructed to use his lifetime office "in everything he touches seeking the shelter and conservation of his subjects."[76] Spaniards also envisioned pan-Pueblo offices as rewards for service, as in the case of Pedro de la Aguila of Isleta Pueblo, who was named "Governor of the said province of the Tiwas [which included several Pueblos] . . . for the rest of his life." His lifetime appointment was a reward for "having served His Majesty on various occasions for more than ten years" as an interpreter and missionary to the Ypotlapigua Indians.[77]

While outsiders controlled Pueblo elections during at least the seventeenth century, and continued their attempts to exert control over electoral processes throughout the colonial period, these elections eventually became indigenized. Exactly how and when this process unfolded is unknown. But, as the traditional history of the Pueblo of Santa Ana recounts, the new system of government "slowly became a part of the people's lives. . . . Once a year, Tamaya [the Keresan name of the Pueblo] chose a group of officers to represent the people before Kastera's [Santa Ana's name for the Spaniards, based on the word *Castilian*] officials."[78] The transition was likely slow, and must have included its fair share of growing pains. Nor did it yield the same results at each Pueblo. But eventually, all of New Mexico's Pueblo nations had implemented some variation of the Spanish town electoral system. At all the Pueblos, the elections mixed Spanish customs with traditional Pueblo practice.

Detailed descriptions of Pueblo elections during the Spanish period simply do not exist. We are left to sift cautiously through the numerous descriptions of Pueblo elections dating from the late nineteenth century to the present. The two best descriptions of Pueblo elections come from Pueblo men intimately acquainted with the process: the aforementioned Alfonso Ortiz of Ohkay Owingeh Pueblo and Joseph Suina of the Pueblo de Cochiti. While the election process certainly changed and evolved between the Spanish period and when these accounts were given in the late twentieth century, the process surely retains enough similarities to render these accounts useful. Suina's rich description states:

> There are two kivas in the village [Turquoise and Pumpkin], two moieties, of which one of them you are born into, and they're the hubs of our government. The moieties, which are religious in nature, take turns providing the leaders for the village. The leaders are in place for one year, and then at the end of the year, they switch kivas furnishing the leaders.
>
> And every year that the leaders are in place, they have a layer of another six to 12 junior officers underneath them—drawn from the opposite kiva. The junior officers do the dog work, if you will, but that's how you learn. What's happening in that process, of course, is that, as a junior officer [Suina himself was chosen to serve as a junior officer four times, each time serving a one-year term], you're privy to council meetings and to ceremonies in the kiva that are only for tribal leaders. So that while you're doing your piddly stuff—sweeping floors, or getting the message out to the people and those kinds of things—you're also learning the way of life and laying the groundwork for governing in the future.... [Later] I was given my first major responsibility of a post within the tribe in 1995. I became lieutenant governor, and that sort of changed my whole relationship to the tribe. Before you're an elder, you can be fairly lax about attendance at events. You can offer an excuse when you miss something, and so forth. But as an elder, which I became, you've got to be there for things; that's expected of you. If you expect the youth to be there, then you better be there first. I had to drop out of university teaching for that period of time in office.... Then in 1998 I became the governor of Cochiti Pueblo.... [Also] in 1995, when I was lieutenant governor [I] went with delegations to Washington to lobby for financial aid for an irrigation project, for a problem with seepage from the dam on our land, and for the construction costs for an elderly center and other projects. Being governor was another level of education for me, which clearly involved my pueblo but not so much on the traditional end. It was more about assisting with the tribe's intersect with the big world, where we dealt with highways, hospitals, social services, schools and much more.[79]

Suina's and Ortiz's accounts, although contemporary, are essential because they are among the only such accounts by Pueblo individuals,[80] and they illustrate many of the characteristics of the Pueblo-Spanish electoral process: an electorate composed entirely of male caciques, moiety leaders, and elders; divisions of leaders into junior and senior officers; the main responsibility of senior officers (the governor, and to some extent the lieutenant governor) to deal with outside entities and protect Pueblo interests; and the overall importance of these offices.

We see these principles in action in the various descriptions of Pueblo elections. A few of Ortiz's observations deserve further attention. For example, the nominations and elections of candidates occur in their absence, and great care is taken that they do not find out beforehand. This is due to the enormous sacrifice of time, commitment, and expense required of a Pueblo officer, one from which certain individuals might flee. Nambé Pueblo oral tradition tells of how ancestors wept when they found out that their male relatives had been elected to office.[81] As the anthropologist Leslie A. White wrote in 1942 after years of work at the Pueblos, "being an officer is a duty rather than a privilege, a burden with no compensation except status; men do not seek office, but, on the contrary, often wish to avoid it."[82]

Ortiz also noted that Pueblo governors received black canes adorned with silver and silk tassels as symbols of their offices, a tradition taken from Spanish towns, where officers similarly carried canes. Today the governor receives three canes: one for the Spanish government; another for the Mexican government; and the third—the so-called Lincoln canes—representing governing authority granted by the President of the United States.[83] According to Ortiz, the junior officers received only a single, shorter cane, which they hung on their walls while in office, while the governor could carry his cane when acting in an official capacity.[84] Spaniards referred to these canes as *varas de justicia* (staffs of justice, or canes of power), and they played an important symbolic role in the confirmation of Pueblo officials.[85]

Yet Pueblo tradition holds that leaders used canes or staffs as symbols of power long before the Spanish invasion. For example, at Ohkay Owingeh the Winter chief holds an Ice Governing Stick as his primary symbol of office, while the Summer chief has a long wooden rainbow (both of these leaders predate the Spanish period).[86] A traditional cane was often viewed as a living entity with a life and heartbeat of its own. Thus, the use of varas was likely easily incorporated since it corresponded with traditional Pueblo practice. Furthermore, a former Tesuque Pueblo governor, Gil Vigil, related that canes simultaneously served Spanish purposes. They were visible symbols of office, thus allowing Spaniards to quickly identify Pueblo civil officers, "instead of having to deal with ten, twelve, fifteen people" or a large group of traditional Pueblo elders in whose hands power traditionally rested.[87] There was Catholic religious significance as well. According to the Pueblo of Acoma, "The good

Franciscan Fathers following the Good Book of Moses impressed upon the Indians the lessons of leadership in Exodus Four and Numbers Seventeen [from the Old Testament]. The rod and staff should be their comfort and strength, and their token against all enemies."[88] As one Picuris Pueblo elder recounted, "There is a lot of respect for the canes to this day."[89] Canes were a ubiquitous symbol of Indian rulers all over Spanish America, and they have remained important in the Pueblos of New Mexico down to the present.

After the electoral process concluded at each Pueblo, and after village leaders confirmed the new officers and distributed canes, one final step in the process remained: Spanish authorities in Santa Fe received Pueblo officials and swore them in. One Spanish document dated 10 January 1706 details the reception and confirmation of numerous officers from the Pueblo repúblicas for the year:

> Captain Don Alfonso Rael de Aguilar, secretary of government and war, *alcalde ordinario* of the villa of Santa Fé, the capital of this kingdom and province of New Mexico, protector-general of the Indians native to its pueblos and frontiers . . . I certify, as is my duty. . . . That on the sixth day of January of the current year, 1706, there appeared before me as their protector-general the Indian governors, chiefs, captains, and the other officials of justice of the pueblos of this kingdom and jurisdiction, of the nations of the Zuñis, Queres [Keres], Teguas [Tewas], Hemes [Jemez], Thanos [Tanos], Pecos, Tiguas [Tiwas], Pecuries [Picuris], and Thaos [Taos]. They had come to this villa for the purpose of being confirmed in the positions to which they had just been elected.[90]

This formal reception and confirmation process persisted throughout the Spanish period. In a letter written a century later, dated 16 January 1811, Ignacio Sanchez, a Spanish official with jurisdiction over Jemez Pueblo, wrote, "The Justices who have been elected in the Pueblos of my care, have gone [to Santa Fe] to be confirmed with their staffs [of justice] and to receive the orders of their office."[91] Religious leaders at those Pueblos would have already sworn in the civil authorities in a scripted, ceremonial manner. But to Spanish eyes, the physical act of traveling to Santa Fe to be confirmed, which served as a sort of colonial inauguration, gave legitimacy to the process as a whole. The Crown, the Church, and their own communities now recognized these men as the civil arm of government at the Pueblo repúblicas.

Ortiz also carefully outlined the various duties of the elected officials. Officers maintained and supervised the Pueblo's irrigation system. This was a considerable undertaking, since the system was shared with neighboring

View in Pueblo Laguna, Inauguration Dance, January 12, 1887. Photo by Ben Wittick, courtesy Palace of the Governors Photo Archives (NMHM/DCA), 002805.

Hispano communities. Officers also oversaw the Pueblo's stock and grazing rights on communal lands, and directed the renting of Pueblo land and property to outsiders. The village *aguacil*,[92] or sheriff, punished minor crimes, but was to bring those who committed more serious crimes to the governor, who had the power to fine such individuals. The fiscales maintained the church grounds and helped the priest with his duties on feast days and during other special religious observances. Ortiz pointed out that during the stricter period of Spanish Catholicism, fiscales forced Pueblo citizens to attend church services under the threat of whipping. They also taught the catechism to village children, and buried the dead in the Catholic manner.[93] The Pueblo governor held perhaps the most important responsibility among the elected officers, that of representing the traditional leadership of the Pueblo in all dealings with "outside polities."[94]

Pueblo officers frequently met with Spanish officials over "matters both large and small." These men—the governor in particular—kept safe the Pueblo's land grant papers and other important documents. When a Pueblo needed additional lands, officers presented their petition to the Spanish governor. If Spaniards trespassed on their lands or otherwise violated their rights, the governor often personally delivered the community's protest to Spanish officials.⁹⁵ Civil officers were also the local arm of tribute collection at the Pueblos. The fiscales and their aides circulated among their villages collecting *primicias* (first fruits) after the harvests. They also oversaw activities on All Saints Day (1 November), when community members brought offerings of wheat and corn to the church in return for pulling the rope that rang the mission bells or chimes. The fiscales placed these items in corn bins and wheat storage boxes to be used by the missionaries during the coming year. Pueblo governors collected other taxes, imposed by alcaldes and Spanish governors in the form of produce and textiles, and delivered them to the Spanish governor's agents.⁹⁶ For example, Father Joseph de Lara reported meeting with Pablo, the Indian governor of Taos Pueblo, in April 1713, who gave to him the inventory book for the mission pantry. The mission stores included bushels of flour, corn, beans, and other foodstuffs, all under the charge of the governor.⁹⁷ New Mexico Governor Juan Bautista de Anza wrote to Pueblo governors in 1779, reminding them to set aside a certain portion of communal crops for the support of the church and the relief of the poor. Governors were to oversee this.⁹⁸

Pueblo governors also had to give permission for community members to leave for any reason, whether hunting, trading, or even gathering salt (which was critical for bartering and the preservation of foodstuffs). A governor mustered men for auxiliary service when Pueblo warriors were needed for Spanish military campaigns.⁹⁹ Dorothy Roman of Jemez Pueblo, who was interviewed in 1968, also recounted the traditional duties of Pueblo officers: "The way I understand [it] . . . my daddy used to tell us that the governors [are supposed] to take care of the Pueblo, to take care of roads, to take care [of] ditches, to take care of water gates and fans and everything like that . . . and then to go to meetings, and whenever they put up a meeting to see what is right or what they want for somebody to do."¹⁰⁰ Pueblo officers thus saw to the well-being of the community as it related to both interactions with the outside world and the quotidian.

After the Spanish electoral system took root in Pueblo communities during the seventeenth century, the Pueblos reached a relatively high degree of autonomy in their electoral processes, perhaps bolstered by Spanish accommodation that occurred in the wake of the Pueblo Revolt and *Reconquista* in the late sixteenth century.¹⁰¹ Still, as a historian of colonial Mexico, Michael Ducey, has pointed out, it would be a mistake to assume that because Spanish law recognized a separate ethnic sphere for the Pueblo repúblicas (and all such semisovereign Indian communities, for that matter), the Pueblos were ever truly politically independent under Spanish rule (aside from the years between 1680 and 1692). Indian republics, Ducey writes, were "sites of power where colonial authorities and indigenous communities negotiated terms of domination."[102] Spaniards persisted in their efforts to influence Pueblo elections throughout the colonial era, and such elections were important sites of struggles over power and sovereignty.

Father Fray Joaquín de Jesús Ruiz penned a short treatise in 1773. Ruiz, who had ministered at both Jemez and Isleta, underscored the importance of the office of Pueblo governor, but also illuminated Spanish Franciscan views on Indian self-government:

> Each pueblo shall have its head, who shall be satisfactory to the missionary father and confirmed by the governor [of New Mexico]. He must be a man who will make himself respected by the Indians and unite us with them, and he must be of temperate disposition.... It is his obligation to join the minister immediately when the bell rings, to see that none of the pupils are missing at catechism, or the married people at mass, without sufficient cause; but shall not be allowed the right to punish without consulting the missionary father or minister, so that the latter may decide whether or not there is sufficient reason for the punishment. It should be the duty of this leader to see that the Indians live in peace.... He should exert himself to make them plant crops, for if they have enough to eat in their pueblos they will not wander about. He should take note of what Indians go out and come in and report to the father; he should see that they keep watch over the country.... Citizens are not permitted to enter the community, nor shall the girls enter it when there are travelers there.... And if this leader becomes sick, or joins in with the Indians [who are engaged in prohibited behavior], the minister shall report it to the prelate, so that the latter may inform the governor [of New Mexico], who will remove him from office.[103]

While the Pueblos came to view their governors as representatives and protectors, missionaries such as Ruiz viewed them more as enforcers of Catholic mission discipline. As Ducey observed, while the Crown developed law and policy for how repúblicas were to function, "in practice each locality had its own traditions specifying how the community elected their officials, what their functions were, and, most importantly, who could hold posts and vote."[104] This was true of the Pueblos, and throughout the colonial period they would use the Pueblo-Spanish electoral system to protect an evolving form of Pueblo nationhood.

The Work of the Governors

A scholarly ambivalence has surrounded commentary on the Pueblo-Spanish governing system and its place in Pueblo society. Sando wrote that it was "a form that the Spaniards understood; and with this kind of government, he saw a way of making village officials conform to his way of doing things." At the same time, the governor system was "superimposed upon the ancient tradition of selecting war captains and their aides to govern the civil aspects of pueblo life."[105] Thus, it is Spanish in form, but could be incorporated into traditional Pueblo practice. The anthropologist Edward Dozier of Santa Clara Pueblo, who wrote extensively on Pueblo history and culture during the second half of the twentieth century, remarked, "It is important to note only that the officers of the civil government system are recognized in all the pueblos today as an imposed set." Still, he added this caveat: "This is not to imply that the latter are unimportant, for these officers are crucial in dealing with profane matters and the outside world." He summed up the views of many scholars and Pueblo peoples when he wrote that secular officers typically masked the identity and obscured the activities of traditional Pueblo religious leaders who oversaw those ceremonies that so angered Spanish authorities, especially the mission priests. In Spanish times, the corps of civil officers was a "convenient façade" that allowed the religious officials to successfully continue the social and religious activities of a Pueblo.[106] As the anthropologist Tracy Brown recently summarized, during the Spanish colonial period, caciques and their assistants retained governing power, with secular officers subordinated to them. Brown went so far as to assert that governors had no real power, but simply followed the directives of religious leaders. The new Spanish system was simply incorporated into traditional structures of governance. Furthermore, this incorporation reinforced male-dominated power structures, buttressing gender and class distinctions.[107]

It is, therefore, a fair critique to say that the Pueblo-Spanish electoral system was not particularly democratic. Yet this system demonstrates the development of sovereignty in practice. The Pueblos decided who would be included within the electorate, which electoral processes would be used, and which powers and responsibilities were associated with office. In addition, that traditional leaders continued to make important decisions for Pueblo communities belies the crucial role played by civil officers, and governors in particular. Pueblo governors were in many ways important political and cultural intermediaries in colonial New Mexico. Without their work, the Pueblos may not even have survived the colonial era. While civil officers were subservient to the traditional leadership, and provided an identifiable front that shielded the ceremonial life of the Pueblo, they operated in a symbiotic manner with traditional leaders, ideally to the benefit of their communities. When the actions of Pueblo civil officers during the Spanish era are viewed in a more holistic light, the importance of the electoral system and officers becomes clear.

An example that illustrates this symbiotic relationship between secular and traditional leaders comes from, of all places, Governor Diego de Vargas's account of the Reconquista in the winter of 1693–94. After brutal clashes around Santa Fe, Vargas's force succeeded in retaking the provincial capital, but the question arose of what to do with Tano Pueblo Indians who had moved into the city's vacant buildings. Vargas required that each group of reconquered Pueblo Indians have a Catholic church. For these Pueblo Indians inhabiting Santa Fe, the logical choice was the San Miguel Mission, located centrally in the city. But the church had been damaged during the Pueblo Revolt and was not in serviceable condition at that time. Vargas demanded that Indians repair the chapel, although this was nearly impossible due to "the many freezes and the snow, [so that they] could not go to the forest to cut the beams necessary [to repair] the roof."[108]

Hearing Vargas's church requirement, José, the governor of the Santa Fe Pueblo, and another Indian leader, Antonio Bolsas, conferred overnight "*with the elders they obey* and the other inhabitants of the walled pueblo they have here in this villa," and proposed that a door be made into one of their kivas, and then the kiva be made into a "chapel." Using this structure, which was attached to their buildings, "it would be more likely that all will be able to attend mass and pray, because they will be able to come down through their pueblo without having to go outside." Governor Vargas inspected the kiva, and found it a satisfactory temporary replacement for the San Miguel Church. He ordered the Indians to "cut a door in it immediately, whitewash it, and also make adobes in order to put up an altar." His final demand was that the Indians make the adjoining building into a residence for the priest.[109] In this illustrative episode, Pueblo civil and religious leaders on one side had collaborated with Spanish religious and secular officials on the other in order to solve a mundane but still pressing problem. But all sides seemed happy, not least of whom the civil leaders, who had proceeded with the necessary blessing of their elders.

Variation certainly must have existed, however, in the independent decision-making power of Pueblo governors. Pedro Pino, for example, who served as governor of Zuni Pueblo from 1830 to 1878 (admittedly, during the Mexican and U.S. Territorial period), is an intriguing example of the melding of religious and secular leadership. Zuni caciques, who chose the Spanish officers, entrusted Pino with the Pueblo's civil government for several decades. But as Pino biographer E. Richard Hart has pointed out, while Zuni Pueblo should be considered a theocracy, after their election Pino and the other officers were given "much personal discretion." Hart asserted, "it was considered a very serious breach of policy for a *cacique* as a religious leader to dirty his hands with secular affairs." Pino's position is made all the more intriguing by the fact that he was a member of the powerful Zuni Priesthood of the Bow, and used his position as governor and priestly leader to allow anthropologist Frank Hamilton Cushing's general intrusion into Zuni culture and initiation into the bow society in the late nineteenth century. This demonstrates the potential vibrancy and variability of the electoral system and the powers of officers from Pueblo to Pueblo.[110]

Another important aspect of the Pueblo-Spanish electoral system was the development of new councils for community government. Councils of elders and traditional leaders had existed since time immemorial, but added to these councils were former civil officers. The Pueblo de Cochiti Tribal Council today consists of some forty male members "who have served in one or more of the top positions of Tribal Government *and by tradition are council members for life.*"[111] Members of these councils, whom Spaniards referred to as principales, were typically society leaders and other men who had served in one of the major civil offices. Leslie White, for example, wrote that any man who had served as one of the important civil officers at Santo Domingo Pueblo "becomes automatically a principale for the rest of his life. The principales are regarded as men of influence in the pueblo. They very frequently advise or collaborate with the officers of the pueblo, including the heads of the two kiva-kachina groups. The principales do not constitute an organization; there is no head principale, no meeting house, no paraphernalia."[112]

However, we must be careful not to place too much emphasis on the role of former governors and officers. Ortiz, for example, stated that while the *punan* (past governors) at Ohkay Owingeh served as advisors to the governor, and with the male heads of the Made People's societies formed a village council, the council traditionally served as the venue whereby Made People—the two moiety chiefs in particular—imposed their will on the governor and his former governors-turned-advisors on important decisions. He asserted that councils "traditionally meant very little," and that many have "exaggerated the importance of the council as the governing body of the Pueblo."[113] Be that as it may, governors, especially good ones, were respected for their work and attained some status from jobs well done. Good governors were often retained in office or called on to serve again, which remains the case today. The documentary record hints at the importance of former governors, as they often show up throughout Spanish American petitions as *gobernadores pasados* (past governors) or simply as *pasados*.[114]

Former governors sometimes wielded their influence negatively, as was the case with former Picuris Pueblo governor Jerónimo Dirucaca. In 1713, the principales of the community asked that he be removed from the Pueblo because of his abusive behavior. They accused him of idolatry, cohabitation, and witchcraft. Apparently, his power was significant enough that he still carried a vara de justicia, which they asked be confiscated. A Spaniard, Juan de Atienza, acted as Dirucaca's legal defense, but ultimately in vain, as Dirucaca agreed to reveal the location of a hidden silver mine in return for a pardon. Dirucaca took the Spaniards to a nearby canyon, where he showed them four veins of silver ore; afterward, he was banned from Picuris, but was allowed to take up residence at one of the Tewa Pueblos and received no punishment other than paying his court costs.[115] That the principales, of whom Dirucaca was one, asked for his removal from the Pueblo, and that he still possessed a cane, demonstrate the considerable potential for entrenched power by former officers.

Conversely, a former officer could use his knowledge and experiences to serve the community long after he had served in office. As Dorothy Roman of Jemez Pueblo stated in the late 1960s, "everybody that [has been] an officer is what they call a councilman. Almost all of the men are councilmens [*sic*]."[116] Pueblo Indian Agent Benjamin H. Thomas wrote in 1879 that while the governor's office is "purely honorary in respect of remuneration . . . the honors do not cease with office, for the dignified position of principal is waiting him at the close of his term."[117] These accounts, spanning several eras of Pueblo history, all point to the presence of former civil officers on governing councils composed of both civil and religious leaders. This suggests a less rigid form of compartmentalization at the Pueblos. There is no such thing as a strictly secular Pueblo person. The holistic nature of Pueblo culture and society means that the secular and sacred are inextricably intertwined. While acting in a secular office, Pueblo officers still needed to keep the sacred foremost in their minds—the land, traditions, and ceremonies of their people—and must act to protect them. Furthermore, the overarching responsibility of any Pueblo leader was the same: to maintain the people's well-being and the sovereignty of the Pueblo. All worked together to this end. While we should heed Ortiz's caution about the relative power of Pueblo councils, some form of power sharing must have occurred in the Spanish period. Similarly, Pueblo governing councils contrast with those found in other areas of Spanish America. Unlike the

Nahua altepetl of central Mexico, for example, which often boasted a full complement of Indigenous officers with Spanish titles and a formal cabildo composed of alcaldes and regidores[118] (as noted above), Pueblo governing councils were more hybrid in nature.

Pueblo civil officers were also crucial to Spain's colonizing project in New Mexico. Spain recognized the key role these officers played in maintaining community order and keeping Pueblo repúblicas in harmony with both Cross and Crown. Well-run, self-governing Pueblos meant fewer administrative headaches. Thus it was clearly a Spanish priority that such structures remain present at the Pueblos. Nowhere is this more apparent than in Governor Vargas's account of the Reconquista. After over a decade of Spanish absence—a time when the Pueblos almost certainly ceased holding annual elections for officers—one of Vargas's first actions was to see to the reestablishment of Pueblo electoral structures. He wrote extensively in his journals of efforts to recommit Pueblo Indians to elections. For example, on 18 October 1692 he gathered all the residents at Pecos Pueblo. He told the community's inhabitants to "freely elect the Indians to serve in the offices of governor, his lieutenant, an alcalde, his alguacil, two fiscales, and two war captains. They did so, presenting them before me. I received their oath to faithfully fulfill the duty of their offices, which ... [I] told them was for the greater service of both majesties [the Spanish king and Jesus Christ]." "Those elected ... were happy with the possession of their offices," he reported. Six days later, at Zia Pueblo, he replaced Governor Antonio Malacate, who "was old and could not perform the duties of his office well." A man by the name of Cristóbal, "a tall, robust Indian," was elected governor by the "elders and Indians of the Keres nation in this place," and Vargas had him "swear the oath to use his office well, making him understand the care I was ordering him to take of the Indians and what is necessary for the greater service of both majesties."[119] In these telling episodes, Vargas ordered Indians to freely elect their officers, and they obliged.

Vargas repeated these actions at each successive Pueblo, and as Spaniards slowly reconsolidated their power in New Mexico, he pursued a sort of Pueblo reeducation program in the 1690s. Again at Pecos Pueblo, this time in 1694, Vargas addressed an assembly of Pueblo leaders for the purpose of overseeing an election:

> Speaking and conferring with their cacique and governor as well as with the captains and elder Indians who are their leaders {*mandones*} and war captains ... [I] told them that in order that they may live in an orderly political manner, recognizing their leader to govern them and administer

justice among them, it was necessary for them to elect freely, meeting together as His Majesty the king, our lord, orders and directs them to do, and to present to me those elected from among those Indians best qualified and required to exercise the said offices and that I would present them with the rods of office and would receive in the name of His Majesty their oath, which they should make in recognition of the law of God our Lord and the holy cross, and which I, said governor and captain general, would confirm and approve so that he {the elected} would be and continue to serve as the head of the government of the said natives, and understanding my wishes, they assented and indicated that this was their true wish. And in fulfillment of the above, today, said day, at two o'clock in the afternoon they appeared before me bringing the rods and requesting that I, said governor and captain general, present them to the said elected persons. They were: for governor of this said pueblo, Diego Marcos; for lieutenant governor, Augustín; for *alcaldes*, Pedro Pupo and Salvador Tunoque; for captain of war, Pedro Lucero Tuque; for *alcalde unfeto, alguacil*, Pedro Cristóbal Tundias; as fiscals, Antonio Quoaes, Pedro Coctze, Diego Ystico, and Augustín Gocho; and as captains of war, Juan Chiuta as chief war captain and Miguel Echos, Juan Ombire, Miguel Himuiro, Juan Diego, Diego Stayo, don Lorenzo de Ye, and Augustín Tafuno. And to all of the said I gave the said rods and canes.... And in this form I carried out these measures and completed the said visit and election.[120]

In this rare account in which *all* the Pecos officers are listed, the formal, almost liturgical, interplay satisfied both Spaniards and Pueblos, demonstrating how the system had become accepted and workable. Vargas wrote of similar visits to San Felipe, Zia, Jemez, Santo Domingo, Tesuque, San Ildefonso, Santa Clara, Cuyamungué, Ohkay Owingeh, and other villages. In some Pueblos, residents had even held elections in anticipation of his arrival. At Santo Domingo, he stated, "And they asked that I accept their officials, whom they had already designated, which I did, and they presented the elected officials, to whom I gave the said rods and canes."[121] It is noteworthy that Vargas nearly always referred to these processes as "elections," and that he repeatedly told the Indians that they must "freely elect" their officers. He seemed almost enthusiastic about the process, and reported cooperative and eager Pueblos. That said, Pueblo compliance must be understood in conjunction with the general deployment of crushing violence on the part of the Spaniards in the 1690s, as well as a Pueblo eagerness to return, as much as possible, to peaceful life.

It is difficult to know the degree of ambivalence that Pueblo peoples felt regarding their imposed civil governments. Yet we find clues in the scores of examples from the documentary record of the actions of Pueblo officers and the communities they represented. Like Indigenous peoples throughout Spanish America, Pueblo Indians became highly skilled at using Spanish law and courts to secure and protect their rights.[122] One of the primary legal activities in which the Pueblos engaged was the protection of land. As the prominent New Mexico historians Malcolm Ebright, Rick Hendricks, and Richard W. Hughes have pointed out, "the ability of an Indian pueblo to maintain its culture and its religious life is closely linked to the pueblo's preservation of its land base."[123] In other words, for the Pueblos, as for all Indigenous peoples, land is life. Without the land within which they constructed their ritual kivas, and on which were situated the sacred landmarks that informed their geographic reckoning, the Pueblo way of life could not exist. As such, the efforts of Pueblo civil officers—governors in particular—to ensure the survival of Pueblo religion, culture, and sovereignty that were inseparably tied to Pueblo land, and the importance of elections and civil officers, become obvious. The electoral process must be viewed not simply as a way to compartmentalize and protect the inner Pueblo leadership from outside forces, or even to appease Spanish colonizers, but rather as a proactive means of securing those leaders best equipped to guarantee survival through the conservation of sacred Pueblo land.

Numerous narratives emerge of Pueblo officers boldly defending the right to control community lands, curbing constant encroachments by Spanish vecinos, and dealing with the myriad problems caused by outsiders living in their midst. These narratives illustrate how, in many cases, Pueblo officials served as powerful advocates for their people, and tell how their efforts made the crucial difference in confrontations with Spaniards. For example, in 1705 several northern Pueblos faced difficulties with Hispanos living inside their land grants.[124] These Spaniards were ostensibly there to take part in the trade with Apaches, Comanches, Utes, and other neighboring tribes. The Pueblos of Taos and Picuris were among the most prominent trading centers because of their location at the mountain passes that controlled access to the Great Plains.

In 1705 Governor Francisco Cuervo y Valdés issued an order regarding Taos and Picuris. In it, he described the "gravest disadvantages, damages, deteriorations and extortions" in the frontier Pueblos of Taos, Picuris, and Pecos that had been brought to his attention. These acts were perpetrated by "the residents of this kingdom . . . living in the pueblos and . . . those who come in from outside to trade with the heathen friends." The complaints originated with a

Pueblo governor, and Cuervo y Valdés took a hard line against these outsiders and the "grave damage" they inflicted. By order of the governor of New Mexico, then, he decreed that "no resident of the said (province), regardless of what state, quality or condition he may be in shall dare to pass to the said pueblos for any purpose whatever, or on any valid or invalid pretext, without my special permission, (under) penalty of life (as a) traitor to the King, with the confiscation of property." Those already living at the Pueblos were ordered to immediately depart. Cuervo y Valdés further ordered that the Spanish alcaldes mayores of the area publish his decree and see that all people were in compliance under penalty of a harsh fine of two hundred pesos.[125]

We can only surmise the nature of the specific "disadvantages, damages, deteriorations and extortions" in this case, but Father Juan Augustín de Morfí's "Account of Disorders in New Mexico, 1778" offers clues. Morfí wrote that while Pueblo Indians living near and frequently interacting with Spaniards were "more civilized, speak our language perfectly, embrace our customs, are more attentive to our religion, have greater respect for their property, and give better obedience to our magistrates," it was still not desirable to have outsiders living at the Pueblos. Such individuals took Pueblo land, and with "a little liquor, a few ribbons, some feathers, and other trifles of this kind, they entice the Indian who sells them his possessions, or they get him into debt. In the latter case, they turn the matter over to an *alcalde* and by using the law take away what the Indian has." They forced the Indians to pay off impossible debts through work and obligations, until the "poor Indian who had title to his lands by the same method becomes a virtual slave."[126]

He also lamented that coyotes (offspring of one mestizo and one Indian parent) and Mulattos (individuals of mixed African and Spanish heritage) living at the Pueblos, "either through an election or through selection by the local [Spanish] magistrate, he gets the job. And then, since he holds the advantage in his hand, he does what he pleases.... This kind of man is given to committing the worst sort of injustices and cruelties." Morfí was unequivocal: "All outsiders in an Indian pueblo should be expelled, as the law requires."[127] With this additional perspective it is easy to see why Pueblo governors fought so hard to expel interlopers from their communities. The abuses they suffered included shrinking homelands, outsider control of internal governance, and sexual violence.[128] Just as war chiefs had protected Pueblo communities before the Spanish invasion, Pueblo governors sought to control borders and mitigate personal outrages suffered by their citizens. These are the hallmarks of independent Pueblo republics, a status Pueblo officers continuously battled to maintain against outside efforts to the contrary.

Such battles to protect Pueblo homelands were often neither swift nor neat affairs. For example, a dispute between the Hispano Tafoya family and Santa Clara Pueblo over lands located near Santa Clara Creek dragged on for nearly two centuries. In 1724 Juan and Antonio Tafoya petitioned Governor Juan Domingo de Bustamante for land within the Pueblo's grant. The Santa Clarans protested, and an agreement was reached that the Tafoyas could only use the land for pasturage for cattle and horses. They were forbidden to use the land for agriculture, as the water from Santa Clara Creek was not sufficient for both Hispano and Pueblo needs. Over the course of the next several decades, Hispanos did not keep to this agreement, farming on the land and funneling off precious water upstream for irrigation. Time and again, Santa Clara officers argued their case, seeking to protect their lands through every means short of armed revolt.

The Santa Clarans won legal victories on a number of occasions, and New Mexico governors and lesser officials ordered Hispanos off the lands. For example, in 1763 Governor Tomás Vélez Cachupín declared the Tafoya grant null and void, quoting the *Recopilación* that grazing grants to Hispanos were to be at least a league and a half from Pueblo grants. Governor Juan Bautista de Anza reaffirmed Vélez Cachupín in 1780 as well, stating that upstream irrigation by Hispanos was forbidden. But these declarations did not stop illegal actions by the Tafoya descendants, and in 1788 the local alcalde finally ordered that Hispanos remove their cattle from Santa Clara Pueblo lands.[129] The governors' and alcalde's orders were likely never carried out, and the problems of Hispano encroachments at Santa Clara continued into the twentieth century. But this example serves to demonstrate that persistent efforts by Pueblo governors and other officers did sometimes yield favorable decisions, though these decisions were difficult to enforce.

Other examples also point to constant and nearly insurmountable battles fought by Pueblo officers to protect land. In 1704, inhabitants of San Ildefonso Pueblo took Captain Ygnacio de Roybal to court in Santa Fe over lands that he claimed to have been granted near their Pueblo. They claimed that his grant encroached on their lands, and crossed the boundaries of their original Pueblo grant. The court took testimony from Pueblo witnesses in the case, which included "Mathias Cuntzi, native governor of the native Indians of this said pueblo of San Yldephonso, and the other ministers of justice of this said pueblo." In their testimony, the elected officers claimed that, "the natives of this pueblo are hemmed in in the same (pueblo) because the Ensign Ygnazio de Roybal has intruded in the lands which belong to this said pueblo and to the natives of the same."[130]

The aforementioned Protector de Indios, Captain Alphonso Rael de Aguilar, acted on behalf of the Indians. He asked that measurements of one league in each of the cardinal directions from San Ildefonso be retaken in order to properly assess whether Roybal's land fell within the Pueblo's four-square-league boundary. The San Ildefonsans also countered Roybal's assertion that the territory under question was not arable and only good for grazing, a tactic frequently deployed by Spaniards to diminish both the land's relative value and their own illegal activities. The Indians insisted that the land was indeed arable, and that there was obvious evidence of their prior cultivation of the disputed land.[131] Spanish Governor Páez Hurtado ordered that four square leagues be measured, but the alcalde, Cristóbal de Arellano, purposely measured a full league to the north, but only a half league in the other three directions. San Ildefonso governor Matías Cuntzi, with the support of Protector Aguilar, pleaded for the correct measurement to be made and respected, but Governor Hurtado rejected the request.[132] In other land disputes, Pueblo officers-as-litigants even took their cases to Durango and Mexico City. In some instances, the Pueblos secured favorable decisions; in others, they lost. The system was unarguably tipped in favor of Spaniards. But even if it would appear that legal actions in their own defense were fools' errands, elected Pueblo officers repeatedly went before Spanish officials and courts, a clear testament to the perseverance of Pueblo peoples and their elected governments. The unfavorable results notwithstanding, elected Pueblo officers more often than not ably sought to secure Pueblo lands before the Crown.

Pueblo officers also used their power to subvert Spanish civil and ecclesiastical control. On 19 March 1748, a frustrated and frightened Fray Juan Bautista Hernández wrote from Zuni Pueblo that during that day's Feast of San José, an Indian named Thomas burst into the church as the missionary read the Mass, yelling that Apaches were attacking. Thomas called all the men to come with him to repel the assailants. But it was all a ruse to keep the Zunians from hearing the Mass. That same day, the fiscal mayor—the head of the church officers—"lost respect for me," and also chased all of the women from the church so that they could not pray. In response, Hernández "took away his staff against the torrent of all," and concluded, "God send his grace because here there is no remedy to straighten out the Indians because they are up in arms."[133] Spaniards reserved special hatred for "disloyal" officers, such as this fiscal mayor. Such actions often brought swift repercussions, as in this fiscal mayor's immediate removal from office. Missionaries were also quick to physically punish any disobedience by an officer.

In an oft-recounted example of Pueblo officers subverting colonial authority, Spanish officials opened up an investigation in 1797 at Sandia Pueblo over the fate of an Indian there named Cristóbal whom the community had accused of witchcraft. Pueblo curing societies traditionally performed specific actions and ceremonies to eradicate witchcraft in their communities. Pueblo law dictated that witches be put on trial and punished, sometimes with death. Sandia Pueblo governor Juan Domingo and War Chief Diego Antonio gathered community members at the kiva. The officers had Cristóbal bound and drawn from the roof beams of the kiva, after which they whipped him numerous times. Cristóbal was accused of using witchcraft to assist Apaches in a raid on the Pueblo, which resulted in the loss of several livestock and other items. He confessed after the lashing, but the abuse continued, leading ultimately to Cristóbal's death. While local Spanish officials submitted reports to Santa Fe, the Pueblo's leadership took action to silence community members, and Spanish officials found their investigation difficult to pursue. New Mexico Governor Fernando de Chacón, who reviewed the case, decided that the evidence was too weak to bring criminal proceedings against the Sandia Pueblo officials, and that the case was not worth the risk of inciting the Indians. Chacón thus ordered the investigation halted.[134] Spanish law allowed governors and war chiefs to punish only minor offences, and never with death. Cristóbal's punishment and death, though unfortunate, must be seen as an effort by Sandia Pueblo to administer its own justice in the traditional way, while incorporating the new civil officers into that practice.

Perhaps the most dramatic use of Pueblo office to oppose Spanish authority came from Esteban Clemente of Abó Pueblo, "the most Hispanicized, honored, and trusted Pueblo Indian east of the Rio Grande." Clemente, who had been educated by Spanish Franciscans and received the honorary title of "don" (*de origen noble*, "of nobility"), was given the pan-governorship of the Las Salinas Pueblos.[135] He had been such a staunch supporter of Spanish goals that he personally penned a letter in 1660 denouncing masked Pueblo katsina dances, which he characterized as "evil."[136] It appears that don Esteban soured of the Spaniards at some point in the 1660s, however, as he reappears in the historical record, having attempted to organize a general revolt of the Pueblos in 1670, ten years before the Pueblo Revolt. It was reported that Governor Clemente intended to drive all Spanish horses to the countryside to prevent the Spaniards from escaping, and then kill indiscriminately, "not leaving a single religious or Spaniard." Spaniards discovered the plot, and hanged don Esteban, while the rest of the rebellion's supporters were "quieted." When they searched his home, they found "a large number of idols and entire kettles full of idolatrous powdered herbs, feathers, and other trifles."[137] In an interesting contrast to the future leader of the Pueblo Revolt of 1680, Po'pay,[138] Clemente was a Hispanicized Pueblo governor and loyal Spanish ally, yet he too seemingly returned to traditional Pueblo practices and hoped to expel the Spaniards, using skills and knowledge he obtained as a governor in the Pueblo-Spanish electoral system.

The Pueblo-Spanish system also created opportunities for collective action by the Pueblos. The previously cited example of Indian governors and officers who traveled to Santa Fe in January 1706 was more than just a confirmation of república officials. In his statement, Captain don Alfonso Rael de Aguilar related that the governors and justices from the Zuni, Jemez, Taos, Pecos, Picuris, and the Keres, Tewa, Tano, and Tiwa Pueblos "all came together, having been incited thereto each by the other, asking me to hear them as their protector-general on certain subjects upon which they had conferred, and which had been dealt with and discussed in their pueblos by the old men, the chiefs, and the men, children, and women." Aguilar summarized statements made by Pueblo officers on this occasion: "Don Domingo Romero [governor of Tesuque] began to speak in our Castilian tongue (in which he is very well instructed)." Romero stated that he had "called together all the governors, chiefs, and other captains who were there present" because they were "exceedingly well satisfied, pleased, and content with [their] good treatment" from then-governor and captain general of New Mexico Francisco Cuervo y Valdez. They praised Governor Cuervo for his swift actions in assisting them, especially the most remote frontier Pueblos, against the Apaches, "who killed many of their people and robbed them of their scant stores," and also against the Navajos, "who had stolen some beasts and cattle from the towns of San Ildefonso, Santa Clara, and San Juan [Ohkay Owingeh]." This invaluable document gives the names of many of the Pueblo governors: Don Felipe Chistoe (Pecos); Don Juan Pacheco (Taos); Don Christóbal Corís (Santo Domingo); Francisco Enjenoe (Nambé); Don Luis Conitzu (Jemez); Don Luis Romero (Cochiti); Don Antonio Cossío (Zia); Don Felipe (Santa Ana, no surname given); and Don Joseph (Acoma, also no surname). These men spoke Castilian and asked that Cuervo be kept in power for a long time. According to Aguilar, those who only spoke their Native languages "said the same thing through their interpreters."[139]

Aside from its value as a rare document that names a great number of the Pueblo civil leadership in a given year, it also speaks to the role played by elected Pueblo leaders. The officers came to Santa Fe to address "certain subjects *upon which they had conferred*," meaning that they had gathered beforehand as Pueblo magistrates to discuss these matters. This can be interpreted as an early example of the All Indian Pueblo Council (AIPC), with governors meeting to counsel on important issues that concerned all of the Pueblos. Pueblo tradition places the founding of the AIPC at 1598, when thirty-eight leaders from the Pueblos met with Oñate at Santo Domingo, although Pueblo oral history asserts that "a semblance" of the organization existed before the arrival of Europeans in New Mexico.[140] In addition, the civil officers related that these issues "had been dealt with and discussed in their pueblos by the old men, the chiefs, and the men, children, and women." Although this account is filtered through a Spaniard, it seems to give a much more inclusive view of Pueblo internal discourse, one where leaders and others, including women and children, had a voice. Clearly, Pueblo office was also at times a cooperative affair, as certain situations required pan-Pueblo action.

Knowing what Pueblo officers did helps to clarify what they must have known and who they must have been, even though the vast majority of them remain anonymous in the conventional historical record. As Ortiz explained, those chosen to serve as war chiefs or war captains oversaw traditional observances and ceremonies. It was essential that they possess "a firm commitment to and knowledge of native ritual." Those who served in the civil offices—governor, lieutenant governor, sheriffs, etc.—had an entirely different set of requirements. As the moiety chiefs gathered to nominate men for these offices, they looked for those with "demonstrated ability in dealing with the outside world. The primary requirements in the past were that the nominees know the Spanish language and Spanish institutions." Similarly, nominees for fiscales were those "well versed in Catholicism, in addition to knowing the Spanish language."[141]

While New Mexico had always been a borderland, where various Indigenous nations met for trade and battled for resources, the presence of the Spanish colonial machine created new types of border crossers. Pueblo officers who met with their local alcalde, or traveled to Santa Fe to petition the governor, were traversing cultural and physical borders that required new bodies of knowledge. Even Pueblo villages became bordered in ways not known before, with the mission complex and its associated church, fields, and buildings creating new delineations in the community.[142] Knowledge of sacred landmarks—mountains, hills, shrines—had previously ordered the Pueblo world and boundaries between the community and the outside, but Pueblos now needed to know the boundaries between their land grants and Spanish possessions, Pueblo and Spanish law, and traditional Pueblo practices and Spanish expectations. It was an evolving world in which the Pueblo and the Spanish became increasingly intertwined and difficult to disentangle, and yet the survival of the community was located within the spaces between the two. A Pueblo election was, therefore, a serious affair. It could not simply be left to chance, or foisted upon an inept or unequipped lackey. With the survival of the community at stake, only men who could navigate the immensely complex cultural, religious, legal, and physical borderlands would suffice. Some did their job poorly and were removed from office, as we shall see. But the majority of these Pueblo border-crossers performed in a workmanlike, anonymous manner, and thereby helped insure the survival of their communities. Their main qualifications were knowledge and a commitment to service.

Violence in the Pueblo Electoral System

The archive is replete with examples of varying degrees of conflict and violence over Pueblo elections and officers. For starters, Pueblo election disputes, though seemingly rare, did occur during the Spanish period. For example, during Governor Pedro Rodríguez Cubero's term (1697–1703), reports came in of a dispute over the governorship at Zuni Pueblo. The cacique, Juan, apparently was upset because "the [governor's] cane was taken from him." A Zuni named Antonio was serving, and Cubero ordered Captain Juan de Ulibarrí to investigate whether Antonio "was elected as governor of Zuni Pueblo with the agreement and at the pleasure of all the Indians or whether this was done based on the opinion of the [Spanish] alcalde mayor, José Naranjo, and not that of the Indians." If the latter was true, Ulibarrí was to return the governor's cane to "don Juan, the cacique of Zuni Pueblo." Spaniards collected testimony from a number of witnesses on the matter, and Captain Ulibarrí found that the people were "very happy [with Antonio as governor] and confess that he fulfills his duties better than don Juan, who, though at first sad to give up control (since because of it, he had been made governor), is today very happy."[143] It would appear that the dispute ended favorably for all, with the cacique relenting even though he might have preferred to retain the governorship.

Pueblo communities also showed a willingness to fight for their elected officers. A relatively brief 1815 letter from the Comandante General of Durango, Bernardo Bonavía, instructs New Mexico Governor Alberto Maynez regarding Pueblo officers. The governor of Cochiti Pueblo, identified as Juan Antonio Ignacio, along with other officials, collectively referred to in the letter as the Pueblo's *Justiciales* (Justices), complained after several of Cochiti's officials had been removed from office. Pedro Bautista Pino, the Hispano statesman who represented the province at the Spanish Cortes at Cádiz from 1810–12, had previously filed the complaint on behalf of the Pueblo officers. The letter does not give the reasons why the Pueblo officers had been removed, but it was made very clear to Governor Maynez that this intervention should not have happened. Bonavía ordered Governor Maynez to "Immediately restore them to the exercise of their responsibilities." He further wrote, "Even if there had been cause [for removal], you should not have removed them from their offices; if this were the case, this would fall under my jurisdiction." A note in the margin indicates that two officials were "put in possession of their jobs," but the names of these officers were Juan Roque and Toribio, indicating that Cochiti's governor was not reinstated. The episode demonstrates that while Pueblo officers had recourse to legal channels, Hispano officials in New Mexico still retained a higher degree of power.[144]

Conversely, Pueblo peoples frequently petitioned Spanish officials for the removal of abusive officers. For example, in 1788 Indians of Santa Clara complained to the provincial government about their governor, Antonio Naranjo. Claiming that he was abusive in the extreme, having broken his staff over the head of his Pueblo's fiscal mayor and assaulted the sacristan. According to the complainants, Governor Naranjo had acted in this manner "since the hour he was elected," and over time his behavior had only worsened, so that he acted "more like a stepfather than a father of that Republic."[145] The language of the complaint is intriguing. The Indians were presenting themselves as citizens of the Indian republic of Santa Clara, and their characterization of Naranjo as a stepfather corresponds with Pueblo tradition that viewed the governor as a sort of father to the community.[146] As a result of their complaint, Naranjo was removed from office and a new election for governor ordered.[147] This episode raises unanswered questions about the power of civil officers. Was Naranjo's power so entrenched that his removal could not be accomplished internally? Was this due to support from tribal members or Spaniards? Would a removal carried out by and at the Pueblo, along with a new gubernatorial installation, not have been recognized by Spanish officials? Perhaps the people of the Pueblo feared further violence and saw Spain as an acceptable power broker.

Conflicts also arose between civil officers and traditional leadership. When Pueblo officers swore allegiance to Church and Crown, receiving canes and the right to govern in exchange, there was always the possibility that this new power could lead to divided loyalties on their part. In 1771, at Isleta Pueblo, a case initially involving stolen sheep at the Pueblo led the governor and war captain to bring complaints against the cacique. He was accused of numerous offenses, including helping his friends escape punishment for crimes they had committed, and—interestingly—taking actions "in the name of all of the Pueblo, without the consent of the governor, the fiscal mayor, or the principals." Spaniards who investigated the complaints wanted to know whether the cacique had acted on behalf of the Spanish king or whether he saw himself as a sovereign. Several Indians gave testimony, and the Spanish alcalde mayor concluded that the Indians of Isleta "probably" saw the cacique as a king. The governor of New Mexico, Pedro Fermín de Mendinueta, ordered that the cacique "no longer use that name," effectively removing him from sacred office and telling the Isletans that they "only have to obey the Governor, and those officials whom they annually elect."[148]

These conflicting loyalties were on full display during the Pueblo Revolt of 1680. As Pueblo scholars have pointed out, those who planned the Revolt were primarily war chiefs and war captains. Governors were not included in the planning because their authority came through the Spanish system and their loyalty and interests were therefore suspect. They also singled out specific leaders seen as disloyal, such as Governor Juan de Ye of Pecos Pueblo.[149] After the Spaniards had been forced to flee, taking up refuge in El Paso del Norte, a witness statement from a Pueblo Indian identified only as Juan related how Po'Pay, the Ohkay Owingeh holy man and leader of the Revolt, communicated with the devil and received his instructions from him. Juan also asserted that Po'pay killed his own son-in-law, a man by the name of Nicolás Bua, who also happened to be the governor of Ohkay Owingeh Pueblo. Juan contended that Po'pay had killed Bua "so that he might not warn the Spaniards of the rebellion, as he intended to do."[150]

Ortiz has disputed this account, stating that Po'pay, as a religious leader, "could not have taken life of any kind—or knowingly participated in its taking."[151] Two facts are not in dispute: governors were generally excluded from planning the Revolt; and there were loyal Pueblo officers in a number of locations. The Revolt nearly failed because Spanish Governor Antonio Otermín had received warnings in the days leading up the rebellion: "[I] received notice of the said rebellion from the governors of Pecos and Tanos... they came to tell me of it and of how they were unwilling to participate in such wickedness and treason, saying that they now regarded the Spaniards as their brothers."[152] Were such Pueblo governors simply sellouts more loyal to Spain than to their own people? Whatever their motivations—whether Spanish clothing and goods, exemption from communal labor, or a coveted seat in church services—some Pueblo officers made the choice to support the Spanish cause, further dividing their communities at a time when the Pueblo world seemed to be coming apart at the seams.

After twelve years of freedom from Spanish colonialism, the Pueblos confronted armed conquest for a second time. They staged a series of revolts in the 1690s in an attempt to maintain their independence. Under these circumstances, Governor Vargas found one of his most loyal allies in Governor Felipe Chistoe of Pecos Pueblo. In 1696, Chistoe appeared before Vargas in Santa Fe. He requested royal permission to hang a number of rebellious Indians present at Pecos, including some from Jemez and Nambé. Vargas wrote of telling Chistoe, "you can summon them to your house at night by reason of speaking about the people of the rebellious pueblos. In this way, you can surely succeed in killing them." He reported that Chistoe expressed that this advice "seemed good to him, and he told me he would do it." In the ensuing episode, Chistoe, an Indian governor loyal to Spain, tricked rebel Pueblo Indians into coming to discuss conspiracy plans and then executed them. Chistoe lured the Jemez, Nambé, and Pecos rebels into the Pecos kiva, where he asked for their opinion of the revolt. One of the rebel leaders, Diego Umviro of Jemez, expressed support for the insurrection because Spaniards "were of a different blood." In response, Governor Chistoe brandished his vara de justicia and announced, "Here [we are] for the king." Chistoe's men seized these leaders, and hanged Diego Umviro and three others.[153]

One rebel escaped, but Chistoe later chased him down and shot him personally. Governor Vargas recorded the grisly events in his journal: "[Felipe brought] his harquebus close to [the escaped rebel's] temple, [and] the governor killed him with a shot. He sent me his head, hand, and foot, so that this may be of record to me. When all the citizens of this villa saw them, they were surprised at this Indian's loyalty. I thanked him and gave him and the others gifts."[154] The episode resulted in two factions at Pecos Pueblo, with the families of Diego Umviro and the other executed Indians attempting to oust Felipe Chistoe in 1700. They failed in their attempt, were jailed in Santa Fe, but escaped. On five occasions, the two parties came perilously close to civil war at Pecos Pueblo. Chistoe's faction won each showdown, thanks largely to Spanish support, but the infighting severely weakened the Pueblo. This was one of the causes of its eventual abandonment in the nineteenth century. This violent example illustrates how, in the extreme, the Pueblo-Spanish electoral system could significantly contribute to the demise of an entire community.[155] That a few Pueblo officers were willing to betray their communities, and even kill for the Spaniards, throws the violence inherent in the system into stark relief.

Genízaros in Spanish New Mexico

Genízaros present a unique dimension to the history of Indian voting and sovereignty in Spanish New Mexico. Although the meaning of the term evolved over the course of the Spanish period, genízaro generally designated captive Indians who had been "ransomed" (bought) by Spanish settlers or officials, and placed in Spanish homes to work off the cost, in a system that featured elements of both slavery and indentured servitude. Spaniards expected genízaros to adopt Spanish culture through Spanish education and Catholic religious instruction. Over time genízaros also came to include Pueblo Christian Indians who, for one reason or another, had left or been forced out of their Pueblos and gone to live with other genízaros or Christian Indians.[156] Genízaros occupied a complicated space between cultures as neither fully Spanish nor fully Indian. It was both an imposed racial category and, over time, an ethnic identity embraced by genízaro communities.[157] In 1744, Fray Miguel de Menchero described genízaros as Indians "of the various nations that have been taken captive by the Comanche Apaches" who would then "sell people of all the nations to the Spaniards of the kingdom, by whom they are held in servitude, the adults being instructed by the fathers and the children baptized."[158] Descendants of captives also held this designation. Morfí wrote that Spaniards designated "the children of the captives of different nations [of] the province" as genízaros. One definition that reduces the term to its essence is simply "detribalized Indian."

With a burgeoning captive trade in New Mexico during the colonial era (and after), large numbers of genízaros lived both in Spanish households and in ethnic enclaves and towns, with some even receiving their own land grants. By the late 1700s, roughly one-third of New Mexico's population was genízaro.[159] Genízaro neighborhoods, or barrios, kept them segregated as a group, and also enabled them to develop a distinctive group identity, particularly as warriors, for they were, according to Morfí, "fine soldiers, very warlike, and most formidable against our enemies."[160] It was more than an expectation that genízaros fight for the Crown; it was an obligation. Menchero wrote that they were "under obligation to go out and explore the country in pursuit of the enemy, which they are doing with great bravery and zeal."[161] Their status as warriors was tied to their position in-between Spanish and Indian worlds: "forced to live among the Spaniards without lands," and without other means, they were forced to subsist "by the bow and arrow."[162] In spite of their unquestioned value as warriors, Spaniards stigmatized genízaros for their Indianness and low social position as household servants, even after they completed their period of indenture.[163] There is also evidence that Pueblo Indians sometimes viewed genízaros unfavorably. Because they came from enemy tribes, the Pueblos, who "bear long grudges, never admit them to their pueblos."[164]

In the face of such challenges, genízaros mobilized as communities in a bid to assert their rights as wards of the Crown and Church, much as Pueblo Indians did during the Spanish period. In so doing, they attempted to sidestep whatever detrimental legal status they occupied.[165] Genízaros had some of the same rights and entitlements as Pueblo Indians, but not all. Genízaro communities were not Indian republics. But, their members could sue in court, and on many occasions they won favorable verdicts. For example, in one case from 1780 a group of thirty-four genízaros complained about a plan that would have removed them from their homes in Santa Fe and sent them to the Comanche frontier. They even threatened to rejoin their former tribes in response: "We find ourselves burdened and without having anything in our favor. This affliction has forced us to have idle thoughts, as to whether we shall suffer our anxieties and hardships or shall leave in order to seek comfort in our domain and tribe."[166] Genízaros had thus successfully petitioned the Commander General of the Provincias Internas in Arizpe, Sonora, when Governor Anza attempted to remove them from Santa Fe.[167]

Genízaros recognized their own leaders, known as *cabesas* (heads), as well as captains. These leaders were the men who argued for genízaro causes in the courts.[168] Examples of formal genízaro petitions and court cases pepper the archival record, illustrating genízaro access to legal redress, but the limitations of that access are also on display. For example, in a 1746 land dispute at the genízaro community of Belén, where genízaros tried to claim land protections as an Indian pueblo, they were referred to as "haughty half breeds, recently converted to the lady of our Holy mother church, and incapable of petitions or demands as judged by affiant, that the said Antonio Casados [who brought suit claiming he had been granted land] is the one that incites them with his captiousness as he is well versed in the castillian language, that he is no chief, captain or any thing else."[169] These remarks notwithstanding, their status as warriors, and their ability to mobilize, did secure genízaros some power in New Mexico.

At the village of Abiquiu, in north central New Mexico, genízaros received a land grant in 1754, and occupied their lands alongside neighboring Hispanos. In 1820, near the end of the Spanish period, by which time constitutional ayuntamientos proliferated in New Mexico (as we shall later see), genízaros participated in these ayuntamientos alongside Hispanos. Abiquiu's genízaros formed a political alliance with their Hispano neighbors in order to protest the actions of the local Franciscan priest, Teodoro Alcina, who had actively sought to buy as much Abiquiu land as possible. Genízaros and Hispanos accused him of a number of additional offenses. The two groups presented a unified front at the local court, but a strange exchange took place in which the friar purportedly damned the District of Abiquiu. The next day, a severe hailstorm destroyed much of the local crops, and then locusts ate what was left.[170] While the courts and Spanish officials had viewed Abiquiu as an Indian pueblo during this time, and this and other genízaro communities attained a relatively high degree of autonomy, their status as self-governing Indian communities with protected land rights were continually questioned. The court cases originating at Abiquiu dragged on well into the Mexican period, and were not resolved until the United States Land Claims Court reached a decision in the first decade of the twentieth century.[171] All of this illustrates the difficult and sometimes fluid status of one of New Mexico's Indian groups. As it pertains to voting and town governing institutions, genízaro and Pueblo experiences diverged in important ways.[172]

Conclusion

The legacy of New Mexico's Pueblo Indian electoral system under Spain is a mixed one. On the one hand, the Pueblos established methods—according to the needs and traditions of the individual community—of electing governors and other officers who served their people in critical ways, securing their rights as semisovereign repúblicas de indios. Pueblo civil officers possessed the knowledge necessary to cross physical, cultural, religious, and legal borders in order to advocate for their communities. In so doing, they largely succeeded in an era of crushing colonial impositions, as Pueblo communities carefully incorporated, indigenized, and subverted Spanish institutions. Civil offices failed to supplant traditional Pueblo leaders, despite persistent Spanish efforts to the contrary. Still, it must be recognized that Spain sought a form of incorporation that proved very sinister. Pueblo Indians were simultaneously forced into colonial spheres and excluded from Spanish society. While they fought to retain much of their culture, language, and institutions, they did so without all of the rights and privileges granted to Spaniards. For generations, Pueblo Indians were forced to provide tribute and labor, while also being dictated what to wear, eat, and ride.[173]

Furthermore, the Spanish system, which envisioned a Pueblo transition to tax-paying citizenship, did not allow Pueblos to make such a transition as Indians. In 1815, a group of Santa Clara Indians by the name of Canjuebes petitioned to retain title to lands at the Pueblo. These Santa Clarans had become "Indios Vecinos," or citizen Indians. The instructions from Durango to New Mexico Governor Alberto Máynez were clear: if the Natives wanted to retain lands within the Pueblo grant, they must once again move back to the Pueblo. If they remained outside the Pueblo and lived as vecinos, they would have to buy whatever lands they needed with cash, "as it is with all Spanish vecinos of this province."[174] In short, they could not have it both ways, and Pueblo Indians did not leave their communities and become vecinos in large numbers. In accepting and modifying elections and civil governing structures only to a certain degree, the Pueblos thereby preserved their land and culture, and avoided total incorporation and subsumption into Spanish colonial society.

It is also noteworthy that at various points over the course of the eighteenth century, the bulwark of local Spanish municipal government in New Mexico, the Santa Fe cabildo, experienced "a demise in its importance." For extended periods during the colonial era, New Mexico's Hispano communities had no popularly elected town councils. This diminution of democratic local government in New Mexico's Spanish towns did not begin to abate until after the Bourbon Reforms of the 1780s and beyond.[175] The Pueblo repúblicas seem to have experienced no such interruptions, excepting, of course, during the Pueblo Revolt, and the Pueblos continued to select officers from year-to-year throughout the Spanish period. The irony is that the Pueblos practiced their form of limited democratic self-government during periods when their Spanish counterparts exercised no such rights. New Mexico's repúblicas de indios withstood the turmoil that unfolded as Spain's empire in the Western Hemisphere unraveled, which is remarkable considering the political and cultural pressures exerted on them by vecinos, military officers, magistrates, and clergy. That this form of civil government, with governors, lieutenant governors, fiscales, and, most importantly, Pueblo electorates, still exists today is a mark of its utility, resilience, and importance throughout the Pueblo world.

CHAPTER TWO

Hopis, Yaquis, and O'odhams in the Spanish Arizona-Sonora Borderlands
Political Incorporation by Degrees

For over two centuries, Spain struggled to successfully congregate, convert, and incorporate the Pueblo Indians of New Mexico. To the west of the province lay another vast landscape of Indigenous nations, one in which myriad peoples had lived and thrived for generations. As with their eastern Pueblo neighbors, these peoples would over time feel the force of Spanish domination, with missions and presidios dotting their river valleys. While the Pueblo sense of shared culture and origin eventually came to include a fairly unified colonial experience, Indigenous peoples in the Arizona-Sonora Borderlands experienced Spanish colonization in a more varied, uneven manner. While many of these Indigenous nations largely escaped Spanish colonialism, the differing locations, civil administrations, and religious orders resulted in a wide spectrum of political incorporation for those who did not. This chapter examines three groups whose experiences in forging Indian electorates vary as widely as their geographical settings: Hopis, Yaquis, and O'odhams. All three of these Indigenous groups fall within the same Uto-Aztecan language family, and align geographically more or less along a north-south axis. But their alignment within the Indian-Spanish political experience could not be more pronounced.

In the northern reaches of the Arizona-Sonora Borderlands, Hopis lived on their high-desert mesas while farming the valleys below. As part of the province of New Mexico, they confronted the same Spanish colonial machinery as the Pueblo peoples to the east. But the Franciscans who ventured into the Hopi homelands in the seventeenth century, seeking to establish mission communities and transform Hopis to Spaniards, failed miserably. Hopis not only violently expelled Spaniards from their mesas, but they also massacred their own people in brutal fashion, thereby destroying nearly all traces of a Spanish Hopi Indian republic. In the far south of Sonora, along the river that bears their name, lived the Yaquis. In many respects, the effort to incorporate Yaquis into the Spanish body politic met with success. They reduced from scores of rancherías to eight principal mission towns, and organized those towns in the Spanish municipal model. But such actions belied a deep Yaqui ambivalence toward the colonial system. In the 1730s and 1740s, elected Yaqui officials confronted

Spanish religious and state power in an unapologetic show of sovereignty, demanding that their rights as Yaqui repúblicas de indios be respected. Occupying a middle ground both geographically and politically, O'odhams experienced the repeated, sputtering attempts at missionization by Jesuits as well as Franciscans. In the harsh region of the Sonoran Desert known as Pimería Alta, O'odhams seemingly welcomed forays by the zealous Father Eusebio Francisco Kino and those who came in his wake. But O'odham incorporation proved elusive. Cross and Crown never accomplished their goal of tax-paying, voting, Catholic O'odhams. The results of the Spanish project aimed at forging Indigenous electorates in the Arizona-Sonora Borderlands were as varied and disparate as the landscapes that these peoples continue to inhabit, and it was these Indigenous peoples who played the biggest part in determining outcomes.

Hopis, the "Most Famous Apostates"

Discussions of Spanish New Mexico sometimes leave out the distant western Pueblo people, the Hopis. They were, administratively, part of the Kingdom of New Mexico. Hopis fell under the jurisdiction of Santa Fe, having dealings with Spanish governors, soldiers, and missionaries. But the various representatives of Cross and Crown only exercised a fleeting hold over Hopi land and peoples, and never fully brought the Hopi mesas under administrative, military, or religious control. Over the centuries, Hopis allied with their eastern neighbors on numerous occasions, enjoying their closest ties with Zuni Pueblo to the southeast. But distance, language, and culture separated the Uto-Aztecan-speaking Hopis from the Tewa, Tiwa, Towa, Keresan, and Zunian Pueblos. Joe Sando wrote that although Hopis were "within the Pueblo family," their "progress in history [has] tended to individualize their social structure, their issues, and their responses to events." Furthermore, while the heritage of the other Pueblos is "freely sprinkled with Hispanic traditions," Hopi heritage is not.[1] Isolation and separation—from both other Pueblos as well as imperial powers—are key factors in understanding the Hopi colonial experience. As we will see, Spain failed to firmly establish a Hopi república, and this failure would deeply influence the course of Hopi history moving forward.

Spaniards invaded the Hopi mesas of what is today northern Arizona as early as the 1540s, during the Coronado expedition. Spanish accounts tell that when Coronado dispatched Pedro de Tovar to Hopi, he met resistance at the outskirts of Kawayk'a on Antelope Mesa. His men charged the Hopi warriors while shouting "Santiago [Saint James]!" The Hopis retreated to the safety of

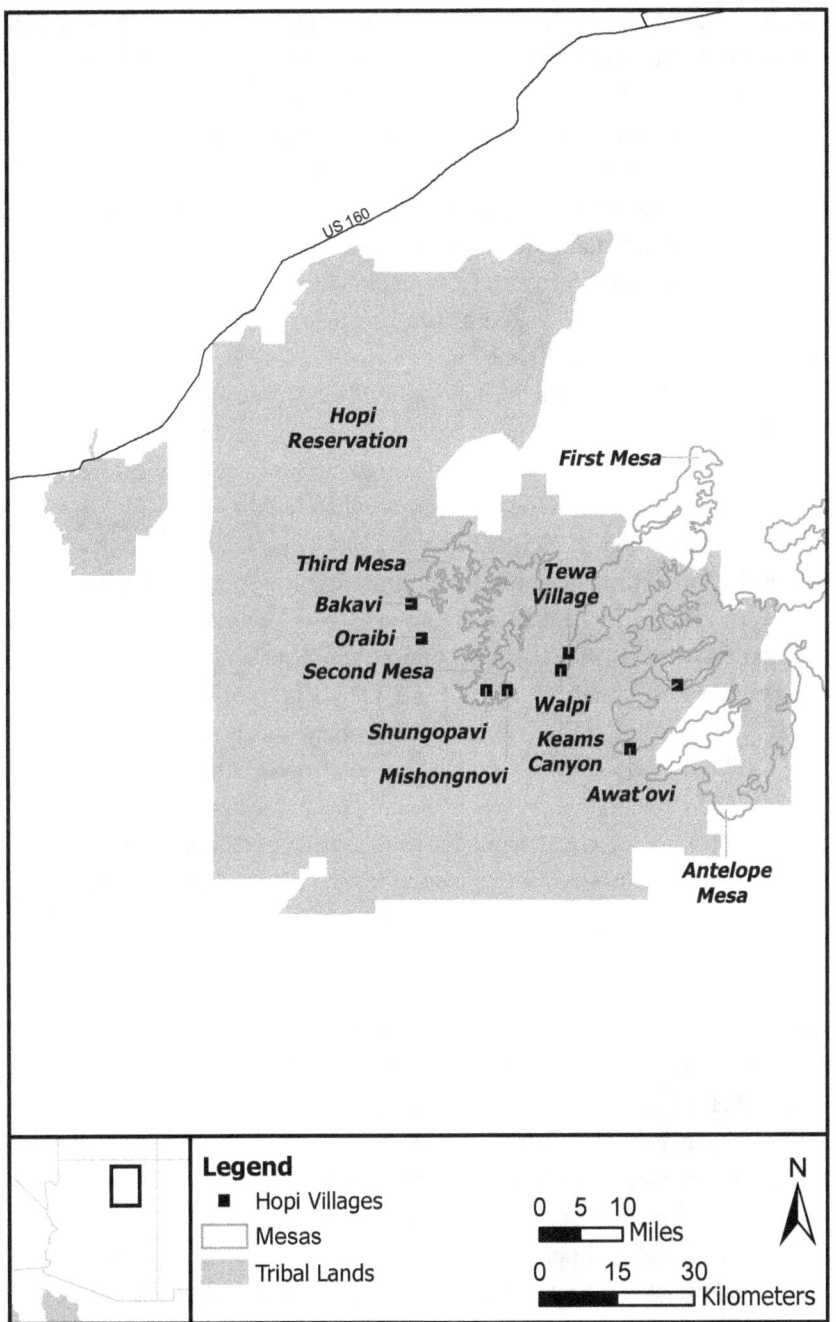

Hopi Territory. Map by Alex Ochoa.

their mesa, but later returned bearing gifts. In observing Hopi villages and their governing structures, Pedro de Castañeda, who was a member of Coronado's party, wrote that the Hopi province was "governed like Cíbola [Zuni] by a council of the eldest people. They have their appointed governors and chiefs." He even used the term "ayuntamiento" to describe the Hopi village council in an early superimposition of Spanish forms. Hopi oral accounts, on the other hand, relate that Spaniards destroyed Kawayk'a after Hopis killed five of their party, and violence characterized Coronado's foray to the Hopi homelands.[2] Hopi-Tewa Albert Yava related in the late 1900s that when the people of Kawayk'a "didn't accept" Tovar, "he attacked that village and destroyed it."[3] There would be more encounters—notably Antonio de Espejo's 1582–83 expedition—but Hopi-Spanish contacts from Coronado through Juan de Oñate did not significantly alter Hopi culture or lifeways. They did, however, foretell the violent Spanish policies that would follow.

When Oñate opened New Mexico to permanent Spanish colonization in 1598, he followed the familiar pattern of ceremonially subjecting Hopis to Spanish royal authority. In a document penned by Juan Velarde, Oñate's secretary, dated 21 February 1599, Velarde recounted the meeting between Spaniards, Hopi leaders, and "common people" from "Oraybi [Oraibi], Xumupami [Shungopavi], Cuaurabi, and Esperiez [it is unknown to which villages he was referring]." Through don Tomás, an Indian interpreter, Oñate declared, "He [Oñate] had come to their lands to bring them to the knowledge of God and the king our lord, on which depended the salvation of their souls *and their living securely and undisturbed in their nation, maintaining justice and order*, secure in their homes and protected from their enemies, and that he had not come to do them any harm.... [I]t was fitting that they should render obedience and vassalage to God and the king." Oñate also declared that he planned to "employ them in many offices and posts in connection with political and economic matters, as would be explained more at length to them later." Spain thus included Hopis in its plan to force Pueblo peoples to adopt a Spanish form of civil governance and to establish repúblicas de indios. Velarde concluded his account of the Hopi-Spanish encounter by stating that the Hopi "chiefs, having heard, understood, and discussed among themselves all the aforesaid, replied, with signs of spontaneous contentment and agreement, that they wished to become vassals of the most Christian king our lord."[4] As with the eastern Pueblos, the extent to which Hopis understood this swearing of vassalage to the Spanish monarch and God is questionable, but Spain clearly intended to place Hopis under the control of Cross and Crown. Hopi actions must be seen as a strategy of first welcoming Spaniards and then sending them on their way,

Burros and Moki Men on the Road, ca. 1900. These Hopis are traveling on the flatlands, while one of the mesas can be seen in the background. Edward S. Curtis Collection, Prints and Photographs Division, Library of Congress, LC-USZ62-112229.

all in an effort to avoid violent conflict and maintain territorial sovereignty. But Spaniards were beginning to see the strategic importance of the Hopi mesas as a stopping point in their expeditions to the west and California.[5]

One might expect that Oñate's visit to Hopi and the subsequent permanent colonizing mission would change life dramatically for the Hopis, but they had little immediate effect.[6] Hopis were the clear exception among New Mexico's Puebloans, as the Pueblo communities to the east experienced immediate and sweeping changes under Spanish political, military, and religious administration. Contacts with Hopis in the wake of Oñate's visit remained infrequent. This was likely a result of the distance from Santa Fe and the nearest Spanish installations, as well as the aridity and lack of permanent streams to support Spanish settlers.[7] Thirty more years passed before Spaniards committed the manpower and resources necessary to bring Hopis firmly into the Spanish colonial sphere.

In August 1629, Padre Fray Francisco de Porras, Padre Fray Andrés Gutiérrez, and lay brother Cristóbal de la Concepción, along with an escort of twelve soldiers, established the first Hopi mission at Awat'ovi. According to a

Spanish report, "an apostate Indian from the Christian pueblos" arrived in advance of the Franciscans, warning the Hopis that the Spaniards soon to appear would "burn their pueblos, rob their haciendas, and behead their children." He also told them that those "with tonsures [shaved heads] and habits were liars; and that [the Hopis] should not allow water to be poured on their heads, because they would die right away."[8] The Hopis were pacified, however, when the friars' escort of soldiers threatened to call on the governor of New Mexico to bring an entire army to their land to burn and destroy them if they made any threatening movements.[9] Spaniards attributed Hopi pacification to the power of the Christian God, yet the threat of destruction must certainly have been the most convincing factor in the Hopi decision not to attack and destroy the small Spanish religious-military party that arrived in 1629. After all, two Hopi men had witnessed the 1599 massacre at Acoma. Spaniards had taken them prisoners and cut one of each man's hands off before releasing them so that they could warn all Indians with whom they came in contact about the deadly seriousness of Spanish intentions. These events were deeply ingrained in the Hopi memory, and likely influenced the decision to allow the Spaniards to remain.

Alonso de Benavides related the events of the previous year in his 1630 account, *A Harvest of Reluctant Souls* (a more appropriate title of the Hopi missionary efforts could not exist). He attributed the pacification, and subsequent permission granted to the Franciscans to stay in the Hopi villages, to miraculous circumstances. According to Benavides, the Hopis at Awat'ovi who greeted Porras in 1629 initially venerated the cross. Hopi "sorcerers" became enraged at this sight, stirring up their people almost to the point of killing the priest and his companions. In an account mirroring the biblical story of Elijah's showdown with the priests of Baal in 1 Kings, the Hopi holy men produced a "boy of twelve or thirteen, blind from birth, born with his eyes shut tight" and challenged Porras, whom they called "an incredible liar," to put their cross to the boy's eyes and heal his blindness. Just as Baal's priests had failed in the Old Testament, so too had the Hopi priests been powerless to help the boy. Porras, playing the part of Elijah, dramatically dropped to his knees, imploring God to "confound those barbarous infidels" and grant him the faith to work this miracle. He healed the boy, who was then hoisted up by the villagers and paraded around with loud cries for all to believe the padre and be baptized.[10]

It made for a great story, one in which King Philip IV of Spain, to whom it was written, would have reveled. But even Benavides commented that the Spaniards were unharmed in 1629 "on account of the vigilance of the soldiers." Then, almost correcting himself, he stated that it was even more "because of divine aid."[11] As entertaining as this episode is, Hopi oral tradition makes absolutely no mention of it. A group of Hopi experts from the Hopi History Project, meeting in October 2009, discussed Porras's alleged miracle. They did not dismiss the possibility of miracles having accompanied the works of the Franciscans, but all agreed that if true Porras's act would certainly have made its way into their oral traditions. They concluded that Benavides's account was "clearly the case of a falsehood becoming enshrined in the Spanish documentary record."[12] The safest conclusion is that a desire to avoid bloodshed led Hopis to allow the Spanish presence.

On the heels of these opening episodes, Franciscans oversaw the construction of three large stone mission churches at Awat'ovi, Shungopavi, and Oraibi. Hopis literally did all the heavy lifting, providing the stones for building and all the labor, even hauling huge trees from the San Francisco Peaks near Flagstaff, a trip that today takes well over two hours by car and covers more than one hundred miles each way. The mission at Awat'ovi was built directly on top of a kiva, thereby announcing the arrival of a "superior" faith.[13] Franciscans also established smaller, satellite churches, called *visitas*, at Walpi and Mishongnovi.[14] Whether the missionary success was due to some combination of kindness, mysticism, threats, punishment, or disruption of the old religious order, as the historian James Brooks has wondered,[15] Hopi oral history overwhelmingly points to the cruelty of the Franciscans who labored there.

Albert Yava recalled that at Awat'ovi, the Franciscans were "pretty successful at converting the people," and "eventually more than half the population allowed itself to be baptized, and the ones resisting were the minority." But the Franciscans were "quite severe" with their Hopi charges, trying in vain to force them to abandon their traditional beliefs and ceremonies. In particular, the priests "frequently took women and young girls into their quarters and seduced them. In order to get the women they sometimes had to dispose of their menfolk." Men frequently "disappeared." A missionary would "send a young man to some distant place to get sacred water from a certain spring, and while he was gone they would take his wife. Some of these young men never returned because they were killed by enemies." Spaniards subjected the people of Awat'ovi to a "rough life." They were forced to "haul stones and timbers, construct church buildings, and do everything they were told to do. It was also like that in the other villages."[16] Hopi elder Clark Tenakhongva related how the mission priests at Oraibi mistreated Hopis. He referred to "sodomy" and "child abuse" by the friar, and said that "all the young ladies that were pretty, anywhere from twelve to sixteen years old, that's who he was abusing." The priest would send the husband of a young woman out, and then "that guy would never see his wife again from that point on." He even referred to the beheading of a Hopi in the middle of the plaza in order to make an "example out of him." Tenakhongva referred to the information that elders told to him about the Spanish period as "horror stories."[17]

Unsurprisingly, perhaps, this violent period witnessed the greatest Spanish influence at the Hopi mesas. From 1629 to 1680, Spaniards made the most religious, cultural, and political inroads, although their successes were still modest. A number of scholars have suggested that this era also saw the development of Hopi repúblicas, complete with Hopi electorates and officers, although how sophisticated these Hopis republics were is impossible to determine.[18] For one thing, no one has located any baptismal, marriage, or death records for the Hopi missions, nor the detailed mission correspondence the Franciscans at these missions must have generated. Only accounts from a few major events have survived.[19] Perhaps more important, virtually nothing remains of the Hopi-Spanish system in structures of governance or oral traditions. This indicates that Hopis themselves consciously and systematically eliminated all vestiges of Spanish political power after expelling these foreigners, including elections to offices and varas de justicia. The Hopi Indian republics are thus incredibly difficult to reconstruct.

The examples in the documentary record that do establish the existence of some aspects of Hopi-Spanish electoral systems are, without exception, tied to violence. For example, in 1665 Padre Fray Salvador Guerra, the missionary at Oraibi, was charged with the whipping and scalding death—by turpentine—of a Hopi named Juan Cuna. Juan Xiveni, a Hopi interpreter from Oraibi, initiated the case when he appeared before Antonio de Ybargaray, the padre custodio of the missions of New Mexico, at Zia Pueblo. Xiveni of Oraibi appeared before Ybargaray "in the name of its governor and the rest of the natives of said pueblo." Xiveni accused Guerra of "terrible and inhuman punishments" against the people of Oraibi, such as "whipping them very cruelly on every part and limb of their bodies, and afterward scalding them and smearing them with burning-hot turpentine." He hoped that by appearing "in the name of the governor of the entire said pueblo of Oraybi," Ybargaray would "prevent similar punishments" and "console" the Hopis of Oraibi by removing Father Guerra.[20]

In the case that followed, Fray Salvador was found guilty of Cuna's death. Numerous Hopi church and civil officeholders took part in the trial. Among them were Joseph Ocheguene, fiscal at Oraibi; Francisco Quera and Juan Cocpi, war captains of Oraibi; Elseario Patui, lieutenant governor of Mishongnovi; Juan Nacuxi, governor of Shungopavi; and other Hopi officers. These

Hopi witnesses told of Guerra's grotesque actions. For example, Oraibi war captain Juan Cocpi told the court that Guerra had given Cuna "many kicks and punches" at the door of the church, which resulted in his being "bathed in blood . . . in the presence of the people." Afterward, he took Cuna inside the church, where he was tied to a ladder, and "he gave him a great many lashes on the back, on the belly, and [on] the other parts of his body." As if this were not enough for the alleged crime of idolatry, Guerra "smeared him on all parts with a large piece of turpentine, and burned him." Guerra ordered the fiscales and war captains of Oraibi to transport Cuna "and other idolaters" to Awat'ovi, but Cuna collapsed en route, "unconscious and speechless," and later died from Guerra's torture.[21]

For his part, Guerra denied the severity of the charges, stating that he had only given Cuna "a slap on the face and about six or seven drops of blood came out of his nose." He said it was true that he had tied Cuna up, but that it was the Hopi fiscal, Ocheguene, who had done the whipping, and that "the lashes did not exceed twenty, and that none of the lashes struck his belly." He said he had thrown "no more than ten or twelve drops [of turpentine], and not all over his body" because Cuna was "old and sick."[22] The trial dragged on, but what emerged in the end was a picture of a sadistic priest guilty of torture and other punishments on numerous occasions. Witnesses from other Hopi villages, primarily officers, testified that Guerra had whipped numerous Hopis and burned them with turpentine. He had also demanded such high numbers of Hopi textiles that the Indians were obliged to spend all their time weaving, unable to tend to their own crops.[23] The trial eventually moved to the Franciscan administrative center at Santo Domingo Pueblo, where Ybargaray and five other Franciscans found Guerra guilty of killing Cuna, abusing numerous Hopis, lying under oath about the number of mantas he had accumulated, disobeying the padre custodio, divulging religious secrets, being "incorrigible, arrogant, and haughty," and exhibiting a lack of "modesty and circumspection that for the sake of religious decency cannot be set down [herein]."[24] He was supposed to go to Mexico City to receive punishment, but there is no record of that occurring. If he did go, he was back in New Mexico by 1659 and went on to serve at Taos, Isleta, Acoma, and Jemez.[25]

This court case illustrates some important facets about the Hopi Indian republics. First, the officers named included both church officers (fiscales) as well as civil officers (governors, lieutenant governors, and translators). While the offices are listed, we have no way of determining the method of selection of such individuals. It is unknown whether an established Hopi electorate chose annual officers, or if missionaries did the choosing. There is reason to believe that Hopis developed their own electoral system, since such systems had developed at all the Pueblos to the east. The república system was obviously in place, and Hopis clearly understood its possibilities and limitations. In this instance, Hopi men successfully used their standing as town and church officers to rid themselves of a priest who had singlehandedly made their lives miserable.[26]

Hopi officers also figure prominently in the events surrounding the destruction of Awat'ovi in 1700. As Hopi oral traditions attest, Franciscan missionaries succeeded in converting a large number of the town's residents—perhaps as many as fifty percent—but the missionary success was more complex than such figures would indicate. Regarding the loss of control of Hopi after 1700, Clark Tenakhongva asserted that "even though maybe forty to fifty percent of the people had been converted into Christianity," Hopis "didn't lose faith in who and what they were," and instead remained true to their Hopi identity.[27] Furthermore, just as the Spanish religious institutions and systems of governance led to divided loyalties at the other Pueblos, they also led to violence between Hopi Spanish sympathizers and those intent on driving all things Spanish from their communities. In 1680, in conjunction with the Pueblo Revolt, Hopis rose up, killing their priests and forcing the Spaniards out of their homeland. The priests were objects of extreme—and justifiable—hatred. Hopis even slit the throat of Father José de Espeleta at Oraibi and threw his body off the mesa.[28]

Still, Spaniards hoped to bring Hopis under colonial domination after the Revolt. In 1692, Governor Diego de Vargas conducted a party of soldiers to Hopi territory. They endured a tense initial meeting at Awat'ovi, thanks in no small part to Vargas's castigation, in which he lamented, "How is it when you are Christians, though such bad ones, that, forgetting what you promised in baptism, you have profaned the churches, destroyed the images, murdered the missionaries, and sacrificed yourselves to the Devil to your own damnation! [How is it that] you do not humbly cast yourselves upon the ground and revere the true Mother of your God and mine who, in the image which ennobles this banner, comes with forgiveness to offer you salvation! Kneel, kneel at once before I consume you all with the fire of my indignation!"[29] The threat of force once again prevailed, as Hopis made signs of penance to the image of the Virgin and pledged loyalty to the Crown. Vargas proceeded to the other Hopi villages and secured similar responses. According to Hopi oral history, "All he [Vargas] was after was for the Hopis to agree that they were still under the authority of the Spanish Crown. I don't know what they agreed to, but the Spanish troops stayed awhile and then returned to Santa Fé."[30]

Nevertheless, Spanish hopes at reestablishing the Hopi missions were soon dashed. The events of 1700 would prove disastrous to Catholic Hopis and their Spanish allies alike. Writing over thirty years after the fact in 1732, José Narváez Valverde gave an account of how Fathers Juan de Garicochea and Antonio Miranda gained permission in 1700 to return to the Hopi villages to minister there. They made their way to Awat'ovi, where they "reduced [gathered] all the natives and baptized many."[31] The recommitment to the Catholic faith of Hopis at Awat'ovi did not sit well with the more defiant Hopis who had only nominally committed to Cross and Crown when the threat of Spanish arms compelled them to do so, returning to traditional ways once the Spaniards left. Now, the devotion of Catholic Hopis at Awat'ovi appeared to go beyond lip service.

Captain John G. Bourke, the famous U.S. Army officer and ethnographer who spent time at Hopi in the late nineteenth century, told of the "legend of Awatovi," which had been related to him in the 1880s. When he and others came upon substantial ruins of a Hopi village, Bourke stated that the "Moquis [the Spanish term for Hopis that saw continued use into the twentieth century] tell the story that this town was destroyed by the people of Mu-shang-newy [Mishongnovi], who came over in the night, got on the top of the roofs, and tossed bundles of lighted straw down upon the people inside and stifled them." Interestingly, his Hopi informants told him "this attack [was carried out because] the town was full of 'singing men,' whom the Moquis did not like."[32] The aforementioned murdered Father José de Espeleta was obsessed with singing. He taught many Hopis to sing the liturgical songs, even exempting Hopi singers from labor or tribute requirements. Navajos referred to Awat'ovi as "the Singing House, or Place of Singers."[33]

The story of Awat'ovi's destruction is clearer when numerous factors are considered. For one thing, archaeological evidence indicates that Catholic practices persisted there during the Pueblo Revolt years. After killing their Franciscan minister and destroying the mission church, Awat'ovi's residents continued to inter their dead at the mission, and included both traditional Hopi items and Catholic objects with the burials.[34] Second, Awat'ovi is the only village in which the selection and installation of a Hopi governor are described in any detail. When Governor Vargas entered Awat'ovi on 19 November 1692, he found its residents friendly although guarded. He identified a Hopi named Miguel, who spoke Castilian, as the head of the village. After a tense first night in which the Spaniards refused to camp at the village, the party baptized 122 children. Vargas was godfather to Miguel's son and daughter. He then related, "Afterward, I appointed Miguel as their governor in their presence, telling them to obey him in every way. I had him swear the oath to properly exercise his office, which he did and I received, before God Our Lord, and the sign of the cross. Then, he asked me to go up to his house and eat, which I did to please him and the Indians so that they might not think I was afraid of them."[35] The oath Miguel was compelled to swear and Vargas's lecture on the duties of office were doubtless the same ones Vargas delivered to the reconquered Rio Grande Pueblos. While this is one of only a few mentions of Hopi governors in the historical record, it was likely that more served. The matter-of-fact way in which Vargas relates these events strongly suggests that Hopis continued to be familiar with this system.

Vargas's retelling of other events surrounding Miguel's selection reveals much about Hopi intentions. Before Vargas went to Hopi, he stopped at Zuni. While there, he sent a letter ahead to Hopi stating his plan to enter their territory. Miguel had received this letter, and notified his own village, as well as Walpi, Shungopavi, Mishongnovi, and Oraibi. The villages hastily called a multivillage meeting, in which they all agreed that they could easily kill the Spaniards, who were few in number. Miguel and others from Awat'ovi did not support such a course, and Hopis from the other villages threatened him, warning that they would kill him once the Spaniards left. In fact, Miguel came to Vargas privately after being made governor, and, "crying a river of tears," said he "was well aware [that Hopis from the other villages] would kill him after [Vargas] left with the men-at-arms."[36]

Vargas had virtually no contact with Governor Miguel after this visit, but he did attempt to write to Miguel and his people in 1694, when many of the Rio Grande Pueblos again rebelled against Spanish colonial domination. He addressed Miguel variously as "governor," "son," and "compadre," thereby harkening to their relationship as fellow officers and fictive kin. Vargas told Miguel that he would come to see him soon, and that he "greatly" wished to "embrace" the Hopi governor. Vargas reminded Miguel that the king of Spain had only sent him "so that you may live as Christians, which you are." Vargas also asserted that he had no intentions of asking Miguel's people for anything or to do them any harm. He reminded him that when he was at Awat'ovi two years earlier, he had paid him for whatever supplies the Spaniards had taken. He closed by telling Miguel and the other Hopis that they were his "children, and I love you, and God, very much. May He keep you, my compadre, for many years."[37] Miguel was likely already a leader before his selection as governor and, barring either some egregious offense to his people or his death, he would have remained in power. Just what the office of governor meant to Miguel or his co-villagers is impossible to ascertain, but it may have been a powerful symbol of everything Hopis hated about the Indian-Spanish political system. A solitary friar was bad enough, but a sympathetic Catholic Hopi governor and other civil officers were likely more imposition than they could bear. Miguel's fear for his own life proved prescient.[38]

Following near-nonexistent contact with Spaniards for the next five years, in 1699 Hopis at Awat'ovi offered to rebuild their mission and permit the Franciscans to return. Perhaps Hopis, who kept continued contact with the Rio Grande Pueblos, wanted to avoid further violence at the hands of Spaniards. Albert Yava related that "some of the people welcomed them because they had already been baptized as Catholics."[39] Hopis sent a preemptive delegation to Santa Fe in 1699 to ask for missionaries. Father Garicochea reported that when he arrived the Catholic Hopis were already rebuilding the mission at Awat'ovi. But as the prospect of the return of Spanish missionaries and soldiers dawned on them, Hopis from other villages grew alarmed. The singing missionary, José de Espeleta, had a protégé to whom he gave the name Francisco. Francisco de Espeleta was baptized and fluent in Castilian. By 1700 he was a cacique at Oraibi, and strongly opposed the growing Spanish influence at Awat'ovi.

Espeleta led a second delegation of Hopis to Santa Fe. They opposed the return of missionaries and hoped to negotiate a peace with Governor Pedro Rodríguez Cubero. Writing at the end of the nineteenth century, Adolph Bandelier insisted that Espeleta and the chiefs at Oraibi, along with twenty other delegates, appeared before Governor Cubero "not as subjects and vassals of the crown, but as delegates of a foreign power sent to conclude a treaty of peace and amity."[40] They went as representatives of independent Hopi sovereignties. Espeleta later masterminded the attack on Awat'ovi. With the assistance of the chief of Awat'ovi, the conspirators, who now included men from Oraibi, Walpi, Mishongnovi, and Shungopavi, planned the attack for a morning when all the men of Awat'ovi would be in their kivas for a ceremony. Early on a December morning in 1700, the attackers greeted the men, who were now in the kivas, from the roofs above. They pulled out the ladders, and threw in bundles of burning wood. The victims below panicked, and in a final show of spite, the attackers threw in Spanish chile peppers, for which their victims had apparently developed a taste. The roof beams burned and collapsed, killing many, while others were shot with arrows. The attackers then poured through the village, killing most of the residents, who may have numbered as many as eight hundred. They took the surviving women and children as spoils of war and divided them among the villages.[41]

It seems that the Hopi villages experienced what anthropologist Matthew Liebmann has referred to as a crisis of "cultural distortion" in which communities under periods of extreme distress begin to change or abandon long-held cultural practices. Moreover, in such circumstances community members often disregard traditional sexual and kinship mores, and defy traditional authority. This results in community upheaval, and is possibly what occurred at Awat'ovi.[42] According to Hopi oral tradition, Ta'palo, who by 1700 was the leader at Awat'ovi, lamented how Spanish influence had corrupted his community. The "sorcerers, those creatures of evil [the Spaniards], do not let anyone go free anymore." He described their influence as "devastating," and stated that they were "destroying people whenever they can," and "seducing the unmarried girls and having intercourse with them wherever they can. It's a lot worse than it ever was before. I'm at my wits' end. I do not know what to do anymore."[43] In an attempt to enlist the help of other village chiefs, Ta'palo told them of his "children" being "out of control. They have no respect for people nor do they listen to anyone." They openly disrespected elders, and had neglected shrines and ceremonies. They also ignored sexual taboos. He feared that the Spaniards, who were "nothing but sorcerers and witches," would settle permanently at Awat'ovi.[44] Nearly three centuries later, Albert Yava told of Catholic Hopis emboldened by the return of Spaniards: "Ever since the uprising they had been kind of quiet, but now they had more courage and were showing themselves and acting in a contentious way. There was a lot of friction in Awatovi." He also spoke of "constant struggle" between traditional Hopis and Catholic converts, who were the majority: "People were getting hurt. The Catholics were ridiculing and interfering with the Hopi religious ceremonies." The only solution in the mind of the traditional religious leader at Awat'ovi was to destroy the village and "wipe the slate clean."[45]

And so one cold December morning, fearful Hopis razed one of their own prominent communities. The violence was said to be so severe that, when a dispute arose after some from Walpi and Mishongnovi took the more attractive women and girls before the attackers from Oraibi got their chance, they angrily grabbed the women and began stabbing them, shooting them with arrows, and mutilating their bodies. Men from the party who tried to intervene on their behalf had their penises and testicles cut off.[46] These extreme acts of violence speak to the depth of the hatred for the Spaniards, their religion, and especially those Hopis who had embraced the colonizers' culture. Some Hopis point to a deeply ingrained guilt for the events of that day. Elgean Joshevama, a former vice-chairman of the Hopi Tribe, stated, "[Spaniards] left us with us having to deal with the guilt of destroying our own people."[47] Yava asserted that "Nowadays the Hopis want to forget that whole Awatovi affair. They're ashamed of what happened, because they were supposed to be the Peaceful

People. But I believe that when the destruction actually took place they were mortally afraid of letting that Catholic thing grow and spread."[48] In short, Hopis even in the present time are still dealing with the trauma of the Spanish period, a time that inflicted deep wounds that "still bleed today."[49]

Furthermore, Hopi oral histories relating to the seventeenth and early eighteenth centuries focus almost entirely on the behavior of Franciscans (and Spanish soldiers, to a lesser extent), while making no mention of any structural changes to Hopi governance. For example, in 1936 Edmund Nequatewa of Shungopavi told of peaceful initial relations between Hopis and colonizers. These soured when the missionary, "who had great power," sent the men of the village away on long trips to fetch him water from a certain spring that had his favorite drinking water, only to seduce their wives while they were away, as confirmed by numerous other oral histories.[50] Wíkvaya, an Oraibi informant, related in 1905 that Hopis there tired of the oppressive priest, even though the Spaniards "were not bad to them at first." After a series of poor harvests, no rain, and the priest's constant demands for tributes of food, the men of Badger clan dragged him out of his house and slit his throat. This signaled the beginning of the Pueblo Revolt at Hopi, and the other villages followed suit.[51]

Curiously, Robert Sakiestewa, interviewed in 1967, was asked, "Did the Spanish actually have a province out here [at Hopi] or a state or something of this kind?" Sakiestewa answered, "Yes, they did," but provided no details as to what it looked like.[52] In these circumstances, it is no wonder that Hopis successfully repressed memories of the Hopi-Spanish electoral system. In a single stroke, recalcitrant Hopis destroyed the village that had been the most fertile ground for reestablishing this system after the Revolt. With the destruction of Awat'ovi, any Hopi survivors who had taken active part in these institutions of governance would have left such concepts to die along with those at Awat'ovi. The Hopi-Spanish Indian republic surely died that day. We are left with only a few scattered references in the historical record of Hopi governors, lieutenant governors, war captains, and fiscales.

In a letter dated 28 October 1775, Father Silvestre Velez de Escalante—who spent a brief period at Hopi—debated how to once again bring Hopis under colonial control. He wrote that although Hopis were "very civilized," they were "rebels" who had once bowed their "arrogant heads beneath the gentle yoke of our Lord, Jesus Christ." For Escalante, "suave exhortations" would not "conquer their obstinacy"; only force of arms and removing them from the mesas would elicit the "necessary compliance." The main obstacle to their conversion and subservience was the "inordinate religious control which the caciques and chiefs have, the absolute dominion which they usurp" over their people. By making "terrible threats" to any who listened to the missionaries and by "reserving to themselves solely the faculty of hearing and speaking on points of religion," the Hopi religious leadership had successfully kept the Franciscans at bay.[53]

Although such hyperbolic pronouncements about the undue influence of traditional religious leaders and medicine people of New Spain's frontier Indian nations were common, Escalante does not seem far off in his summary of their power at Hopi. The lengths to which Hopis were willing to go to eliminate Spanish influence—including the structures, offices, and elections of government—served notice to those who may have been sympathetic to the Spaniards and their colonial system. Perhaps we must revisit the words of anthropologist Richard Clemmer, who in 1995 wrote, "The Hopi are one of the few groups to have endured prolonged domination by the Spaniards—more than 50 years—without being influenced even a little bit by Spanish culture, unlike their Puebloan cohorts to the east, who were influenced to some degree."[54]

Yaquis, Jesuits, and a Borderlands Voter Rebellion

The Yaqui colonial experience is one of diaspora, return, and reimagining homelands. Mobility has been a key Yaqui cultural component over the last five centuries. Today Yaquis reside primarily in the Mexican state of Sonora, as well as in southern Arizona.[55] The following section will examine Yaqui voting and civil government from 1617 to the early 1740s, focusing on the eight Yaqui pueblos along the Río Yaqui: Pótam, Vícam, Tórim, Bácum, Cócorit, Huírivis, Bélem, and Ráum.[56] Yaquis speak a dialect of Cahita, a group of mutually intelligible languages spoken by Yaquis, Mayos, Fuertes, and other Indigenous groups in northern Mexico. It is part of the Uto-Aztecan family, thus making Yaquis, Hopis, and O'odhams linguistic relatives. If it is difficult to cobble together the nature of a Hopi Indian republic, the Yaqui experience under Spanish Jesuit and civil authority is very well documented. In stark contrast to Hopis, Yaquis seem to have "Hispanicized" quite readily, eventually becoming the most prosperous mission in northern Mexico.[57] But the success of the Yaqui Jesuit mission and the Yaqui reduction to eight principal mission towns belie a deep ambivalence that developed over the decades between the 1610s and 1730s. Yaquis adopted Catholicism, mission life, and civil government, but they also violently revolted in favor of a Yaqui-Spanish electoral system that conformed to their ideals. Their anger was due, at least in part, to Jesuit

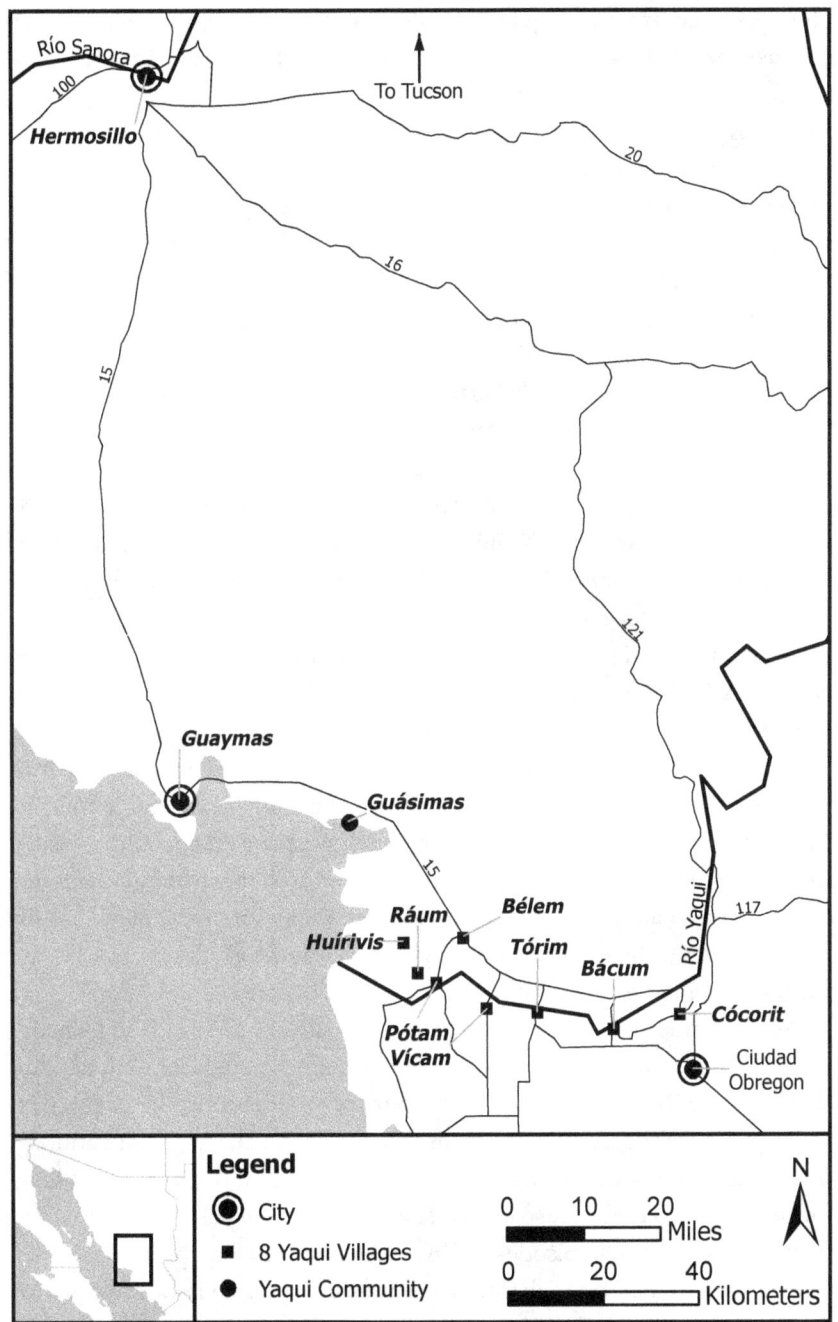

Yaqui Territory along the Río Yaqui. Map by Alex Ochoa.

attempts to control the Yaqui electorate and officers. Yaquis rebelled in 1740 because their república broke down, and they sought to maintain village sovereignty within novel Yaqui-Spanish institutional frameworks.

Yaquis, known as the Yoeme in their own language, traditionally occupied the area around the river bearing their name, at the extreme northwestern edge of New Spain. The Río Yaqui, which flows from nine-thousand-foot highlands to the coastal plain, emptying into the Sea of Cortés, provided the water needed for Yaquis to cultivate maize, beans, squash, amaranth, and cotton. Because of frequent flooding and an ever-shifting river course, Yaquis were traditionally mobile out of necessity.[58] While on a slaving mission along the coast of the Sea of Cortés in 1533, Diego de Guzmán became the first Spaniard to reach the Yaqui River Valley and encounter its Indigenous occupants. An anonymous chronicler of the time recorded what happened in that first meeting. Although not seeing any Yaquis during the first part of the expedition, the Spaniards eventually spied a group of Yaquis at a distance, arrayed for battle and intimidating, "shaking their fists in the air, with bows trembling and making menacing faces." The chronicler made special note of one Yaqui, set apart by his elaborate dress and regal appearance: "This Indian who governed the others came ahead of the group and with his bow made a very long line in the ground, knelt down and kissed the ground." He then stood, and the Spaniards understood that if they crossed the line "they would kill all of us." Captain Guzmán told the Yaquis that they meant no harm, desiring only peace and friendship. Predictably, Guzmán's party crossed the line, and a violent encounter ensued in which twelve Spanish horses were wounded and one man killed out of a party of seventeen. The chronicler praised the Yaquis for their abilities as warriors, stating that he had seen "none fight as well as they."[59] It was a fairly typical encounter in the annals of Indian-white first contacts.

And yet, this account initiated the oft-repeated epithet of "the bellicose Yaquis."[60] This trope peppers the Yaqui historiography to the present day. Andrés Pérez de Ribas, the first Jesuit missionary to minister to the Yaquis over an extended period, referred to them as a "bellicose, and arrogant nation."[61] In his classic 1905 study of armed conflicts with the Yaquis, the Mexican army officer Francisco P. Troncoso characterized Yaqui history as "extremely abundant in wars, in bloody episodes and in scenes of savagery, perpetrated by them and on them."[62] Pérez de Ribas tersely expressed Spanish views on Yaqui barbarism with these words: "I found hardly a single Indian who did not have a name derived from or signifying the murders he had committed, such as he-who-killed-four or -five or -ten, he-who-killed-in-the-monte or -on-the-road or -in-the-field."[63] But Yaquis of course were never one-dimensional, and nei-

Río Yaqui. Severely dammed in recent times, the Río Yaqui once flowed much larger than today. Photo by author.

ther were their responses to Spanish colonialism. At times they used accommodation and diplomacy, while at other times they deployed violence. Yaqui actions in the late 1730s and early 1740s constitute a complicated response to Spanish religion, politics, and economics and must be understood as signifying a fierce commitment to independence and sovereignty, even within the confines of colonialism. Yaquis would repeatedly demonstrate this same commitment over the course of the following two centuries.

Yaqui-Spanish interactions accelerated in the first decades of the 1600s. During the entradas of Captain Diego Martínez de Hurdaide in 1607–8, Yaquis repeatedly defeated Spanish soldiers and their Indian auxiliaries, which strengthened their renown as a savage, fearsome people. Spaniards experienced their worst setback in 1610, which unexpectedly paved the way for Yaqui evangelization. Captain Hurdaide again invaded Yaqui territory, this time at the head of forty mounted Spaniards and two thousand Indian allies, many of whom were from the neighboring Mayos, close cultural relatives of the Yaquis but also their fierce enemies. Yaquis almost killed Hurdaide in battle, but he somehow managed to escape back to the base of Spanish operations at the Villa of San Felipe. Captain Hurdaide then planted a rumor that Spaniards planned to bring overwhelming military force to the Yaqui homelands, with three squadrons of ships making their way up the Río Yaqui to attack.[64]

Although Pérez de Ribas arrived a few years after the battles between Hurdaide and the Yaquis, he surmised that since the Yaquis had been unable "to take the head" of Hurdaide, nor any of his captains, and "when the threats of this brave man, of whom they had heard a great deal, reached their ears from the villa [of San Felipe], some of the caciques of the nation decided to negotiate peace with him and the Christians."[65] The Jesuit scholar Francisco Javier Alegre (1729–88) asserted with similar conceit that Yaquis sued for peace after "Seeing... men battle without any break for an entire day, without losing a soldier and finding a way to escape in the midst of more than seven thousand enemies who had encircled them, they were frightened by such heroic valor, and did not want such valiant men for enemies."[66] The fact is that Yaquis made a strategic decision to negotiate. There is the possibility that Yaquis saw Hurdaide, who was rumored to be short in stature, as some sort of wizard or dwarf. The supernatural, powerful Surem, the ancestral Yaquis, were also believed to be small beings. Yaquis had beaten Hurdaide back, but they "recognized that the captain and his allies represented a formidable enemy... cunning in battle and [possessing] skill in negotiations over captives." But Hurdaide also knew how close he was to losing the war. In the end, peace benefited both parties.[67]

Whatever their motivations, a complicated diplomatic mission followed, in which Yaquis first sent small, female-led delegations to the Mayos, whose territory they had to traverse in order to reach the Villa of San Felipe. As previously mentioned, Mayos had served as Spanish auxiliaries. One Yaqui delegation brought two female Mayo captives taken years before as a sign of peaceful intentions. Acting as go-betweens, the Mayos traveled to San Felipe and informed Hurdaide of the Yaqui peace overtures. Pleased with these developments, Hurdaide and the Jesuits at the Villa initiated direct contacts between the Spaniards and Yaquis. Two Yaqui caciques arrived at San Felipe and, according to Pérez de Ribas's account, informed Hurdaide that after having suffered many casualties in their battles with the Spaniards they "recognized that their neighbors, the Mayo, and other Christian nations were at peace, happy, and content—protected by the captain and cared for by the priests, who treated them as their children." Yaquis desired the same. Yaquis reportedly gave these as the reasons for their peace mission.[68]

A much larger delegation, consisting of 150 Yaquis, signed a formal peace agreement with the Spaniards at San Felipe on 25 April 1610. Although they had bested Hurdaide in battle, Yaquis possibly chose accommodation over a violent struggle in the hopes that they could endure the presence of a few "peaceful" missionaries.[69] There was also a strong coercive element in this peacemaking process. For example, after one exchange with a small group of Yaquis, Hurdaide ordered them to return with a larger delegation and to bring back any stolen horses, silver items, weapons, or other treasures. He told them that they must never fight any Indigenous nations under Spanish control, and demanded that they kill any rebels from other tribes hiding among them. The Yaquis did return stolen silver and weapons, and left "a good number of their sons" to live with the priests at San Felipe to learn Spanish and absorb the Christian gospel, "so that their seriousness in seeking peace and their will to receive the instruction of the Gospel and become Christians would be understood."[70] Such actions indicate a people desiring peace but also under considerable duress. It is possible that they did not realize the power of their own position. With a total population estimated at perhaps 30,000, Yaquis greatly outnumbered whatever forces the Spaniards could marshal in this remote northern borderland. Pérez de Ribas admitted that the Yaquis "could have been much more daring and arrogant than they had been in the beginning."[71]

Yaqui oral history offers important insights into why they negotiated with the Spaniards. Ramón Hernández of Pótam told of a Yaqui tradition from "about 5,000 years ago," in which "there appeared a wooden pole" on the sacred *Kawi Omteme* ("Angry Mountain"). The pole began to make a noise: "It sounded off in this way. And no one understood what it said." None of the Surem present—not even the wise among them—could understand what it said, yet they knew that it was giving them a warning of some sort. Later, they summoned the "wisest person in the land," Maapol, a woman "poetess" who lived by the sea. She told them that "other people are going to come. They will come from the other side of the sea. People . . . like us. The same. It's just that they are from over there, and we are from here." These other people would bring "a change, another way of life. They are going to bring a thing called religion. They shall bring an upright pole, crossed with another." They would bring knowledge of Jesus Christ, "a person who died for all the people." Furthermore, these other people would bring their "customs" and "knowledge to us, so that we might learn it." But Yaquis must also be vigilant, having their bows ready so they would not be surprised and could guard their territory.[72] The Talking Tree Prophecy, which has seen many iterations, often foretold the splitting of Yaquis into two groups: the baptized and the unbaptized. The unbaptized Surem would go to live in the mountains, caves, and hills of the Yaqui homelands, almost in a parallel universe, where they were to remain mostly unseen but could make themselves known to Yaquis. The baptized would go on to live in the eight towns. Thus the Yaqui negotiation with Spaniards was in fulfillment of prophecy—they knew baptism was coming.[73]

Jesuits opened the Yaqui mission on 20 May 1617. Pérez de Ribas was one of the two missionaries assigned there, and his account serves as an important resource in assessing early developments in the Yaqui-Spanish electoral system. He first came to Mexico in 1602, and from 1604 to 1619 he labored among several groups of northern Mexican Indians, eventually returning to Mexico City due in large part to poor health. His account of Jesuit missionary activities among these Indigenous peoples, first published in 1645, is similar to the *Relations de Jésuites de la Nouvelle-France*. As one of the most comprehensive and authoritative primary sources on the Indigenous peoples of northern Mexico, it addresses many dynamics of Indian-Spanish relations in the seventeenth-century Arizona-Sonora Borderlands.[74] Pérez de Ribas highlighted, among other things, important political changes that occurred within Yaqui society.

In his classic 1980 study of Yaqui history, Edward Spicer asserted that the 1617 arrival of the Jesuits brought Yaquis "into the state of citizens of Spain," and that Yaquis "embarked on remodeling their existing military, political, and ecclesiastical organizations in ways suggested or required by the Spaniards." Over the next 150 years, "the process of incorporation proceeded with increasing intensity, always with members of the highly organized Society of Jesus playing a major role . . . [and therein occurred] a vitalization that extended through all aspects of native life."[75] Conversely, historian Rafael Folsom cautioned that change was "slow, piecemeal, fraught with violence and loss, and very much on Yaqui terms." Yaquis dictated the pace, and Jesuits were forced to accept only a "precarious foothold" among them.[76] The Jesuit arrival was certainly transformative, but whether it represented a "revitalization" is questionable. Yaqui life did change significantly over time, and political reorganization and voting figured prominently in the change.

Jesuits had two immediate goals for the vast Yaqui population: baptism and reduction. As the prophecy had foretold, they quickly baptized thousands of Yaquis. Reduction took considerably more work. While the Franciscans labored among Pueblo peoples, many of whom lived in fixed apartment blocks, Jesuits encountered a Yaqui population spread over a vast homeland in scores of rancherías. Instructions laid out by the Council of the Indies for all Indian towns were straightforward. There was to be a large, elevated central plaza lined with the church and administrative buildings, surrounded by rectangular blocks and streets intersecting at right angles. The town perimeter was stockaded or walled off, and the area outside the perimeter contained the pasture and farmlands. Jesuits adapted their reductions to suit their own needs: the priest's house and church lined an entire side of the plaza, with adjoining storehouses for food and other goods, as well as workshops for various trades.[77]

The Franciscan Estevan de Perea had commented excitedly about the New Mexico Pueblos: "Their pueblos have streets, and the houses are in rows like those of Spain."[78] No such luck for the Jesuits laboring among the Yaquis. While Pérez de Ribas did not believe Indians were inherently inferior or lacking in intelligence, he insisted that they nevertheless required reduction. He described Yaquis as a ranchería people living in small villages of one to several families. He stated that they lived in some eighty rancherías along the Río Yaqui, with an estimated total population of around thirty thousand. According to his account, the prospects of their reduction had been good even before Jesuits opened the mission: the Yaquis who formed the 1610 peace delegation to San Felipe "offered to reduce their rancherías to large pueblos, where they could build churches when the priests came to instruct them." Again, when he arrived in 1617, "they offered to bring their rancherías together in the form of pueblos and to make enramadas [open-sided structures with roofs made of branches] for churches, just as other nations had done to receive us."[79] Yet Jesuit enthusiasm for the Yaqui reductions glosses over an extremely messy process. Even after many Yaquis had been reduced to the principal mission towns, many more remained in the countryside.[80] Even so, once a large number of Yaquis had been congregated in the towns, the work of religious, political, and social reforms intended to make Yaquis into Spanish citizens began in earnest. And while reduction paved the way for Yaqui-Spanish Indian republics, it also fostered the Yaqui political consciousness that would eventually lead to violent revolt.

Pérez de Ribas said relatively little about the role of civil government in the converting, civilizing mission. He spoke generally about traditional Indigenous government, but described it in derisive terms. Indians he encountered had "no laws or kings among them to chastise their vices and sins, nor was there any kind of authority or civil government that could punish them." He recognized that they had "some principle caciques" among them, but "their authority consisted only in organizing for war or attacks against their enemies or working out peace agreements with other nations." For Pérez de Ribas these Indigenous leaders were lazy: "At their houses . . . the well-known drunken war revels were held . . . [and] their subjects helped cultivate their fields, which were usually larger than those of others." He could scarcely grasp the nature of their authority: "[They] acquired this authority not so much through inheritance, but rather through their bravery in war, the number of children, grandchildren, and other relatives they had, or at times because they were orators or preachers."[81]

Clearly, what Pérez de Ribas observed as a lack of law or civil authorities was instead a complex meritocratic system of government with leaders and a keenly developed sense of action by consensus. What he was actually seeing was the absence of coercive religious or social control, the hallmarks of the Spanish-Catholic system. In a revealing encounter at the village of Tórim, an unbaptized Yaqui angrily fired arrows at Pérez de Ribas. When the Jesuit asked the baptized cacique of the pueblo to punish the offender, he replied, "He could not punish it, for one thing because the Indian who shot the arrow was not yet reduced to his kin group [or baptized, as he was, perhaps]. Moreover, these caciques . . . do not have authority over their people to punish them for the offenses they commit."[82] In short order, Spaniards would grant Yaqui officers such powers, but always under Jesuit supervision, of course.

While Pérez de Ribas oversaw the spiritual conquest of Yaquis, Captain Hurdaide laid the roots of Yaqui-Spanish officers and elections. In 1618, the year after the Yaqui mission opened, Hurdaide decided that a peaceful visit to the Yaquis was advisable, "to win them over with affection and friendship and to establish political government in their numerous pueblos." The captain "appointed governors and alcaldes [mayors] for the pueblos" so that they could have "some type of government and civility" and could "receive with pleasure and esteem that which the priests preached to them."[83] These selections were completely Hurdaide's; Yaqui elections did not yet take place. Furthermore, once Hurdaide and his soldiers returned to San Felipe, Jesuits were left with wide powers over Yaqui officers. Such officers were, theoretically, directly answerable to the military officials at San Felipe, but in practice Jesuits defined the duties of officers, appointed their assistants, and exercised direct supervisory powers.[84] The Jesuits sought to take full advantage of these powers, controlling Yaqui government as they saw fit, and in the absence of significant royal power they enjoyed a great deal of autonomy over the next roughly 150 years.

Generally speaking, in many ways Indigenous civil government in Sonora functioned in a manner similar to that of colonial New Mexico. Yet there were also key differences. The town governor was the most important Indian official, and was to be elected annually by the Indian residents. His powers included maintaining community order, adjudicating disputes, and punishing guilty parties. He was also to organize town communal work, and give authorization to those who needed to leave the town for whatever reason. Indigenous governors in Sonora could administer punishments, which included warnings, lashings, detention in stocks, and cutting offenders' hair. The Sonoran Indian alcalde was the functional equivalent of a Pueblo lieutenant governor. He took over in the governor's absence and served as a second in command. But an alcalde was also a judge of the first instance, giving testimony, defending the boundaries of Indian pueblo lands during property surveys, and signing written petitions and legal complaints. Alguaciles and topiles served as town constables, enforcing attendance at Mass and public meetings, overseeing work assignments in communal fields, and supervising church and mission complex upkeep and repairs. Fiscales were the church officers who oversaw ecclesiastical obligations and notarial records of baptisms, marriages, and burials. Temastianes taught the catechism. Major officers received the customary canes, a baton, a wooden cross, or the keys to the warehouse and chapel, all of which symbolized their authority and duties. Missionaries were to direct the elections of the governors and alcaldes, who then appointed the alguaciles and topiles. In pueblos where officers and institutions were well developed, these officers formed an Indian cabildo. Priests often used the Indian cabildo to rule over their communities indirectly, keeping a close eye on religious observance and work assignments through informants on the council. The sovereignty that Indigenous officers enjoyed would greatly depend on the Jesuits, and in many cases they were merely the priests' auxiliaries.[85]

Pérez de Ribas asserted that introducing Catholicism, towns, and civil government "not only made them Christians, but also taught them a rational and human way of life," remaking them into civilized Indians. He commented with pride that "it is . . . true that the Yaqui nation provides the greatest and clearest evidence of this change" from base heathens to civilized Christians. While Yaquis were one of the most "savage" Indian nations he had encountered, he was satisfied with their political development at this early stage, succinctly describing the nascent system in which Indigenous officers, Jesuits, and military officers conveniently operated within their spheres:

> [The Yaquis'] bravery and ability to reason exceeded that of many [others], and with cultivation, their moral and political life have improved greatly. In all of their pueblos there are governors, alcaldes, church fiscales, and their own ministers of justice. These individuals govern with order, respect, and obedience. Some of these officials are appointed by the captain [meaning Hurdaide], although he is more than fifty leagues away. The missionaries appoint the fiscales of the church. The latter are responsible for keeping the priest informed of all matters that pertain to the church (as has been described previously), including marriages that Christians wish to contract, newborns who need to be baptized, the

celebration of feast days, and those who become ill and are in need of the sacraments. The civil governors likewise inform the captain of matters that require his attention. Because the missionary is right there and everyone regards him as a father, the people normally go to him with everyday complaints, which usually concern land or similar things. The priest settles these disputes, and they obey him and are satisfied.[86]

But it was never as tidy as Pérez de Ribas would have readers believe. On the one hand, the fact that military officers initially selected Yaqui officials, and saw these Indian leaders as answerable to them, portended future conflict with Jesuits over the authority of Yaqui officials. Pérez de Ribas described the arrangement in which captains of militias of Sinaloa were "actually responsible for civil justice." Such an arrangement "avoided burdening the Indians," largely because it kept significant political power out of their hands.[87] Further complicating things was the fact that Jesuits saw Indian officers as integral both in facilitating conversion and in building mission economies. In "Rules for the Government of the Missions, as Approved by the Father Visitor Rodrigo de Cabredo, 1610," Rule 12 reads: "Ours ought to encourage and introduce the Indians to beneficial works which will eradicate laziness that is the root and mother of all vices; *in this way they can live a more politically organized life.*"[88] Representatives of Cross and Crown would clash over the proper place of Yaquis within the developing regional economy. And in the middle of all of this were Yaquis who desired community sovereignty, including the ability to choose their own officials.

Scholars have frequently commented on the rapidity with which Yaquis converted to the Spanish municipal system and on the scale of the change. Spicer wrote that Yaqui "secular government"—governors "elected by the general populace" as well as church government—"developed steadily," and eventually "became fully accepted by Yaquis," with both "under Jesuit influence into a single local government unit."[89] How fully Yaquis accepted these institutions, offices, and elections is debatable, although real structural changes undoubtedly occurred. But even after they transitioned from appointments to elections, as the Borderlands scholar Susan M. Deeds has pointed out, "Jesuits introduced a new political-religious hierarchy, in which they were the final arbiters.... For many decades, Jesuits were successful in manipulating the election of Yaqui officials who were effective in brokering conflicting interests. Even more significantly, they were able to minimize the demands of Spanish secular society on Yaqui peoples for nearly a century."[90] Such control and manipulation simply could not go on indefinitely without consequences.

Without question, Yaqui civil officers were an important part of the political reorientation along the Río Yaqui. As it evolved over time, the Yaqui political organization at each pueblo included both civil officers and *los basorium*, a council of important men from the villages, prominent among whom were ex-governors who served on the council until their death. These councils, still present today, "represent the voice of the people and solve problems due to their great experience and ensure the transmission of traditions."[91] Similar to the Pueblos, a Yaqui governor's service was without pay and at great personal sacrifice. The oath of office states, "Without saying a word, you offer your body to the service of your people. . . . From this day on you have neither father nor mother, children, nor brothers." The governor also represented the voice of the sacred Yaqui homelands: "You know that the sierra does not have a voice but you do[.] The territory does not have a voice but you do[.] The sea does not have a voice but you do[.]"[92] Yaqui governors received canes, although they were not considered living entities; they are symbols that come from Moses's rod in the Old Testament.[93]

As Yaquis incorporated Spanish concepts of electoral town government, making certain adaptations while also indigenizing the system, Jesuit dismissiveness of Yaqui sovereignty eventually became untenable. The Yaqui Revolt of 1740 best illustrates these competing Yaqui institutional strains. In 1733, Manuel Bernal de Huidobro was appointed lifetime governor of the Provinces of Sonora y Sinaloa, the first and only lifetime appointment of this sort in New Spain.[94] Conflict between Jesuits and *vecinos* (high-status neighbors) had been brewing for decades, with Yaquis in the middle of the two feuding sides. The conflict was due to the growth of mining in Sonora and Sinaloa and the attendant need for Indian labor, a desire by Spanish civil and military officials to exercise more control over the missions, and the push by Indians for changes in the mission system.[95]

Governor Huidobro, who represented the interests of the Crown and vecinos, argued that Jesuits overstepped their ministerial powers by controlling Yaquis. He also agreed with vecinos that Jesuits illegally monopolized Indian labor.[96] Huidobro reported to superiors in Mexico City that very few, if any, Indians in his province were actually paying taxes, which should have been the case after ten years of missionization. He also reported that Yaquis were not holding regular elections for their officers. Jesuits had kept town leaders in office for extended periods, in one case up to seventeen years, while they had also arbitrarily removed officers after only three or four months. Jesuit Padre Cristóbal de Cañas, the missionary at Arizpe and rector of San Francisco Javier de Sonora, strongly contradicted Huidobro. He stated that while the work of evangelization had proceeded well among the Yaquis, many were still holding to heathenish and heretical practices, and the very men the Yaquis had elected as civil officers were encouraging or allowing such nonconformity.[97] For his part, Governor Huidobro supported a policy of reform that included ending indolence, vagrancy, and idolatry; forming militias; building infrastructure; overhauling systems of labor and finance at the missions; and curtailing Jesuit abuses. He believed it was high time for Yaquis to take their place in mainstream political and economic life.[98] Obviously, this pitted him sharply against the Jesuits.

In September 1735, Pedro Álvarez Acevedo, a vecino militia captain and miner from Río Chico, complained to Spanish authorities that he could not keep the mines running because he lacked Indian workers. In response, the alcalde mayor of Ostimuri, Miguel de Quiroz, ordered Cristóbal de Gurrola, captain general (the highest officer in the Yaqui auxiliary forces) of the Yaquis and an Indian magistrate from Pótam, to send workers to the mines. Gurrola would soon emerge as one of the main objects of Yaqui complaints. He was one of their own, yet he had been chosen by the Jesuits and always supported their interests. Gurrola ignored Quiroz's order, because it would have taken labor away from Jesuit fields and workshops. Acevedo complained again in October and November. Huidobro eventually became involved, ordering a *tapisque*, or work detail, of twenty Yaquis each fortnight. The required workers again failed to report. Vecinos complained that Pótam's priest, Diego González, told Yaquis not to work in the mines, thereby directly defying Huidobro's orders and hurting the regional economy.[99]

When Indians mustered for work duty, Father González reportedly asked a Yaqui officer, "Where do you think you're going? Are you the alcalde mayor's sheriff? You don't know your place. I'll give him an answer for all of you."[100] Quiroz wrote to Huidobro in frustration: "[The] cause for the Indians' failure to obey the [civil] authorities [is] because these missionaries so dominated them that they only did what the padres wished, and the padres wanted to be despotic lords, who install and depose [Yaqui] gobernadores at their whim ... as if each padre in his station was so absolute that there were no sovereign power than he alone."[101] In addition to obstructing Yaqui labor outside the missions, Jesuits had completely undermined the Yaqui electoral system, installing governors who were favorable to their own aims and policies and deposing those who were not.

In the ensuing months and years, a strange alliance emerged in which Yaquis, Spanish civil-military authorities, and miners combined forces to remove Yaquis from Jesuit tutelage. The important actors in this dispute included Governor Huidobro and his associates, assorted vecino miners, Ignacio María Nápoli (the Sicilian Jesuit priest of Pótam, Ráum, and Huírivis), and the Yaqui governors of Ráum and Huírivis, Juan Ignacio Usacamea (known as Muni) and Bernabé Basoritemea (known as Bernabé), respectively. Muni and Bernabé were related and had authority in their pueblos as war chiefs, as well as their elected offices. Muni had been elected ensign of Yaqui auxiliaries during the famous campaign of the elder Juan Bautista de Anza (father of New Mexico Governor Anza) against the Seris and Tiburones. Bernabé had worked as a mule driver, traveling widely across the region.[102] They led the Yaqui resistance movement, demanding that Jesuits respect the Yaqui electoral system and allow greater village sovereignty. With their military service and travel, both men were highly experienced with life outside the missions. They would use their experience and external contacts in the service of the revolt.[103]

On 13 March 1736, Muni and Bernabé appeared before Quiroz to complain about Gurrola, who they said had improperly wielded his power over the Yaquis as captain general, with the Jesuits' blessing. They also complained about a number of mestizos and coyotes (offspring of one mestizo and one Indian parent) living in the Yaqui pueblos who they alleged had used their friendships with Gurrola and the Jesuits to appropriate lands and extort money from the Yaquis.[104] Jesuits responded by sending a convoy of their own, consisting of loyal Yaqui officials under Gurrola's command and accompanied by Father José Roldán. They told Quiroz that all was well, and that Yaquis and Jesuits had been reconciled. Quiroz's term concluded in the middle of this mounting controversy, and the new alcalde mayor, Francisco Ordóñez, did nothing to resolve the matter. It was soon clear that both Quiroz and Ordóñez supported the Yaqui side and felt unfavorably toward the Jesuits.[105]

Complicating matters, for much of this volatile period Governor Huidobro was away attending to affairs in California, over which he also had authority. In his place was Lieutenant Governor don Manuel de Mena. The disgruntled Yaquis, unsatisfied with both Jesuit and Spanish responses to their complaints, began making their way to Sinaloa in October 1736 to visit Lieutenant Governor Mena. Mena's messengers intercepted Muni and Bernabé and told them and their party of more than twenty Yaqui leaders to return to their villages and await his visit, promising resolution to the conflict. Mena seemed amenable to the Yaqui cause. With the Yaqui leaders back in their villages, Mena arrived, as promised, and was greeted with celebrations. But what happened next was the opposite of what Muni and Bernabé expected. After meeting with the Jesuits, who bribed him with pearls and other riches, Mena changed his stance on the developing conflict, throwing Muni, Bernabé, and other leaders, including Muni's father, in the Pótam town jail. He harassed the Yaqui governors, telling them to admit that Quiroz had put them up to their agitation, which they denied, but when he threatened to take them to Guadalajara to be executed, they relented.[106]

Quickly responding to this escalation of tensions, Muni's nephew Luis Aquibuamea led a group of more than 2,000 Yaqui warriors to the scene. Dressed for battle with banners and weaponry, they surrounded the jailhouse and began shouting threats at the terrified Spanish jailers. It looked as though a battle would follow, one in which the heavily armed Yaquis would have easily overpowered the handful of Spanish soldiers. Muni decided to pacify the surrounding Yaquis, asking Mena to allow him to speak to his compatriots. He convinced his Yaqui supporters to disperse as long as Mena promised to release him and the other prisoners the next day. They agreed and duly scattered, and Muni and Bernabé were released. This was a resounding victory for the elected Yaqui governors, and among Muni's greatest moments as a leader of his people.[107] Muni, Bernabé, and the others clearly viewed themselves as the legitimate Yaqui leadership, possessing sovereign political authority that had been officially sanctioned through proper electoral processes, and they felt bolstered by their victory. Both Muni and Bernabé were restored to office by the Spaniards in October 1736.[108]

Yaqui-Jesuit relations further soured after the Pótam prison incident, which marked a point of no return. Father Nápoli despised Muni and Bernabé, accusing them of countless infractions and crimes. For example, Nápoli accused Yaquis of stealing various items intended for the California missions, and questioned Muni and Bernabé about the missing items. They told him that the Spanish king was rich and would not miss the goods, and flippantly opined that since the king had stolen so much from Yaquis in the past, it was only right that they steal a little bit from the king. When Nápoli attempted to reprimand them, they slapped the table and told him that they feared no man. The friar was enraged at their insolence. Nápoli hated Bernabé in particular. When the Jesuit called in the governor of Huírivis for questioning, he refused to appear, telling Nápoli that the priest knew where to find him and that Nápoli should come to his house if he needed him. Nápoli also had seen Bernabé wearing silk stockings and high heels from the looted goods, and accused Bernabé of shielding other accused thieves.[109]

In a strange turn of events, Muni and Bernabé unexpectedly left their offices as governors. What motivated this action is unknown. By this time Muni had apparently begun advocating that Yaquis pay tribute to the Crown, which would place them under Spanish civil jurisdiction and outside Jesuit authority and would signal the long-awaited secularization of the missions. Nápoli had called Muni to his residence, and the pair had argued fiercely. Muni reportedly placed his vara on a chair. Nápoli took this as a sign that Muni was giving up his civil authority, and even alleged that Muni had said that he no longer wanted to be governor of Ráum. Nápoli then held an election for a new governor of Ráum a few days later, and at this election only a few men turned up to vote. Women cast most of the votes, which was not typical of a Yaqui election, as women were not part of the Yaqui electorate. Juan Turimea succeeded Muni as governor. Bernabé left office around this same time, ostensibly because his one-year term was up. Nápoli once again oversaw an election in which Bernabé's nephew Diego Marquina was elected. Bernabé was unhappy with the result and vandalized his nephew's home, taking back his vara.[110] Nápoli had thus single-handedly subverted the entire Yaqui electoral system in the towns under his jurisdiction.

Muni and Bernabé refused to acquiesce, instead walking to Sinaloa on 29 November 1737 to lodge a formal complaint with Lieutenant Governor don Martín Cayetano Fernández de Peralta. They claimed that Nápoli had removed them from office for refusing to abuse other Yaquis, and said that their replacements were unfit for office. They asserted that Turimea was a cruel adulterer, while Marquina was a backstabbing gossip who had threatened to cut off their heads if they went to Spanish authorities.[111] Lieutenant Governor Peralta took swift action. He immediately sent word to Huidobro in California, informing him of all the Yaqui developments. He also commissioned don Manuel Gaspar de Flores, a vecino civil officer from Baroyeca, to go to Ráum and Huírivis, reinstate Muni and Bernabé, and inform Gurrola that he was not to mistreat the Yaquis any longer. Peralta also wrote to the vice-rector of Sinaloa about Nápoli's misbehavior, but he was careful to declare that Nápoli remained a most beloved son of the Society of Jesus.[112] Peralta still feared the Jesuits, who had threatened him with excommunication if he misstepped.[113]

The disputes escalated over the ensuing months, with Nápoli, Muni, Bernabé, and Spanish officials locked in a back-and-forth battle of accusations and counteraccusations. At both Ráum and Huírivis, small groups came out in support of the new governors, calling their elections legitimate, while hundreds of Muni and Bernabé's supporters disputed the elections.[114] On 14 January 1738, Muni, Bernabé, and thirty-one other Yaqui leaders arrived at the Villa de Sinaloa. As a show of strength, they went attired in battle clothing, with drums beating and flutes blowing. Muni rode at their head on horseback (technically, another breach of Spanish law that barred Indians from riding horses). It was a dramatic scene, one that undoubtedly made an impression on the Spaniards.

Muni and Bernabé had not been reinstated, but Peralta intimated that they were still governors, merely temporarily suspended from the exercise of their office. Peralta also convinced the Yaquis to return to their villages, and somehow coaxed them into apologizing to Nápoli, who for his part immediately questioned their sincerity.[115] Peralta was paralyzed by the decisions before him. He knew that the Yaqui grievances were real and that the Spaniards depended on the Yaquis to help defend the northern borderlands against O'odhams, Seris, and Apaches. But he was also terrified of being excommunicated. In the end, he hoped to leave the mess to Governor Huidobro to sort out on his return.[116]

Huidobro finally returned from Baja California in June of 1738. In his twenty-month absence, events had deteriorated significantly. He received a letter while away, purported to be from Gurrola and the three Yaqui replacement governors of Pótam, Ráum, and Huírivis. It contained accusations against Muni, Bernabé, and fifteen others: they openly carried arms, disobeyed the Yaqui captain general (Gurrola), stole items from the churches, did not attend Mass, Muni aspired to be captain general of the Yaquis, and Bernabé intended to make himself the perpetual governor of Huírivis. Huidobro questioned Nápoli, the new governors, and others, and realized that the Jesuits and some coyotes living in the villages had penned the accusations, since Captain General Gurrola and Governors Marquina, Turimea, and Buimea were all illiterate. On 21 July, Nápoli appeared before Huidobro, claiming that the Yaquis had demonstrated a clear pattern of insubordination for two years. He repeated the charges in the fake letters he had helped author. Nápoli was indignant that Muni and Bernabé had dared to act as "gentlemen" in his presence. Furthermore, Muni had entered Nápoli's church with his hat on and seated himself as Nápoli's equal at the Jesuits' mission dwelling.[117]

Some of the charges were true. Muni had indeed carried a weapon—since he had a military background—and they despised and disobeyed Gurrola. But Nápoli's final action bespoke desperation, as he claimed that Muni was possessed by the devil. He also claimed that from the day of his arrival, Yaquis had told him that he would have to obey them, that they would not consent to outside leaders, and that they would name their own pages and mission servants. The deeper Huidobro probed, the more obvious it was that Nápoli was caught in a lie. Still, he remained firm in his opposition to Yaqui political independence, and he clearly had powerful allies.[118] Taken as a whole, his claims, though exaggerated, indicated that Yaquis had a keenly developed electoral-political identity. They intended to choose their own civil and church officers. While they had every reason to believe in the power of their threats—after all, they had recently broken out of the Pótam jail—Muni and Bernabé would continue to engage legal channels as officers of Yaqui republics.

Huidobro held public meetings in which he heard Yaqui complaints: they had been forced to work on Jesuit mission lands for little or no pay; they had not been allowed to work in the mines or elsewhere; they did not see any of the profits from their mission labor, which they said all went to the unprofitable Jesuit missions in Baja California; and they had often been subjected to severe corporal punishment with little or no cause. Governor Huidobro showed signs of favoring the Yaqui side of the dispute. He decided that this was the perfect moment to read a letter that had conveniently arrived from the viceroy, Archbishop Juan Antonio de Vizarrón, dated March 1737. It exonerated the Yaquis for the Pótam prison incident and invited Yaqui leaders to Mexico City for a private audience.[119] Support from the viceroy, himself a cleric, must have been troubling for the Jesuits. On 30 July 1738, Huidobro accompanied Governors Marquina, Turimea, and Buimea to see Nápoli. They resigned their posts, and new elections were held at Pótam, Ráum, Huírivis, and Vícam. Huidobro likely viewed this as the best option, since the previous elections had been so heavily disputed. Yaquis were purportedly happy with the results.[120]

The accounts of Huidobro's visit provide a fascinating window into the Yaqui electoral process. It was somewhat similar to those in place at the Rio Grande Pueblos, but there were differences. For example, in the middle of December, the outgoing governor went before the leadership of the pueblo and stated that he had completed his duties, asking to be relieved. He returned the cane, and it remained at the church in the possession of no single person.[121] At each pueblo, an electorate consisting of forty to fifty Yaqui men—los basorium—met at the *casa de comunidad* (community house), where they presented approximately three candidates for governor. They then voted on the candidates. If a tie occurred, they drew lots to determine a winner. The Jesuit who was present at the proceedings could oppose their choice, but when this happened, the captain of the Villa de Sinaloa would select a replacement, always subject to the consent of the Yaqui electorate and the Jesuit. After the governor was duly elected, Yaquis named lesser officials such as teniente, alcalde, topil, alguacil, and others. This delicate balance required cooperation from Yaquis, Jesuits, and Spanish officials alike.[122] Consensus was important to this process, although a split vote was possible. While there were "candidates" for office, these names were put forward by los basorium. Men could protest their selection, although such protest was futile, as it was at the Pueblos of New Mexico. In addition, the new Yaqui officers were announced on 24 December, thereby being symbolically "born" with the Christ child. The officers became official through a feast and ceremony on 6 January, Three Kings' Day.[123] In some ways, the Yaqui electoral model conformed more closely to the Spanish ideal, although it clearly had its own nuances. By the 1730s, Yaquis had claimed ownership of the electoral process to the extent that they would not allow significant tampering. The Ráum election of 1737, for example, was so objectionable because women had comprised the bulk of the electorate and Nápoli had controlled the entire affair. Such sham elections, which they viewed as invalid, were consistently at the top of Yaqui complaints.

The Yaqui diplomatic mission to the capital of New Spain departed in October 1738. Muni and Bernabé traveled with an interpreter and five other Yaqui compatriots. They stopped in Sinaloa, where Huidobro gave them passports, and then traveled on to Mexico City.[124] Certainly, Huidobro was using the aggrieved Yaquis for his own political purposes. He disliked the Jesuits, thought Yaquis should be politically and economically integrated, and saw the economic interests of miners and vecinos as more important than the Jesuit mission enterprise itself. Still, his actions also indicated at least some measure of sympathy for the Yaquis' cause, and he was willing to put his political career on the line on their behalf. He was eventually relieved of his position for his handling of the Yaqui Revolt, and was universally criticized by the Jesuits in the wake of the revolt. But it was at his urging that Muni and Bernabé made the long trip to the capital; ostensibly, he respected their office and status as Indian magistrates, even if only to serve his own ends against Jesuit interests.

It was a long journey, and in their absence the situation at home worsened. Yaquis lacked reliable leadership, and Jesuits persisted in their mistreatment. After a terrible crop yield, Jesuits hoarded what food remained, selling it to starving Yaquis at inflated prices.[125] Yaquis reached their breaking point and revolted in 1740. During that time, though, the actions that Muni and Bernabé took as two former elected officials of the Yaqui Nation were quite remarkable. Their role had transcended their previous offices as governors of Ráum and Huírivis. Yaquis had developed a sense of nationhood, and as circumstances required this Yaqui national political voice could and would be marshaled, and was in fact marshaled on numerous instances in the coming centuries. In the late 1730s and early 1740s, Yaqui republics had coalesced within the Spanish colonial system as a Yaqui nation. But it is important to recognize that such a political move served certain immediate ends. Yaquis would function mostly as independent republics, while uniting for national causes under extreme circumstances, much as Pueblo Indians had done in 1680.

The Yaqui petition, which Muni and Bernabé presented to Viceroy Pedro de Castro in Mexico City, and which was widely distributed at the time, confirmed the Jesuits' worst fears about the Yaquis, their leaders, and their demands. The document presented the viceroy with a number of requests, not least of which was that Muni and Bernabé have their names cleared (particularly for the Potám prison incident) and their lands restored. The Yaquis condemned padre Nápoli and other Jesuits for their poor treatment of Yaquis and asked that the hated Yaqui Captain General Gurrola be replaced. They demanded that the coyotes brought in by the Jesuits be expelled, and that Yaquis be allowed to carry arms. They insisted they be paid for their work for the Jesuits, that the Padres not impede Yaquis from working in the nearby mines, and that their vecino ally Miguel de Quiroz be named their Protector. Their most important political demand, number nine, was encapsulated in a single, brief phrase: "Que se guardase dicho auto, en quanto a la livertad de las elecciones" (That the before mentioned order be kept, regarding freedom of elections).[126] Among a litany of other complaints, this one spoke to the Yaqui desire to self-govern and to have the final say in choosing their own leaders. In sum, the Yaquis wanted to make it clear in whose hands the ultimate political power at the local level rested. While they stopped short of demanding independence from both Spaniards and Jesuits, the Yaquis demanded an electoral system with free elections, which could only happen when Jesuit political hegemony had been broken.

The Yaqui Revolt raged while Muni and Bernabé were away in Mexico City. Governor Huidobro acted indecisively, and Jesuits saw this as complicity with a Yaqui plot to overthrow their power. Word of the revolt spread to neighboring Indian nations, some of which became involved. The Mayos offered particularly fierce resistance to Spanish power. O'odhams, too, joined in the cause. Jesuit Philipp Segesser, who was laboring at the O'odham mission of Tecoripa during the revolt, and whose charges became involved in the fighting, wrote in 1741, "About two years ago, ten or twelve Indians named Jacquis (Yaquis) had traveled to Mexico in order to take care of some grievances with the viceroy, and at the same time to promise to pay tribute to the king, which secured them some freedom."[127] Unfortunately, the sympathetic Viceroy Pedro de Castro died in office in 1741. His replacement, Pedro Cebrián, grew impatient with Huidobro, replacing him that same year with Sonora's sargento mayor, Captain Agustín de Vildósola, first as interim governor and then on a permanent basis. Vildósola was much more sympathetic to the Jesuit fathers, and acted decisively to put down the growing pan-Indian revolt. On 22 June 1741, after the events of 1740 had largely subsided, the new governor had Muni and

Bernabé executed and then decapitated, sending their heads on tour to all the Yaqui villages as a warning against further rebellions. His actions were all the more outrageous considering that since returning to Yaqui territory the pair had encouraged Yaquis to stop fighting and lobbied for a peaceful resolution of the conflict.[128]

On the surface, it would appear that the Yaquis and their allies had lost on every front: Muni and Bernabé were first deposed and then executed; Huidobro was removed from office; and the revolt failed. Still, Viceroy Cebrián did directly address two central Yaqui demands: Jesuits were expressly forbidden to name or depose Yaqui governors; and coyotes, lobos (those of African and Indigenous descent), and mulattos were expelled from the Yaqui pueblos.[129] The importance of the actions undertaken by Muni and Bernabé, first as governors of their pueblos and then as representatives of a united Yaqui political consciousness, cannot be overstated. The Yaqui Revolt, which spread throughout the northern borderlands of New Spain in the 1740s with sustained conflagrations for years to follow, destabilized the mission system. The Jesuits of the region never recovered. Spain eventually expelled the order from the New World in 1767 after prolonged fears of disloyalty to the Crown. Yaquis, though, continued to maintain their fierce political independence, fighting a number of wars against Spain and Mexico well into the twentieth century, when many fled Sonora as political refugees and settled in what is today southern Arizona. It was a steep price for a Yaqui electorate, free elections, and sovereignty. But it was one that Yaquis were willing to pay.

The Incomplete Political Incorporation of Pimería Alta

For millennia, numerous Indigenous peoples have inhabited the region that today encompasses the U.S.-Mexico Borderlands, which Herbert Eugene Bolton referred to as the "rim of Christendom." One of the most prominent groups of this region is the various Indigenous nations collectively referred to as O'odhams (historically, Pimas). They have included Tohono O'odhams, Akimel O'odhams, Sobaipruis, and others, inhabiting a large territory that today falls within the U.S. and Mexican states of Sonora, Arizona, and California. Spaniards used various names for these groups, and generally distinguished between Upper and Lower Pimas. Thus the Upper Pima homeland was Pimería Alta. In the simplest terms, Akimel O'odahms (River O'odhams) and Sobaipuris lived in far northern Sonora, while Tohono O'odhams, known as Papagos or Desert Pimas, lived to the far northwest.[130]

This section focuses mainly on these three groups of Pimería Alta, which I collectively refer to as O'odhams. In particular, I will make frequent reference to the communities of San Cayetano de Tumacácori, San Gabriel de Guevavi, and San Xavier del Bac, among others. The boundaries of this O'odham region are the Gila River to the north, the Santa Cruz and San Pedro Rivers to the east, the Colorado River and Gulf of California to the west, and the Magdalena and Altar Rivers to the south.[131] It is important to point out that since the arrival of the Spaniards in the seventeenth century, these peoples have experienced cataclysmic population shifts and been subjected to a process of political, religious, and cultural incorporation that at various points sputtered, stalled, and then advanced. One of the foremost experts on Tohono O'odham history, Bernard Fontana, summarized the fraught process of Tohono O'odham colonization in the far northern borderlands in this manner: "For three centuries Papagos [Tohono O'odhams] have been encouraged directly . . . and indirectly . . . to become Spaniards, Mexicans, and Anglo-Americans. The results to date have been very uneven; the process continues and perhaps always will."[132] Spain failed to mold O'odham communities into Indian republics for sustained periods of time, and O'odham electorates were fleeting and underdeveloped. Still, the reverberations of Spain's attempts continue to be felt today.

In the second half of the seventeenth century, the Crown tasked the Society of Jesus with bringing the various groups of Pimería Alta into the sphere of the Kingdom of Spain and the Catholic Church. Much as Pérez de Ribas had labored to open the Yaqui missions, that tireless "padre on horseback" Eusebio Francisco Kino opened up O'odham lands to missionary work. Kino established his headquarters in Pimería Alta near the O'odham village of Cosari, founding the Mission Nuestra Señora de los Dolores on 13 March 1687. Situated at a strategic point on the San Miguel River, it had a number of O'odhams living in the vicinity. An important headman by the name of Coxi also lived there, who was influential among the region's O'odhams.[133] Kino followed the tried-and-true method of befriending and converting the headman, baptizing Coxi, his wife, and more than forty other adults and children on 31 July 1687, thereby becoming their godparent and fictive kin. The padre related that he was received very well by all the Indians in his early encounters at Dolores and the outlying areas: "In all places they received with love the Word of God for the sake of their eternal salvation."[134]

After a few years of ministering to the O'odhams of northern Sonora from his base of operations at Dolores, Kino embarked on many expeditions to the Indians of today's southern Arizona, in the land "más allá."[135] During

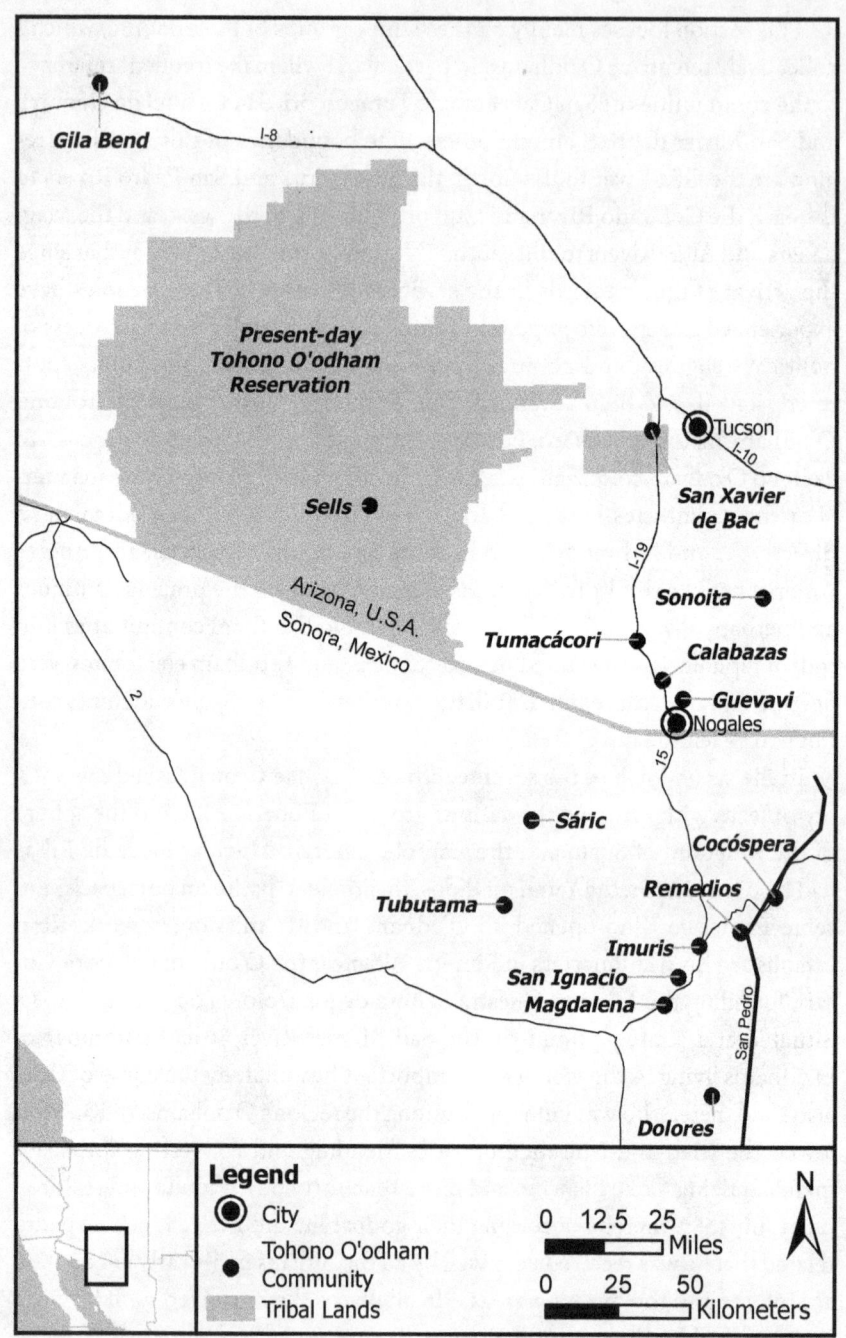

Tohono O'odham Territory. Map by Alex Ochoa.

Undated Photo of Baboquivari Peak. Sacred to Tohono O'odhams, Baboquivari Peak is where I'itoi, the creator god, resides. Bonaventure Oblasser, O.F.M. Collection, 1901–1977 MS 543, box 10, folder 12, courtesy of University of Arizona Libraries, Special Collections.

Kino's numerous visits to O'odhams at the far north of Pimería Alta, he assessed the feasibility of missionary work in their communities, and began the process of political incorporation, although political organization was always secondary to his missionary efforts. In a 1691 journey with a travel companion, Father Visitor Juan María Salvatierra,[136] Kino visited the villages of San Cayetano de Tumacácori and San Gabriel de Guevavi and met with Indian representatives from San Xavier del Bac. Kino reported that the Indians asked him to come to visit them at his earliest convenience. The padres delivered the customary orations on Catholic theology, and baptized several individuals, including children. They also distributed gifts and promised that priests would come in the future to live in their villages. They began the process of political incorporation that took place in so many Indian-Spanish encounters before and after by identifying Native leaders and conferring on these men the titles of gobernador, alcalde, and *mador* (herald). They distributed the tasseled ebony varas de justicia, and informed the O'odhams that they were now subjects of His Most Catholic Majesty, King Charles II of Spain.[137]

Captain Juan Mateo Manje, the lieutenant alcalde mayor of Sonora, escorted Kino on nine of his expeditions to Pimería Alta in the late 1690s and early 1700s. These expeditions of "discovery" and "exploration" covered thousands of miles and featured interactions with thousands of Native peoples. Manje recorded many of his activities as they related to the political implications of these O'odham-Spanish encounters. His narrations frequently contain descriptions of meetings in which he distributed varas de justicia all over Pimería Alta. But he also recorded his awkward attempts at explanations to Indian leaders of the meaning of such titles and authority. For example, on 9 February 1694 at the O'odham village of Tupo, during Kino's and Manje's first voyage, Manje wrote, "We counted 100 Indian men and the corresponding number of women and children. Father Eusebio Kino requested me to distribute staffs of justice, ribbons and other trinkets, and he explained to them the obligation of the government and the meaning of Lord and King."[138]

Later in the voyage, Manje related an encounter at the village of Caborca of the Soba Nation, located on the Río Altar in northern Sonora: "We gave them [the Indian officials] staffs of justice showing them how to govern their people and to take an interest in the public welfare," as if O'odhams did not know how to self-govern or see to their own general welfare. He also narrated the ideal scenario in which Native rulers and their people came under Spanish dominion. He described Chief Soba of said Soba Nation, who lived in the south of Pimería Alta, as a "vigorous, strong and valiant Indian . . . [who, along with his people,] heard the Word of God and His Sacred Law and submitted to His Royal Majesty." According to Manje, thanks to this brief interaction, "in a short time this nation was subdued . . . and indicated their willingness to serve God and to become loyal subjects of His Majesty."[139] Manje repeated these actions during subsequent voyages almost ad nauseam. During their second voyage, at the village of San Andres, Manje gave the leaders "staffs of justice as insignia of authority to establish their own government." On this same voyage, at the villages of Bac, Tumacácori, and Guevavi, Kino and Manje found that the Indians had built houses for priests to live in, apparently hoping that resident missionaries would soon be sent. Of all of the O'odham villages without missionaries, Manje wrote, "They are asking for missionary priests."[140]

In some cases, leaders they had previously designated and to whom they had given canes had died. In such instances, Spaniards appointed new leaders and redistributed canes. Lieutenant Cristóbal Martín Bernal, who traveled along the San Pedro and Santa Cruz river valleys in November 1697, wrote that at the village of San Joaquin, Don Domingo Jaravilla,[141] the previous Indian governor, had died. Bernal named "a nephew of his as Governor at the request of the entire village and they were very pleased."[142] Bernal's narration seems to indicate he had at least attempted to ascertain the opinion of the O'odhams, but this was not a formal election. During Kino's and Manje's sixth voyage in late 1699, they returned to Tumacácori, where they had previously visited. Manje "gave them two staffs of justice, explaining to them how to govern themselves and describing the loyalty, fealty and obedience they are to render unto our King and natural Lord."[143] Manje makes no mention of the previous governor's having died, so we are left guessing why they selected new officers at some villages and not at others.

In all likelihood, because the act of designating governors and distributing canes had questionable significance to O'odhams of Pimería Alta, in most cases the Spanish representatives were forced to repeat these actions time and again. Still, in some places the office of governor seems to have taken root rather quickly. At Bac, for example, Bernal described the governor in 1697, Eusebio, as "an old man, a good administrator, and well liked. In the rest of the rancherías they obey him promptly."[144] It is also difficult to know what to make of statements by Kino and Manje that they were continually met by throngs of happy Indians who welcomed them and begged for missionaries to be sent. Certainly, O'odhams saw some material benefit in what the Spaniards had. But they likely only desired the tools, animals, foodstuffs, and gifts, not the changes to their traditional forms of government. The lack of significance of the canes and offices at this early stage is confirmed by Manje's statement from 1697 that they had to distribute loads of gifts wherever they went, for "Benevolence is the only thing with which you can attract these Indians." In spite of the lack of real religious or political transformation, Manje and Kino felt that, thanks to their voyages, these O'odhams were "ripe to be initiated into the science of [Spanish] government and politics."[145]

Spaniards understood that initiating O'odhams into the colonial political realm required a constant Spanish presence at or near Indian towns. In some instances, the colonizers quickly established missions and presidios, while in other areas they were many, many years in coming. Kino constantly demanded more help—more Jesuits to minister to Pimería Alta—with mixed results. Despite Kino's assertion that he was always well received and that the Indians greatly desired resident priests, things did not always go smoothly. In some cases Spanish attempts at political incorporation resulted in violence, just as they had at the Pueblos. For example, in October 1694, after much lobbying from Kino, Jesuits established a Soba mission at La Concepción de Nuestra Señora de Caborca and assigned Francisco Javier Saeta to serve there. Although Saeta was young and ambitious, his mission was beset with problems from the beginning, including the father's own physical difficulty with the harsh environment. Less than six months later on 2 April 1695, Saeta was dead.

What is fascinating is that, according to Kino, his killers were none other than the Native civil leaders of the neighboring town of San Antonio de Oquitoa. Kino related that when Father Visitor Salvatierra visited Oquitoa in 1690, he had promised them a resident priest. The Oquitoans waited patiently for a number of years, and even "appointed officials—a governor, a mayor, a legal officer, a clerk, a minor judge, sheriffs, etc." But when Father Saeta was sent to Caborca instead of to their village, they could bear it no longer. Jealous of both the spiritual benefits and the "inner and outer clothing, cattle, sheep and goats, horses, mules, a farm, cow-hands, pack-trains and drivers" that a resident priest brought to Caborca, many from Oquitoa left their town and went to live at Caborca, "leaving the [Indian civil] officials almost alone, etc., with all their dissatisfactions and other grievances." The acalde of Oquitoa, with fifty to sixty followers from the surrounding area, traveled to Caborca, shot Saeta with arrows, and clubbed the father, while "the Captain and Governor of [Caborca] responded immediately . . . [but] were defenseless . . . so they turned and fled in fear with all of the people of the pueblo, the officials, etc."[146] Kino placed the blame squarely on Oquitoa's Indian officers, who were jealous of Caborca's new status and their own lack of power when town residents moved away.

As Kino awaited missionary reinforcements to support his vision of a borderlands empire of O'odham installations, he continued the work of periodic ministering and the installation of officers. In 1698, he wrote: "Two Governor's batons of authority were presented; one to the Governor of Guevavi and one to the Governor of Los Reyes, in place of those of the two Governors who had died during the previous months."[147] But all involved knew that these were only stopgap measures; missionaries were needed. Finally, in 1701, Jesuits were assigned to the far north of Pimería Alta. Father Valenciano Francisco Gonzalvo was selected for Bac, while Father Juan de San Martín went to Guevavi. Within a short time, both Gonzalvo and San Martín had left their posts as a result of illness.[148] San Martín had only lasted a few months at Guevavi, while Gonzalvo died in 1702 of an illness he contracted at Bac.[149] Another thirty years passed before fathers again took up residence at the O'odham towns. In 1730, the viceroy gave instructions for missionaries in Pimería Alta to once again proceed to the far northern O'odham missions: "For the conversion of those heathen Indians to our holy Catholic Faith and for their education, three missions are to be erected and planted in northern Pimería Alta and entrusted to three religious of the Sacred Company of Jesus." The towns of Bac, Guevavi, and Santa María Soamca were chosen, and missionaries arrived there in spring 1732.[150]

This began the first period of extended missionization among these O'odhams, as well as the beginning of attempts to fashion O'odham mission communities into Indian republics. At the center of this work for the next half-century were the Jesuit missionaries whose names loom large in the history of northern Sonora, including Ignaz Pfefferkorn, Jacobo Sedelmayr, Joseph Och, and Juan Nentvig. While the missions at which they labored experienced a great deal of instability, and even periods without priests (at Bac, for example, between 1692 and 1767 the padre's house stood vacant four out of every five years on average[151]), their relatively sustained presence led to a more formal establishment of O'odham-Spanish electoral governments. But O'odhams and Spaniards faced immense challenges in this endeavor: the mission communities were remote, often underpopulated, constantly exposed to Apache attacks, and administered by Jesuits who cared very little for O'odham sovereignty. Thus the institutions of colonial government that developed there, as well as their Indigenous electorates, were rather anemic when compared to those found at the Pueblos of New Mexico or among the Yaquis.

While O'odham missions did mirror Iberian town governments, with the election of officials such as gobernador, alcalde, fiscal, topil, mador, and temestián, the complexity of the organization likely depended on the size of the settlement. O'odham mission communities were supposed to hold elections each year, overseen by the Jesuit in residence. But with extended periods lapsing without missionaries, many communities reverted to other methods of selection for leaders, such as heredity. In the end, the various villages worked out their own electoral methods.[152] Many of the familiar elements were present—an election process adapted to the customs and needs of the community, a formal installation process, and travel to the provincial capital at Pitic (now Hermosillo) for confirmation at the hands of Spanish officials.[153] Jesuit chroniclers at the far northern O'odham missions left valuable clues about the electoral processes they instituted. Ignaz Pfefferkorn, who served at Guevavi from 1761 to 1763, offered perhaps the best summary of Indian town government in Sonora from a Jesuit perspective:

Certain Indian magistrates were put at the head of each village. . . . Indians who were best fitted for the position and who seemed also to be true and pious Christians were appointed as magistrates.

The first and most distinguished of these magistrates was the *govenaar* [gobernador]. . . . His duty it was to pass judgment on disputes which occurred in the village, to see that the laws were obeyed, and to punish transgressions according to their seriousness. However, he was not permitted to punish anyone without the pastor's knowledge and consent, lest passion cause him to misuse his power.

> The second in command bore the name *alcalde* [similar to a Pueblo lieutenant governor].... The alcalde carried out the governor's orders and filled his office during the governor's absence.
>
> Every community had also a fiscal ... who was, so to speak, a summoner. He was obliged to assemble the people when a community enterprise was to be undertaken or when a general announcement was to be made.... Similarly, he reported ... misdeeds which he discovered among the people....
>
> In each village there were also one or two ... *madores*, who supervised the grown children and also cared for the sick. This office was filled by Indians, who from their reputations could be expected to be faithful, careful, and diligent.[154]

Ignaz Pfefferkorn also referred to special clothing worn by Indian magistrates while performing the duties of their office, such as scarlet shirts and pants with silver borders, a decorated hat (which had so angered Nápoli), and their "silver-knobbed" varas de justicia.[155] But for all of his detail about the magistrates and duties of office—and Pfefferkorn certainly was observant—he was not describing a democratic system where Indians chose their own leaders; rather, Jesuits simply selected the officers.

Joseph Och, who labored among O'odhams and Opatas in the 1750s and 1760s, similarly described the officers and their duties. The governor was the "first person of the village" who reported to the missionary "once or twice daily" on "everything of a political as well as a military nature ... and receive[d] orders and guidance" from him. He echoed many of Pfefferkorn's statements: "The Indians' actual superiors [magistrates] in the villages are mainly chosen by the father, who knows them best, and then approved by the provincial governor. These Indian magistrates may become somewhat conceited and consider themselves of the nobility or as caciques; yet it lies in the father's power, if they conduct themselves badly, to depose them along with a public whipping, and reduce them to common folk. Others are then elevated in the name of the King, and receive the staff of authority. Such a staff is often fitted with a silver knob weighing a pound."[156] Pfefferkorn and Och reveal a deep Jesuit bias against the ability of O'odhams to choose their own leaders and administer their own affairs. In his own words, Och "mainly chose" O'odham officers, and then whipped or deposed those who misbehaved. He went so far as to assert that "The Indians recognize the King of Spain as their overlord, or much more; they believe he is the man who can give them orders."[157]

Juan Nentvig, who also labored in Pimería Alta in the 1750s and 1760s, differed from Pfefferkorn and Och in his 1764 account, observing that "The governor is a native *selected by the inhabitants of the pueblo* in the presence of the missionary who directs the inhabitants to be sure that the *elected man* is one who leads a good life thus setting an example that will stimulate and spur them to be good." His narrative stands out in that it refers to an Indigenous electoral process and to the governor as an "elected man." He also wrote that the temastián "also serves as scribe for the town council," thereby pointing to the existence of Indian cabildos with at least some literate councilmembers.[158] Since Jesuits wielded a great deal of power within the O'odham-Spanish electoral system, it stands to reason that a more enlightened missionary could have put greater faith in an O'odham electorate and thus allowed more political autonomy. But real electoral power in Indian hands was the exception; these were typically *not* free elections.

Most Jesuits seem to have followed the early lead of Kino, who lamented that "the Indian governors do not know how to obey the missionary fathers nor how to command their own subjects. Their rather uncouth subjects, in turn, do not know how to obey the governors or officers."[159] Jesuits shared many of the same negative views of their charges that Franciscans in New Mexico held. For example, Philipp Segesser wrote that O'odhams at Caborca in the 1730s had "neither laws nor kings, and even God is not known here. Therefore there is much work to shape the heathens and also those who are already converted into a form." He displayed little trust in the men he had a hand in selecting for positions of government at Guevavi and Tumacácori. In one instance the O'odham governor, to whom he referred as "the most noble person in the mission," had told the father of strange men appearing to the Indians during nights of traditional dances. Segesser concluded that these figures were the devil disguised as Spaniards, coming to frustrate the work of the Jesuits.[160] It is not surprising that Jesuits were loath to allow the sort of electoral freedoms inherent to Indian republics, since they believed the O'odhams to be unintelligent, godless, devil-worshiping children with no concept of government.

Yet Jesuits were not solely to blame; other factors also played a part in the failure of O'odham electorates to take root. In 1767, King Charles III expelled the Jesuits from the Spanish Empire and attempted mission reform. At first, the reformers tried to rid the missions of paternalism, instead favoring policies that granted civil rights to Indians and put mission economic activities in the hands of government agents. Spaniards hoped to secularize these missions and place Indians under the obligation to pay tribute. But these actions proved disastrous. Indians fled the missions in droves, tax revenues were not as expected, Franciscans sent to replace the Jesuits could not survive on their meager salaries, mission property disappeared, and church structures fell apart.[161]

Another major factor was population decline and the political instability it caused in the missions. For example, hundreds of Sobaipuris from the Santa Cruz missions, who had been under constant attacked from Apaches, were relocated to Bac and its visita at Tucson. Francisco Garcés, the first Franciscan assigned to serve there, wrote in 1768 of the difficulty of staffing these in-flux missions with officers. He even had difficulty getting the Indians just to stay at the missions. He attempted to have the O'odham governor bring in reluctant Indians, who "by force or by free choice ... must come." He was forced to deal with three governors from three of the relocated Sobaipuri pueblos, who attempted to manipulate and flatter him so that he would leave them alone. In exasperation, Garcés wrote to his superiors on 23 July 1769, "Although in other areas the Indians can govern themselves, it is not so here unless the priest should govern."[162]

The mobility of the Indians in particular was a problem, as O'odhams died off and Tohono O'odhams from the desert were brought in to replace them. Diego Manuel Bringas, a Franciscan who came to the Pimería Alta missions in the wake of the Jesuit expulsion, reported that when the Indians were "made aware that the royal order left them at complete liberty," they "lived in perpetual idleness and continual wanderings in the brush and in the various pueblos." He concluded that "the Indians ... are incapable of governing themselves for many years after their conversion. They are always children." Spaniards were forced to continually fill the missions with "gentiles who join the reducción every year.... The old time Indians of these missions have died out due to the continual deaths caused by the Apaches, sickness, and fighting when there is an uprising.... Of what importance is it, then, that these missions have been here for more than a hundred years while their population has the characteristics of one that is barely ten years old?"[163]

Decades had passed since the establishment of the O'odham missions, and yet to Franciscans they seemed as politically unorganized as ever. Fray Pedro Font, writing of the Franciscan missionary efforts in Sonora in the late 1770s, commented, "In all the pueblos there are usually more deaths than births," and the missions "daily advance toward complete extermination."[164] Mixed communities existed in which O'odhams, Sobaipuris, Tohono O'odhams, and even Akimal O'odhams were packed into a one-size-fits-all setting. Many of the O'odhams who did not die from disease or Apache raids simply fled to the countryside, where they felt much safer. Fray Bartolomé Ximeno, who served at Tumacácori in 1773, reported that Tohono O'odhams were hesitant to settle at his mission in large numbers "because they say that in the missions the Apaches kill them, but that in their own lands the Apaches do not fall upon them as often. These then are the reasons for the backwardness of the missions and why the heathens are not converted."[165] Furthermore, as the historian Juliana Barr has pointed out, many Indians simply incorporated the missions into seasonal cycles of migration, living at the missions only part of the year.[166] It would have been extremely difficult to choose and install an Indigenous officer corps under which this in-flux, heterogeneous population could unite.

And yet, within this framework we can discern acts of political power and resistance by O'odham officers. Och went into great depth describing the punishments meted out at the missions under his watch. He commented, "Each offense has its prescribed punishment in blows and specific penalties set by the King himself, or in his name. The missionary alone can moderate them, as he almost always does." He was vehement: "Never did I permit a punishment to be meted out during my absence." In one instance the Indian governor, an "old, upright man, violated this rule." While Och was away, the governor administered a punishment to his own wife, who had violated some mission rule, shouting repeatedly, "No matter who it is, justice must be done!" After this, his "cunning" wife took the governor's vara de justicia and stated, "I am the *gobernadora*, justice must be done. You cannot deny that eight years ago I also apprehended you, and that you have not received punishment, and must now endure it." The "stupid old one" stated, "You are right." He removed his shirt and allowed himself to be lashed. The priest rebuked him for this "stupid and laughable" affair, but "he nevertheless rose in the esteem of the entire community who followed his example. Nevertheless, the woman had to make a public apology because she had arrogated authority to herself, and the other magistrates had to be displaced as useless and faint-hearted fellows because they had permitted their authority to be questioned."[167] Both the governor *and* his wife had subverted mission rules and the priest's authority, and while they were both punished, for that brief, humorous moment Indian humanity shone through within the O'odham-Spanish electoral system.

Missionaries expressed interest in educating future Indian governors and leaders, but such efforts to train young Indians for future service could backfire. Antonio Barbastro, a Franciscan who labored for a number of years in both O'odham and Opata missions, recalled actions he took at the Opata mission of Aconchi, where he called the people to his house and separated all the boys who were under the age of twelve. He told the people that these boys would remain in his home, which was the school, and there they would learn to read and write, among other things he would teach them. He did this because "These boys, after twenty years, will be governors, alcaldes, and hold other offices, and they will be people and will know what books say."[168] Och apparently attempted the same at his missions, describing the boys as "eager to learn, to the point of being indiscretely curious." He taught those boys "who worked with me how to read and write, which they did more avidly from natural zeal than would a European child with blows or coaxing." Unfortunately, he "soon ceased my schooling, for no book was secure from them, and suspicion moved them to open letters and betray the contents to their compatriots."[169] It could very well be that these officers-in-training were uncovering sensitive mission information and passing it along, thereby subverting mission discipline and order.

The vast majority of O'odham officers, regardless of whether empowered through a formal election or appointed to office, were involved in the many day-to-day activities associated with Indian officials throughout the Spanish empire. For example, they had a crucial hand in the work and supply of the missions. As Barbastro explained, "This work, this harvest, these sales and these purchases and the distribution are run directly by the hand of the Indian Governor, but with the announcement, advice and direction of the minister, to avoid frauds that could intervene."[170] O'odham governors also led their towns' auxiliaries in battle, as was the case at Bac in 1768, when Apaches raided the mission. The two Spanish soldiers stationed there, augmented by O'odham warriors led by the governor, engaged the Apaches, recapturing some stolen cattle. They were ambushed as they gave chase to the Apaches. Despite fighting "with great valor," the governor and two soldiers "gave up their lives in battle."[171]

Governors also gave testimony in court, in cases both serious and inconsequential. In Tucson's first murder trial, a vecino by the name of Francisco Xavier Díaz was accused of killing his wife, María Ignacia Castelo. The murder took place at San Xavier del Bac, where Francisco was employed as a "cowboy." The accused murderer claimed that his was a crime of passion, after he had witnessed his wife having an affair with an O'odham named Juan. Bac's governor, Eusebio, gave testimony at the trial that he and Díaz had been drinking together on the day of the murder. But he said he had not seen Juan in the village that day, nor at any other time, and did not suspect that María had been unfaithful to Francisco. With the testimony of the governor and other individuals, both O'odhams and vecinos, Díaz was found guilty and in all likelihood was garroted at the Tucson garrison toward the end of 1814.[172]

In another example of legal actions taken by O'odham officers, Father Narciso Gutiérrez encouraged Tumacácori's justicias to travel to the administrative capital at Arizpe in 1806 to ask for a formal land grant, which the Indians of the mission did not have. In fact, no one knew Tumacácori's actual boundaries, and vecino ranchers and others had frequently encroached on Indian lands. By then many Tohono O'odhams from the west had relocated to the mission. The priest told Tumacácori's governor, a Tohono O'odham named Juan Legarra, and the other justicias to petition for a formal land grant. The legal proceedings that ensued lasted from 1806 to the next year. The Indians of Tumacácori won their land grant, and none too soon as ranchers on all sides increasingly encroached on their land. The justicias made statements in court on behalf of their people, called witnesses, and generally handled all the important parts of the case.[173]

Nevertheless, the political incorporation of O'odhams into the Spanish electoral sphere can only be described as incomplete. While they did not reject the system outright, as Hopis had, neither did they embrace and incorporate the franchise, as Yaquis had. This was due to the factors already mentioned, and in the end, as the historian John Kessell pointed out:

> The annual mission "election" was never intended to be free and open. The missionary provided close supervision, seeing to it that indios ladinos, the most hispanicized of his neophytes, were chosen. At Tumacácori cooperative Indians were elected over and over. As mission *justicias*, they maintained order and assisted the Father in his relations with the people. In turn they learned something of how [so-called] civilized men governed themselves. [Franciscan Antonio María Reyes wrote in 1772 that] "The missionaries must . . . teach and make the justicias understand the obligation, love, and veneration they owe our beloved Sovereign, and that in his name they must punish the bad in moderation and serve as protectors of the good."[174]

With Spaniards retaining much of the power of governance at the fledgling O'odham republics, often the best they could hope for was the selection of a leader who commanded their respect and also had the community's best interest at heart, but a tyrant was also possible, as had arisen at the Pueblos. Writing in 1778, Juan Agustín de Morfi described an election in Pimería Alta: "The annual election of these officials should be in the community house by vote and with the assistance of the Spanish justice of the district. But ordinarily they yield to the proposition which is made at the door of their house, and immediately that they are admitted, he [the justice] places them in possession [of the office] without any other formality than to inform those present that so and so are the officials."[175] Morfi's language would indicate a certain routineness in Indians' yielding to the selections made by Spaniards, not to mention a rather unceremonious installation process. The rhetoric of Indian self-government in Pimería Alta thus rang hollow, even while O'odhams made the most of a flawed system.

Conclusion

The history of Indian voting in the Arizona-Sonora Borderlands, viewed through the experiences of Hopis, Yaquis, and O'odhams, is replete with the unfulfilled promises of colonial Indian voting and self-government. The plan to politically incorporate Indigenous peoples in this borderlands region hinged on efforts by clerics, military officials, civil governors, and Indian officers. Clearly, the goal to complete this incorporation within one to two decades was unreasonably optimistic. In all three cases—Hopi, Yaqui, and O'odham—violence accompanied the new political realignment. At the northern extreme, Hopis endured the arrival of Spanish civil and religious representatives, followed by the establishment of Franciscan missions at Awat'ovi and other villages. They implemented a system of civil government, although we do not know exactly what form it took. The record contains fleeting mentions of Hopi governors, fiscales, and other officers going about their work in the often-violent sphere of Franciscan missionization. Perhaps such political realignment was too much, as Hopis twice expelled Spaniards and their allies in order to restore balance to their world. One can imagine that Hopis working within a tenuous Hopi Indian republic were silenced or murdered at Awat'ovi that fateful December morning in 1700, and whatever memory remained of Hispanicized Hopis wielding varas de justicia died with them. Perhaps the Castilian-speaking Miguel had met such a fate after accepting the governorship at Awat'ovi. The image of Hopis killing other Hopis over power and Christianity is one of the darkest illustrations of the destructiveness of colonialism and of how Spanish efforts to realign the politics and religion of Indian communities could result in unimaginably brutal consequences.

At the southern edge of the Arizona-Sonora Borderlands, Yaquis confronted Spanish political-religious power in a manner that reflected an adaptive culture, but one that always had as its primary goal the maintenance of political independence. Yaquis, who knew of the arrival of the Spaniards through sacred prophecy, incorporated and adapted Spanish electoral institutions. But Yaquis always viewed these institutions as their own and did not countenance Jesuit interference or disrespect. Muni and Bernabé, the quintessential Yaqui governors, navigated complex legal, economic, and religious boundaries, but also displayed strident and forceful sovereignty when they thought it necessary. While Yaquis appear the most "Hispanicized" and politically accommodating of the three groups, they insisted that all political realignment be done on their own terms.

Residing in the middle of this complex geographical-ideological borderlands, O'odham peoples experienced more than a century of missionization, and yet mission officials lamented over the last decades of the eighteenth century and the first decades of the nineteenth that their charges seemed habitually at square one. They never truly approached being incorporated into the Spanish body politic, or forming sovereign republics. The project to transition the O'odhams of Pimería Alta into tax-paying Spanish citizens mostly failed. Missionaries there proved unwilling to place control of political affairs squarely in O'odham hands, which, coupled with epidemics, borderlands warfare, and an unwillingness on the part of O'odhams themselves to commit to living at the missions, resulted in the failure to establish colonial O'odham electorates. Still, some O'odhams recognized their lack of political power and engaged in armed revolt on several occasions. In 1751, O'odhams, who were "dissatisfied over certain abuses in the exercise of civil authority,"[176] mirrored many of Muni and Bernabé's actions during the Yaqui Revolt of 1740. Luis Oacpicagigua, who was both the O'odham governor of Sáric and the captain general of the Pimería Alta, complained bitterly in the aftermath of the revolt that he had been severely mistreated by the Jesuit Father Ignacio Keller. Keller had insulted him for wearing Spanish clothes and going on military campaigns as an Indian auxiliary leader, and questioned his authority as a town officer.[177] Father Provincial Juan Antonio Baltasar asserted that Oacpicagigua was solely to blame for the revolt, because of his conceit brought on by the honors and titles that had been bestowed on him.[178] This O'odham officer, surely like many others, yearned for the autonomy and sovereignty of his people, even while he cooperated with Spanish authorities in military campaigns and other actions. Yet the vote was not central to this revolt, as it had been for Yaquis.

Taken as a whole, the history of Indian electoral politics in the Arizona-Sonora Borderlands during the Spanish period is much more varied than the experience of New Mexico's Pueblo peoples. Still, both areas would share in the further promise of secularization and expansion of civil rights for Indigenous peoples that accompanied Mexican independence during the pivotal first half of the nineteenth century. And while secularization, tribute-paying, and an end to the mission system would appear to be solutions to ending the minority of Indigenous peoples first in New Spain and later in Mexico's far northern borderlands, these policies would bring their own set of problems, centering on Indigenous electorates and the position that Indians would occupy in the colonial state.

CHAPTER THREE

Pueblo Contestations of Power in the Mexican Period

From Spanish Twilight to Mexican Republic

The years from 1821, when Mexico formally gained its independence from Spain, to 1846, when the United States began a war of conquest against the Republic of Mexico, are remembered as politically, socially, and culturally chaotic for Mexicans of all races and classes. For Indigenous peoples, that chaos did not simply begin with the Treaty of Córdoba in 1821, in which Spain formally recognized an independent Mexico, or even with Miguel Hidalgo y Costilla's "Grito de Dolores" in 1810, which called on *criollos* (Mexicans of Spanish descent born in the New World), mestizos, and Indians to throw off the yoke of Spanish oppression. While James Brooks has correctly identified the years from 1810 to 1846 as the period of Mexican nationalism in the Southwest Borderlands,[1] the roots of the profound change that engulfed the Indians of New Mexico and the Arizona-Sonora Borderlands are to be found in the latter half of the eighteenth century, culminating in the events of the 1840s, when yet another colonial power forced its administration on the Indians of the territory.

The Mexican period in what became the U.S. Southwest would mark the final stage of colonial administration in the Hispanic model, a model that agents of New Mexico and the United States would later attempt to alter drastically in favor of their own vision. For Indians, this brief interlude was a period marked by the high ideals of independence, racial equality, and opportunity promised by those who heralded an independent Mexico. But the reality was that New Mexico's Indian peoples found Mexican promises as empty as those offered by the Spaniards who had preceded them. Government officials in Mexico City were far too preoccupied with the upheavals that accompanied independence to fully implement the reforms intended to bring political and social equality to Indians. Furthermore, the rhetoric of independence also opened up Pueblo lands to alienation and encroachment, as protections extended to repúblicas de indios were dropped in favor of "equality." It was a difficult time for the Pueblos, who sought to confront colonial power and its abuses with assertions of their own sovereignty, while navigating a tricky landscape of citizenship in the Mexican state.

For all its faults of colonial administration, Spain did allow a relatively high degree of political autonomy on the local level in its New World colonies. By the mid 1700s, in many areas *criollos*, mestizos, and Indians all enjoyed some degree of political power. With a declining empire and numerous wars that left the Crown reeling and in search of funds, Spain sold political offices—from corregidores and ayuntamiento members to the viceroy—to the highest bidder. As a result of this policy, criollos and mestizos who could afford it had access to some upward political mobility. Contemporaneously, many Indians at the missions enjoyed semisovereign political and economic powers within the system of repúblicas de indios. But as Habsburg rule of Spain came to a close in the early 1700s, and after nearly a century of imperial decline, Spain needed drastic reform. Bourbon King Felipe V instituted a series of measures aimed at centralizing government in Spain, restoring royal finances and a depleted treasury, and reorganizing the military. These Bourbon reformers hoped such actions would modernize a desperately inefficient system of tax collection, provide for more competent provincial government, and speed up the development of regional economies.[2] More important for Indians, the colonial government took greater fiscal control of Indian pueblos in 1766, which left Indian rulers under more extensive oversight and with less autonomy in dispensing community funds and determining budgets.[3] In the waning days of its empire, Spain began the process of phasing out repúblicas de indios, a process that Mexico would continue once it had achieved its independence.

In the midst of the Crown's desperate eighteenth century attempts to reform its colonial administration, inhabitants of Spanish America began to develop a strong American identity. Criollos in particular became increasingly disillusioned with *peninsulares* (Spaniards born in Iberia), or *gachupines*, as they called them. Spain responded to this heightened, politically strident American identity by attempting to reduce New World possessions to their former colonial status, referring to them as *colonias* (colonies) as opposed to *reinos* (kingdoms), which had become common practice. Spain replaced the sale of provincial offices with regular paid officials chosen by the Crown, which significantly diminished the power of criollos. There was pushback, particularly in Mexico, where prominent criollos and their supporters agitated for greater autonomy and home rule.[4]

Events came to a head in the early nineteenth century when Napoleon Bonaparte's armies invaded Iberia. King Charles IV abdicated the throne in March 1808, and Napoleon replaced him with his own brother Joseph Bonaparte. In response, Spaniards rallied around Charles's son, Ferdinand VII. They called for him to be king, and a movement in support of Ferdinand became synonymous with the movement against the French presence in Spain. In addition, emerging political players in the Americas saw the collapse of the Bourbon Crown as the perfect opportunity to push for more power in New Spain's politics.[5] Peninsulares, criollos, mestizos, and Indians in Mexico City and elsewhere all watched anxiously to see how the Spanish struggle against Napoleon would unfold. Pueblo Indians in New Mexico continued with their seasonal, cyclical lifestyle, largely unaware of the political turmoil that would come to grip even the far-flung borderlands. The events that followed 1808 marked the beginning of a political revolution in the Americas that would significantly change Pueblo Indian rights, electorates, and political participation.

In America, many criollos initially rallied around the embattled Ferdinand VII. Others argued that with the Crown in chaos under a virtually powerless monarch, sovereignty reverted to the people and their institutions, such as the powerful ayuntamiento of Mexico City. With the Spanish government hemmed in by the French at the port city of Cádiz, in the southern Spanish region of Andalucía, a national congress, or *Cortes*, was called to deliberate on political reforms that resulted in a new constitution for Spain and the restoration of Ferdinand to the throne. The Constitution of 1812 transformed Spain into a constitutional democracy.[6] In the deliberations that resulted in a constitutional state, participants engaged in spirited debate over the place of non-Iberians in the nation. Spain needed the support of persons residing outside the Iberian peninsula in order to defeat Napoleon, but such support was almost certainly contingent on access to greater political participation for those residing in overseas possessions. Many peninsulares at the Cortes of 1810–12 could not stomach the prospect of full political participation for some sixteen million American and Philippine residents.[7] Still, non-peninsulares played a part at the Cortes. In fact, don Pedro Bautista Pino traveled to Spain as New Mexico's representative, but played a rather anonymous part in the proceedings.[8]

In Cádiz, the struggle between peninsulares and non-peninsulares over representation and political participation played out over a frenetic year-and-a-half. Dionisio Inca Yupangui of Perú, a highly educated and celebrated military veteran, was the lone Indian representative at the Cortes. Despite its low Indigenous representation, the American contingent pushed for political equality. A leader of this contingent, José Mejía Lequerica, delivered an impassioned statement on 2 October 1810, calling for the Cortes to "grant equality . . . to all the free castes." He even got down on his knees in a bit of dramatic flair, reportedly drawing tears from the gallery. Unfortunately, the peninsulares at the Cortes made up the majority of the delegates, with their seventy-five deputies greatly outnumbering the thirty American and Philippine deputies. They refused to grant full political participation to all free men, in spite of the impassioned pleas offered by the Americans.[9]

On 15 October 1810, the Americans presented a list of eleven demands, the most important of which called for equal representation between Spain and its overseas possessions. The language of this list stipulated representation for "natives derived from both hemispheres, Spaniards as well as Indians, and the children of both."[10] Iberians put up particularly stiff resistance to the proposal for Indian political rights. A statement was read on 11 September 1811, declaring that more than 200 years of efforts to Christianize and civilize Indians had accomplished little. Indians simply were not fit for self-government. This statement, called the *Representación del Consulado de México*, read: "[The Indian] is endowed with a laziness and languor. . . . He never moves unless hunger or vice drive him. Congenitally stupid, without either innovative talent or strength of thought, he despises both the arts and work; they are not necessary to his way of life. He is a drunkard by nature. . . . Sensual because of lascivious thoughts and bereft of chaste ideas about physical closeness, modesty or incest, he takes his fleeting pleasures with the woman closest at hand. As careless as he is insensitive to religious truths . . . and lacking love for his fellow-creatures, he only avoids those crimes which will bring him immediate punishment." American representatives were so outraged by this characterization that they attempted to leave the proceedings, but the president of the Cortes ordered the guards to bar the exit doors.[11] The peninsular desire to completely exclude Indians from political representation ultimately proved impossible, since the nominal freedom and equality of Indians had already been too firmly established in the Leyes de Indias to pursue such a course. Furthermore, peninsulares simply could not overlook these demands while still seeking the loyalty and support of criollos, mestizos, and Indians, which they desperately needed.[12]

In the end, the Constitution of 1812 represented a compromise between American demands and peninsular fears. Article 5 read, "Of those who are Spaniards, and lawfully considered as such: 1. All free-men, born and bred up in the Spanish dominions, and their sons." This meant Indians were considered Spaniards under the law. Article 18 granted citizenship to "Those who, by both lines, are of Spanish parents, of either hemisphere, and have resided ten years in some village of the Spanish dominions." Article 23 stated, "Those who are citizens can obtain municipal employments; and elect for them, in the cases pointed out by law."[13] The constitution allowed all municipalities with 1,000 or more inhabitants to establish constitutional ayuntamientos, with significantly expanded political participation. For purposes of representation, one deputy to the Cortes was granted for every 70,000 inhabitants. But the Cádiz Constitution left out all Spaniards of African descent. On paper, it seemed that the long fight for Indian citizenship and voting rights in Spain had finally been resolved. The granting of the franchise to all adult males (except persons of African ancestry), without a literacy test or property requirement, made Spain the most politically open society in the Western world to date.[14]

The first large-scale popular elections in New Spain were held in Mexico City in 1812–13. These elections for Spanish Congressional Deputies represented the first direct participation in national politics by large sectors of the population. It was a complicated process, but electoral *juntas*, or assemblies, chose electors, who then chose the deputies to the Cortes. Among the electors were former Indian governors of Mexico City's Indian communities, such as Dionisio Cano y Moctezuma, who had been the governor of the San Juan section of the city. Nevertheless, many were excluded from the elections, since the constitution did not grant citizenship to women and people of African descent, and also suspended the voting rights of debtors, domestic servants, the unemployed, and those who were under criminal indictment.[15] Yet these elections represented an important development in electoral reform: the first Indian participation in politics beyond the town level.

These sweeping political concessions failed to stave off turmoil in the Americas. Criollos who favored home rule in Mexico, led by Father Miguel Hidalgo y Costilla, the priest of the mostly Indian parish of Dolores located in the central Mexican state of Guanajuato, sought to assemble a broad coalition of support. Criollos, mestizos, and Indians all had a part to play.[16] Hidalgo and his supporters planned a revolt for October 1810. When it was discovered in mid-September, the rebels decided to strike early, much like Pueblo Indians had done in 1680. What happened next is steeped in legend, and it is impossible to know what Hidalgo actually said when he reportedly called his parishioners, many of them Indians, to join the revolt.[17] The popular retelling of what became known as the "Grito de Dolores" has a distinctly Indigenous feel. In the most common version of the Grito, Father Hidalgo stated: "My Children: a new dispensation comes to us today. Will you receive it? Will you free yourselves? *Will you recover the lands stolen three hundred years ago from your forefathers by the hated Spaniards?* We must act at once.... Will you not defend your religion and your rights as true patriots? Long live our Lady of Guadalupe! Death to bad government! Death to the gachupines!" Hidalgo embraced la Virgen de Guadalupe as a symbol of the revolt. By employing the Virgin as a symbol—an Indigenous representation of the

Virgin Mary who first appeared to the Indian Juan Diego in 1531—Hidalgo thereby appealed to Indians.[18] He also called for an end to tribute, which burdened Indians disproportionately. The early propaganda of Hidalgo's movement was aimed at criollos, mestizos, and Indians. Printed materials were popular with literate white Mexicans, while slogans, songs, and banners prevailed among Indians and mestizos.[19] Thus, while the Cortes in Spain debated citizenship for people of color in Mexico and elsewhere, Father Hidalgo led an independence movement that specifically called on Indians to expel the colonizers and reclaim their lands. By this point independence seemed inevitable, as Spain only reluctantly granted citizenship and voting rights to all non-African Spaniards, while Father Hidalgo called on Indians to unite with him to cast off Spanish government. During Hidalgo's rise and the decade that followed, a new language of nationalism and citizenship emerged in which Indians played a prominent role.[20]

The independence movement gained further traction after Hidalgo was executed in 1811, and sustained the rhetoric of racial equality and civil rights for mestizos and Indians. General Augustín de Iturbide, who inherited Hidalgo's mantle, championed the *Plan de Iguala*, which became independent Mexico's first governing document. The Plan attempted to balance the interests of the Church, the army, and the Mexican nation. It proposed a constitutional monarchy, and suggested that Ferdinand VII come to Mexico to rule as emperor. When Mexican forces finally defeated royalist armies and seized Mexico City, the Spanish *jefe politico superior* (the office replacing that of viceroy in the final years of Spanish rule) Juan O'Donojú signed the Treaty of Córdoba on 24 August 1821, thereby accepting the Plan de Iguala and recognizing Mexican independence.[21] The Plan called for the *Tres Garantías* (Three Guarantees) of Catholicism, Union, and Independence. The ideology of equality is clear from its preamble: "When I speak of Americans, I speak not only of those persons born in America, but of the Europeans, Africans, and Asians who reside here. May they all have the good grace to hear me! . . . For three hundred years . . . Spain educated and aggrandized [North America], forming its opulent cities, its beautiful villages, its remote provinces and kingdoms. . . . [A] general union between Europeans, Americans, and Indians, is the only solid basis upon which our common happiness can rest." Article 12 related to the political status and rights of Indians: "All of the inhabitants of that Empire, with no considerations except those of merit and virtue, are citizens qualified to accept any employment."[22] Thus, Mexico continued the trend toward racial equality begun in the twilight of Spanish rule, but carried it one critical step further by also extending full citizenship to all Mexicans, even those of African descent. It remained

New Mexico Spanish-Mexican Constitutional Reform

By November 1812, Spain had instituted a number of reforms, such as abolishing personal servitude by Indians and giving them control of communal lands in order to encourage agriculture, industry, and population growth. One of the biggest reform measures of the Constitution of 1812 was its establishment of ayuntamientos in all towns with more than 1,000 residents. This change marked the virtual elimination of repúblicas de indios. Constitutional ayuntamientos lumped Spaniards, mestizos, and Indians together in a single voting body—in "ethnically neutral municipal governments"—thereby replacing the traditional cabildos and town governments of Indian republics.[23] Indians were no longer to vote for leaders solely of their own race. Even in larger urban areas with Indian neighborhoods, they had traditionally elected their own town governments. But now, Indians were swallowed up in the larger Mexican population. Circulars emanating from Mexico City declared that repúblicas de indios would be closed down with no more local elections beyond those for the new constitutional ayuntamientos. Many Indians grew disillusioned, believing their participation in the new ayuntamiento system was useless. In large villages with multiracial populations—especially where they were a minority—Indians had essentially lost their political power.[24]

Constitutional changes made their way to New Mexico's Pueblo Indians in some forms. As alluded to previously, in 1812 the Cortes had established the elaborate system of indirect democracy whereby voters chose *compromisarios* (delegates), *escrutadores* (scrutineers), and a secretary. It was a convoluted process, but delegates elected one or more parochial electors, and then the parochial electors elected a *partido* (district) elector, and then partido electors met to elect a provincial *diputado* (deputy).[25] As the historian Gary Van Valen has shown, Pueblo Indians did take part in these elections, although only sparingly. For example, in 1814 at the partido of Alameda, which included several Pueblos, Sandia parish (representing both the Indians of the Pueblo and neighboring Hispanos) elected sixteen compromisarios, with Juan Roque Perico, a Pueblo Indian, among them. Cochiti parish (which also had Pueblo Indians and Hisapanos) elected twenty compromisarios, of which two were Cochiti Pueblo Indians, Juan Antonio Ignacio Baca and Juan José Quintana. San Felipe parish chose eleven compromisarios, but none of them were Indians. These compromisarios then chose all Hispanos for parochial electors, and the parochial electors also chose an Hispano for partido elector. In all, Pueblo participation in the Alameda partido represented just three Pueblo Indians. Other locales had little or no Pueblo Indian participation in choosing partido electors. Tesuque had the highest proportion of Indian participation, where three of the five compromisarios chosen were Pueblo Indians. Yet they still elected an Hispano parochial elector, who was ultimately rejected by the electoral junta in Santa Fe on the grounds that Tesuque lacked enough vecinos to hold elections and the man they ultimately selected was not old enough to serve. As Van Valen aptly demonstrated, "Limited Pueblo participation [in Cortes-era elections] was the rule throughout New Mexico."[26]

Perhaps more important, it proved extremely difficult to completely eliminate the repúblicas de indios across Spanish America. Even though they had been legally abolished, residents in rural areas populated almost solely by Indians continued to elect Indian town governors and officials. In some places Indians constituted as much as 70–90 percent of the population. In such places, the old Indian republics simply continued. Depending on the proportion of Indians to non-Indians, there were three possibilities for the compositions of town councils: ayuntamientos or cabildos without a single Indian; those with some Indians; and those that were entirely Indian.[27] While many of New Mexico's Pueblo Indians lived in villages that were geographically, culturally, and linguistically separated from Hispano populations, others lived in close proximity to people of Spanish descent. Indian elections of town officials in the Pueblos persisted into the Mexican period, even while the Republic of Mexico sought to eliminate special Indian status, a trend that had begun in the final years of the Spanish colonial period.

But in many ways, the developments of the previous decades remained distant to New Mexico's Indian and Hispano populations alike. New Mexico remained one of the most remote territories in the Spanish Empire. Despite now living in an independent Mexico with no legal distinctions between Indians and non-Indians, life for New Mexico's Indians went on much as it had before. New Mexicans had not taken an active part in the independence movement, instead observing the unfolding events from a distance. Word of Iturbide's victory arrived relatively late, with a mounted courier bringing the news to the Palace of the Governors in Santa Fe on 26 December 1821. The courier presented a circular demanding that New Mexico Governor Facundo Melgares and other leaders officially swear their allegiance to the Mexican nation. A quiet, somber celebration followed on 31 December, in which Melgares and others hailed the Tres Garantías on a stage built in the center of the plaza.[28]

New Mexicans held a second celebration on 6 January. This time the spirited festivities lasted several days and nights. Governor Melgares later recounted the January celebrations for Mexico's official state newspaper, the *Gaceta Imperial*. His description demonstrates that Pueblo Indians helped usher in a new national government. Melgares wrote, "Ending the parade which terminated at the main church of the parish, the crowd, which in spite of the severe inclemency, was very large, and moved to the main plaza: awaiting them was a magnificent dance, [performed] by the natives of the Pueblo of San Diego de Tesuque which lasted until one o'clock in the afternoon, and after it ended, the participants divided up to [go to] the various public games which had been set up around the plaza."[29]

An Anglo-American also witnessed the day's celebration. General Thomas James, a soldier and frontiersman, was sent from St. Louis in 1821 to open up trade with Mexico. He was present in Santa Fe in late 1821 and early 1822, and wrote about what he observed. Although clearly biased against Mexicans— they "abandoned themselves to the most reckless dissipation and profligacy"—he also referenced Pueblo Indian participation in the celebration of the new national political order: "[A] large company of men and women from San Felipe, an Indian town forty miles south of Santa Fe, marched into the city, displaying the best-formed persons I had yet seen in the country.... This Indian company danced very gracefully upon the public square to the sound of a drum and the singing of the older members of their band.... About the same time the Peccas [*sic*, Pecos] Indians came into the city, dressed in skins of bulls and bears." Interestingly, James commented on the fitness of New Mexico's Indians for self-government: "I saw enough during this five days' revelry to convince me that the republicans of New Mexico were unfit to govern themselves or anybody else. [But] the Indians acted with more moderation and reason in their rejoicing than the Spaniards." He also wrote that New Mexico's Indians—referring not only to Pueblos but also to Utes and Navajos, all of whom he described as "Mexican Indians"—were "a nobler race of people than their masters ... generally far in advance of the Spaniards around them, in all the arts of civilized life as well as in the virtues that give value to national character."[30] Putting aside his attempt to discredit New Mexico's Hispano population, it is noteworthy that more than one source mentions a Pueblo Indian presence at the Santa Fe festivities celebrating the new nation.

It is difficult to determine how Indians might have viewed these political changes, based solely on brief accounts by non-Indians of the festivities accompanying Mexican independence. A significant hemispheric geopolitical shift, Mexican independence had repercussions that continue to reverberate to the present, but what did it mean for Indians of the time? The historian David Weber, writing about the events of early 1822, concluded that "the reaction [to Mexican independence] of Pueblo Indians [cannot] be assessed. Although [they] participated in the Independence festivities, there is no way of knowing what meaning it held for them."[31] The succinct asides by Melgares and James are significant, nonetheless, because they show that Indians at least took some active part in celebrating Mexican independence in New Mexico. It remained to be seen how they would participate in Mexican national politics, but their presence demonstrates at least a passing interest in—and awareness of—these developments.

New Mexico's Indians in the New Republic

That some of New Mexico's Native peoples helped celebrate the dawn of an independent Mexico is without question. But precisely how the high ideals of the new Republic of Mexico filtered down to the Pueblos is an entirely different matter. The most important change was that Indians were now unquestionably Mexican citizens. This citizenship should have carried with it the right to vote and hold office. Yet changes in civil rights appear to have been rather slow in coming. Ward Minge, a prominent scholar of Acoma Pueblo history, described the changeover from colony to independent nation for the Pueblos in the following manner:

> On September 16, 1821, Mexico won her independence from Spain, a political change of some magnitude for America in general, but one so distant that the Ácomas would not be affected by it. Over the years the pueblos' mode of living did not change perceptibly. Mexican authorities accepted the agrarian and peaceful Indians as citizens and with a few changes in the old Spanish laws, their life went on as before. They continued farming, hunting, and grazing their own lands. Likewise, there were no apparent changes in administrative procedures when the Mexicans took control of New Mexico in 1821. If there were changes which affected the Pueblo Indians, other than those of citizenship and national loyalty, they went unrecorded.[32]

Minge's point is clear: although the Pueblos had become Mexican citizens, their lives did not change overnight after 1821.[33]

Unfortunately, much of our ignorance regarding changes during the Mexican era and Pueblo perceptions of the new republic are the result of an absence of Pueblo Indian sources. As such, one way to make sense of these developments is to again cautiously turn to the documents of the colonizers, where the Pueblo voice appears at times. Decrees issued during the years leading up to 1821 illustrate that New Mexico's Spanish authorities received directives from the Crown regarding the protection of Indian civil liberties. For example, a decree from Alejo García Conde, the "Governador Comandante General y Gefe Superior Politico" of New Spain, reiterated the civil rights of Indians throughout New Spain. Conde called attention to the actions taken in the Cortes, and stated that he wanted to "avoid any doubt" about the question of the status of Indians. The decree contained eight articles, among them that personal servitude by Indians be eliminated; that opportunities for Indians to attend religious colleges be provided; that communal work such as the maintenance of public houses, road construction, and building of bridges be distributed among Indians and vecinos of all classes; and that land be given to Indians who were married or over the age of twenty-five.[34]

Still, we must be careful not to overstate the attention that New Mexico officials paid to New Mexico's Indians at the time. For example, when don Pedro Bautista Pino, New Mexico's deputy to the Cortes in the 1810s, received instruction from his superiors at home, none of these instructions dealt specifically with Indians.[35] In his classic *Exposition on the Province of New Mexico*, prepared for royal officials in Spain, Pino pointed to the lack of ayuntamientos in New Mexico, thus necessitating an alternative electoral system for choosing their deputy.[36] Pino scarcely referenced Indians in his *Exposition*: "Spaniards and pure Indians (that are hardly distinguishable from ourselves) are the ones who make up the total of [New Mexico's] 40,000 inhabitants," and "New Mexico counts 40 thousand [persons], all citizens."[37] In Pino's statement—and he must be viewed as representing prominent Hispanos in New Mexico—we can see the roots of the pervasive myth of New Mexico's peaceful race relations, which persists to this day. He and others at times ignored or glossed over challenges faced by Indians. By flatly stating that Indians were indistinguishable from Hispanos, and that all were equal citizens, he asserted that New Mexico had succeeded in the mission of civilizing and incorporating its Indians into the body politic. Whether this was true for New Mexico's Pueblo Indians is a complex issue, to put it mildly.

Pueblo Indians before, during, and after the period of Mexican independence found themselves in the throes of frequent and complex political changes, which would, in turn, affect their exercise of the rights to vote and to participate in politics beyond the town level. Only one "official" cabildo or ayuntamiento was appointed in New Mexico before the first decades of the nineteenth century. It was naturally located in Santa Fe. However, as has been demonstrated, the Pueblos had their own Indigenous ayuntamientos where civil officers worked in conjunction with village elders and religious leaders to make important decisions on behalf of the communities. But as the historian Marc Simmons has pointed out, New Mexico's sole cabildo ceased functioning around 1725, with local civil authority thereafter resting in the hands of appointed alcades mayores and their assistants through the first decade of the nineteenth century. This began to change when the Cortes ordered that all towns with 1,000 or more inhabitants were to have a constitutional ayuntamiento composed of *alcaldes constitucionales* (mayors), regidores, a *procurador-síndico* (attorney), and a secretary. Towns that did not possess the requisite population, but were economically significant, could also select municipal councils. During these elections, which were held in December of each year, citizens voted first for electors, who then selected the magistrates. Alcaldes served for one year and regidores for two. The only requirements for holding office were that a man be at least twenty-five years of age and have resided in his town for five years. In an unexpected turn of events, when Ferdinand was restored to power after Napoleon's defeat in 1814, he issued a July 20 order that did away with the newly established constitutional ayuntamientos and reestablished the old system of town magistrates. He ordered all existing municipal councils dissolved. But in the typical seesaw action of the late Spanish period and the era of Mexican independence, this decision was reversed in 1820, thus restoring constitutional ayuntamientos in New Mexico's towns. The laws of the Cortes and the Cádiz constitution were once again formally recognized.[38] These constitutional ayuntamientos adopted local ordinances for the area under their jurisdiction, supervised local elections, verified land exchanges, and functioned as the court of first resort for both civil and criminal cases in their boundaries.[39]

But what of Indian participation in municipal affairs in New Mexico? The central question is not whether the rights to vote and to participate in government applied to Indians after Mexican independence; they did. The Indian program that Mexico pursued was based on the fundamental pillar of Indian citizenship. Adult Indian males could vote in elections and hold office, and Indian towns were to become participating units of larger municipalities that included Hispano communities as well. But Indian citizenship also implied the division of Indian communal lands and their subjection to taxation. Officials vigorously pursued these ends in Sonora during the Mexican period.[40] Nuevomexicanos also targeted Pueblo lands during the Mexican period. Even before independence, Hispano leaders favored the privatization of communal Pueblo lands. Pedro Pino lamented that Indian populations had not grown, which he attributed to the refusal of Indian women to give birth to more than four children (clearly, other factors were at play: hunger, disease, violence, and other threats to women's health). As a result, Indian towns were small, leaving "the larger part of the territory... uncultivated." Pedro Pino believed that the ayuntamientos called for in the 1812 Constitution should be authorized to correct this by taking Indian land and redistributing it to Spaniards.[41]

But the tradition of the Pueblo "four square leagues," an area measuring one league (approximately 2.6 miles) in all four cardinal directions from the central plaza of each Pueblo, was still in force in the 1820s, and stood in opposition to such plans. When New Mexico officials sought to privatize Pueblo land grants, and redistribute "surplus" lands to Hispanos, the Pueblos fought back as best they could. At Pecos Pueblo, for instance, a long dispute between Indians and neighboring Hispanos—which began during the administration of Governor Bartolomé Baca (1823–25)—persisted until 1829. Initially, Baca favored the interests of land-hungry Hispanos who had received grants of Pecos land and also bought land from individual Pecos Indians. Following years of court battles and the administrations of several New Mexico governors, Pecos secured the rights to its league. New Mexico's principal legislative body, the territorial deputation, declared, "Since time immemorial the land in question was the property of the Indians of Pecos." The Mexican Supreme Court agreed, leaving such cases of Pueblo land adjudication under the jurisdiction of New Mexico. The New Mexico deputation ordered the return of Pecos land granted to Hispanos, but not lands sold by the Indians, since they were now citizens and could alienate their land, making this a pyrrhic victory for the Indians. Unfortunately for Pecos, one of their own unscrupulous citizens by the name of José Cota, who had served as an alcade at Pecos Pueblo in the 1820s, went on to sell the best Pecos land to an Hispano for "eleven cows with calves and three bulls" in 1829. In short, even with Mexican courts protecting their land, Pueblo losses could not be fully prevented.[42]

Providing a Pueblo Indian perspective on their experiences during the Mexican period, Joe Sando has suggested that what some have seen as a lack of meddling by Hispano officials in Pueblo affairs under independent Mexico was actually quite the opposite: "Mexican influence in Indian life consisted largely of confusing Indian land title, ignoring the illegal taking of Pueblo land, and responding passively when Indian boundaries were violated. Thus were twenty-five years under the rule of Mexico spent." Furthermore, Sando asserted that the Plan of Iguala and Mexican rhetoric of equal rights "soon became the right for all equally to take Pueblo land."[43] Alfonso Ortiz concurred with Sando's statement, pointing to the attitudes of leaders such as Pedro Pino who, as previously indicated, "began to argue that because of the long decline in the Pueblo population ... the leagues were too large to be needed or advantageously used by the Pueblo villages and should thus be opened up for [Hispano] settlement." Like Sando, Ortiz concluded that one of the net results of Mexican independence for New Mexico's Pueblo peoples was "unauthorized encroachment upon Pueblo leagues and the filing by non-Indians of a number of formal petitions requesting titles to communally held Pueblo property."[44]

In extreme cases, Mexico's extension of citizenship to Pueblos even resulted in factionalism at Pueblo communities. For example, some Pueblo Indians at Cochiti used their new status as citizens to sell portions of the Pueblo's land to Hispanos, setting off a controversy that gripped the community during the first decades of the nineteenth century. Competing factions in favor of and opposed to citizenship and land alienation rights traveled to Mexico to present their cases, which historian Gary Van Valen asserts was behind the removal of the aforementioned Cochiti Governor Juan Antonio Ignacio Baca in 1815.[45] Armed with a more balanced perspective on what Mexican "neglect" meant in the lived experiences of Pueblo peoples, we can more fully understand the nature of Indian participation in New Mexican electoral processes and governance during the Mexican period.

Whether the constitutional changes of the late Spanish and early Mexican periods resulted in more Pueblo ayuntamientos is a matter of interpretation. Simmons asserted that by the time of Mexican independence, most New Mexican towns, including the Pueblos, had ayuntamientos. He also stated that changes to Spanish law from the 1810s through independence ended the "minority" of New Mexican Indians, and that they would thereafter be regarded as "Spaniards in all things, exercising especially their rights to vote and stand as candidates for office." He concluded definitively: by late 1821, most of the Pueblos had installed formal municipal governments.[46] Such statements may overlook the fact that the Pueblos continued with mature political institutions that had developed over the course of the previous two centuries. As Lansing Bloom pointed out, the Pueblos were "nominally under the jurisdiction of the federal government as Mexican citizens, but each pueblo had its own *cacique* and *principales*, and also its own 'governor' and other civil officers for each year, who were named by the cacique and approved by the people."[47] These institutions of Pueblo government would now have to balance Mexican citizenship with existing Pueblo-Spanish governing traditions.

While independent Mexico carried on the system of constitutional ayuntamientos after it had won independence, the assertion that most Pueblos had ayuntamientos by 1821 is difficult to verify. For example, according to the historian Daniel Tyler, "Although *ayuntamientos* (town councils) had been dissolved in the late colonial period in 1820, the King of Spain was forced to restore the Constitution of 1812 and recall the Cortes. In so doing, the *ayuntamiento* system was reestablished, and by 1821, most New Mexican towns and Indian Pueblos had their own *ayuntamientos*." Tyler further pointed to the problematic nature of determining which Hispano towns and Indian Pueblos had ayuntaminetos during the Mexican period, resulting from a lack of good recordkeeping: "Records of *ayuntamiento* activities are incomplete. Some collections were destroyed during the Mexican War and subsequent uprisings, but the general carelessness of officials in the Mexican and early territorial periods resulted in lost records. In some places, records were not even kept because of the illiteracy of the officials, the high cost of paper, or infrequent meetings. Although Governor Armijo listed sixteen *ayuntamientos* in 1828, a few years later Antonio Barreiro counted only four and noted that the majority of towns and pueblos were under the control of an alcalde."[48]

In Mexico's most remote provinces, with low populations and isolated villages and towns (which often lacked even paper for proper recordkeeping), it is simply impossible to know whether many locales had continuously functioning ayuntamientos during this period. In reality, the Pueblos likely had the most stable town governments in New Mexico and they had been in operation for decades. Outside observers did not understand this fact. To wit, a noted Anglo-American trader, Josiah Gregg, dismissed the Pueblos thusly: "Although the Pueblos are famous for their hospitality and industry, they still continue in the rudest state of ignorance, having neither books nor schools among them, as none of their languages have been reduced to rules, and very few of their children are ever taught in Spanish."[49] Such statements undermine general knowledge of the successful manner in which the Pueblos had governed their communities throughout the Spanish and Mexican periods. Pino, though he favored the redistribution of Pueblo land, contradicted Gregg, asserting, "Many Indians can read and write." Furthermore, "All of them have good reasoning power, keen judgment, and a natural, persuasive eloquence. They are slow to deliberate; they act in everything by common accord; and in their dealings they are extremely honest and truthful. These pueblos have different languages, but all the residents speak Spanish."[50]

The fact remains that ayuntamientos in the Mexican period were almost ephemeral institutions, seemingly popping up one year and then vanishing the next. Determining their number can at times feel like an exercise in futility. Governor Armijo put the number at sixteen in 1828. Scarcely five years later, the *administrador principal de correo* (head postal administrator) of Chihuahua, the location through which all of New Mexico's mail was delivered, listed the main cities, villas, Pueblos, missions, mines, ports of mark, presidios, plazas, haciendas, ranchos, and ayuntamientos in the territory. He reported that there were ayuntamientos only at Santa Fe, Abiquiú, Bado, Cochiti, Belen, San Agustin de la Isleta, San José de la Laguna, and Socorro, making eight in total. All the locations listed as ayuntamientos also received the designation of "Pueblo," which in this case simply meant "town."[51] Cochiti, Isleta, and Laguna were Indian Pueblos (with large Hispano populations nearby, as well), while Abiquiú, Belen, and Socorro did have many genízaro residents, but were not necessarily Indian Pueblos. Bado, or San Miguel del Bado, was located near Pecos Pueblo, but Pecos was nearly depopulated by this point. A report completed by Antonio Narvona in 1829 and subsequently sent to the government office of the Mexican Republic, listed alcaldías (locations with alcaldes, but not necessarily ayuntamientos) at thirty cities and towns. Among these, Indian Pueblos with alcaldes were Tesuque, Pecos, Cochiti, Santo Domingo, Jemez, Zia, Santa Ana, Sandia, San Felipe, Isleta, Laguna, Acoma, Zuni, Santa Clara, San Ildefonso, Pojoaque, Nambé, Ohkay Owingeh, Taos, and Picuris, for a total of twenty.[52] These Pueblos had an alcalde, and where a formal ayuntamiento was in place an elected alcalde worked in consultation with the body.[53] But the presence of an alcalde does not necessarily mean that a formal ayuntamento was in place as well.

Don Antonio Barreiro wrote an account of New Mexico in 1832. Barreiro was an attorney sent from Mexico to serve as *asesor*, or legal advisor, to New Mexico territorial authorities. Young and ambitious, he was elected New Mexico's deputy to the Mexican Congress in 1833, and then reelected in 1834. He published New Mexico's first newspaper, *El Crepúscolo de la Libertad*. His short account, or *Ojeada sobre Nuevo Mexico*, was published in Puebla.[54] In Barreiro's summary of New Mexico, he addressed, among other things, the territory's ayuntamientos. He included a table that showed where ayuntamientos were in place in the early 1830s, and where there were only alcaldes with no councils. Furthermore, he stated, "The illiteracy which prevails generally in this Territory causes these bodies, in which the law has deposited a great part of the common happiness, to be null and insignificant; so it will be evident that this, by no means the least of ills, is curable only by time and by such protection as the government may give to education." Thus Barreiro blamed governmental deficiencies on the lack of literacy among New Mexico's inhabitants and called the condition of public education in the territory "distressing."[55] While Pino pointed to literacy among Pueblo Indians, issues of illiteracy surely affected them. In the end, Barreiro listed only four ayuntamientos in New Mexico in

1832: Santa Fe, Cañada, Taos, and Albuquerque. Cochiti, Jemez, Sandia, Ohkay Owingeh, Isleta, and Laguna are listed as having a judge (alcalde) and an attorney (procurador-síndico).[56]

How, then, do we account for the discrepancy between assertions that all or perhaps most of New Mexico's Pueblos had ayuntamientos by 1821, and later reports that none of them did in 1832? The number of Indian ayuntamientos clearly fluctuated during the chaotic Mexican period, but to proceed from a majority in 1821 to none in 1832 seems strange. The answer, perhaps, is that formal ayuntamientos—those that Hispanos in positions of power would have acknowledged as such—may have infrequently existed at the Pueblos. Nor does it seem likely that the Pueblos simply dominated ayuntamientos, even in municipalities where they made up a significant part of the population.

A number of factors would have impeded, or at least complicated, the establishment of ayuntamientos in the Pueblos. Within the framework of the old república system, the Pueblos chose civil leaders through an electoral process that in many ways did not follow Hispanic democratic principles. Still, the system persisted and Mexican leaders continued to recognize elected Pueblo officers after 1821. Since the governor system continued, did it coexist alongside a Mexican ayuntamiento structure? Did citizens of Pueblos that had formal ayuntamientos elect their officers with candidates and vote tallies? Or did the village elders simply select regidores and other administrators, as they had the governors and officers? And what happened at Pueblos where there were only an alcalde and a procurador-síndaco? Did the powers of ayuntamiento officers coexist alongside or perhaps exceed those of the governor and the old Indian town council?

All these questions force us to examine the existence of Pueblo ayuntamientos more carefully. Due to the lengthy persistence of the governor system, and the relatively short lifespan of formal ayuntamientos during the Mexican period, it is a safe assumption that formal ayuntamientos never attained a place of prominence in all Pueblo communities. Instead, they continued in their reliance on Indian town councils in the older Spanish model. As one scholar has summarized it—and this seems particularly apt in describing Pueblo civil governments in the Mexican period—municipalities in the new republic failed to eliminate repúblicas de indios. The new state and local governments found these bodies to be useful intermediaries between the new mechanisms of the state and Indigenous peoples. Furthermore, Indians supported their repúblicas because they stood against new challenges to village land and sovereignty. In this way, Indians remained "sons of the town" as they became citizens of the

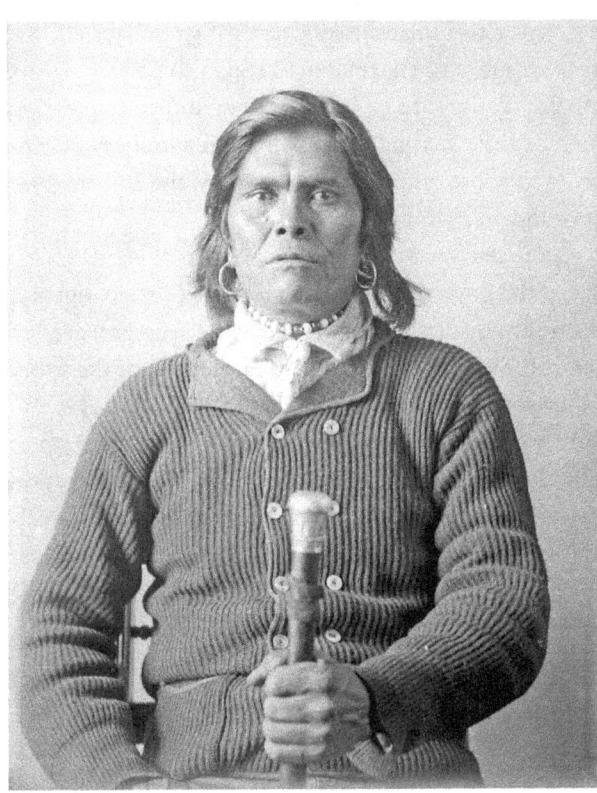

Portrait (front) of Governor Jesus Antonio Moya with Ornaments and Holding President Lincoln Cane, Nov. 1899. BAE GN 02208A 06366500, National Anthropological Archives, Smithsonian Institution.

nation, thus preserving Indigenous national identities and community resources.[57]

In addition, Mexican-era documents refer to formal ayuntamientos at locations such as Isleta, Jemez, Santa Clara, and Cochiti—all Indian Pueblos. This can be cause for some confusion. Such references do not necessarily indicate formal Indian ayuntamientos, or that Indians participated in ayuntamiento politics. An ayuntaimiento was, in theory, the governing council for a geographical area with more than 1,000 residents, but that area could include several towns or villages. Census figures for the Mexican period, though at times unreliable, display a wide disparity between Indians and Hispanos in a number of jurisdictions. For example, a church census of 1821 gave closely matched Indian-Hispano populations in a few locations, with Indians outnumbering Hispanos in a handful of others, but then Hispanos greatly outnumbering Pueblo Indians elsewhere. For example, Zuni Pueblo counted 1,597 Indians with no non-Indian population, while Cochiti Pueblo had 339 Indians to

359 non-Indians. In Isleta, 2,313 non-Indians resided, against 511 Indians.[58] Governor Facundo Melgares, writing at the tail end of the Spanish period in 1820, reported a total Hispano population of 28,436, with a total Indian population of 9,923.[59] In ayuntamientos representing areas with large numbers of Hispano residents, or likely even those with population parity, the Indian voice was likely drowned out or Indian participation was low.

Take, for example, a report sent in 1832 to the Jefe Politico of New Mexico (the position that replaced the governor for a time in New Mexico, but was essentially a change in name only) and then forwarded to the Secretary of State in Mexico City. The report brought to light an election dispute for the ayuntamiento of Isleta. This jurisdiction included the Pueblo of Isleta, but it also included a number of other towns and villages nearby. In the detailed set of documents, several individuals brought complaints against the alcalde, don José Chávez, who was described as an "hombre rico," or rich man. Individuals accused Chávez of manipulating the ayuntamiento elections for 1833 so that candidates to his liking won positions of power. The documents also provide insight into the electoral process: voters cast by ballots and voted by *manzana*, or neighborhood. In the complaint, it was further alleged that Agustín Beitia, who was acting as president of the ayuntamiento, tore up the ballots when he did not like the results for manzanas nine and ten.[60]

On the surface, the report could be taken as proof of Pueblo participation in the electoral process, since it refers specifically to the "pueblo de la Isleta." But, examined more critically, it becomes clear that this is likely not a reference to the Indian Pueblo. For one thing, there is the matter of population referenced earlier. In 1821, as stated earlier, the mission at Isleta served 511 Indians and 2,313 Hispanos.[61] Thus, Hispanos outnumbered Indians nearly five to one in this jurisdiction. It would likely have been difficult for Indians to assert their political voice in the face of such numbers. On the other hand, part of the complaint references a lack of individuals able to read or write, and thus to serve as suitable voters.[62] High rates of illiteracy prevailed among both Hispanos and Pueblo Indians, so the lack of literate individuals to serve as electors applied to both groups. Still, although the documents name the Pueblo of Isleta, they also reference locations outside the Pueblo. For example, the alcalde under complaint, José Chávez, is described as a "vecino de la plaza de los Padillas."[63] Los Padillas is a neighborhood in Albuquerque's South Valley, some 4½ miles from Isleta Pueblo. In searching for an Indian voice in this report, one finds none. This 1832–33 election dispute at Isleta was between vecinos of the pueblo of Isleta. This is a case of an ayuntamiento in which Hispanos firmly controlled the affairs of the council. If Indians did participate, they did so as a vastly outnumbered minority and were likely relegated to the sidelines.

Frequent administrative changes in New Mexico under the Mexican regime further complicated Indian participation in ayuntamiento elections and politics. The Mexican Constitution of 1824 demoted New Mexico from provincial to territorial status. The territory was divided into two *distritos* (districts)—northern and southern—with these districts further subdivided into *partidos* (subdistricts). Taos and San Ildefonso (not the Indian Pueblos, but rather the Hispano towns near them) were the northern partido capitals, while Albuquerque and Los Padillas were the southern capitals.[64] The Constitution of 1836 then changed the designations from provinces to departments, whereupon New Mexico was made a department. The departmental junta was located in Santa Fe, with the department divided into two districts, each governed by a *prefecto* (prefect). The districts were again subdivided into two precincts each, or partidos, overseen by subprefects. The northern district was the Río Arriba, while the southern district was the Río Abajo, with Cochiti Pueblo as the dividing line.[65]

The New Mexican governor held broad executive powers, able to suspend common councils in the districts, and he was the arbiter of disputed election results. He cast the deciding vote in case of an electoral tie, and he could accept or reject resignations of council members. He also responded to personal petitions from New Mexico's Hispanos, Indians, and religious officials, who recognized him as the ultimate arbiter of justice. In spite of all this, local politics were more "elective" under Mexico, since alcaldes were voted on and worked closely with their ayuntamientos, having previously been appointed under the Spanish system. By contrast, under Mexico the local political system played a greater role in the administration of judicial matters, local economies, and land distribution.[66] Minge pointed out that under political reorganizations that took place in 1837, each Pueblo had a local judge, who was frequently a member of the Pueblo. Still, all these judges were the governor's appointees, and by 1844 "there were indications of gross incompetence and corruption among these local officials." Further reform came in 1844, when Governor Mariano Martinez created *jueces de barrio* (ward justices), with each Pueblo receiving a justice from among the tribal membership.[67] Yet the existing officer corps from the old Pueblo-Spanish system still persisted.

With population decline and frequent complicated changes in political administration during the decades of Mexican rule in New Mexico, it is understandably difficult to decipher the extent to which Indians participated in systems of local politics, especially in mixed-ethnic settings. But even with these extenuating factors, formal Indian ayuntamientos did exist. As G. Emlen Hall and David Weber have shown, "Following the liberal reforms some Pueblos operated their own municipal governments, paid taxes, and served in the militia with other 'citizens.'"[68] The location of one such formal Pueblo municipal government was Pecos. The Pueblo reported on an ayuntamiento election on 3 January 1821, during the murky changeover from Spanish to Mexican administration. The short letter is addressed to Governor Facundo Melgarez and signed by one Manuel Duranes. It is written in a barely legible hand, with significant spelling errors. It reads, "Por parte ha ellos havere mudado el ayuntamiento que continuaba en el pueblo de pecos los que ocupan el lugar por elesion es el yaman [G]uanima de alcalde y regidor el que yaman Rafael." For the ayuntamiento of Pecos Pueblo, those who lived there elected for alcalde "he whom they call guanima," and for councilman "he whom they call Rafael."[69] The informal tone of the document, coupled with the use of first names only for the elected alcalde and regidor, point to Indian officials for an Indian ayuntamiento. The fact that there was an ayuntamiento at the Pueblo is somewhat surprising, given the facts that Pecos had a reported 54 Indians to 738 Hispanos in 1821,[70] and that the Pueblo Indian inhabitants of Pecos would relocate to Jemez Pueblo by the end of the 1830s. By the 1820s, the Hispano settlement of San Miguel del Vado had come to overshadow Pecos Pueblo in importance. While we can identify a formal Indian ayuntamiento at Pecos, it can be difficult to decipher, overall, where and how constitutional ayuntamientos were established in New Mexico, and who sat on these councils.[71]

Without question, Pueblo Indians appealed to ayuntamientos—even those controlled by Hispanos—for redress on many occasions. Numerous accounts document Indians appearing before ayuntamientos for help in matters large and small. In a seemingly trivial account of Pueblo Indians working through their ayuntamiento, an Hispano official named Juan Armijo filed a formal complaint to the governor of New Mexico on behalf of the ayuntamiento for the Indians of Cochiti Pueblo "and the neighborhood." In his complaint, he spoke of the priest at the Pueblo mission saying Mass without first ringing the bell, stating, "On one hand it is true that he says the mass on the Festival days, and even during the week, but he does so without ringing the bells, as has been the custom, and for this cause they don't hear it, and nobody goes [to mass] for two months.... He says the mass every day, but he says it to himself... he doesn't wait for anyone, and only he who hears it is the one who says it."[72] While the episode borders on the comical, to those Indians who had converted to Catholicism, the actions of the Franciscan threatened the welfare of their souls, since they were unable to receive one of the holy sacraments. It was serious enough for these Indians to take their case to the ayuntamiento, which then elevated the complaint to the attention of higher authorities.[73] Pueblo Indians clearly viewed their ayuntamientos as a legitimate space for redress in some cases.

In 1830 residents of Laguna Pueblo, with Vicente Romero speaking on behalf of his fellow Lagunans, complained directly to the governor of New Mexico about the actions of Alcalde Marcos Baca and a vecino, Joaquin Pino. In the complaint, the Indians expressed their sense of hopelessness after years of mistreatment by Pino, who with the support of Alcalde Baca (Pino was, incidentally, Baca's grandfather-in-law), had "intended to disturb our tranquility . . . [and] in the interest of exasperating us and getting us to abandon, to cede, or renounce the small possessions [of land], which, although with enough penury, give us moderately the necessary support and also are open so that we may be able to have our few little animals on them." They also claimed "[Pino] has imposed fines, taken animals, and despoiled as many as show up around those environs of the most value and usefulness . . . these injuries received being much greater when under the protection of being Alcalde, as [Pino also] has been several times."[74]

The Indians of the Pueblo took the case directly to the governor of New Mexico, complaining against their highest local authority, the alcalde, and his vecino ally. In the 1821 mission census, Indians in the vicinity of Laguna outnumbered Hispanos 779 to 463.[75] The local ayuntamiento would have been the court of first resort in this instance. Perhaps the governing body had come under vecino control and was not responsive to Indian needs. Furthermore, an ayuntamiento was answerable to the alcalde, who clearly did not have Laguna's best interests at heart. Whatever the particulars of the relationship between Indians, ayuntamiento, and alcalde at Laguna, a link had been broken between the local officials and the Indians they were supposed to represent. Interestingly, Laguna oral history recalled this dispute between the Pueblo and Joaquin Pino, which lasted well into the American territorial period. Former Laguna Governor Robert Anaya and Mrs. Walter K. Marmon, interviewed in November 1968, stated, "They [the Pinos] said they were granted the land, but they never were; it was just a permit. But they needed a grant, and said it was a grant. They were there until . . . say in the 1890s . . . and they vacated. They had very influential friends in Santa Fe . . . who helped them hold onto the place. But finally when research was made, it was found that their land was only a permit, and not a claim."[76]

The Pueblos also disputed ayuntamiento jurisdiction, at times expressing a preference for one municipal council over another. In the early 1820s, the

Mexican government, under the principle of privatizing "unused" Pueblo lands (a policy the United States would later pursue with Indigenous lands within its territorial boundaries under the Dawes Allotment Act), issued the Río de Picurís grant to Hispanos from Santa Cruz de la Cañada. Citizens of Picuris Pueblo strongly opposed the granting of this land to these Hispanos, who claimed the "unused" land in order to expand their own agriculture and pasturage. The Indians stated that the land in question from the new Río de Picurís grant was already in use as part of their *ejido* (common land) to pasture and water their animals in the summer. The original Hispano petition for the grant, which was filed with the territorial deputation, was referred to the ayuntamiento of Santa Cruz de la Cañada. In addition to arguing that they were already using the land, the Picuris Indians, along with some Hispano allies, asserted that the land was under the jurisdiction of the ayuntamiento of Taos, not Santa Cruz. Unfortunately, things did not end well for Picuris Pueblo, as the grant to the Hispanos was eventually upheld, and the Indians found themselves completely surrounded by non-Indian settlements and land within their league occupied by outsiders.[77] Even with Pueblo leaders adept at finding a favorable governing body in the Mexican period, it proved difficult to maintain the integrity of the Pueblo land grants, as both Ortiz and Sando have pointed out.

In another example of Pueblo involvement in ayuntamiento politics, the ayuntamiento of Santa Clara included the Pueblo of Santa Clara and a number of non-Indian towns in the vicinity. A seemingly mundane document reporting the results of an ayuntamiento election on 4 December 1836 gives no mention of Indians or indeed anything of significance to Indian voting in the jurisdiction. It simply states that electors from among the ayuntamiento members were selected. Jose Miguel Naranjo, president of the ayuntamiento, signed the report.[78] The document assumes greater significance when coupled with another dated 19 April 1837. In the later missive, the same Jose Miguel Naranjo and another man by the name of Marcos Tafoya presented a formal complaint to the governor of New Mexico on behalf of Santa Clara Pueblo against Joaquin Castellana, a member of the Pueblo. Castellana, according to Naranjo and Tafoya, fraudulently sold lands to three Hispanos. The lands he sold fell within the Pueblo's leagues, and they stated that there was no evidence that the community had consented to the sale. They asked that the land be returned to the community and the guilty party be punished "immediately."[79]

This type of document concerning land disputes between Hispanos and Pueblo Indians is found frequently in both the Spanish and Mexican Archives of New Mexico. What makes this one significant is that both Naranjo and

Tafoya identify themselves as representatives of Santa Clara Pueblo speaking on behalf of the principal chiefs, but they also present themselves as "natives of the pueblo of Santa Clara."[80] In other words, Naranjo, who here represented his people in a land dispute, had served the previous year as the president of the ayuntamiento of Santa Clara. This jurisdiction included several Hispano communities. Even in 1821, Hispanos purportedly outnumbered Santa Clarans 1,205 to 180.[81] In an ayuntamiento where Hispanos greatly outnumbered Pueblos, an Indian was elected to the ayuntamiento and served as its president. This would appear to be a clear example of an ayuntamiento in which Pueblo Indians and Hispanos worked side by side, and Pueblos, although a minority, had a voice and even held positions of power.

More examples of interethnic political cooperation are likely to be uncovered. As Alfonso Ortiz asserted, the period of isolation and neglect by the central government in Mexico City "strengthened the cooperative bonds forged between the Pueblo and rural Hispanic communities." Furthermore, the groups "frequently worked together to maintain and regulate the use of irrigation ditches [which neighboring Pueblo and Hispano communities shared for their crops and livestock]. Hispanic families were welcomed visitors at feast days and Pueblo dancers performed at Santa Fe in full regalia at the annual independence day celebrations" each September.[82] In some areas, such as Santa Clara Pueblo, permeable cultural borderlands allowed the Native voice to be heard in New Mexico's multiethnic democratic governing bodies. As Mexican law stated, Indians possessed these rights as citizens. Writing in the spring of 1821, on the eve of Mexican independence, Governor Melgares noted that Indians "should be considered Spaniards in everything and enjoy their rights to elect and be elected."[83] Nevertheless, the highly idealistic guiding principles of Mexican equality and the Tres Garantías were extended to New Mexico's Pueblo Indians in an uneven manner, and Pueblo Indians found frequent obstacles in their path to formal democratic political participation. It would be left to Native peoples to find alternative forms of asserting their political voice.

Indian Voting and the Politics of Rebellion in Mexican New Mexico

Outside formal channels of democratic political participation during the Mexican period, there exist intriguing examples of extra-constitutional and alternative Pueblo voting from the 1820s to 1840s. In particular, when the events of the Río Arriba Rebellion of 1837 (also referred to as the Chimayó Rebellion) are viewed in the context of Indian electoral participation, they take on added significance. Although they were ultimately unsuccessful, during this brief period of violent upheaval New Mexico's Pueblo Indians voted with their voices as well as with force of arms, greatly influencing the political landscape of the territory. Hispanos and Indians selected José González of Taos, who was either a Pueblo Indian or a genízaro, as the governor of their short-lived state. The Río Arriba Rebellion thus represents a political maturation of sorts for the Pueblo peoples of New Mexico, who played a prominent part in the group that took control of the territory's affairs for a brief time.

Political chaos gripped the Mexican state after independence. From 1821 to 1837, for example, the Mexican presidency changed hands a staggering twenty-one times. And yet New Mexico remained relatively stable, albeit neglected. The main threats to New Mexico's stability came from raids by Apaches and other Indigenous groups. The province responded much as it had for decades: with its militia. Hispano farmers and Pueblo auxiliaries comprised the bulk of New Mexico's fighting units. They were often poorly armed and forced to serve for extended periods, paying for their own weapons and supplies out of their own pockets, at that. Because of this frontier military service, New Mexicans had been exempted from paying direct taxes to the national government. In particular, the residents of northern New Mexico had two fundamental rights: to select their own town governments, and to pay no taxes.[84]

But events combined in the mid-1830s to bring Mexico's political upheaval to its far northern frontier. A worldwide economic crash and depression, which began in many places in 1836, spread to much of Europe and the Americas by 1837. Nearly bankrupt, Mexico scrambled to generate funds. In 1835, during his fourth term in office, President Antonio López de Santa Anna openly displayed his authoritarian centralist tendencies. Frustrated with the degree of autonomy afforded to Mexican provinces and municipalities under the 1824 constitution, Santa Anna implemented a centralized form of government called the Departmental Plan, which would reign in the provinces, especially those that did not share in the tax burden. Under that plan, provinces were changed to departments. Each department had a jefe politico, or governor, who answered directly to the central government. Five-man appointed councils replaced provincial legislative assemblies. When a governor's term ended, the departmental council would draw up a list of three candidates, from which the government in Mexico City would choose one. Santa Anna's plan aimed to centralize all branches of the Mexican national government, at the expense of local self-government. On the local level, communities were now subject to the authority of prefects who answered directly to the governor. Santa Anna appointed Albino Pérez governor of New Mexico. Pérez, a military officer from Veracruz, carried himself as both an aristocrat and an autocrat, thereby antagonizing New Mexico's more provincial population. Hispanos had grown accustomed to native New Mexican governors, which Pérez was not, and viewed him as an outsider.[85]

Problems quickly arose when Pérez, though seemingly well intentioned, failed to grasp the unique characteristics of New Mexico's people. Although the evidence was all around him, he did not understand the importance they placed on local autonomy. He was also unquestioningly loyal to Santa Anna's centralist government, and intended to fully implement the president's reforms. Pérez hoped to transform New Mexico from an isolated outlier into a department in Santa Anna's model. Part of Santa Anna's Departmental Plan was that all Mexicans in all departments would pay equal direct taxes to the central government. In 1835, Pérez's government began directly taxing New Mexicans, and he duly replaced the old provincial assembly with a provisional five-man departmental council in Santa Fe. New Mexicans became truly worried about their local government and tax-exempt status. He again enraged New Mexicans in 1835–36 when he sought to end the lucrative illegal arms trade with Apaches, Navajos, Comanches, and Utes; required licenses for New Mexicans to trade with Indians or to trap beaver; levied taxes on all wagons arriving from the United States; implemented new taxes for combating raiders; and generally regulated the actions of all those involved in the Santa Fe trade.[86]

New Mexicans chafed under these new policies. They asserted, and rightly so, that they had never received any benefits from the Mexican government, such as schools, hospitals, roads, bridges, soldiers, or arms. The Anglo-American trader Josiah Gregg, who spent much of the 1830s on the Santa Fe Trail, wrote of New Mexicans' response to the new taxation: "It was now found necessary for the support of the new organization, to introduce a system of direct taxation, with which the people were wholly unacquainted; and they would sooner have paid a *doblon* through a tariff than a *real* in this way." As galling as these economic changes were under the Departmental Plan, it was the threat it posed to self-government that tipped the scale in favor of rebellion in New Mexico. Gregg said as much: "Yet, although the conspiracy had been brewing for some time, no indications of violence were demonstrated, until, on account of some misdemeanor, an *alcalde* was imprisoned by the *Prefecto* of the northern district." In 1836, the ayuntamiento of La Cañada in northern New Mexico was made up of seven regidores. The majority of these men were related, as was the norm in many municipalities. This was technically against the law, but it was rarely enforced since a few select families often made up the core of leadership in New Mexico's towns. Governor Pérez dissolved the ayuntamiento of Santa Cruz de la Cañada and ordered new elections, thus threatening local autonomy. The residents of Santa Cruz were incensed. Pérez had grounds for removing the alcalde, Juan José Esquibel, who often flaunted his authority and disobeyed orders from superiors, including the governor. Esquibel was arrested and jailed for bribery and disobedience, but a mob of his relations and supporters freed him in July 1837. Esquibel then openly challenged New Mexico's departmental government by forming a twelve-man governing council that he called the *Cantón*. This council then masterminded a rebellion against the governor and other authorities.[87]

When Esquibel made overtures to New Mexicans to join him, both Hispanos and Pueblo Indians flocked to the Cantón. Hispano support was particularly strong in the Santa Cruz valley, which included many genízaro descendants. Indians from Taos and San Ildefonso Pueblos also joined the cause. They were involved in such large numbers from the outset that Gregg commented, "The most active agents in this desperate affair were the Pueblo Indians." Alarmed by these rapid developments, Pérez finally mobilized a fighting force, but he had been dangerously slow in doing so. Several weeks passed before his army of a few hundred militiamen—mostly Indians from Cochiti, Santo Domingo, and Sandia Pueblos pressed into service—moved to confront the rebels. The two sides met on 7 August 1837. To their horror, Pérez and his men found an opposing force of 1,500 to 2,000 men, both Hispanos and Indians, waiting for them at La Mesilla, just north of San Ildefonso. As the battle began, Pérez's Indian troops deserted to the opposing side, as did several of his Hispano soldiers and officers. Pérez and twenty-three of his men fled south for their lives. They were eventually caught and killed by Indians from Santo Domingo Pueblo.[88]

One Nuevomexicano account, probably written in the fall of 1837, makes several interesting points about the rebellion. The author wrote that Pérez was not able to raise a large enough force to subdue the insurrection because he moved too slowly, and because the alcaldes from the various New Mexico jurisdictions did not help him raise his force. They withheld their support because they recognized the threat that Pérez's administration posed to their local political power. The writer also stated that when the fighting began, "all the Indians *with their alcaldes* passed over to the other side." These alcaldes may have been Indians themselves, demonstrating how Indian self-government also crossed into military affairs. And in one final gory detail—which may be fabricated—the author told how Pérez "was killed by two Indians in its suburbs [Santa Fe], and his head carried to the camp and jeered [at] by the perverted villains."[89]

As important as these events were at the beginning of the Río Arriba Rebellion, the political maneuverings that took place after the battle at La Mesilla truly demonstrated the Indian nature of the revolt, and revealed how the Pueblos played a crucial role in directing its affairs. After defeating and killing Pérez, the rebels moved the Cantón from Santa Cruz to Santa Fe, forming a new government. They met first on the outskirts of town, and on 10 August "[Held] the election of governor which devolved on a farmer named José Gonzales whose only talent was knowing how to kill buffalo."[90] This election included voting by both Indians and Hispanos. The new government then entered Santa Fe, and what became known as the *Junta Popular* (People's Assembly) proclaimed itself the legitimate governing body of New Mexico. The Junta differed from New Mexico's previous departmental, provincial, and territorial assemblies in that its rhetoric and membership were far more inclusive. The Junta's minutes were frantically written, with motions scribbled onto the pages and then scratched out. Writing crowds the margins of the minutes as well. Whole paragraphs are deleted at times. Junta members made few decisions, but agreed to send a delegation to Mexico City. The Junta declared in plain language, "They are met under the portal of the palace [of the governors] of our city [as] all of the citizens that compose the respectable Junta popular." This was a governing body for all New Mexicans, regardless of race or class. Rich and poor from Pueblo Indian and Hispano communities all participated in the new government and fought on the battlefield together.[91]

The rebels demonstrated by their actions that they comprised an inclusive entity. They sent letters to the Pueblos inviting their leaders to participate in the Junta Popular. A letter dated 21 August 1837 to Josecito Archibeque, the Indian governor of Cochiti Pueblo, informed him of threats to the rebellion and invited him to come to Santa Fe. The letter, signed on behalf of Governor González by José Esquibel and Juan Vigil, reads, "Let us as compatriots and good Mexicans purify our native land so that we can live in peace and quiet."[92] González wrote to Tesuque Pueblo on 31 August 1837, stating, "Two Indians from the Pueblo of Tesuque must present themselves . . . so that they can accompany [leaders] from other Pueblos and march to . . . El Paso . . . and leave . . . for the Capital of the Republic with the objective of representing our rights."[93] As the rebellion took root, two principles guided its actions: governmental power resided in leaders at the village level, and Pueblo Indians were to be included in all governing councils.[94] It was the most inclusive government New Mexico has ever seen—past or present.

It is important to clarify the identity of the man chosen to lead the Cantón, which since 1837 has been shrouded in confusion. First, here is what is known about José González: he was from Taos, he was a buffalo hunter, and he was illiterate. Those unsympathetic to the rebellion used his background to criticize both González and the revolt. For example, a caravan of merchants who were in Santa Fe when the rebellion broke out then traveled to El Paso, bringing news and providing legal testimony about the events of August 1837. Guadalupe Miranda testified, "José María Gonzales . . . is an idiot not worthy or capable of filling the position he has usurped, and even less for having been enthroned over the cadavers of the true and legitimate authorities." Gregg, who also had accompanied this merchant party, testified that "José Gonzales was in command of the government . . . a man without civil virtues and so ignorant that he does not even know how to sign his name." Another Anglo-American trader who was in Santa Fe during the rebellion wrote that "the triumphant army having declared their leader, Jose Gonzales, an inhabitant of Taos, governor, made the entrance into the town, where he assumed the government." Writing years later, Gregg elaborated further on González. He observed that he was "one of the boldest leaders [of the rebellion]" and that he was "a good honest hunter but a very ignorant man, [and] was elected for governor."[95] To detractors, he was an ignorant hunter with no business managing the affairs of New Mexico.

Scholars have long contested González's ethnic origin. The historian Janet Lecompte argued that he was a vecino from Taos.[96] The New Mexico historian William H. Wroth stated that González may have been a Taos Indian, a genízaro, or a vecino.[97] Lansing Bloom wrote that González was "reputed to have been a Taos Indian and buffalo hunter by trade."[98] Philip Reno commented that his mother was a Taos Pueblo Indian and his father was a "genízaro of non-Pueblo Indian lineage with some admixture of white blood." Reno went on to conclude, rather unkindly, that it is "no wonder that such a government was brief, or that it achieved only *de facto* status. The wonder is that José González ever became governor at all—a singular aberration in the long succession of governors of New Mexico from other geographical areas and other classes of society."[99]

Fray Angélico Chávez wrote the definitive work on José González. He sought to uncover the man's identity, which he called "unimportant but intriguing." Using parish records and genealogical sources, Chávez convincingly concluded that José González was the son of a genízaro father and a Taos Pueblo mother, and that the terms *vecino* and *genízaro* were often interchanged in describing him. Any of these descriptions, including vecino, could have been used to describe virtually any Pueblo Indian who married a Hispano and moved away from the Pueblo, as Chávez argued that González had. He wrote,

"From his close connections with Taos Pueblo, especially through his mother, we can assume that he was conversant [in] the North[ern] Tigua language. His arousing of various Pueblos to follow him in his bloody spree shows his influence, and also sympathies, with the indigenous inhabitants of New Mexico." González proved invaluable to the Río Arriba Rebellion. Its initial success was owed to widespread Indian support, which would not likely have coalesced without an Indian at its head. As Chávez concluded, "The upshot of the whole matter is that New Mexico did have an Indian Governor, even if by savage usurpation, in the same manner that Mexico [had] an Indian President in Benito Juárez. But neither of these two revolutionaries wore loin-clouts and war-bonnets."[100]

It is also noteworthy that Padre don Antonio José Martínez, who served as the parish priest at Taos and played an important role in New Mexico in the nineteenth century, was present at the end of the rebellion when González was defeated and killed. The man in charge of the army that finally crushed the Cantón is reported to have said to the father, "Padre Martínez, hear this genízaro's confession so that he may be given five bullets."[101] The safest conclusion, therefore, is that González was of Indigenous ancestry. The significance of this cannot be overstated: for the first and only time in the history of New Mexico, its duly elected governor was an Indian.

The quality of González's leadership, however, was unremarkable, and the rebellion ultimately failed. The Cantón had issued its set of five demands just before González's election as governor. Its primary demands were an end to the Departmental Plan and no direct taxation. In response to the rebellion, a former governor, Manuel Armijo, led the pro-centralist party against the rebels. Armijo's forces gathered in the Río Abajo, adopting the *Plan de Tomé* on 8 September 1837, which neatly encapsulated their aims and rhetoric in ten points, two of which directly addressed Indians. Point 5 stated, "As it is fitting that the Pueblo [Indians] remain tranquil and do not mix in the affairs of the Mexicans, they will be instructed to take part in favor of no party, as the war is not, nor is it directed, against them; and that, until the supreme government name a governor [of New Mexico], they are to govern themselves without regard to any authority which may not emanate from themselves." And point 6: "In order that the preceding article may take effect, three natives of Isleta who are present were informed of all the just reasons which exist and which they are to explain to their fellows." Armijo knew that the early success of the revolt had largely been thanks to Pueblo support, so he implored them to sit out the hostilities and appealed to their desire for self-government. He also believed that it was a good strategic move to use the Isletans to explain their reasons for opposing the Cantón.[102]

Armijo led his force north from the Río Abajo and met with the rebels. By early September, the Cantón no longer supported González as governor. The center of the rebellion had shifted to Taos, and it was now under the leadership of Pablo Montoya, the former alcalde of Taos (and later a key instigator of the Taos Revolt in 1847). Montoya and other rebel leaders met with Armijo, and the rebels signed a treaty in Santa Fe on 21 September 1837. Writing later to explain his actions, Armijo laid much of the blame for the revolt on the Pueblos, whom he described as a "weak, credulous, ignorant people very addicted to the sack and spoils of war" who had been "easily seduced" into believing that the Departmental Plan would "take from them a third part of the fruits of their labor, taxing heavily the common benefits of water, wood, pastures, and even their own children and wives." The rebellion, he opined, had caused the Pueblos to debase themselves to the level of the "savage tribes."[103] In keeping with his statements in the Plan de Tomé, he saw the Indians as ignorant victims of persuasive Hispanos. He failed to recognize the fact that he was denigrating politically mature Pueblo Indians who were committed to local autonomy, just like the Hispano rebels from La Cañada and Taos.

Despite the treaty, hostilities flared once again in early 1838. This time the conflict centered on the town of Truchas, and Armijo moved quickly to dissuade any Indians who might support it. He issued a circular on 19 January 1838, addressing the Indians specifically:

> I want the Indians of the country to know that my aim is none other than to sustain the law, punishing only the truly culpable, protecting the ignorant even when they have cooperated with previous revolutions, having been motivated by the seductions and deceits of the promoters. I want them to suffer no hostile treatment however light, nor especially do I want their poor families to suffer the terrible scourge of war to which they are provoked by the rebels of Las Truchas at those *reuniones*, as criminal as they are insignificant, so that they forget the clemency and commiseration they have enjoyed until now; but once they are freed from their obstinacy and backsliding, one must work in another manner, and therefore I am convinced that the blame always falls on the poor ignorant Indian who knows not what he does. I am warning them, so that they may not be deceived, so that they may close their ears to the invitations, and so that they may live in peace in the confidence that the government values them, but if in spite of this they take part in the revolution, they may not

afterwards complain nor plead ignorance, for then the rigor of the law will fall equally on everyone.[104]

Armijo and his men eventually put down the rebellion. Bolstered by a force of Mexican cavalry regulars sent from Veracruz—thereby demonstrating the resolve of the Mexican republic to crush the rebellion—the pro-centralist forces defeated the Cantón at Pojoaque on 27 January 1838. Although no longer holding power, José González was present. In the aftermath of the battle, he presented himself to Armijo at Santa Cruz, asking one last time that no direct taxes be imposed on the people. Armijo refused to make any guarantees, whereupon he condemned González to be shot. Hispano and genízaro leaders of the rebellion such as Esquibel were also executed. The multiethnic coalition had failed to stop President Santa Anna's dictatorial reforms. Still, within another ten years New Mexico would be further weakened and would be placed under the control of another colonial power.[105]

Conclusion

In his circular of 19 January 1838, Manuel Armijo referenced the "poor ignorant Indian who knows not what he does." Yet Armijo pleaded with New Mexico's Pueblo Indians to refrain from supporting the Cantón. He asked them to stay at their Pueblos and govern themselves until a proper New Mexican government could be reestablished. Armijo at once belittled and praised the Pueblos. On the one hand, they were ignorant children who had been misled and needed correction. On the other, he feared the strength they provided to the rebellion both on the battlefield and in its leadership ranks. Furthermore, in the Plan de Tomé, issued four months before Armijo's warning to the "ignorant" Indians, he unknowingly affirmed the Native tradition of self-government. He requested that they remain in their Pueblos and govern themselves—something they had already done for centuries—while he attempted to sort out the chaos in Santa Fe and Santa Cruz. For Armijo, politics at the departmental level were the concern of Hispanos, not Indians; it would be better that they remain at their Pueblos and not concern their supposedly simple minds with these things.

Yet the actions of Pueblo Indians throughout the Río Arriba Rebellion showed that they were anything but children. By 1837–38, New Mexico's Pueblo Indians had become politically astute and well versed in the complexities of both Spanish and Mexican electoral politics and town governance. They had weathered numerous policy changes over several chaotic decades. In some ways, Indian actions in the rebellion represented a coming of age in the political landscape of New Mexico. These were Indians who for two hundred years had annually elected their village officials in a manner adapted to community needs. Some had also taken part in constitutional ayuntamientos in the late Spanish period as well as throughout the Mexican era, and in some of these instances even held positions of power. Pueblo Indians continued to traverse territorial, legal, and political boundaries to protect the land and rights of their people. Furthermore, they had formed an important block in the Junta Popular that elected José González, whose ascent represented the single most significant Indian action in the history of New Mexico's electoral politics up to that point. With an Indian governor at the helm, the Pueblos assumed a large part of the leadership that directed the affairs of New Mexico during those fateful months in 1837–38. Pueblo Indians were simultaneously citizens of the Republic of Mexico, of their own Pueblo republics (which remained distinct political entities throughout the Mexican era), and of the short-lived multiethnic Cantón.

Indian electoral participation was, nonetheless, constrained by localized conditions during the Mexican period, as it had always been in the Spanish era. In one locale, Indians and Hispanos could work in an effective, mutually beneficial manner. In other areas, Indians viewed ayuntamientos as bodies that addressed their needs and concerns, even if they did not take an active part as council members. They petitioned these governing councils time and again, occasionally with favorable results. But in other areas, the Indian presence in ayuntamientos is conspicuously absent. This could be due to several factors, not the least of which was that Hispanos significantly outnumbered Pueblo Indians. Furthermore, Hispano communities only continued to expand during the Mexican era. Pueblo republics also continued their important day-to-day functions of governing their communities in the 1820s through the 1840s.[106] And, as ever, the powers of the administration in Santa Fe cannot be overlooked. A favorable or unfavorable governor could greatly affect the degree to which Indians were secure in the exercise of their rights. On the whole, from 1821 to 1846, Pueblo Indians would become more familiar than ever with the colonially imposed politics of town government. This would be both a benefit and a hindrance during the Anglo-American colonial administration that soon followed.

CHAPTER FOUR

The Politics of Inclusion/Exclusion in the Arizona-Sonora Borderlands during the Mexican Period

In 1821, officials in Tucson officially swore allegiance to the Republic of Mexico. While New Mexico Governor Facundo Melgares had orchestrated two celebrations in Santa Fe—one of which included public revelry and Indian dances—Pimería Alta witnessed a simple affair. On 3 September, the *comandante* of the presidio of Tucson swore allegiance to the Mexican government. Aside from the nature of these celebrations, Pimería Alta differed from New Mexico during the late Spanish and Mexican periods in two significant ways. First, while officials in Mexico City had neglected New Mexico during this time, the tradition of self-government remained strong in that territory's Pueblo Indian and Hispano communities.[1] In his classic study of Arizona under Spanish and Mexican administration, James E. Officer provided a useful contrast of the degree to which residents of Pimería Alta had grown accustomed to self-government before the region came under U.S. control: "Relatively little that the Hispanic residents of the Pimería Alta experienced during the years of Spanish and Mexican rule prepared them for participation in the political life of the region after it became a part of the United States. In this respect, they differed somewhat from certain of their neighbors in California and New Mexico, where the Spanish founded towns with civil governments."[2] Second, as the Mexican government was stretched to its limits in both resources and political capital, missions and military installations in the Arizona-Sonora Borderlands decayed considerably.[3]

The decline of these institutions had a direct effect on the Indians of the Arizona-Sonora Borderlands. For example, when Mexico inherited control over Hopi territory from Spain, Hopis came under only nominal control of the new republic. Isolation and increased raids on their territory exacerbated their tenuous plight. Farther south, Yaquis continued to adapt the Yaqui-Spanish model of town government, and remained in command of much of their own internal affairs. They pushed against colonial authority, and once more turned to revolt in the 1820s under the leadership of the charismatic Juan Banderas. Elections of Yaqui officers again played a part in this rebellion, although not as prominent a role as in the 1740 Revolt. Still, at the heart of their grievances was control of Yaqui governance.

Much like Yaquis, O'odhams in Pimería Alta saw more Hispanos encroach on their territory, while simultaneously receiving fewer protections from these trespasses. For all their other flaws, the Jesuit and Franciscan missionaries who ministered to them were at times among their most vocal defenders. The system of Indian civil government in Pimería Alta, which had been so unevenly instituted and rarely under the control of Indians themselves, continued into the Mexican period. But as the Catholic Church abandoned its northern Sonora missions, the selection of Indian officers fell completely to Indian communities. In the end, the system bore little resemblance to the Spanish municipal town model, as Indians turned to their own methods of selection and as the cadre of officers shrank to a few men in many locations, and only a governor in others. While the Yaqui-Spanish electoral system persisted into the Mexican era, it was nonexistent at Hopi and was significantly weakened in Pimería Alta.

Thus no single summary of Indian voting during the Mexican period can be easily applied to the Arizona-Sonora Borderlands. Indian participation in electoral politics varied from group to group. In some areas, the diminished vecino presence created opportunities for greater control of internal affairs, including the selection of community leaders. Even absent substantive coercive power from without, some Indigenous groups continued under officers carried over from the Spanish town electoral model. But in other areas, Mexican officials sought to exert greater control over highly independent Indian villages, resulting in significant pushback from their inhabitants. What is certain is that for the Indigenous peoples of the Arizona-Sonora Borderlands, the brief decades of Mexican independence were chaotic and unpredictable, holding a promise of greater sovereignty as well as a prospect of dangers posed by outsiders looking to exert control over community governance.

Hopis under Mexican Rule

Mexico had little or nothing to do with Hopis from 1821 to 1846. Interactions between Hopis and Spaniards in the seventeenth century slowed significantly after the Pueblo Revolt and the destruction of Awat'ovi in 1700. Thereafter, Spaniards made infrequent attempts to reestablish missionary work among the Hopis, such as that undertaken by Father Francisco Silvestre Vélez de Escalante in 1775, along with the occasional military foray into Hopi territory. By the time of Mexican independence, contacts between Hopis and outsiders were nearly nonexistent. An almost-prohibitively long distance separated Hopis from the Rio Grande Pueblos and the government at Santa Fe. Moreover, raids by groups such as Apaches and Navajos increased markedly during the late Spanish period and Mexican era. After significant human and material losses in the particularly violent 1810s, Hopis sent a delegation to Santa Fe in 1818 to request military assistance against the Navajos. Spaniards recognized the urgency of the situation, and saw that it represented an opportunity to reestablish contacts with Hopis. Unfortunately, Santa Fe could do nothing, lacking the manpower and money to invest in a large military operation to Hopi. The raiding and warfare impeded Hopi-Mexican relations even more than the distance separating the two sides. According to Edward Spicer, "The widespread warfare which took place with increasing frequency during those years between the settled Pueblos and the far-ranging, marauding Navajos and Apaches—and which the Mexican troops were unable to prevent—virtually stopped all travel in the northern area.... Hopis [simply did not feel] the touch of Mexican political authority."[4] As evidence of this bureaucratic inattention, a search by a team of Hopi and non-Indigenous scholars of the Mexican Archives of New Mexico in Santa Fe, with findings published in 2015, yielded no "significant documents about the Hopis" from the period. The group concluded, "After Mexican independence from Spain, the beleaguered province of New Mexico simply did not have the funds or manpower to concern itself with the faraway Moquis."[5]

The violence in the region grew to a level not previously seen under Spain, as various Indigenous groups clamored to fill the vacuum that an administratively weak Mexico had created. The introduction of increasing numbers of firearms to non-Pueblo Indians through the Santa Fe trade (which expanded dramatically in the Mexican period) amplified the violence. Navajos penetrated deeper than ever before into the Hopi homelands, wreaking havoc on those communities. For example, a massive 1837 Navajo raid on Oraibi, which was the largest of the Hopi villages at that time, purportedly resulted in the deaths or scattering of nearly the entire village. But Hopi troubles were not limited to bloody encounters with Navajos. Apaches, Comanches, and Utes all ventured onto Hopi lands, taking captives and seizing livestock. Hopis commanded a premium on the Indian slave market, and thus were prime targets for the slave raiders who ranged over the Southwestern Borderlands.[6]

That Hopis essentially had to fend for themselves against violent attacks was nothing new; it was the nature and frequency of the attacks that had changed. If there was any upside to their isolation-induced vulnerability, it was that Hopis essentially remained in a state of complete political independence. This political situation, originating in the eighteenth century, continued after 1821. Hopis paid no taxes to Mexico, nor did the Mexican Republic count them in its censuses.⁷ Josiah Gregg wrote of this time, "The 'seven pueblos of the Moqui' (as they are called) . . . formerly acknowledged the government and religion of the Spaniards, but have long since rejected both, and live in a state of independence and paganism. . . . [But] they are . . . industrious and agricultural, and . . . ingenious in their manufacturing."⁸ The Mexican government was unable to place Hopis under its jurisdiction, but it failed not so much because of Hopi resistance but for a complete lack of effort on the part of the Mexican government. Hopis remained citizens of their own independent Indian nation-villages, and participated in none of the Mexican political developments of the 1820s–40s.

Hopi oral tradition, however, tells of at least one instance in which Hopis sought and secured the support of Mexican officials. Edmund Nequatewa, who heard the story from one of his elders, related that in 1846 a party of Mexican traders (or raiders) supposedly visited Oraibi. Hopis feared such visits "because they were never sure but that the Mexicans were coming to take revenge on them for killing the Spanish priests in 1680."⁹ At the same time that the Mexicans arrived, three Hopi men from Oraibi were troubled with their own personal lives to the point of desiring to die. Yet a Hopi man could not kill himself, "for he would lose his reputation of being a brave man." The arrival of the Mexicans came at a fortuitous moment, and the three Hopis made arrangements with the Mexicans to kill them so that their reputations would not be tarnished. The plan was for the Mexicans to shoot the three men while they were in a kiva for a ceremony. But since the Mexicans could not distinguish the three men from the others inside the crowded kiva, the three Hopi men with a deathwish—not wanting to be responsible for disgracing the kiva—exited the chamber one by one. The Mexicans shot each man after he exited. By this time, a large number of Hopis had gathered on their rooftops and saw what had happened. After the third Hopi was killed, another Hopi, unaware of the arrangements, shot one of the Mexicans.¹⁰

A pause at this point is useful to suggest that it is unlikely that Hopis would have made such arrangements with Mexicans. But a few oral histories *do* confirm that Mexicans came to Hopi and kidnapped a Hopi woman and children in this episode. Regardless of how the violence started, the Mexicans were forced to flee for their lives as a melee ensued. In their flight, the killers grabbed a Hopi woman and several Hopi children.¹¹ They tied the children to their own bodies to use as human shields. The Mexicans killed more Hopis while attempting to escape, and also stole a number of Hopi sheep. They raped the Hopi woman nightly, to the horror of the children. A party of Hopis attempted to track the Mexicans, but turned back after three futile days of pursuit. The

Plaza Where the Snake Dance Is Held, Oraibi, n.d. The entrance to the kiva is visible. Photo Lot 90-1, number 1499, National Anthropological Archives, Smithsonian Institution.

captive woman's husband, Wíkvaya, set out on his own, determined to find his wife and the children, or to die trying.[12]

He eventually made his way to one of the Rio Grande Pueblos, where a Hopi living there took him to the village chief. The chief insisted that Wíkvaya's story be written down, and so they located a literate Indian, who recorded the account. The chief also insisted that they travel to Albuquerque, where they "found someone who had the authority to look into the matter."[13] The officer heard Wíkvaya's story, and sent him to see the governor in Santa Fe, with some sort of document in-hand. The governor listened intently to Wíkvaya's story and then, to his surprise, sent a large group of men to locate the children and his wife. It took some time, since the children had all been sold as genízaros to Hispano families, but the governor's men found the children and Wíkvaya's wife, all of whom made their way back to Oraibi. The governor also had the Mexican raiders executed in brutal fashion, but not before the condemned men had lied by saying that their captives were Navajos, about which no one had cared "because the Navajos were enemies of most everyone at that time."[14]

While no Mexican documentation of this episode seems to exist, another Hopi oral account confirms the general events of the Mexican raid, kidnapping, and return of the captives. Uwaikota of Moencopi told of "Spaniards" coming to Oraibi for slaves, who were then transported to Santa Fe, which the headmen of the village visited in order to free them. Uwaikota stated that the Hopis brought "prayer sticks" to "whoever was in charge there," who examined the sticks and knew their meaning. A search was made for any Hopi captives, who were then returned to their people. As punishment for the slavers, Mexican officials "tied them to logs and whipped them to make them pay."[15] Hopi-Tewa Albert Yava also related in 1970 that "the Spanish gave us hard times. They captured Hopi women and children and made slaves out of them." This phenomenon was common, and happened "right down to the time of the Treaty of Guadalupe Hidalgo in 1848, maybe even later." One of Yava's uncles had a cousin who was kidnapped and transported to the Mexican interior, but "one day he reappeared." Yava's ancestor had indeed been kidnapped, and became a sheepherder for a man he came to call his "Papá." The man treated the kidnapped Hopi kindly, and when he "worked for him" he "wasn't a slave anymore."[16] This man was clearly a Hopi genízaro, illustrating one possible outcome of Hopi enslavement.

And yet many Hopi captives were not so fortunate, and never returned to their homes and families. These episodes of kidnapping and liberation illuminate the tenuous nature of Hopi-Mexican relations during the brief Mexican administration. Hopi territory was vulnerable to attack, and not only by Navajo, Apache, Comanche, and Ute raiders. Mexicans also made clandestine forays to Hopi, killing villagers, kidnapping women and children, and stealing their property. Those Hopis who attempted to retrieve their loved ones, or who wanted redress for these wrongs, had to make their own way to Santa Fe, a long and dangerous journey. In at least one instance Hopis treated with Mexican authorities, both on the local level and with the governor in Santa Fe. When Indian complaints were deemed legitimate, Mexican authorities meted out swift and severe punishments. Still, the essentially independent Hopis had to seek this justice in Santa Fe themselves. Such justice was difficult to obtain, since they had no elected governors, alcaldes, regidores, or justices of the peace in their communities who could easily link up with Mexican authorities. The Hopi villages remained independent, autonomous Indian nations, largely untouched by Mexican decrees of Indian citizenship and of voting rights.

Sonoran Electoral Politics and the Breaking of the Colonial Compact

Electoral politics came to the northernmost towns of the Arizona-Sonora Borderlands later than did their New Mexican counterparts. For example, civil government on the ayuntamiento model arrived at the Tubac presidio and Tucson in early 1825, when elected officers assumed their positions. The elections had been held a few weeks earlier. In the beginning, both Tubac and Tucson had only an *alcalde de policía* (essentially a mayor) and a *síndico procurador* (a sort of treasurer-attorney). The title of the main officer was changed in December 1831 to a *primer juez de paz* (first justice of the peace). Also noteworthy is that neither Tucson nor Tubac had the necessary 1,000 residents for an ayuntamiento constitucional. Tucson met the requirement only when the tally included both Apaches de Paz living there and some nearby O'odhams. In these first ayuntamiento elections, held 19 December 1824, José de León became the first alcalde de policía of Tucson, while León Herreros served in the same office for Tubac. Both men took office on 1 January 1825.[17]

Since Indians were included in population counts for Tucson (and possibly Tubac as well), the question is whether they took part in these elections, or served in office at either location. As the historian James Officer pointed out, "Record keeping was a responsibility of the first justice of the peace and the treasurer-attorney, meaning they had to be literate, a requirement that severely limited the pool of candidates." This would have precluded large numbers of Hispanos and most Indians, given that the overwhelming majority of the Natives of Pimería Alta were illiterate. He concluded, "The result was circulation of these offices among a handful of individuals from the elite families of the region. Such persons were closely bound by kinship and the godparent system, or *compadrazco*, to the *comandantes* and to civil and military officials at higher levels." This does not leave out the possibility that an individual of Indian origin would rise to a position of prominence. Both soldiers and settlers served as godparents to Indians baptized at the missions. In 1818, the Pima lieutenant of the Tubac presidio even married his commander's daughter, who was strictly considered a Spaniard.[18] Such "indios ladinos," or acculturated Indians, often spoke Spanish and were familiar with Hispano cultural norms, having sometimes intermarried with vecinos. While the chances of Indians' serving in positions of power were small, it is possible that at least some of them participated in the elections of ayuntamiento officials.

As election mandates filtered out from Mexico City to state assemblies, these bodies instituted the qualifications for voting. The 1825 Constitution of the Estado de Occidente (a state that combined Sinaloa and Sonora) defined citizenship and set voting guidelines. To be considered a citizen of the state, Section Three, Article 13, stated, "Sonorans are: 1. All those born in the territory of the state." This meant that Indians were citizens, since the article did not differentiate between Hispanos and Indians. Citizenship was granted to all who were over the age of eighteen if married, and over twenty-one if unmarried. Furthermore, Section Three, Article 21, read: "Sonorans are equal before the law.... [A]ll citizens may obtain employment by the state with no other motive of preference than merit, virtue, the aptitude for the discharge of the office, and the talents required by each one." As with Mexican national law, Indians who qualified for employment or office on merit held that right. The rights of citizens could be taken away for specific causes, but only one of these was Indian-specific. Section Four, Article 28, No. 6, stated that the rights of Indian citizens could be stripped "For having the custom of going about shamefully nude; however, this clause is to have no effect on the indigenous citizens until the year 1850."[19] On paper, Occidente granted its Indigenous peoples citizenship, and they could participate in all political activity there.

While Mexican liberalism and legal developments paid lip service to equality and inclusion, clearly something more sinister was afoot, perhaps even more so than what occurred in New Mexico during the Mexican period. As the ethnohistorian Cynthia Radding has summarized, in the wake of Mexican independence, "Sonoran oligarchs changed the terms of negotiation with the ethnic communities in their province and, in so doing, altered irretrievably the operative legal definition of property and the relations between the state and these Serrano *naciones*. The new regime pushed aggressively to privatize the land and to change both the civic status of Indians and the internal governance of their pueblos." Between 1825 and 1835, leaders in Occidente and Sonora (the latter became its own state in 1831) enacted legislation that made Indians and Hispanos equal before the law. Yet Mexican leaders sought to extend their jurisdiction over Indian towns through municipal government and the dividing up of Indian communal lands. As Mexico had attempted in New Mexico, and as the United States would later pursue during the Allotment era, the State of Occidente implemented legal protections for Indian lands, but moved to sell off "vacant lands" for the "benefit" of Indians. Whether Indians actually saw any of the proceeds of these sales is unknown still today. Indian communal lands were severely depleted, as vecinos continually constricted the Indian land base. This policy was further strengthened by the expulsion of Iberian priests from the missions in Pimería Alta. Occidente and Sonora then passed laws that subordinated Indian towns to local municipal governments. Since Indians no longer had any special status, they were included in municipal governing bodies dominated by Hispanos.[20] The powers of Indian governors diminished significantly as Indian landholdings in Sonora shrank and as municipal government was transformed.[21] It was, in short, a great Indian land grab, sanctioned by changes in municipalities and Mexican liberal ideals, whereby much of the land that had remained under Indian ownership by way of royal protections during the Spanish period changed hands during the Mexican era.[22]

In a sense, Mexico attempted to solve its "Indian problem" by ignoring it. Indians became citizens under the law, with the mere mention of "Indian" dropped from official documents. In the case of laws in which it was absolutely necessary to refer to Indians, the term *indigene* was used instead. Mexican officials did make some efforts to ensure that Indians were treated fairly under Mexican law, but not nearly enough. The state government charged its representatives with guaranteeing that democratic elections of municipal officers begin immediately in all areas, thereby establishing an Indian electorate. Regarding the question of communal lands, officials were to keep in mind that lands had been illegally and unjustly stripped from Indians in the past. Mexican representatives were to administer the public lands in partnership with commissions composed of Indians. Finally, arbitrators were to decide disputes over land between Indians and non-Indians in favor of Indians. With justice and equality as guiding principles, a slight preference would be given to Indians, although they would not retain their previous status as members of Indian republics possessing distinct rights and protections.[23]

The Yaqui Response

What policymakers failed to realize was that their actions, however well intentioned, attacked the foundations of a system to which Indians had long been accustomed, and which some groups, such as Yaquis, had incorporated into their own Indigenous lifeways. In the first decades of the nineteenth century, Yaquis continued to practice—and further develop—a system of democratic town government loosely based on the Spanish model, with the customary elections and definite ideas of both political sovereignty and corporate land control. Yaqui village sovereignty was a keystone of their political system, with each village electing its own officer corps that oversaw village governance, military affairs, and relations with the outside world.[24] When Yaquis were pushed—as in the previous century—they once again pushed back. Mexican reforms brought a return of Yaqui violence, with the two sides unable to reconcile. Mexicans viewed Yaqui attempts to maintain entrenched and preferred methods of local governance and land control as the actions of spoiled children, too long accustomed to a "privileged" status as Indians. To the Mexican government, opposition to reform posed by Yaquis and other Indigenous groups was simply "resistance to a loss of special privilege—the exemption from citizenship responsibilities."[25]

During the Mexican period Yaquis lived within a complex electoral landscape that included village governors and other officers. The governors, elected by community members, remained particularly important, wielding the customary varas de justicia. They were inducted on 6 January each year, and their powers included the ability to settle family disputes and manage land boundaries within their communities. Mexican officials had only a nominal presence in the governing of Yaqui communities through the office of captain general, whom the Mexicans appointed and regarded as a liaison officer between the government of Occidente and the Yaquis. But individuals used this office to mobilize Yaqui resistance and to align Yaquis with Mexican interests at various times. The net result was a set of institutions and governing principles perfectly suited to Yaqui life. Yaqui voting, along with the obligation of all community members to participate in the town political sphere (which included the civil, military, and religious), was central to this system. It is not difficult to understand why Yaquis violently resisted the Mexican incursions of the 1820s and 1830s. They were not simply opposing taxation and the division of land; they were safeguarding their own political and cultural sovereignty, not to mention their very survival as a distinct Indigenous nation.

When the Constitution of Occidente (1825) declared all Indians to be citizens, it thereby subjected Yaquis to direct taxation for the first time. Moreover, Yaquis were increasingly called on to render military service for the republic, though one in whose independence movement they had played no part. Much like Nuevomexicanos, Yaquis abhorred the idea of paying direct taxes, and felt uncomfortable with military service to the new nation, although they had served previously as auxiliaries under the Spanish and Yaqui flags. When Occidente officials came to Yaqui territory in 1824–25 to survey Yaqui lands, begin taxation, and establish new municipal governments, the Yaquis became deeply concerned. When they ignored new taxes and troop levies, Mexico took action. The new republic hoped to deal with the Apache threat to the north, and needed Yaqui manpower to do so. In September 1825, the federal commander general of Occiente, José Figueroa, ordered Yaqui captain general Nicolás María Alvarez to mobilize Yaqui auxiliaries to fight Apaches along the Colorado River. Yaquis refused. Not only that, but they deposed Alvarez as captain general, placing Juan Buitemea, Huírivis's militia commander, in his place. To complicate matters even further, the priest of Huírivis, José María Melquiades Villaseñor, had actually encouraged the Yaquis to depose Captain

General Alvarez in favor of Buitemea.[26] Mexico's response to the Yaqui actions of 1825 precipitated a war that persisted well into the 1830s.

An enraged Commander General Figueroa sent Captain Ramón Mier to the Río Yaqui to arrest both Father Villaseñor and Buitemea. On 25 October 1825, Captian Mier's soldiers entered the Yaqui town of Ráum.[27] The Yaquis refused to stand down, and a clash ensued in which a number of Mexican soldiers, vecinos, and Yaquis were killed. Panic quickly spread in the wake of this encounter, fanned by Mexican fears of a pan-Indian alliance of Yaquis, Opatas, and Pimas, like the one from 1740, and by the rumor that Yaquis would indiscriminately kill any Mexicans they encountered.[28] On 27 October 1825, only two days after the initial encounter, the governor of Occidente offered a pardon to Yaquis if they gave back stolen goods, returned to their villages, assisted in hunting down any Yaquis who continued armed resistance, and reinstated Alvarez as captain general. In their counterdemands, Yaquis insisted that all troops depart the Yaqui River Valley, that vecinos who had fled the fighting not return, and that Mexico recognize Yaquis as the sole owners of their land.[29]

Mexican civil and military officials disagreed on how to handle the situation. Occidente governor Elías González favored amnesty and meeting Yaqui demands, while General Figueroa favored decisive military action to subdue the Yaquis once and for all. In the end, they decided on a diplomatic solution, meeting with the elected Yaqui governors and captains at Guaymas on Christmas Day, 1825. Governor González trod the familiar path of lecturing the Indian officers on their new responsibilities to the government of Occidente, while Figueroa secretly hedged his bets by sending some two hundred Mexican soldiers to Belém on 8 January 1826. Yaquis there were generally peaceful, but he knew that the more resistant Yaquis were still hiding in the hills. As a precautionary measure he left three detachments of seventy men each at Tórim, Guaymas, and Buenavista to monitor the situation and surveil the Yaqui villages. General Figueroa believed that he had succeeded in suppressing Yaqui resistance, but he was mistaken. He wrongly believed that Yaquis were motivated by race hatred and simply wanted to kill all Mexicans. He also incorrectly believed that Yaquis had neither morals nor politics, so he refused to recognize their right to self-govern.[30] Figueroa and other Mexican officials failed to see Yaqui resistance for what it was: a struggle to maintain both sovereignty and an ordered electoral system adapted to Yaqui needs. Taxation, the division of lands, and a new system of town government eroded Yaqui sovereignty and their ability to govern themselves and were thus deemed unacceptable.

The individual at the head of Yaqui resistance in the 1820s to 1830s was Juan Ignacio Jusacamea,[31] commonly known as Juan de la Cruz Banderas, or

Bells at Tórim, with Bacatete Mountains in the background. Tórim was one of the major sites of Mexican military occupation in Yaqui territory. Photo by author.

simply Juan Banderas. He had initially led only a few hundred Yaqui holdouts during the struggle against Figueroa. The group successfully hid in canyons and forested areas, and raided villages for subsistence. But Banderas began to attract more Yaqui adherents as resistance to the Mexican occupation grew, and some Mayos also joined the cause. General Figueroa, who had set up his headquarters at Buenavista by June 1826, decided to offer amnesty to Yaquis who turned themselves in. He distributed passports to those who came in from the hills and valleys, certifying that they were "friendly" Yaquis. But Figueroa's forces had a difficult time hunting down the resistant Yaqui bands, and Mexicans living in the countryside began to panic at the possibility of another Yaqui, or even pan-Indian, uprising. Figueroa made some headway in June and July 1826, when his forces defeated Yaquis in a few engagements and a number of Yaquis turned themselves in.[32]

It was at this point that Banderas's unique leadership style emerged. Very little is known about Banderas before his war with Occidente and Mexico. What *is* known is that he served in the position of *alférez*, or flag bearer, of the military organization of Ráum. He carried the flag bearing the image of the Virgen de Guadalupe, thus the name "Banderas."[33] The flag was to assume special significance in his message. Alférez was an important position in the village military organization, but not that of the top commander. Thus Banderas, the most significant Yaqui leader since Muni and Bernabé, was neither a governor nor a traditional religious leader.

It would seem that Banderas attained his status through his leadership skills and charisma. Primary accounts from the period corroborate this theory. For example, Lieutenant R. W. H. Hardy, an officer in the British Royal Navy who was in Sonora in the 1820s during the Yaqui War, recorded his impressions of Banderas. Although he clearly harbored an anti-Mexican bias, Hardy had much to say about the Yaqui leader and the events surrounding the resistance he led. He spoke highly of Banderas, calling him "a man of extraordinary talent and character," and remarked that "it [is not] easy to foresee how his career will terminate, or where the revolution, which he so ably manages, will stop." Hardy wondered how long the protracted struggle would continue with Banderas at the head of the Indians: "[Banderas is] endowed with a natural flow of eloquence quite extraordinary, and with a talent and activity which have kept up the revolution for two years, in spite of every effort of General Figueroa to subdue it." The Briton also believed that Banderas was a leader who exercised restraint, seeking only to protect the sovereignty of the Yaqui Nation and the rights of his people: "It cannot be denied that he might have captured Fuerte, Alamos, and Pitic [all major towns in the region], if he had chosen so to have done; but his object seems throughout merely to obtain redress for his suffering nation, by convincing the Mexican government that, although unarmed and undisciplined, the Yaqui is not so impotent as he has always been supposed. Indeed, *he sent delegates to remonstrate with the President*, General Victoria, and the government, with orders to state the grievances of the nation, and with assurances, that, so soon as they should be redressed, he would immediately disband his warriors, and they should all return to their homes on the instant."[34] Banderas's actions were those of a leader representing a sovereign people, even treating with President Victoria on a nation-to-nation basis. To Hardy, Banderas provided a stark contrast to Mexican leaders, with his charisma and integrity.

Even some Mexican commentators of the time grudgingly admired Banderas's gifts as a leader, and believed him to be representative of Yaqui characteristics in general. Ignacio Zuñiga, who traveled to the Arizona-Sonora Borderlands in the 1830s, was concerned with consolidating a defensive frontier line from New Mexico to Arizona that would provide a bulwark against both Apaches and the expansionist United States. He believed that the definitive integration of "pacified" Indians would help guarantee peace and internal security. While Zuñiga wrote disparagingly of O'odhams, calling them "phlegmatic and lazy," he was complimentary of Yaquis, saying that they possessed "a lively and vigorous imagination: they are men of ideas and clear powers." But Zuñiga also fell into the "warlike Yaqui" trope when he referred to them as "fierce in war, audacious and intrepid." Zuñiga felt a begrudging sense of admiration for Banderas, whom he complimented as "a genius at managing and exciting his followers, blessed with spirited imagination, eloquence, and a rare talent, with which he could have done a lot more bad." But, like other Mexicans, he did not understand Yaqui motivations for resisting the Mexican Indian program: "This people has thus far perpetrated bloody and disastrous uprisings ... due to the extraordinary genius displayed by their bosses." He failed to recognize that their highly developed political institutions and system of land tenure were in fact the result of the enterprising spirit of which he wrote. Zuñiga urged an increase in Mexican colonization of Yaqui territory and advocated for the division of their lands, at the same time lamenting, "At no time has the Yaqui nation been governed by anyone other than their own governors and captain general."[35] While he offered faint praise for Yaquis and their leaders, Zuñiga fell in line with Mexican political thinkers of the day who argued for an end to Indian status, the division of Indian lands, and the mainstreaming of Indigenous political institutions. Men such as Zuñiga believed that the security of Mexico's vulnerable north depended on full Yaqui political incorporation through whatever means necessary.

While Banderas's rise to prominence outside traditional Yaqui channels of power was somewhat unique, his political ideology was nothing short of singular. A report from 1827 asserted that Banderas was illiterate, but fortunately someone in his inner circle could read and write. This individual was most likely another Yaqui. Four of Banderas's manifestos have survived, as well as one of his purported religious visions and also several letters that other Yaqui leaders wrote to him. The Yaqui linguistics expert John M. Dedrick transcribed these manifestos and letters in the 1980s, shedding light on Yaqui thought from the period and how Yaquis viewed Banderas's leadership.[36] For example, a letter Banderas received from José de Jesús and Juan Felipe de Jesús of Ráum, dated 18 August 1832, states, "People! Yaqui Nation! The time has arrived in which we must mutually help one another. Great harm is coming to us. We who are all brothers, who are of the brotherhood of Yaquis, we must join together for our mutual defense.... United we will cry our war cry, launching the attack against our enemies. God will help us." The ideology adopted by Banderas's supporters, calling on Yaquis and other Indians to join the struggle against the Mexicans, often invoked God, and Banderas would do similarly. Banderas and his followers believed that they would have divine help in their fight. Yet Yaquis were by no means unified behind Banderas, and many supporters felt that those who did not follow him completely simply lacked the necessary faith to throw themselves wholeheartedly into the cause.[37]

Other letters from Yaqui supporters demonstrate that Banderas, though primarily a military leader, also wielded significant influence in diplomatic affairs. This influence even extended outside the Yaqui villages, when Mayos and other groups joined in the war. In a letter dated 28 September 1832, Governor Manuel Ozuna of the Mayo village of Tesia wrote to Banderas in an obvious attempt to assuage Banderas's anger with him. Governor Ozuna referred to complaints that had reached Banderas of how he, Ozuna, had whipped his people (something well within his power as an Indian governor). Ozuna admitted to punishing some individuals, but insisted that he took no pleasure in it. He was worried about what Banderas had heard, and insisted that those who had spread rumors about his severity as a governor were simply troublemakers. He asserted his loyalty to the cause, and said that he was ever at Banderas's service. He went so far as to state that he respected and loved Banderas, and that he kissed his hand three times.[38] Governor Ozuna's fear of Banderas was evident in his letter. While Banderas's appeal as a leader must have motivated many supporters to join his side, others clearly feared him and were not as dedicated to the cause. One letter, signed by Alcalde Juan Gerónimo Marquín, Síndico Ysidro Juan Maria Jusacamea, and Juan Zacaria Armenta—all Yaqui civil officers—described complaints by a number of civilians who "told us of the bad and misery that Banderas and his soldiers had caused them."[39] Disunity among Yaquis, including questions about Banderas's leadership and fear of his army, would ultimately prove disastrous to his efforts.

Each of Banderas's four manifestos is brief and written in a simple, phonetic manner. Along with the account of Banderas's vision, all were penned by the same hand, which Dedrick insisted is "characteristic of a manuscript of the seventeenth or early eighteenth century rather than one of the nineteenth century." Although undated, the manifestos were submitted with other documents to the central government, and are believed to date from approximately 1826.[40] More than the letters to and about Banderas, his own statements in the manifestos and his vision provide an intriguing lens into the mind of an influential Yaqui. They indicate how he viewed both Yaqui leadership and the source from which power ultimately derived. In the first manifesto, he began by referring to himself as "the flag of our sovereign Montesuma [sic].... I come sent by my Lady of Guadalupe to win this crown." He went on to state that it was she who bade "all of the Governors of the Towns, to win this crown of Our King Montesuma that they have inherited from our Lady of Guadalupe." He assured the people that he had not come to harm Indians or criollos. He claimed to have 1,000 men under arms from the Yaqui and Mayo Nations, and even twenty men of razón (vecinos) under his flag.[41]

A few items in this manifesto are particularly noteworthy. First, Banderas asserted that his power flowed from the Aztec emperor Moctezuma. Further, he combined this with the Virgen de Guadalupe. Banderas's power was thus both hereditary and otherworldly, since it originated from the important line of Aztec kings along with the Mother of God. Banderas did not come up through typical Yaqui avenues of power—he was neither an elected major town official nor part of the religious leadership, so he did not possess conventional civil or religious authority. But he ingeniously satisfied both needs by appealing to Moctezuma (political authority) and the Virgen (religious authority). Furthermore, he covered all the necessary bases by enlisting the support of "the Governors of the Pueblos." Banderas must have realized the tenuous nature of his position as a leader, unlike Muni and Bernabé, who both came up through "proper" leadership channels, because he took great care to affirm his own legitimacy.

The second manifesto echoed many of these statements, but closed by stating, "All that which the Gachupines had will be for those who will help me win this crown of King Montesuma." In his third manifesto, Banderas offered little variation, except that this time he explicitly called on other Indian nations to join what had been primarily a rebellion of Yaquis and Mayos. He implored Yaquis, Mayos, Opatas, Eulaves, Apaches, O'odhams, and Seris to join his band, which, he asserted, had grown to over 2,000 strong. General Figueroa sent the third manifesto to the central government in Mexico City, along with his own thoughts on its contents. He saw nothing of value in Banderas's message and cause, calling his proclamation "bastante ridiculo" (rather ridiculous), yet he still wanted to bring it to the attention of authorities because it was circulating among the Indian towns and fanning fires of discontent.[42]

In the fourth and final manifesto, which also contained Banderas's vision, we see the coalescence of his leadership rhetoric. In the last manifesto he referred to himself as "Yo el Rey y Emperador" (I the King and Emperor). He called on various Indian nations to "get themselves ready" to support him and serve under his flag.[43] Banderas was also a visionary, though only one reliable account of a vision exists, as it was written in the same hand as the manifestos, and on the reverse side of the paper containing the fourth manifesto. In his vision, which differed from the manifestos in that it was written in the third person, Banderas told of reclining as if dead for an entire day. He revived at a certain point, and then went up to a mountain, staying there with no food or drink. Jesus Christ, the Virgin Mary, St. Bartholomew, St. John, and other angels then visited him. The angels lifted him by his armpits, and carried him back to his own land so that buzzards and foxes would not eat him. One of his relatives found him three days later and over the next month nursed him back to health. At the end of this period, Banderas led the people in a festival for the Apostles, after which they launched their war against the Mexicans.[44] This vision has clear similarities to the visions of Native revivalists such as the Lenni Lenape prophet Neolin, the Shawnee prophet Tenskwatawa, and the Seneca visionary Handsome Lake. Unlike these other visionaries, who usually functioned as the religious leaders in conjunction with a military arm of their movements (such as Pontiac, Tecumseh, and Cornplanter), Banderas was both a civil-military and a religious leader. His power was ultimate because it came from God as well as from a hereditary line of Indigenous Mexican kings. Yet it was his assumption of power outside proper channels that would ultimately prove his undoing.

As for the war itself, Banderas met with mixed results in his calls for followers, especially among nations apart from the Yaquis and Mayos. His movement never gained the traction with other groups that he would have liked. Even among his own people and his closest Mayo allies, support was unreliable. Lieutenant Hardy related events surrounding raids by Banderas's band and the looting they undertook in these attacks: "A great deal of plunder was taken, of which Bandéras made division. He would give a portion to his present followers; another part he sent into the Yáqui and Mayo country, for the purpose not only of raising recruits, but of also keeping up the spirits of the old men of the different towns which had elected him for their Generalissimo."[45] Hardy, who we must recall admired Banderas and his leadership, indicated with his statement that Banderas gained at least some of his adherents, and maintained the confidence of influential elders, through the goods that he sent to them. And while Banderas may have had some support among Yaqui and Mayo elders, he did not necessarily have a mandate from the Yaqui people, a group characterized by government based on popular support. It is possible that a council of elders selected Banderas as their leader, although his mandate was far from universal. Nor did he have the widespread support of other Indian groups. As Spicer summarized, "Juan Banderas's authority had foundations outside the traditional Yaqui governmental system."[46]

The fighting was sporadic from the time of Banderas's emergence in 1826 to his capture in 1832. Episodes of intense warfare were followed by periodic truces. Banderas's actions during the rebellion are illuminating. By late 1827, the manifestos ceased and he no longer declared himself the heir of Moctezuma, empowered by the Virgen de Guadalupe, nor did he refer to himself as emperor and king. In fact, on 13 April 1827, Banderas made one of his surrenders, to the priest of Pótam. In return for his submission and assurances of peace, Banderas was promised the position of captain general of the Yaqui Nation, or leadership power through a recognized channel, although this office was appointed by Mexican officials and not achieved through popular election. Furthermore, as Banderas periodically resisted and accommodated Mexican incursions, officials sought to tighten their control of Yaqui civil affairs. For example, after some Yaqui villages surrendered to Mexican soldiers in late 1826, Lieutenant Colonel Romero appointed captains and governors there. Yaqui captains were placed in command of twenty-five men each and ordered to hunt down rebels.[47] This followed the well-established Hispano tradition of appointing "agreeable" Indians to positions of leadership.

In the midst of these developments, the government of Occidente sought to address Indian discontent by issuing a series of decrees concerning both fundamental Yaqui grievances and those of neighboring Indian nations: among them, citizenship, taxes, land, and voting. The documents show a certain degree of naïveté on the part of the state government, as if legislation alone could solve the problems manifesting themselves in an alarming number of Indian rebellions flaring up during this time.[48] Decree 44, issued 6 February 1828, addressed Occidente's desire to regain control over Yaqui territory. Article 1 of the decree stated that a new *partido* (subdistrict) would be formed out of the eight Yaqui villages under the control of the presidio of Buenavista. Occidente intended to remove Yaqui independence by placing their villages under the administrative control of a military presidio. Article 4 called for the immediate elections of *alcaldes de policía* (mayors) and of *síndicos procuradores* (attorneys) for the towns, who would report to the state government on any abuses and would "jealously seek the unity and equality of those called whites and indigenes." Article 6 encouraged Hispano settlement on Yaqui lands by exempting vecinos who settled on Yaqui lands from taxes for a period of six years. But the government also sought to appease Yaquis by declaring in article 7 that the ayuntamientos of Buenavista and other towns in this new subdistrict "will very scrupulously watch over the integral conservation of the common lands of the pueblos and the private properties of the Indians." The ayuntamientos were also to oversee the restitution of any Indian lands or goods lost to outside parties, "whether through sale, exchange or donation."[49]

The government of Occidente thus attempted to pursue contradictory ends in its dealings with Yaquis. It simultaneously encouraged Hispano settlements in the area, while calling for the restitution of Yaqui lands and goods. In addition, Occidente placed control over lands and issues of governance squarely in the hands of the ayuntamientos of Buenavista and other prominent Mexican towns. Yaquis had enjoyed a great deal of political autonomy up to this point, particularly in electoral matters. Through these decrees, the state government stripped them of control over their own national affairs and attempted to incorporate them into the system of mixed-ethnicity ayuntamientos.

More decrees followed. Decrees 88 and 89, both dated 30 September 1828, sought to clarify once and for all the status of Indian towns, addressing how they were to be governed and their lands administered. One can clearly see the motives of Occidente officials in these decrees. For example, Decree 88 stated in its introduction that it was "law for the particular government of villages of the indigenes." The very first article reaffirmed that Indians were to be protected in their rights of "equality, liberty, property and security." After this generic pronouncement of Indian rights, it went on to state "that in every popular election they be called on to vote and be voted for, both for council jobs, or for any other they be capable of performing."[50]

The language of this decree as it pertains to Indian voting is critical. It affirmed that the "rights" associated with citizenship were, in reality, obligations. Indians were not encouraged to vote; rather, they are called on to vote and also to hold office. This meant being part of ayuntamientos that were inclusive, and not exclusively Indian. In addition to the voting obligation, the decree specified that Indian militias were a thing of the past. From that point on, the "civil Militia" was to be composed of all citizens in common, another erosion of Indian sovereignty, this time over military affairs. The motivation for this action was obvious. With Indian militias, Mexicans found an established, experienced, disciplined enemy under Indigenous leadership. Even though they had refused to send troops for the Apache campaign, Yaquis had fielded large companies of soldiers on numerous occasions. By integrating Yaqui soldiers into Mexican militia units, Occidente hoped to eliminate potential sources of organized resistance.[51]

Decree 88 also addressed the issue of Indian lands, of particular interest to Yaquis. Article 5 reaffirmed that land distribution was to proceed, but stated that lands and goods subject to the new redistribution laws were to be "administered with the knowledge of the indigenes, under the inspection of the ayuntamientos and alcaldes." Article 6 declared that both Indians and vecinos had the same obligation to cultivate their lands and partake in the fruits of these labors with equality. Article 7 established an administrative position to oversee the communal lands. This administrator was to serve for a five-year term, and Indians were "preferred" for the position. Regarding how funds were to be used from the sale of "excess" lands, Article 8 listed the appropriate expenditures: paying for teachers of Indian children; creating and encouraging schools; repairing churches, jails, and municipal buildings; beautifying and cleaning churches and municipal buildings; and making any expenditures conducive to public education. The final portion of Decree 88 took the previous articles one step further, addressing questions of Indian education. Articles 10 through 15 called for establishing schools, for both boys and girls, where Indians would be taught "to read, write and count, [and] they will be instructed in the principles of our religion and their civil and political rights."[52]

Decree 88, in its totality, was a calculated, comprehensive plan for Indian towns that attacked the fundamental pillars of Indian sovereignty. First, Indians would be obligated to perform their "civic duty" in voting and holding office through elections that would replace the established Indian town democratic practices. Second, Indians would no longer muster their own militia units, a measure that would weaken their ability to offer organized military resistance to Mexican soldiers and policies. Third, lands would be distributed and the excess sold off. Only the absolute minimum care would be taken to ensure that Indians were part of the process. Vecinos would be incentivized to occupy excess lands, thereby hemming in Indian communities on all sides. Lastly, Indian children would be removed from traditional teachings and educated in the Mexican way, with special emphasis on their duties as citizens. If all went according to plan, the ever-troublesome Yaquis would be incorporated into the political mainstream in short order.

Understandably, Yaqui resisters did not accept these legal measures. With Bandaras and his supporters still offering armed resistance, Mexican leaders found their ideal candidate for a sympathetic Yaqui leader and intermediary in Juan María Jusacamea. Throughout the late 1820s and early 1830s, Banderas and Jusacamea were mired in a power struggle for Yaqui leadership. When more Apache threats flared up in 1831, Sonora—which was once again a separate state—accepted a political solution to the Yaqui War in May of that year. The Yaqui demands were threefold: first, that a single, popularly elected alcalde be made the chief governing figure over the Yaqui Nation; second, that each Yaqui pueblo be allowed to elect its own regidor, or gobernador, answerable only to the Yaqui alcalde; and third, that Yaquis be permitted to elect a captain general and a lieutenant general of the Yaqui Nation. The government of Sonora accepted these three measures, but added a few items to the agreement. Returning to old mission policy, Sonora granted priests direct supervisory power over the alcalde and village governors, in hopes that the priests would have better luck than Mexican military and civil officials with the Yaquis. In addition, the Yaqui alcalde and town governors were to serve one-year terms, as they had in the old Yaqui-Spanish system. They oversaw civil matters, but could only punish minor crimes. All other jurisdiction reverted to the Buenavista ayuntamiento.[53] This arrangement, though it represented a compromise, was similar to the old república system. All three of the Yaquis' major demands aimed at securing the right to choose their own officers on both town and national levels. But in a final measure the Sonora state government established a director position for Yaqui affairs. This non-Indian director outranked the Yaqui alcalde and reported directly to the governor of Sonora. He was to guarantee that Yaqui leaders did not exercise *too* much autonomy and sovereignty.[54]

Even though these developments held some promise for Yaqui sovereignty, they ultimately failed to satisfy Banderas and his followers. At Yaqui elections for alcalde, town governors, and other officers on 1 July 1831, overseen by the non-Indian director, Banderas did not run for office. Instead, at a general meeting held at Bácum on 30 August, he deposed the newly elected alcalde, governors, and officers, proclaiming himself captain general of the Yaqui Nation. Banderas attempted to rally Yaquis, Mayos, and other Indians to his cause one final time, but these were the last actions of his political and military career. On 6 December 1832, soldiers captured Banderas and a number of his men. He was tried by a military tribunal in Arizpe and executed on 7 January 1833. Mexican reports claimed that Banderas spoke to a confessor in his last days, imploring Yaquis not to follow his "bad example." He also purportedly invited all Yaquis to live in peace with non-Indians. He then reportedly begged forgiveness for his crimes against vecinos—and left his family in the care of a priest.[55]

With Banderas gone, Mexican authorities seized the opportunity to prop up their man in the Yaqui government. Yaquis elected Juan María Jusacamea, Banderas's fiercest Yaqui opponent for the previous several years, to the position of captain general of the Yaquis. From the Mexican point of view, Jusacamea was the perfect captain general, since he was content to allow Mexican authorities to control Yaqui affairs. Jusacamea did not have the support of the Yaqui people, nor did he seem particularly fond of them. In a report to the governor of Sonora in 1833, he stated, "[Yaquis] are resentful against me for having been obedient to the government and to the laws." He then went a step further, characterizing the Yaqui spirit as "generally inclined towards evil." By the summer of 1836, four Yaqui villages openly opposed Captain General Jusacamea. The governor of Sonora refused to hold new elections, even though Jusacamea had been in office for several years, and since serving successive years in office was expressly prohibited in the Indian election laws of 1831. A full-fledged rebellion did not ensue, but Yaquis continued to resist efforts by Mexican authorities to make them full citizens of Mexico and to subject them to civil and military jurisdiction.[56]

As Spicer has summarized, "The Mexicans had not foreseen the depth of the Indian devotion to the institutions which had developed out of the fusion of Spanish and native forms."[57] They had not imagined they would show such fierce loyalty to the Yaqui-Spanish electoral system that had developed over the course of two centuries. Even so, it is difficult to assess Banderas's contribution in defending an autonomous Yaqui Nation dedicated to the maintenance of distinct institutions of governance. On the one hand, there is no doubting Banderas's commitment to Yaqui autonomy. He envisioned a Yaqui Nation free from Mexican meddling. On the other hand, when Yaquis and Mexicans reached a compromise in 1831, allowing Yaquis to elect their own officials—a compromise Banderas supported at the time—he was unwilling to relinquish power and allow those elected by fellow Yaquis to serve in their offices. In the end, this was Banderas's undoing. He was a chameleon of sorts. His power came from the Virgen de Guadalupe, from Moctezuma, or perhaps from his right to rule as the supreme leader of the Yaqui Nation. Yet his power never came from popular elections and national consensus, principles crucial to Yaqui electoral politics. Banderas, a man whom Yaquis and outsiders admired and praised for his eloquence, forcefulness, resoluteness, and even restraint in some instances, ultimately failed his people—because he could not fully reconcile himself to those very Yaqui electoral practices that could have threatened his power. These institutions would weather the years of upheaval and would continue to provide a foundation for Yaqui governance in the decades of terror that followed.[58]

O'odham Governors, Mexican Administrators, and the Decline of Pimería Alta

The decline of the mission system in Pimería Alta before and after Mexican independence was the single most important factor affecting Indian voting and town governance in the region. The Mexican era was a time of complete collapse for the missions of northern Mexico.[59] The Indian population of Pimería Alta had been steadily declining for decades. As early as 1776, Friar Pedro Font reported that "in all the pueblos there are usually more deaths than births."[60] An 1820 count gave a total Indian population at the eight missions of Pimería Alta of only 1,127. The vecino population of the same area was 2,291. Although the vecino population was not particularly large, it had doubled since 1800. By 1820, only San Xavier del Bac, Tumacácori, and Caborca had more Indians than gente de razón. The only reason that significant Indian populations remained at the missions at all was that Franciscan missionaries had actively recruited so-called "desert Pimas," or Tohono O'odhams, to take the place of those Sobaipuris and O'odhams who had steadily died off.[61] The weakening of Indian electoral politics in Pimería Alta during the Mexican period is closely linked to the atrophy of the mission system, shrinking Indian populations, and the growth of vecino communities.

Regardless of whether Jesuits or Franciscans administered the missions of northern Sonora, the ultimate goal of transforming Indians into tax-paying citizens was always a painfully slow process. But, after Mexican independence, conditions seemingly combined to expedite this process. The political incorporation of Indians required the secularization of missions. For this to occur, the state-supported friars from the orders had to be replaced with parish-supported priests, or *curas* (secular clergy). Indians would no longer be under the control of missionaries; they would become parishioners and taxpayers. Indian parishioners would support the priest through *diezmos* (tithes) and other fees, thus ending the government's responsibility to provide financial support for the missions. With treasuries severely depleted from years of instability, during the 1820s and 1830s Mexican officials turned to secularization as both a revenue source and a relief from decades of maintaining the burdensome mission business. They sorely needed the funds that could be gathered from Indian taxation. Vecinos also favored secularization because, as mentioned previously, the protected communal mission lands, or the *fondo legal*, would be converted to private property for individual Indians. "Excess" lands reverted back to the public domain, making them available to vecinos.[62]

Those who embraced the liberal humanistic ideology of the late Spanish colonial period and Mexican independence also supported secularization as a moral imperative. Liberals argued that Indians were not inferior. The time had come for their inclusion as equal citizens. But Franciscans, who in theory also wanted Indians to achieve the status of "civilized" persons and citizens, strongly resisted secularization. They believed that Indians still did not sufficiently understand private property, thrift, and hard work as means to protect themselves from greedy vecinos who would steal Indian land once the friars were gone. Regardless of what the law stated, missionaries failed to see Indians as full citizens and doubted their potential to attain that status. Indians, government officials, missionaries, and vecinos were all locked in a difficult situation. In 1833, a Franciscan serving in the California missions engulfed by similar upheavals wrote, "The [government] wants the Indians to be private owners of lands and of other property; this is just. The Indians, however, want the freedom of vagabonds. The [non-Indians] want the absolute liberation and emancipation of the neophytes ... in order that they may avail themselves of their lands and other property as well as of their persons. I do not see how these opposing interests can be harmonized."[63] But the secularization that vecions and politicians desired—and that Indians and Franciscans feared—proceeded in the mission communities of the Arizona-Sonora Borderlands, due as much to happenstance as to conscious policy decisions.

As Indian populations declined in Pimería Alta, so too did the number of priests in the region. Missionary numbers did not diminish solely because of the depopulation of the missions. The College of Santa Cruz de Querétaro, which supplied the Pimería Alta missions with Franciscans, had difficulty staffing its installations. The vast majority of Franciscans sent to the northern missions were Iberian-born Spaniards. While the war for independence raged in Mexico, it was nearly impossible to find Spaniards willing to serve in the distant outposts. The church failed to replace the old, infirm, and dying priests in the northern missions. Actions by the Mexican government on 20 December 1827 compounded the situation when it ordered all Spaniards to leave the country. This measure drastically affected the missions of Pimería Alta. The expulsion of Spaniards from Mexico has been called, somewhat melodramatically, "Armageddon in the Missions."[64] The northernmost region of Pimería Alta, already scarce with missionaries, became completely devoid of them.

In addition, by the late 1820s the Pimería Alta missions had evolved into northern and western, with northern missions at Cocóspera, Tumacácori, and Bac. Santa Cruz, Tubac, and Tucson served as presidios. As administrative boundaries shifted and orders came in from the central government, Pimería Alta's civil leaders hesitated to enforce an expulsion order that would leave both Indians and vecinos without priests indefinitely. As they hesitated, military leaders stepped in and took the lead. One of the missionaries, Padre Ramón Liberós of Tumacácori, was told to leave in the second week of April 1828. He was given only three days to get mission affairs in order, which he felt was not nearly enough time to see to the mission goods, livestock, stores, books, and Indians. Officials informed him that these things were no longer his concern. Father Rafael Díaz was similarly expelled from San Xavier del Bac. Díaz was a bit more fortunate in that he had become a naturalized Mexican citizen. He weathered the storm of anti-peninsular sentiment, and returned to Pimería Alta in the summer of 1828 after his expulsion in the spring of that year, and went on to serve as chaplain of Tucson. Father Díaz rode the circuit in the Santa Cruz

River Valley over the ensuing years, administering sacraments to the Indians at the priest-less missions. Much like Kino, Díaz visited Bac and Tumacácori, "where a few Indians hung on." When he died in 1841 at age forty-six, he was the last Spanish Franciscan to serve in Pimería Alta. Neither Tumacácori nor Bac had resident priests from 1828 through the end of the Mexican period.[65] In the absence of priests, mission buildings deteriorated, mission fields lay fallow, orchards became overgrown, and those livestock herds not seized by Indians diminished or dispersed.

Inexplicably, some Indians remained at the missions. The old Spanish system of village governors and other officials, which had been in place for over one hundred years, persisted in some form even in the absence of missionaries. Tohono O'odhams brought to the missions during the previous decades continued to select governors during the Mexican period, but seem to have made no distinction between Spaniards and Mexicans, and were largely unaware of Mexico's war of independence.[66] The system did not include democratic elections by means of votes or ballots—which it never really had at the Pimería Alta missions—so, as was the case in New Mexico, individual tribal communities developed their own selection methods, which resorted to more traditional forms.

Interestingly, one of Ramón Liberós's final actions as the missionary at Tumacácori was to instruct his namesake, Ramón Pamplona, the longtime governor of the village, to pay off the mission debts still owed to workers who had labored on its unfinished church. Father Ramón seemed to have preferred that mission affairs be placed in Indian rather than vecino hands. When Commissioner General of Pimería Alta Fernando Grande went to Tumacácori in late summer 1828, he found that Governor Pamplona had performed respectably in administering the affairs of the mission. He begged Pamplona to remain in office as governor and continue in charge of the mission, but Pamplona refused, even after he was offered a salary. A vecino was put in his place to oversee the mission, after which Pamplona shared control of mission affairs with the Mexican civil administrator. These secular overseers, who administered mission lands and properties, were known as *mayordomos*.[67]

Grande continued on to Cocóspera, where he deposed the Native governor, Nicolás Martínez, who apparently had not been as adept as Pamplona at administering a mission. For their part, vecino mission administrators were notoriously corrupt, making every effort to steal mission lands and goods.[68] For example, the Indians of Tumacácori saw their vecino overseer, a resident of the Tubac presidio, as a "no-good white." Commissioner General Grande wrote on 1 November 1828:

The friars continually and consistently impressed upon the Pimas that all mission properties are the legal and rightful possession of the Indians alone. Three centuries of Spanish domination and the degrading and dehumanizing exemptions granted the Indians have made these people incapable of ever accepting our present system of government. They are irremediably prejudiced in favor of monarchy, and their lack of intelligence will always prevent them from understanding anything else. . . . At this very moment the native governors of Tubutama and Saric are here in Magdalena complaining against my civil subcommissioners at those missions and demanding the right to control their own mission properties. . . . I am insisting now on only one central administration for the wealth of all the missions, instead of an individual civil commissioner in each mission, precisely to delay reaction on the part of the Pimas. Only in this way can we gain time to sell off gradually the effects of these missions. Only in this way can we ever refill the depleted treasury of our state.[69]

While Grande lamented the actions of civil administrators, his primary goal was to fill up the state treasury with money and goods from the Pimería Alta missions. Overall, civil administration of mission lands and goods was an unqualified debacle. On 13 January 1830, Manuel Escalante y Arvizu, jefe político of the department of Arizpe, wrote to the governor of Occidente, Francisco Iriarte, that, even though only four Franciscans remained in Pimería Alta, mission lands must be returned to them "before the totality of mission wealth is either squandered by the civil commissioners or destroyed by the Apaches." In January 1830, mission lands in Pimería Alta were again placed under the control of Franciscans. In the absence of resident missionaries this solution also fell short.[70]

Under these chaotic circumstances, Native governors and officers in Pimería Alta, even those outside the missions, continued to govern their communities as best they could, often with "assistance" from the vecino administrators. Ever faithful in recording the condition of the Pimería Alta missions, Grande wrote about San Xavier del Bac to the Father Superior of Pimería Alta, José María Pérez Llera. In a letter dated 25 May 1830, he described the fertility of the fields around the mission, and told how Indians from other locations frequently came to Bac, with its imposing mission church, during harvest and at other festive times, only to return to their own villages later. He discussed how the furnishings for the priest's quarters and tools were handed over to the Native governor, Juan Ignacio Zapata. He observed, "Justice is exercised in this village by a representative of the mayor of law and order of Tucson," a vecino administrator. But the actual keys to the priest's quarters were entrusted to Governor Zapata.[71] Thus, Native governors retained certain powers, such as administering some of the mission properties, but the ultimate authority clearly resided in the hands of the vecino administrators.

Even after control of mission administrations was returned to the Franciscans in 1830, the lack of missionaries and the declining power of those few who remained troubled many Indians. For example, the O'odham governor of Caborca, Francisco Neblina, commented on the mission's alarming decline. Governor Neblina's 28 February 1835 letter, which he penned in his own hand, retains a rather nostalgic tone regarding the old mission days. Writing to the Father Prefect, José María Pérez Llera, he noted that their missionary father, Faustino González (who by virtue of being an old man in 1828 had escaped the expulsion order), had been able to sell the mission's crops at a higher price than they themselves could now obtain, and with the profits he "was able to maintain schools in our three villages and care for the widows, the sick, and the neophytes among the baptized, as well as giving something to the unbaptized."[72]

Despite the governor's loyalty to the priest, it was the Franciscan who stopped these O'odhams from lodging official protests against both vecino encroachments on mission Indian lands and the denial of their civil rights: "Often we have wanted to go ourselves and present our problems personally before these higher superiors. Our missionary himself, however, has stopped us. Being a Spaniard, he is sure they would blame him for our action." He proceeded to lament the state of the Tohono O'odhams, many of whom had settled in the missions although many others were unable to do so. He reported that significant numbers of them wanted to come in from dispersed rancherías, be baptized, and settle on mission lands, but could not do so, since much of the land had been snatched up and privatized. With no place for them, Tohono O'odhams wandered around, "free from the control of mission regulations and *free from guidance by their native governors.*"[73] Overall, the letter expressed many of the central concerns of O'odhams in Pimería Alta in the decades following Mexican independence: land dispossession, mission decay, an influx of vecinos, and the uprooting of many Indigenous peoples in the region. With the degeneration of the O'odham-Spanish system of mission governance, which was tenuous even in the best of situations, conditions worsened.

Governor Neblina's position—and that of O'odham and other Indigenous leaders more generally—was complicated. Mission administration by civil authorities, which officially ended in 1830 but actually continued after that date,[74] depleted the missions of lands and goods. Vecinos continued to encroach on Indian communal lands as more and more of the fondo legal became private property, particularly after the Mexican Congress declared on 16 April 1834 that all missions were to be secularized, followed by a 10 February 1842 law that allowed "abandoned" Indian land valued at $500 or less to be sold at public auction.[75] While Franciscans had oppressed the Indians in many ways and enriched the church and themselves at Indian expense, Neblina and others could point to schools and care for the needy in villages under Franciscan control, along with some limited protection of Indian land. The Franciscans' refusal to allow the Indians to travel to the seats of Mexican government to air legal complaints was not universal, as many records tell of Indians' using the colonizers' legal system to protect their rights and lands. As for the issue with Tohono O'odhams, vecino encroachment largely prevented Franciscans from distributing mission lands to the desert O'odhams. More importantly for Neblina, vecino land grabs inhibited the ability of Native governors to incorporate Tohono O'odhams into the mission Indian body-politic, where they might have had a say in both the governing of the villages and the selection of Native officers in a strengthened O'odham-Spanish village-governing structure. Neblina surely recognized that the mission system had its weaknesses, but to the mission Indians of Pimería Alta, the secularization of missions and the administration of mission lands and goods by civil administrators had proven to be the worst possible options.

Native governors, a few Franciscan missionaries, and a handful of sympathetic vecinos could not stem the tide of mission decay, secularization, abandonment, encroachment, and the loss of Indian land. An anonymous report dated 11 May 1843 depicted the bleak condition at San Xavier del Bac: "The communal agricultural lands of the mission are no longer cultivated and lie barren. Only about an eighth part of these lands and of the garden are kept up by the native governor. The rest of the planting land is used by the natives of this village and those of Santa Ana, a remote village subject to the authority of the missionary at San Xavier. No non-Indians are involved. The majority of even the native residents are without sustenance and unable to farm."[76]

The satellite mission at Tucson fared no better: "Our native governor sold the door to the sacristy and the door to an upper room of the missionary's residence for a yoke of oxen. The missionary himself sold the door to the baptistery to a settler for a saddletree.... The mission agricultural fields, both communal and those apportioned to the Indian families individually, and the plentiful water corresponding, are maintained by only six Indians, who are all that are left. The abundant land left over is farmed by the settlers of this presidio." O'odhams at Bac and Tucson saw none of the products or profits from their efforts. Settlers farmed on Indian lands without paying rents. The anonymous author of the 1843 report pleaded that a missionary come to Bac, which was an ideal location with ample land and water. Plus, "many unbaptized Papagos would come in from the desert and settle here" if there were a priest. Most alarming to the author was the fact that "For lack of religious attention, many Indians have abandoned religious practice, left the missions, and returned to the open desert."[77] By the 1840s, secularization had accomplished the near-destruction of O'odham missions to the far north of Pimería Alta.

The complete decline of the Pima missions did not go unnoticed by Anglo-American travelers at the time. Yet they made very little, if any, mention of O'odham officers from the old república system. Cave Couts, a U.S. Army officer who traveled through southern Arizona in the late 1840s, wrote of Tumacácori, "Today we passed quite a nice Indian village 2½ miles from Tubac. The church looked very well." He was relatively impressed by O'odhams at Tumacácori and Bac:

> The churches in this [Santa Cruz] valley are remarkable. At Tumacacori is a very large and fine church standing in the midst of a few common conical Indian huts, made of bushes, thatched with grass, huts of most common and primitive kind. . . . This church is now taken care of by the Indians, Pimas, most of whom are off attending a jubilee, or fair, on the other side of the mountain.
>
> No Priest has been in attendance for many years, though all its images, pictures, figures &c remain unmolested, and in good keeping. No Mexicans live with them at all.
>
> The Church at *Xavier del Bac*, which we left this morning, is said to be the *finest* in Sonora. 'Tis truly a noble and stupendous building. Its domes and spires which projected above the thick mesquite growth as we approached was of itself sufficient to guarantee a City with *many* churches and other large and fine buildings. But when we came up, found it standing solitary and alone, not another building nearer to it than *Tucson*, save the few old Indian huts of the most rude description, whose inmates (Pimas) had charge of the fine old church. . . . It is kept by these Pimas with incredible care and neatness.[78]

Couts offered a terse summary of the condition of the Indians, which could also be applied to O'odhams in Pimería Alta: "The unfortunate redman! unsuspicious and unsuspecting of the cunning and politic white flatterer, little thought of their days being numbered! of the day when the white man would see the last red warrior drowning in the Pacific, and rejoice when his rifle ball took the last breath of life from him!"[79]

United States Boundary Commissioner John Russell Bartlett was far less admiring than Couts in his own narrative. Traversing the same region in the early 1850s, he referred to Tumacácori and Guevavi as "two depopulated towns, in both of which were churches." He admired the church at Bac, but wrote disparagingly of its Indian inhabitants: "[It was] truly a miserable place, consisting of from eighty to one hundred huts, or wigwams, made of mud or straw, the sole occupants of which are Pimo [sic] Indians, though generally called *Papagos*. In the midst of these hovels stands the largest and most beautiful church in the State of Sonora.... [One building adjacent to the church] is occupied by the only Mexican family in the place." He even insulted the Indians who took care of the church and worshiped there: "The poor Indian doubtless believed them all [statues in the church] to be saints, and made his offerings accordingly, although about one half are statues of old Spanish cavaliers and figures of Chinese mandarins.... This church was built towards the close of the last century from the produce of the Mission lands, and is throughout in a good state of preservation." Bartlett's final piece of soliloquy was reserved for the failure of Mexican Indian policy generally: "A more thoroughly lazy set of people, I never saw.... Whether a proximity to the church and the worthless half-civilized Mexicans has reduced them to this state of indolence and poverty, I know not; but if so, they would better have remained in their native valleys, and never seen the faces of white men."[80] What Bartlett and Couts failed to recognize was that it was the destructive power of the upheavals of the period of Mexican independence, depopulation through disease and warfare, and struggles between near-powerless Native officers, vecinos, military leaders, and Franciscans that precipitated this decay.

Even under these chaotic circumstances, O'odhams continued to select governors as a remnant of the O'odham-Spanish electoral system. In the absence of missionaries or civil administrators to oversee elections or select Indigenous officers, such activities fell exclusively to O'odhams. It is safe to assume that the selection process varied from village to village. As it evolved during the Mexican period, the O'odham governor system looked less and less like those systems of the Pueblos of New Mexico or of other communities with stronger mission administrations. Still, O'odham officers proved their worth by navigating the increasingly complicated lines between missionaries, vecinos, and other Indians during the Mexican period. O'odham governors focused their efforts increasingly on encroachments by Mexican settlers. As Mexican landholdings grew, O'odhams became a dependable source of labor and partici-

Undated Photo of O'odham Chapel at San Ignacio. While many visitors commented on the splendors of the San Xavier del Bac mission church, most O'odhams worshipped at more modest chapels like this one. Bonaventure Oblasser, O.F.M. Collection, 1901–1977 MS 543, box 10, folder 19, courtesy of University of Arizona Libraries, Special Collections.

pated in the developing regional cash economy. They often traveled long distances from their villages to engage in this work, thereby keeping their own homes and families at arm's length from vecino farms, ranches, and communities. But in many locations, O'odhams found it difficult to push against increasing encroachment. In particular, Mexican cattlemen moved onto O'odham lands, after which disputes arose over water and grazing.[81]

In addition to farmers and ranchers, miners also complicated O'odham-Mexican relations. The late Spanish and Mexican periods marked an era of economic growth in the region. When gold was discovered on Tohono O'odhams lands in the 1830s, Mexican gold seekers poured into the area. Violence nearly erupted around Altar between miners and O'odhams. Santiago Redondo, the Mexican political chief of the Altar district, wrote to the Federalist Governor of Sonora José Urrea on 12 May 1838, "We were saved from further incident through the good graces of Tónolic, governor of Cubó and a prominent Papago leader."[82] The picture that emerges is one of Mexican settlers and Tohono O'odhams on the brink of war in the late 1830s, with only Native governors standing in the way of full-scale conflict on several occasions.

Tónolic demonstrated masterful diplomacy throughout this period, as many Tohono O'odhams agitated for both armed conflict with the Mexicans and the forceful repossession of their lands. He acted as the head of Indian officers in their diplomatic forays. Redondo and other Mexicans were met at Soñi on 27 April 1838 by "Tónolic, the Papago governor of Cubó, and the governors of Carricito, Ayoma, and Tac, all accompanied by constables, alcaldes, and other officials of their government." As Tónolic and others voiced their complaints "through Francisco Carro, our state-appointed captain general of the Papagos, [we] tried to make him understand that there are legal procedures he can follow when others try to steal Papago lands. Most important, these procedures would avoid armed invasions to seek out dissident Papagos and even enlist the powerful aid of our state governor against the enemies of the Papagos."[83] These Tohono O'odham leaders shouldered an enormous burden. Fortunately, their diplomatic relations with Mexicans did not completely collapse at this time, because Indian governors and other officers continued representing their communities under nearly impossible circumstances.

Unfortunately, conflicts between Mexicans and Tohono O'odhams did not cease in the late 1830s, despite the best efforts of skilled governors such as Tónolic. Mexicans also attempted to ease the pressures in the region during the 1830s, believing that the appointment of a greater number of civil officials for O'odhams would solve some of the problems created by Mexican land grabs and Apache raids. For example, the Sonoran Congress issued Decree 19 in 1831, mandating that each major Indian settlement in Pimería Alta have two civil officials (besides governors and previous officials). These two officers included a *juez económico* (economic judge), who was a tribal judge and overseer of communal property. The other was the alguacil, a constable who enforced law and order. In addition, on 1 April 1832 the ayuntamiento of the Mexican town Altar petitioned for the establishment of an O'odham Captain General for all of Pimería Alta. In the end, they created two captains general—one for the northern region and one for the southern.[84] The aforementioned Francisco Carro was one of these, referred to in a document as "our state-appointed captain general of the Papagos." The fact that the Mexicans referred to the captain general, who was Native, as "our" official, and that he attempted to persuade his fellow O'odhams to seek redress through legal channels, indicates that Carro grappled with a difficult intermediary relationship between O'odhams and Mexicans, much as the Yaqui captain general, Juan María Jusacamea, had found himself at odds with Yaquis in the 1830s.

Such stopgap measures could not prevent violence, and a Tohono O'odham revolt was in full swing by 1840. It spread all the way to the northernmost settlement of San Xavier del Bac and to its Tucson satellite village, El Pueblito. Tensions between O'odhams and Apaches also flared, as O'odham auxiliaries stationed in the Tucson presidio clashed violently with Pinal Apaches de Paz living in the vicinity. Mexican military forces finally arrived in April 1843, and Tohono O'odhams sued for peace the following summer. In the June 1843 negotiations, Pedro, the governor of Santa Rosa, led the Tohono O'odham delegation. Mexican officials offered pardons to the Indians, for which Pedro expressed thanks on behalf of all the villages he represented. The governors of Gácac and Pirigua joined Pedro as well. In his official account of the day's proceedings, Antonio Comadurán reported that the governors asked the Mexican delegation to "present them once again with the wands of office that they had brought with them and reappoint them as governors of their respective villages." In return, the Tohono O'odham officers vowed to "respect in the future only those communications channeled through the presidio so as forever to avoid the grief brought upon them recently by lying to emissaries from elsewhere." Comadurán then collected their varas, or canes of power, which he "adorned with new ribbons, and requested that they prepare to receive them in the accustomed fashion." The governors "immediately knelt down, and as I presented each with his wand I reminded them of their obligations to both their own villages and our government."[85]

After the customary lecture on their duties and responsibilities to both their own villages and Mexico, the Tohono O'odham officers made a "profound bow" and kissed the varas. Comadurán gave each of the three governors a certificate of "temporary appointment as village governor," but requested in his report that permanent appointments be issued as soon as possible for governors Pedro (Santa Rosa), José (Pirigua), and Juan Cuate (Gácac). He gave Pedro eight yards of broadcloth for his "special services as . . . emissary to the western Papago villages," then closed the proceedings.[86] The episode demonstrates the continued importance of Tohono O'odham governors, even as the mission system collapsed, Mexican settlers appropriated Indian land, and Apaches raided their communities. In addition to varas and official, albeit temporary, certificates, the ceremony included gift giving, one of the ubiquitous hallmarks of Indian diplomacy. That the Mexican official asked for permanent appointments for these Tohono O'odham governors demonstrated the adaptability of the system within Pimería Alta, where exigency proved more important than the letter of the law. Clearly, these governors were not chosen for office after a formal election; rather, the process reflected localized tradition that had evolved since the days of Eusebio Kino, coupled with necessity.

Although open hostilities in the early 1840s between Mexicans and Tohono O'odhams subsided, vecino encroachment did not. In a letter dated 18 October 1846, Indian officers from the towns of Oquitoa, Átil, and Tubutama purportedly complained to Mexican officials from the prefecture of Altar that vecinos had taken Indian lands. Hearkening back to pleas from previous O'odhams that Franciscan authority to administer Indian communal landholdings be upheld, they asked that the sale of Indian lands be handled by their priest, and that the proceeds from such sales be used for "the repair of our churches, the material needs of divine worship, compensation for the religious instruction of our children, and with even more reason, the repair and reconstruction of the residential rooms within the mission buildings themselves." They were angered that "all these benefits are [instead] going to the private citizens usurping the rights to our own lands. Justice demands that these lands immediately be returned to the administration of our missionary."[87]

In reply, two justices of the peace from the Altar district wrote "to the native governors of Oquitoa, Átil, and Tubutama," making clear that priests no longer had the power to administer Indian lands in former mission communities. The justices stated that the departmental assembly had decided to deposit the proceeds from the sales of all Indian lands into a fund for an Indian school and teacher. It further cited a Mexican national decree of 5 March 1845 that relieved all missionaries of their jurisdiction over mission lands "and their emoluments."[88] This exchange between Indian governors and Mexican officials underscored the erosion of the power held by Indian governors and their former Catholic overseers. Indian and missionary authority to administer Indian lands had become almost nonexistent.

The Sonoran political arrangement no longer favored Indian governors and officers, if it ever truly had. Within the framework of Sonoran politics, O'odham town governors and civil officials continued to handle some local affairs, but found themselves powerless to regulate the sale of their common lands and to successfully stanch the flow of settlers, miners, and ranchers. This condition persisted even after the United States took control of the region following the Gadsden Purchase in 1854. In addition, as the missions declined and Hispano settlers poured into the region, eventually comprising the majority population, O'odhams were increasingly drawn into the regional cash economy, which favored the privatization of Indian communal lands and drove an increased demand for Indian labor, all to the detriment of communal subsistence patterns and former mission community solvency. Ultimately, these policies failed to accomplish the goal of Mexicanization of O'odham peoples in the Arizona-Sonora Borderlands.

From the 1820s through the Gadsden Purchase, Mexico thus attempted to accomplish the incorporation of O'odhams through a strange, paradoxical amalgam of intrusive legal measures mixed with a policy of complete neglect, which combined to devastating effect.[89] O'odham mission populations decreased sharply because of outmarriage, relocation for economic opportunities, raids and warfare, and disease, eventually leading to what the anthropologist and prominent authority on pre-Columbian Native American demographics Henry F. Dobyns referred to as "Indian Extinction in the Middle Santa Cruz River Valley." Raids and depopulation compelled the last one hundred or so O'odhams at Tumacácori to flee to San Xavier del Bac in 1848. This small group "constituted the entire surviving native Indian population in the Middle Santa Cruz River Valley and beyond." By the first decades of the 1800s, this region in particular had experienced a depopulation ratio of 23/24ths of the population in 1700. Of course, such dramatic demographic declines were not limited to the Santa Cruz Valley. At San Ignacio, farther south, by the mid-1820s only a few dozen Indians were left, compared to some 1,500 vecinos.[90] Such staggering losses demonstrate how the old O'odham-Spanish electoral model simply could not continue—there was nobody left to govern.

Still, O'odhams did participate in Mexican political life in some limited ways. For example, Hispano residents at the presidial town of Tubac and O'odham residents from Tumacácori shared close relationships. Tubaqueños and O'odhams from Tumacácori drew from the same irrigation water and ran their livestock herds together. Soldiers and settlers even served as godparents for the Indians baptized at the mission. In the words of the U.S.-Mexico Borderlands anthropologist Thomas Sheridan, "Cultural differences blurred between O'odham and non-O'odham as Spanish Sonora leapfrogged north." O'odhams served as both auxiliaries and professional soldiers during the late Spanish and Mexican eras. For example, O'odhams of the Compañía de Pimas, also called the Compañía de San Rafael de Buenavista, were professional soldiers during this time. Furthermore, dating from the first establishment of military outposts in the Arizona-Sonora frontier, soldiers were encouraged to fraternize and intermarry with O'odhams and to settle at nearby presidios. This helped to keep the peace, to some degree, and aided Mexico in holding the frontier line.[91]

O'odhams who served in military capacities participated in military democracy, such as the electing of officers and other activities. In 1832, combined vecino and Indian forces campaigned against Apaches in Pimería Alta, the same military forays in which Yaquis hesitated to participate. In May of that year, leaders from the so-called "patriotic pueblos" of Cucurpe, Tuape, San Ignacio, Magdalena, Ímuris, Cocóspera, Tumacácori, San Xavier del Bac, and Tucson met at Cocóspera as the guests of Father Rafael Díaz, while they readied for the military campaign. They formed an organization called La Sección Patriótica, and elected don Ignacio Elías to preside over their meeting. They then named Joaquín Vicente Elías as its chief. They even drew up military articles, with Father Díaz signing the pact on behalf of the aforementioned O'odham leader Francisco Carros, who was listed as lieutenant general of the Pima Nation. The mixed O'odham-vecino force defeated an Apache group on 4 June 1832 (mostly from the Apaches de Paz establecimientos), with La Sección Patriótica killing seventy-one Apache fighters and capturing thirteen Apache children, while suffering only a single death in their own ranks, a Mexican. The battle was a resounding success, but it also engendered the resentment of some Mexican regulars, who saw La Sección Patriótica as "a bunch of farmers and breeds." Even O'odhams felt ambivalent about the victory, with some reported to have stood by indifferently during the engagement.[92] As previously stated, it is also possible that acculturated O'odham soldiers, especially those who had married into prominent Mexican military families, had access to political channels and the vote in mixed-ethnic communities such as Tucson.

Conclusion

Indigenous peoples in the Arizona-Sonora Borderlands found themselves at a crossroads when Mexico at last expelled imperial Spain from its territory. Independence could have signaled a new era in Indian affairs. The rhetoric of the Tres Garantías promised Indian political and social equality, and paved the way for Indian incorporation into the political mainstream. But things did not pan out as Indians and Mexicans might have hoped. The Mexican era left Hopis, Yaquis, and O'odhams alike with no more access to the franchise and political equality than they had enjoyed under Spain. Hopis, as a group, felt increasing pressures within their position on the extreme edge of Mexican territory. That they faced warfare and slave raids with other more-mobile Indian nations presented the possibility of strengthened Hopi-Mexican ties and cooperation, and perhaps even the return of Hopis to the Hispanic political sphere. Yet the opportunity passed without bearing fruit. The young republic, stretched thin monetarily and militarily, lacked both the resources and the manpower to dedicate to the Hopi frontier, Hopi overtures for assistance notwithstanding. Under these circumstances, Hopis remained politically independent, with no established electoral system linked to Iberian models. Their democratic institutions remained Indigenous. It would be left to United States policymakers to take up the cause of Hopi voting and political inclusion, and Anglo-Americans would face similar challenges in dealing with these isolated and independent peoples.

Yaquis found themselves at the other extreme. The degree to which they incorporated Spanish democratic town institutions was so thorough that attempts by Hispano religious, civil, and military authorities to limit Yaqui electoral freedom within that system led to violent conflict on several occasions. Yaquis continued to develop a town-governing system based on consensus and popular sovereignty over the course of the second half of the eighteenth century and the first decades of the nineteenth. By the time of Mexican independence, Yaquis had created institutions that extended beyond governors, lieutenant governors, sheriffs, and the like. The Yaqui town was in fact governed by a complex system in which numerous branches formed an integrated whole. The Yaqui vote stood paramount within this framework.

When Mexico declared Yaquis to be citizens of the republic, signaling an end to Yaqui communal land-tenure practices and tax exemptions, Yaquis felt alarmed at these attacks on community sovereignty. Division of land and the sale of excess lands to vecinos, along with the establishment of multiethnic ayuntamientos, meant that Mexico considered the Yaquis part of the larger municipalities in which their voice would be only one of many. To Yaquis, the idea of outsiders' having the final say in their governance was insufferable. So the Yaqui flag bearer, Juan Banderas, took up the mantle of Muni and Bernabé. Eloquent and charismatic though he was, Banderas's frenetic leadership failed to unite Yaquis and surrounding Indian nations in a manner that would decisively push the Mexicans out of their territory. Further, he failed to abide by the central Yaqui principles of unity and popular sovereignty. At the very moment when Yaquis had won concessions that would preserve some degree of autonomy in village affairs, Banderas chose to stand on his own, rather than behind elected Yaqui officials. That decision would lead to the end of his power, and eventually to his own capture and execution. Although Yaquis had failed, as in 1740, Mexico would still have to repeatedly confront the specter of Yaqui independence in the future. Yaquis had once again demonstrated their fierce commitment to self-government and a hybridized Yaqui-Spanish democracy.

O'odhams experienced significant population decline over the course of missionization and Mexican independence. With shrinking—or even vanishing—populations, a number of the O'odham missions were closed, and community members relocated to other missions or returned to a more mobile life in the desert rancherías. In communities outside Mexican control, O'odhams used their own models to select governors and other officers who dealt with outsiders. In the Pimería Alta of the 1820s and 1830s, as the secular initiative attacked the foundations of the mission system, O'odhams saw whatever remnants existed of Indian republics at the missions erode away, as well. As Sonoran authorities pursued a policy of Hispano settlement on former mission lands, while claiming to ensure that lands were equitably administered to Indians, O'odham governors and civil authorities saw their powers dismantled, while missionaries experienced a similar diminution of their influence.

Surrounded on all sides by Mexican encroachment, and without the backing of Jesuits or Franciscans, O'odham authorities were left in tenuous positions. In some mission communities where priests no longer served, much of the power to administer mission lands, moneys, and goods fell to Indian governors, which was an unprecedented development. But the governors held very little leverage in confronting Mexican and Apache threats. In other areas beyond Mexican control, Indian governors and civil leaders continued to exercise diplomatic authority and sought to protect the land and sovereignty of their people. Still, in other communities, Mexican authorities simply ignored O'odham leaders, as they divided communal Indian lands and oversaw the Mexican resettlement of "excess" lands. It must also be recalled that Indian elections and civil governance had always been varied and uneven in Pimería Alta, with O'odhams in mission communities controlling electoral processes to a much lesser degree than their Yaqui and New Mexican Pueblo counterparts. In the decades that followed, Hopis, O'odhams, and Yaquis would all deploy distinctive strategies in confronting and negotiating Anglo-American conceptions of town governance, the franchise, citizenship, and the place of Indigenous peoples within the expanding U.S. nation-state.

CHAPTER FIVE

Refusing Citizenship
Pueblo Indians and Voting during the United States Territorial Period

When Brigadier General Stephen Watts Kearny's Army of the West entered Santa Fe on 15 August 1846, New Mexico's Pueblo peoples could not have imagined the extraordinary pressures that the Anglo-American conquerors would bring to bear on their hybridized political systems. During the Spanish period, the Pueblos had enjoyed a relative degree of autonomy in the selection of their own officers and internal governance; although there were major disruptions during the Mexican period, much of that autonomy remained. Overall, while the Pueblos were under the domain of the two previous colonial administrations, some things had remained constant. The Pueblos continued to follow the cycles of nature, tend to ceremonial obligations, farm ancestral lands, and elect men to represent their communities in dealings with the outside world. If previous experience was any indicator, the change of power from Mexico to the United States would be in name only, with very little substantive change on their everyday lives.

But the reality was that the Pueblos were forced to confront a colonial power with an altogether different conception of Indian status and political rights. From its inception, the United States had never considered Indians as citizens, and the right of Indians to vote in an election, municipal or otherwise, would have been unthinkable to many Americans. During the first half of the nineteenth century, the United States had enacted a policy of removal or extermination of its Native peoples in its march toward a "manifest destiny." But it had little to no experience with Southwestern Native peoples who were in possession of land and citizenship rights established under Spain and Mexico. As the U.S. pursued successive waves of Indian policies—treaties, reservations, President Ulysses S. Grant's Peace Policy, an influx of Christian reformers, assimilation, allotment in severalty, boarding school education— the Pueblos never fit neatly into those plans. As Charles F. Lummis, a Progressive-era journalist and Indian rights activist summarized it, the Pueblos were "indeed very different in every way from the average eastern conception of an Indian."[1]

The change of power thus posed far more questions than answers. Principal among these concerns was the citizenship status of the Pueblo Indians. Would they be citizens, as they had been under Mexico (even if that citizenship was nominal)? Would they become wards of the federal government, like other Native peoples in U.S. territory? Would the system of semi-sovereign Pueblo republics continue? No simple solutions presented themselves. Federal, territorial, municipal, and Pueblo officials all grappled with these questions, and the Pueblo vote played a central role in this debate. Soon after their transition to American rule, the Pueblos realized that they were confronting an entirely different sort of colonial overlord. During New Mexico's territorial period, from 1846[2] to 1912, the Pueblos saw their lands and political rights—even their very existence—threatened by countless foes.

Pueblo Status during the U.S.-Mexico War and after the Treaty of Guadalupe Hidalgo

After leading the army that seized New Mexico in the summer of 1846, Stephen Watts Kearny issued the so-called Kearny Code for governing the territory. The code began with a Bill of Rights based loosely on that of the U.S. Constitution, guaranteeing such liberties as peaceable assembly, jury trial, freedom of religion, and freedom of the press. It also established laws relating to property, criminal offenses, and voting. Yet the Kearny Code made no mention of Indians, Pueblo or otherwise.[3] This is not to say that Kearny and his men were unconcerned with the Pueblos; they clearly were. And Pueblo Indians were equally interested in sizing up the invaders. The two sides experienced tense initial encounters, including an episode in which Pueblo leaders went to Santa Fe to meet with U.S. officials. The scene was reminiscent of the one that took place in early January 1822, when Pueblo leaders had sworn allegiance to an independent Mexico. On the morning of 14 August 1846, these Pueblo leaders pledged their allegiance to the United States. They also sought to understand what the transition of power would mean for them.[4]

William H. Emory, an American military officer in Kearny's army,[5] kept a record of early U.S.-Pueblo encounters. As the Army of the West entered Santa Fe, the soldiers feared an attack by a combined Mexican and Pueblo force, and Emory believed that "The Mexicans to a man were anxious for a fight, but . . . half the Pueblo Indians were indifferent on the subject, but would be made to fight." He was correct that the Pueblos had no desire to fight for the Republic of Mexico. He went on to describe the meeting between American military officials and Pueblo leaders:

The next day, the chiefs and head men of the Pueblo Indians came to give in their adhesion and express their great satisfaction at our arrival. This large and formidable tribe are amongst the best and most peaceable citizens of New Mexico [Anglo-Americans repeatedly mistook the nineteen separate New Mexico Pueblos for a single tribe]. They, early after the Spanish conquest, embraced the forms of religion, and the manners and customs of their then more civilized masters, the Spaniards. Their interview was long and interesting. They narrated, what is a tradition with them, that the white man would come from the far east and release them from the bonds and shackles which the Spaniards had imposed, not in the name, but in a worse form than slavery.

They and the numerous half-breeds are our fast friends now and forever. Three hundred years of oppression and injustice have failed to extinguish in this race the recollection that they were once the peaceable and inoffensive masters of the country.[6]

These seemingly innocuous encounters were among the first in unfolding (and complicating) the relationships between Anglo-Americans and Pueblo Indians.

At the aforementioned meeting, representatives from Santo Domingo Pueblo invited the Americans to visit their community. The newcomers agreed, and Emory again provided an account of the visit. The American party traveled to Santo Domingo early the next month, and Emory's narration of events offers a description of the Indian political status quo in 1846. He called their 3 September visit a "great day." His party encountered "ten or fifteen sachemic looking old Indians, well mounted, and two of them carrying gold-headed canes with tassels [varas de justicia], the emblems of office in New Mexico." The leader of the party from Santo Domingo told him, "We shall meet some Indians presently, mounted, and dressed for war, but they are the young men of my town, friends come to receive you, and I wish you to caution your men not to fire upon them when they ride towards them." While at Santo Domingo, they also had a conversation with the village priest, whom Emory described as a "fat old white man." He similarly disparaged the women of the community, describing them as "fat and stupid," and he "delivered a speech to the assembled people of the town, which was first interpreted into Spanish, and then into Pueblo."[7]

Other military officers described similar interactions during the first months of the occupation. Lieutenant J. W. Abert, who stopped at Santa Ana Pueblo on 11 October 1846, wrote of meeting a "Spanish schoolmaster who teaches the

Santiago Naranjo with Governor's Cane (left) and a Man Dressed as Colonel Stephen W. Kearny (right) in Front of Crowd at Corner of Palace and Lincoln during Fiesta, 1919. This reenactment commemorated the initial meeting of Pueblo officers and Kearny. Photo by Wesley Bradfield, courtesy Palace of the Governors Photo Archives (NMHM/DCA), 052422.

children of the Indians of Santa Ana." On 21 October, while at Laguna Pueblo, he recounted being surrounded by "crowds of children . . . all day long." He and his companions were "loath to repulse our new fellow *citizens*."[8] A group of about twenty Pueblo warriors even came to Colonel Alexander William Doniphan's camp on 22 September, asking to join the Americans in fighting Navajos. They were told, "This of course could not be permitted."[9] In all these encounters, Pueblo Indians interacted with American officials in a manner to which they were accustomed, with duly chosen leaders of autonomous Pueblo republics carrying staffs of office and treating with the Americans largely on a government-to-government basis.[10]

In December 1847, during the administration of Governor Donaciano Vigil,[11] the New Mexico government took its first substantive action toward establishing the legal standing of Pueblo Indians in the territory. The government enacted a law that formally incorporated the Pueblos as legal entities. The law recognized that the Pueblos lived on lands "granted to such Indians by the laws of Spain and Mexico," and that these previous colonial administrations had "conced[ed] to such inhabitants certain lands and privileges, to be used for the common benefit." The territorial government declared that the Pueblos were "hereby created and constituted bodies politic and corporate," like other communities within the territorial boundaries of the United States. Pueblo Indians could now "sue and be sued, plead and be impleaded, bring and defend in any court of law or equity," and take actions to "recover, protect, reclaim, demand or assert the right of such inhabitants, or any individual thereof, to any lands, tenements or hereditaments, possessed, occupied or claimed contrary to law, by any person whatsoever," as well as "bring and defend all such actions, and to resist any encroachment, claim or trespass made upon such lands, tenements or hereditaments, belonging to said inhabitants, or to any individual."[12] This measure was to have far-reaching consequences. While it provided legal protections for encroachment or trespass, as corporate entities Pueblo lands *could* be alienated. And the burden was also on the Pueblos to defend their own lands.

The following year, the U.S. and Mexican governments took up the matter of the political status of Mexican citizens residing in the territory conquered in the U.S.-Mexico War. Article VIII of the Treaty of Guadalupe Hidalgo stipulated that Mexican citizens could continue living where they were, or they could sell their property, free of taxes and charges, and relocate to territory within the new Mexican borders. Those who chose to remain in New Mexico and the other newly conquered lands could "either retain the title and rights of Mexican citizens, or acquire those of citizens of the United States." But such an election had to be made within one year of the ratification of the treaty, and those who failed to explicitly retain Mexican citizenship would be "considered to have elected to become citizens of the United States." Furthermore, the property rights of those who remained in the United States would be respected. These stipulations applied to Indians as well as Hispanos, since all were citizens of the Republic of Mexico. Article IX stipulated that those who elected to become U.S. citizens would be "incorporated into the Union of the United States, and be admitted at the proper time (to be judged of by the Congress of the United States) to the enjoyment of all the rights of citizens of the United States, according to the principles of the constitution."[13]

The wording of these articles could not be clearer: Mexicans—a designation that included Indians—who remained in New Mexico, and who did not declare their intentions to retain Mexican citizenship, would become citizens of the United States, with their rights and properties secured to them. Joe Sando stated, from a contemporary Pueblo perspective, "Clarity of purpose is certainly expressed in the language of the treaty." Regarding whether the

Pueblos desired to remain citizens of Mexico, he was similarly unequivocal: "Not a single Pueblo Indian elected to retain Mexican citizenship."[14]

And yet the United States wasted no time in making a mess of Pueblo citizenship. Two questions plagued territorial officials, Indian Service employees, and Congress: were Pueblo peoples Indians? And did they have the right to protections granted to Indians under federal law? These questions remained unresolved throughout the territorial period, as the Pueblos were subjected to one lawsuit after another and eventually won respect and admiration while simultaneously being denied the rights granted both to other Indians in the United States and citizens of the nation.[15] In the decade following the Treaty of Guadalupe Hidalgo, citizenship was often tied directly to voting. Before that time, the Pueblos had participated almost exclusively in electoral processes solely on the village level. Even during the Mexican period, when Pueblos were legally given the right to vote and to hold office, relatively few cases were recorded in which they went beyond the limits of their own communities to vote in elections or serve in office. Further, governors and lieutenant governors had the job of dealing with outsiders, thus diminishing interactions between common Pueblo people and Hispano officials. Pueblo Indians did not generally seek the vote or hold office before the territorial period.[16] While Pueblo lands were certainly subjected to assaults during the Mexican period, unlike Indigenous peoples in Sonora, the New Mexican government made no widespread effort to force the Pueblos into the political mainstream. Thus, when the United States assumed control of New Mexico, the Pueblos continued long-established practices of tending mostly to internal affairs and retaining a relatively high degree of village sovereignty.

James S. Calhoun (not to be confused with the former vice president and senator from South Carolina), whom President Zachary Taylor appointed Indian Agent at Santa Fe in April 1849, framed much of the early debate around the Indian vote during his time in New Mexico. His policies profoundly affected the Pueblo vote and citizenship through the duration of the territorial period. In one of his earliest letters as an Indian agent, Calhoun wrote to Commissioner of Indian Affairs William Medill on 29 July 1849: "The Pueblo Indians . . . are entitled to the early, and especial consideration of the government of the United States. They are the only tribe in perfect amity with the government, and are an industrious, agricultural, and pastoral people, living principally in villages, ranging North and West of Taos South, on both sides of the Rio Grande, more than two hundred and fifty miles. By a Mexican statute these people . . . were constituted citizens of the Republic of Mexico, granting to all of mature age, who could read and write the privilege of voting. But this statute had no practical operation."[17] As Calhoun gained more experience with the Pueblos, he began to see the pressing problems they faced, including raids by Navajos, against whom he led an expedition with fifty-four Pueblo soldiers. He also traveled to Zuni Pueblo, commenting that the Indians there "are, in every sense of the word, *excellent* people, and ought to be immediately protected." He met with leaders from twelve Pueblos—Jemez, Laguna, Acoma, Santo Domingo, Ohkay Owingeh, Santa Clara, San Ildefonso, Nambé, Pojoaque, Zia, Santa Ana, and Sandia—and began to understand how local Hispano officials such as alcaldes and prefects did not "use their authority, whatever it may be, without abusing it. Contributions upon their labor, and property, are frequently made by the law, or laws, which Alcaldes and Prefects *manufacture* to suit the occasion."[18]

In fact, the Pueblos needed protection from a number of groups. Weakened Mexican frontier defenses and the change of power from Mexico to the United States had left Pueblo communities vulnerable, and Navajos and other groups were all too eager to step up their raiding activities. Calhoun noted that under Spain and Mexico, Pueblos had been permitted to launch reprisals against such raiders, but he turned down requests to continue this practice, commenting in late 1849, "It has not been deemed advisable to accede to their request."[19] More pressing was their need for protection from land-hungry Hispanos and Anglo-Americans. The Pueblos had confronted threats to their lands from Spain and Mexico, even when such lands had been "granted" to them, but the issue became more pressing after 1847, when New Mexico law declared them corporate communities that could sue and be sued, and whose land could be alienated. Delegations of Pueblo officers visited Calhoun in an almost unending stream, complaining of these encroachments and begging for relief from both settlers and local officials. For example, Calhoun wrote of a visit by the "Governor, Lt. Governor, and an Indian of less repute, of the Pueblo of Santo Domingo," who came "to enter a formal complaint in reference to encroachments upon their planting grounds, and asking for a redress of grievances." Aware of the crucial importance the Pueblos placed on their lands, Calhoun saw the foolishness of attempting to remove or consolidate them onto reservations as a solution to the encroachments, stating, "To remove and consolidate the Indians of the various Pueblos at a common point, is out of the question—the general character of their houses, are superior to those of Santa Fe—they have rich valleys to cultivate—grow quantities of corn and wheat, and raise vast herds of horses, mules, sheep and goats." He referred to them as "valuable," and as "firmly fixed in their homes, as any one can be in the United States." While he recognized that they possessed Spanish and Mexican land grants, he conceded "to what extent is unknown." They had been on their lands for innumerable generations, and "their concentration is not advisable."[20]

In reality, Calhoun confronted something wholly outside the experience of most Indian Service administrators up to that point. Spanish and Mexican Indian policy had been founded, at least in theory, on the principle that Native peoples, when ready, should be incorporated as full citizens and allowed unrestricted participation in mainstream political life. For Calhoun and those who followed, U.S. policy must of necessity both stress extending protection to the Pueblos as Indians and allow the maintenance of their self-sufficiency and peaceful relations with outsiders.[21] It would undoubtedly be a fraught process, but Calhoun seemed invested in the Pueblo plight and even empathetic to it.

Calhoun quickly came to articulate a stance that linked Pueblo citizenship with voting. Under the terms of the Treaty of Guadalupe Hidalgo, Pueblo Indians were entitled to U.S. citizenship, along with all its associated rights and privileges. The new Indian agent admitted to Commissioner Medill on 15 October 1849 that Pueblo Indians were entitled to the vote: "One born in Mexico, was a Mexican Citizen, and, as such, is a voter; and therefore, all the Pueblo Indians are voters." He also noted, however, that Pueblo participation in New Mexican elections had not been the norm: "But, still, the exercise of this privilege was not known." He felt ambivalent about their status as American citizens. While it was true that they had been Mexican citizens, granting them blanket citizenship was a complicated matter. Calhoun asserted that they "must become Citizens, sooner or later of the United States," and did "not hesitate to say that the Pueblos are entitled to all the rights and privileges of citizens of the United States, *as mere voters*."[22]

As for the rights conferred in Article IX of Guadalupe Hidalgo, he would "venture not an opinion. . . . If the Pueblo Indians are to be taxed, *they are from their general intelligence, and probity as much entitled to select their agents*, as the mass of New Mexico." He concluded that it was "easier to dispose of the tribes of roving Indians, than the better, and more civilized Pueblo Indians."[23] Thus, Pueblo voting was one matter, but granting all the rights guaranteed under Article IX was another. Calhoun would only go so far as admitting the Pueblo right to suffrage when he wrote, in the following month, "A more upright and useful people are no where to be found; fit to be associated with, and to have—all the rights and privileges, of the body politic, *at least, so far as the right of suffrage is concerned*." He even suggested to his superior, "If it should be preferable, you may colonize them, without risking a convulsion."[24] Calhoun foresaw the difficulties associated with the Pueblo vote, citizenship, and taxation. That he wished they were more like "roving Indians," or that they could simply be colonized and the matter settled, was a testament to the trickiness of both the circumstances and his own prejudices.

Willing to grant only that Pueblo Indians were voters, although not ready for full citizenship, Calhoun began to favor wardship and federal protection for the Pueblos. At this point in American Indian policy, Calhoun and other administrators were unable to envision a policy that granted Indian status and protections while affirming citizenship rights. Either the Pueblos were wards of the federal government, subject to special protections stemming from that status, or they were citizens of the United States, subject to all the laws and obligations of non-Indians. From Calhoun's perspective, the issues of encroachment and abuse of power by petty officials would only continue if the Pueblos were declared full citizens. In late 1849, he therefore argued that the Pueblos should be brought under the care of the federal government, according to the provisions of the Nonintercourse Act of 1834, which aimed to protect tribes from non-Indian trespassing by prohibiting settlers from entering or settling on Indian lands.[25] Inclusion under the protections offered through the Nonintercourse Act also meant that the Pueblos would be lumped with other Indians considered to be "less civilized." Calhoun, as well as the Pueblos for that matter, were likely not particularly concerned with such a designation, but opponents would later cite the degree to which the Pueblos had become "civilized" as an argument against wardship and in favor of the ability of Pueblo Indians to sell their lands.

The inspiration for the wardship concept came from decisions relating to the Cherokees handed down by the U.S. Supreme Court under Chief Justice John Marshall. In *Cherokee Nation v. Georgia* (1831), Marshall wrote that the Cherokee Nation was "a distinct political society separated from others, capable of managing its own affairs and governing itself." But while the court ruled that the Cherokee Nation and other Indian nations were indeed states unto themselves, they must be considered "domestic dependent nations." Furthermore, they were "in a state of pupilage. Their relation to the United States resembles that of a ward to his guardian."[26] Over the coming decades, agents attempted to apply this principle to the Pueblos. They were considered to be independent political entities capable of governing themselves, yet their incomplete state of civilization, coupled with the need for protection from Hispano and Anglo-American land grabs, entitled them to federal protection as wards, whether or not the Indians actually wanted it.

But if the federal government were to consider the Pueblos wards and extend to them protection under the Nonintercourse Act, the question of voting in municipal, state, and federal elections would have to be resolved. To

Calhoun, the solution was simple: Pueblo Indians would forego voting in such elections. He set to work in early 1850, attempting to convince the Pueblos that wardship was preferable to citizenship and civil rights, especially the franchise. In addition to the issue of land theft by non-Indians, Calhoun also recognized that full citizenship would pose a threat to the system of internal government that the Pueblos had enjoyed for over two centuries. Writing in November 1849, Calhoun argued that wardship would protect Indigenous civil government for the Pueblos: "There are a few, and at present, but few, who advise the immediate blending of these Indians with the mass of the people of this territory, with common laws, and institutions for the government of all alike—The execution of this plan would in my opinion produce terrible results." He correctly noted that under previous administrations, "each Pueblo has had, from time immemorial, a separate and distinct political existence," but that in the current climate, prefects and alcaldes were "extending the operation of some of the laws of this territory over these people—a matter they can not comprehend, and of which, they daily complain, and beg for relief." He did not dispute the importance of "mak[ing] these people as worthy and useful Citizens as will be found in this territory; but, this is not the labor of a day."[27] Thus, if the Pueblos were granted wardship status, Calhoun believed, he could solve the twin problems of land encroachments and interference in internal Pueblo politics.

In January 1850, Calhoun traveled north from Santa Fe. That he made the trip in January, when conditions can be treacherous in the Sangre de Cristo Mountains, demonstrated the increasing severity of the Pueblo political situation. At Taos, he found the Indians in a "moody and dissatisfied State." For one thing, the previous fall an election had been held for delegates to a territorial convention, accompanied by accusations that Taos Indians had been "brought to the polls and induced to vote." They also complained of "Mexican" encroachments on their lands. They lamented that Hispano authorities had "subverted" the laws of the Pueblo, "laws by which they had been governed from time immemorial." Worst of all, their officials "were now appointed by the Governor at Santa Fe, instead of the annual elections to which they had been accustomed." The Indians of Taos Pueblo "pray for protection, and the extension of the United States Indian laws over them," since "Mexican Alcaldes, sheriffs &c &c. appointed by American authority, are demanding just such contributions *as they may desire*, for their own use—and many of the Pueblos have yielded to these unjust demands, and for which there is not the shadow of a law."[28]

Calhoun made the case for wardship to the Taoseños, "explain[ing] to [them] the character of the laws of the U. S. regulating trade and intercourse with Indians, and made them understand how such laws might affect them." But he also made it clear that they could advocate for their rights as American citizens: "I also told them, if they preferred to be a part of all the people of New Mexico, they might have the right of voting for Governors, Member of Congress, and all of the officers of a State, or territory." But, if they chose this condition, then they would lose their status as an autonomous community. Calhoun explained:

> If they should determine to ask the President of the United States *to secure them in an independent government*, and to extend to them the benefits of the laws regulating trade and intercourse with Indians under the protection of the Government, they ought not to allow themselves to be used by Americans or Mexicans in voting for at elections for officers out of their Pueblo—that in said elections they should take no part, but quietly attend to their own business. [Other American officials present echoed what he said], and closed with a full endorsement of my advice as to voting, unless they preferred to yield their identity as a distinct people.[29]

It was the clearest articulation to date of Calhoun's position on wardship and the Pueblo vote. If the Indians voted in territorial, state, congressional, and national elections, he believed he would be unable to offer any protection from further encroachments and abuses, since they would be under territorial jurisdiction, not that of the federal Indian Service. Furthermore, he recognized that New Mexico's courts offered no support for the embattled Pueblos.[30] Such developments, if unchecked, would eventually result in their losing their status as a distinct people.

For Taos Pueblo, this was an unthinkable result. Calhoun correctly recognized that their identity, culture, government, and religion—in short, everything that they were and held dear—were all at stake. The Indians met at council for some time, and then returned with their reply. The governor and principales asked Calhoun if the Nonintercourse Act could be extended over them immediately. He told them that he did not have the power to do so, but that he would lobby the "great Father"—the term by which many Indian nations referred to the federal government in general, and the president in particular—to extend the provisions over them as soon as possible. After returning to Santa Fe, Calhoun wrote a letter to the Taos Indians reiterating what they had discussed in council. He reminded them that they could "take your chance to become citizens" like other New Mexicans, and "be governed, not by your own laws, but by such as the Americans and Mexicans here may make for you." He did not think that the president would object, but felt it was his "duty" to give his personal advice to them: "Be quiet, attend to your own business pursuits, and dont [sic] listen to the talk of bad men, and in due time, your great Father, the President of all the Indians, and all the people, of the United States," would order his agents to "act as to secure, to you happiness and prosperity." Calhoun reminded them that they had told him during his visit that they understood his proposal, and that they "did not wish to be New Mexicans, that you wished to live as a separate community, and to make your own laws, and to execute them in your own way, and to select your own Officers, all in the same way that you, and your fathers, and fathers' fathers have done, since the Great Spirit sent you into this country."[31]

The episode at Taos Pueblo was representative of other exchanges between Calhoun and the Pueblos, in which he continued to press the case for wardship, federal protection, and foregoing the vote, whether in person at their villages, to their governors and representatives who came to call on him, or in letters. He reported in late 1849, "Of the twenty two Pueblos, east of the Mochies [sic, Hopis], *Sixteen* have asked for the extension of the laws which regulated the intercourse with the Indian tribes of the United States prior to the late treaty with Mexico." In the same letter, he related that the Indians of Santa Clara Pueblo had reminded him "they were permitted, each, a separate government for every Pueblo—a separate and undisturbed political existence."[32] Next to retaining their sacred lands, this separate and undisturbed political existence was important above all else.

Overall, in the wake of the U.S. takeover of New Mexico, Hispanos and Anglo-Americans made a conscious effort to dispossess Pueblo Indians of their land. They also sought to bring the Pueblos under outside jurisdiction and control, similar to the actions of Sonora officials during the Mexican period who subjected Indians to foreign laws and wrested internal control. Such a condition had not existed to this extent before 1846. Furthermore, Calhoun spearheaded an effort to remove Pueblo suffrage, not necessarily because he felt it was misplaced in Pueblo hands, but because he believed that in so doing it would offer the surest protection to continued Pueblo existence. Finally, the Pueblos themselves chose to forego suffrage in territorial New Mexico. This is not to say that Pueblo Indians did not attempt to vote in elections from time to time; they did. But, as the Pueblos understood it, and as it was presented to them, their greatest chance of preserving their existence as distinct communities, with ancient (and some not so ancient) customs and practices, rested in becoming wards of the federal government. When viewed in this manner, it becomes much clearer that most Pueblo Indians did not truly "fight" for voting rights in territorial New Mexico. By foregoing the vote and U.S. citizenship, they preserved their best possible chance at maintaining Pueblo village electoral institutions and citizenship in autonomous Pueblo republics.[33] It was a tradeoff they were willing to accept, given the strictures of the post–U.S.-Mexico War political landscape.

Electoral Developments after 1850

Although Calhoun had suggested the inclusion of Pueblo Indians in the Nonintercourse Act of 1834, and the Pueblos had largely accepted this idea, he did not actually have the power to effect this change on his own. Calhoun awaited further instructions from federal officials while seeking to put out proverbial fires. A convention in 1850 to decide the immediate political future of New Mexico severely tested his resolve. The question was whether it would be admitted to the Union as a state, with its own elections for governor, congressmen, and other officials, or whether it would be a territory, with federal appointments of territorial officials. New Mexico had been under military administration since 1846, but in 1849 some Hispanos began agitating for statehood.[34] Nuevomexicanos favored statehood because it allowed for greater home rule, and, as the majority population in New Mexico, they stood to gain a greater share of power. The territorial party consisted mainly of Anglo-Americans who sought to preserve their tenuous grip on New Mexico affairs through official appointments from Washington.[35] Both sides sought the support of Pueblo Indians, and reports of questionable dealings began to stream in. Cyrus Choice, the Indian Agent at the Abiquiu Agency, which administered Utes and Jicarilla Apaches in northern New Mexico, wrote to Calhoun on 8 May 1850 that a Pueblo Indian had come to him to report that an Hispano constable by the name of Pedro Solisair "had been all around the Pueblo, requesting the Mexicans to meet at his house, on the day of the Election for Deligates [sic] to the Convention." Apparently, Solisair had warned Indians and others that a large Mexican army was on the march from "Old Mexico," and he wanted to know if the Indians would support them or the Anglo-Americans.[36] Rumors of a Mexican reconquest had circulated at various times after the U.S.-Mexico War, such as before the Taos Revolt, but on this occasion the rumor was clearly calculated to scare the Indians into supporting the Hispano for fear of being punished when the imaginary Mexican army arrived.

Calhoun wrote to Commissioner Brown on 19 June 1850, the day before the vote on statehood. He reported, "The Pueblo Indians are excited, the Mexicans are excited, and a *certain class* of Americans are greatly excited.... The contest is extremely violent. The Pueblo Indians have been called upon by both parties, and during the week past, various deputations have called upon me for advice." Calhoun believed it was the "general disposition, upon the part of the Indians, to have nothing to do with the elections, and I approved, most heartily, their determination."[37] In fact, Calhoun had offered a strong caution to the Pueblos the previous month. He wrote to them as their "Agent and friend sent to you by the President of the United States," and advised them to "not take part in the elections . . . for delegates to form a state constitution for New Mexico, if you do not want to lose your character as a <u>separate people</u> and abandon your old customs and your own laws and become citizens of New Mexico, subject to its laws." If they voted, then they were taking the actions of citizens, and he could offer no federal protections, as they had forfeited their Indian status.[38]

Remarkably, the sitting military governor of New Mexico, John Munroe, sent a proclamation to the Pueblos, telling them that they could not be prevented from voting. This directly contradicted what their Indian agent had told them. Pueblo Indians were understandably confused, just as Calhoun had indicated in his letter. In Governor Munroe's Spanish language document, dated 6 June 1850 and addressed "To the Pueblo Indians of New Mexico," he stated that his purpose was to avoid a situation where any Indian was being pressured to vote a certain way in the upcoming election. He declared that Indians could either vote or stay in their homes; it was up to them. Furthermore, he asserted that "no official agent of the government is authorized to attack, govern, direct, or in any other manner influence you in the free and independent exercise of this right."[39] Pueblo Indians apparently participated in that convention, which overwhelmingly approved a constitution and statehood. Despite the efforts of Calhoun and Munroe, some New Mexicans enticed Indians to vote, while others threatened to take away their property if they *did* vote, which was likely the real reason for Munroe's letter.

After the election, the Pueblos feared retaliation for having participated. Calhoun and Munroe apparently put their differences aside, coauthoring a letter to the Pueblos in late June. The letter represented a clear attempt to ease Pueblo fears after heavy solicitation of their votes in the statehood debate:

> We having learned, that, malicious representations have been made to you. In order that you may not be deceived [we think] it proper to say; That neither are you abandoned or ruined. We say to you, that you and your people are in the same position and security, that you had prior to the election, and the same protection to your persons and right of posses-

sion of your houses, lands and all other property, will be maintained as formerly. And until other news be Agency made, or until the President of the United States provides otherwise, the internal affairs of your Pueblos shall be governed by your laws and customs and by the same authorities which each Pueblo has elected as their Governors and other officials.[40]

Calhoun obviously found himself in a difficult situation. As he had told the Pueblos on so many occasions, if they voted—and thereby acted like citizens—then they would be treated like citizens. Since some Pueblo Indians had voted in 1850, he and Governor Munroe had to perform damage control by assuring the Pueblos that all was not lost. He still advocated that they abstain from voting and see only to their own internal affairs. Ironically, these events turned out to be much ado about nothing. As the historian Marc Simmons pointed out, "In the end the constitutional election was without meaning since Congress ignored it and created a territorial government for New Mexico. . . . Their brief participation in the new political structure had . . . soured [the Pueblos] on the democratic process."[41]

At the same time, Calhoun also attempted to shore up the status of the Pueblos as Indians under federal protection by concluding a treaty with ten of the nineteen Pueblos in July 1850. In the treaty, the Pueblos placed themselves "under the exclusive jurisdiction and protection of the Government of the United States." They also agreed to the terms of the Nonintercourse Act regulating affairs with Indian tribes, thereby affirming their status as Indians. The federal government promised, for its part, to settle, "at its earliest convenience . . . the boundaries of each pueblo which shall never be diminished, but may be enlarged whenever the Government of the United States shall deem it advisable." Importantly, the treaty affirmed the right of the Pueblos "to be governed by their own laws and customs, and such authorities as they may prescribe, subject only to the controlling power of the Government of the United States."[42] Unfortunately the treaty went unratified by the Senate, and the problems the Pueblos faced persisted.

Although the Pueblos may have soured on the democratic process after the convention debacle in 1850 and the unratified Pueblo treaty, the question of their political status remained unresolved. Calhoun and other Indian Office employees continued to push for inclusion of the Pueblos under the Nonintercourse Act. New Mexico Indian Agent E. H. Wingfield, who wrote to Commissioner of Indian Affairs Luke Lea on 6 Febraury 1852, perfectly encapsulated the complexity of the debate over Pueblo citizenship and voting rights. He declared that the "Pueblo Indians [are] a very interesting tribe, possessing many of the amiable elements of character, without the savage features of other races—and well worthy of the consideration of the Government of the United States." He went on to state, "They approach nearer to civilization" than Indians of other tribes. They were "virtuous," "intelligent," "honest," and "industrious," and they held their lands by virtue of Spanish land grants. He felt that it was "evident" that the Pueblos "should be regarded by us either as Indians, or like ourselves as citizens of the United States [and] entitled to all the privileges springing from that relation." But Wingfield believed that "as the latter position would be obnoxious to their own wishes—the Government should view them as Indians in all future legislation."[43]

In 1851, the lobbying by Calhoun and others evidently paid off, when Congress officially included all territory conquered in the U.S.-Mexico War under the terms of the Nonintercourse Act. Such inclusion would provide a number of specific protections for the Pueblos and their lands. While it made them wards of the federal government, it also forbade the sale of alcohol to Indians and prevented all non-Indians from purchasing Indian lands. It strictly prohibited encroachments on Indian lands, and named the federal government as the sole entity with the right to purchase or regulate these lands. In essence, the Nonintercourse Act was a powerful measure that would make any unauthorized settlement or seizure of Pueblo lands a federal offense.[44] As the historian of Indian-federal relations Francis Paul Prucha pointed out, measures to regulate trade and intercourse with Indians were the actions of a young, expanding republic that was seeking "conciliation of the Indians by negotiation, a show of liberality, express guarantees of protection from encroachment beyond certain set boundaries, and a fostered and developed trade." The federal government hoped these laws would "prevent the steady eating away of the Indian country by individuals who privately acquired lands from the Indians."[45] Alas, this would not be the case with the Pueblos.

Had the Nonintercourse Act been strictly enforced in New Mexico, future encroachments by Hispanos and Anglo-Americans could have ended or been significantly slowed. Furthermore, the previous law of 1847 that declared the Pueblos corporate bodies subject to lawsuits would have been ineffectual, since such suits could not be brought against the Pueblos under federal protection. The Pueblos themselves had also clearly expressed their desire to be placed under the act. Writing to Commissioner Lea on 30 June 1851, Calhoun reported that a three-day council had been held at his office. Representatives came from the Pueblos of Sandia, Santa Ana, San Felipe, Zia, Santo Domingo, Cochiti, San Ildefonso, Santa Clara, Tesuque, Nambé, Ohkay Owingeh, and Taos. These Pueblo leaders drafted a report that was subsequently forwarded to

Washington. The governor of Sandia Pueblo acted as voice for the group. Calhoun characterized him as an "exceedingly clever Indian." The delegation made itself clear: "Not one of the Pueblos, at this time, desire to abandon their old customs and usages."[46]

Unfortunately, the trade and intercourse law was not strictly enforced, so questions about the status of the Pueblos persisted. Calhoun wrote in desperation to Commissioner Lea on 29 February 1852, stating, "Differences between the Pueblos and the Mexicans will continue until the end of time unless the Government of the United States shall provide for their adjustment."[47] President Millard Fillmore appointed Calhoun governor of New Mexico in late 1850, and he went on to serve for a brief time as both governor and superintendent of Indian Affairs, in which office New Mexicans with an interest in Pueblo land and resources (but with little respect for the law) continually dogged him. His health deteriorated in 1852 and he left New Mexico for Washington, D.C. Ill with scurvy, he died on 6 May 1852, near Independence, Missouri.[48] His tenure had set the stage for relations among the Pueblos, the federal government, and territorial officials. Yet he had failed to clarify the political status of Pueblo Indians.

William Carr Lane, who succeeded Calhoun as governor, served for a relatively brief period. Governor Lane was hardly sympathetic to the Pueblo cause. Writing to his son-in-law, William Glasgow, on 26 February 1852, Lane mocked Pueblos and Hispanos for their ongoing disputes, to which they gave voice on frequent visits to his office: "And the 'Dignitat' consists in one eternal round of appeals, written & verbal, from Mexicans & Indians, & sometimes from Americans, for reparations, of every description of wrongs, - in which you hear, or read - 'Governor,' or 'Gobernador,' every 5 minutes, - besides getting at least 50 embraces, from Indians & sometimes from Mexicans, daily. I'll tell you all about it by & by. These people *embrace*, with much grace & dignity; but the custom does not suit the taste of one of us." Lane obviously had no patience for Indian diplomacy, and from his letter it is clear that he was not responsive to Indian complaints of Hispano aggression. But Lane's poor qualities did not end there. In addition to his lack of sympathy for the Indian cause, he also had no idea as to the parameters of his power and how they related to civil, military, and Indian affairs. An exasperated Governor Lane wrote to Glasgow: "There is such a strange state of things, in every Dept of the Govt. of this Ter.— civil, military & Indn; & so ill-defined [regarding] the line of offl. duties, in both the civil & Indn. Dept., that we are compelled to grope in the dark, in discharging our duties."[49] Lane faced many of the same difficulties Calhoun had, but he was far less inclined to sympathize with the Pueblos.

Governor Lane left office in 1853 to campaign for New Mexico's sole congressional territorial delegate seat. Lane's opponent was the prominent Hispano José Manuel Gallegos, a Catholic priest who had served in the legislative assembly of New Mexico during the Mexican departmental period. Gallegos spoke no English, and chiefly represented New Mexico Hispanos. Given the demographics of the territory, Lane had his campaign work cut out for him, and he recognized as much. Writing to his wife on 30 August 1853, he lamented the "Rabidity" infecting New Mexico. He was told by Nuevomexicanos that they "have no personal objection to me, but they are determined to elect one of their own race: that I am the most acceptable, of all the Americans; but that they must try a Mexican." He patronizingly pointed to "how very little the very best informed [among them] know."[50]

While he recognized the uphill battle he faced, Lane could not have imagined the source of his eventual undoing. Gallegos won the election, but Lane and his supporters claimed that it was only because Pueblo Indian votes in Lane's favor had not been counted. They claimed that sixty Taos Indians had attempted to vote in the election but had been turned away. To the south, 202 Laguna Pueblo Indians had succeeded in voting. Lane believed that the Indian vote had swayed the election in his favor, and he should have been declared the rightful winner. He sent a memorial to Congress laying out his case before the body. In response, the House Committee on Elections issued a report declaring Gallegos the winner. Congress declared that Indians were not citizens and could not vote in New Mexico. The New Mexico election judge who had initially handled the case was criticized for accepting "illegal" Indian votes. According to the House report on the contested election, the 202 Laguna votes should be discounted because the election was held at the Pueblo under the direction of the "chiefs" and "without authority from the probate judge." Laguna cast all 202 votes for Lane. Declaring these votes illegal, the House sided with Gallegos. The irony was that Lane, so obviously prejudiced against Indians, lost his bid for congressional delegate as a result of the Indian vote. Dejected, he penned these words to his son-in-law after his unsuccessful protest to Congress: "My contest has ended, this day, adversely."[51]

David Meriwether, who succeeded Lane as governor and superintendent, entered office oblivious to the seriousness of the situation. In his annual report for 1853 to Commissioner of Indian Affairs George W. Manypenny, Meriwether asserted:

> The Pueblo, or half-civilized Indians of this Territory, are in a satisfactory condition in every respect. They reside in villages situated upon grants

made to them by the governments of Spain and Mexico, and subsist themselves comfortably by cultivating the soil and rearing herds and flocks of various kinds. Each tribe or pueblo has a separately-organized government of its own, though all fashioned after the same model. They annually elect their respective governor, lieutenant governor, and various other minor officers.... When disputes arise between two pueblos, or between them and their more civilized neighbors, the matter is invariably laid before the territorial governor, and his decision is invariably regarded as final.[52]

Meriwether was naïve to believe that the Pueblos were "in a satisfactory condition in every respect." They were not. At the same time, he understood the basic political organization of the Pueblos, and seemed to grasp the importance of their governing structures and officers. Still, he referred to the Pueblos as "half-civilized Indians" who engaged in disputes with their "more civilized neighbors."

Casting Pueblos as half-civilized was a stance that could be used for a variety of purposes, both good and ill. On some occasions, officials denied the vote to Pueblo Indians because they were not deemed civilized enough. On other occasions, a lack of Pueblo civilization was used to support wardship and federal protection. The franchise was duly withheld, with wardship offering important legal protections for Pueblo land. On still other occasions, individuals employed the degree of Pueblo civilization in support of their citizenship. American officials believed that while not as civilized as whites, the Pueblos had achieved a level of civilization sufficient to be granted citizenship. This would open up their lands to sale, alienation, encroachment, and a host of unfair legal maneuvers. In a letter contained in the same 1853 annual report in which Meriwether characterized Pueblo Indians as half-civilized, Meriwether's subordinate, Indian Agent E. A. Graves, complained of the failure to implement the Nonintercurse Act, "which was adopted and applied to this Territory by an act of Congress of 27th February, 1851." He reported having visited Taos and the Río Arriba region, and found Pueblo Indians there to be "friendly, and well disposed towards the government and the citizens of this Territory." He reiterated the "half civilized" stance, but also believed that the Pueblos "merit the attention of the government, and should receive its fostering care and watchfulness," which obviously was not occurring.[53]

Within a short time, Governor Meriwether began to recognize the contradictions embedded in official policy, if indeed there was one. On the one hand, the Pueblos were corporate bodies that could sue, be sued, and alienate their land. On the other hand, they were under the protection of the federal government. Some felt that they could and should vote, as in the case of William Carr Lane's failed election. On 5 December 1853, Governor Meriwether rose before the New Mexico legislative assembly and proposed that the question of the status of Pueblo Indians be settled once and for all. In his address, he told lawmakers, "The right of suffrage is a privilege held dear by every American freeman, and great care should be had that this inestimable right be not abused or trenched upon by such as are not legally entitled to its exercise." He lamented the fact that New Mexico voting laws were not clear enough on who was entitled to the vote. Referring to the Lane-Gallegos debacle, he stated, "It appears that in some parts of the Territory the Pueblo Indians were permitted to vote at the late election whilst in other parts they were excluded. And I would recommend express legislative actions upon this point."[54]

On 16 February 1854, the territorial legislature acted to resolve the issue of Indian voting. It passed an act with exceedingly clear language that could not be misinterpreted: "That the Pueblo Indians of this Territory, for the present, and until they shall be declared, by the Congress of the United States, to have the right, are excluded from the privilege of voting at the popular elections of the Territory, except in the elections for overseers of ditches to which they belong, and in the elections proper to their own pueblos, to elect their officers according to their ancient customs."[55] From this point forward, Indians could only vote under two circumstances: the elections of their own Pueblo officers; and the selections of those mayordomos of irrigation ditches shared with Hispano communities. After this date, Indians rarely attempted to vote outside of their own Pueblos, although there were occasional cases, such as a contested election between José Manuel Gallegos (him again) and Miguel A. Otero for congressional delegate for New Mexico in 1855. On this occasion, Gallegos alleged, "in the precinct of Los Lentes, in the county of Valencia, fifty Pueblo Indians voted for [Otero], and that said fifty votes were counted for you." These Indians would have come from Isleta Pueblo.[56] The 1854 law essentially closed the book on Pueblo Indian voting in New Mexico elections for nearly a century. The next order of business was an assault on the protected status of Pueblo Indians.

Judicial Assaults on Pueblo Indian Political Status

Even with legislative action specifically prohibiting Pueblo Indians from voting, their citizenship status still remained in question. Part of the "problem" was that they were unlike Indians previously encountered by Indian Service employees. For example, in his annual report to the Commissioner of Indian Affairs for 1854, Governor Meriwether pointed out that the Pueblos acted like independent sovereignties in administering justice: "The Pueblo of Nambe in March last actually executed several of their own people, who were charged with being witches." He was appalled by these actions, and prevented further executions. But he failed to recognize that this was a community enforcing its own criminal code, however unpalatable he may have found it. He also stressed the importance of the annual elections of a "governor, war captain, and various other minor officers." He even conceded, "It has been contended that the Pueblo Indians were recognized as citizens by the Mexican government, and hence are citizens of the United States under the Treaty of Guadalupe Hidalgo." But, after a "full investigation," Meriwither was "clearly of [the] opinion that this is not the case. Having visited several of these pueblos ... [I believe] that these people differ in some respects from any other Indians to be found on this continent. ... I can but recommend them and their possessions to the protection and fostering hand of the government."[57] Meriwether acknowledged the elements that made the Pueblos autonomous, self-governing communities, but was unable to reconcile the tribal, communal elements of Pueblo Indian life with nineteenth-century American conceptions of "civilization." From this perspective, Pueblo Indians did not fully meet the civilization requirement for citizenship, although many New Mexico officials opposed their protection as federal wards. Thus the Pueblos remained in a state of political limbo.

The same circumstances plagued the Indian administrators who followed in the 1850s and 1860s. As Hispanos and Anglo-Americans continued their assaults on Pueblo lands, officials blamed these problems precisely on their "partially civilized" state. In his 1855 annual report, Meriwether wrote, "These Indians are ignorant, and but little removed from a savage state, and interested persons stir up litigation between the different pueblos and between the Mexican population and the pueblos."[58] The Anglo-American view held that the loss of Pueblo lands was a casualty of their own ignorance. In actuality, of course, the Pueblos had been using the courts to protect their lands for centuries. In the territorial era, with control of the courts in the hands of corrupt Hispanos in many instances, coupled with an erosion of legal protections for Indians, they were simply unable to secure their lands and rights in the courts. The New Mexico Superintendent of Indian Affairs J. L. Collins, who had replaced Meriwether, wrote in 1857, "These Indians [Pueblos] can, at no distant day, be made useful and intelligent citizens." But in order for that to happen, they needed schools, vocational training, and a "speedy" resolution of Pueblo land grant disputes.[59]

Pueblo Indian Agent Samuel M. Yost asked in his 1857 annual report, "Must the territorial laws have precedence over the laws and regulations of your department [the Indian Office], or must I carry out the instructions embraced in those regulations?" The Pueblos were "far too advanced to be recognized as Indians . . . and not sufficiently civilized to assume the responsibilities of *bona fide* citizens." Deeming their position "anomalous," he called for resolution, "the sooner . . . the better," for Pueblo Indians were "constantly" visiting his office, asking for "adjustment," which he did not feel empowered to grant.[60] Yost highlighted the crux of the problem: New Mexico wanted to treat the Pueblos as non-Indian (read: nonvoting) citizens, while the Indian Office viewed them as semicivilized Indians under federal protection. Unfortunately, the Indian Office and the U.S. Congress provided insufficient direction on the matter.

By 1858, Superintendent Collins had come to the conclusion that the Pueblos' status in political limbo could not be solved solely through Indian Service policy. In his annual report, he "deem[ed] it proper to mention that the laws and regulations of the Indian department are not suited to the conditions of these Pueblos." He hoped that the approaching session of Congress, by some "special enactment," would resolve the issue. He opined that they were "not citizens in the true sense of the term, and yet are too far advanced in civilization to come under the laws and regulations that are intended for the government of the wild tribes." What was also needed was a "central school" for the Pueblos, which was "all that [was] wanted to make them useful and obedient citizens."[61] The New Mexico Superintendent of Indian Affairs thus called on Congress for a new set of policy guidelines, designed specifically for the Pueblos. The call for education also became a rallying cry for Indian agents and others, who viewed schooling as the means for accomplishing full citizenship for these "partially civilized" Indians.[62]

While Indian Service employees grappled with questions of Pueblo legal status, Superintendent Collins also recognized factional disputes present within Pueblo internal elections. These disputes were the latest incarnation of the factionalism that had flared up from time to time during the Spanish and Mexican periods, and are often described, rather simplistically, as battles between "traditionalists" (those who favored traditional Indigenous practices) and "progressives" (those who supported accommodating American cultural practices). Factionalism arose as Pueblo peoples sought various ways to confront Anglo-American and Hispano power during the territorial period. As

Collins wrote in 1859, "The officers are elected annually, by a vote of the people. In these elections, party divisions [do] not unfrequently create much excitement among the Indians, and questions arise that have to be referred to this office for settlement. They are always submissive, and acquiesce without further trouble." As an Isleta Pueblo informant named Juan Abeita told the anthropologist Elsie Clews Parsons in the early twentieth century, "Smart young boys who know more than old people in some ways" came into positions of power in the late nineteenth and early twentieth centuries. These new leaders were those educated in American schools and trained in American culture and ways. This represented the culmination of the trend toward factionalism, one that American officials began to observe as early as the 1850s.[63]

The United States symbolically confirmed the Pueblos' status as sovereign communities in 1864 when Dr. Michael Steck, serving as Superintendent of Indian Affairs for New Mexico, issued nineteen silver-tipped canes to Pueblo leaders. The canes, which bore President Lincoln's engraved signature, were integrated into the existing Spanish and Mexican varas carried by Pueblo leaders, becoming important symbols of Pueblo civil authority. The arrival of the Lincoln canes also coincided with long-promised confirmation of Pueblo land patents from Washington, D.C.[64] Despite their significant symbolic power, the Lincoln canes alone did little to change the political situation of the Pueblos vis-à-vis the territorial government. Viewed in this manner, Steck's actions only highlight the impasse between Indian Service employees, who viewed Pueblo Indians as being under protective wardship, and territorial officials, who hoped to further alienate Pueblo lands and deny Pueblo rights. Territorial courts and officials continued their onslaught against Pueblo lands and sovereignty after 1864. Even with patents from the federal government protecting Pueblo lands formerly granted by Spain and Mexico, the Pueblos faced overwhelming challenges to their sovereignty and territorial integrity. Writing in 1864, New Mexico Supreme Court Chief Justice Kirby Benedict wrote that the "savage" tribes of northern New Mexico (Apaches, Utes, Navajos) would need to be fed and clothed in order to "save the citizen and protect his rights." Once such Indians were "colonized, governed and taught," they would "within a short period, become self-sustaining, *as are now the Pueblo Indians*."[65] Such a view of the Pueblos would be used to justify a series of disastrous court decisions.

In 1866, on the eve of an important case involving Hispano encroachments on Pueblo lands that would ultimately prove detrimental to Pueblo Indian rights and status, New Mexico Superintendent of Indian Affairs A. B. Norton wrote to the commissioner, suggesting that Congress act so that "all suits against these Indians [Pueblos] shall be brought only in the United States district court." The Pueblos were "continually imposed upon and harassed by vexatious prosecutions brought before [local] alcaldes, who always decide in favor of the Mexicans and against the Indian, no matter how meritorious may be the case of the latter." He further asked that Congress act so that "the sale of the lands granted to these Pueblo Indians be absolutely forbidden, and that all sales heretofore made be declared null and void." He proposed that Hispanos and Anglo-Americans living on Pueblo lands gained from such sales be made to vacate those lands.[66] It was an ambitious proposition, and one that non-Indians in New Mexico would never support.

Collins and the Pueblos suffered a stark reversal the following year. Pueblo Agent John Ward summarized the events surrounding an 1867 case concerning outsiders illegally residing on Pueblo lands. According to Ward, in June 1866 he had received a letter from Stephen B. Elkins, district attorney for New Mexico, with a request for a list of "all persons residing upon and occupying lands belonging to the Pueblo Indians." Agent Ward went to Tesuque, San Ildefonso, Nambé, and Pojoaque, and made a list of over two hundred names of persons illegally residing on Pueblo lands. Ward reported that "most of [them] were indicted and brought before the district court." U.S. District Attorney Elkins initiated approximately thirty lawsuits against these individuals, one of who was Benigno Ortiz, an Hispano squatter on Cochiti Pueblo land. Elkins attempted to have Ortiz pay a $1,000 fine for settling on the Pueblo's territory. Ward asserted, "This case, it was supposed, would settle and decide all the other cases."[67] The United States used the terms of the Nonintercourse Act as the basis for its argument.

Unfortunately, the District Court of the First Judicial District of New Mexico disagreed, ruling that the act did not apply to the Pueblos of New Mexico. Justice John P. Slough, who would be murdered by a political opponent later that year, ruled that the Pueblos were citizens of the United States and not entitled to the protections of the Nonintercourse Act. In his decision, Justice Slough argued that "the Pueblo Indians . . . were recognized as citizens of Mexico . . . [and] as late as the year 1851, the Pueblo Indians of this territory, without question or interruption, not only voted, but held both civil and military offices. . . . They should be treated not as under the pupilage of the government, but as citizens, not of a State or Territory, but of the United States of America." William Arny, Indian Agent for New Mexico, vehemently disagreed with Slough's conclusions. The decision, he argued, "will open the door for the despoiling of the Pueblo Indians of their property . . . [and] they will soon be swindled out of their lands by designing men, and 7,000 pauper Indians will be thrown upon the government to be fed and clothed, who for years have supported themselves upon the lands granted them, without any appropriations from the government." He concluded that "These Indians have never claimed citizenship." In addition to losing their land, Ward believed the Pueblos would ultimately lose all faith in the United States government, toward which they had acted fairly and amicably up to that point.[68]

The *Ortiz* decision was devastating to Pueblo status and rights. In affirming Pueblo citizenship, Justice Slough gave official sanction to encroachments on Pueblo lands, forcing Pueblos to seek redress in New Mexico's judicial system, with courts controlled by non-Indians in which Pueblo peoples had little to no chance of receiving justice. But even more sinister was the fact that Slough affirmed Pueblo citizenship when the laws of New Mexico said otherwise. By judicial action, they were citizens, yet legislative measures had taken away the cardinal right of citizens: the vote. The only liberty they now possessed was the "right" to lose their land. Slough went to great lengths to praise the Pueblos, stating that crime was practically unknown among them: "The criminal records of the courts of the Territory scarcely contain the name of a Pueblo Indian." As such, the 1851 extension of the Nonintercourse Act over Indians in the Mexican Cession could not apply to them; they were not "wild Indians," and they had voted.[69] Calhoun had questioned the ability of the Indian Bureau to protect Pueblo Indians who voted. Such fears had become a reality.

A case of a similar nature followed in January 1869. The United States again brought suit against an Hispano, one Juan José Lucero, who had moved onto Cochiti Pueblo land. The New Mexico Supreme Court handed down a decision very similar to the one of two years before, agreeing with Justice Slough that Indians were citizens and not entitled to any special protections. The long decision, which read like a biased history lesson, stated that "[Indians] were as much and fully citizens of the republic of Mexico as Europeans and Africans." The same argument was made that through the Treaty of Guadalupe Hidalgo, the Pueblos were U.S. citizens. Citizens were supposed to possess the right to vote, Chief Justice John Watts conceded, but he wrote, "Whether the right to vote shall be . . . given to the pueblo Indian or taken away from him [is a question] not properly before us, and [is] to be judged of by the congress of the United States. It is to be presumed that congress has the right, if congress thinks proper to exercise it, to . . . disfranchise all the citizens . . . but it is the right and duty of the courts to see that every citizen of the territory of New Mexico, in conformity with the ninth article of the treaty of Guadalupe Hidalgo, 'shall be maintained and protected in the free enjoyment of their liberty and property.'"[70] In other words, while the Pueblos were not entitled to federal protections, they were indeed citizens and should be allowed to vote because of the Treaty of Guadalupe Hidalgo. But it was up to Congress to see to it that this right was upheld. It was a hollow victory with only one possible outcome: more Pueblo land losses.

Indian Agents were quick to criticize *Lucero*. Pueblo Special Agent Lieutenant George E. Ford wrote in September 1869 that Chief Justice Watt's decision had "given rise to much uneasiness if not dissatisfaction among the Pueblos, and opens up a way by which much injustice is done." According to Lieutenant Ford, by deciding that Pueblo Indians were "citizens under the treaty of Guadalupe Hidalgo, no action can be taken by their agent against parties for violation of the 'intercourse act' in locating upon Pueblo [lands]." The Pueblos had brought many complaints to him, but he was "unable to give them the assistance it is their right to expect." Pueblo Agent Charles L. Cooper wrote that same year that by "placing these Indians on the footing of citizens, and allowing them to sue and be sued, vote, hold office, &c. they are continually imposed upon and harassed by vexations [sic] prosecutions brought before the [Hispano] alcales, (justices of the peace,) who generally decide in favor of the Mexicans. These alcaldes are elected by the Mexicans, (*the Indians not being allowed to vote*)." The Pueblos were "not being allowed to vote [for alcaldes and local officers]," and they "do not want to become or be considered as citizens." Pueblo Special Agent Ford had also concluded his report by reaffirming the importance of Pueblo citizenship and civil government, which trumped all other forms of citizenship in importance to the Pueblo peoples: "These people have their own laws and form of government. When any question arises among them it is decided by their own governor and head men, to the satisfaction of all parties."[71]

As Ford pointed out, the Pueblos were growing particularly concerned about the state of affairs. Yet the right to vote was no longer of primary importance. Judicial decisions had gone far beyond that right. As the Pueblos now understood, they were engaged in a life-or-death battle for their survival as distinct peoples. If they were to retain the status of United States citizens, they had little to no chance of being able to protect their lands, communities, cultures, religion, and government. The vote could do very little to change that, even if they could exercise that right. A delegation of Pueblo leaders traveled to Washington in 1868 to address these concerns. Special Agent Ward accompanied two Pueblo leaders, Alejandro Padilla and Ambrosio Abeita, to the capital, where they lodged an official complaint with the Indian Office about the recent court decision that they feared would "unmake them as a distinct and separate people, and dispossess them of their ancient customs and rights, and will also deprive them of their land." A letter recounting the visit of this Pueblo delegation, written by Acting Commissioner of Indian Affairs Charles E. Mix, was addressed to New Mexico Superintendent of Indian Affairs L. E. Webb, who likely then forwarded a copy to Pueblo leaders from Isleta.[72] Mix instructed Webb to tell the Pueblos that even though the court had decided in an unfavorable manner, in the meantime the Indian Office would do what it could to protect the property and the observance of their customs. Mix also ordered Superintendent Webb to instruct Special Agent Ward to inform the Pueblo delegates that their grievances and requests "will receive the attention they deserve in regards to this office all will be done to increase your happiness."[73]

Eventually, Commissioner of Indian Affairs Ely S. Parker took it upon himself to write to Juan Andres Abeita and Juan Rey Lucero of Isleta Pueblo in order to reassure them that the federal government still cared about them. Parker, who was Seneca, told them that he wanted to help them "to advance [their] material and intellectual prosperity." How and when would this be accomplished? "In a day not too distant they will be put in a position so that they can exercise all of their pertinent Rights and privileges." He desired that all Indians "progress to agriculture and other trades and literacy, so that they can be qualified to be citizens of the Unites States. And have an equal voice with Whites in the making of laws for the benefit of the entire country."[74] Commissioner Parker's promises must have rung particularly hollow in light of the desperate nature of the Pueblo struggle.

Parker's statements also demonstrate that in 1869 the Indian Office did not view Pueblo Indians as U.S. citizens. He placed conditions on the granting of citizenship. They must first progress in agriculture, the mechanical arts, and literacy. Then, they would be adjudged ready for citizenship and the full enjoyment of their rights, and be able to take their place alongside whites in framing laws for the benefit of the nation. In addition to its condescending tone, Parker's letter also showed no real understanding of what the Pueblos truly needed at that moment. Full citizenship was a disastrous step backward. The besieged Pueblos needed the protection of the Indian Service, and needed their laws and customs to be respected. The Pueblos and their agents understood this fact, but it seems clear that Commissioner Parker did not truly grasp the seriousness of the Pueblos' plight. Perhaps his own struggles as a noncitizen Indian clouded his understanding. He had trained as a lawyer, but was denied the opportunity to sit before the bar because he was not a U.S. citizen.[75] Perhaps he viewed citizenship as the ultimate good.

The *Ortiz* and *Lucero* decisions did little to clear up the citizenship status of Pueblo Indians, even if Justices Slough and Watts asserted that they were indeed citizens of the United States. Just two years after *Lucero*, New Mexico Superintendent of Indian Affairs Nathanial Pope wrote, "A vexed question in this superintendency is, whether or not the Pueblo Indians are citizens of the United States." He mentioned the regular issues of land, but also made reference to electoral problems that resulted from encroachments, and competing authorities. Hispanos elected their own alcaldes and officers, while the Pueblos chose governors, lieutenant governors, war captains, and other officers, "whose duty it is to consult with their agent and superintendent in the management of the affairs of the village." He indicated that elected Hispano officials and elected Pueblo officers often clashed, and, "in consequence of this conflict of authority, differences often arise, and street fights are not uncommon." Superintendent Pope asked that schools be established among the Pueblos, and concluded by characterizing the Pueblos "as law-abiding, industrious, and self-sustaining."[76]

Pope wrote in his 1872 report, "The question of citizenship, I regret to say, has not yet been satisfactorily settled, and every year renders it more difficult to solve. The courts of this Territory have decided upon several occasions that the Pueblo Indians are citizens of the United States." He also indicated that "during last summer two Pueblo Indians were placed on a United States jury at Albuquerque, in this Territory, in accordance with these decisions, but it is doubtful if this action will be sustained till their status is finally and definitely fixed by the Supreme Court of the United States."[77] Once again, the Pueblos had all the characteristics of "good" citizens and civilized people, but were they or were they not citizens? There were token actions such as occasional Indian jury participation, but Hispano and Anglo-American encroachments and disputes over jurisdiction continued to threaten Pueblo sovereignty.

The 1871 report also contained Pueblo Agent William Arny's fascinating in-depth report on the condition of the Pueblos at that time. He provided a glimpse into the disputes between Pueblos and outsiders. Early in his report, he pointed to a Pueblo characteristic that outsiders had noted throughout centuries of contact: "They do not like to be questioned on subjects which they believe to concern none but themselves." Or as Susan E. Wallace, the wife of New Mexico Governor Lew Wallace (1879–81), stated, less generously, "The Pueblos jealously guard their wretched little chapels (*estufas*) from the prying eyes of strangers, and the gentlest of visitors is rebuffed by their dumb secrecy." While many saw the Pueblos as mostly civilized and self-sustaining, they were also perceived as backward, secretive, and tribal. Non-Indians failed to recognize that they were, and would ever remain, a very private people with an acute sense of propriety with regard to internal matters. Arny's findings highlighted the precarious nature of the Pueblos' existence in territorial New Mexico. For example, at San Ildefonso, he counted 156 Indians and 373 non-Indians, while at Nambé there were 78 Indians and 175 non-Indians. In total, he put the number of non-Indians living on Pueblo lands at 5,543, with a total property value of $434,677. Realistically, this was "too much for the government to pay for the breaking up of some of the best settlements of [non-Indian] citizens within the Territory of New Mexico." Arny believed that non-Indians should be allowed to stay on Pueblo lands, thus foreshadowing the Bursum Bill of 1922, which would have allowed non-Indians to claim "squatters' rights" on Pueblo lands. Arny also claimed that the overwhelming majority of Pueblo Indians were willing to let the squatters stay on their land. But he went on to pen an insightful summary of Pueblo political status. He asked, "What shall be done with them in reference to our body politic?" They were surrounded by outside communities and forces, "without any authority to mingle in our political affairs." He pointed out, correctly, that they were "independent sovereignties in the midst of one of the Territories of the United States," who had always been "self-sustaining." That they had not become full citizens was due to the fact that they had "never received until now any aid from the Government of the United States to qualify them to become citizens." He called for the implementation of a system of "industrial education."[78] Yet what the Pueblos needed more than citizenship rights, access to political participation in the territory, or educational programs, was protection. Only the Nonintercourse Act would accomplish this in the second half of the nineteenth century.

Further cases involving Pueblo land, political status, and citizenship would be decided in the mid-1870s. In the lead-up to these cases, New Mexico Superintendent of Indian Affairs L. Edwin Dudley reported that the attempts by non-Indians to solicit Indian votes had continued into the 1870s, long after New Mexico court decisions had declared the Pueblos nonvoting citizens: "[Pueblo Indians] have often been solicited by aspiring candidates to exercise the right of suffrage, but in every instance they have refused, preferring to remain as wards of the Government."[79] The Pueblos had refused to vote in order to protect their status as distinct, sovereign peoples. The year after Dudley's report, another case involving encroachment on Pueblo land made its way to the New Mexico Supreme Court. *United States v. Santistevan* turned on a familiar scenario: an Hispano had moved onto Taos Pueblo land. With the help of the Indian Office, Taos Pueblo attempted to evict him under the terms of the Nonintercourse Act. The New Mexico Supreme Court dismissed the case, reaffirming the *Ortiz* and *Lucero* decisions. Once again, the Pueblos were too civilized to be grouped with the other "wild Indians," so were left to fend for themselves.[80]

While the New Mexico courts repeated themselves with regularity, the Supreme Court of the United States finally heard a case involving Pueblo land. In *United States v. Joseph* (1876), the nation's highest court reaffirmed what the New Mexico courts had stated on so many occasions. The court held that the Nonintercourse Act of 1834 did not apply to the Pueblos. The decision stated:

> At the time the act of 1834 was passed there were no such Indians as these in the United States.... The pueblo Indians, if, indeed, they can be called Indians, had nothing in common with this class ["wild" Indians]. The degree of civilization which they had attained centuries before, their willing submission to all the laws of the Mexican government, the full recognition by that government of all their civil rights, including that of voting and holding office, and their absorption into the general mass of the population (except that they held their lands in common), all forbid the idea that they should be classed with the Indian tribes for whom the intercourse acts were made, or that in the intent of the act of 1851 its provisions were applicable to them.[81]

Thus repeating the misguided history lessons offered by *Ortiz, Lucero,* and *Santistevan*, the court declared that the Pueblos held undisputed title to their lands. With said title, they could dispose of their lands at will. The court did not question the right of Pueblos to petition for redress on land issues in the courts, but it was quite clear that this was the responsibility of the Pueblos themselves, not of the federal government. What further complicated this case and others like it was that these judicial matters often involved non-Indians who had obtained some sort of title to the land they occupied. The Pueblos claimed that lands had actually been stolen, or that such "sales" and "transfers" of title were done without proper approval from Pueblo leadership, and were thus illegal.

The court declared that ejecting trespassers, or imposing fines, was possible "according to the laws regulating such matters in the Territory" if such individuals were living on Pueblo lands "without the consent of the inhabitants." But "if he is there with their consent or license, we know of no injury which the United States suffers by his presence, nor any statute which he violates in that regard." In a puzzling move, the court declared, "We have been urged... to declare that they are citizens of the United States and of New Mexico. But... we leave that question until it shall be made in some case where the rights of citizenship are necessarily involved." Yet, in summarizing all the rights of citizens that the Pueblos enjoyed under Mexico, as well as the United States' obligation to extend the same rights, the court *did* declare them de facto citizens. As the historian Richard N. Ellis has explained, the net result of all these developments, from the entry of Kearny's Army of the West through the *Joseph* decision, was that "in practice . . . Pueblo people were denied suffrage because they were Indians [under the 1854 New Mexico voting statute] and . . . they were also denied protection that the federal government provided other Indian people" because they were too civilized for such protections.[82]

Pueblo Political Status after *Joseph*

With the sanction of the U.S. Supreme Court, Hispanos and Anglo-Americans continued their Pueblo land grabs. The Pueblos took their place alongside African Americans and women as the United States' nonvoting citizens, and saw their lands under attack for the coming decades. While these negative court decisions eroded Pueblo status as Indians, and excluded them from federal protection, Indian agents undertook a conscious effort to bring the Pueblos from their "half-civilized" state to "full civilization" and citizenship. Pueblo Agent B. M. Thomas summarized the Indian Office's position in August 1876: "The Pueblo Indians are worthy of every effort that can be bestowed upon them to lead them up to citizenship."[83] For the agents, "every effort" mainly meant education, with agriculture also forming an important component of the civilizing mission. Writing earlier, in September 1865, Superintendent Felipe Delgado told Commissioner of Indian Affairs William P. Dole, "But few of them can read, and the number is growing less every year from deaths. I regret to say that there is not a school in the Territory for the education of the Indians . . . [which would] prepare them to become useful and worthy citizens."[84]

As the historian Brian Dippie has pointed out, for African Americans "agriculture would define a humble role in life as a member of a permanent American peasant class; for the landed Indian, it would facilitate eventual mergence with white society." Through agriculture—which the Pueblos already practiced—and education, "yesterday's savages" would become "tomorrow's citizens."[85] Since allotment in severalty was deemed impracticable for the Pueblos, and because, as corporate entities, they held title to their communal lands, education was pursued in earnest. As the United States embarked on the era of assimilationist Indian policy, it employed schools and vocational training to meet these goals. In their reports, Pueblo Indian Agents spoke constantly of education and training in the industrial arts such as farming, carpentry, and blacksmithing. In addition to establishing schools at the Pueblos, agents began sending Pueblo children to off-reservation boarding schools. Agent B. H. Thomas reported in 1880 that he had "collected ten Pueblo children to be taken to the 'Carlisle Indian training-school'" in Pennsylvania, the first and most (in)famous of such institutions.[86]

Progress in establishing schools was slow, and was met with considerable resistance from the Pueblos. Pueblo Agent Pedro Sanchez's 1884 report oozed with disdain for Pueblo resistance to the civilizing project: "I am, indeed, extremely sorry to state that these Pueblos ... are debased and *idiotized* by the effects of ignorance, indolence, and superstition, to which they abandon themselves to excess." They had not taken upon themselves the uplifting traits of white society, and "instead of identifying themselves with it, they hate and fear it, because it attacks their superstition, loathes their vices, and punishes them for their crimes. To this indigenous race the conquests of civilization are unknown and the law of progress utterly void." Sanchez believed that mandatory education of their youths was the only way to combat Pueblo "superstition." He blamed their elected leaders for their state, and attacked those agents who argued that the Pueblos were "independent" and that their "councils for the administration of justice are composed of wise men." In his opinion, "It is only the civilized, educated, and energetic man that is independent. What wisdom is there in men who for centuries have lived among civilized people and are not yet ashamed to go naked?"[87] Sanchez's background as a New Mexico Hispano during the period of fierce Pueblo-Hispano land disputes clearly colored his opinions.

As U.S. Army officer and Carlisle founder Richard Henry Pratt envisioned the boarding school program, Indian children would be separated from their tribal environments, but they would also be forced to interact with mainstream white society by working on white farms and in white businesses—termed the "outing program." In this manner, Indian pupils would receive industrial training while interacting with whites in close quarters, thereby learning the superiority of mainstream American culture.[88] Understandably, the Pueblos offered staunch resistance to the project of assimilation through education (what one historian has termed "education for extinction").[89] They despised having their children taken away to boarding schools far from home, and especially disliked the influence such an arrangement could have on traditional culture and ceremonial life. They had worked far too long and too hard to allow outside influences to creep in.

In 1897, Acting Pueblo Agent C. E. Nordstrom reported extensively on Pueblo school attendance, noting that many of the Pueblos had day schools on their land. But even those schools attracted few pupils. At Santa Clara, for example, there were 78 children, of whom only 38 were enrolled, with an average daily attendance of 7 boys and 10 girls. At Ohkay Owingeh, there were 84 children with 23 enrolled and an average attendance of 7 boys and 5 girls. Taos had 76 children, with only 31 enrolled and an average attendance of 11 boys and 5 girls. Laguna Pueblo fiercely opposed children's being taken off-reservation for education. In their efforts, the Lagunans even had the support of a progressive missionary stationed there, about whom Nordstrom complained: "According to his dictum the Indian should be taught in his own language [Keres] and children should never be separated from their parents; the transfer of children to nonreservation schools is therefore a 'cruelty.'" When the agent reported that ten pupils had been found eligible for transfer from this school . . . not a single case of 'consent' was recorded. And Laguna is considered as being among the foremost in 'advancement' of all the pueblos."[90] Interestingly, one visitor to the school at Cochiti Pueblo in the mid-1890s noted that when the teacher, a Mrs. Grozier from Boston, left the room, the students began "laughing and talking in their wonderful threefold language, a mixture of Indian, Spanish and English, sometimes in one sentence using the words from all three languages."[91] If nothing else, some Pueblo children were becoming multicultural.

Agent Nordstrom also reported a darkly comical episode at Santo Domingo Pueblo. Santo Domingo—which today remains one of the more conservative Pueblos—turned away a female headmaster sent by the federal government. Pueblo leaders eventually allowed a male teacher, but the governor refused to turn over the key to the schoolhouse and bring the children to school. The governor told Nordstrom that he could not send the children, since "this was a feast week." Nordstrom remarked that "there is always a feast or a fast among these people." The agent eventually threatened to bring in a cavalry troop and arrest the governor and headmen and take them to Fort Wingate if the children were not sent to school. The governor relented, but sent only the boys to school. When asked why he had not also sent the girls, the governor "coolly and with a nonchalant shrug of the shoulders" replied, "Education might be all very well for the boys, but it wouldn't do for the girls, who as soon as they got educated wanted to run off." Nordstrom was incensed at the governor's lack of gratitude for the school and the agent's efforts on his behalf. When he could not enforce his threat, Nordstrom wrote that the governor was "astonished to find his official head still attached to his official shoulders, and knowing that it was occupying anything but its proper place, could only reconcile the fact with the belief that I was afraid of him, that I did not dare give the order he knew in his heart I ought to give him." For the agent, the situation was "infinitely humiliating."[92]

Pueblo agents also reported disputes between Pueblo Indians who supported education and those opposing its introduction. Indian Agent John H. Robertson wrote in 1892 that there were instances in which "for one year a progressive man (Indian) has been elected governor, favoring all the modern ideas of improvement." But with the yearly elections of the governor system, "the following year a man of totally different ideas succeeds, and by his influence and position undoes to a very great extent the work of progression previously started, in the way [es]pecially of education." Agent Robertson proposed empowering Indian Agents to remove any governor who "proves to be a stumbling block in the way of his people's improvement." Robertson wanted Pueblo citizenship tied directly to education, recommending that "all graduates, on attaining their majority and passing a satisfactory examination, such as may be prescribed by the Indian office, shall have the privilege offered them of becoming citizens of the United States." He felt that too many "returned to the blanket," as it were, but that if they were granted citizenship, "they would be on an equality in this regard with the outer world, and would be more likely to act independently of their tribal relations and government, and to mix among the general population and follow the avocations they have acquired at school."[93]

As Indian policy in New Mexico evolved, Indian Service officials pointed to three conditions for full Pueblo U.S. citizenship: (1) Pueblo Indians had to be educated in the American way; (2) "progressive" Pueblo leaders who favored education and assimilation must be elected; and (3) Indian Agents must exercise more control of Pueblo internal affairs to ensure that the requisite progress was made. Underscoring all of this was the belief of Office of Indian Affairs (OIA) officials that the Pueblos had to "earn" citizenship and the vote. While the most ignorant and uneducated white person was a citizen by birth, a Pueblo Indian, legally a citizen under the terms of the Treaty of Guadalupe Hidalgo, had to become educated and shake off centuries of "superstition" and "backwardness" in order to take his place as a citizen of the United States. And in none of this did the Indian agents take into account the wishes of the Pueblo Indians themselves.

Acoma Pueblo seemingly met many of these conditions between the late 1880s and early 1890s. In 1885, the principales of Acoma elected Solomon Bibo to serve as governor of the Pueblo. Bibo, a German-Jewish entrepreneur, first secured a license to trade at Acoma and then married into a prominent Acoma family. He was fluent in Spanish, Keres, and a number of other Indian languages. Acoma elders apparently welcomed him, in part, because he did not display the type of anti-Indian prejudice that was common among other whites who had come to their community in the past.[94] Bibo, who was among the few non-Indians ever chosen as governor of a Pueblo, supported education and progressive policies for Acoma. After his term in office, Bibo retained a great deal of influence at the Pueblo.

The governor who followed Bibo strongly opposed sending Acoma children to off-reservation boarding schools. He came into conflict with Bibo and the so-called progressive faction. The dispute quickly escalated, and, according to Bibo's account, which he wrote about in a letter to Richard Henry Pratt, the governor had men and boys horsewhipped and left hanging from whipping posts on the Pueblo's annual feast day—September 2, the Feast of San Estevan.[95] Pratt wrote to the Commissioner of Indian Affairs, urging him to take immediate action to break the power of the governor. As long as such men were in office, he asserted, Acoma children would not be educated, the tribe would not become civilized, and they would never take their place as American citizens. The commissioner ordered the governor arrested and held by an Albuquerque sheriff, and the Pueblo Indian Agency placed Juan Rey, a young, progressive Indian, as interim governor until the elections of January 1890.[96]

We must, therefore, acknowledge the distinct possibility that more Pueblo Indians may have attempted to vote in elections outside their communities, had there not been the strong coercive power of civil and religious officers. Severe corporal punishments, or the threat thereof, were likely to keep many of the more "progressive" individuals away from the polls. Taken as a whole, these events demonstrate the destructive nature of Pueblo factionalism, and that if the Pueblos would not willingly accept education, civilization, and citizenship, the Indian Service would take drastic steps to force them to do so.

At the same time, economic as well as other external forces began to converge on the Pueblos, speeding up the pace of Pueblo life. For example, in 1880 the Atchison, Topeka, and Santa Fe Railroad extended its line though five Pueblos, while the Denver and Rio Grande completed its grading through four others. The Atlantic and Pacific had begun grading its own line, which would cross through three more Pueblos. While many Pueblo Indians viewed the railroads with suspicious apprehension, some Pueblo men found employment with the railroad companies. They worked the rails at the Pueblos of Acoma, Laguna, and Zuni, in particular. Agent Nordstrom cited Laguna as an example of how the railroad and education aided in the work of civilization, asserting they had "made more rapid strides on the road to civilization than any of the Pueblos." He linked education and railroad work, pointing out that

"Between 125 and 150 of the young men have been educated at Carlisle and other industrial institutions provided by the Government," and were nearly all "employed in some capacity or other by the Atlantic and Pacific Railroad, which runs through the village, the authorities of the road informing me that they prefer Indian labor to that furnished by the native Mexican."[97]

In this regard, the Anglo-American work of assimilation could be viewed as a success in some select cases. In some instances Pueblo Indians even demanded their citizenship rights during the territorial period, although they were a minority. One such individual was a Laguna man by the name of Charles Kie, who worked as a train car inspector for the Atchison, Topeka, and Santa Fe Railroad. Over a several-year period, Kie, who had been educated at Carlisle, wrote numerous letters to Special Attorney for the Pueblo Indians A. J. Abbott, in which he pointed to the injustice of New Mexico's denial of his right to vote, since he was a citizen of New Mexico and the United States. Abbott wrote to the Commissioner of Indian Affairs on Kie's behalf, and even initiated a lawsuit for Kie. Kie reported mixed results in his voting attempts—he succeeded on some occasions, while on others he was denied the franchise.[98] Kie wrote to Commissioner of Indian Affairs Francis Leupp in October of 1908: "What I want is to be permitted to exercise the duties of a citizen of [the] United States." He told the commissioner that he had been "denied these right[s] just because I am an Indian. That does not sound right." Nevertheless, his mistreatment was a reality. He complained that he knew of individuals who were not proficient in English, whom he considered "not fit for citizenship" but who were "allowed to vote every year in town elections." He asked how much longer he would have to wait to be considered a citizen and exercise his rights. On 2 April 1912 Kie attempted to vote in a Gallup town election, where he was a resident. He and two other Laguna Indians were arrested and, in Kie's words, "handled pretty rough."[99]

New Mexico had become a state in January of 1912, and had constitutionally barred Indians from voting. Kie and other would-be Indian voters were probably a small minority. The Pueblos voiced their opposition to American citizenship and largely did not ask for the vote. As Superintendent C. J. Crandall wrote in 1904, the Pueblos "have never been permitted to vote or exercise the right of citizenship. *Neither have the Pueblo demanded this nor asked for it.*"[100] Pablo Abeita of Isleta Pueblo, who served as governor of Isleta, was secretary of the All Indian Pueblo Council, and frequented the highest political circles in New Mexico before and after statehood, commented in the 1930s, "I don't care about politics, but I hope I will be seven feet under the ground when my people start voting."[101]

Still, a significant number of progressive Pueblo Indians may have desired the franchise or supported Western ideas of democratic government. For example, a Hispano county judge related to Adolph Bandelier, a Swiss-born archaeologist who spent considerable time at the Pueblos, that he had been called to Santa Clara Pueblo on the first of January 1883, during the annual elections, "to settle a dispute between the young and the old men of the Pueblo about the election of a new governor. The young men claimed to elect through a majority of votes; the old people claimed the usual form of nomination by the cacique!" The judge decided in favor of the young men.[102] Santa Clara Pueblo was famously split between Summer and Winter moieties for several decades, each having its own governor. While the Santa Clara dispute has sometimes been framed as a simple feud between "progressives" and "traditionalists," the fact remains that in the latter half of the nineteenth century and into the twentieth, there were groups of men, many of them young and educated at boarding schools, like Charles Kie, who would have been influenced by, and potentially favored, democratic elections and majority rule. But the power of the leadership likely would have discouraged voting among tribal members, as evidenced by Pablo Abeita's statement.

United States Citizenship and the Pueblo Refusal

The question over the Indian vote in the United States had been at issue since at least the 1850s, and was not limited to the Southwest. For example, a letter to the editor titled "Can an Indian Vote?" appeared in the *Indianapolis Weekly Indiana Sentinel* on 5 April 1855. The article reported that on the previous day, during a township election, the election judge had accepted the vote of an Indian. The author pointed out that Article II, Section 2, of the Indiana Constitution stated, "Every *white* male *citizen* of the United States, of the age of twenty-one years and upwards . . . shall be entitled to vote in the township or precinct where he may reside." The author went on the ask, "Is a *red* man a *white* man? and is an *Indian* a *citizen*? Under our Constitution and laws he is clearly not, and has no right to vote."[103] As with New Mexico elections of the 1850s, in a Michigan election in 1859, losing candidate George W. Peck accused the victor, A. M. Fitch, the Indian Agent for the Mackinac Agency, of winning the election through a "large fraudulent Indian vote." Peck asked that Fitch's victory be nullified.[104] In 1889 the *Reno Weekly Gazette and Stockman* reported that the "bribing of Puyallup Indians to vote to put a railroad through their reservation" was the "latest sensation at Tacoma, W. T. [Washington Territory]."[105] Thus, competing groups across the United States strategically deployed the

Indian vote, with various parties questioning the validity and legality of such votes.

The developments in Pueblo citizenship and voting in the latter part of the nineteenth and early twentieth centuries took place within a framework of national calls for citizenship by Indian reformers and their allies, who viewed citizenship as the logical and necessary next step in the progression of the nation's Indigenous peoples. The Friends of the Indian, a small group of wealthy, reform-minded philanthropists who met at Lake Mohonk, New York, for example, adopted Indian citizenship and legal equality with whites as one of their principal proposals.[106] Organizations that mobilized on behalf of Indian rights in the last quarter of the nineteenth century, such as the Indian Rights Association and the Women's National Indian Association, were composed of evangelical Protestants from comfortable economic backgrounds. They hoped to Christianize Indian men, grant them citizenship, and transform them into the yeoman farmers envisioned by Thomas Jefferson. Through missionary work and education, they would hasten civilization, Christianization, and enfranchisement.[107] But it was extremely difficult for an Indian to attain citizenship, and thereby the possibility of enfranchisement, during this period. John Elk, an Omaha who had abandoned his tribal membership and farmed on his own land, sued for his citizenship rights in 1884. A Nebraska voting registrar, Charles Wilkins, refused to allow Elk to vote since he was an Indian and therefore not a citizen. The U.S. Supreme Court ruled in *Elk v. Wilkins* that Elk had not become a citizen simply because he had left a tribal way of life and farmed his own land. Indians would need a congressional statute or some other official action to obtain citizenship.[108]

Again, Indians were regarded as "noncitizen nationals." The only way to overcome this status was for an Indian to receive a special certificate from the U.S. Secretary of the Interior stating she or he was a citizen.[109] Some federal policies aimed, at least in part, to grant Indian citizenship. Initially, under the terms of the Dawes Act of 1887, Indians who received trust patents for their allotments[110] became U.S. citizens. When the Burke Act amended the Dawes Act in 1906, eliminating the granting of citizenship until the end of the twenty-five-year trust period, individual Indians could still petition the Secretary of the Interior to be declared "competent" and to be granted citizenship before the quarter-century waiting period was up. Still, the process of transforming Indians into citizens proved cumbersome. Plus, allotment did not apply to the Pueblos. Furthermore, vocal critics of Indian citizenship and of the vote frequently sounded the alarm. The *Rochester Weekly Republican* (Indiana) of 2 January 1890 lamented, "Hereafter every Indian male who consents to take a separate farm ... is entitled to vote. New complications of American politics! Cannot the Indian vote easily become a factor of importance in some of the western states? Doubtless it will."[111] The *Atchison Daily Globe* (Kansas) of 14 August 1890 pointed out that "the Indian vote in Tishimingo County is larger than the white vote."[112] Some news outlets were downright derisive of the thought of Indians' voting, such as when the *Alton Telegraph* (Illinois) commented, "Give the Indian a vote, says the New Orleans Picayunne, and he would soon hold the balance of pow-wow in politics."[113] The question of U.S. citizenship for Indians would not be resolved until the Indian Citizenship Act of 1924, and even then Indians in New Mexico and Arizona would not be allowed to vote.

When Carlos Montezuma (Yavapai), Charles Eastman (Santee Dakota), Thomas Sloan (Omaha), Laura Cornelius Kellogg (Oneida), Henry Standing Bear (Oglala Lakota), and Charles Dagenett (Peoria) gathered in Columbus, Ohio, in spring 1911 to establish the Society of American Indians (SAI), they represented the most progressive, educated, and influential Indians of their day. Not surprisingly, they made citizenship for the Indian their prime objective. As the historian Frederick Hoxie pointed out, the "Red Progressives," as they came to be called, believed that citizenship would "empower their members to become forceful actors in the nation's democracy." As an organization, they declared, "The open plan is to develop race leaders, to give hope, to inspire, to lead outward and upward.... We ask every Indian to speak, to voice his wrongs, to tell of injustice." The SAI solicited, and received, the support of Richard Henry Pratt, who applauded their call for citizenship, referring to it, rather morbidly, as "your good citizenship gun." These SAI founders believed that citizenship could be a powerful tool (or gun, in Pratt's telling), which they could then wield to help them live outside the control of the Indian Office, turn back the various and constant assaults of their white neighbors, or even join whites as fellow citizens.[114] The calls for citizenship and the vote from non-Indian allies could be equally loud. Herbert Welsh, who served as Corresponding Secretary of the Indian Rights Association, wrote in 1885, "The right of suffrage [must] be conferred upon the Indian speedily" if the "complete civilization" of the Indian was to be accomplished.[115] Such vocal calls for Indian civilization, education, allotment, citizenship, and enfranchisement by Red Progressives and their allies dominated much of the debate on the "Indian Problem" during this time.

But a simple search of the names of prominent Indian reformers in the second half of the nineteenth century and the first decades of the twentieth yields virtually no Pueblo Indians. Pueblo leaders continued their diplomatic missions to colonial seats of power, as when the aged governor of Zuni Pueblo, Pedro Pino, traveled to Washington, D.C., in an effort to secure protections for Zuni territory. Encroachments increasingly diminished vital grazing range for Zuni herds and flocks, and curtailed access to crucial springs.[116] In addition, the Pueblos certainly desired to secure their rights vis-à-vis their position in the face of ongoing legal assaults and land encroachments, but they displayed little desire to make their political mark on the national scene as voting citizens. There was no Pueblo Eastman, Montezuma, or Cornelius. Instead, elected Pueblo officers filed petitions, traveled to Santa Fe to meet with New Mexico governors, and occasionally made the trek to the nation's capital to lobby the "Great Father" and his representatives. The Pueblos had survived nearly four centuries of invasion and colonization partly through adaptability and legal efforts, on the one hand, but primarily by maintaining fiercely independent and closed societies, on the other. When Governor of New Mexico Territory James Calhoun wrote to the Pueblos in May 1850, on the eve of the ratification vote for a state constitution, he was offering them a choice: vote and become citizens of New Mexico and the United States, or refrain from voting and remain a separate and distinct people, governed by their own laws, customs, traditions, and leaders. It is hardly surprising that the Pueblos chose the latter when such an approach had proven its utility time and again.

From the late 1840s through the 1910s, some Indian agents, superintendents, and others largely respected the Pueblo stance: they controlled their own internal affairs and did not want to become part of mainstream American political society. Indian Service representatives and the Pueblos had worked out an arrangement whereby, in exchange for largely staying out of New Mexico and United States politics, including elections, the federal government would protect the Pueblo right to self-govern. As Pueblo Agent Silas F. Kendrick wrote in 1860, "Each village, or 'Pueblo' . . . is a political community of itself, has its own complete organization; its own laws; its own tribunals; and its own officers for their enforcement. Probably there is no people, enlightened or otherwise, among whom the laws are enforced with greater regularity and efficiency." In 1859 New Mexico Superintendent of Indian Affairs J. L. Collins summarized this arrangement matter-of-factly: "The internal government of these Pueblos is left entirely to themselves."[117]

While an element of coercive power was certainly woven into this arrangement, with the federal government ever as the colonizer, the Pueblos clearly sought their own ends within this framework. The system of village government, which had evolved and been adapted over the centuries, remained similar to the república de indios system that the Spaniards had instituted in the early seventeenth century. Deeply ingrained in Pueblo political organization, it had attained a status as an almost "traditional"—or at least customary—element of Pueblo society.[118] The Pueblos fiercely clung to the governor system throughout the territorial period; Indian agents and others repeatedly noted Pueblo resentment of any outside meddling in internal Pueblo affairs. On the list of Pueblo grievances, this meddling in internal politics was second only to land encroachment. Superintendent Crandall summarized the Pueblos' desire for complete village autonomy, stating, "This is . . . one . . . of the traits of the Pueblo. They desire to be independent of all white people, to have nothing to do with them. . . . There is a greater desire among the Pueblo to live apart and be independent and have nothing to do with the white race than among any other Indians with whom I have worked." While the governor system was one of the forces that had allowed the Pueblos to maintain their existence for so long, Crandall referred to it pejoratively (and mistakenly) as a "one-man domination."[119] Fortunately for the Pueblos, the governor system, together with some relatively unobtrusive Indian agents, allowed for the persistence of a degree of autonomy in Pueblo governance.

What, then, did Pueblo "internal control" look like during the U.S. territorial period? In short, it resembled that in the Spanish and Mexican eras. Each Pueblo elected its own officials on an annual basis, and these officials exercised the duties of their offices. In addition, the Pueblos largely continued to administer internal justice in the traditional way. Pueblo Agent José Segura wrote to the Commissioner of Indian Affairs in 1890, "There is no court organized to try Indian offenses at this agency, and it is impracticable to establish one. On account of the location of the villages being so distant from the agency office and from each other each Pueblo has some kind of tribunal in which they try offenders against their customs, rules, and regulations and mete out punishment to the convicted; and if reports are to be believed the punishment is sometimes quite severe. But these matters are never officially reported to the agent; he only hears of them incidentally. I can not possibly estimate the number so tried and punished. Some offenses that to civilized man is [sic] very trivial are considered heinous crimes by them, and the guilty party is severely punished."[120] Coupled with yearly elections of officers—the true Pueblo vote—the administration of internal justice was one of the most prominent displays of Pueblo sovereignty.

Further examples are illustrative. The anthropologist Elsie Clews Parsons, who wrote extensively on Isleta Pueblo during the first half of the twentieth century, related events that took place at the Pueblo in 1904. One night, an intoxicated Isleta man was "being baited by some boys." The man became angry, and "took a strap and then grabbed [one of the boys] to choke him." The boy grabbed a rock with which to defend himself, and struck the intoxicated man in the head. The man died from the blow. The boys panicked and fled the scene. Someone in the village saw the body later that night, and reported it to the dead man's father, who in turn alerted Isleta's sheriffs (who were among the annual officers). They combed the village, arresting all men they found roaming the Pueblo. The next day, they found the man's killer hiding in a bush. The governor, acting within his powers to dispense justice, levied a fine on the boy of $350 and a team of oxen. These items then went to the deceased man's wife. When the Indian agent later found out about the events, he could have insisted that the killer be brought up on charges in a New Mexico court. Instead, he agreed with the Isletans that the decision was fair and did not pursue the matter further.[121] Such an internal handling of justice had satisfied all involved, and was in line with the agreement to allow the Pueblos to see to their own internal affairs as an autonomous community, even in the case of a capital offense.

Isleta Pueblo offers another revealing example, originally related by Father Anton Docher, the French Franciscan who labored at Isleta from the 1890s to the 1920s. Once, as he traveled by wagon performing his priestly duties, a severe sandstorm arose. Father Docher came across Vicente, the governor of Isleta, traveling alone in the storm. The father told of giving Vicente a ride, and also recalled the governor's words at his installation as governor: "I want no one to say when I surrender the Lincoln Cane of Authority, that I failed to lead the ... People [of the sixteen clans] in the right direction." While the pair traveled in the storm, Vicente asked Docher if he had heard anything of a certain Isleta man in the village of Peralta, where the father had been earlier to minister. The man in question had been gone for three days, and his wife had come to the governor because she was concerned for his safety. The governor feared the man might be dead. Vicente planned to employ the "Town Crier, the War Captain, the First and Second Lieutenant-Governors, and the two sheriffs on the job of hunting for the missing Isletan, after consulting of course, the *cacique* and the Business Council of Twelve."[122]

When the missing man, Pedro Lucero, still did not turn up, the people of Isleta Pueblo searched for several days. The governor eventually announced that they had found a man by the name of Juan Montoya, who was the last person seen with Lucero. Montoya was suspected of foul play. Apparently, villagers had seen him by the river bridge "looking at the water in a very suspicious manner." After Docher again traveled to Peralta for the funeral of a tribal member, he returned to Isleta to find the governor and other secular officials, along with some Anglo-Americans who had been surveying for a new bridge, standing along the riverbank. Nearby was an object on the ground, covered in canvas. The governor said, "It is the body of Pedro Lucero. The white men found it in the river this morning. His head was smashed, and his hands and feet tied. We will have to lock up Juan Montoya again. I think he is the only one who has something to do with Pedro's death." They did not discipline him, though, and when Docher later saw Governor Vicente carrying out one of his duties of office—supervising men cleaning the *acequia* (ditch)—Juan Montoya was among the workers. The governor said to the father, "You see we let him out of jail. Some one has to support Pedro's family. We might just as well let Juan do it."[123] Once again, Pueblo leaders had administered traditional justice, to the apparent approval of all involved. The Territory of New Mexico dispensed no justice; there was no trial in a New Mexico court, imprisonment of the accused, or eventual punishment (capital or otherwise).

Interestingly, these accounts contradict a short article penned by Father Docher himself for *The Santa Fe Magazine* in 1913, titled "The Quaint Indian Pueblo of Isleta." In the piece, Docher summarized systems of power then in place at Isleta: "The village of Isleta, like all other Indian pueblos, has a special administration which is recognized by the United States government. A cacique, appointed for life, has supreme power over his subjects. A governor, elected yearly by the people, is the judge in civil cases only. He has two assists, and, if the occasion demands, a grand council." But it is Docher's final statement regarding the administration of justice that belies the previous summary: "*All criminal cases are turned over to the district courts*, but criminality is almost unknown among the Indians of Isleta."[124] According to official Indian Service policy as well as the Major Crimes Act of 1885, Pueblo officials were to have jurisdiction over civil cases only. But in practice, as in the Spanish and Mexican periods, they exercised jurisdiction in criminal cases, as well. They did so at times with the tacit approval of federal officials. In these instances, the Pueblos approximated sovereign Indigenous nations.

An episode that culminated during the term of Pueblo Agent Leo Crane, who served in New Mexico for most of the 1920s, provides a final example of how the Pueblos exercised sovereignty in internal electoral affairs with the support of Indian Service employees, all at the expense of territorial and state power. According to Crane, during Harold F. Coggeshall's time as Superintendent of Pueblo Day Schools during the early 1910s, intense factionalism had gripped Ohkay Owingeh Pueblo. The "worth-while Governor was deposed [so] that a very doubtful one should reign in his stead." The deposed governor complained to the superintendent that "the election had not been conducted in strict accordance with the customs of the people." The governor also "refused to yield the symbols of his office." An intriguing situation developed in which the "pretender" governor filed suit in the New Mexico Territorial Court to force the deposed governor to give up both his Lincoln and his Mexican canes,[125] Ohkay Owingeh's land grant patent, and the archives of the Pueblo as well. Before the Territorial Court's writ to deliver the items could be served, the governor deposited them with Coggeshall, who passed them on to his successor, Phillip T. Lonergan, who then gave them to his own successor, Leo Crane. The case lasted until 1919, during which time the state court decided in favor of the "pretender" governor. Lonergan had refused to comply with the state court, citing its lack of jurisdiction over a federal official, and he was even jailed for a time before resigning. Eventually, the Federal Court sided with the Indian Service employees in the case of the deposed Ohkay Owingeh governor. Crane observed, "Naturally, the Federal Court decided that *the State Courts [and Territorial Court before them] had no jurisdiction over questions of internal government of the Pueblo Indians*, and the state did not appeal the case."[126] Thus, in at least one case, federal law supported and even protected Pueblo internal sovereignty in the late territorial period through the late 1910s, with territorial and state courts unable to interfere in such matters.

Conclusion

In their numerous statements and actions, federal authorities repeatedly recognized that Pueblo communities were ordered, distinct sovereignties with systems in place for electing leadership and administering justice. In some cases, Indian agents intervened in internal Pueblo affairs, especially as factionalism expanded during the territorial period. They also inserted themselves at times when serious criminal offenses occurred. But in the majority of cases, the Pueblos resolved their own disputes, administered justice to those who violated Pueblo law, and saw to their own internal affairs. Furthermore, it was largely the Pueblos themselves who ultimately decided on voting and citizenship. They passed on the franchise and New Mexico or U.S. citizenship in favor of protecting citizenship in distinct Pueblo republics. By maintaining their culture, religion, and institutions against an overwhelming tide of encroachment, competing jurisdictions, and unfavorable courts, the Pueblos were committed to the same persistent struggle that had begun under Spanish domination. Armed not with the weapon of the "good citizenship gun" but with stable, proven systems of electoral politics and civil governance, Pueblo communities did all they could to maintain autonomy and sovereignty. Considering the obstacles, they succeeded to a surprising degree.

In the decades preceding its admission to the Union as a state in 1912, New Mexico launched another attack on Pueblo sovereignty in the form of taxation. The territory had attempted to collect taxes on Pueblo lands for decades, since previous territorial statutes and court rulings had classified Pueblos as citizens having title to their lands. This once again pitted the Indian Office against territorial officials. In 1885, for example, New Mexico Governor Edmund G. Ross wrote to the territory's tax collectors, informing them of a directive he had received from Interior Secretary L. Q. C. Lamar. The secretary, quoting his own commissioner of Indian affairs, declared that the Pueblos were not, at that time, "prepared for the duties of citizenship [taxation and the franchise], and do not desire to be so considered." Secretary Lamar concurred with the commissioner, and asked Governor Ross to hold off on collecting property taxes form the Pueblos. Governor Ross informed his tax collectors to "suspend all further purpose to collect the taxes assessed upon the lands of these Pueblos 'until such a time as the matter can be fully considered by congress and their status defined.'"[127]

Yet the issue went unresolved, and proved to be the final assault on the status of Pueblo Indians as citizens of the United States in the territorial period. In 1900, New Mexico eventually took the Pueblos, collectively, to court. *Territory of New Mexico v. Delinquent Taxpayers* reached the New Mexico Supreme Court in 1904. In his ruling, Associate Justice J. W. Crumpacker stated, "Among other property on which taxes were delinquent, were the land grants." The decision contained another lengthy summary of Pueblo rights and history; a history always told from the conqueror's point of view. Invoking *Lucero*, the court held that "it seems clear that [the Pueblos] have ... [the] right" to alienate their lands. Furthermore, "The right of alienation is one of the chief elements of property values, and is possessed by all citizens," who are thus "subject to taxation."[128]

The defendants argued that the Pueblos were in a state of wardship, especially since "they have been deprived of the elective franchise." The court overlooked this, asserting, "Never has congress assumed to reduce them to a state of tutelage and their status has never been attempted to be changed by any act of the government," which was patently false. In terms of Pueblo property, the court pointed out that the "United States has never assumed to take control of their property ... [but] it has quitclaimed to them and issued its patent for all their lands." The Pueblos were delinquent on their property taxes "for fifty years." In its conclusion, the court felt perfectly comfortable arguing two contradictory sides. While Indian agents and others had for decades pointed out that even though the Pueblos were "civilized" or "semi-civilized," they were still Indians in need of the protections granted to the Indian peoples of the United States. The court, by contrast, stated, "It is true, no doubt, that the fact that these people live in communities, separate from the rest of the people, and have local self-government, and thus preserve, in a large measure, the characteristics of their ancient civilization, is the fact which appeals most strongly to the mind and causes it to rebel against the conclusion reached here; but when their history is seen and understood and their legal status examined, they are found to possess all the qualifications and rights of citizenship. They are not unlike, in this respect, the Shakers and other communistic societies in other parts of the country." Having considered all these points, the court ruled "that the Pueblo Indians of New Mexico are citizens of New Mexico and of the United States, hold their lands with full power of alienation, and are, as such, subject to taxation."[129]

Thus, the decision by the New Mexico Supreme Court on the citizenship status of the Pueblos supported all the previous statutes and decisions, and firmly rejected both Indian Office determinations and the desires of the Pueblos themselves. Furthermore, Justice Crumpacker reaffirmed the status of the Pueblos as nonvoting citizens. The fact that Pueblo lands and property were deemed taxable only underscored the unfair position of the Pueblos. The supreme irony was that a period of more than three hundred years of colonization looked to have ended with the achievement of the goal that the Spaniards had originally pursued: to turn Indians into taxpaying citizens. But these taxpaying citizen Pueblo Indians did not possess the gold standard of citizenship: the franchise. American policymakers had found a way to legally deny full citizenship rights, while still preserving both the right of Hispano and Anglo-American access to Pueblo lands and the right of the Territory of New Mexico to tax their sacred ancestral lands. Pueblo Indians had little or no legal recourse in the adversarial courts, as evidenced by one negative decision after another.

The next year, Congress finally took action on the issue of Pueblo taxation. In its Appropriation Act of 3 March 1905, which covered financial year 1906, Congress definitively excluded the Pueblos from property taxes. In fact, the act excluded "lands now held by the various villages or pueblos . . . or by individual members," as well as "all personal property furnished said Indians by the United States, or used in cultivating said lands, and any cattle and sheep now possessed or that may hereafter be acquired by said Indians shall be free and exempt from taxation of any sort whatsoever, including taxes hereafter levied, if any, until Congress shall otherwise provide."[130] This act resolved neither the citizenship matter nor voting issues, but at least it potentially provided some relief from territorial officials' attempting to collect taxes on Pueblo property.

While this congressional action protected Pueblo Indians from property taxes, it opened the door for their continued disenfranchisement when New Mexico entered the Union. Perhaps stinging from Congress's move to exempt the Pueblos from taxation, delegates to the New Mexico Constitutional Convention in 1910[131] moved to prohibit Indian voting once again. Article 7, Section 1, of that constitution reads, "Every male citizen of the United States, who is over the age of twenty-one years, and has resided in New Mexico twelve months, in the county ninety days, and in the precinct in which he offers to vote thirty days, next preceding the election, except idiots, insane persons, persons convicted of a felonious or infamous crime, unless restored to political rights, *and Indians not taxed*, shall be qualified to vote at all elections for public officers."[132] For decades, the Territory of New Mexico had battled to legally designate Pueblo Indians as citizens of both New Mexico and the United States, while also denying their voting rights. Now Indians were kept from the franchise because of the tax-exempt status of their lands. The New Mexico Constitution also grouped Indians in the same class as "idiots, insane persons, [and] persons convicted of a felonious or infamous crime." Delegates ratified the constitution on 21 November 1910, and the voting male citizens of the territory—Indians not included, of course—approved the document on 21 January 1911. President Taft signed New Mexico's admission document early the next year, and New Mexico officially became the forty-seventh state on 6 January 1912.[133]

The inclusion of the "Indians not taxed" clause in the New Mexico State Constitution would prove critical over the next nearly-four decades, as Indians were completely barred from voting. And while individual Indians or small groups of Indians had occasionally tried to vote during the territorial period, by 1912 the issue of Indian voting was essentially moot. Framing the years from 1846 to 1912 as a struggle to secure the Indian vote would be a mischaracterization. Rather, we should view the period as a continuing struggle by the Pueblos to retain their autonomy, sovereignty, and control of internal affairs. Pueblo Indians actively rejected citizenship, telling their Indian agents repeatedly that they did not desire to become citizens. They were already citizens of Pueblo republics, and it was this citizenship that mattered most to them. They were already voters, as well, participating in the annual elections for Pueblo officials. For them, citizenship and voting rights in New Mexico and the United States held little appeal, since these endangered their sacred land, their religion, and their institutions.

A statement from Pueblo representatives dated 24 March 1904 best summarizes the Pueblo position. The New Mexico Supreme Court had just handed down the *Delinquent Taxpayer* decision, and the Pueblos were alarmed at the prospect of heavy property taxes. Representatives from the Eight Northern Indian Pueblos Council[134] met at the office of Ohkay Owingeh Pueblo Governor José Ramon Archuleta, and drafted a letter, in Spanish, to the Southern Pueblos to enlist their support in opposition to *Delinquent Taxpayer*. They were stridently opposed to taxation of their lands, but they carried it a step further. The representatives stated, "It was decided that all of the pueblos that were there represented were opposed to participating as citizens in the public affairs of the Territory, and that we want to protest against the taxation of our lands." They concluded definitively with the following statement: "We ask all the Pueblos of the Territory to join together and consider these matters and take some action to make known to officials in Washington, and in this Territory, and to Congress that is now in session, *that we do not want to be citizens* and that we protest against the taxation of our lands."[135] The document lists the participating officers—governor, lieutenant governor, and war chief—from Taos, Ohkay Owingeh, Santa Clara, San Ildefonso, Nambé, Pojoaque, Tesuque, and Picuris. We can only assume that the ten Southern Pueblos, and Zuni, were in agreement. The Pueblos had no desire to become citizens or to exercise the associated franchise. The overwhelming majority of Pueblo Indians chose to forego both the vote and participation in any public affairs outside their villages to preserve their stable, traditional, and ordered way of life.

To further complicate matters, after Justice William H. Pope of the New Mexico Supreme Court ruled in 1907 that an 1897 federal law forbidding the sale of alcohol to Indians did not apply to the Pueblos, Congress had required that New Mexico insert into its Enabling Act of 1910 provisions that prohibited such sales to the Pueblos. The act, which the *Cuervo Clipper* (Guadalupe County) of 8 July 1910 reprinted in full, promised that New Mexico would forbid the sale of alcohol to Indians, which "shall also include all lands now owned or occupied by the Pueblo Indians of New Mexico . . . [and such sales] are forever prohibited." Furthermore, it read, "the terms 'Indian' and 'Indian country' shall include the Pueblo Indians of New Mexico and the lands now owned or occupied by them."[136] This was highly significant, as it marked the first admission by New Mexico that Pueblo Indians were indeed Indians—an action the Pueblos had demanded for decades.

Pope was not yet finished. After being appointed the first Judge for the U.S. District Court of New Mexico, he ruled that Felipe Sandoval could not be prosecuted for selling liquor to Indians in Santa Clara Pueblo. *The New Mexican*

Review of 18 July 1912 lauded Pope's decision, calling his ruling "exhaustive" and "very important . . . far reaching from a political standpoint as well as from the standpoint of establishing finally the status of the Pueblo Indians as citizens of the United States." *The New Mexican*'s reasoning was clear: "The Indian population of New Mexico, of the Pueblo tribes, is from 4,000 to 5,000. That . . . gives New Mexico two congressmen to be chosen the coming fall instead of one." The editorial concluded, "The effect of this decision, if sustained by the supreme court of the United States will be to make the Pueblo Indians citizens in the fullest sense of the word."[137] Once again, lawmakers and those in power demonstrated that they did not care for Pueblo Indians and their rights—caring only how they could be used to strengthen New Mexico's political status. But the case made it to the U.S. Supreme Court, and in 1913 the court overturned Judge Pope, ruling definitively in *United States v. Sandoval* that Pueblo Indians were Indians and that the terms of the Nonintercourse Act applied to them, thereby overturning *United States v. Joseph*. It was a landmark ruling, finally affirming the federal government's responsibility to protect Pueblo lands and that the Pueblos could not be compelled to pay property taxes nor to vote. It represented a delayed—yet sorely needed—victory for Pueblo peoples.

CHAPTER SIX

Disparate Designs
Indian Voting in Territorial Arizona

During the territorial period in New Mexico, in many ways individual Pueblo nations faced similar challenges regarding issues of education, assimilation, voting, and citizenship. In Arizona, by contrast, Native peoples confronted differing dilemmas from one Indigenous nation to the next. The inroads made by Spanish and Mexican systems of democratic town government and mainstream political participation varied, sometimes drastically, from group to group. To the far north, Hopis had mostly evaded colonial control since 1700. When U.S. officials inserted themselves into the region, they encountered a people whose lives were still dictated by strict ceremonial cycles, traditional leadership, and a reluctance to accept any changes brought by the colonizers.

Hopis would prove a worthy adversary to the panoply of Americans—Indian Service employees, military officers, missionaries, educators, and reformers—who came to their territory after the late 1840s. These outsiders eventually focused their assimilationist agenda on schooling for Hopi children and land allotment for individual Hopi farmers in an effort to prepare them for citizenship and voting. Many Anglo-Americans who labored at Hopi reported enthusiastically about progress made by the "peaceful" and "tractable" Hopis. One went so far as to suggest that progressive young Hopi men who had received allotments—thus qualifying for citizenship under the Dawes Act of 1887—were on the cusp of claiming their right to the franchise as full U.S. citizens. But such pronouncements and progress proved a hasty mirage. Hopis resisted U.S. influence just as they had that of Spain and Mexico. The much-anticipated Hopi citizen voter did not materialize as Arizona transitioned to statehood in 1912. Hopi villages largely continued to operate as sovereign, Indigenous nations, only allowing the degree of Americanization with which they were comfortable.

To the south in Sonora, Yaquis endured the most violent period of their existence during the decades following Mexican independence. The eight Yaqui villages, once the wellspring of Yaqui cultural and political development, suffered steep depopulation. Mexico exterminated Yaquis wholesale or deported them to the plantations of Yucatan, some two thousand miles from their homeland. Under these intolerable circumstances, many Yaquis moved to the cities of Sonora, where they changed their names in an attempt to "pass" as Mexicans, thereby protecting both their identity and their lives. Others began a trek north to relative safety in Arizona. The resulting Yaqui exodus saw thousands of Yaqui refugees cross the porous Mexico-U.S. border. While Yaquis found some degree of safety in these newly formed communities in southern Arizona, the horrors of Mexico were still too fresh to forget. Yaquis did not transplant the governor system and complex pillars of village civil government from the eight villages. Fearful of deportation, Yaquis kept a low profile. In addition, Arizona and federal officials did not view Yaquis as Indians; they were unlike Hopis, Navajos, or Apaches. They had no reservation, no trust land, no Indian agent, and no Indian status. Their only protection came from their status as refugees. Thus, added to the tragedy of their experience was the fact that the intricate systems of democratic town government that existed on the Río Yaqui were not to be found in southern Arizona; and neither was the right to the franchise in federal and territorial elections.

Spain began colonizing the O'odhams of the Arizona-Sonora Borderlands as early as 1687, the year of Eusebio Kino's first mission to the area. Throughout the Spanish and Mexican periods, the region experienced significant ebbs and flows in the degree of missionization and outside interference. When the U.S. territorial period began, Tohono O'odhams had already experienced intimate interactions with colonizers for nearly two hundred years. The governor system had declined sharply during the Mexican era, which meant that most Tohono O'odham communities had restored traditional modes of leadership, even if they retained a tribal office similar to that of the old O'odham-Spanish village governor. The United States did not encounter well-organized cadres of Spanish-style Tohono O'odham officers wielding varas de justicia. Even in the absence of an O'odam-Spanish democratic system, federal officials still viewed them as "civilized" or "half-civilized," much as they had the Rio Grande Pueblo peoples. The United States believed it could transform Tohono O'odhams of San Xavier del Bac, in particular, into "civilized," voting citizens who farmed land in severalty. But the allotment of Tohono O'odham lands at San Xavier did not produce voters. John M. Berger, who served as the Indian Service farmer at San Xavier, reported year after year during the period of Tohono O'odham allotment that they had consistently failed to embrace the franchise. For Hopis, Yaquis, and Tohono O'odhams in Arizona, voting remained a right withheld, or unclaimed, or undesired. Change would only come on the wings of the post–World War I and post–World War II political climate, when Arizona Native peoples more actively pursued citizenship and voting.

The United States and the Hopis

When the United States assumed control of the Hopi homelands in 1846, all of the current state of Arizona was part of New Mexico. Arizona did not become its own territory until 1863. Not only did Arizona remain under New Mexican control for nearly twenty years, but Anglo-American contacts were delayed, as well. Bill Williams was probably the first U.S. trapper to visit Hopi lands in 1827, and it is likely that Williams guided Captain Joseph Walker's 1834 exploration that led to the deaths of twenty Hopis, shot dead in the so-called "cornfield incident." In that episode, trappers attempted to steal corn from Hopi fields. The Hopis, already accustomed to Navajo and Apache raids, attempted to defend their precious fields. Twenty Hopi men were shot dead by the trappers.[1] James Calhoun was the first U.S. administrator of Hopiland. While Calhoun met frequently with the governors and other representatives of the Rio Grande Pueblos, he had difficulty negotiating with Hopis. What made meeting with them so difficult was the fact that both Navajo and Apache territory lay between Santa Fe and the Hopis. In addition, the military was reluctant to provide Calhoun with the protective escort he deemed essential to safely visit the Hopi villages.[2] This established a years-long pattern of infrequent contacts between Hopis and U.S. authorities.

Calhoun had every intention of visiting the Hopis and establishing political ties with them. Yet he was simply unable to do so during his brief tenure in office. Voicing his desire to visit Hopi in 1850, Calhoun reported that he was "extremely anxious to visit these Indians; but it would be unsafe to do so, without sufficient escort, as the Apaches are upon the left, and the Navajos on the right in traveling . . . to the Moquies [sic]." Feeling unsafe visiting the Hopi villages without a military escort, and desperately short on information relating to Hopi customs and political protocol, Calhoun felt that he could not recommend that an Indian agent be sent to them without his first visiting in person, to ascertain their condition and disposition.[3] Thus territorial officials failed in their efforts to bring Hopis into the political mainstream, following the familiar pattern set first by Spain and later by Mexico.

Somewhat surprisingly, Hopis initiated the first contact when they went to Santa Fe to visit Calhoun, who reported receiving the first official Hopi delegation to the United States in October 1850: "The Seven Moqui Pueblos sent me a deputation who presented themselves on the 6th day of this month. Their object, as announced, was to ascertain the purposes and views of the Government of the United States towards them. They complained, bitterly, of the depredations of the Navajos—The deputation consisted of the Cacique of *all* the

Pueblos, and a *chief* of the largest Pueblo, accompanied by two who were not officials. From what I could learn from the Cacique, I came to the conclusion, that each of the seven Pueblos, was an independent Republic, having confederated for mutual protection."[4] Calhoun's report to the Commissioner of Indian Affairs, Luke Lea, contains a number of telling statements. First, he explained that Hopis were still smarting from Navajo raids and depredations, a situation that had persisted since at least the Mexican period. At this time, Navajo aggressions remained the foremost Hopi concern.[5] Second, he stated that an envoy consisting of a "cacique," "chief," and two other individuals had demonstrated to him that, unlike the Rio Grande Pueblos, Hopis had no religious-secular division of government. Third, he described the seven Hopi villages represented by the delegation as "independent Republic[s]." Whether this was a nod to the earlier designation of the Pueblos as repúblicas de indios is difficult to say, but Calhoun and other New Mexico officials certainly had access to, and pored over, Spanish and Mexican records at the Palace of the Governors, documents that frequently referred to Pueblo republics.[6]

U.S. officials thus initially viewed the Hopi Pueblos as independent political units. Despite his failure to visit the Hopi villages, James Calhoun wrote again to Lea in 1851: "These Indians seem to be innocent, and very poor, and should be taken care of."[7] In the absence of firm political ties between the United States and Hopis, a status that persisted for several decades after the 1840s, issues of Hopi voting would not trouble Calhoun or many of his successors. While federal and territorial officials focused on issues of Rio Grande Pueblo citizenship and voting during this era, such concerns did not surface at Hopi until a later date.

By the time the Indian Office had established an agency among the Hopis in 1869,[8] a number of visitors had already entered their territory. One important visitor, U.S. Army Lieutenant Joseph C. Ives, directed a party dispatched to explore the Colorado River by steamboat in 1857–58. Despite the ugly cornfield incident and the lack of any response by the United States to Hopi pleas for assistance against the Navajos, when Ives's party reached the outskirts of the Hopi villages on 11 May 1857, it was met by two mounted Hopis "arrayed ... in their best attire." The two Hopis were extremely friendly, "each insisting upon shaking hands with the whole company." Ives identified one of the pair as the leader, recalling that, in spite of his friendliness, his "pleasant, intelligent face ... expressed, however, misgivings as to our character and object in coming into that unvisited region." After the group was directed to the first Hopi village, a "pleasant looking middle-aged man" approached the Americans. Aside from being adorned with a "handsome shell" around his neck, Ives noted that he had "a kind of baton in his hand." Ives surmised that he was a "chief." Despite the fact that the Hopis had fed, watered, accommodated, and guided Ives, his party, and their numerous animals, he concluded that Hopis were quick to "lounge and gossip." Although they were honest and did not steal, "their promises are not to be relied upon. They want force of character and the courageous qualities which the Zuñians and some other Pueblo Indians have the credit of possessing." Like the Spaniards and Mexicans who preceded him, Ives failed to grasp the complex structure of Hopi government and its machinations: "Their chiefs exercise a good deal of authority, but by what tenure they hold their power, or how many there are, we could not learn."[9]

Ives held long conversations with his host, who, among other things, indicated that "Comanches and Navajoes had driven off a great deal of their stock during the previous year. The Moquis do not look warlike, and but for their natural and artificial defences would doubtless long ago have been exterminated by their powerful and aggressive neighbors." He also encountered the more-resistant group of Hopis at Oraibi, whose chief he described as "the senior of all," "out of humor," and "ill temper[ed]." The chief refused to allow any of his people to guide the party on its trip north toward to Colorado, and when one of the junior Hopi leaders expressed a desire to accompany the Americans, the man, who "was friendly in his manner . . . said that he could not go while his superior objected." Ives may or may not have understood the unanimous nature of Hopi leadership. Even though he might have disagreed with his superior, the junior Hopi leader stood aside in favor of group unity. Surprisingly, when the Americans left unaccompanied the next morning, the Oraibi chief sent a guide after them, and without his help they would not have found a trail north leading to the next watering hole. Ives said that he and his companions "began to think the old fellow less churlish than he had appeared, and gladly availed ourselves of his civility and the new-comer's knowledge." Ives referred to Hopis as "citizens" of their individual villages, but the many-layered nature of Hopi government would remain a mystery to Anglo-Americans for some time.[10]

Another U.S. visitor to the Hopis arrived at the very moment of the agency's establishment. Quoted in Thomas Edwin Farish's eight-volume *History of Arizona*, published from 1915 to 1918, Dr. Edward Palmer,[11] an ethnobotanist and archaeologist who visited Oraibi in May of 1869, stated that during his visit, "The Governor [of Oraibi] invited Mr. Colyer, Lieut. Crouse and myself to dine with him at his house. He received us cordially, showing us a silver headed ebony cane, a gift from President Lincoln."[12] The Hopi headman was apparently in possession of one of the famous Lincoln canes. It is also noteworthy that Dr. Palmer referred to the leader at Oraibi as a "Governor." Perhaps his reference to a Hopi governor was colored by experiences with the Rio Grande Pueblos, but there can be no mistaking a Hopi leader's possessing a Lincoln cane—either Palmer fabricated the story, or the village chief at Oraibi had somehow actually received such a cane, or the Hopi leader had manufactured a fake Lincoln cane. There is no record of Superintendent Steck's having a cane made for Hopi.[13]

In the 1860s, when Arizona was separated from New Mexico Territory, the new territory took a decidedly different tone than its neighbor regarding Indian voting and citizenship. As we will see, individual Anglo-Americans, such as Indian Service employees, may have had their own opinions on the current or potential political status of Hopis and Tohono O'odhams, but the law was clear from the mid-1860s forward. The Howell Code, the legal apparatus approved by Arizona's first legislative assembly in 1864, stated in Chapter 24, Section 6: "Every white male citizen of the United States, and every white male citizen of Mexico, who shall have elected to become a citizen of the United States under the treaty of peace exchanged and ratified at Quintero on the 30th day of May, 1848, and the Gadsden treaty of 1854, of the age of twenty-one years, who shall have been a resident of the Territory six months next preceding the election, and the county or precinct in which he claims his vote ten days, shall be entitled to vote at all elections which are now, or hereafter may be, authorized by law."[14] Arizona thus differed from New Mexico in that it made whiteness a requirement for voting from early on. In short, only white former citizens of the Mexican Republic could vote in Arizona. Later developments, particularly around the allotment of Indian lands, finally raised the question of the right of Indians to the franchise. But the agents who labored at Hopi during the early years of the territorial period did not have to quickly establish Hopis' citizenship and voting status; that would come later.

When an agency for the Hopis finally opened in 1869, federal officials chose Fort Wingate for its location. After visiting the Hopi villages, Special Agent A. D. Palmer, writing to Commissioner Ely Parker in 1870, reported that Hopis were anxious to receive smallpox vaccinations. He duly vaccinated some four hundred and seventy-eight Hopis, and revaccinated three hundred and forty more. Special Agent Palmer also commented, as many before him had, that "the Moquis are not progressive in their work, clinging strongly to their traditional customs in everything they do. They are much attached to their villages and country, and extremely jealous of innovation." Palmer surmised that a general lack of Hopi enthusiasm at his arrival was due to the fact that "several Americans, who formerly visited them, counted their people and promised them aid,

[but] failed to fulfil their promise." He summarized the American stance on Hopis with the following statement: "They are the most ignorant and superstitious tribe I have ever seen, due, I believe, to their isolated position."[15] What Palmer had actually noted was a longstanding resistance to colonial control, and, like his predecessors, Palmer discerned nothing substantive regarding traditional patterns of Hopi governance and power structures.

From the 1870s on, federal agents began to speak of a strategy for civilizing the Hopis. Just as agents were attempting to establish schools among the Rio Grande Pueblos during the era of federal expansion in Indian schooling, the Indian Office moved forward with similar plans for the Hopis. Unfortunately, the difficulty of reaching the villages proved a constant concern. Writing in 1872, Agent W. D. Crothers commented, "Their locality is so remote from civilization, that in order to make much progress in civilization there must be a greater number of schools established among them." He also noted the reluctance on the part of Hopis at Oraibi to cooperate with American officials.[16] Resistance to education by Hopis at that village would persist for decades and would attain an almost legendary status. Regardless, Crothers held firm to the American belief that education would do much of the work of Hopi civilizing. The U.S. was convinced that Hopi education would eventually lead to Hopi citizenship and, potentially, Hopi voters.

Initially, the Hopi Agency had an exceedingly high turnover. But by 1875, Agent W. B. Truax became perhaps the first OIA official to make specific references to Hopi citizenship. By this time the agency had a boarding school, which had finally been moved close to Hopi lands ("some fifteen miles from the nearest Indian [Hopi] village"). According to Agent Truax, "All the pupils are boarded, clothed, and furnished lodgings here." He reported enthusiastically that parents had requested more schools at the villages, since a boarding school proved to be an inconvenience for many of them. He also recommended two additional teachers for a school "located as to be within convenient reach of six of the villages . . . [which] would afford facilities to almost the whole tribe for educating their children." Truax believed that if such measures were implemented, "These Indians, living in permanent abodes, far removed from all disturbing causes, *and to some extent civilized*, furnish a most hopeful field for missionary and educational effort." But, he cautioned, "The Bible and the common school must be given them, *if they would ever rise to the true position of citizens*. I believe that no nation or people ever did or ever will, by their own efforts, lift themselves out of a state of degradation and barbarism into a permanent civilization."[17] Truax believed that Hopis could "rise to the true position of citizens," but, repeating the mantra of his cohort, he inserted the common claim that only schools and the Bible would accomplish this goal. The agents who followed him carried Traux's ideas to the next step, suggesting that Hopis become voters, as well.

Before that happened, though, the Indian Office would have to resolve the question of Hopi land title. Hopis were not in possession of land grants from the Spanish or Mexican governments. One federal official did not doubt that such titles had been granted by Spain and Mexico, but Hopis had not applied for a confirmation of such title, which had been granted to the nineteen Rio Grande Pueblos, perhaps because "they did not know it was necessary and because they have no money." He even suggested that Hopis qualified for title to their land through so-called squatter's rights.[18] In addition, Hopis had no official reservation. As Agent Traux indicated in his 1876 report, with "no reservation or title to the country they are now occupying, consequently they are . . . liable to be imposed upon in various ways." The agent also believed that the soil near the mesas was approaching the critical point of exhaustion, so he recommended that Hopis farm a river valley some fifteen miles from their villages. He even supported the idea of possible Hopi removal to Indian Territory, but conceded, "They told me emphatically they would never leave their present abodes, unless forced to do so." He suggested that in order to solve the issues of encroachment, and to avoid further degradation, a Hopi reservation needed to be set aside. The school was already proving successful, and "A good portion of the scholars have a strong desire to obtain an education 'that they may be like Americans.'"[19]

The issue of land title was not the only challenge facing the Hopis, as the first Hopi school closed down in September 1876 after only a few years in operation. Agency turnover continued, and a frustrated Agent William R. Mateer reported in 1878 that the Hopis were "an exceedingly superstitious people." He suggested that "six of the brightest Moquis boys, sixteen years of age, be sent to a State normal school for four or five years. . . . These young men upon their return would make competent teachers . . . [and] certainly do much toward educating, civilizing, and christianizing these Indians."[20] In spite of the recommendations of the Hopi agents, Americans saw little Hopi progress toward "civilization" as the 1880s began. But in a positive development, on 16 December 1882 President Chester A. Arthur finally set aside a Hopi Reservation through an Executive Order. A reservation provided some degree of protection for Hopi lands. While Americans had viewed the Rio Grande Pueblos as either "civilized" or "half-civilized," they did not necessarily consider Hopis in the same class. They saw quite a bit of work left to do in turning Hopis into voting citizens.

Beginning in the early 1880s, Hopis endured a rocky period with the Indian Office. By 1882, the Presbyterian Board of Home Missions had opened a day school with a staff of two teachers, but it was sorely underfunded and supplied.[21] In addition, the OIA abandoned the Hopi Agency for five years (1882–87). From 1882 to 1889, the Indian Service jointly administered Hopis and Navajos. It was an administrative mess, to put it lightly. The United States finally sent James Gallaher to serve as Hopi Agent in 1887. Based at Keams Canyon, located in the far southeast of Hopi territory and at a town where the agency had been moved in 1873, Gallaher and his staff ushered in the opening of a school at Keams Canyon on 1 October 1887, with an initial enrollment of fifty-two pupils.[22] The work at Hopi would take on a decidedly different air after the late 1880s, as agents ramped up their efforts to civilize the Hopis and even attempted to transform a select few of them into voting citizens.

The redoubled efforts by Hopi agents had dire consequences. The Indian Service touted its successes at Hopi—failing to see, or ignoring altogether, the negative consequences of its work there. Beginning in the late 1880s, Hopi agents worked "with a determined dedication to do everything within their power to make the Hopi over into an imitation and second-class white man, rather than the best type of Hopi citizen."[23] Furthermore, officials actively sought to undermine or sidestep traditional patterns of Hopi leadership and governance, whereby clan leaders, and the village *kikmongvi* (chief), were the customary holders of power.[24] OIA officials were only too happy to completely ignore the Indigenous system of Hopi governance, and thus made no efforts to work through these leaders.[25] The Indian Office aggressively employed numerous tactics in its attempt to civilize Hopis: education, allotment and private property, employment, and religion. All four were intertwined, and it was believed that these tools would function to bring Hopis, who were perceived to be at a lower stage of social development, into the American mainstream. With such measures successfully deployed, it was thought that Hopis would naturally evolve in their degree of civilization, with citizenship as the inevitable conclusion.[26]

When the General Allotment (or Dawes) Act passed in 1887, which corresponded with the reopening of the Hopi Agency, the Indian Service saw a perfect opportunity to transform those "superstitious" and "overly communal" Hopis. The Hopi allotment plan, which aimed to break up village lands, as well as dismantle their social and political structures, began to crystallize in 1891. The Indian Office contracted an outsider to survey Hopi lands for possible individual allotments, while Indian Service officials promised lumber and other supplies to those Hopis who accepted their parcels. They hoped to move the

Hopis off the mesas and onto the valley floors to farm. Hopis had successfully practiced agriculture for centuries, yet Indian Office bureaucrats reasoned that if Hopi farming communities could be modeled after Anglo-American patterns, their difficult charges could be much more easily educated, surveilled, and controlled. American officials surveyed some 120,000 acres of Hopi land, and then proceeded to make individual allotments. Agents reported enthusiastically that they had equipped twenty houses on individual land allotments with stoves, beds, and other modern conveniences, but the reality was that it was difficult to find Hopis who would accept them. OIA employees pointed out that even allotted Hopis continued with traditional subsistence patterns, moving from their valley homes to the mesas during certain parts of the year. Hopis simply incorporated their allotments into traditional, seasonal subsistence patterns.[27]

The allotment work was "completed" by 1894, but for a number of reasons it had not gone according to plan. Thomas Donaldson of the U.S. Census Bureau had commented in 1891 that to attempt to allot Hopi lands would "work them a grievous injury." There simply was not enough water. "[O]ne man with one tract of 80 acres of land will be likely to get all the water now used by the inhabitants of any one of the several towns." He concluded that it was "cruel to deprive these people of their ancient homes, their lands, and their means of livelihood."[28] Commissioner of Indian Affairs Daniel N. Browning reported to the Secretary of the Interior that the work had to be discontinued in 1894. While some Hopis had made their allotment selections, as per the terms of the Act, he reported persistent opposition to the allotment work from both Hopis and "Friends of the Indians," which led to discontinuing the efforts prematurely.[29] Agent E. H. Plummer wrote flatly to the commissioner in 1894 that "There is little, indeed no, improvement in the condition of the Moquis in the past year."[30]

The plan to move allotted Hopis off the mesas had simply not worked. They had no desire to move, and resisted all efforts to that end. While they were generally "very friendly to the whites and appear anxious to learn and have their children educated"—except at Oraibi, of course—enrollment at the Keams Canyon boarding school was down, and the day schools averaged only around thirty pupils in attendance. Plummer concluded that allotment was not feasible. Hopis, with the support of Anglo-Americans sympathetic to their cause, such as Charles F. Lummis, had petitioned for an end to Hopi allotment, and Plummer favored this action.[31] This episode effectively closed the book on Hopi allotment at that time, although there was another effort made in 1910. Hopi allotment had failed. It might have accomplished the U.S. goal

Moki Melon Eaters, ca. 1900. Hopi children enjoying a melon. Edward S. Curtis Collection, Prints and Photographs Division, Library of Congress, LC-USZ62-112226.

of citizenship for Hopis, because Indians holding trust titles to allotted lands at this time automatically became U.S. citizens, but Hopis and their allies rallied in favor of their traditional village structures and way of life. Without allotted Hopi citizens, there were simply no Hopi voters for the time being.[32]

The Hopi education project similarly struggled. Reporting in 1897, Agent Constant Williams wrote to the Commissioner of Indian Affairs, "There are not sufficient school accommodations for the Moqui children."[33] Williams elaborated during the following year: "The school plant at Keam's Canyon is old and the buildings are in bad order." He suggested that a new school be built.[34] In 1899, Williams's replacement, G. W. Hayzlett, was a bit more positive about the situation. He commented, "The Moqui is quite provident. . . . They are industrious and appear to be a very quiet and peaceful people." Hayzlett concluded, using a familiar measuring stick of civilization: "All dress mostly in citizens' clothing."[35] The subsequent arrival of School Superintendent Charles E. Burton would signal a sea change at Hopi. Burton pursued a forceful assimilation policy with Hopis, one that earned him infamy in Hopi history. He remains notorious for having Hopi children dragged away from their families, beating parents and leaders who opposed this policy, and ordering the forced haircutting—at gunpoint—of many Hopis. He was also the first Anglo-American official at Hopi to take seriously the prospect of Hopi citizen voters at the turn of the twentieth century.

When Superintendent Burton reported to Commissioner of Indian Affairs William A. Jones in 1902, he proudly listed the schools at Hopi: Moqui Training School at Keams Canyon, Polacca Day School, Second Mesa Day School, and Oraibi Day School. More Hopi children were being educated in American schools than at any time in the past. As pleased as he was with the schooling, Burton was more enthusiastic about Hopi involvement in the operation of trading posts and other establishments. He wrote, "There are now five stores on the reservation run entirely by Indian young men on their own capital.... *No other features of my work here has [sic] had better tendencies toward civilization*. These young men are learning to be keen traders and to compete successfully with the white man instead of cowering in servile obedience to him."[36] In 1902, after decades of work by federal and denominational representatives at Hopi, officials could count some successes as measured by American standards. But Burton was categorical that *nothing* had worked more toward civilizing Hopis than young Hopi men themselves working in the trading posts and stores. He again referred enthusiastically to these endeavors in 1904. In these young Hopi men, School Superintendent Burton believed he had finally found the ideal Hopi candidates for citizenship *and, significantly, voting*: "Several young Indians [Hopis] will vote this coming election, being able to fulfill every requirement of the law. They can read and speak well in the English language, they can hold their own in commercial pursuits, they can make a good living for themselves and their families, and why should they not vote?"[37]

Burton believed these Hopis were worthy of the vote because they could read and speak English, displayed commercial savvy, and could successfully provide for their families. These young men were likely boarding school graduates, or at the very least had attended day school at Hopi. They might also have been allottees, as this would have fulfilled the citizenship requirement. If they were not allottees, Burton felt they qualified for the franchise based on the above criteria.[38] Fortunately for the Hopis, the OIA replaced Burton the following year.[39] His dismissal makes uncovering the fate of these Hopi young men more difficult. It is possible that they in fact exercised the right to vote at that time, but they would have been the exception, as were the few Rio Grande Pueblo voters. Furthermore, whether election officials would have allowed "qualified" Hopis—through allotment or having attained a certain level of civilization—to vote is difficult to tell.

The year after Burton's dismissal, Moqui Superintendent Theodore G. Lemmon wrote, "Progress has necessarily been slow as these Indians are loath to part from old tribal customs."[40] Lemmon proved more insightful than his cursory first report suggested. In the following year, 1906, he addressed the seemingly never-ending issue of how Hopi religious practice and culture interfered with the civilizing mission directed toward these Indians: "The Hopi's religion, ceremonies, dances, and other customs pertaining to his final and future salvation are, I maintain, not of political nature or of Government concern except as any of these may interfere with good citizenship.... When the Hopi quits the earth he goes beyond the jurisdiction of the United States and beyond Government concern, and may as well belong to the missionary as to another. The Government deals with him as present or prospective citizen, and while the best Christian is probably the best citizen, his religious belief and practise is sacred so long as it does not lead him to violate a reasonable standard of public morals or personal decency."[41] He concluded, "I have faith in my ability to work to good results along lines of good citizenship, with the support of the Office, and without that no man may succeed."[42] Much has been written about the Hopis' fierce maintenance of religious practice and customs. Lemmon did not seem to particularly care about this matter, though he certainly preferred Hopi Christians. It was more important to him that Hopis be made into good U.S. citizens, a work he believed he could accomplish.

In the decades leading to Arizona statehood, many concurred with assessments by men like Charles Lummis, who believed that Hopis were of good character and could be led to citizenship peacefully. Some even argued that Hopis were already citizens of the United States. Thomas Donaldson, writing in the Eleventh Census of the United States in 1893, argued that "the Moqui Pueblos of Arizona and Pueblos of New Mexico are citizens of the United States by virtue of the laws of the Mexican republic." He referenced the Indian citizenship arguments made regarding the Treaty of Guadalupe Hidalgo. But, in terms of Hopi voting, he stated, "neither the Moqui Pueblos nor the Pueblos [of New Mexico] have exercised the right of suffrage to any extent since they became citizens of the United States. This fact should have no weight against their right of citizenship, especially in the case of the Pueblos of New Mexico. Suffrage is not a natural right; it is a privilege, and is conferred by the state. The citizen need not vote; there is no law to force him to vote; neither does he lose any rights or remedies for wrong by not voting. He can vote or not, as he likes. Thousands of American citizens do not vote, but they are citizens nevertheless."[43] In Donaldson's estimation, Hopis were citizens of the United States, since they had been classed with the Rio Grande Pueblos during Spanish and Mexican times. Although they had not voted, this fact had no bearing on their citizenship. Furthermore, the right to vote was conferred by the state, not by citizenship status alone. Hopis were thus nonvoting citizens, like their Rio Grande Pueblo neighbors to the east.

The view that Hopis were U.S. citizens seems to have been fairly common at that time. Joseph A. Munk, an Arizona doctor, rancher, and collector of books who amassed a large and important collection on Arizona history that he later donated to the University of Arizona Library, wrote in 1905 of disagreements over American education in this way: "When the school [at Keam's Canyon] was opened the requisition for a specified number of children from each pueblo was not filled until secured by force. As free citizens of the United States, being such by the treaty made with Mexico in 1848 and, indeed, already so under a system of self-government superior to our own and established long before Columbus discovered America, they naturally resented any interference in their affairs but, being in the minority and overpowered, had to submit."[44] In Munk's view, Hopis were "free citizens of the United States" under the Treaty of Guadalupe Hidalgo with inherent rights of sovereignty and self-government, who had been forced to submit to the U.S. Government. In the era of nostalgia for the "vanishing American" during which the photographer Edward S. Curtis captured Hopis and other Pueblo Indians before their feared extinctions (which, fortunately, never materialized), Munk praised the Hopi system of government. He did not comment on whether or not they were entitled to vote, but believed they certainly had the right to self-govern.

Charles Francis Saunders, a botanist who traveled through New Mexico and Arizona around the turn of the twentieth century, also wrote that Hopis were U.S. citizens. He believed that Hopis had been incorrectly considered as separate from the Rio Grande Pueblo group, and that this had damaged their rights and citizenship status. Since they were not considered Pueblo Indians, Hopis and their land received no special protection. They were simply considered "reservation Indians," like other tribes. Commenting on Pueblo Indians in general, Saunders wrote that they were "already as good citizens as their neighbour whites," which was scant consolation.[45] But as with their Rio Grande Pueblo neighbors, there is no record of Hopi clamoring for the franchise during the territorial period. Similarly, no Hopi Charles Eastman or Carlos Montezuma had emerged, and Hopis seemed largely focused on community sovereignty and continuity.

Hopis clearly had their allies among Indian advocates, but still occupied a difficult physical and political terrain in terms of citizenship and voting. Decades of aggressive efforts to civilize them had met with mixed results. In many cases, such as at Oraibi, officials dragged reluctant Hopi children to school through the cold winter snow, and even imprisoned parents and leaders who resisted these efforts. In other cases, educated young Hopi men engaged in business and commerce, appearing to Indian Service employees to be on the very cusp of voting in outside elections. Some observers saw in the Hopis an inherent right to self-govern, much like their Pueblo neighbors to the east, and still a few individuals saw Hopis as nonvoting U.S. citizens.

Whether Hopis themselves had voted or even expressed a desire to claim the franchise and other citizenship rights is difficult to determine. Small numbers of "progressive" Hopis seemingly subscribed to the American plan of civilization and assimilation, just as some individuals had at the Rio Grande Pueblos. But this would have been a distinct minority, since even those Hopis who supported schooling saw its potential as a tool to protect Hopi rights, sovereignty, and culture. No significant Hopi electorate crystalized during the territorial period. A search of Navajo County voter registrations from June 1906 to November 1911 yielded no registered Hopi voters.[46] That the Hopis maintained their ancient forms of governance and traditional lifeways throughout the territorial period and into statehood is without question. Furthermore, in their struggle with the invasive forces of assimilation that converged on their homeland, Hopis somehow managed to keep much of their traditional territory intact and their culture viable, all without a clear citizenship status that many would deem essential to securing rights in American society. Hopis did so as citizens of their own sovereign villages. Yaquis, by contrast, confronted an enemy determined to wipe them off the map. At a time when Hopis rejected citizenship and voting, Yaquis had to flee for their lives to the north, forming expatriate communities in southern Arizona. For Yaquis, the struggle for survival would mean the demise of the town-governing system in these Arizona communities, along with no possibility of either U.S. citizenship or the franchise. Such a loss of a defining feature of Yaqui political organization would have far-reaching consequences.

Yaqui Refugees in the Time of Terror

In 1909–10, the Norwegian explorer and ethnographer Carl Lumholtz undertook one of his many expeditions to Pimería Alta. Like many such adventurers of his day, Lumholtz was fascinated with "primitive" cultures. During this particular expedition, funded by the American Museum of Natural History, Lumholtz wrote briefly about his encounters with Yaquis in northern Sonora:

The State of Sonora is, as is well-known, the home of the Yaqui Indians and the scene of war for, more or less, one hundred and sixty years between these extraordinary able-bodied and very intelligent Indians and the masters of Mexico on the other hand. It is the old question occurring all over the world, whether the country belongs to the native of the soil or to the conqueror.... The Yaqui, besides their own language, speak Spanish and are Roman Catholic, although they keep up many aboriginal customs and beliefs. As miners and laborers they are preferred by Americans to Caucasians or other races. They have, which for Indians is a singular gift, great mechanical ability and learn to work machines quicker than the whites.[47]

In this relatively brief passage, Lumholtz outlined some of the major impressions of Yaquis that were in wide circulation during the territorial period: their protracted, bloody struggle with Mexican forces; their adoption of many Spanish cultural and religious elements; their maintenance of traditional Yaqui lifeways; and their reputation as skilled laborers. All these factors played a part in Yaqui political status from the 1840s through the 1910s.

More than ever, in the late nineteenth century Yaquis would become a people without a homeland in their native Sonora. Many of them would eventually find relative safety in southern Arizona, where they formed communities and revived some elements of traditional Yaqui culture. But, since they remained essentially visitors in a foreign land, U.S. officials came to view Yaquis as members of a distinct group that was separate from other Indians. They were neither citizens of the United States nor wards of the federal government. Yaquis were viewed more as akin to refugees, and in their attempt to maintain safety and anonymity in their new home they would necessarily abandon much of their fierce political independence and systems of village governance and elections. Yaquis did not transplant the sophisticated system of civil government of the eight villages along the Río Yaqui to southern Arizona. They were, in the words of historian Eric Meeks, the quintessential "border citizens," meaning "people whose rights of belonging were in question, leaving them on the margins of the national territory and of American society and culture."[48]

In the decades following the death of the Yaqui leader Juan Banderas in 1833, large landholders came to dominate Sonora under a hacienda system. These hacendados controlled the land and politics of the region, and Yaquis bitterly opposed their policies, which put Yaqui autonomy, sovereignty, and lives at risk. This hacendado politico-economic system eventually broke down in 1910 with the onset of the Mexican Revolution, but not before the powerful landholders had succeeded in killing countless Yaquis and forcing thousands of others to flee the region. In particular, during the reign of Mexican President Porfirio Díaz (1876–1911), state officials from Sonora and federal leaders teamed up to implement the Porfirian policy of "order and progress," which favored the pacification of dissenting groups, pushed economic development (in the north especially), and implemented tight control of the legal system. Hu-Dehart referred to the men who controlled Sonora state politics as a "closely-knit clique of federal generals and local civilians. The state and national power structures were so intertwined at times that it was difficult to separate the two." Perhaps the most important figure in this civilian ruling class, Ramón Corral served as governor of Sonora several times, and also rose to the vice presidency of Mexico under Díaz. Two other prominent leaders in this clique were General Luis E. Torres and a relative, General Lorenzo Torres. They arrived in Sonora from neighboring Sinaloa in 1879 to help institute the Díaz government. Corral, the two Torres men, and the civilian leader Rafael Izábel took turns serving as governor during most of the Porfiriato. Between them they essentially monopolized Sonoran political power.[49]

These leaders pursued goals that directly conflicted with Yaqui interests. They took the railroad to Sonora and opened up the state for economic exploitation by foreign firms and governments. The new railroads naturally passed through Yaqui lands. They also reopened the region to mining, which had lain dormant for years. Historically, there had been many mines on Yaqui lands worked by Yaqui miners. Much of the investment capital for these new railroad and mining ventures came from the United States, as Díaz desperately sought to inject foreign investments into the heavily indebted Mexican economy. Furthermore, Mexican officials pushed for agricultural development in Sonora. Yaqui land was the best in the state, and the Indians would thus need to be dispossessed or eliminated if their land was to be properly "utilized."[50] In order to subdue the Yaquis, the Sonoran and federal governments tried legal maneuvers, military campaigns, offers of land, and, finally, deportation and even extermination.

While the historiography, both in Spanish and English, relating to important political and social developments during this period in Mexican history—and even how they relate to Yaquis—is rather broad, this summary will be relatively brief. As Hu-DeHart aptly described:

> For three-quarters of the nineteenth century, the chaotic, divisive and problem-torn state of Sonora was unable to dominate the Yaquis. In a series of civil wars in Sonora, they became the allies of any side that would

promise them autonomy and independence in the Yaqui Valley. Thus they were found fighting alongside the Federalists, the Centralists, the Liberals and even the French Imperialists. Although they were merely used by these various political factions as a fighting force, their active participation contributed to the instability and impotency of the state government. For most of this period the Yaquis enjoyed a *de facto* independence, and were able to keep incursions into the Yaqui territory at a minimum.[51]

The chaotic and violent second half of the nineteenth century saw a number of prominent Yaqui leaders in the tradition of Muni, Bernabé, and Banderas. One such leader was José María Leyva, commonly known by his Yaqui name, Cajeme (*he who does not drink water*). Born in Hermosillo in 1837, Cajeme spent part of his youth in California, where his family unsuccessfully sought their fortune in the gold fields. He later became a soldier in the Mexican Army, fighting in various conflicts against enemies that included French filibusterers, and fighting both for and against Emperor Maximilian von Hapsburg. He even took up arms against other Yaquis.[52]

By 1872, federal officials had appointed Cajeme—who had distinguished himself as a soldier under the Mexican flag—as first alcalde of the eight Yaqui villages, or the chief Mexican official in the zone. They saw Cajeme as an important piece in finally solving the "Yaqui problem." But in 1875 Cajeme murdered the Yaqui Captain General Julio Mayoroqui (known by the nickname "El Jaguali," or "the harelip"), and declared himself captain general. He initiated a revolt against the Mexicans, proclaiming himself "head of the Yaqui nation."[53] It could be argued that this was one of Cajeme's early flaws: he violated the traditional basis of power in the eight villages—the governors, civil leaders, and religious society heads—and tried to consolidate political and military power with himself as figurehead. Cajeme was accused of self-interest and nepotism, but as Spicer pointed out, he apparently learned his lesson (unlike Banderas before him): "Once he learned that he had to accept a position subordinate to the civil government, he began to develop an effective working relationship, and his enthusiasm spread among young and old." By 1884 Cajeme's reorganization of the Yaquis proceeded at a rapid pace.[54]

Ramón Corral, Sonora governor-turned-vice president, became Cajeme's biographer while the defeated Yaqui leader awaited trail and execution in his last days. He linked Cajeme's success to this political reorientation, writing that Cajeme had "organized the towns with their Governors, Alcaldes, Captains and

Temastians," and, "for resolutions that affected the common interests of the tribe, he established a system of popular assemblies that met every time he believed it necessary to consult them on some matter." The Yaqui assemblies consisted of "all of the Indians in general," and they did not meet at a regularly fixed time and place. Instead, Cajeme, "through the town governors, convened the meeting at a determined location, and exposed the business which needed to be addressed and put it before the resolution of the crowd." Cajeme thus cultivated a sense of Yaqui nationhood, one that was contingent on the civil governing structure. Corral also pointed out that "The administration of justice in each town was in the hands of the alcaldes and governors." Power thus remained firmly with the civil leaders.[55] Yaquis flocked back to Cajeme's flag from cities such as Hermosillo and Guaymas, hoping that the decades of Yaqui dispersal were at an end, and that they would finally achieve their dream of complete autonomy. From his rise to power until his capture and execution in 1887, Cajeme defeated numerous Mexican foes, including officers under whom he had fought.[56]

Cajeme's demise opened the door for other Yaqui leaders to fill the void, and Yaqui resistance fighters waged a protracted guerilla campaign. The Yaqui Juan Maldonado, known as Tetabiate, led guerilla forces after Cajeme's death. Yaquis hid in the mountains—particularly the sacred Becatete Mountains—and the surrounding countryside, mixing with noncombatant Yaqui ranchers and farmers. Skilled Yaqui guerilla fighters eluded detection and capture time and again. In 1897, after a decade of fighting, a pragmatic Tetabiate attempted to negotiate with Luis E. Torres's Sonoran state government. The "Peace of Ortiz," as it was called, included quite a bit of pomp and circumstance, calling to memory the incident at the Pótam jail in 1736, when Yaqui forces successfully forced Spanish jailers to release Muni and Bernabé.[57] Four hundred Yaquis reportedly turned up for the ceremony. The official Act of Submission, which Torres himself drew up, included a number of guarantees for the Yaquis. Mexican officials promised Tetabiate and his companions that both they and their property would be protected, and the government offered those who had been displaced in the hostilities new lands on the Río Yaqui. The government also promised to supply these men and their families with some animals and provisions for a period of two months, while they readjusted to life in the villages.[58] Díaz had expressed his desire to see every Yaqui behind a plow, and Mexican officials believed that this peace would help make that vision a reality. But Yaquis understood the peace quite differently. They believed that the document guaranteed their autonomy, and that federal soldiers would finally leave the Yaqui River Valley.[59]

Interestingly, at no point does the Act of Submission mention village politics or elections. Muni and Bernabé had traveled to Mexico City to secure, among other things, express guarantees of autonomy in town politics. By the late 1890s, Tetabiate and his followers were fighting for their very survival. While they must have hoped to keep town structures intact, one can only imagine the disruptions caused by the constant warfare. Still, Spicer stated that the annual elections of town officers continued, and while town life "may have been constricted and even choked off at the peak of the conflict . . . the Yaquis' memories of what town life had been like were not far in the background." This was one of the great ironies of the Yaqui-Mexican conflict. Yaquis fully believed in the superiority of their system of town governance. Yet their town governments had elements in common with other Mexican towns of the time, such as elections aimed at the transfer of office without military force. Yaquis also appeared selectively open to the incorporation of elements of Mexican society,[60] as evidenced by opportunistic transnational leaders like Cajeme. While their incorporation into the Mexican political sphere would have certainly meant Yaqui land losses, it also could have potentially led to Yaqui participation in regional politics and coalition-building. But as was consistently the case with Indigenous peoples of New Mexico and Arizona, Yaquis flatly rejected such participation. Through continued resistance to Mexican control, and their maintenance of town politics—even if only by keeping the memory alive—Yaquis actively resisted Sonoran or Mexican citizenship. Instead, they focused on citizenship in the sovereign Yaqui community.

Unfortunately, Tetabiate's peace was short-lived. Since both sides had misunderstood the intentions of the other form the very beginning, fighting resumed in 1899–1900. Mexican soldiers relentlessly pursued Yaqui holdouts into the Becatete Mountains, and at the battle of Mazocaba on 18 January 1900, Tetabiate's army suffered a crushing defeat. Federal troops killed more than four hundred Yaquis and took eight hundred prisoners. The Díaz government considered the Yaqui campaign to be closed by the summer of 1901.[61] Although Tetabiate survived the Battle of Mazocaba, he was eventually killed in the summer of 1901. U.S. news outlets took note of Tetabiate's death, as it signaled a shift in the Yaqui wars, and potentially an end to the violence that had gripped northern Sonora and occasionally spilled over into the United States. The 31 July 1901 *Los Angeles Herald* reported, "Tetabiate, the formidable warrior chief of the Yaquis, was ambushed and slain several days ago near Potam, Mexico. The victory of the Mexican troops has caused general rejoicing throughout that portion of Mexico lying east of Guaymas, and it is considered by all that the Yaquis, the bravest and most intelligent race of Indians that ever trod on

Mexican soil, have made their last stand." Another portion of the short piece pointed to a change in Mexican policy in dealings with Yaquis: "All [Yaquis], whether peaceful or hostile, who have been captured since the commencement of the rebellion, have been sent to Yucatan, on the east coast of Mexico.... The general policy is to get the Yaquis out of their native country."[62] While pockets of Yaqui resisters remained in the mountains, the government undertook what it considered the final solution to the Yaqui problem. Sonoran Governor Rafael Izábel, with federal support, spearheaded a policy of deportation during the first decade of the twentieth century. In the simplest terms, Yaquis were made to pay dearly for maintaining sovereignty during decades of resistance.[63]

Before turning to Yaqui deportation, it is important to underscore the remarkable fortitude shown by Yaquis in their fight to protect sovereign rights. Manuel Balbás, a Mexican medical doctor who had lived among the Yaquis while serving as an army surgeon in the Yaqui campaigns of 1899–1901, recorded many of his observations on Yaqui life on the eve of the mass deportations. He wrote that numerous Yaquis still remained outside Mexican control, stating that "These Yaqui towns remain at present in the same state of abandonment and backwardness in which they must have been before the conquest. One meets in them not a single detail of civilization." Furthermore, he reported that few Yaquis spoke Spanish, and "Among them there exist no schools and the few which there are in the region have been established by the government, which has not concerned itself sufficiently with this point, the most important among all the problems of the Yaqui." Still, he conceded, "The intelligence of the Yaquis is perhaps superior to that of all the other Indians of the country." His most revealing comments, though, referred to Yaqui self-government at that time:

> The form of government of the tribe is very rudimentary; it reduces itself to arming among themselves with no more formula than the opinion of whatever group (meets together) a chief who almost always has the double character of governor and military [officer].
>
> This chief remains in his post the whole time [during] which his ascendancy among the Indian lasts. If the dominance which he exercises is great, either for his bravery, for his strength, or for his audacity, he can remain many years [in office]. But if he shows the slightest weakness, they remove him immediately.
>
> They have various chiefs or "governors," according to the towns that they live in, although among all these chiefs they always recognize one as the superior.

The "governors" dispense justice, aided by a council formed of the eldest men of the people.

The decisions of this council are final, conforming with true religiosity, from punishment by whipping to the penalty of death. Generally the sentences of the council are just.[64]

Remarkably, Yaquis still retained much of the old Yaqui-Spanish system of democratic town government. At the turn of the twentieth century, Yaquis continued to hold elections and meet in governing councils. Unfortunately, the deportations and disruptions of the first decade of the twentieth century were so severe that these tried-and-tested institutions would finally break for a time, and would not be revived in the Yaqui communities of southern Arizona.

After suffering through years of brutal military campaigns and the subsequent state-sanctioned diaspora, Yaquis became "the most widely scattered native people in North America."[65] The preferred destination for Yaquis was the henequen (agave) plantations of Yucatán, far to the south. The deportation figures differ, depending on the source. One put the number of Yaquis deported to Yucatán between 1903 and 1908 at two thousand,[66] while a source from the period posited a much higher number. The U.S. author and reporter John Kenneth Turner traveled to Yucatán and published an exposé on the Yaqui deportations in 1910. Posing as a rich investor, he found the conditions there deplorable, with rich landowners controlling huge numbers of laborers. Turner claimed that there were "8,000 Yaqui Indians imported from Sonora, 3,000 Chinese (Koreans), and between 100,000 and 125,000 native Mayans, who formerly owned the lands that the henequen kings now own." He also claimed that planters paid the government $65 for every Yaqui deported. He had scathing words for "President Diaz's sweeping order of deportation": "The Yaquis are being exterminated and exterminated fast. There is no room for controversy as to that; the only controversy relates to whether or not the Yaquis deserve to be exterminated.... The extermination of the Yaquis began in war; its finish is being accomplished in deportation and slavery."[67] While the number of deportees may be debatable, there is no question that the government pursued the policy with gusto. General Torres concluded, "I don't see any other solution for these *indios*." While many Yaquis had been forced into work camps on the haciendas of Sonora in a form of peonage, numerous Yaquis still held out in the remote mountain fastnesses. Any Yaqui under the slightest suspicion of aiding the fighters or showing sympathies for the cause was rounded up and deported. Whole families were shipped south.[68] This represented the nadir of modern Yaqui history: extermination, deportation, and slavery.

By 1910, the Yaqui diaspora was so widespread that the types of Yaqui communities that had once dotted the Río Yaqui until the latter part of the nineteenth century had largely ceased to exist. Total Yaqui international population was still perhaps as high as 15,000, although they were dispersed widely throughout Mexico and the United States. Many were in Yucatán, while others lived in barrios in southern California. Some even took up residence at Zuni Pueblo. But the most famous Yaqui refugees were those who formed communities in southern Arizona. By 1887, when Cajeme was executed, a group of Yaquis had already established a community across the international border on the outskirts of Nogales. They worked on the railroads linking the mines with Tucson. They also passed through the Altar Valley and into the Baboquivari Mountains. It was not uncommon for Yaquis to even find refuge among Tohono O'odhams as they migrated to southern Arizona, and a high degree of cultural exchange and even some intermarriage took place between these two peoples.[69] Since the United States did not patrol the border during the first decade of the twentieth century, no official Yaqui immigration numbers are available. But by 1910 at least five Yaqui communities existed in southern Arizona: Nogalitos (on the outskirts of Nogales), Mezquital (south of Tucson on the east bank of the Santa Cruz River), Barrio Anita (on the Santa Cruz in the northern part of Tucson), Tierra Floja (a large farming area north of Tucson), and Guadalupe (south of Phoenix in present-day Tempe on the Salt River).[70]

The Yaquis who went to Arizona did so out of necessity. Their lives were no longer safe in Mexico, so crossing into the United States offered relative protection from death, deportation, slavery, and peonage. Octaviana Valenzuela Trujillo, a former chairwoman of the Pascua Yaqui Tribe, stated that many Yaquis were forced "clandestinely across the U.S. border into Arizona and into a life of self-imposed exile ... [which at least saved them] from the threat of annihilation." She also commented that the cultural adaptations that had characterized Yaqui life in Mexico continued in Arizona: "By the time the Yaqui began to migrate across the border into the United States in the late 1800s, their lifeways had undergone drastic changes from earlier times. Cultural adaptations continued as small Yaqui communities were established in Arizona." While Yaqui oral tradition tells of their presence in Arizona since "time immemorial," the "major migration of the historical era came during the years 1900 to 1910."[71] Yaquis soon came to inhabit a unique place in Arizona's cultural landscape.

Fearing the same violence that Mexico had perpetrated against them in Sonora and elsewhere, Yaquis acted with caution in Arizona. Many had changed their identities while hiding in Mexico. The common Yaqui surname "Husacamea" became "Valenzuela," for example.[72] As Trujillo pointed out, fear led Yaquis in Arizona to operate "primarily within their own microcosmic cultural enclave as a defense mechanism to the perceived threat of deportation." Part of this retrenchment included the outward suppression of Yaqui identity, language, and religious practices. Continuing the lessons Yaquis had learned in Mexico, "They had as little contact as possible with government officials so that nearly fifteen years passed before the Yaquis became aware that they had been afforded political asylum, and that in the United States religious freedom was upheld regardless of political or social status."[73] Yaquis were less politically organized during this time, as well.

Yaqui refugees who crossed over into Arizona in the late 1800s and early 1900s left a number of written accounts. One comes from Rosalio Moisés, whose grandfather had fought by Cajeme's side and whose father crossed over into Arizona in 1904 and then brought the family into Arizona the following year. In his autobiography, Moisés related that many of his mother's relatives were killed at the massacre that followed Tetabiate's defeat at Mazocaba. His family was working at the Colorada Mine in Sonora, when "Mexican soldiers came from Hermosillo to tell all Yaqui men they had to register with the government [for work at the haciendas]. From this time on, our lives changed." When Moisés finally crossed into Arizona with his family, an "American inspector" questioned the group. He asked for letters of recommendation, but they had none. Moisés's grandmother told the inspector that she was taking the group to her son, who was already in Tucson. He asked for the son's name, and they told him it was Miguel Valenzuela. He had changed the family name while still in Mexico to avoid detection and identification as a Yaqui.[74] Fortunately, Moisés and his family found relative safety and anonymity in the United States.

Some of Moisés's more interesting comments refer to relations between Yaquis and other groups, and with U.S. authorities in particular. As Trujillo stated, Yaquis avoided contact with government officials at all costs, and one episode from Moisés's life illustrates this fear. He told the story of a Yaqui man who caught his sixteen-year-old daughter talking to a boy by the river. The man, Juan Buichileme, was so angry at his daughter's impropriety that he beat her severely. She died one week later. Moisés stated, "No one ever reported this to the American police because no one spoke English." A fear of government officials, coupled with the language barrier, caused Yaquis to refrain even from reporting murders. Moisés and his family lived in Barrio Anita on the outskirts of Tucson, on land owned by a certain "Mr. Nash." On a number of occasions,

Moisés's family provided assistance to Yaqui guerillas in Sonora, even participating in military actions. They received frequent visits from a Yaqui general based in the Sierra who sometimes stayed for months at a time. It was a truly transnational setting, with Yaquis from Sonora coming to buy arms, ammunition, and supplies in Tucson, and then transporting them, along with Yaqui fighters, back to Mexico on horseback. At one point in 1912 Moisés's father bought a .30-30 rifle and three ammunition belts, then returned to Sonora to fight. In Moisés's words, "He was very happy."[75]

Refugio Savala was another of the Arizona Yaqui refugees. Around 1900, before Refugio's birth, his family, accompanying a donkey cart, slowly plodded north through Sonora to safety. He was born in 1904 in the town of Magdalena, which has served for generations as a destination for O'odham and Yaqui Catholic pilgrims, south of the international border. His grandparents had fled to the mountains to escape deportation to Yucatán, and his father "drifted to Arizona to work on the Benson-Nogales branch of the Southern Pacific Railroad." As in the case of Rosalio Moisés, Savala's father returned from Arizona to Sonora to retrieve the family: "He brought good news to our people about himself and other Yaquis who had accompanied him on his first trip and about the opportunities to work freely for a good wage. Many Yaquis, learning of this, started drifting on their way north." More than any other commentator on the Yaqui refugees, Savala, who was a poet by trade, perfectly encapsulated Yaqui motivations: "The Yaquis did not go to Arizona because of ambition or to seek riches, but went in search of peace and freedom and to escape from heartless killers. We hail the Southern Pacific for having provided all these Yaqui refugees shelter, wage work, and food." Refugio Savala's life is a testament to the resilient, transnational borderlands nature of Yaqui existence at that time: he worked in Tucson and Yuma, Arizona; Deming, New Mexico; California; and a number of other locations.[76]

The Yaqui deportation policy officially ended in 1910, with the advent of the Mexican Revolution. Yaquis also participated in this struggle, with many fighting for Álvaro Obregón, President of Mexico from 1920 to 1924. By this time Yaquis could again live a relatively secure life in Mexico, and many returned, although the violence in Mexico was not over. The Yaqui communities in southern Arizona were there to stay.[77] Rosalio Moisés, Refugio Savala, their families, and other Yaqui refugees inhabited some of the more unusual towns then in existence in the United States. Although several Yaqui communities were situated in southern Arizona, and there were areas of Yaqui settlement elsewhere, the community of Pascua on the outskirts of Tucson, and Guadalupe in Tempe, are particularly instructive to understanding Yaqui political sta-

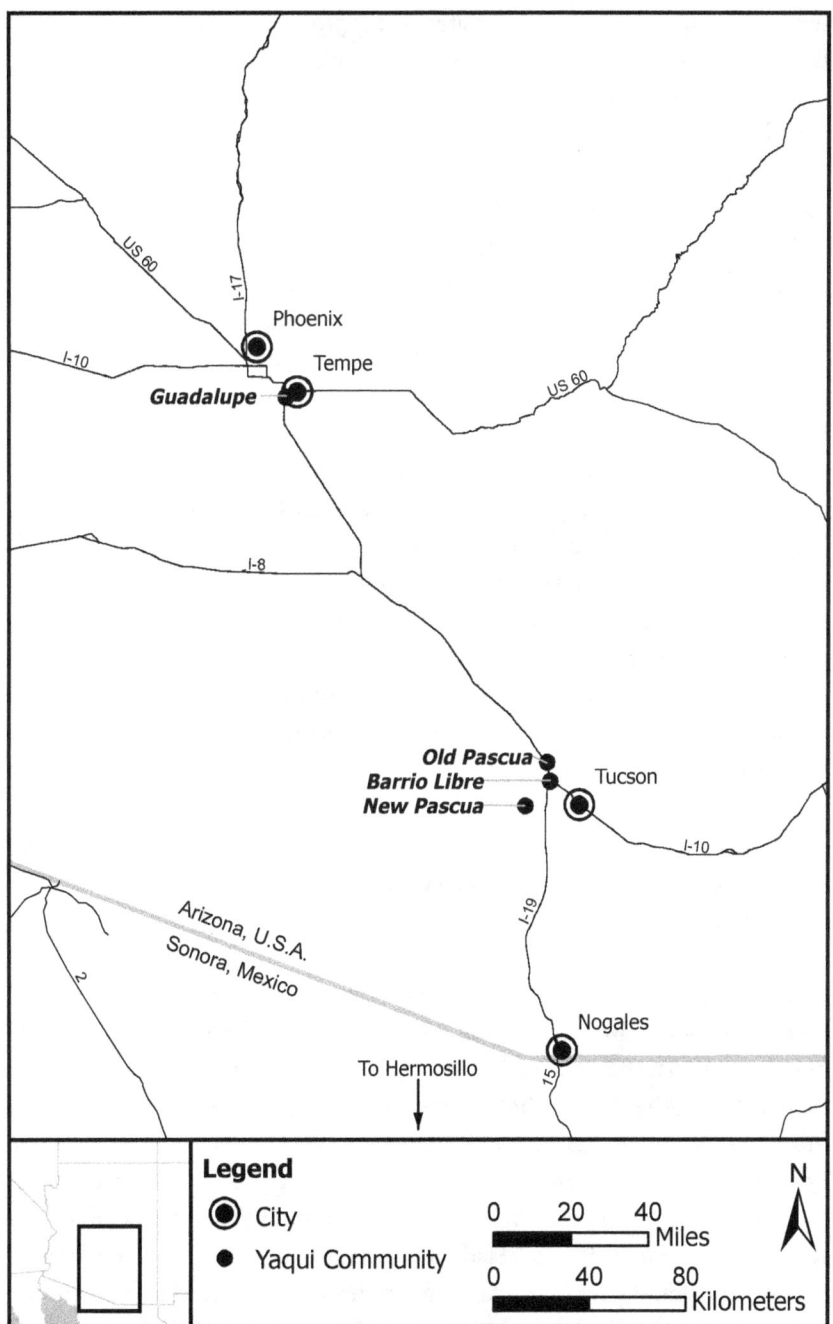

Southern Arizona Yaqui communities. Map by Alex Ochoa.

tus and voting rights as Arizona statehood approached in the first years of the twentieth century. These Yaqui refugees were encountering a non-Hispanic culture and form of government for the first time in their history. As they adjusted to this new, transnational existence, their tendency was to turn inward, seeking to preserve both traditional and Yaqui-Spanish lifeways that had sustained them in Sonora for nearly three hundred years.

Edward Spicer, who spent many years living and researching in the Yaqui village of Pascau in the middle of the twentieth century (and who remains one of the foremost experts on Arizona Yaquis), summed up their political status at that time: "The Yaqui population of Arizona consists of immigrants from the Mexican state of Sonora and their descendants. Other than those born in the United States, there are few, if any, citizens of the United States. The immigrant basis of the population has entered this country at various times from 1882 to the present. As early as 1904 there was a settlement of Yaquis at a place called Guadalupe, about seven miles east of Phoenix."[78] Many Yaqui mothers in Arizona, such as Refugio Savala's, returned to ancestral towns in Sonora for the births of their children, further diminishing Yaqui births in the United States—and the number of potential citizens—around the turn of the twentieth century. The vast majority of Yaquis in southern Arizona were simply not U.S. citizens. Furthermore, Spicer elaborated that they did not behave as citizens: "It is a rare Yaqui who has the sort of stake in his community that goes with the ownership of immovable property. Yaquis do not ordinarily own the land they live on, nor do they have even the well-established connection with it that comes from paying rent. The typical Yaqui is a squatter."[79]

While they may have been squatters, they did form connections to the lands on which they lived. Their squatter status was largely through no fault of their own. At the same time, Yaquis had no reservation, and thus were not viewed as Indians similar to Apaches, Tohono O'odhams, or Hopis: "They are marked off thus from other Indians in their own and in Anglo-American eyes." When Spicer conducted his research at Pascua, he estimated that "90 percent of the heads of Yaqui families are not citizens of the United States. This means that this proportion has been born in Mexico and has not become or signified intention of becoming citizens." Had they expressed a desire to become citizens, the process would have been extremely complicated. According to immigration guidelines enforced in Arizona during the first half of the twentieth century, all persons who entered from Mexico before 1924 and had no papers were in the United States illegally. But they could not be deported because "there [was] no legal provision for starting deportation charges." They needed first to return to Mexico and then reenter the United States legally in order to become citizens.[80]

As if this were not complicated enough, Spicer recognized that a large number of Yaquis in Arizona by the 1940s were U.S. citizens by virtue of having been born in Arizona. But this was not the case in the first decade of the twentieth century. In addition, there was the issue of Yaquis born in Mexico, who entered the United States in the first half of the twentieth century and decided to apply for citizenship. If they declared that they were Yaqui Indians, then they could be denied citizenship because the Arizona constitution itself denied citizenship rights—namely, voting—to all persons "under guardianship, non compos mentis or insane." Indians living on reservations in Arizona were considered wards under the guardianship of the federal government, and thus could not vote.[81] But since Yaquis had no reservation, were they truly federal wards? Furthermore, if on entering the United States they simply declared themselves Mexicans, then theoretically they *could* have become citizens and voted. Spicer asserted unequivocally, "Up to 1940 there had been no record of a Yaqui attempting to register for the purpose of voting in an election, at least a Yaqui who called himself a Yaqui in his registration. There seem as yet no evident advantages as recognized by Yaquis in citizenship except that of freedom from fear of deportation, which is one of the ever-recurrent fears among Arizona Yaquis."[82]

Spicer's assertion that no Yaquis attempted to vote before 1940—at least not without "passing" as ethnic Mexicans—seems bold, but the theme of Yaqui political nonparticipation motivated by fear is also supported by former Pasqua Yaqui chairwoman Octaviana Valenzuela Trujillo.[83] Spicer noted in 1937, "There are many Yaquis in Tucson who do not admit that they are Yaqui. They live apart from the other Yaquis and do not go to Yaqui fiestas. They say that they are Mexican."[84] As the anthropologist George Pierre Castile succinctly stated, "Fearing deportation, few Yaqui appear to have put their status to the test by attempting to claim civil rights, such as the vote, which was not granted to Indians in Arizona until 1948."[85]

Regardless of their political status in the United States, Yaqui transplants found work wherever they could: railroads, smelters, mines, and irrigated farms. They made permanent settlements largely according to the work patterns they established. These settlements were constructed around a plaza with a church, a communal kitchen for preparing food for religious celebrations, and a ramada (an open shelter roofed with branches) for Pascola and Deer dances. Leadership in these early communities fell to officers in the religious organizations of the Yaqui communities that predated the diaspora.[86] In the towns of southern Arizona, Yaquis did not transplant the Yaqui-Spanish governor system. They did not institute annual elections or establish the same town officers and systems of government. There are several reasons for this. For one, as Trujillo pointed out, the town that refugees established at Guadalupe around the turn of the century was a "small one-square-mile desert settlement" that was more akin to a "refugee camp, an innocuous cluster of extremely humble dwellings on the lightly populated Valley's periphery." Their location on the periphery was "symbolic of the Yaquis' lack of cultural and social integration in their new homeland."[87] These refugees, worn out from years of fighting, hiding, and a long journey to a new and unfamiliar place, focused primarily on survival. Complex, strident political institutions along with assertions of sovereignty were simply out of the question at that particular historical moment.

Furthermore, as Trujillo indicated, "Most Yaquis came to the United States as individuals without any kin or social grouping to help them survive. Usually they were unrelated individuals who had fallen in with one another. During the early years of residence in Arizona, they gradually developed new family groupings through reunion of separated families and the starting of new families. Ritual kin groups, based on baptismal godparents and ceremonial sponsors, further extended the basic family organization."[88] This is another critical observation. At various points in their history, Yaquis had felt a strong sense of nationhood and a collective struggle for a Yaqui Nation. But Yaqui political identity was much more closely tied to village identity. Yaquis identified as citizens of Bácum, or Ráum, or Cócorit, and they tied their allegiance to local, elected civil officials. Since the Yaquis who fled to the United States were "without kin or social grouping," that sense of village identity would have blurred. Yaquis would have remembered their individual villages, but reconstituting the traditional village civil government would likely have been difficult among refugees hailing from multiple communities. Finally, many residents of Arizona Yaqui settlements did not reside there full time. They worked on railroad lines or at mines far away from their settlements and families, returning for special ceremonies or to visit families.[89] A stable leadership corps of elected men would have been nearly impossible to achieve under such transitory employment and settlement patterns. These three factors, among others, combined to stymie the reestablishment of Yaqui democratic civil government and voting in Arizona.

At Guadalupe, for example, we can observe these issues at play in its early history. Around the turn of the twentieth century Yaquis established a community in Tempe when railroads first began connecting the area's farms to larger markets. Railroad companies and large farming enterprises needed cheap, reliable labor, and Yaquis ably filled this need. Canals made fields in this area particularly fertile, and the railroads brought their crops to market. After their arrival in the area in the 1880s in the wake of the Cajeme wars, some thirty Yaquis established ties with Franciscans, who helped secure five acres of homestead land for the Indians in 1898 for a single dollar. They named their newborn village after their homeland's patron saint, Nuestra Señora de Guadalupe. Initially, Guadalupe's Yaquis considered themselves temporary, but by 1906, they had come to understand themselves as refugees. This meant that the United States had no plans to extradite them, so they initiated a cultural revival. This revival mostly centered on the church and religious celebrations and dances. As explained by the historian Leah S. Glaser, who wrote extensively on the history of Guadalupe, "Yaqui communities did not develop the same types of social or political institutions as other immigrant groups, including Mexicans."[90] Spicer concurred on the lack of political development among the Arizona Yaquis, stating in 1940 that two of the Arizona Yaqui villages had attempted to set up some form of village political organization, but, according to his observations, "none has any purely political government. . . . Village organization is entirely in terms of the ceremonial groups."[91]

This not to say that the Yaquis in communities such as Pascua and Guadalupe were wholly without political organization during the territorial period. While they generally lacked access to U.S. citizenship, or failed to claim such a status as Yaquis, they did have some form of political organization. As Spicer wrote of Pascua in 1967, "The founders of Pascua brought not only religious and social traditions, but also the genius for organization and the spirit of independence which marked their ancestors in Mexico." These traits had "given the distinctive character to Yaqui life in Arizona and have provided the foundations on which rest their present efforts to develop their community."[92] What form this organization took is difficult to decipher. Dane Coolidge, an American reporter who visited Guadalupe in 1909, reported on a town election for a "captain." He wrote, "The *pueblo* of Guadalupe, duly organized, has elected its *capitan*, a ruler and leader among the people, half a chief and half a mayor, the *Jefe politico* of the Mexicans. If you would succeed in your desires, whether it be to see the church or hire a ditch cleaner, call on the *capitan* first, for his good will carries with it that of the whole village, and his word is law among the people. The *capitan* at Guadalupe is a Mayo Indian, near neighbor and kindred to the Yaqui in Sonora, Teodoro Ramos, a man of great force of character and of tremendous physical strength. He has been in Arizona since 1886 and is an example of the peaceful Indian, driven from Sonora by the long years of war."[93] This raises the possibility that Arizona's Yaqui refugee communities

Pascua Yaqui Deer Dancer, n.d. Bonaventure Oblasser, O.F.M. Collection, 1901–1977 MS 543, box 10, folder 13, courtesy of University of Arizona Libraries, Special Collections.

also included other Indigenous Mexicans. But what form this election for capitan took is difficult to determine.

Spicer also reported on some rudimentary political organization at Pascua in the 1930s, and the *maestro* (a lay reader in the church) in particular. But Spicer's Yaqui informant, Lucas Chaves, told him that the maestro (Chaves was one himself) at Pascua "does not participate in politics because he is afraid. This is a result of the fear developed in all Yaquis to reveal themselves as such during their residence in Sonora."[94] His fears were justified. An official publication of the State of Sonora from the first decade of the twentieth century described Yaquis as having an "inextinguishable hatred" for the white race, and stated that "Such a race must sooner or later disappear, and the sooner the better."[95] Furthermore, Chaves was clear: "There is no elected group of old men at Pascua now." He spoke of the need "for someone to bring the people together into unity." They had not elected such a leader, "yet."[96] Thus, while there seems to have been some form of loose governing structure in the Arizona Yaqui towns before statehood,[97] a Yaqui-Spanish system was not in place, nor did Yaquis participate in outside elections. The Yaqui electorate in Arizona was restricted to this rudimentary town organization whose parameters are still difficult to define.

Yaquis engaged in deeper discussions about village government in the 1920s and after, and some favored re-creating the structures of civil government from the Yaqui Valley. But they eventually concluded that since there was no actual Yaqui land to manage—Yaquis did not own the land on which they resided—and since federal and state officials already fulfilled the functions of the old officers, they should not try to completely reestablish their traditional posts.[98] From the first Yaqui refugees in the 1880s through statehood, Yaquis remained noncitizens in Arizona. In addition to this status, Yaquis had no reservation. They lacked the Indian status of other Indigenous nations in both Arizona and New Mexico. Not only could they not vote in municipal and territorial elections like other Indians, but also, because of disruptions caused by decades of warfare and forced diaspora, they no longer possessed many of their previous governing structures. Among all the Indian groups of Arizona and New Mexico, the Yaqui right to vote had perhaps seen the most interruptions, culminating in limited sovereignty even on the village level for the Yaquis of southern Arizona. The Tohono O'odhams, with whom the Yaquis shared cultural ties, would face challenges to their own sovereignty, as well. Yet Tohono O'odhams, much like the Hopis and the Pueblos, failed to embrace the franchise, preferring instead to participate in their own internal forms of governance. Such a refusal was a luxury the Yaquis did not possess.

Tohono O'odhams and the Franchise in Territorial Arizona

Two O'odham groups, in particular, stand out because of their long history of interaction with the U.S. government and its agents: Tohono O'odhams and Akimel O'odhams. Descended from various groups, including Sobaipuris who originally inhabited the missions, and the later "desert Pimas" or Papagos—as Spaniards referred to them—who increasingly moved to the mission in the late Spanish and Mexican periods, Tohono O'odhams endured some of the longest and most sustained interaction with government officials during the territorial period. I will refer almost exclusively to the Tohono O'odhams of San Xavier del Bac, with occasional references to Akimel O'odhams (Gila River Pimas) and Piipaash (Maricopas) and to how they interacted with the government officials who largely dictated the development of O'odham political incorporation.[99] More than Hopis and Yaquis, San Xavier Tohono O'odhams came closest to the ideal of voting American Indian citizens. But they would also ultimately fall short in this regard, as citizen Tohono O'odhams never embraced the franchise in significant numbers.

The instability and turmoil of the Mexican period resulted in extreme neglect of O'odham peoples and lands. A number of Catholic missions had once dotted O'odham territory, but an independent Mexico mired in internal problems could no longer fully fund the presidios and missions of Pimería Alta. This drastically affected those O'odhams who had previously been attached to the missions, as they increasingly found themselves at the front line of the decades-long war against surging Apaches. Even so, as the historian Winston P. Erickson has pointed out in his work, "The O'odham were not concerned with the problems of Mexican politicians most of the time."[100] The abandonment of the missions during the Mexican period adversely affected O'odhams because the missions, in spite of their troubled history, had often served to protect Indian rights guaranteed under Spanish and Mexican law. When the church placed the missions in the hands of civilian administrators in the 1830s, these administrators liquidated much of the valuable property, sold or consumed mission livestock, and generally drove O'odhams from mission lands through their abusive treatment. These policies effectively destroyed the tenuous mission system and imperiled the Mexican towns surrounding them. O'odhams further retreated to desert and mountain hideouts to avoid incursions by Apaches as well as by Mexican settlers.[101] Thus, when the United States began to exert control over Tohono O'odham lands in the 1840s and 1850s, American authorities encountered a people with *centuries* of experience in dealing with government and church officials. Tohono O'odhams had seen these dealings diminish significantly over the course of the previous decades, while experiencing a simultaneous increase in encroachments by Mexican settlers. Hemmed in on all sides, Tohono O'odhams had essentially been forced to hold their own against a veritable invasion of squatters and Apaches.

With the ratification of the Gadsden Treaty in 1854, the United States "acquired" the homelands of thousands of O'odham peoples. The treaty also split Tohono O'odhams into two groups living on different sides of an international boundary. Several decades passed before the revised U.S.-Mexico border was strictly enforced, and Tohono O'odhams on both sides maintained strong ties into the early twentieth century, and continue to do so today, in spite of the challenges imposed by the border. In addition, many of the Mexican Tohono O'odhams, who probably numbered no more than 1,000 individuals, began moving north as more Mexicans moved onto the best lands along the Altar River, much as they had done to Yaquis along the Río Yaqui. Erickson summarized: "Life for the O'odham continued much as it had. A new government meant little to them." O'odhams simply "remained at peace with whatever government they had to deal with."[102] A Tohono O'odham calendar stick—calendars that recorded important village or tribal events on an annual basis—dating from 1841–1939 did not even record the war between the United States and Mexico.[103]

While Mexico considered the Indigenous peoples of Pimería Alta citizens of the republic with all the rights of citizenship, their attempts to incorporate O'odhams were halting and had never truly gained traction. After the U.S.-Mexico War and the Gadsden Purchase, Anglo-American influence did grow in Papaguería (the Tohono O'odham homeland). But unlike some other Native groups, they never received the protection of their land and liberties guaranteed almost a decade earlier under the Treaty of Guadalupe Hidalgo.[104] As Erickson pointed out, "The O'odham had few or no rights as the intruding Anglos took whatever they wanted and ignored the rights of native peoples." Since O'odhams still lived in a communal manner, intruding settlers and government officials alike assumed that sparsely populated O'odham lands without proper documentation were ripe for settlement. Since O'odhams were not hostile, did not fight against the U.S. Army, and did not raid American settlements, the United States saw no need to send troops in order to protect their land, interests, or rights. Quite simply, "the federal government basically ignored the O'odham and their rights."[105]

Agents of the U.S. government thus began their dealings with O'odhams in a subdued manner. During the early years of the U.S. administration of Pimería Alta, the two sides tried to feel one another out, as it were, and to understand each other's characteristics and intentions. O'odhams began to appear in official reports sent from New Mexico Territory to the Commissioner of Indian Affairs in the middle of the 1850s. New Mexico Governor David Meriwether, who oversaw dealings with these O'odhams, sent what sparse information he had gathered to the commissioner in 1856:

> From the most reliable information in my possession, we have acquired, by the Gadsden treaty with Mexico, about five thousand Indians in addition

to those heretofore under the charge of this superintendency. A large portion of this accession to our Indian population consists of Pueblos, situated near Tucson.... These recently acquired Pueblo Indians are represented to me as being in a similar state of civilization as the other Pueblos of this Territory. They reside in permanent villages, have comfortable houses built of adobes, have flocks and herds around them, and rely upon the cultivation of the soil for a subsistence—raising wheat, corn, cotton, and other vegetables. They are divided into six pueblos, or villages, but whether or not they hold their lands under grants from the former governments of their country I am not informed; but presume that they do, as they have been permanently settled for a great number of years.[106]

Since Meriwether never actually visited Pimería Alta, he based his information on accounts from military officers and others who had traveled through southern Arizona. He described O'odhams in terms that he understood: as another type of Pueblo Indians.

Officials commonly used this characterization during the early years of U.S.-O'odham interactions, but it would fade as the territorial period progressed. There were those who began to provide reliable, firsthand information on Tohono O'odhams. Julius Froebel, a German geologist and journalist who visited San Xavier del Bac in 1854 just as the area was transitioning from Mexican to U.S. rule, described the Tohono O'odhams there as "good-natured, quiet, honest, and inoffensive people," who maintained "strict discipline, which they may have acquired from a mixture of Jesuit discipline and the remains of old Indian customs." They understood Spanish "tolerably well," but "refused to speak it with us."[107] Andrew B. Gray, an Anglo-American surveyor, visited Sonoita, a Tohono O'odham village just across the Mexican border, in 1854. He reported that the leader of the village was referred to as a "Governador," indicating that the term was still in usage in the 1850s, even if annual elections were not.[108] The above accounts underscore the fact that detailed information on Tohono O'odhams of the Arizona-Sonora Borderlands was in short supply.

Official reports to the commissioner over the next few years began to describe O'odhams in more detail. Reporting in 1857, Lieutenant Sylvester Mowry described the Indians of the Gadsden Purchase lands as having "extensive buildings, irrigating canals, and broad cultivated domain." In particular, he singled out Akimel O'odhams and Piipaash[109] along the Gila as "undoubtedly the most interesting and docile tribes of Indians on the continent." He asserted that they possessed Spanish title to their lands and that their territory "is intersected in all directions by 'acequias,' or irrigating canals, through which water from the Gila is drawn for purposes of cultivation." He concluded that they were living on lands that were already like reservations, and that "By proper management, the condition of these Indians may be much improved, and their villages be made of great service to the Territory by supplying large quantities of breadstuffs." But he warned, "Injudicious management would bring on contact with the white population, and cause infinite trouble. They are at present extremely anxious about the tenure of their lands, and inquire of all Americans who have visited their villages whether they will be allowed to remain."[110] To American observers, the Indians of this newly acquired territory seemed to fall under the category of more "civilized" Indians; they lived in permanent dwellings, farmed, used irrigation, and were peaceful. But even American observers could sense the anxiety the O'odhams felt over the future of their sacred homelands.

Other Army officers who interacted with O'odhams in the 1850s echoed these high estimations. Lieutenant A. B. Chapman of the First Dragoons reported, "About ninety miles from Tucson, and directly on the route from Fort Buchanan to Fort Yuma, are the Pima villages, occupied by the Pima and Maricopa Indians. . . . These Indians, even before their country came into possession of the United States, were exceedingly friendly to the Americans." Referring to Akimel O'odham and Piipaash support for the Mormon Battalion, a group of Mormon volunteers during the U.S.-Mexico War that traversed their territory in 1846–47, he wrote, "From the time they refused to assist the Mexicans in cutting off Colonel Cooke's command, in 1847, they have ever been loyal to us. . . . Their chief recently boasted that 'the Maricopas had not yet learned the color of the white man's blood.'" He recommended that their lands be secured for them "at once" so as to maintain the longstanding peaceful relations between them and the United States. In addition to reporting on the Akimel O'odham–Piipaash settlements, he also reported on the Tohono O'odhams of San Xavier del Bac: "They occupy an unproductive tract of country lying west and southwest of Tucson, their principal village being in the vicinity of San Xavier del Bac. . . . They are represented as being very poor, and indeed destitute."[111] These tropes would be repeated frequently: Akimel O'odhams and Piipaash were agricultural, peaceful, and industrious, while Tohono O'odhams were also peaceful, although destitute.

When William H. Emory of the Boundary Survey team visited the Tohono O'odham homelands in 1855, he understood—and sought to communicate to the Indians—the rights guaranteed them under the Treaty of Guadalupe Hidalgo. Emory reported being visited in his camp at Nogales on 29 June 1855 by

José Victoriano Lucas, "Head chief of San Xavier," and "Captain" José Antonio, "chief of San Xavier." The pair came to ascertain "in what manner the cessions of the territory, under the treaty with Mexico, will affect their rights and interests." He told them, "by the terms of the treaty, all the rights that they possessed under Mexico are guarantied to them by the United States; a title to lands that was good under the Mexican government is good under the United States government."[112] Whether Emory believed those rights included citizenship and the franchise is unclear, but he certainly was convinced that Tohono O'odhams had a right to their lands. Yet he also assumed that they held title to their lands, which was not the case. A Tohono O'odham calendar stick recorded an 1856 encounter between Tohono O'odhams and Anglo-American officials in which Tohono O'odham "chiefs" took a firm stance, stating, "The White people must not bother us." One of the elders told the whites that everything they saw belonged to the Tohono O'odhams: "These mountains, I say, are mine and the Whites shall not disturb them."[113]

By 1859, Indian Agent John Walker had been in Tucson for two years, administering the affairs of both Tohono and Akimel O'odhams. He reported enthusiastically that all was well and that the Indians were busy with agricultural pursuits. But he stated that the Tohono O'odhams in his agency needed more tools. He made no comment on Indigenous governance or the rights of these peoples, concluding simply, "I find the condition of these people very much improved indeed since I first came among them, two years since: now their confidence being established in the kind intentions of government towards them, I consequently have no fear of their future conduct towards all good Americans, and in their success and prosperity in a pecuniary point."[114] Lieutenant Mowry submitted another report in 1859 after meeting with a large group of Akimel O'odham and Piipaash leaders. He feared the possibility of an O'odham war, and went so far as to consult with Governor Alberto Cubillas of Sonora, who confirmed, along with "the archives of the State and of the capital of Mexico, that the Pimos [sic] and Maricopas were entitled to fifty leagues of land by actual grant." Ironically, even though he referred to them as a "friendly and semi-civilized people," he did not believe in the civilization project for them: "The idea of civilizing and christianizing them, exposed as they are to all the influences of a frontier people, is the idle dream of a pseudo-philanthropist. The rapid development of the mineral resources of Arizona and the settlement of the Territory will bring them soon enough in contact with 'the humanizing and civilizing influence of the white man,' and the result will be the same inevitable one that has followed its contact with other tribes: the men will become drunkards, the women prostitutes, and disease will soon leave only the name of their race."[115] Fortunately, Lieutenant Mowry's vision of O'odham-Piipaash doom did not pan out. Unfortunately for Tohono O'odhams, Akimel O'odhams, and Piipaash, however, the civilization program would move forward in future years.

Tohono O'odham sources fill in some of the gaps for this period. For example, the above-mentioned calendar stick told of a Tohono O'odham governing council, with representatives from constituent villages. Four headmen had died of natural causes in 1855, leaving the tribe "without councilmen." In response, "a general meeting was called and two were elected." Two more were chosen in 1858, "thus filling the council." The entry for 1861 recorded that the four new councilmen "proved unsatisfactory and were recalled. This was noteworthy because, while the councilmen serve at the pleasure of the tribe, they usually die in office. Four others were selected." The four new replacements were given a "vote of confidence" in 1862, and two of these men, who were unmarried, were "given wives."[116] While these records do not describe the elections of Tohono O'odham councilmen in detail, they do indicate a form of functioning national, representative government in the 1850s, and show that Tohono O'odhams had mechanisms for selecting councilmembers and recalling those who did not perform satisfactorily. This took place largely out of the view of Anglo-Americans. But we should be careful not to carry this sense of Tohono O'odham nationhood too far. Surely there was intervillage cooperation, but as Eric Meeks has stressed, as late as the 1930s O'odhams fought hard to protect village autonomy, with each community conceiving of itself as an independent unit.[117]

As the 1850s drew to a close, U.S. representatives continued to work among Akimel O'odhams, Piipaash, and Tohono O'odhams. A report compiled from records culled from the Surgeon General's Office on sickness and mortality in the Army described the three groups—collectively classed as "Pueblos"—as "semi-civilized or tame Indians." The report referred specifically to Tohono O'odhams as a "mute, inoffensive race, industrious and capable of being made good, peace-loving, law-abiding citizens." They were also the "best laborers in the country."[118] Agent Walker shared this enthusiasm, reporting in 1860 that there was "a very perceivable advance in civilization among [Akimel O'odhams]." He again registered the need for farming implements and tools for Tohono O'odhams at San Xavier, and observed that they were "the best Indians in the Territory . . . as easily managed as the Pimos [sic]."[119]

While Arizona moved into its final year as part of the New Mexico Superintendency, Superintendent Michael Steck reported in 1863 that many O'odhams in southern Arizona had participated in the emerging economy of the region as shepherds. He also commented that "A number were educated at the mission of San Xavier."[120] American agents soon began to understand what this "education" entailed. The new Superintendent of Indian Affairs for Arizona, Charles D. Poston, noted that Tohono O'odhams had been baptized, cut their hair short, wore Western-style clothing, and were generally "modified by civilization." He began to discern a system of government at San Xavier, with a "captain" by the name of José Victoriano Solorse, a "highly intelligent Indian ... exercising a beneficent influence on the tribe." Superintendent Poston also called for a reservation of two square leagues, plus additional aid so that they could "colonize the straggling members of the tribe within this reservation."[121]

J. Ross Browne, the nineteenth-century author, journalist, traveler, and government employee who accompanied Poston in Arizona, wrote about the Tohono O'odhams he encountered at San Xavier during his 1863 visit. He described them as a "peaceable, industrious, and friendly race. They live here, as they lived two centuries ago, by cultivating the low grounds in the vicinity, which they make wonderfully productive by a system of irrigation." He also commented, "They profess the Catholic faith, and are apparently sincere converts. The Jesuit missionaries taught them those simple forms which they retain to this day, though of late years they have been utterly neglected. The women sing in the church with a degree of sweetness and harmony that quite surprised me." Brown also mentioned the governor, José, and stated that Mexicans living nearby had intruded on him and his people. They entreated Poston for assistance, and he "ordered the Mexicans to leave" O'odham lands.[122]

In 1865, Papago Agent M. O. Davidson wrote at length to Commissioner of Indian Affairs William P. Dole about the conditions of Tohono O'odhams around San Xavier. While he echoed Superintendent Poston's praise of the Tohono O'odham "'gobernador' or head chief, Don José Victoriano Solesse [sic] ... an intelligent and worthy man," Davidson did not agree that more Tohono O'odhams should be congregated at San Xavier, and neither did he believe that such a measure would "contribute most to their welfare," owing to their "local attachment to their homes, nor can they be made readily to understand why such a measure should be proposed. So far as I can learn, they will be better pleased to retain possession of their own little valleys and villages."[123] What Davidson proposed instead was the formation of an O'odham republic, with San Xavier at the center.

Davidson's treatise on potential Tohono O'odham democratic government is lengthy, but portions of it bear repeating to show that one agent, as early as 1865, envisioned a Western-style O'odham electorate and representative government. He advised that the federal government "unite [them] in forming a central government at San Xavier, to which each community will send delegates yearly, to deliberate upon the common welfare, and pass such laws and ordinances as the condition of the people may require." This sounded very much like an O'odham national council with delegates elected annually. Clearly, Davidson was unaware of the fact that Tohono O'odhams already had a council with village representation. He believed that Tohono O'odhams should be given the choice between remaining in their dispersed communities or congregating at San Xavier, and that this should take place in a national referendum:

> Before acting upon any policy, I would suggest that a convention of the people be called to deliberate, and give expression to their wishes by a decisive vote. They are disposed to agriculture and the arts of peace. Again, it may be reasonably doubted whether the limits of the proposed reservation will embrace sufficient arable land to sustain the whole people. If it should not be the case, and the voice of the people shall be in favor of concentration, then the surplus population that cannot be advantageously located at San Xavier, may be allotted a reservation not far distant, and selected from the tillable lands now in the power of the hostile Apaches, when the latter shall be conquered and removed.[124]

Davidson did not stop there. He believed that these Tohono O'odhams should be considered citizens of the United States with all the appertaining rights:

> In my opinion, we must regard them as American citizens, and under certain conditions entitled to all their privileges. Many are sufficiently advanced to understand their duties and exercise their rights as such. It is my humble opinion that it is the duty of the government to educate the remainder to a degree that will qualify them also to fulfil all the obligations and perform all the duties of citizenship. I will venture to say that these people, from their intelligence, their morality, and the manifestation of all the requisite qualifications, are quite as much entitled to the privileges referred to as the majority of the Mexican population. . . . In a few words, confirm their possession to the lands they occupy, by the title of pre-emption, establishing suitable metes and bounds thereto, not interfering with the white settlements or mining claims; and it may be confidently asserted that, with the aid of schools, the rising generation of

Papagos will not discredit the country or the institutions by which they are allowed to profit.¹²⁵

As enlightened as these statements sound for 1865, they demonstrate the limitations of what was observable to Anglo-American eyes in the second half of the nineteenth century. Accepting the accounts from their own calendar sticks, Tohono O'odhams already had set up structures for intervillage cooperation and governance. Still, if the United States had established a national council, or even recognized existing governing structures, that would have signaled its recognition of a sovereign O'odham nation, as well as its respect for the right of Tohono O'odhams to choose whether to remain in small communities stretched throughout Papaguería or concentrate at the mission. Davidson's plans obviously did not take into account Tohono O'odham desires and ideas of governance, although they did convey a clear sense of Tohono O'odhams as deserving of the franchise and rights as U.S. citizens.

Davidson's suggestions caught the attention of the Indian Bureau. In response to Davidson's recommendations, Acting Commissioner of Indian Affairs Robert B. Van Valkenburgh¹²⁶ wrote back in the fall of 1865, instructing Davidson to "convene the Papagos at the earliest convenient day, and [set] before them the advantages which will accrue to them from a settlement upon certain defined reservations within which their rights will be exclusive." If the Tohono O'odhams accepted, Davidson was to "make selection for them of one or more reservations of reasonable extent for their wants." Davidson was also empowered to employ a teacher for the Indians, "who must read and speak both the English and Spanish languages." Finally, he notified Davidson that "Provision will be made for the payment of a salary of $500 per annum to the duly elected head chief of the Papagos, and to three subordinate chiefs of $350 each per annum, to be paid so long as they shall continue friendly and efficient in aiding the United States authorities in preserving the peace and in the improvement of their people." Acting Commissioner Van Valkenburgh also hoped that the reservation and a steady advancement in "education, civilization, and the arts of self-sustaining industry" would cause them, "[eventually] as citizens of the United States, [to] lose their separate tribal character and become merged in the general population of the Territory."¹²⁷ As a result of these instructions, Many Skirts of San Xavier del Bac was appointed head chief of the Tohono O'odhams. While he was the main leader at San Xavier, Many Skirts would not necessarily have been recognized as head chief by all the other Tohono O'odham villages.¹²⁸

Despite these developments, the Tohono O'odham republic envisioned by American officials failed to materialize, at least not for many years, and not one that Americans could observe. There was constant turnover in O'odham administrators, hindering stability in policy for southern Arizona. The agents who followed Davidson spoke frequently of establishing schools among Akimel O'odhams, Piipaash, and Tohono O'odhams. Schooling became the main focus of the assimilationist goal of turning these Indians into self-sufficient farmers in the Anglo-American mold. Levi Ruggles, for example, was special agent for the Akimel O'odhams and Piipaash in the late 1870s. As part of this office, he also administered Tohono O'odhams. He commented on the benefits of education and a perceived willingness among the Akimel O'odhams and Piipaash to embrace it: "They desire to have a school established here, where a few of their youths can be taught the English language. I think that they fully appreciate the advantages to be gained by education, and would cause a portion of their children to attend school constantly; and there is no doubt of their capacity to learn." He believed that Tohono O'odhams would benefit as well: "Critics might doubt that great good had been derived from [their] conversion [to Catholicism], but without doubt these people are capable of receiving and are anxious to obtain moral, religious, and scientific authors. A school for the education of a few of these youths in the elementary branches of an English education should be established at the Old Mission church of San Haver del Bec [sic]."[129] The idea that education would ultimately civilize O'odhams was in line with federal Indian policy of the era.

By 1869 officials had also begun to distinguish between Akimel O'odhams/Piipaash and Tohono O'odhams. Akimel O'odhams and Piipaash, who received annuities and other assistance, were "cared for to a greater or less extent by the government, are located on reservations, or who live in their own villages, receiving clothing, seeds, and agricultural implements from Indian agents or superintendents." Tohono O'odhams, by contrast, "live in pueblos or villages, and cultivate the soil, or otherwise support themselves by their own labor exclusively, receiving no support from the government, but who are at peace with the whites." The author of these statements, Lieutenant Colonel R. Jones, also observed, "Of late years this industrious tribe has been utterly ignored by the Indian department, and it is not known that any reservation has ever been designated for them, though a former agent, named Lyon, assigned to them the country in the vicinity of San Xavier del Bac, and while they remained under his charge he protected them in their rights, but since then the Whites and Mexicans have been encroaching on and taking up their best lands, and the Papagos are being gradually crowded across the line into Mexican

Territory." Jones, whose report was endorsed by none other than General William Tecumseh Sherman, felt strongly that Ruggles should be removed as the Pima-Maricopa agent: "In a word, he is a mere nullity, for whom the Indians have no respect." He felt that Ruggles only took an interest in these Natives when it came time to distribute goods.[130] Tohono O'odhams, who received no annuities and very few goods, were in a situation similar to that of the Pueblos of New Mexico. Their peaceful, agricultural characteristics simply led many federal agents to ignore them, believing that all was well. This neglect also included nonrecognition of their status as citizens. William H. Jackson, one of the foremost photographers of the American West, wrote in 1877, "At the close of the Mexican war [Tohono O'odhams] were Mexican citizens, and partly civilized, but were not recognized as such by the United States, and were left without an agency or a reservation."[131]

In the 1870s, various groups opened schools among Akimel O'odhams, Piipaash, and Tohono O'odhams. For example, a Presbyterian missionary, Charles Cook, began his work ministering among the Akimel O'odhams in 1870, and soon established a school.[132] This work would continue well into the twentieth century. Among the Akimel O'odhams, Piipaash, and Tohono O'odhams, several day schools were operated by Presbyterians, Catholics, and Indian Service employees, as were industrial boarding schools in both Tucson and Phoenix. Agents grappled with the common conundrum of the benefits and drawbacks of day schools as opposed to boarding schools, and the relative merits of schooling under the various denominations. Acknowledging that this important history of the education of O'odham children requires its own volume, our focus now turns to important events surrounding allotment, citizenship, and voting among the Tohono O'odhams of San Xavier del Bac.

In the early 1870s, still no Tohono O'odham Reservation had been established. Federal officials had discussed the issue ad nauseam, but had not taken the necessary actions to establish such a place. Special Agent R. A. Wilbur reported in 1871 that Tohono O'odhams at San Xavier were "peaceful, comparatively intelligent," and even commented on their participation in the regional economy: "[They are] very industrious, being of great assistance to the farmers of the Santa Cruz Valley in harvesting and as herders." Referring to years of neglect and many broken promises by U.S. officials, Wilbur pleaded for action on the O'odhams' behalf. They were "ready and willing to conform to any proposition the Government may wish to extend them." They desired "something permanent" that would help them to "take care of themselves under an improved and civilized organization." They had been promised schools, agricultural implements, and livestock, although very little had been

Gila Bend—Teacher—Jose Lopez, n.d. The Office of Indian Affairs hoped to educate and "civilize" Tohono O'odhams, who in turn brought civilization to their people. Bonaventure Oblasser, O.F.M. Collection, 1901–1977 MS 543, box 10, folder 1, courtesy of University of Arizona Libraries, Special Collections.

delivered. Furthermore, Wilbur pointed to the fact that many Tohono O'odhams participated in Tucson's cash economy: "From their employments and associations they have become more intelligent in regard to these matters than any other Indians."[133]

The situation was exacerbated by settler encroachments around San Xavier. Wilbur reported in 1872, "Little by little settlers are hedging them in, using the water for irrigating their own fields, until now they are so crowded they come continually with complaints." Wilbur had seven suggestions: (1) put them on a reservation; (2) give them agricultural implements, seeds, carts and oxen, and breeding-stock; (3) establish schools and provide instructors; (4) increase the salary of the physician there and give him enough supplies; (5) give them clothing, blankets, and shoes; (6) provide the agent with a light wagon and team of horses for traveling to their dispersed villages; (7) consider sinking artesian wells for them.[134] Agent Wilbur believed these would all mitigate the situation, but establishing a reservation was the most pressing issue.[135] Tensions were further compounded by the 1871 massacre of Pinal and Aravaipa Apaches at Camp Grant by a combined force of Anglo-Americans, Mexican Americans, and Tohono O'odhams. The United States had continued many of the Spanish/Mexican practices relating to Tohono O'odhams, such as recognizing village governors—although they were frequently referred to as "captains"—and using Tohono O'odhams as military auxiliaries against Apaches. Americans even encouraged a trade in Apache scalps, ears, and other body parts, giving Tohono O'odhams tools, cloth, tobacco, beads, and other useful goods in return.[136]

In the massacre at Camp Grant on 30 April 1871, scores of Apache men, women, and children were slaughtered, many as they slept in their camp along the banks of the San Pedro River. A murder trial was held late that year, with the Tohono O'odham captain of San Xavier, Ascención Villas, the only O'odham testifying.[137] R. A. Wilbur, who had been appointed Special Agent for the Papago Agency in July 1871, saw the massacre as part of a larger pattern of violence in the U.S.-Mexico Borderlands, and wrote after the massacre that Tohono O'odhams were in a "destitute condition," with many crossing "over the border to Sonora in search of work to keep from starving." He also wrote of efforts to locate Apache captives, many of whom were eventually sold into the Sonoran slave trade.[138] On the last day of 1871, Wilbur wrote to his superior, Superintendent of Indian Affairs for Arizona Herman Bendell: "I again would call your attention to the necessity of some immediate steps being taken in regard to a Reservation for these Indians. The settlers are fast crowding them around San Xavier del Bac and taking up the best portions of land." Tohono O'odhams experienced violent relations with Mexican American and Anglo settlers, and also with Apaches, so Wilbur believed their security depended on having a reservation. He concluded, "It would almost be a sacralidge [sic] to take them away from the church which their ancestors built hundreds of years ago and which owes its present state of remarkable preservation to their care and interest alone."[139]

One more positive development in May 1872 was a peace council between Tohono O'odhams, Akimal O'odhams, Piipaash, and surviving Apaches, all overseen by General Oliver O. Howard, prominent for his work as Commissioner of the Freedmen's Bureau from 1865 to 1874. Representatives from the Indian groups met along the San Pedro River and agreed to make peace.[140] Howard succeeded in bringing "these chiefs to agree to perpetual peace with each other and with the whites." In a meeting on 30 May, the general dramatically picked up a stone and said, "I want you all to be at peace as long as that stone lasts." In one of the understatements of the nineteenth century, he said, "I have heard that you have some trouble among yourselves," and restated, "I want you now to live in peace as long as this stone lasts."[141] In another coup,

Howard convinced Ascención Villas to go with him to Washington, D.C. Agent Wilbur wrote that the Tohono O'odham leader returned impressed from his trip to the East, telling his people of all the marvels of American society. He "impressed them in his rude way of the advantages of education and civilization."[142] Yet Tohono O'odhams were still far from secure in their territory, and their situation became more precarious as the months and years passed.

In the wake of these tumultuous times, the long-awaited reservation finally materialized through an Executive Order issued on 1 July 1874. Encroachments by outsiders, and the Apache threat, had brought Tohono O'odhams to the breaking point. The Executive Order set aside 69,200 acres. Once established, the San Xavier Reservation fell primarily under the jurisdiction of the Pima-Maricopa Agent, save for a few years when there was a Papago Agency.[143] Papago Agent John W. Cornyn reported in 1875 that the Tohono O'odhams at San Xavier were very happy to finally have a reservation. He also asserted that education among them had been a "great success," and that he found them to be a "civilized, moral, and virtuous people." While other agents had urged that they be moved north to the Gila River Reservation, he strongly protested such a course; he thought that the Akimel O'odhams would corrupt the "gentle, virtuous Papagos."[144] Such bias aside, it was clearly the correct decision to leave Tohono O'odhams at San Xavier on their own land, just as it had been to keep Hopis and Rio Grande Pueblos in their territory.

With the San Xavier Reservation established, agents turned to what they believed was the next logical step in their development: individual land ownership and title. O'odhams had gained a reservation, but no agent. Pima-Maricopa Agent Charles Hudson administered the San Xavier Reservation from Gila River. He found O'odham affairs "somewhat complicated." While many Tohono O'odhams successfully contributed to the regional economy, having secured "considerable employment among the settlers," he noted that "Mexicans are occupying farms and using the water-privileges belonging to and absolutely necessary to the Indians, without a shadow of title except occupancy." As a solution, Hudson proposed 160 acres to each family and inalienable title: "Such action would encourage them to renewed efforts, allow them to assume a position by the side of their civilized brethren, and to join in the march of progress."[145]

Hudson based his vision on congressional Indian Homestead Acts, which extended the terms of the 1862 Homestead Act to Indians at various times. The original Homestead Act had opened O'odham lands to Anglo-American settlement in 1866,[146] and it is a remarkable irony that Hudson wanted to encourage Tohono O'odhams to take up homesteads on their own ancestral lands.

His thinking also preceded the Dawes Act by more than ten years. By the following year, 1877, Pima-Maricopa Agent J. H. Stout updated the Pima Agency's recommendation. He suggested giving heads of family a minimum of forty acres in severalty, and as much as eighty acres if forty did not suffice. Accepting a homestead would grant citizenship, and the government would retain title until the Indian homesteaders "become somewhat familiar with their responsibilities as citizens." He also regretted to report that the Mexican-American encroachments he had mentioned the previous year had not abated, with adverse impact on Tohono O'odham water and trees.[147] It seems that this proposal failed to gain momentum, and it would be over a decade before allotment in severalty came to the Tohono O'odhams.

By 1885, Pima Agent Roswell G. Wheeler reported that Tohono O'odhams on the San Xavier Reservation had been "harassed, cheated, bulldozed, by lawless whites and Mexicans. Troubles about land and water have continually called for the interference of the agent. The intruders have finally been ejected and temporary quietness prevails." Still, he feared that the ejected parties would not hesitate to "create a disturbance" and seek Tohono O'odham land once again.[148] In 1886, Agent Wheeler actively "endeavored so far as possible to arouse an interest in and to induce them to avail themselves of the homestead law.... Many of them have gladly embraced this opportunity and roughly outlined their homesteads." He also stated, "The Papagos need an agent badly.... No better Indians than these there are known, and a great field is open and waiting for the harvest."[149]

While agents called for O'odham homesteads, the passage of the Dawes Act paved the way for Tohono O'odham allotment. Agents were anxious to begin allotment at San Xavier, but Pima Agent Claude M. Johnson reported in 1889 that "No land has been allotted in severalty to them."[150] This would all change in 1890, when the government began to allot land to Tohono O'odhams at San Xavier. Agent Cornelius W. Crouse mentioned allotment almost in passing: "During the year the Papago Reservation was allotted to 363 Indians."[151] In the end, ninety-four heads of family each received 160-acre allotments. They were all men, as married women shared their husbands' tracts. A single 160-acre allotment contained twenty acres of farmland and fifty to eighty acres of mesquite "timberland," with the rest being mesa fit only for grazing. All single adults—male and female—received forty or eighty acres of mesa. When the allotting at San Xavier was complete, 42,000 acres of the 71,090-acre reservation had been divided into individual plots.[152] Unfortunately for the O'odhams, on average, each allottee received only about ten acres of irrigated land.[153]

Crouse's casual approach and the seemingly tidy allotment work belie the complexity of allotment at San Xavier. For one thing, Tohono O'odhams had long practiced seasonal migrations, even those individuals and families who had permanent homes at San Xavier. When the allotting agent counted resident Tohono O'odhams, he put the number at 363. He considered all of them residents. Some were, in fact, descendants of the original Sobaipuris who had lived in the vicinity for centuries. Others were in the area only temporarily to visit family members or for economic reasons. Carl Lunholtz reported on San Xavier at the end of the 1910s: "The church is at present surrounded by a reservation of the Papago Indians.... Owing to the half nomadic habits of the tribe, natives of the interior districts are constantly to be found there."[154] It made no difference; all who could be found received allotments. Many residents of San Xavier were away at the time for various reasons and did not receive allotted lands.

Tohono O'odham Peter Blaine Sr., whose biography, *Papagos and Politics*, remains one of the best Tohono O'odham accounts of life in the late nineteenth and early twentieth centuries, reported that his aunt had married an allottee, but that the man was originally from Caborca, toward the Gulf of California. His allotment was one of those made at San Xavier in the early 1890s, close to the mission church. He stated that some people who lived there had been away and therefore missed being allotted, while others who were clearly nonresidents received plots. Blaine commented, "I really didn't understand how the Papago lands were allotted to just certain people. I never could get that straight." He also related that his father-in-law held an allotment at San Xavier. He had chosen a plot of land he liked, cleared it, and begun farming it. When the allotting agent came, "he got that piece of land."[155]

A Tohono O'odham calendar stick did not mention the allotments made in 1890, but did refer to an allotment being completed on the Akimel O'odham Reservation in 1910, stating, "The Pima reservation was surveyed for allotment of individuals." But it asserted, "The Papago reservation was also surveyed but not for allotment because it is totally grazing land, while the Pima lands can be irrigated and farmed."[156] Tohono O'odhams seemingly ignored the new allotment boundaries, continuing with their traditional agricultural practices, and few may have even been aware that the reservation at San Xavier had been allotted, as evidenced by the calendar stick. But as time wore on, more people moved onto individual plots. These allottees seldom made wills, nor did they understand Arizona land inheritance laws. When allottees died, their lands were divided among heirs. Because of this, land ownership at San Xavier became fragmented and confusing over the years. Amazingly, OIA officials asserted that some Tohono O'odham allottees had "progressed" enough after the twenty-five year trust period, so they gave them fee-simple title.[157] Most would likely have received trust patents for their allotments, as the lands were held in trust for twenty-five years under the Dawes Act. Trust patentholders were, nonetheless, immediately eligible for citizenship and, potentially, the franchise.

As historian Eric Meeks has shown, "One of the central tools of the assimilation policy was allotment.... Any Indian who received an allotment would become a U.S. citizen with 'equal protection under the law,' echoing the language of the Fourteenth Amendment." San Xavier was the *only* reservation allotted by the Bureau of Indian Affairs in south-central Arizona during the nineteenth century.[158] While Indian agents considered the Tohono O'odhams of San Xavier to be (half) civilized, and to be citizens under the terms of the Dawes Act—or at the very least well on their way to citizenship—the dream of voting Tohono O'odham citizens was not a reality in the 1890s or early 1900s. A key figure in these developments, or lack thereof, was John M. Berger, the Indian Service farmer in charge of the San Xavier Reservation. Berger, a Swiss-born naturalized U.S. citizen, had worked initially as a jeweler in Tucson. After he married an Hispana, he took up ranching on traditional Tohono O'odham land. Agent Wheeler forcibly removed Berger and his wife from the ranch in 1875, when it was included in the San Xavier Reservation boundaries of 1874.

Somehow, Berger later became deeply enmeshed in the Indian Service bureaucracy at San Xavier, serving variously as farmer, agent, and subagent for more than twenty-five years.[159] Berger began his work among the Tohono O'odhams in 1890. In 1893, the Pima Agent Crouse was already regretting allotment at San Xavier, which he felt was a mistake. He explained, "So many nonreservation, nomadic, homeless Papagoes [sic] were and are yet needing it [allotment]." He thought that it had been done hastily and did not extend to enough Tohono O'odhams.[160] In his report that year, Berger painted a rosy picture of an allotted, civilized people, stating, "All the Indians on this reservation without a single exception, wear citizen's dress and the greater part of them live in more or less comfortable houses built of sun-dried bricks of large size (here called adobes)." He also commented, "About three-fourths of the allottees are devout Catholics and attend regularly the mass held in the church every two weeks by a priest of that denomination." Most interesting of all, he wrote, "With the exception of a few malcontents, found in every community, all the allottees appreciate fully the privilege they enjoy in the ownership of land in severalty. It gives them a greater inclination toward farming and especially toward a more careful clearing and cultivating of their land than they ever had before, a fact clearly shown by the increase in the number of farmers among them."[161] Berger obviously exaggerated Tohono O'odham enthusiasm for allotment, although his report for that first year enunciated the government's plan for Tohono O'odham civilization and citizenship—one that he hoped would culminate in the franchise.

The following year, Berger reported at length on the Tohono O'odhams under his care. First, he noted two classes of O'odhams at San Xavier. One consisted of those who descended from Sobaipuris, and had "always lived upon this reservation. They are a better kind of Indian, more advanced in civilization, live in better houses, dress better, are more honest, and generally more amenable to good advice than the others. They send their children to school." The other class consisted of more recent immigrants from the desert rancherías. They had a more "nomadic disposition," he suggested, and were, "as a rule, opposed to civilization in any manner, and will not send their children to school." In a critical insight from his report, Berger stated, "The Papago allottees have not yet claimed any of their rights as citizens, but at the same time they have done their duty as citizens in this respect, that they have worked on the public roads under the supervision of the county road overseer from the village of San Xavier to Tucson, 125 allottees having each given one day's work for that purpose. This was done to comply with the Territorial law exacting this duty from every male citizen between the ages of 21 and 50 years, or in default of said labor a payment of $2."[162] In other words, Tohono O'odhams had not claimed any of their rights as citizens—voting, for one—but they behaved as good citizens, participating in public works projects required of citizens.

Even after some eight years of service at San Xavier, Berger maintained his positive attitude, attesting that "The Indians of this reservation live much better than they did formerly. They have better houses, wear better clothing, have more to eat and of a better quality, and they are more cleanly in their habits, consequently their sanitary condition has improved." He was the proud patriarch in his paternalistic little empire. Returning to the idea of citizenship, he wrote, "In making a review of the year's work I can see much to encourage, for in many things that go to make up a prosperous people and good citizens, great progress has been made."[163] Such grand statements of progress toward civilization by Indians under any given agent's care were common, but in this case Berger had a valid point. There were hundreds of allotted O'odhams.[164] Every one of them was technically a citizen of the United States. They farmed, wore citizen dress, lived in mostly permanent housing, sent their children to school, could lease their land to outside parties, and by law were entitled to all the rights of citizens, including the franchise. Berger must have been frustrated to report in 1899: "As yet no land has been leased, nor has any application to that effect been made, *nor has any allottee exercised his right to suffrage.*"[165]

Berger was clearly consumed with ideas of progress and civilization, measuring his own performance with the degree to which he was able to "lift" Tohono O'odhams to the status of good American citizens. The pinnacle of citizenship in the late nineteenth and early twentieth centuries was suffrage. Berger proudly reported in 1890, "I am pleased to state that reasonable progress has been made in civilization among the Papagoes [sic] under my charge during the past year. Every step made by them has been a step forward. On the whole there has been manifested a better appreciation of the value of the occupations pertaining to civilized life and a greater earnestness and persistence in pursuit of them. They are getting more progressive and self-sustaining every day and many of them are abundantly able to manage their own affairs. The allottee plainly shows that he is proud to be the owner of a piece of land which he knows belongs to him and his family, by the many improvements he is continually making thereon."[166] Berger saw what he wanted to see. What were longstanding Tohono O'odham traditions of participation in the transnational labor and cash economy appeared to him as examples of progress in "the occupations pertaining to civilized life." Tohono O'odhams had long been self-sustaining, a fact noted by the earliest Anglo-American observers, so again, Berger's point was moot. Further, it is difficult to ascertain the level of enthusiasm each allottee truly displayed for land in severalty. What *is* clear is that Berger was trying to justify his own work, and to show in every way possible that Tohono O'odhams were truly on the cusp of citizenship and suffrage.

Berger summarized his eleven years at San Xavier by asserting that the O'odhams had made significant progress. But, as he noted, there was still room for improvement: "They have not only considerably advanced in civilization, but they are also in a far more prosperous condition than they ever have been."[167] He must have been extremely disappointed when his charges, who qualified for citizenship in every way, apparently never undertook that culminating step of claiming the franchise. His frustration is apparent in a 1902 report, when he was removed from his position for a short time and then reinstated. Tohono O'odhams misunderstood this action, believing that they were no longer under federal control. According to Berger, "The subsequent behavior of a great number of them fully demonstrated that they were not yet ready for self-government." He laid the blame on the traditional Tohono O'odham leadership, which thwarted his efforts: "A few old Indians and medicine men," who were "troublesome and opposed to civilization and progress, thought that their time had come again." These men called meetings and "selected new chiefs of their own kind and sentiment," informing the chiefs supported by the Indian Service "that they had no further use for them, etc."[168]

When Berger was reappointed, it was a "great relief to the good Indians," since it stopped the "injurious proceedings" perpetrated by the "bad element." Tohono O'odhams, jubilant at the prospect of actual self-government, had gathered to select new leadership in the traditional manner, ridding themselves of the "very good and progressive" leadership that the Indian Service supported. In actuality, this episode demonstrated that Tohono O'odhams at San Xavier were readier than ever for self-government. Berger concluded this 1902 letter with a familiar statement, "As yet no land has been leased by the allottees, nor has any allottee exercised his right of suffrage."[169]

The same rang true in 1904: "As yet no land has been leased by the allottees to whites, nor has any application to that effect been made, nor has any allottee exercised his right to suffrage."[170] No contrary report surfaced in the remaining years of Berger's tenure, which terminated with his death in 1910. Voter registrations from Pima County in the first decades of the 1900s yield no significant numbers of Tohono O'odham voters, if any at all.[171] Although Berger noted the progress made by Tohono O'odhams during his years of service, he failed in the final goal of fashioning them into citizen voters. His report from 1902 speaks volumes about the Tohono O'odham vision of leadership and citizenship, at least at San Xavier. The simple fact is that they wanted to select their own leaders in the manner of their choosing, and they did not exercise the right to suffrage because they did not desire to. As with the Pueblos of New Mexico, citizenship in the O'odham community was far more important than U.S. citizenship, and the allure of gaining supposed "rights" could not convince them otherwise.

Furthermore, the Burke Act of 1906 largely closed the door to Tohono O'odham citizenship and voting. According to the terms of the Burke Act, which amended the Dawes Act of 1887, allottees must receive fee-simple title in order to become citizens. They either had to pass the twenty-five-year trust period, or had to be individually assessed by the Secretary of the Interior as competent and capable of managing their own affairs.[172] No Tohono O'odhams from San Xavier had voted as of Berger's 1904 report, and there is no reason to believe that significant numbers of them voted in the years immediately following. While some O'odhams qualified for citizenship before the Burke Act, and could potentially have been declared competent afterward, there is no record of significant Tohono O'odham voting. Still, a few accounts of Tohono O'odham voting activity come from anecdotal newspaper sources. It would appear that attempts were made to induce Tohono O'odhams and possibly Hopis to vote at various points during the territorial period. For example, the notes section of the *Weekly Arizona Miner* (Prescott) of 3 May 1878 stated, "An effort will be made to vote the Papago Indians living in Pima county, at the coming November election. All right, Yavapai [County] must see that the Moquis, who are very superior, intelligent Indian[s], have fair play.s [sic]."[173]

Similarly, the *Arizona Citizen* (Tucson) of 10 December 1870 reported on the election between Peter R. Brady and Richard McCormick. McCormick was reelected Delegate to the U.S. House of Representatives for the Arizona Territory, defeating Brady. A Democrat, Brady contested his loss, which the Republican *Citizen* welcomed, as there were allegations of Tohono O'odham votes being cast. The paper hoped that election officials "will commence by throwing out the seventy-five Papago Indians and newly arrived Sonorianian's [sic, possibly Yaqui?] votes that were cast at Phoenix, for Brady."[174] Such allegations were made as early as the election for Arizona's first Territorial Delegate in 1864, when Charles D. Poston, a Southerner and a Republican, defeated the Democrat, W. H. Bradshaw. Individuals accused Poston of having "rung in" the O'odham vote.[175] Such instances were the exception, similar to what happened on occasion in New Mexico, whereby Indians were induced to vote in hotly contested races.

Berger and other officials administering Tohono O'odhams, as well as other outside observers, occasionally noted Tohono O'odham forms of government, but they failed to recognize their importance. The *Arizona Weekly Citizen* (Tucson) of 12 December 1896 referred to the election for a Tohono O'odham chief: "Even the Papagoes [sic] are burdened with politics. Today is the date of their election of a chief." The author applauded the Tohono O'odham tradition of political consensus: "There is no record of a contested election in the Papago tribe, so the logical conclusion is that they do not indulge in the civilized custom of ballot-box stuffing."[176] Alden Jones, an Indian Office employee who served as the Sells Agency Superintendent during the first half of the twentieth century, reported, "Papagos really do argue long enough to convince one another, and that the unanimity is real and not merely an agreement that majority decision shall prevail."[177] These observations indicate that Tohono O'odhams chose their leaders mainly through traditional methods of consensus.

The office of village governor had persisted among Tohono O'odhams, but resembled Spanish forms less than in the Rio Grande Pueblo villages. As mentioned previously, the calendar sticks recorded the deaths[178] or removals of Tohono O'odham councilmen and the selections of their replacements. Jose

Lewis, a bilingual Tohono O'odham who accompanied William John McGee on his 1894 expedition to the Seri Island of Tiburón, penned a short treatise on Tohono O'odham government in 1897. It is the best Tohono O'odham primary source on governance during the territorial period. According to Lewis, each jurisdiction, which consisted of one or more villages, had a "Ká-ve-nä'l"[179] (a clear O'odhamization of the Spanish word "gobernador"), who was the "chief ruler" of said jurisdiction. He had an "assistant chief," who "if good may succeed him in case of the death of the Ká-ve-nä'l." The primary duty of the Ká-ve-nä'l was to "look after the welfare and rights of the people, and to correct so far as lies in his power any disorder or injustice." It was an unpaid position, and he consulted with elders and medicine men. In addition, Lewis described the position as "elective or rather one of appointment."[180]

Lewis also delineated the lesser offices. The Ká-ve-nä'l's assistant saw to it that "all persons attend the councils," and "[told] the people what is desired by the Ká-ve-nä'l." He had two or three assistants, and his office was "hereditary in the family. Usually descending from father to son." His two or three assistants oversaw the fires at the meeting places "to enable the people to light their cigarettes easily."[181] The office of O'sä gä'gäm (O'sä-gä means "cane" in O'odham) was involved with advocating for the rights of the people. He "carried in his hat a plaited raw-hide whip used to punish offenders against various rules of conduct," such as "stealing, rape, adultery, etc." He served without pay, and was selected by the Ká-ve-nä'l "with the consent of the people."[182] These structures of village government, which blended some of the old O'odham-Spanish system, remained the most important governing institutions for Tohono O'odhams, and bore some resemblance to the Spanish model of democratic town governance.

Writing about the Tohono O'odhams in the 1940s, after they had organized under the Indian Reorganization Act, a group of authors commented, "The Papago tribe as a political unit has existed for less than ten years. Before this time, *each village handled its own affairs, and related villages cooperated economically and socially, but there was no tribal government as such.*"[183] While there was intervillage cooperation during the territorial period, the federal government did not recognize a Tohono O'odham national government before the 1930s. The local reigned supreme throughout this time. Tohono O'odhams of San Xavier del Bac handled their own affairs for decades, even while federal officials focused their efforts on securing Tohono O'odham citizenship and enfranchisement. But Tohono O'odhams at San Xavier had repeatedly spurned the franchise. The project of transforming Tohono O'odhams into citizen voters had failed. Peter Blaine's philosophy perfectly encapsulated their view of governance and politics, one that resisted change by the Bureau of Indian Affairs. Although Blaine became politically active in the 1920s, this idea had guided Tohono O'odham thought during the territorial period. He stated, "I started working more closely with the old San Xavier people. I had already been an interpreter for them to the Agency, so when my godfather went to the San Xavier village council meetings, I went along. Most all of the council were older men, some young, but most were old. Being young, I never wanted to fail my people." As Blaine's biographer summarized, he was "committed to the traditional concept of leadership: a head man, chief or chairman must always go to the people and ask what they want done before making a decision. This is 'the Papago way.'"[184]

The last year of the territorial period also saw the establishment of the Good Government League. Formed in 1911, the GGL supported Progressive Era reform and campaigned forcefully for, among other things, more day schools in Papaguería, declaring, "We want to become good and useful citizens of our great country, but how are we to become so if means for securing an education is not provided?" They were supported by the Indian Rights Association, and wanted more federal involvement in Tohono O'odham affairs. The IRA vociferously called for schools and the federal government to give Tohono O'odhams "at least a white man's chance."[185] GGL members were mostly Presbyterian Tohono O'odhams who were graduates of the Tucson Indian Training School, a Presbyterian-run boarding school. Their main opposition was the League of Papago Chiefs, who were predominantly Catholics dedicated to more-traditional concepts of Tohono O'odham governance.[186] Blaine fell squarely into the latter group, and the two groups battled long and hard over control of O'odham leadership. This conflict precipitated O'odham political realignment during the Indian Reorganization period, which occurred mostly in the 1930s. The territorial period saw the beginnings of Tohono O'odham factionalism, yet the people largely lived under traditional village governance, with hardly an eye to U.S. citizenship and the franchise.

Conclusion

In 1928, Peter Porter, a citizen of the Gila River (Akimel O'odham) Indian Community, attempted to register to vote in Pinal County. The county registrar denied him. Porter filed suit, and the Arizona Supreme Court eventually decided against him in *Porter v. Hall* (1928). In Arizona, those opposed to Indian voting argued that Indians could not vote because Indian reservations did not fall within the state's political and governmental boundaries. Furthermore,

Indians were wards of the federal government. The court decided against Porter on the grounds of his status as such a ward. While New Mexicans denied voting through constitutional means by way of the "Indians not taxed" clause, Arizona opponents of Indian voting deployed wardship in a different way. Article 7, Section 2, of the Arizona Constitution read: "No person under guardianship, non compos mentis or insane, shall be qualified to vote at any election."[187] Indians in Arizona were thus classed with institutionalized persons in the denial of their voting rights.

Yet it had not been impossible for an Indian to gain the right to vote in territorial Arizona, although it was certainly difficult. Mike Burns (*Hoomothya* in Yavapai), a Yavapai taken captive as a child and forced to witness the massacre of his family and hundreds of tribal members by Crook's 5th Cavalry on 28 December 1872 in a remote stretch of the Salt River Canyon, was taken east and educated at Carlisle. On 15 July 1908, Burns, who had returned to Arizona as an adult and worked as an interpreter for the BIA, appeared before the Yavapai County recorder and registered to vote.[188] Burns had been declared "competent" by the secretary of the interior and given his citizenship rights. He wrote to his first cousin, Carlos Montezuma (*Wassaja* in Yavapai), himself a famous Yavapai captive and one of the first Native American medical doctors, "I was up to Mayer on the election Day ... I voted for a friend of mine: named Judge Ed. W. Wells of Prescott and the Republican, for Governor. For, as yet, we learned he got beat: by whole lots of Majority: and I am kindly sorry to hear it: as he had promised me a good job, if he ever gets in power."[189] Like Charles Kie in New Mexico, Burns was one of the rare Indian voters in Arizona during the territorial period, although he seemed to have less difficulty exercising the right than Kie. There may have been others like Burns, but he was certainly the exception to the rule.

The Arizona Constitution of 1912 actually made no specific mention of Indians in its sections on voting, but the state still found a way to disenfranchise Indians. By the time Peter Porter brought his case to court, scores of Arizona Indians had fought in World War I, and the Indian Citizenship Act of 1924 granted birthright citizenship to all Indians, although it left voter requirements up to the individual states. More than anything else, Indians did not vote in Arizona during the U.S. territorial period in any noteworthy numbers because they had no desire to do so. Indian agents seemed willing to extend this right and even encouraged those Indians they deemed "civilized" enough to seek the franchise. The Dawes Allotment Act granted citizenship to Indian allottees who held trust titles to their lands, which included Hopis and Tohono O'odhams. Even after the Burke Act of 1906 amended Dawes, some Indians in Arizona could have met the citizenship requirement and been deemed "competent" by the secretary of the interior, as Mike Burns had. But Hopis did not embrace citizenship and voting, even after a number of them had been allotted, turning instead to internal affairs, as they had done for so many centuries. One is left wondering about the fate of the "promising" young Hopi men who seemed poised to vote in Arizona elections.

As tentative refugees in a foreign country, Yaquis tried to stay away from any situation that would potentially lead to trouble and the horrors of deportation. Furthermore, their reconstituted communities in southern Arizona did not possess the same town electoral systems for which Yaquis had fought so valiantly in the eighteenth and nineteenth centuries. For the Yaquis, as refugees in a new colonial nation-state, voting was simply out of the question. The Tohono O'odhams of San Xavier del Bac, who seemed the ideal subjects for the civilizing project, also did not exercise their right to the franchise in any substantive way. Although they had been allotted land in severalty, and had met the qualifications for citizenship and voting under the law, they frustrated agents by showing no interest in voting. While they participated in the regional economy and interacted with Anglo-Americans, Mexicans, and Mexican Americans, they also labored to keep their communities strong, basing their leadership on traditional structures that had existed for centuries, while retaining some vestiges of the old O'odham-Spanish system. For all these reasons, the entire territorial Indian voting project bore no significant fruit—and Arizona's Indians would not participate in the electoral politics of the outside world for almost the next thirty years.

Conclusion

In 1948, Frank Harrison and Harry Austin, both citizens of the Fort McDowell Yavapai Nation (FMYN), attempted to register to vote in Maricopa County, Arizona.[1] Harrison had served honorably in the U.S. Marine Corps in World War II, but found that his family and other tribal members lived as second-class citizens in the country for which he had recently fought. Harrison recalled that when he and Austin, who was tribal chairman at the time, went to fill out their voter registrations, Roger Laveen, the young county registrar, refused, telling them, "You're under the ward[ship] of [the] government."[2] The pair were classed with those under institutionalization or otherwise deemed mentally incompetent, and were summarily denied the vote. Harrison and Austin first sued in Maricopa County Superior Court, where they lost. Nevertheless, they persisted, appealing to the Arizona Supreme Court. With the help of amicus briefs filed on their behalf by the National Congress of American Indians and the American Civil Liberties Union, they eventually won a favorable decision in *Harrison v. Laveen* on 15 July 1948.[3]

Yavapais from Fort McDowell retell this story and commemorate the event each July. The poster from the 2014 edition of this celebration reads, "Celebrating the 66th Annual American Indian Right to Vote" and "Exercise Your Right to Vote."[4] The *Harrison* decision remains a point of pride for Yavapais and other Arizona Indians. My own cousin Paul Russell, a long-serving tribal council member at Fort McDowell, who, as of this writing is vice president of the FMYN, speaks admiringly of his predecessors and their successful efforts to secure the franchise. Descendants of Harrison and Austin are often invited to speak at tribal commemorations. Even non-Indians in Arizona have increasingly recognized the importance of the men's actions.

The experiences of Frank Harrison and Harry Austin link with a prominent story in the history of New Mexico's Pueblo Indians. An Isleta Pueblo citizen, Miguel Trujillo Sr., had also served in the Marine Corps in World War II. He attended the University of New Mexico, where he earned both BA and MA degrees, after which he worked as a Bureau of Indian Affairs schoolteacher at Laguna Pueblo. In 1948, he attempted to register to vote in Valencia County, New Mexico. The county recorder, Eloy Garley, refused to allow Trujillo to register, citing Article 7, Section 1, of the New Mexico Constitution and its

"Indians not taxed" clause.[5] Not only did New Mexico group Indians with "idiots, insane persons, [and] persons convicted of a felonious or infamous crime," it was patently false that Pueblo Indians were untaxed. They paid nearly all the same taxes other New Mexicans paid, save for property tax on reservation trust land. Trujillo sued the county recorder, and Felix Cohen, called the "father of federal Indian law," served as his attorney. On 3 August 1948, mere weeks after the Arizona Supreme Court handed down the *Harrison* decision, the federal court in Santa Fe ruled in *Trujillo v. Garley* that Indians in New Mexico could no longer be kept from voting in municipal, state, and federal elections.[6] These events are commemorated among New Mexico's Pueblo Indians and other Native peoples. A poster celebrating Miguel Trujillo and the "Indian Vote" hangs in the hallway of the Indian Pueblo Cultural Center in Albuquerque.

The previously referenced Peter Porter of the Gila River Indian Community was another figure who rose to prominence in the fight for Indian voting during the first half of the twentieth century, preceding the *Harrison* and *Trujillo* cases by twenty years. A story printed in 2012 in the Gila River Indian Community's newspaper read, "To not vote is a disservice to those who fought for decades to win that right for Native peoples."[7] Such stories are important to Native peoples because they help us to remember. Through the act of remembering we reaffirm our identity and history, our connection to our ancestors, and thereby our very existence. The stories of individuals such as Harrison, Trujillo, and Porter are repeated, their power grows, and they become foundational narratives for Native American civil rights. I have heard them repeated many times throughout the course of my life; I have retold them many times, as well. It is tempting—even rewarding—to frame the narrative as one of a long struggle for Indian voting rights in New Mexico and Arizona, finally culminating in victory in the middle of the twentieth century. Consider the following passage from a recent work on the history of New Mexico:

> The Indian Citizenship Act of 1924 ... granted full U.S. citizenship to America's indigenous people. By 1947 states with large Indian populations, *except Arizona and New Mexico*, had extended voting rights to the nation's newest citizens.... Trujillo, a schoolteacher from Laguna Pueblo and former staff sergeant in the U.S. Marine Corps, refused to be denied his right to vote. Trujillo ... became a dissident voice representing twenty thousand Indian people in New Mexico.... In a stunning reversal on August 3, 1948, a federal triumvirate ruled that the New Mexico statute violated the Fifteenth Amendment and was, therefore, null and void.

Thirty-six years after gaining statehood, New Mexico finally granted the right to vote to its American Indian citizens.[8]

The heroic actions of all these individuals are worthy of our highest praise. We should retell these stories to our children and communities and should attend the yearly commemorations. We should never forget the efforts and sacrifices of those who came before us and secured the Indian vote for future generations.

But we must also not forget those individuals—many of them in the more-distant past—who labored to secure the Indian vote within a different set of circumstances. Under the incredibly constraining conditions of colonialism, which in a number of ways still persist, Pueblos, Hopis, Yaquis, and Tohono O'odhams all fought to secure the right to vote and to govern their communities as they saw fit. This meant instituting and adapting colonial ideas of electoral politics that may seem incongruous with Indigenous practice. Yet the people of these communities, together with the governors, lieutenant governors, and other officers who frequently represented them, were all involved in the crucial work of protecting their Indigenous nations' sovereignty. Elected officers, for example, repeatedly confronted colonial power as stand-ins for their own people. Their intense focus on their communities, so often in the face of the incessant demands of the colonizers, preserved their status as sovereign Native nations for future generations.

Describing the centuries-old efforts by Mohawks of Kehnawà:ke to preserve their sovereignty, the Mohawk scholar Audra Simpson has argued: "The Mohawks of Kahnawà:ke are nationals of a precontact Indigenous polity that simply refuse to stop being themselves. In other words, they insist on being and acting as peoples who belong to a nation other than the United States or Canada. Their political form predates and survives 'conquest'; it is tangible (albeit strangulated by colonial governmentality) and is tied to sovereign practices.... As Indigenous peoples they have survived a great, transformative process of settler occupation, and they continue to live under the conditions of this occupation, its disavowal, and its ongoing life, which has required and still requires that they give up their lands and give up themselves."[9] Much the same can be said of the Indigenous peoples of New Mexico and the Arizona-Sonora Borderlands. Through an ingenious mixture of Indigenous tradition and colonially imposed practices, these groups simply refused to stop acting like sovereign Indian republics.

We must thus see the history of Indigenous electorates in its totality—not as a process with a definite ending. Recent legal victories have been crucial to securing and protecting the Indian franchise, although we must be careful not to promote a certain historiographic agenda: that Indigenous peoples truly suffered under the unjust system of previous colonial administrations, but in the courts of the United States of America everyone can seek, and ultimately win, justice. This is simply not the case. The narratives of struggle and success—both personal and communal—extend much farther into our past. We must, therefore, celebrate and tell stories about the elected Cochiti Pueblo officers who traveled all the way to Mexico City—some 1,400 miles—in an attempt to protect the Pueblo's lands. We must retell the story of the Yaqui governors who challenged the authority of Jesuits, eventually giving their lives in the fight to preserve their communities' status as sovereign Indigenous nations. We must relate the stories of Tohono O'odhams at San Xavier del Bac who subverted the allotment process, instead maintaining their traditional subsistence and economic practices. Those O'odhams refused to embrace either U.S. citizenship or the franchise at a time when their baffled Indian agent saw no reason why they did so. We cannot know their exact motivations, but through this simple act they sought to protect their communities from settlers and bureaucrats seeking to allot and alienate Tohono O'odham lands, and thereby to decrease community autonomy.

Further, we must tell the stories of the Yaqui founders of the southern Arizona communities, who left their beloved Río Yaqui in the hopes that their people might find sanctuary across the international boundary with Mexico. We must tell the stories of elected Pueblo officers who repeatedly took Hispano and Anglo-American squatters to court to have them ejected from Pueblo lands. These same officers expressed their desire to officials in Santa Fe and Washington, D.C., to *not* become citizens of the United States. To accept citizenship, they believed, would open the floodgate to forces they likely could not turn back. They would have been further compelled to recognize the rights of squatters within their territory or the titles of those who had illegally purchased Pueblo land. They also fought against so-called delinquent property taxes on Pueblo land, which could have initiated additional, crushing land loss. Surely many more stories are part of the hidden transcript that Pueblo, Hopi, Yaqui, and Tohono O'odham peoples tell one another. These stories need to be shared repeatedly.

We must also realize that, historically, the Indian vote was far from perfect and was replete with many hazards. Imposed ideas of democracy caused friction within communities, and on a number of occasions even violently pitted those who supported such ideas against those who vehemently opposed them. Such ideological clashes, among which the vote figured, contributed to the deaths of numerous individuals at places such as Pecos Pueblo and Awat'ovi. This violence is also part of the legacy of the Native vote.

But through such stories we come to understand that the Indigenous peoples of New Mexico and the Arizona-Sonora Borderlands were not simply colonized peoples having no rights during the Spanish, Mexican, and U.S. territorial periods. On the contrary, they were enfranchised Native nations who simply refused to relinquish control of their own communities, and who continued to function as sovereign nations to the fullest extent possible. The vote was often an act of refusal. Through this defiance, those Indigenous peoples refused to forget their past, abandon their traditions, or bow their heads under a colonial yoke. The Nuevamexicana historian Deena J. González similarly wrote of the refusal by New Mexico Hispana women to abandon their identity, thereby "stav[ing] off complete colonization." Like the Indians of New Mexico and Arizona, "Their resistance efforts were not always visible to the newcomers who wrote about them, nor are they visible to contemporary historians who continue today to interpret these events." Like the Hispana women who confronted the U.S. takeover of New Mexico, the Indians in this work stood up to three separate colonial powers and "refused the favor."[10] Through the vote, or their opposition to it, Pueblos, Hopis, Yaquis, and O'odhams all refused to relinquish their status as sovereign nations—ones that remain strong today.

Still, in many other ways, the actions of these Indigenous groups were visible to the colonizers. In practical terms, the Spanish arrival brought a system of town government that included the vote as one of its central components. While the Franciscans and Jesuits who oversaw the elections of Indian officers were frequently dismissive of the Indian vote, the franchise brought real power to these Indigenous communities. The Pueblos used the vote to continue precontact traditions of town government, as well as to fight to protect their land, water, and culture. The degree to which Hopis implemented the Spanish colonial governing system is still unknown. What *is* known is that they successfully eradicated this system from among their communities. For their part, Yaquis accommodated concepts of voting and town government to the degree that they were willing to revolt when such rights were infringed upon. The vote kept their communities strong, providing a bulwark against Spanish colonial authority. In Pimería Alta, O'odhams lived under Jesuits who impeded their right to freely vote. Nevertheless, O'odham officers fought for their people and land as best they could, while also battling population decline and increasing land encroachments.

In many ways, the vote also remained important during the Mexican era. While Mexico's declarations of political equality for all ethnic groups brought little substantive change in some Indian communities, in certain cases it heralded unprecedented joint participation in governing bodies by both Pueblos and Hispanos. In a singular episode of Pueblo-Hispano cooperation, the two groups ousted the governor and briefly established an independent state—the Cantón—with an Indian serving as its governor. But Indians in the Arizona-Sonora Borderlands did not fare as well. Mexican officials there had not embraced a spirit of coexistence, and instead viewed the collapse of the mission system as a means to take away O'odham lands. O'odham officers' authority decreased significantly and, with the colonial pact broken, the Indian vote faded. Yaquis found themselves similarly assailed by Mexican state power. They would again revolt, and would again fail, as they had in 1740. Yaquis had, perhaps, become too adept at governing their communities and manipulating the institutions of the colonizers. Yaqui political power and sovereignty simply had to be broken.

In the distant north, Hopis had, for the most part, successfully evaded colonial control since that fateful winter morning at Awat'ovi in 1700. But the transition from Mexico to the United States initiated an unprecedented influx of outsiders. These newcomers brought American schooling, trading posts, and an insistence on Hopi "progress" and assimilation. As Indian agents touted their success, believing they were on the cusp of ushering in a Hopi electorate who would vote in territorial elections, the effort seems to have stalled. Hopis failed to embrace the franchise. To the far south, Yaquis came under unprecedented assault in the second half of the nineteenth century. Mexico waged wars of extermination, killing many Yaquis, forcing others to flee, and deporting the rest to slave plantations. Many Yaquis found safety in the United States, but such refuge came at a cost. The Yaqui vote, which had sustained their communities for over two centuries, struggled to make the trip north. Yaquis kept a low profile to avoid state violence. Yaqui political reconstitution in Arizona was a slow process that took decades.

Pueblos and Tohono O'odhams similarly refused to embrace U.S. citizenship and voting during the U.S. territorial period. Although some Pueblos went to the polls at various times during this era, the U.S. takeover of the region pitted Pueblos and Hispanos against one another. Within this setting, citizenship and voting served to decrease Pueblo sovereignty, and so they refused, turning to the vote on the community level to protect their individual Pueblo nations' autonomy. In Pimería Alta, the Tohono O'odhams of San Xavier del Bac also refused to exercise the franchise, but it is difficult to know their specific motivations. Like the Pueblos, they likely saw little material benefit to taking their place as citizens of Arizona and the United States. Local, internal needs took precedence. For all these groups, full enfranchisement in the U.S. model did not come until the post–World War II period, when the growth of federal power in the West had increased the need for political participation and voting in the American system. I emphatically repeat: through all these changes, the element that remained constant was *the desire by Pueblos, Hopis, Yaquis, and Tohono O'odhams to protect their rights as sovereign Native Nations*. It remains so today.

And so I come full circle with another story. In the fall of 2016 I sat in the familiar confines of a shady area near Montezuma Well—the Yavapai place of emergence—with my mother, sisters, brother, aunties, uncles, cousins, and other relatives and friends. Even more familiar than the setting were the day's activities: sitting around the table, sharing food, listening to family stories, and laughing. We had gathered to celebrate an election day. The chair, vice chair, and one council seat were up for grabs. The governing structure of my people, the Yavapai-Apache Nation, includes a seven-person tribal council, an executive branch with a chair and a vice chair, and a judicial branch with a chief judge and tribal court.[11] Under the terms of the Indian Reorganization Act of 1934, we adopted a tribal constitution and three-branch governing structure on 24 October 1936, which were approved by the U.S. Secretary of the Interior on 12 February 1937.[12] Tribal politics are in fact messy, with council members frequently removed from office—sometimes deservedly so, but other times not—resulting in emergency elections to fill vacated seats, in addition to regular election cycles. We have learned well from our colonizers. In this particular election, my mother had run for tribal chair, and a cousin for the vacated council seat. Both women won their elections. Even though our nation is small in number—some 2,500 citizens—our elections generate great excitement. We realize that through our officers and our political activities, we continue the fight to maintain our status as sovereign Indigenous nations in an imperfect system.

As I sat in council chambers while the votes were tallied that evening, I felt both joyful and sad. Joyful because I knew that my mother would serve our people wholeheartedly and well, but sad because I knew that this new position would be difficult and time-consuming, frequently taking her away from the family to travel to seats of power both near and far to protect the rights of all our people. This is the legacy of Indian voting.

Notes

Introduction

1. A note on terminology: throughout this work, I use *Indian, Indigenous, Native American,* and *Native* interchangeably. All four terms are used in various settings. *Indian* is common in informal conversations with Native North Americans, as is *Native* (or *Native American*). *Indigenous* is more standard in academic settings, and is seeing increased usage in other settings as well. I have, at times, favored *Indian*, not because I believe it best describes the Indigenous nations and peoples of the Southwest Borderlands, but because it is the term I am most accustomed to hearing and using in my interactions with family members and other Natives, especially in informal storytelling situations.

2. Herman, *Rim Country Exodus*, 149.

3. A large smelter was located in Clarkdale, which smelted the copper ore from the Jerome copper mines. These mines were once among the largest in the world. See "The History of Clarkdale," Town of Clarkdale website, http://www.clarkdale.az.gov/history.html, accessed 28 September 2015.

4. Crandall, "The Early Life of Ned Russell," 4.

5. Crandall, 40–44.

6. Wunder, *"Retained by the People,"* 50.

7. Wunder, 15.

8. Cohen, *Cohen's Handbook of Federal Indian Law*, 157.

9. In New Mexico's 2nd Congressional District, Xochitl Torres Small defeated Yvette Herrell, a citizen of the Cherokee Nation of Oklahoma. Had Herrell won, it would have resulted in three Native American women in Congress.

10. Stuart, "Meet Deb Haaland."

11. Jones, "Inside Deb Haaland's Historic Bid." While the 2018 midterms were a significant milestone for Native American political participation, they also brought to light many of the obstacles Native American voters have faced for generations. A controversial North Dakota voter ID law, which the U.S. Supreme Court refused to overturn in October 2018, required state residents to present an ID with a current street address; P.O. boxes did not qualify as valid addresses. Many North Dakota Native Americans live on rural reservations and have no street addresses. The law and the subsequent Supreme Court decision left tribal nations scrambling to issue new IDs with street addresses. See Reilly, "North Dakota's Voter ID Law."

12. McCool, Olson, and Robinson, *Native Vote*; and McDonald, *American Indians*.

13. Venturini, "The Fight for Indian Voting Rights in New Mexico"; Dunbar, "A Study of the Suffrage of the Arizona and New Mexico Indian"; and Mangusso, "A Study of the Citizenship Provisions of the Treaty of Guadalupe Hidalgo."

14. See Wunder, "Retained by the People"; Stubben, Native Americans and Political Participation; Wilkins, American Indian Sovereignty; Hoxie, Final Promise; Rosier, Serving Their Country; Cohen, Cohen's Handbook of Federal Indian Law; and Deloria and Lytle, American Indians, American Justice.

15. Cohen, Cohen's Handbook of Federal Indian Law, 157; Venturini, "The Fight for Indian Voting Rights in New Mexico," 2–4.

16. See Haskett, Indigenous Rulers; Lockhart, The Nahuas after the Conquest; Spalding, Huarochirí, esp. pp. 216–22; Ducey, A Nation of Villages; Tanck de Estrada, Pueblos de Indios Y Educación; Wasserman, Capitalists, Caciques, and Revolution: 1984; and Hackel, Children of Coyote, Missionaries of St. Francis.

17. Regis Pecos, in Sando, Pueblo Nations, xi.

18. Morrow, A Harvest of Reluctant Souls, 37, emphasis my own.

19. Scott, Domination and the Arts of Resistance, 15.

20. Joseph "Woody" Aguilar, "Postcolonialism in Borderlands and Pueblo Histories," Joe Sando Symposium for Pueblo Indian Studies, Albuquerque, N.Mex., 5 March 2015.

21. Many Indigenous communities in what became the U.S.-Mexico Borderlands had long traditions of farming through irrigation. They constructed elaborate ditch systems, which the Spaniards later copied and termed *acequias*. These ditches were often shared by neighboring Spanish and Indian communities, and "ditch captains" were selected to administer these important irrigation works, deciding who received water, both when and how much.

22. Many of New Mexico's Pueblos are divided into halves, or moieties, with each having its own chief. For example, Santa Clara Pueblo is divided between Summer and Winter People, with Summer and Winter Chiefs.

23. See Brooks, Mesa of Sorrows.

Chapter One

1. A. Ortiz, The Tewa World, 3.

2. In Ortiz's work, *Fiscales* are one of the three groups of officers at Ohkay Owingeh. In other cases throughout this book, however, a *fiscal* may be an individual (*fiscales* is the plural), not the same as Ortiz is referring to. *Fiscal* as an office also has some variation among Indigenous communities. I have capitalized the term when referring to the specific context of Ortiz but have left it lowercase at other occurrences.

3. Ortiz, The Tewa World, 62.

4. Ohkay Owingeh Pueblo is divided into Summer and Winter moieties, exhibiting what many have referred to as the dual organization. This is typical of the Tewa Pueblos (Ohkay Owingeh, Santa Clara, Nambé, Tesuque, Pojoaque, and San Ildefonso). The nominating order would be reversed the following year.

5. A. Ortiz, The Tewa World, 63.

6. Ortiz, 64.

7. Ortiz, 64.

8. Ortiz, 64–65.

9. Ortiz, 64–65.

10. Ortiz, 65.

11. Ortiz, 65.

12. Ortiz, 65.
13. Ortiz, 65–66.
14. Ortiz, 66.
15. Ortiz, 66.
16. Ortiz, 66–67.
17. Ortiz, 67.

18. Charles F. Lummis, who lived at Isleta Pueblo for a time in the early twentieth century, wrote of officeholding there, "There are no office seekers—and no salaries. It is one place where in very truth the 'office seeks the man.'" Lummis, *Mesa, Cañon and Pueblo*, 401.

19. A. Ortiz, *The Tewa World*, 61.

20. The Cuban scholar Fernando Ortiz referred to this phenomenon as transculturation. It is not simply the acquisition of a new culture, or acculturation, nor the loss or uprooting of a previous culture, or deculturation, but instead a process similar to the reproductive process between individuals. The resulting phenomena have traits from both "parents" but are distinct and different from each one. See Fernando Ortiz, *Cuban Counterpoint*, 102–3.

21. Adams, *Indian Policies in the Americas*, 21–22.

22. The use of the term naturales for Indians under Spanish colonial control indicated that they were more natural or normal, as opposed to the barbarian savages outside of Spanish dominion. This process of classifying and "othering" was also ongoing and evolving during the colonial era. See Weber, *Bárbaros*, for a superb discussion of Spain's late eighteenth century dealings with Indians and the concept of indios bárbaros.

23. L. B. Simpson, trans., *The Laws of Burgos of 1512–1513*, 2.

24. The encomienda system was first established on the island of Española. Under this system conquistadores and other influential individuals known as encomenderos were granted specific numbers of Indians, from whom they extracted tribute and labor. Theoretically, these payments of tribute and labor were in exchange for protection and Christianization, and Indians were supposed to receive wages for their labor. By 1503, the crown altered encomienda so that Indians received their own inalienable lands in permanent villages with the encomenderos as their "protectors." Encomenderos were supposed to see to the teaching, indoctrination, and suppression of Native culture, as well as some intermingling of Indians and Spaniards. All profits from this system were to be shared with the crown. Encomienda often degenerated into a form of Indian slavery. See Hackett, *Historical Documents*, 1:26–27.

25. L. B. Simpson, *Laws of Burgos*, 14.

26. Simpson, 45.

27. "[Royal order] commanding that the Indians of Nueva Galicia be gathered into towns, where they may live under an organized government [1570.]," in Hackett, *Historical Documents*, 1:101, 103.

28. Hackett, *Historical Documents*, 1:20.

29. Hackel, *Children of Coyote, Missionaries of Saint Francis*, 231.

30. It was also referred to as the *cabildo secular*. See Cruz, *Let There Be Towns*, 5; generally, in larger cities the council was called an ayuntamiento, while in smaller towns it was a cabildo. See Hackett, *Historical Documents*, 1:25.

31. Cruz, *Let There Be Towns*, 5–6.

32. Hackett, *Historical Documents*, 1:25.

33. S. Lyman Tyler, *The Indian Cause in the Spanish Laws of the Indies*, 51–52.
34. Haskett, *Indigenous Rulers*, 20.
35. Hackett, *Historical Documents*, 1:25.
36. Borah, *Justice by Insurance*, 224.
37. Haskett, *Indigenous Rulers*, 27; Tanck de Estrada, *Pueblos de Indios Y Educación en el México Colonial*, 30.
38. Haskett, *Indigenous Rulers*, 30; Hackel, *Children of Coyote, Missionaries of Saint Francis*, 234–38.
39. Lockhart, *The Nahuas after the Conquest*, 32.
40. Haskett, *Indigenous Rulers*, 30.
41. "Solórzano Pereira," accessed 15 November 2014. It is sometimes spelled "Pereira" and sometimes "Pereyra."
42. Capítulo 24, nos. 2, 5, 48, 49, 53, 55, 58 in Juan Solórzano Pereyra, *Política Indiana*, Tomo I, 512–13, 524–25, translation my own.
43. The Marquis to the Magistrate of Otumba, 29 December 1589, MSS 867, box 4, folder 182, rec. 182, transcription, Archivo General de la Nación, Center for Southwest Research, University Libraries, University of New Mexico (hereafter cited as AGN CSWR), translation my own.
44. Haskett, *Indigenous Rulers*, 32. See also Tanck de Estrada, *Pueblos de Indios*, 37.
45. Don Luis de Velasco to the Magistrate of Otumba, 29 November 1590, MSS 867, box 3, folder 147, rec. 204—DF, transcription, AGN CSWR, translation my own.
46. Don Luis de Velasco to the Magistrate of Ozolotepec, 31 July 1591, MSS 867, box 4, folder 112, rec. 848—DF, transcription, AGN CSWR, translation my own.
47. New Spain, and later New Mexico, was divided into *alcaldías*, or districts, headed by an alcalde, who was the head of the cabildo and the judge of first instance. This local magistrate met with Indian leaders, hearing and resolving disputes that arose, supervising land matters, and delivering royal notices to Indian towns. He was the first link in a chain of government that stretched from Indian town to provincial governor, then to the viceroy, and eventually to the Spanish king. See Bayer, *Santa Ana*, 53, 88–89.
48. Haskett, *Indigenous Rulers*, 60–61, 63, 69, 77–78.
49. Tanck de Estrada, *Atlas Ilustrado de los Pueblos de Indios*, 32.
50. Taylor, *Drinking, Homicide, and Rebellion in Colonial Mexican Villages*, 23, 165.
51. Dozier, *The Pueblo Indians of North America*, 31, 36–37.
52. Sando, *Pueblo Nations*, 8.
53. Sando, 23–24.
54. Sando, 13, 24. Many of the Pueblos maintain these traditional forms of government today; these are living, vibrant structures.
55. A *manta* is a large square cotton cloth worn over one shoulder and tied at the waist with a sash, typically worn by Pueblo women.
56. Flint and Flint, *Documents of the Coronado Expedition*, 306.
57. "Gallegos' Relation of the Chamuscado-Rodríguez Expedition," in Hammond and Rey, *The Rediscovery of New Mexico*, 84–86.
58. "Report of Antonio de Espejo," in Hammond and Rey, *The Rediscovery of New Mexico*, 220, 223, 230.
59. Simmons, *New Mexico*, 11; Cutter, *The Protector de Indios in Colonial New Mexico*, 29.

60. "Castaño de Sosa's 'Memoria,'" in Hammond and Rey, *The Rediscovery of New Mexico*, 280–81.

61. Interestingly, Oñate recounted meeting with these leaders "in the great kiva of this pueblo." This sacred space for Pueblo ceremonial activities normally would have been off limits to outsiders. We can only guess as to why the meeting took place there. See "Act of Obedience and Vassalage by the Indians of Santo Domingo," in Hammond and Rey, *Don Juan de Oñate*, 338.

62. Hammond and Rey, *Don Juan de Oñate*, 338–40.

63. "Act of Obedience and Vassalage by the Indians of San Juan Bautista," in Hammond and Rey, *Don Juan de Oñate*, 343.

64. "Act of Obedience and Vassalage by the Indians of Acolocu," in Hammond and Rey, *Don Juan de Oñate*, 349.

65. "Act of Obedience and Vassalage by the Indians of Acoma," in Hammond and Rey, *Don Juan de Oñate*, 355.

66. Dr. Joseph Henry Suina in *Canes of Power*, DVD.

67. Bayer, *Santa Ana*, 36.

68. Ortiz, *The Tewa World*, 61.

69. Marc Simmons, "History of Pueblo-Spanish Relations to 1821," in Ortiz, *Handbook of North American Indians*, 183.

70. Sando, *Nee Hemish*, 53.

71. Scholes, "Church and State in New Mexico," 146, 148–49.

72. Scholes, *Church and State in New Mexico, 1610–1650*, 78.

73. Franciscans repeatedly lobbied for exemptions for Pueblo officers from paying tribute or providing personal service to the governor of New Mexico. For example, in 1635, Fray Alonso de Benavides asked that "caciques, chief captains, governors, alcaldes, and fiscales of the churches . . . be exempt from tribute and personal service while they hold these offices." He asked for this dispensation "on account of the big tasks they perform for the republic and the service of your Majesty," and noted that "They are so busy in their offices that even their planted fields are cared for by others, as they are unable to do it themselves. The native lords and chieftains resent very much that they are compelled to pay tribute." See "Petition of Benavides Regarding Tribute and Personal Service by the Indians" in Hodge, Hammond, and Rey, *Fray Alonso de Benavides' Revised Memorial of 1634*, 170–71. Benavides also asked that New Mexico's governors not be allowed to take from the missions Pueblo children whom they deemed "orphans" in order to put them to work in Spanish households.

74. "Diego Fernandez de Cordova to Juan de Eulate," 10 March 1620, in Bloom, "A Glimpse of New Mexico in 1620," 360.

75. Bloom, 362–63.

76. "Appointment of Mateo Pacheco, Indian, as Governor of Jemez Pueblo," 9 February 1665, MSS 867, file 24, box 5, folder 5, rec. 64—DF, transcription, AGN CSWR, 1–2, translation my own.

77. "Appointment of Pedro de la Aguila, Indio, as Governor of the Tiguas, Isleta Pueblo," 9 February 1665, MSS 867, file 24, box 5, folder 4, rec. 63—DF, transcription, AGN CSWR, 1–2, translation my own. Jack Forbes noted that Ypotlapigua probably referred to Opatas. See Forbes, *Apache, Navaho and Spaniard*, 127. It is also worth noting that during the Pueblo

Revolt, a number of individuals at Isleta Pueblo fled with or were taken by the Spaniards to El Paso. Perhaps de la Aguila, if still alive, was among this group of Isletans.

78. Bayer, *Santa Ana*, 88.

79. "Joseph Henry Suina: Cochiti, N. Mexico," North Dakota Study Group Oral History Project, http://www.ndsg.org/oralhistory/jsuina/index.html, accessed 26 July 2015. I met informally with Dr. Suina and he graciously spoke with me about some of his experiences as a Pueblo civil officer and the challenges he faced. I held a number of such informal conversations with current and former Pueblo officers, but I do not quote directly as these matters are private affairs for the Pueblos, and issues of governance are to be kept confidential.

80. Numerous anthropological and ethnographic accounts of Pueblo elections exist. Some are more reliable than others, and the information in some was likely obtained in unethical ways. For example, working in the first half of the twentieth century, Elsie Clews Parsons courted great controversy with her work on Isleta, Jemez, Taos, and other Pueblos. The charge was that her work revealed Pueblo sacred knowledge. The matter is complicated, but Parsons, who somehow managed to coax sensitive information out of her informants, received death threats on a number of occasions over her work. See Gutiérrez's introduction in Parsons, *Pueblo Indian Religion*. I have flatly avoided any Pueblo sacred or ceremonial knowledge, and I have approached anthropological sources with great care. For other descriptions of Pueblo elections, see Sando, *Pueblo Nations*, 13–15; Adler and Dick, *Picuris Pueblo Through Time*, 26–28; White, *The Pueblo of Santo Domingo, New Mexico*, 33–48; White, *The Pueblo of Santa Ana, New Mexico*, 188–201; White, *The Acoma Indians*, 40–61; Dumarest, *Notes on Cochiti*, 197–202; Lange, *Cochiti*, 191–213; Hill and Lange, *An Ethnography of Santa Clara Pueblo*, 188–90; and Aberle, "The Pueblo Indians of New Mexico," 5–65. Aberle, who served as General Superintendent of the United Pueblos Agency from 1934 to 1943, described in some detail the officers and their method of selection for all the Pueblos. These various anthropological sources show the variations in elections and civil government at the Pueblos, but also indicate the degree of unity among them in these secular governing institutions.

81. Lela Kaskalla, former governor of the Pueblo of Nambé, "Coffee and Conversation with Verna Teller, Former Governor of Isleta Pueblo, and Lela Kaskalla, Former Governor of Nambé Pueblo." Public speaking event, Indian Pueblo Cultural Center, 14 March 2015. I was also told by a man from Cochiti Pueblo, who had served as a sheriff for a year, that he had a feeling he would be chosen for office again the year after. He said that he would not be returning home around the New Year. In another story related to me, an Acoma man chosen for a major office intentionally stayed out of town. The village elders found out where he was and had someone drive there to pick him up. He was informed that he had no choice in the matter.

82. White, *The Pueblo of Santa Ana, New Mexico*, 184.

83. LaCroix Dailey, "Symbolism and Significance of the Lincoln Canes," 129. The number of canes the governor receives can vary. Some Pueblos seem to have lost their Mexican canes, retaining only the Spanish and Lincoln canes. There is also the cane given by New Mexico Governor Bruce King—"the king of New Mexico"—to the Pueblos in 1981, recognizing Pueblo sovereignty and celebrating the 300th anniversary of the Pueblo Revolt.

84. Ortiz, *The Tewa World*, 62–67.

85. Simmons, *Spanish Government in New Mexico*, 161. The tradition of receiving varas de justicia was not limited to Pueblo Indian officials; Spanish municipal officers in the Western Hemisphere and Iberia also received varas as symbols of authority on entering office (see Cruz, *Let There Be Towns*, 149).

86. Ortiz, *The Tewa World*, 34–35.

87. *Canes of Power*, DVD. As living entities, sometimes even considered family members, canes are offered food, sacred cornmeal, and other objects.

88. "Canes of Power," official website of the Pueblo of Acoma, http://www.puebloofacoma.org/canes-of-power.aspx, accessed 27 July 2015.

89. Adler and Dick, *Picuris Pueblo through Time*, 27.

90. "Certification of Captain Rael de Aguilar, Santa Fé, Jaunuary 10, 1706," in Hackett, *Historical Documents*, 3:366. Don Alfonso Rael de Aguilar, who names himself as the "protector-general of the Indians," was pointing to his office as *protector de indios* (protector of Indians). Those who held this office acted as intermediaries for the Pueblos and assisted them in land cases, election disputes, and other important matters. See Cutter, *The Protector de Indios in Colonial New Mexico*.

91. "Election of Jemez Officials," 16 January 1811, Spanish Archives of New Mexico II, 2391, roll 17, fr. 350. Santa Fe: New Mexico State Records Center and Archives (hereafter SANM II), translation my own.

92. This spelling may be unique to Ohkay Owingeh; the spelling is normally "alguacil."

93. Ortiz, *The Tewa World*, 71–72.

94. Adler and Dick, *Picuris Pueblo through Time*, 26–27. Women are absent from nearly all historical accounts of Pueblo elections. Brief mention is made in Adler and Dick's account of women's being appointed to help the fiscal with the maintenance of the saints in the mission church, but it is unknown whether this practice extends back to Spanish times. See p. 27.

95. Bayer, *Santa Ana*, 88.

96. Sando, *Pueblo Nations*, 60. In cases where the Pueblo did not have a missionary in residence, the fiscales kept the keys to the church, maintained the church and its grounds, and readied the mission for periodic visits by the priest. See Dozier, *Pueblo Indians of North America*, 49.

97. "Fragment, inventory book. Pantry provisions," Loose Documents, Mission (1680–1850), Archives of the Archdiocese of Santa Fe (hereafter AASF) 51, 1712 no. 12, fr. 834. In his 1630 report on New Mexico, Fray Alonso de Benavides wrote that, "although over half of this nation [of Jemez Pueblo] has died, Your Majesty may still count on more than three thousand newly assembled taxpayers." Morrow, *A Harvest of Reluctant Souls*, 25.

98. "Governor Don Juan Bautista de Anza to all Indian pueblo governors," Loose Documents, Mission (1680–1850), AASF 51, 1779 no. 1, fr. 495.

99. Bayer, *Santa Ana*, 88. Permission to travel outside one's community was not limited to Indians; this applied to Spaniards as well. Travel required the local magistrate's permission, or in his absence that of the friar or parish priest. See Simmons, *Spanish Government in New Mexico*, 183.

100. Dorothy Roman, interview by Ronald Switzer, 5 March 1968, tape #33, American Indian Oral History Collection (MSS 314 B.C.), Center for Southwest Research, University Libraries, Albuquerque: University of New Mexico (hereafter AIOHC CSWR).

101. Former New Mexico State Historian Robert J. Torrez wrote that the Pueblo Revolt "did force changes in Spanish attitudes which enabled the Pueblos to maintain their language and ancient religious practices. After the reconquest, it became apparent that the Spanish would have to demonstrate tolerance towards Pueblo religious and cultural ceremonies and cooperate with their neighbors." Although the idea of the "bloodless reconquest" is a complete fabrication, it is possible that more freedom in the selecting of officers was among the changes in Spanish practice after the Revolt. See Robert J. Torrez, "A Cuarto Centennial History of New Mexico," ch. 4, available online at the New Mexico Genealogical Society website, http://www.nmgs.org/artcuar4.htm, accessed 27 January 2014.

102. Ducey, *A Nation of Villages*, 6–7.

103. "The form of government used at the missions of San Diego de los Jémez and San Augustín de la Isleta by Father Fray Joaquín de Jesús Ruiz, their former minister." [Undated. 1773?] in Hackett, *Historical Documents*, 3:506.

104. Ducey, *A Nation of Villages*, 12, 24.

105. Sando, *Nee Hemish*, 52–53.

106. Dozier, *The Pueblo Indians of North America*, 68.

107. Brown, *Pueblo Indians and Spanish Colonial Authority*, 27, 21.

108. "Diego de Vargas, Campaign journal, 20 September 1693–20 January 1694, DS," in Kessell, Hendricks, and Dodge, *To the Royal Crown Restored*, 483.

109. Kessell, Hendricks, and Dodge, 483, emphasis my own.

110. Hart, *Pedro Pino*, 2, 14.

111. "Pueblo Government," official website of the Pueblo of Cochiti, http://www.pueblodecochiti.org/government.html, accessed 15 July 2015, emphasis my own.

112. White, *The Pueblo of Santo Domingo*, 45.

113. Ortiz, *The Tewa World*, 156.

114. Ducey, *A Nation of Villages*, 12.

115. Ebright and Hendricks, *Advocates for the Oppressed*, 9; Brown, *Pueblo Indians and Spanish Colonial Authority*, 46.

116. Dorothy Roman interview, AIOHC CSWR.

117. "Report of B. H. Thomas, Pueblo Agent," 14 August 1879, in *Annual Report of the Commissioner of Indian Affairs to the Secretary of the Interior for the Year 1879*, 119.

118. Lockhart, *Nahuas after the Conquest*, 35–36. A complex altepetl could have multiple officers in varying combinations. For example, Coyoacan in 1553 had a governor, two alcaldes, twelve regidores, two majordomos, two accountants, two notaries, eight alguaciles, and one *alcaide* (jailer). See Lockhart, 38. The Pueblo Spanish civil governing structures did not reach this level of development.

119. "Diego de Vargas, Campaign Journal, 16 October 1692–27 December 1692, DS," in Kessell and Hendricks, *By Force of Arms*, 511, 519–20.

120. "Extracts from Governor Vargas's Journal on the Reestablishment of the Missions, September 18–October 7 and November 1–December 21, 1694," in Espinosa, *Pueblo Indian Revolt of 1696*, 93–94.

121. Espinosa, 109.

122. Cutter, "The Administration of Colonial Law in New Mexico," 106.

123. Ebright, Hendricks, and Hughes, *Four Square Leagues*, 86.

124. The Pueblo land grant consisted of four square leagues, or one league in each of the cardinal directions from the Pueblo's central plaza. One league measures approximately 2.6 miles, and an area of four square leagues totaled approximately 17,350 acres. See Ebright et al., *Four Square Leagues*, 11.

125. "Spaniards in Indian Pueblos. Decree of Governor Cuerbo y Valdes prohibiting the entrance into Indian pueblos of any Spaniards, and ordering the departure of any 'found at present in said pueblos.'" 25 August 1705. WPA Translations of Spanish Archives of New Mexico I, 1340, rl 9. Works Progress Administration, Historical Records Survey (hereafter cited as WPA SANM I). Parenthetical insertions in original.

126. Father Juan Agustín de Morfí, "Account of Disorders in New Mexico, 1778," in Simmons, *Coronado's Land*, 147–50. Morfí went so far as to describe the Pueblos as "well-ordered," "prone neither to thievery nor drunkenness," and that with their agricultural lifestyle "they freely harvest their crops and live in abundance." For Morfí, the only way that Spanish communities could enjoy such benefits was by "putting their towns in similar order" (Morfí, 132).

127. Morfí, 147–50.

128. Morfí, 155. Morfí described Pueblo women forced to serve in the homes of Spaniards, who suffered "personal outrage, a fact that causes their fathers and husbands perpetual sorrow," and asserted, "There is scarcely a single soul who escapes abuse" (Morfí, 155).

129. Ebright, Hendricks, and Hughes, *Four Square Leagues*, 155–62.

130. "Lawsuit. San Ildefonso pueblo vs. Ygnacio de Roibal. Proceedings in a dispute over lands situated 'on the other side of the Rio del Norte opposite the pueblo of San Ildefonso,' held by the defendant and claimed by the plaintiff as Indian land." 16 September 1704, WPA SANM I, 1339, rl. 9. Parenthetical insertions in original.

131. "Lawsuit."

132. Ebright, Hendricks, and Hughes, *Four Square Leagues*, 18.

133. Marriages—Zuni (M-45 Box 42, 1705–1775), AASF 33, 1748, fr. 1299, translation my own.

134. Simmons, *Witchcraft in the Southwest*, 32–33; Brown, *Pueblo Indians and Spanish Colonial Authority*, 32.

135. Kessell, "The Ways and Words of the Other," 32.

136. "Letter of Esteban Clemente, Pueblo of Humanas, November 30, 1660," in Hackett, *Historical Documents*, 3:165.

137. "[Declaration] of Diego López [Sambrano. Hacienda of Luis de Carbajal, December 22, 1681]," trans. Charmion Clair Shelby, in Hackett, *Revolt of the Pueblo Indians of New Mexico*, 2:299–300.

138. The Ohkay Owingeh Pueblo leader's name appears as both Popé and Po'pay. Scholars from the Pueblo, such as Herman Agoyo, have preferred the latter, and so I have chosen to use this spelling.

139. "Certification of Captain Rael de Aguilar, Santa Fé, Jaunuary 10, 1706," in Hackett, *Historical Documents*, 3:366–69.

140. Sando, *Pueblo Nations*, 263.

141. Ortiz, *The Tewa World*, 69.

142. The mission complex included the church, the missionary's dwelling, a kitchen, administrative offices, rooms for instruction, and workshops where "all the trades and arts useful to humans are taught, such as those of the tailor, cobbler, carpenter, smith, and all the

rest, in which the Indians have proven themselves most adept" (Benavides in Morrow, *A Harvest of Reluctant Souls*, 79). The mission complex could be quite massive.

143. "Bartolomé Lobato, Opinion, Cochiti Pueblo, 25 February 1702, DS," 143; "Pedro Rodríguez Cubero, Order, Zia Pueblo, 28 February 1702, DS," 150; "Juan de Ulibarrí to Pedro Rodríguez Cubero, Zuni Pueblo, 8 March 1702, DS," 179, in Kessell et al., *A Settling of Accounts*.

144. Bernardo Benavía to Alberto Maynez, 20 October 1815. SANM II, 2630, rl. 18, fr. 252–53, translation my own.

145. "Complain [sic] of Santa Clara Indians against their governor, Santa Fe," SANM II, 1004, rl. 12, fr. 50–53.

146. In one contemporary account, Santo Domingo Pueblo scholar Estefanita Lynne Calabaza told of an episode where her aunt's father asked the governor's permission for his daughter to leave the Pueblo to attend nursing school. Calabaza related, "The governor was and still is responsible for the well-being of his 'community' children. This included protecting the community from external institutions that may negatively affect the collective whole. He needed to know where each 'child' was." Calabaza, "Through Pueblo Oral Tradition and Personal Narrative," 152–53.

147. "Complain [sic] of Santa Clara Indians against their governor," fr. 54.

148. Isleta Indians vs. Mariano Beitia, Santa Fe, with judgment of Fermín de Mendinueta. SANM II, 662, rl. 10, fr. 678, 681, 685, translation my own.

149. Sando, "The Pueblo Revolt," 21.

150. "Declaration of the Indian, Juan. Place on the Rio del Norte, December 18, 1681," in Hackett, *Revolt of the Pueblo Indians*, 2:232.

151. Ortiz, "Po'pay's Leadership," 88–89.

152. "Letter from the Governor and Captain-general, Don Antonio de Otermín, from New Mexico," 8 September 1680, in Hackett, *Historical Documents*, 3:328–29. Another statement of Otermín's in the same letter relates how he summoned an Indian before him in the besieged capital, before the Spanish evacuation. According to Otermín, this Indian had lived in Santa Fe for many years. When he came to see the governor, "I asked him how it was that he had gone crazy too—being an Indian who spoke our language, was so intelligent, and had lived all his life in the villa among Spaniards, where I had placed such confidence in him—and was now coming as a leader of the Indian rebels. He replied that they had elected him as their captain" (Hackett, 330). The practice of electing military officers was one the Pueblos had followed as auxiliaries in New Mexico's many military actions against more "barbarous" Indian neighbors. Whatever the circumstances of this election, this Indian was clearly speaking in terms that the Spanish governor would understand.

153. "Diego de Vargas, Campaign Journal, 12 June 1696, DS," in Kessell, Hendricks, and Dodge, *Blood on the Boulders*, 747–49.

154. "Diego de Vargas, Campaign Journal, 30 August–6 September 1696, DS," in Kessell, Hendricks, and Dodge, *Blood on the Boulders*, 1008.

155. Kessell's detailed narration of the Pecos virtual civil war can be found in *Kiva, Cross, and Crown*, 288–97.

156. Horvath, "The Social and Political Organization of the Genízaros," 1–2.

157. Brooks, *Captives and Cousins*, 123.

158. "Declaration of Fray Miguel de Menchero. Santa Bárbara, May 10, 1744," in Hackett, *Historical Documents*, 3:401–2.

159. Albert H. Schroeder, "Rio Grande Ethnohistory," in Alfonso Ortiz, ed., *New Perspectives on the Pueblos*, 62.

160. Morfí, "Account of Disorders in New Mexico," 157.

161. "Declaration of Fray Miguel de Menchero," in Hackett, *Historical Documents*, 3:402.

162. Morfí, "Account of Disorders in New Mexico," 156.

163. Horvath, "The Social and Political Organization of the Genízaros," 21; Brooks, *Captives and Cousins*, 128.

164. Morfí, "Account of Disorders in New Mexico," 156.

165. Brooks, *Captives and Cousins*, 133–35.

166. "Protest made by Lieutenant Benture Bustamante at the order of Captain Juan de Armijo in the name of thirty-three companions, half-breed Indians, against being removed from Santa Fe to the Comanche frontier," 20 June 1780, WPA SANM I, 1138, rl. 8.

167. "General Description of New Mexico, written by the Reverend Preacher Fray Juan Agustín de Morfí, Reader Jubiliado and son of this province of Santo Evangelico Mexico. Year of 1782," in Thomas, *Forgotten Frontiers*, 91–92.

168. Horvath, "The Social and Political Organization of the Genízaros," 132.

169. "Antonio Casados and Luís Quintana. Indios Genízaros vs. Barrera, Diego de Torres, and Antonio Salazar," 1746, WPA SANM I, 183, rl. 2.

170. Ebright and Hendricks, *The Witches of Abiquiu*, 95–96.

171. Ebright and Hendricks, 96–105.

172. Another Indian group that came under Spanish control in the eighteenth century was the *Apaches de paz*, or peace Apaches. In the latter decades of the eighteenth century, thousands of Mescalero, Chiricahua, and Western Apaches moved onto reservation-like areas, known as *establecimientos*, or peace establishments. Spaniards believed it would be easier to feed, clothe, and surveil these Apaches than face them in battle. But Apaches de paz differed from Pueblo Indians in that they were under military, not church, authority. Spaniards designated leaders among the Apaches de paz, but there were no annual elections or system of village democracy in place in the Spanish model among the Apaches de paz. Their leaders did have some of the same powers as elected Pueblo officers, such as acting as judges in minor cases and meting out punishments. They could also travel to provincial seats of government to advocate for their people in some cases. For more, see Babcock, *Apache Adaptation to Hispanic Rule*, and Pedro de Nava, "Instructions for dealing with the Apaches at peace in Nueva Vizcaya, Chihuahua, 14 Oct. 1791," in Hendricks and Timmons, *San Elizario*, 102–9.

173. Adams, *Indian Policies in the Americas*, 35.

174. "Bernardo Bonavilla to Alberto Máynez," 27 December 1815, SANM I, 1280, rl. 16, fr. 1055–56.

175. Cruz, *Let There Be Towns*, 147–48.

Chapter Two

1. Sando, *Pueblo Nations*, 9.

2. Sheridan et al., *Moquis and Kastiilam*, 31–32; "The Account of Pedro de Castañeda de Nájera (1560s)," in Sheridan et al., *Moquis and Kastiilam*, 45 and 252n19, for discussion of the

use of the term "ayuntamiento"; see "Coronado's Soldiers Encounter the Hopis and the Grand Canyon, 1540," pp. 30–62, for the entire discussion of the violence of this episode.

3. Yava, *Big Falling Snow*, 89.

4. "Act of Obedience and Vassalage by the Indians of Mohoqui [sic]," in Hammond and Rey, *Don Juan de Oñate*, 1:360–61.

5. Sheridan et al., *Moquis and Kastiilam*, 86.

6. Iverson, "The Enduring Hopi," 144.

7. Clemmer, *Roads in the Sky*, 28.

8. Fray Estevan de Perea, "Second Report of the Grand Conversion that has taken place in Nuevo México," in Sheridan et al., *Moquis and Kastiilam*, 133.

9. Eleanor B. Adams, "Hopi-Spanish Relations in the Colonial Period," unpub. typescript, Eleanor B. Adams Papers, box 1, folder 7, Center for Southwest Research, University Libraries, University of New Mexico (hereafter EBA CSWR), 5.

10. Benavides, *A Harvest of Reluctant Souls*, 37–38.

11. Benavides, 37. Three main accounts exist of the events at Awat'ovi: Benivides's 1630 *Memorial*, Fray Estevan de Perea's 1633 account, and Benavides's *Revised Memorial of 1634*.

12. Sheridan et al., *Moquis and Kastiilam*, 126.

13. Clemmer, *Roads in the Sky*, 28–29; Malotki, *Hopi Tales of Destruction*, 125.

14. Montgomery et al., *Franciscan Awatovi*; Reports of the Awatovi Expedition, 13.

15. Brooks, *Mesa of Sorrows*, 49–50.

16. Yava, *Big Falling Snow*, 89.

17. "Interview with Clark Tenakhongva," 21 November 2002, in Sheridan et al., *Moquis and Kastiilam*, 51, 53.

18. See Clemmer, *Roads in the Sky*, 29, and Spicer, *Cycles of Conquest*, 191.

19. Sheridan et al., *Moquis and Kastiilam*, 11. Nearly all the records relating to the Hopi missions were destroyed in the Pueblo Revolt. Only a handful survive.

20. "The Investigation of Padre Fray Salvador de Guerra for Whipping and Scalding a Hopi Man to Death with Turpentine, 1655," in Sheridan et al., *Moquis and Kastiilam*, 145.

21. Testimony of Juan Cocpi, in Sheridan et al., *Moquis and Kastiilam*, 148.

22. Testimony of Salvador de Guerra, in Sheridan et al., *Moquis and Kastiilam*, 149.

23. Sheridan et al., *Moquis and Kastiilam*, 143.

24. "Sentence of Padre Fray Salvador de Guerra," in Sheridan et al., *Moquis and Kastiilam*, 167–69.

25. Sheridan et al., *Moquis and Kastiilam*, 144.

26. It must also be noted that Hopi oral tradition tells of a man named Sitkoyma, who was tortured and killed for holding a *Niman* (Home Dance) ceremony at Oraibi. This crucial ceremony made a Hopi wedding official, culminating in the new bride's presentation to the community at the Niman. The priest at Oraibi, who in the oral tradition is referred to as *Tota'tsi* (dictator or tyrant), forbade such ceremonies. While the Franciscan was away at a meeting in Santa Fe, Hopis at Oraibi held a Niman for those wedded in the previous years, during which time the ceremony had been brutally suppressed. When the missionary returned, he found out about Sitkoyma, who was the primary sponsor of the dance and whose daughter and son-in-law had participated. Sitkoyma was tied to a pole in the plaza and flogged with a horsewhip until he was "literally covered in blood from throughout his body." The priest then had "the military people" (meaning Spanish soldiers stationed at the village) pour

turpentine on Sitkoyma's wounds. He died in the plaza, still strapped to the pole. It is impossible to know whether Sitkoyma and Juan Cuna were the same man, but this oral history confirms the methods the Franciscans employed at Hopi. The tradition also relates that this episode convinced the Hopi chiefs and leaders to join the Pueblo Revolt. See "Leigh Kuwanwisiwma Talks About the Torture and Death of Sitkoyma of Orayvi for Holding a Niman Ceremony for Hopi Brides," in Sheridan et al., *Moquis and Kastiilam*, 169–77.

27. "Interview with Clark Tenakhongva," in Sheridan et al., *Moquis and Kastiilam*, 60.

28. Brooks, *Mesa of Sorrows*, 64.

29. Sigüenza Y Góngora, *The Mercurio Volante*, 82.

30. Yava, *Big Falling Snow*, 91.

31. José Narváez Valverde, "Notes upon Moqui and Other Recent Ones upon New Mexico," Senecú, 7 October 1732, in Hackett, *Historical Documents*, 3:385.

32. Bourke, *The Snake-dance of the Moquis of Arizona*, 90.

33. Brooks, *Mesa of Sorrows*, 59–60.

34. James F. Brooks, "Women, Men, and Cycles of Evangelism," 761.

35. "Diego de Vargas, Campaign Journal, 16 October–27 December 1692, DS," in Kessell and Hendricks, *By Force of Arms*, 561–62.

36. Kessell and Hendricks, 562, 564–65.

37. "Don Diego de Vargas to Miguel and the People of Awatovi, Santa Fe, 28 April 1694, DS," in Kessell, Hendricks, and Dodge, *Blood on the Boulders*, Book 1, 216–17.

38. It is unknown if Miguel was alive in 1700, since he is not named in the accounts of Awat'ovi's destruction. If he was, and had remained faithful to the Spaniards, he was almost certainly killed that day.

39. Yava, *Big Falling Snow*, 91.

40. Bandelier, *Final Report of Investigations among the Indians of the Southwestern United States*, 2:371–72.

41. James, *Pages from Hopi History*, 62–64; Malotki, *Hopi Tales of Destruction*, 126. See also Brooks, "Women, Men, and Cycles of Evangelization," 742–43.

42. Liebmann, *Revolt*, 46.

43. Malotki, *Hopi Tales of Destruction*, 176. It is possible that Miguel had been killed, deposed, or both. American-Danish scholar Armin W. Geertz, who wrote on Hopis and religion, posited that it was possible that Miguel and Ta'palo were one and the same and that Miguel's prior actions were simply done as political expediency. But he also stated that Ta'palo was actually Christian and the destruction of the village was brought on by the Catholic-traditionalist rivalry. See Geertz, *The Invention of Prophecy*, 30–36. Whatever his fate, and if Ta'palo and Miguel were the same individual, the facts remain that Awat'ovi was violently destroyed and that Miguel had held the Spanish title of Indian governor for some time.

44. Malotki, *Hopi Tales of Destruction*, 182.

45. Yava, *Big Falling Snow*, 91.

46. Malotki, *Hopi Tales of Destruction*, 188–89.

47. Elgean Joshevama quoted in Sheridan et al., *Moquis and Kastiilam*, 8.

48. Yava, *Big Falling Snow*, 95.

49. Sheridan et al., *Moquis and Kastiilam*, 8.

50. Nequatewa, *Truth of a Hopi*, 34–35.

51. Wíkvaya, quoted in Voth, *The Traditions of the Hopi*, 269–70.

52. Robert Sakiestewa, interviewed by Charles Peterson, 13 September 1967. Doris Duke Indian Oral History Project (Salt Lake City: J. Willard Marriott Library, University of Utah), 17.

53. "Escalante to Mendinueta, October 28, 1775," in Thomas, *Forgotten Frontiers*, 151–52.

54. Clemmer, *Roads in the Sky*, 27.

55. Yaquis today reside all over the world, but the largest groupings of Yaquis live in Arizona and Sonora.

56. Spellings for the eight principal Yaqui pueblos vary greatly. The original Spanish names were the customary Spanish length: Espíritu Santo de Cócorit, Santa Rosa de Bácum, San Ignacio de Tórim, La Natividad del Señor de Vícam, La Santísima Trinidad de Pótam, La Asuncíon de Ráum, Santa Bárbara de Huírivis, and San Miguel de Bélem. Hu-DeHart, *Missionaries, Miners, and Indians*, 33.

57. Hu-DeHart, 60.

58. Spicer, *The Yaquis*, 5.

59. "Segunda relación anonima de la jornada que hizo Nuño de Guzman á la Nueva Galicia," in García Icazbalceta, *Coleccíon de Documentos*, 2:301–2, translation my own.

60. West, *Sonora*, 29.

61. Pérez de Ribas, *History of the Triumphs of Our Holy Faith*, 327.

62. Troncoso, *Las Guerras con las Tribus Yaqui y Mayo*, 20, translation my own.

63. Pérez de Ribas, *History of the Triumphs of Our Holy Faith*, 328–29.

64. Hu-DeHart, *Missionaries, Miners, and Indians*, 27.

65. Pérez de Ribas, *History of the Triumphs of Our Holy Faith*, 337.

66. Alegre, *Historia de la Compañia de Jesus*, 2:36, translation my own.

67. Folsom, *The Yaquis and the Empire*, 83–84.

68. Pérez de Ribas, *History of the Triumphs of Our Holy Faith*, 339–40. For other examples of women's involvement in Indian diplomacy, see Juliana Barr, *Peace Came in the Form of a Woman: Indians and Spaniards in the Texas Borderlands* (Chapel Hill: University of North Carolina Press, 2007).

69. Hu-DeHart, *Missionaries, Miners, and Indians*, 28.

70. Pérez de Ribas, *History of the Triumphs of Our Holy Faith*, 340–41. It is possible that Yaquis allowed Jesuits into their village as a sort of ransom for their children. They agreed to send their children to the Villa de Sinaloa over the ensuing decades, but held Jesuits in their villages both as "hostages" and as a sort of insurance policy for their children. See Folsom, *The Yaquis and the Empire*, 58–64. While this is an intriguing theory, no direct evidence for it has been found, and it may overlook the element of Spanish coercive power.

71. Pérez de Ribas, *History of the Triumphs of Our Holy Faith*, 338–39.

72. Ramón Hernández, quoted in Erickson, *Yaqui Homeland and Homeplace*, 27–30.

73. Erickson, 32; Shorter, *We Will Dance Our Truth*, 119–22. Edward Spicer, the foremost authority on Yaqui ethnography, confirmed the importance of the Talking Tree. He contended that the story predated colonial contacts, but the baptism element was inserted after the Spaniards came. He pointed to the prophecy, as it was told to him in the first half of the twentieth century, which included communication by telephone and human flight and other elements, as proof that it had been added to over the centuries. See also Evers and Molina, "Haikim."

74. Pérez de Ribas, *History of the Triumphs of Our Holy Faith*, 3.

75. Spicer, *The Yaquis*, 4, 13.
76. Folsom, *The Yaquis and the Empire*, 73.
77. Caraman, *The Lost Paradise*, 131, 133. Reductions varied in scale. Some of the largest and best-known Jesuit reductions occurred among the Guaraní of Paraguay.
78. Father Estevan de Perea, "True Report of the Great Conversion," 1632, in Hammond and Rey, *Fray Alonso de Benavides' Revised Memorial of 1634*, 214.
79. Pérez de Ribas, *History of the Triumphs of Our Holy Faith*, 4–5, 328, 341, 344.
80. Folsom, *The Yaquis and the Empire*, 73. Jesuits complained as late as 1738 that the majority of Yaquis still lived outside the eight villages (p. 104).
81. Pérez de Ribas, *History of the Triumphs of Our Holy Faith*, 92.
82. Pérez de Ribas, 357.
83. Pérez de Ribas, 361.
84. Hu-DeHart, *Missionaries, Miners, and Indians*, 32–33.
85. Ortega Noriega, "El Sistema de Misiones Jesuíticas," 69–70; Radding, *Landscapes of Power and Identity*, 168–70, 172.
86. Pérez de Ribas, *History of the Triumphs of Our Holy Faith*, 374–75; parenthetical insertion in original.
87. Pérez de Ribas, 459.
88. "Rules for the Government of the Missions, as Approved by the Father Visitor Rodrigo de Cabredo, 1610," in Polzer, *Rules and Precepts of the Jesuit Missions*, 64, emphasis my own.
89. Spicer, *The Yaquis*, 27–30.
90. Deeds, "Indigenous Rebellions on the Northern Mexican Mission Frontier," 40–41.
91. "Organización Política-Religiosa" [*Political-Religious Organization*], Museo de los Yaquis (Yaqui Nation Mueum), Cócorit, Mexico, translation my own.
92. "Consagración de un Gobernador Yaqui (Juramento)" [*Consecration of a Yaqui Governor (Oath)*], Museo de los Yaquis (Yaqui Nation Mueum), Cócorit, Mexico, translation my own.
93. Notes from conversation with Juan Silverio Jaime León, 22 June 2018.
94. Navarro García, *La Sublevación Yaqui de 1740*, 16.
95. Hu-DeHart, *Missionaries, Miners, and Indians*, 60.
96. This was forbidden under Jesuit mission rules, particularly when Indian labor was used to generate a profit, which it was among the Yaquis. The Sonoran mission guidelines in 1662 stated, "The Indians should be persuaded with gentleness but never harassed with tasks and duties in order to make a profit or engage in business because this is strictly forbidden." See Rule 8 in "The Regulations Made by the Visitors General for the Whole Province, and by the Provincials for the Missions, 1662," in Polzer, *Rules and Precepts of the Jesuit Missions*, 68.
97. Navarro García, *La Sublevación Yaqui de 1740*, 22–23.
98. Folsom, *The Yaquis and the Empire*, 121, 127.
99. Hu-DeHart, *Missionaries, Miners, and Indians*, 61. Book 6, Title 15, Law 2 of the *Recopilación* permitted Indians to "voluntarily go to labor, and work in gold, silver, and mercury mines, if they are paid fair wages." See S. L. Tyler, *The Indian Cause in the Spanish Laws of the Indies*, 325.
100. Navarro García, *La Sublevación Yaqui de 1740*, 26, translation my own.

101. Quiroz to Huidobro, 11 December 1735, in Hu-DeHart, *Missionaries, Miners, and Indians*, 61.

102. Navarro García, *La Sublevación Yaqui de 1740*, 27–28.

103. Folsom, *The Yaquis and the Empire*, 128.

104. Navarro García, *La Sublevación Yaqui de 1740*, 28. They were well within the law in airing their complaints to civil officials. Book 6, Title 10, Law 18 of the *Recopilación* stated, "If Indians of Seigniory suffer any wrong from the Alcalde Mayor, the Justicia or any other person, they may go freely to the Royal Audencia of the district to make their complaint and to request satisfaction for the wrong done to them. They shall be dealt justice, and they shall not be restrained." S. L. Tyler, *Indian Cause*, 259.

105. Navarro García, *La Sublevación Yaqui de 1740*, 28; Hu-DeHart, *Missionaries, Miners, and Indians*, 63.

106. Navarro García, *La Sublevación Yaqui de 1740*, 29; Hu-DeHart, *Missionaries, Miners, and Indians*, 63–64; Folsom, *The Yaquis and the Empire*, 129.

107. Navarro García, *La Sublevación Yaqui de 1740*, 31. Interestingly, in his 1743 account of events leading up to the Yaqui Revolt, Mateo Ansaldo, the Jesuit Provincial Father of the Yaqui region from 1739 to 1743, placed the blame for the prison incident on the Spanish authorities. He stated that Muni was riled up by Quiroz, and "became impudent and lost respect for his minister, the rector, Padre Diego Gonzalez . . . [and] the Indians began to be insolent and to lose respect for the missionaries and the *justicias*." See Meredith, "The Yaqui Rebellion of 1740," 229. Ansaldo claimed that Huidobro's ire for the Jesuits came from the fact that he was surveying Yaqui lands to appropriate for both his own and vecino use, which the Jesuits opposed (pp. 228–29). He also asserted that the Jesuit Padre Reynaldos had freed Muni and the other prisoners when the Indians became "stirred up" (p. 230).

108. Folsom, *The Yaquis and the Empire*, 130.

109. Folsom, 133–34.

110. Navarro García, *La Sublevación Yaqui de 1740*, 34; Folsom, *The Yaquis and the Empire*, 134–35. Spanish and Indian town elections were typically reserved for a male electorate, so the Yaqui claim that women had primarily voted in this election was an attempt to delegitimize its results.

111. Folsom, *The Yaquis and the Empire*, 135.

112. Navarro García, *La Sublevación Yaqui de 1740*, 35.

113. Hu-DeHart, *Missionaries, Miners, and Indians*, 66.

114. Folsom, *The Yaquis and the Empire*, 136–37.

115. Navarro García, *La Sublevación Yaqui de 1740*, 37.

116. Folsom, *The Yaquis and the Empire*, 139.

117. This directly violated laws in the *Recopilación* that Indian leaders not use the title of "Señor." See Book 6, Title 7, Law 5 in L. S. Tyler, *Indian Cause*, 189. The term Nápoli used was *hombrearse*, or to make oneself a gentleman.

118. Navarro García, *La Sublevación Yaqui de 1740*, 38–41; Folsom, *The Yaquis and the Empire*, 139–42.

119. Hu-DeHart, *Missionaries, Miners, and Indians*, 67.

120. Navarro García, *La Sublevación Yaqui de 1740*, 43–44; Folsom, *The Yaquis and the Empire*, 144.

121. Notes from conversation with Juan Silverio Jaime León.

122. Folsom, *The Yaquis and the Empire*, 144–45.
123. Notes from conversation with Juan Silverio Jaime León.
124. Folsom, *The Yaquis and the Empire*, 145.
125. Meredith, "The Yaqui Rebellion of 1740," 254.
126. Petition to Viceroy de la Conquista, July 1739, Pastells Collection, Sevilla, Secretaria de Nueva España, Audencia de Mexico y Guadalajara, Knights of Columbus Vatican Film Library, Saint Louis University, St. Louis, Mo., reel 22 (vol. 32), pp. 354–56.
127. "Letter to Brother Franz Joseph Segesser, San Francisco Broja [sic] de Tecoripa, 13 August 1741," in Classen, *The Letters of the Swiss Jesuit Missionary Philipp Segesser*, 180; parenthetical insertion in original.
128. Hu-DeHart, *Missionaries, Miners, and Indians*, 75. Jesuit padre provincial Mateo Ansaldo laid the blame for the revolt squarely on the shoulders of Yaquis, Huidobro, and vecinos. Among other things, Ansaldo accused Huidobro "of not having trusted the good Indians." He also listed the Yaquis' "false" accusations against the order, one of which was "mistreating the Indians," but did not include the denial of voting rights specifically. In fact, he did not once mention Yaqui complaints of political meddling by Jesuits, or a Yaqui desire for sovereignty and free elections as a major cause of Yaqui unrest. Meredith, "The Yaqui Rebellion of 1740," 247, 243. Interestingly, this was not Huidobro's only confrontation with Jesuits during his tenure. He also had problems in Baja California. For example, when Huidobro and civil officials fought with Jesuits over Aripes (who occupied the southern tip of Baja California) accused of stealing church valuables, Huidobro wrote to the viceroy on 26 October 1738 that unsanctioned Jesuit punishments needed to stop, "so that it be recognized in those dominions who is the sovereign and whom they must obey." See MSS 867, Reel 103, Provincias Internas, Legajo 29, Exp. 2, MF, AGN CSWR. It also must be seen as at least a partial admission of wrongdoing that Padre Nápoli was eventually expelled from the order sometime after the 1740 revolt (the preceding expulsion trial is dated 1736, and the trial immediately after his is dated 1744). See MSS 867, Vol 41A, Historia, Legajo 295, Parte 1, AGN CSWR. In addition, some Yaquis refused to join the revolt. For example, when dissident Yaquis attempted to enlist the help of the village of Belém, its people refused. In response, they stole Belém's church ornaments and then danced the matachín in front of the priest there while wearing the stolen church cloth and vestments (Folsom, *The Yaquis and the Empire*, 146).
129. Folsom, *The Yaquis and the Empire*, 179.
130. Fontana, *Of Earth and Little Rain*, 34–35.
131. Lewis, *Neither Wolf nor Dog*, 118.
132. Fontana, *Of Earth and Little Rain*, 47. On p. 130 of *Cycles of Conquest*, Spicer asserted: "Upper Pima history through the Jesuit period is a story of a people whose interest in and demand for elements of Spanish culture was never fully satisfied. It contrasts with the histories of the Opatas, Mayo-Yaquis, and Lower Pimas.... The Upper Pimas ... did not divide sharply into pro-mission and anti-mission groups. As far as we can tell there was throughout the Jesuit period a genuine demand for missionaries all through the Pima country," although this demand was never fully satisfied.
133. Bolton, *Rim of Christendom*, 252–53.
134. Kino, *Kino's Historical Memoir of Pimería Alta*, 112.
135. Bolton, *Rim of Christendom*, 261.

136. As Father Visitor, it was Salvatierra's responsibility to visit the Upper Pima missions and potential mission sites, assess their strengths and weaknesses, and consider sites for future missions.

137. John L. Kessell, "Peaceful Conquest in Southern Arizona," in Smith, Kessell, and Fox, *Father Kino in Arizona*, 63.

138. Manje, *Unknown Arizona and Sonora*, 8.

139. Manje, 18, 21–22.

140. Manje, 90, 93–96.

141. Bernal referred to Jaravilla as a "Don."

142. "Diary of Lieutenant Cristóbal Martín Bernal," November 1697, in Smith, Kessell, and Fox, *Father Kino in Arizona*, 36.

143. Manje, *Unknown Arizona and Sonora*, 136.

144. "Diary of Lieutenant Cristóbal Martín Bernal," 45.

145. Manje, *Unknown Arizona and Sonora*, 75, 128.

146. Kino, *Kino's Biography of Saeta*, 51, 87–91.

147. Eusebio Kino, "Relasión diaria de la entrada Norduesta . . ." quoted in Kessell, "Peaceful Conquest in Southern Arizona," 74.

148. Kessell, "Peaceful Conquest in Southern Arizona," 89–90, 92. The forbidding desert landscape and climate of Pimería Alta took their toll on many Catholic priests.

149. Kessell, *Mission of Sorrows*, 31–32.

150. "El Marqués de Casafuerte, México, April 27, 1730," in Kessell, *Mission of Sorrows*, 40; Kessell, *Mission of Sorrows* 43, 45.

151. Kessell, 65.

152. Radding, "The Colonial Pact and Changing Ethnic Frontiers," 57; Underhill, *Social Organization of the Papago Indians*, 85–86.

153. Underhill, *Social Organization of the Papago Indians*, 87.

154. Pfefferkorn, *Sonora*, 266–67.

155. Pfefferkorn, 275.

156. Och, *Missionary in Sonora*, 167.

157. Och, 166.

158. Nentvig, *Rudo Ensayo*, 111, emphasis my own.

159. Kino, *Kino's Biography of Saeta*, 187.

160. "Letter to the Brother Ulrich Franz Joseph Segesser, San Ignacio de Cabo'rca, 10 September 1732," 152; "Letter to the Brother Ulrich Franz Joseph Segesser, Los Santos Angeles de Gue'vavi and San Xavier del Bac, 7 May 1734," 157–58. Both in Classen, *The Letters of the Swiss Jesuit Missionary Philipp Segesser*.

161. Bringas, *Friar Bringas Reports to the King*, 19.

162. Francisco Garcés, quoted in Dobyns, *Spanish Colonial Tucson*, 21, 27–30.

163. Bringas, *Friar Bringas Reports to the King*, 44, 57. Dobyns referred to such rapid population decline at the O'odham missions and to the need to continually replenish numbers with Tohono O'odhams as "not a matter of Black Legend hyperbole." It was very real displacement, epidemic, and conquest. It was, in short, a "grim story of rapid population decline." See Dobyns, *Spanish Colonial Tucson*, 140.

164. Font and Matson, "Letters of Friar Pedro Font, 1776–1777," 278.

165. Kessell, "San José de Tumacácori," 311.

166. Barr, "Geographies of Power," 21.

167. Och, *Missionary in Sonora*, 168–69.

168. Antonio Barbastro, "Informe del P. Barbastro," 1 December 1793, in Canedo, *Sonora hacia fines del siglo XVIII*, 88.

169. Och, *Missionary in Sonora*, 120.

170. Barbastro, "Informe del P. Barbastro," Canedo, *Sonora hacia fines del siglo XVIII*, 55.

171. "Juan de Pineda to the Viceroy, Marques de Croix, 17 October 1768," in McCarty, *Desert Documentary*, 12.

172. "Tucson's First Murder Trial," in McCarty, *Desert Documentary*, 103.

173. See Kessell, *Friars, Soldiers, and Reformers*, 207–14.

174. Kessell, 72.

175. Juan Agustín de Morfi, "Duties of Officials in the Frontier of New Spain," in Smith, Kessell, and Fox, *Father Kino in Arizona*, 126.

176. Salmón, "A Marginal Man," 67.

177. Rentería-Valencia, "Colonial Tensions," 353–54.

178. "El padre provincial Juan Antonio Baltasar, en respuesta al virrey, en carta de 1752 . . ." in Juan Antonio Baltasar, "Información de los padres missioneros de la provincial de Sonora, como se hallen acabar esta visita de el año 1744," in Burrus and Zubillaga, *El Noroeste de México*, 270.

Chapter Three

1. Brooks, *Captives and Cousins*, 36.
2. Rodríguez O., *The Independence of Spanish America*, 19–22, 25–26.
3. Tanck de Estrada, *Pueblos de Indios en el México Colonial*, 581.
4. Rodríguez O., *The Independence of Spanish America*, 19, 23.
5. Rodríguez O., 51–53.
6. Rodríguez O., 73, 82.
7. King, "The Colored Castes," 33.
8. Sánchez, Spude, and Gómez, *New Mexico*, 70.
9. King, "The Colored Castes," 37, 41–42, 35–36.
10. King, 47.
11. Rodríguez O., *The Independence of Spanish America*, 85.
12. Peninsulares instead turned to Spanish Americans of African descent, both free and enslaved, as their targets of exclusion. Those of African ancestry, known collectively as *castas*, proved easier to marginalize than Indians and mestizos. See King, "The Colored Castes," 43–44.
13. *The Political Constitution of the Spanish Monarchy*.
14. Rodríguez O., *The Independence of Spanish America*, 89, 92.
15. Guedea, "The First Popular Elections in Mexico City," 39–40, 42–43, 45, 49.
16. Meyer, Sherman, and Deeds, *The Course of Mexican History*, 127.
17. Hamill, *The Hidalgo Revolt*, 118–119, 121.
18. Meyer, Sherman, and Deeds, *The Course of Mexican History*, 276.
19. Hamill, *The Hidalgo Revolt*, 123, 127. Hamill also shows that revolutionary plotters included Indians and castas in their plans from the early stages of the revolt. For example, José

Mariano Michelena, a Spanish military officer and early revolutionary, along with his co-conspirators, planned to recruit peasants in Morelia (at the time called Valladolid), to combine them with militia regiments, and then hoped to attract 18,000 to 20,000 Indians and castas to their army with the promise of the abolition of the levy. See Hamill, "An 'Absurd Insurrection'?," 69.

20. Ducey, *A Nation of Villages*, 60.

21. Anna, "Iguala," 3, 5. The plan to bring in Ferdinand VII as emperor was dropped immediately after Mexico gained its independence. It made little sense to begin with and was mostly meant to attract conservatives to the cause.

22. "Plan de Iguala," in Joseph and Henderson, *The Mexico Reader*, 192–93.

23. Ducey, *A Nation of Villages*, 96.

24. Tanck de Estrada, *Pueblos de Indios*, 545, 547–48, 565–66.

25. Van Valen, "In Search of Juan Antonio Ignacio Baca," 71.

26. Van Valen, 73–74.

27. Van Valen, 548–49.

28. Sánchez, Spude, and Gómez, *New Mexico*, 74–75.

29. Facundo Melgares, *Gazeta Imperial de México* (*Imperial Gazette of Mexico*), 26 March 1822, Mexico City. vol. 2, no. 12, p. 92. In Santa Fe, New Mexico Records (MSS 76 B.C., box 1, folder 1), Center for Southwest Research, University Libraries, University of New Mexico.

30. James, *Three Years among the Indians and Mexicans*, 88–90. James's account, written in 1846, is a prime example of anti-Mexican propaganda during the U.S.-Mexico War.

31. Weber, "An Unforgettable Day," 34.

32. Minge, *Ácoma*, 42. Minge was granted unprecedented access to Acoma Pueblo archival materials in the possession of the Pueblo.

33. Minge had also made a similar, though slightly truncated, statement about changes in Pueblo life under Mexico, in an undated document prepared for the Bureau of Indian Affairs: "The Pueblos mode of living had not changed perceptibly over the years. Mexican authorities accepted these agrarian and peaceful Indians as citizens with few changes in the old Spanish laws, living went on as it had. They continued farming, hunting, and grazing their own lands. There were no apparent changes in administrative procedures when Mexicans took control of the Territory of New Mexico in 1821 and if there were changes which affected the Pueblo Indians, other than citizenship and loyalty, these went unrecorded." Minge, "A History of the Pueblo Indians," 50.

34. "Decree of Indian Civil Liberties," 9 September 1820, SANM II, 2886, reel 20, fr. 196, translation my own.

35. Pino, *The Exposition on the Province of New Mexico*, 25–28. The official instruction had four specific items, calling for such things as uniformity in military service for New Mexicans, and more presidios in the territory.

36. Pino, 35–37.

37. Pino, 40, 56. Pino also asserted, "In New Mexico there are no castas of African origin" (p. 40). Perhaps Pedro's picture of harmonious race relations in New Mexico was also colored by the fact that a Zuni Pueblo young man, the aforementioned Pedro Pino, lived for a time in his home as a genízaro.

38. Simmons, *Spanish Government in New Mexico*, 206–7, 209–11.

39. Daniel Tyler, *Sources for New Mexican History*, 7.
40. Spicer, *Cycles of Conquest*, 396.
41. Carroll and Haggard, *Three New Mexico Chronicles*, 137.
42. Ebright, Hendricks, and Hughes, *Four Square Leagues*, 36–43; quote from "una propiedad immemorial de dichos naturales" (minutes of the deputation meeting, 29 November 1829, Mexican Archives of New Mexico, Santa Fe: New Mexico State Records Center and Archives [hereafter MANM], r. 42, f. 631) in *Four Square Leagues*.
43. Sando, *Pueblo Nations*, 83–84.
44. Ortiz, *The Pueblo*, 79–80.
45. See Van Valen, "In Search of Juan Antonio Ignacio Baca," 65–88.
46. Simmons, *Spanish Government in New Mexico*, 212–13.
47. Bloom, "New Mexico under Mexican Administration," 26.
48. D. Tyler, *Sources for New Mexican History*, 6, 7–8.
49. Gregg, *Commerce of the Prairies*, 191.
50. Carroll and Haggard, *Three New Mexico Chronicles*, 30.
51. Bloom, "New Mexico under Mexican Administration," 14–15.
52. Antonio Narvona, "Detailed report of the cities, villas, and pueblos within the territory of New Mexico," 8 April 1827, in Carroll and Haggard, *Three New Mexico Chronicles*, 48–49.
53. Sánchez, Spude, and Gómez, *New Mexico*, 83.
54. Bloom, *Antonio Barreiro's Ojeada sobre Nuevo Mexico*, 29.
55. Bloom, 29, 45.
56. Bloom, 44–45.
57. Ducey, *A Nation of Villages*, 97.
58. Fr. Jose Pedro Ruben de Celis, "Report of the Missions occupied by the 'Religious' of the Regular Observance of Our Lord Father San Francisco pertaining to said *Custodia* which is subordinate to the Province of the Holy Evangel, their gains in the Year 1821, number of Ministers who serve them, Stipends which they enjoy, and the total of Souls distinguished by Classes and Sexes," in Bloom, "New Mexico under Mexican Administration," 28.
59. Bloom, 29.
60. "Ayuntamientos. Sobre no haberse verificado la elección para renovación del Ayuntamiento del pueblo de la Isleta, en el territorio del Nuevo Mexico," Año de 1833 (hereafter "Isleta Ayuntamiento Complaint"), MSS 867, box 1, folder 1A, transcription, Archivo General de la Nación, Center for Southwest Research, University Libraries, University of New Mexico, 2, 8–9. This is another complicating factor, as Abeita, Beitia, and similar surnames were, and still are, common at Isleta Pueblo.
61. Celis, "Report of the Missions," 28.
62. Isleta Ayuntamiento Complaint, 6.
63. Isleta Ayuntamiento Complaint, 11.
64. Sánchez, Spude, and Gómez, *New Mexico*, 77.
65. Sánchez, Spude, and Gómez, 78–79.
66. Sánchez, Spude, and Gómez, 79–80, 83; D. Tyler, *Sources for New Mexican History*, 4–5.

67. Minge, *Ácoma*, 45–47.

68. Hall and Weber, "Mexican Liberals and the Pueblos Indians," 8.

69. Election report for Pecos Pueblo, 3 January 1821, SANM II, 2954, reel 20, fr. 620. Although this document falls right on the cusp of the switch from Spanish to Mexican rule in New Mexico, it is in keeping with the establishment of constitutional ayuntamientos in New Mexico in the last years leading up to Mexican independence, as well as with the continuation of this practice after independence.

70. Celis, "Report of the Missions," 28. Pecos had become severely depopulated by the 1820s, with the surviving members eventually moving to Jemez Pueblo.

71. Other ayuntamientos are referenced in which the officials may have been Indians. One document, for example, refers to the election of Rafael Cordova as president of the ayuntamiento of Nambé in 1831. Nambé was one of the locations in the 1821 census in which Indians purportedly outnumbered Hispanos, so it is possible that they controlled the ayuntamiento there. See Sender Collection, Doc. 118, CSWR.

72. Complaint of Cochiti Pueblo against Fr. Manuel Bellido, MANM, 4 December 1821, vol. 4 (1821), doc. 3092, 845–47, translation my own.

73. Cochiti Pueblo presents a difficult case for deciphering Hispano vs. Pueblo populations. The 1821 mission census gives totals of 339 Indians to 359 Hispanos, for a total of 698. This is the same year the complaint was filed. Yet an 1829 census prepared by the alcalde of Cochiti gave a total population for the alcaldía of 1,746, only 372 of whom were Indians from the Pueblo. See Cochiti Census, MANM, November 1829, vol. 4 for 1829, 803.

74. "Petition from Pueblo of San José de la Laguna to Governor of New Mexico, 16 July 1830," Bureau of Indian Affairs Collection, Museum of New Mexico, The Palace of the Governors, Fray Angélico Chávez History Library, Santa Fe (hereafter BIA Collection), fol. 4, doc. 1, transcription, 1–2.

75. Celis, "Report of the Missions," 28.

76. Robert Analla (Anaya), interview by David E. Buge, Mrs. Walter K. Marmon interpreter, 21 November 1968, tape #19, American Indian Oral History Collection, Center for Southwest Research, University Libraries, University of New Mexico.

77. Ebright, Hendricks, and Hughes, *Four Square Leagues*, 97–99.

78. "Election of primary and secondary electors at pueblo of Santa Clara, 4 December 1836," BIA Collection, fol. 1, doc. 4, transcription, 1.

79. "Asking annulment of illegal sale of Santa Clara lands," 19 April 1837, BIA Collection, fol. 1, doc. 10, transcription, 1. The Naranjo name has long been an important one at Santa Clara Pueblo, most notably for the famous Naranjo potters.

80. "Asking annulment of illegal sale of Santa Clara lands," 1.

81. Celis, "Report of the Missions," 28.

82. A. Ortiz, *The Pueblo*, 83. Ortiz was uniquely equipped to make an assertion about cooperation between Hispanos and Indians. After all, as his obituary stated, "Dr. Ortiz was part Hispanic—an uncle, Emilio Naranjo, was for years the boss of the Democratic political machine in Rio Arriba County, which surrounds San Juan Pueblo." See Johnson, "Alfonso Ortiz, 57, Anthropologist of the Pueblo, Dies."

83. "Governor Melgares to the provincial junta," 18 April 1821, in Simmons, *Spanish Government in New Mexico*, 213.

84. Lecompte, *Rebellion in Río Arriba*, 7, 10, xi.

85. Wroth, "1837 Rebellion of Rio Arriba"; Lecompte, *Rebellion in Río Arriba*, 17; Reséndez, *Changing National Identities at the Frontier*, 175–76.
86. Sánchez, "It Happened in Old Santa Fe," 268–70.
87. Lecompte, *Rebellion in Río Arriba*, 17, 19–20; Gregg, *Commerce of the Prairies*, 92. The doblón, or doubloon, was far more valuable than a *real*. As Andrés Reséndez has pointed out, the new tax code was not nearly as onerous as rumor had made it out to be, but New Mexicans were more opposed to the idea of direct taxation, and Pérez did not communicate the actual terms of the taxes. See Reséndez, *Changing National Identities*, 176–77.
88. Gregg, *Commerce of the Prairies*, 95; Lecompte, *Rebellion in Río Arriba*, 21–22, 31–34.
89. "An Account of the Chimayó Rebellion, 1837," attributed to Albino Chacón, in Lecompte, *Rebellion in Río Arriba*, 99–100. It is possible that the alcaldes mentioned were actually village governors, since governors traditionally played a part in Pueblo militia affairs.
90. Chacón, "An Account of the Chimayó Rebellion," 101.
91. Minutes of the Junta Popular, 27 August 1837, William G. Ritch Collection, 1539–1901, Huntington Library, San Marino, Calif. (hereafter Ritch Collection), reel 2, doc. 161, translation my own; Lecompte, *Rebellion in Río Arriba*, 45.
92. José Esquibel and Juan Vigil to Josecito Archibeque, 21 August 1837, in Reno, "Rebellion in New Mexico," 205.
93. José González, Letter to Tesuque Pueblo, Ritch Collection, reel 2, doc. 163, translation my own. González was illiterate, so the letter was obviously written in his behalf.
94. Reno, "Rebellion in New Mexico," 210.
95. "Testimony of Merchants, August 28, 1837," in Lecompte, *Rebellion in Río Arriba*, 115, 118; "Letter from Santa Fe, August 12, 1837," in Lecompte, 122; Gregg, *Commerce of the Prairies*, 94.
96. Lecompte, *Rebellion in Río Arriba*, 36–37.
97. Wroth, "1837 Rebellion of Rio Arriba."
98. Bloom, "New Mexico under Mexican Administration," 24.
99. Reno, "Rebellion in New Mexico," 197.
100. Chávez, "José Gonzalez, Genízaro Governor," 190, 191–94.
101. Pedro Sánchez, *Recollections of the Life of the Priest Don Antonio José Martínez*, 54.
102. Lecompte, *Rebellion in Río Arriba*, 20; "Plan de Tomé," in Bloom, "New Mexico under Mexican Administration," 26.
103. Lecompte, *Rebellion in Río Arriba*, 46, 56; "Letter of Manuel Armijo, October 11, 1837," in Lecompte, 139.
104. "Circular of Manuel Armijo, January 19, 1838," in Lecompte, *Rebellion in Río Arriba*, 145–46. An obvious reference is made to Christ's crucifixion when he pleaded with his father to forgive his crucifiers, who knew not what they did.
105. Lecompte, *Rebellion in Río Arriba*, 72–74; P. Sánchez, *Recollections of the Life of the Priest Don Antonio José Martínez*, 54.
106. An 1845 letter from Ambrocio Abeita, governor of Isleta Pueblo, outlined the bad state of repairs at the mission church and convent, which the Indians, through their "Justicias," agreed to repair. See "Letter from Father López and Governor Abeita, July 1845, AASF 27, Marriages Isleta (1726–1846), fr. 704.

Chapter Four

1. Weber, *The Mexican Frontier*, 4.
2. Officer, *Hispanic Arizona*, 17.
3. Weber, *The Mexican Frontier*, xviii.
4. Spicer, *Cycles of Conquest*, 196–97.
5. Sheridan et al., *Moquis and Kastiilam*, 14.
6. James, *Pages from Hopi History*, 71–72.
7. David J. Weber, "Hopi Land and Water Rights under Spain and Mexico," Prepared for the Hopi Tribe for General Adjudication of All Rights to Use Water in the Little Colorado River System and Source Superior Court of Arizona Case No. CV-6417, March 2009, 43.
8. Gregg, *Commerce on the Prairies*, 188n, 193.
9. Hopis made no distinction between representatives of Spain and Mexico—to them, they were one and the same, just as O'odhams regarded them, as we have seen.
10. Nequatewa, "A Mexican Raid on the Hopi Pueblo of Oraibi," 45–46. The events may have taken place in the winter of 1845–46, since New Mexico was under United States control in the winter of 1846–1847, but it also could have been earlier. I was unable to locate any Mexican records of the episode.
11. The account also claims that the Hopi men who made the arrangements with the Mexicans had promised the woman and children as rewards for helping them commit suicide. I find this portion of the story questionable in the extreme.
12. Nequatewa, "A Mexican Raid on the Hopi Pueblo of Oraibi," 48–52.
13. Likely an alcalde or justice of the peace.
14. Nequatewa, "A Mexican Raid on the Hopi Pueblo of Oraibi," 48–52. According to the account, some of the Mexican raiding party were executed by being dragged by ropes around their necks behind horses until they were strangled, and the others were stoned. Nequatewa relates that the story was told to him by Masavema, an elder at Oraibi who was one of the kidnapped children. He states that Masavema died in 1939, which would have made him well over eighty years old.
15. Uwaikwiota, "Hopi Slaves in Santa Fe," in Courlander, *Hopi Voices*, 114–15.
16. Nuvayoiya (Albert Yava), "Homecoming of a Hopi Slave," in Courlander, *Hopi Voices*, 115–16.
17. Officer, *Hispanic Arizona*, 17, 88, 103.
18. Officer, 17; Dobyns, *The Papago People*, 34; Sheridan, *Landscapes of Fraud*, 60. When he passed through Tucson in 1848, Cave Couts commented that Tucson was "Indians and Mexicans together, probably the largest place we have met since leaving Chihuahua." See Dobyns, *Hepah, California!*, 62.
19. Faulk, *The Constitution of Occidente*, 11–12, 14; Spicer, *Cycles of Conquest*, 60.
20. Radding, "The Colonial Pact and Changing Ethnic Frontiers," 63–65.
21. Refugio de la Torre Curiel, *Twilight of the Mission Frontier*, 101.
22. Dobyns, *The Papago People*, 34.
23. Spicer, *Cycles of Conquest*, 336.
24. Hu-DeHart, *Yaqui Resistance and Survival*, 19.
25. Spicer, *Cycles of Conquest*, 337–38. Hu-DeHart makes the following statement regarding Yaqui allegiance to independent Mexico: "Yaquis . . . perhaps sensing that what little pro-

tection they had enjoyed as 'Indians' under the colonial system would be lost, continued to feel little pride or stake in the new nation of Mexico that was born in 1821" (*Yaqui Resistance and Survival*, 19). What was referred to as "special status" could also be seen as sovereignty. Above all else, Yaquis wanted to retain village sovereignty, which was guaranteed to a far greater extent under the old Yaqui-Spanish electoral system.

26. Spicer, *The Yaquis*, 130; Spicer, *Cycles of Conquest*, 60; Hu-DeHart, *Yaqui Resistance and Survival*, 20–21.

27. Juan Ignacio Usacamea, known as Muni, who had led the Yaqui Revolt of 1740, was governor of Ráum. The town had a history of being at the forefront of Yaqui struggles for sovereignty.

28. Hu-DeHart, *Yaqui Resistance and Survival*, 22. Mexicans frequently characterized the Yaqui-Mexican conflict of the 1820s–1830s as one of indiscriminate killing by Yaquis. It was the newest incarnation of the savage Yaqui trope; Mexican historian Francisco P. Troncoso wrote of these events in his classic work, *Las Guerras con las Tribus Yaquis y Mayos del Estado de Sonora*, that "los indios perpetraron horrorosos asesinatos de mujeres y niños" (Indians perpetrated horrific murders of women and children). He made little attempt to understand Yaqui motivations. See Troncoso, *Las Guerras con las Tribus Yaquis y Mayos*, 50–51.

29. Hu-DeHart, *Yaqui Resistance and Survival*, 22.

30. Hu-DeHart, 23–24.

31. Note the addition of the "J" to the beginning of the surname, but it is still the same surname as Muni from the 1740 revolt.

32. Hu-DeHart, *Yaqui Resistance and Survival*, 25–26.

33. Hu-DeHart, 24; Spicer, *The Yaquis*, 130.

34. Hardy, *Travels in the Interior of Mexico*, 201, 389, 411, emphasis my own. Hardy also clearly saw that the causes of Yaqui discontent lay in issues of taxation and political autonomy: "At length, the Revolution overset the dominion of Spain; a Republican form of Government was established; and the Yaqui nation, in common with many other tribes of Indians, were declared free citizens, and equal participators in the benefits of Mexican liberty. But the gaudy trapping was a dead letter, since they were not allowed to elect deputies from among themselves to represent their nation, in either the General or the State Congresses. The Causes of tyranny, and with them the vicious friars who resided amongst them, and lived upon their substance, were by no means removed; but as an equivalent for this liberty and equality which had been ceded to them, an additional tax was laid upon every article of food, &c. which they might supply to the town of their co-citizens, whether it were sold or taken back again!" (439–40).

35. Zuñiga, *Rapida Ojeada al Estado de Sonora*, 28–29, 33, 35, 37–38, 96, 101, translation my own.

36. Dedrick's article, "Las Cartas en Yaqui de Juan 'Bandera,'" is a unique piece of scholarly writing. Most of these primary documents, dating from the 1820s and 1830s, were written in the Yaqui language, although Banderas's manifestos and vision were penned in Spanish. Dedrick did the painstaking work of transcribing these documents into Yaqui (in the case of those written in Yaqui originally), phonemic Yaqui, and Spanish. Banderas's manifestos, along with many official military documents dealing with the war against the Yaquis, can also be viewed digitally at the Archivo Histórico Militar del Secretaría de la Defensa Nacional de Mexico (Archive of the Mexican Secretary of Defense), http://www.archivohistorico2010.sedena.gob.mx/home. Dedrick's Yaqui language documents came from the Bancroft Library and date from the latter part of the war, 1830–32. Dedrick is uncertain how these Yaqui documents made their way into the Bancroft's collections (see "Las Cartas

en Yaqui de Juan 'Bandera,'" 119, 122). The translations from Spanish to English for all the documents in Dedrick's article are my own.

37. "Carta 7," in Dedrick, "Las Cartas en Yaqui de Juan 'Bandera,'" 160, 121.
38. "Carta 8," Dedrick, 164–65.
39. "Carta 11," Dedrick, 175–77.
40. "Carta 11," Dedrick, 178.
41. "Manifesto A," Dedrick, 178–79.
42. "Manifesto B," Dedrick, 180; "Manifesto C," Dedrick, 180–81.
43. The flag was an obvious symbol that served Banderas well as a rallying tool, since his very name meant "flags" and he had carried the flag of the Virgen de Guadalupe.
44. "Vision," in Dedrick, "Las Cartas en Yaqui de Juan 'Bandera,'" 184.
45. Hu-DeHart, *Yaqui Resistance and Survival*, 26–27; Hardy, *Travels in the Interior of Mexico*, 394.
46. Spicer, *The Yaquis*, 213.
47. Hu-DeHart, *Yaqui Resistance and Survival*, 30–31.
48. Yaquis were not the only ones to revolt in the 1820s and 1830s; Opatas also rebelled en masse in the mid-1820s for some of the same reasons as Yaquis.
49. "Decree of the State of Occidente re: treatment of Indians and whites," Decree No. 44, 6 February 1828, Don Jesus José Aguiar Collection, 1825–1878, Arizona-Sonora Documents Online, University of Arizona Libraries Digital Collections (hereafter DJJAC), http://content.library.arizona.edu/cdm/compoundobject/collection/asd/id/1537/ rec/1, accessed 10 October 2014. All translations of the Occidente decrees are my own.
50. "Decree of the State of Occidente re: Indian towns," Decree No. 88, 30 September 1828, DJJAC, http://content.library.arizona.edu/cdm/compoundobject/collection/asd/id/1537/rec/1, accessed 11 October 2014.
51. "Decree of the State of Occidente re: Indian towns."
52. "Decree of the State of Occidente re: Indian towns." Decree Number 89, which dealt specifically with the distribution of the common lands, also clarified some parts of Decree 88, stating that lands previously taken from Indians were to be returned to them and that the common lands were to be distributed "only to the natives of each pueblo in equal parts." Furthermore, Indians could not sell or transfer these lands for six years. The decree was to be posted in all the churches and in all the Indian towns so that they would be familiar with land distribution policies. See "Decree of the State of Occidente," Decree No. 89, 30 September 1828, DJJAC, http://content.library.arizona.edu/cdm/compoundobject/collection /asd/id/ 1537/rec/1, accessed 11 October 2014.
53. Hu-DeHart, *Yaqui Resistance and Survival*, 37.
54. Hu-DeHart, 38.
55. Hu-DeHart, 39–40, 44, 47.
56. Juan María Jusacamea, report to José Lucas Pico, 22 June 1833, quoted in Hu-DeHart, *Yaqui Resistance and Survival*, 49; Hu-DeHart, 51.
57. Spicer, *Cycles of Conquest*, 397.
58. Other unforeseen consequences resulted from Banderas's revolt: one was the creation of a strong state militia in Sonora capable of confronting, and in some cases subduing, Indian resistance; another was the decision to maintain the mission system among the Yaquis. See Vidargas del Moral, "Sonora y Sinaloa Como Provincias Independientes," 455. Regard-

ing Banderas's legacy, Spicer wrote, "[He] widened an individual leader's scope." Spicer also pointed to Banderas's introduction of Moctezuma, or the return of an Indigenous leader, and the mixing of Yaqui and Christian elements, both of which corresponded with other Indian revivalist and pan-Indian movements of the period (see Spicer, *The Yaquis*, 133). Scholars should be more critical in their analysis of Banderas. His voice represented a Yaqui yearning for sovereignty in their own affairs, although his seeming failure to understand the fundamentals of Yaqui leadership and popular politics contributed to the collapse of his revolt.

59. This period of mission decay affected California as well as Pimería Alta and New Mexico.

60. Letter from Font, 30 November 1776, Font and Matson, "Letters of Friar Pedro Font," 278.

61. Weber, *The Mexican Frontier*, 50–51; Kessell, *Friars, Soldiers, and Reformers*, 246.

62. Weber, *The Mexican Frontier*, 45–46.

63. Weber, 45–46; Fray Narciso Durán, *Alta California, 1833*, in Weber, *The Mexican Frontier*, 43.

64. Weber, *The Mexican Frontier*, 44–45. The order expelling *peninsulares* (Iberian-born Spaniards) nearly led to the closing of the College of Querétaro in the late 1820s; Kessell, *Friars, Soldiers, and Reformers*, 269; McCarty, *A Frontier Documentary*, 16.

65. Kessell, *Friars, Soldiers, and Reformers*, 270, 277; Weber, *The Mexican Frontier*, 52–53.

66. Underhill, *Social Organization of the Papago Indians*, 87.

67. Kessell, *Friars, Soldiers, and Reformers*, 277–79. The name "mayordomo," which essentially means "steward," was also given to ditch captains in New Mexico, and is still used there today. It also gives us the modern term *majordomo*, the person who runs an enterprise.

68. Kessell, *Friars, Soldiers, and Reformers*, 289–90.

69. Letter from Fernando María Grande, Commissioner General of Pimería Alta, 1 November 1828, in McCarty, *A Frontier Documentary*, 17–18.

70. Escalante to Governor Iriarte, 13 January 1830, in McCarty, *A Frontier Documentary*, 21.

71. Fernando Grande to Fray José María Pérez Llera, 25 May 1830, in McCarty, *A Frontier Documentary*, 23–24.

72. Francisco Neblina to Llera, 28 February 1835, in McCarty, *A Frontier Documentary*, 25–26.

73. Francisco Neblina to Llera, 27, emphasis my own.

74. There simply were not enough Franciscans to administer Pimería Alta in the 1830s. In the eight mission districts during this period, only one or two had a missionary even in temporary residence. See McCarty, *A Frontier Documentary*, 25.

75. Mattison, "The Tangled Web," 75.

76. Anonymous Report, San Xavier del Bac, 11 May 1843, in McCarty, *A Frontier Documentary*, 89–90.

77. Anonymous Report, San Xavier del Bac, 89–92.

78. Dobyns, *Hepah, California!*, 59, 61–62.

79. Dobyns, 68.

80. Bartlett, *Personal Narrative of Explorations and Incidents in Texas, New Mexico, California, Sonora, and Chihuahua*, 1:392; 2:298–300.

81. Spicer, *Cycles of Conquest*, 133.

82. Wilson, *Islands in the Desert*, 59; Santiago Redondo to José Urrea, 12 May 1838, in McCarty, *A Frontier Documentary*, 62; see p. 60 for a general description of mining incursions by Mexicans and the resultant hostilities.

83. Rafael Moraga to José Urrea, in McCarty, *A Frontier Documentary*, 63–64. Desert O'odhams also faced pressures from raiding by Pinal Apaches, which compounded the Mexican land incursions.

84. Fontana, *Of Earth and Little Rain*, 57–60.

85. Antonio Comadurán to Colonel José María Elías González, 15 August 1843, in McCarty, *A Frontier Documentary*, 86–87.

86. Comadurán to González, 86–87.

87. Letter from Benito Valverde, General Juan Tereso Álamo, and Governor Cristóbal Aliso, 18 October 1846, in McCarty, *A Frontier Documentary*, 117–18. Given the fact that all of the items asked for in the letter would directly benefit missionaries, it is reasonable to assume that the letter was written by a priest. Still, Indian complaints over the manner in which mission lands were administered were surely valid.

88. Reply from Diego Moreno and José María Bustamante, 20 October 1848, in McCarty, *A Frontier Documentary*, 118.

89. Fontana, "The O'odham," 27.

90. Dobyns, "Indian Extinction in the Middle Santa Cruz River Valley, Arizona," 166, 181; Kessell, *Friars, Soldiers, and Reformers*, 259.

91. Sheridan, *Landscapes of Fraud*, 58–60; Jackson, *Tumacacori's Yesterdays*, 11–12.

92. Kessell, *Friars, Soldiers, and Reformers*, 284–86.

Chapter Five

1. Lummis, *A Tramp across the Continent*, 142.

2. Although New Mexico did not officially become a territory of the United States until 1850, it was under the control of the United States from the late summer of 1846.

3. "Laws of the Territory of New Mexico, Santa Fe."

4. A. Ortiz, *The Pueblo*, 87.

5. William H. Emory was born into a slaveholding Maryland family. He was a gifted mapmaker and observer of the human inhabitants and plant life of the American Southwest. He served as a brigadier general in the Union Army during the Civil War. See "Gen. William H. Emory (b. 1811–d. 1887)."

6. Emory, *Notes of a Military Reconnaissance*, 22, 33.

7. Emory, 37–38.

8. Galvin, *Western America in 1846–1847*, 43, 47, emphasis my own.

9. Robinson, *A Journal of the Santa Fe Expedition under Colonel Doniphan*, 32.

10. Early Pueblo-U.S. encounters also held the potential for violence. For example, in 1847, a group of Nuevomexicanos with close ties to the Mexican military and the church allied with Taos Pueblo Indians. In their violent rebellion, Taos Indians shot new New Mexico Governor Charles Bent full of arrows and scalped him, and killed a number of other Anglo-Americans and Hispanos. The U.S. military crushed the rebellion in brutal fashion, killing scores of Taos Indian and Hispano rebels. The church at Taos Pueblo, where the rebels had sought refuge, was set afire and blasted with cannons at point-blank range. In the aftermath

of the rebellion, sixteen Taos Indians were executed for murder and treason, even though their status in New Mexico had not been clearly established.

11. Governor Vigil was crucial in the transition from Mexican to U.S. government in New Mexico. He assembled the first territorial legislature in 1847. Although this legislative body was advisory in nature, it marked serious efforts by Vigil and others to establish a functioning government in the wake of the U.S.-Mexico War. See Sánchez, Spude, and Gómez, *New Mexico*, 110–11.

12. "Pueblos constituted corporate bodies," Section 1875 (December 1847), in Victory, *1897, Compiled Laws of New Mexico*, 500–501.

13. Victory, 31–32.

14. Sando, *Pueblo Nations*, 86.

15. Sando, *Pueblo Nations*, 86–88; see also Mangusso, "A Study of the Citizenship Provisions of the Treaty of Guadalupe Hidalgo," 77. Mangusso pointed out that Pueblos were not the only Indians in ceded Mexican territory who confronted issues of citizenship. A small number of Indians and people of Indian descent living in Upper California had also been considered Mexican citizens. The California Constitutional Convention in 1849 engaged in a debate on whether to extend citizenship to these Indians. Delegates grappled with how to grant citizenship to "civilized Indians" who "deserved" it while simultaneously withholding it from "wild Indians." The convention eventually decided that the state would grant citizenship to Indians on a case-by-case basis, when they deemed it proper to do so (Mangusso, 77–79).

16. Exceptions would have been those Pueblo Indians who moved out of the Pueblos and into Hispano communities, becoming "indios ladinos" and living as Hispanos did.

17. "Calhoun to Medill," 29 July 1849, in Abel, *The Official Correspondence of James S. Calhoun*, 18. At the time of this letter, Calhoun had not yet had a chance to visit the various Pueblos under his charge, but the information he had received indicated that they had been Mexican citizens with the right to vote, and that they were civilized and peaceful.

18. "Calhoun to Medill," 1 October 1849, 38; "Calhoun to Medill," 13 October 1849, 46, in Abel, *Official Correspondence*. The previous year, military officials had concluded a treaty with Zuni Pueblo, signed by, among other officials, the elderly governor, Pedro Pino. Although the Senate did not ratify the treaty, it established friendly relations between the United States and Zuni, as well as promising that Zuni would be "Protected in the full enjoyment of all its rights of Person Property and Religion By the authorities Civil and Military of New Mexico and the United States." "Treaty with Zuni, July 1, 1848," in Deloria and DeMallie, *Documents of American Indian Diplomacy*, 2:1266.

19. "Calhoun to Brown," 7 November 1849, in Abel, *Official Correspondence*, 73. Orlando Brown replaced Medill as Commissioner of Indian Affairs in 1849.

20. "Calhoun to Brown," 20 November 1849, 87; "Calhoun to Medill," 15 October 1849, 53–54, both in Abel, *Official Correspondence*. There is some bitter irony in this situation as it developed after the U.S.-Mexico War. As Edward Dozier indicated, the Pueblos and Hispanos had enjoyed relatively amenable relations over the centuries. He pointed to the high degree of Indigenous blood in the Hispano population of New Mexico, and noted that the two peoples had far more in common than their differences. In fact, "The differences between the two people might have disappeared altogether, but Anglos and the United States government intervened." See Dozier, *The Pueblo Indians of North America*, 113.

21. Marc Simmons, "History of the Pueblos since 1821," in A. Ortiz, *Handbook of North American Indians*, 209.

22. "Calhoun to Medill," 15 October 1849, 53–54; emphasis my own.

23. Abel, *Official Correspondence*, 53–54, emphasis my own.

24. Abel, 80, emphasis my own. In the same letter, Calhoun urged that a printing press be established among the Pueblos, "which should publish matter, both in English and in Spanish—There are those who can read Spanish, but not one who can read English. This suggestion would afford them a proper facility for acquiring of our language, and ultimately they would give us a written language of their own" (Abel, 80).

25. Sando, *Pueblo Nations*, 90.

26. The Cherokee Nation v. The State of Georgia, 30 U.S. 1 (1831).

27. "Calhoun to Brown," 16 November 1849, in Abel, *Official Correspondence*, 79.

28. "Calhoun to Brown," 2 February 1850, 132; "Calhoun to Brown," 25 January 1850, 103, both in Abel, *Official Correspondence*.

29. "Calhoun to Brown," 2 February 1850, in Abel, *Official Correspondence*, 134–35; emphasis my own.

30. The Pueblos could not receive a fair trial if they took Hispanos or others to court. Calhoun even suggested that the courts hear no civil suits against Pueblo Indians, which would have negated the 1847 incorporation of the Pueblos. See "Calhoun to Brown," 28 January 1850, in Abel, *Official Correspondence*, 120. To defend land claims in court had always been a hugely expensive endeavor for the generally impoverished Pueblos, one that required travel to distant seats of government. The Pueblos were faced with a catch-22 dilemma of potentially having to sell off lands to cover the costs of defending their lands in court. See Mangusso, "A Study of the Citizenship Provisions of the Treaty of Guadalupe Hidalgo," 83.

31. "Calhoun to the Indians of the Pueblo of Taos," 2 February 1850, in Abel, *Official Correspondence*, 136–38.

32. "Calhoun to Brown," 15 November 1849, in Abel, *Official Correspondence*, 77–78.

33. As Marc Simmons has explained, "As Anglo influence became more pervasive and signs of disintegration of Indian culture appeared, the Pueblos hastened to define boundaries of their traditional lifestyle by way of preserving it from total erosion. In the process many Spanish elements, since they were rooted in the past, not only persisted but also were identified as part of the Pueblo cultural framework." Simmons, "History of the Pueblos Since 1821," 211. The república system is clearly one of these Spanish elements. But it would be overly simplistic to assert that the Pueblos held onto it simply because it was rooted in the past. Instead, within the colonial context, it offered the greatest possibility for Pueblo autonomy and sovereignty.

34. This was the election to which I previously referred, in which Taos Indians were coerced by Hispanos to vote for convention delegates in favor of statehood.

35. Simmons, "History of the Pueblos Since 1821," 209.

36. "Choice to Calhoun," 8 May 1850, in Abel, *Official Correspondence*, 194.

37. "Calhoun to Brown," 19 June 1850, in Abel, *Official Correspondence*, 213.

38. "Calhoun to the Pueblos," 20 May 1850, reel 1, no. 388, Ritch Collection, translation my own.

39. "A los Indios de Pueblo de Nuevo Méjico," 6 June 1850, in Abel, *Official Correspondence*, 213–14, translation my own.

40. "Letter from John Munroe and James S. Calhoun Calhoun to Pueblos concerning election. June 25, 1850," box 1, folder 2, Indian Affairs Collection, CSWR.

41. Simmons, "History of the Pueblos Since 1821," 209.

42. "Treaty with the Santa Clara, Tesuque, Nambe, Santo Domingo, Jemez, San Felipe, Cochiti, San Ildefonso, Santa Ana, and Zia Pueblos," July 7–16, 1850, in Deloria and DeMallie, *Documents of American Indian Diplomacy*, 2:1267.

43. "Wingfield to Lea," 6 February 1852, in Abel, *Official Correspondence*, 470–71.

44. Ellis, "Hispanic Americans and Indians in New Mexico State Politics," 362–63; Minge, *Ácoma*, 58.

45. Prucha, *The Great Father*, 31.

46. "Calhoun to Lea," 30 June 1851, Abel, *Official Correspondence*, 369–70. Calhoun included a note that he was including the letter from the Pueblo delegation. My efforts to locate this report in the National Archives proved unfruitful.

47. "Calhoun to Lea," 29 February 1852, in Abel, *Official Correspondence*, 489.

48. "James S. Calhoun," New Mexico Office of the State Historian website, newmexicohistory.org/people/james-s-calhoun, accessed 12 January 2015. Interestingly, the biographical information on the New Mexico State Historian's website also points out that Calhoun was "popular with the Mexican population because of his efforts to secure them full citizenship rights and appointment to office." It is noteworthy that Calhoun supported full citizenship for Nuevomexicanos, but not for Pueblo Indians.

49. "Lane to William Glasgow," Santa Fe, 26 February 1852, in Bieber, *Letters of William Carr Lane, 1852–1854*, 186; "Lane to William Glasgow," Santa Fe, 30 September 1852, 189.

50. "Lane to His Wife," Las Vegas, 30 August 1853, in Bieber, *Letters of William Carr*, 198.

51. Mangusso, "A Study of the Citizenship Provisions of the Treaty of Guadalupe Hidalgo," 89; Venturini, "The Fight for Indian Voting Rights in New Mexico," 8; 33rd Congress, 1st Session, 1854, "House Report No. 121," *United States Congressional Serial Set 742*, 2; "Lane to William Glasgow," 27 February 1854, Bieber, *Letters of William Carr Lane*, 201. The House report also gave its justification for throwing out the Pueblo votes: "[T]hey retain their tribal characteristics, form a distinct community from the whites, make their own local and separate laws, are governed by their own chiefs, and do not differ essentially from other savage tribes. For the same reason 202 Indian votes, cast by the Pueblos at Laguina [sic] precinct... were rejected by the committee and deemed illegal" ("House Report No. 121," 2).

52. "Report of Governor D. Meriwether, superintendent *ex officio*," 31 August 1853 (Meriwether to Manypenny), in *Annual Report of the Commissioner of Indian Affairs...1853* (hereafter *Annual Report*, and year), 189.

53. "Report of agent E. A. Graves" ("Indians in New Mexico"), 31 August 1853, *Annual Report*, 1853, 197, 200.

54. "Address of Governor Meriwether to the Territorial Legislature," 5 December 1853, reel 1, folder 136, State Department Territorial Papers, New Mexico, 1851–1872, Washington, D.C.: National Archives.

55. "Act of 16th February, 1854. Pamphlet, p. 142," in Davenport, *Revised Statutes of the Territory of New Mexico*, 302.

56. 34th Congress, 1st Session, 1855, "House Miscellaneous Document No. 15" ("New Mexico Contested Election"), *United States Congressional Serial Set 866*, 11.

57. "Report of Governor D. Meriwether, superintendent *ex officio*," 1 September 1854, *Annual Report*, 1854, 173–74, 176.

58. "Report of Governor David Meriwether, superintendent *ex officio*," September 1855, *Annual Report*, 1855, 189–90.

59. "Report of J. L. Collins, superintendent," 30 August 1857 (J. L. Collins to J. W. Denver, Commissioner of Indian Affairs), *Annual Report*, 1857, 276.

60. "Report of Samuel M. Yost, agent for the Pueblos," 30 August 1857, *Annual Report*, 1857, 283. Agent Yost also indicated that he had met several Pueblo Indians who could read and write Spanish, but none with comparable English skills. He also urged education and literacy, stating that if such actions were taken, "it would not be long before the Pueblo Indians ... would become intelligent and useful citizens of the United States" (*Annual Report*, 1857, 284).

61. "Report of J. L. Collins, superintendent," 27 September 1858, *Annual Report*, 1858, 192.

62. Reverend Samuel Gorman, a Baptist missionary, wrote from Laguna Pueblo in 1858, urging the federal government to institute off-Pueblo boarding schools, because, "by our long and intimate acquaintance with this people, mingling with them in their councils and customs, we are fully satisfied that, with their present form of government, and under their present circumstances, centuries might roll away, and the posterity of this people would remain essentially the same ignorant, superstitious people that they are now." "Report from the Reverend Samuel Gorman, relative to the condition of the Pueblo Indians," Pueblo de Laguna, 2 October 1858, *Annual Report*, 1858, 202.

63. "Report of J. L. Collins, superintendent," 17 September 1859 (Collins to A. B. Greenwood, Commissioner of Indian Affairs), *Annual Report*, 1859, 340; Parsons, *The Pueblo of Isleta*, 250–51.

64. LaCroix Dailey, "Symbolism and Significance of the Lincoln Canes," 133, 127, 142.

65. Letter, 15 April 1864, in Benedict, *A Journey through New Mexico's First Judicial District*, 56, emphasis my own.

66. "Annual report of Superintendent Norton (extracts)," 28 September 1866 (A. B. Norton, Superintendent of Indian Affairs to Cooley), *Annual Report*, 1866, 146.

67. "Annual report of John Ward, special agent, Pueblos agency," 2 August 1867 (Ward to Norton), *Annual Report*, 1867, 207.

68. "Annual report of John Ward," *Annual Report*, 1867, 207–8; "Letter of Agent Arny relative to the opinion of the chief justice of New Mexico, respecting the status of the Pueblo Indians," 11 March 1867 (W. F. M. Arny, United States Indian Agent for New Mexico to Charles E. Mix, Acting Commissioner of Indian Affairs), *Annual Report*, 1867, 215–16; "Opinion on Chief Justice Slough," The United States vs. Benigno Ortiz, *Annual Report*, 1867, 219–22; Rosen, *American Indians and State Law*, 189–90.

69. "Opinion on Chief Justice Slough," The United States vs. Benigno Ortiz, *Annual Report*, 1867, 219.

70. Rosen, *American Indians and State Law*, 190; Mangusso, "A Study of the Citizenship Provisions of the Treaty of Guadalupe Hidalgo," 91–92; *United States v. Lucero*, 1 N.M. 422 (1869).

71. "Annual report of Lieutenant George E. Ford, U. S. A., special agent for the Pueblo Indians," 8 September 1869 (George E. Ford to Major William Clinton), *Annual Report*, 1869, 251; "Annual report of Lieutenant C. L. Cooper, U. S. A., agent for the Pueblo Indians," 8 Sep-

tember 1869 (Charles L. Cooper to Major William Clinton, Superintendent of Indian Affairs, Territory of New Mexico), *Annual Report*, 1869, 249–50, emphasis my own.

72. The word they used in the letter was *desaser*, which essentially means to unmake. The notes for the letter indicate that the copy was translated into Spanish for Commissioner Mix by New Mexico Congressional Delegate José Francisco Chaves.

73. "Spanish translation of letter from Acting Commissioner of Indian Affairs C. E. Mix, to Superintendent of Indian Affairs for New Mexico L. E. Webb," 7 May 1868, box 1, folder 23, Arthur Bibo Collection of Acoma and Laguna Pueblo Documents, New Mexico State Records Center and Archives, Santa Fe (hereafter Arthur Bibo Collection), translation my own. The Arthur Bibo Collection is a singular set of documents relating to Pueblo land claims and history. Arthur Bibo was a descendant of Solomon Bibo, one of only a few white men to ever be chosen governor of a New Mexico Indian Pueblo. Solomon Bibo, who served as Acoma Pueblo governor in 1885, likely kept many of these items after he had served as governor and left Acoma in the late 1890s. The provenance of the other papers from after his time at Acoma is unknown. These documents are among the only ones of their type available in public archives and are likely representative of documents in the possession of Pueblo governors.

74. "Copy of letter from Ely S. Parker, Commissioner of Indian Affairs, Washington, to Juan Andres Abeita and Juan Rey Lucero," 23 December 1869, box 1, folder 24, Arthur Bibo Collection, translation my own.

75. "Ely Parker—Chief, Lawyer, Engineer, and Brigadeer General," Appomattox Courthouse website, National Park Service, http://www.nps.gov/apco/parker.htm, accessed 16 September 2015. See also Armstrong, *Warrior in Two Camps*.

76. "Annual report of N. Pope, superintendent of Indian affairs," 25 September 1871 (Pope to the Honorable Committee on Indian Affairs), *Annual Report*, 1871, 371–72.

77. "Nathaniel Pope, *New Mexico Superintendency*, Santa Fé, New Mexico," 10 October 1872 (Pope to Honorable Francis A. Walker, Commissioner of Indian Affairs), *Annual Report*, 1872, 300.

78. "Annual report of W. F. N. Arny, agent of Pueblo agency," 18 August 1871 (Arny to Pope), *Annual Report*, 1871, 382, 387, 389, 393–94; Wallace, *Land of the Pueblos*, 262.

79. "Annual report of L. Edwin Dudley, Superintendent," 15 November 1873 (Dudley to Honorable Edward P. Smith, Commissioner of Indian Affairs), *Annual Report*, 1873, 269–70.

80. Mangusso, "A Study of the Citizenship Provisions of the Treaty of Guadalupe Hidalgo," 94.

81. *United States v. Joseph*, 94 U.S. 614 (1876).

82. Simmons, "History of the Pueblos Since 1821," 214; Mangusso, "A Study of the Citizenship Provisions of the Treaty of Guadalupe Hidalgo," 94–95; *United States v. Joseph*, 94 U.S. 614 (1876); Dozier, *The Pueblo Indians of North America*, 108; Ellis, "Hispanic Americans and Indians in New Mexico State Politics," 363. In Deloria and Lytle, *American Indians, American Justice*, the authors argued that New Mexico was the only territory in which the territorial courts took an active role in deciding Indian cases, due to the perceived "civilized" and "sedentary" nature of these Indians; in the overwhelming majority of locations, such cases came under the jurisdiction of the federal courts (113–14).

83. "Annual Report of B. M. Thomas, Pueblo agent," 24 August 1876 (Thomas to the Commissioner of Indian Affairs), *Annual Report*, 1876, 111.

84. "Report of F. Delgado, superintendent," 10 September 1865 (Felipe Delgado to Dole), *Annual Report*, 1865, 164.

85. Dippie, *The Vanishing American*, 108.

86. "Report of B. H. Thomas, Pueblo Agent," 1 September 1880 (Thomas to Commissioner), *Annual Report*, 1880, 133.

87. "Report of Pedro Sanchez, Pueblo Agent," August 1884 (Sanchez to Commissioner), *Annual Report*, 1884, 138–39.

88. Dippie, *The Vanishing American*, 116–17. See also Fear-Segal, *White Man's Club*.

89. See Adams, *Education for Extinction*.

90. "Report of C. E. Nordstrom, Acting Pueblo Agent," 16 August 1897 (Nordstrom to Commissioner), *Annual Report*, 1897, 196–98. Besides the schools at the Pueblos, there were the larger boarding schools, Santa Fe Indian School and Albuquerque Indian School, established in 1890 and 1881, respectively. See Hyer, *One House, One Voice, One Heart*; and Gram, *Education at the Edge of Empire*.

91. Eickemeyer and Eickemeyer, *Among the Pueblo Indians*, 82.

92. "Report of C. E. Nordstrom," 16 August 1897, *Annual Report*, 1897, 197–98.

93. "Report of John H. Robertson, Indian Agent," 30 August 1892 (Robertson to Commissioner), *Annual Report*, 1892, 335–36.

94. Nabakov, *How the World Moves*, 141–42.

95. Punishing or whipping criminal offenders had been among the customary powers given to Pueblo governors. The case involved James Miller, an Acoma Carlisle graduate who openly condemned traditional dances and refused to participate, and others. Miller was dragged out of bed in the middle of the night, bound and gagged, and taken to a kiva where the governor harshly interrogated him. When he remained obstinate, he was flogged with a rawhide whip until he passed out. After this episode, Miller retuned to traditional ways and was observed enthusiastically dancing at the Pueblo. See "The Story of a 'Civilized' Indian" by James, in *A Little Journey to Some Strange Places and Peoples*, 119–22. Adolph Bandelier reported a similar case dating from the summer of 1885 in which a young man at San Felipe Pueblo, who had also attended Carlisle, was accused of wearing "American dress" and having "grossly insulted his uncle (one of the principales), but also the other principales, [and had] given out false reports about the priest and other matters." He was brought before the cacique and principales at the home of the sacristan, and given the choice of begging for forgiveness or being banished from the tribe. He chose the former, kneeling shirtless and asking forgiveness from the aggrieved. Although he did so "with bad grace," he was forgiven. See Lange, Riley, and Lange, *The Southwest Journals of Adolph F. Bandelier*, 3:72.

96. Minge, *Ácoma*, 71, 79.

97. "Report of B. H. Thomas, Pueblo Agent," 1 September 1880, 133; Minge, *Ácoma*, 65; "Report of C. E. Nordstrom, Acting Pueblo Agent," 16 August 1897 (Nordstrom to Commissioner), *Annual Report*, 1897, 201.

98. Venturini, "The Fight for Indian Voting Rights in New Mexico," 59–62.

99. Charles Kie, quoted in Frost, *The Railroad and the Pueblo Indians*, 162, 168.

100. "Report of School Superintendent in Charge of Pueblo [Santa Fe Indian School]," 17 August 1904 (C. J. Crandall to Commissioner), *Annual Report*, 1904, 261, emphasis my own.

101. Sando, *Five Ancient Pueblo Warriors*, 31.

102. Story related by Don Juan García to Adolph Bandelier in Lange, Riley, and Lange, *The Southwest Journals of Adolph F. Bandelier*, 172.

103. "Can an Indian Vote?," *Indianapolis Weekly Indiana Sentinel*, 5 April 1855, emphasis in original.

104. "Peck After Fitch—A Characteristic Move," *Grand Traverse Herald*, 11 February 1859.

105. "Brevities," *Reno Weekly Gazette and Stockman*, 28 March 1889.

106. Prucha, *Americanizing the American Indians*, 6.

107. Valerie Sherer Mathes, *The Women's National Indian Association*, 24; Valerie Sherer Mathes, "Mary Bonney, Amelia Quinton, and the Formative Years," in *The Women's National Indian Association*, 32. Indian women also received considerable attention from Indian reformers, particularly women reformers. But they were not singled out for citizenship and enfranchisement, as Indian men were. Instead, Pueblo women were targeted for gendered work, as the tendencies of mainstream American politics toward gender inequality were reflected in Indian reform work, as well.

108. McCool, Olson, and Robinson, *Native Vote*, 6.

109. Wunder, *"Retained by the People,"* 45–46.

110. The Dawes Act typically gave individual Indian heads of families 160-acre allotments to be held in trust by the federal government for a period of twenty-five years. Allottees were issued trust patents for these allotments, and eventually received fee-simple patents at the end of the trust period.

111. Editorial, *Rochester Weekly Republican*, 2 January 1890.

112. Editorial, *Atchison Daily Globe*, 14 August 1890.

113. "Gleanings," *Alton Telegraph*, 27 September 1883.

114. Hoxie, *This Indian Country*, 225–27.

115. Welsh, *Report of a Visit to the Navajo, Pueblo, and Hualapais Indians*, 48.

116. For an account of the Zuni party's visit to Washington and the East Coast, see Hart, *Pedro Pino*, 119–27.

117. "Report of Silas F. Kendrick, agent for the Pueblos," 25 September 1860 (Kendrick to Greenwood), *Annual Report*, 1860, 166–67; "Report of J. L. Collins, superintendent," 17 September 1859, *Annual Report*, 1859, 340.

118. See Simmons, "History of the Pueblos since 1821," 211.

119. "Report of School Superintendent in Charge of Pueblo [Santa Fe Indian School]," 19 August 1905 (C. J. Crandall to Commissioner), *Annual Report*, 1905, 272–73; "Report of Superintendent of Santa Fe School [Pueblo]," 17 August 1906 (C. J. Crandall to Commissioner), *Annual Report*, 1906, 283.

120. "Report of José Segura, Pueblo Agent," 25 August 1890 (Segura to Commissioner), *Annual Report*, 1890, 174.

121. Parsons, *The Pueblo of Isleta*, 252.

122. Keleher and Chant, *The Padre of Isleta*, 79–80. By this time, Isleta had established a governing council of twelve men, called the Business Council of Twelve.

123. Keleher and Chant, 82.

124. Rev. A. Docher, "The Quaint Indian Pueblo of Isleta," 32, emphasis my own.

125. Crane only lists the two canes, but it is possible that he had a Spanish cane, as well.

126. Crane, *Desert Drums*, 293–94. Crane is not remembered as one of the more enlightened Indian agents. In the early 1920s, when the issue of Indian citizenship was being

debated in national circles, Crane questioned the utility of the Pueblo franchise. But his stance was not a particularly progressive one. The Pueblo vote in Bernalillo County, he pointed out, would comprise only seven percent of the general electorate, and thus would prove ineffectual. Furthermore, the Pueblo vote "would have been for years a confused and ignorant vote" (see Crane, *Desert Drums*, 319).

127. "Taxation of Pueblo Indian lands, 1885," Territorial Archives of New Mexico, 1846–1912. Santa Fe: State of New Mexico Records Center and Archives, roll 102, folder 671–73.

128. *Territory of New Mexico v. Delinquent Taxpayers*, 12 N. M. 139, 76 Pac. 316 (1904).

129. *Territory of New Mexico v. Delinquent Taxpayers*.

130. Congressional Appropriation Act of March 3, 1905, quoted in Cohen, *Cohen's Handbook of Federal Indian Law*, 386.

131. The convention's one hundred delegates came from all twenty-four of New Mexico's counties. Seventy-one delegates were Republicans, and twenty-nine were Democrats. There were thirty-two Hispano delegates, all of whom were Republicans. There was not a single Indian delegate. See Sánchez, Spude, and Gómez, *New Mexico*, 194.

132. Article 7, Section 1, "Message from the President of the United States Transmitting Copy of the Constitution of New Mexico with Formal Approval Thereof, and Recommending the Approval of the Same by Congress," 61st Congress, 3rd Session, Senate Document No. 835, 24 February 1911 (Washington, D.C., Government Printing Office), 25, emphasis my own.

133. Venturini, "The Fight for Indian Voting Rights in New Mexico," 48–49; Mangusso, "A Study of the Citizenship Provisions of the Treaty of Guadalupe Hidalgo," 97–98.

134. Although they did not identify themselves as such, the representatives listed in this document come from the same Pueblos that are currently part of the Eight Northern Indian Pueblos Council, Inc.

135. "Officials of the northern Pueblos of Taos, San Juan, Santa Clara, San Ildefonso, Nambe, Pojoaque, Tesuque and Picuris to the officials of the Pueblo of Acoma. Statement of united opposition to Territorial Supreme Court decision declaring the Pueblo Indians citizens and their land subject to taxation and requesting united action of all Pueblos to oppose the decision with federal and territorial authorities," 24 March 1904, Arthur Bibo Collection, box 1, folder 31, translation and emphasis my own. The document was addressed to Acoma Pueblo, and was on typed paper. Each of the eleven Southern Pueblos likely received an identical letter. How this copy came into the hands of Arthur Bibo is unknown, but the Bibo family's influence at Acoma and Laguna continued long after Solomon Bibo's term as governor. The Pueblo desire to remain noncitizens, and nontaxpayers in particular, angered some Anglo-American officials. The Rev. H. O. Ladd, who served as president of the University of New Mexico in the 1890s, wrote—incorrectly—in 1891, "It is said that the Pueblos of New Mexico do not vote at elections in New Mexico. They might if they wanted to, in spite of a territorial law that they shall not." The Charles Kie case disproved this assertion. He further argued that the lack of Pueblo voting did not mean that they were not U.S. citizens: "The negligence of a citizen to exercise the right to suffrage is no evidence that he is not a citizen." He observed, correctly, that "if he [a Pueblo Indian] were to vote he might be taxed, and this the Pueblo wants the last of all things." Ladd understood that the Pueblos opposed voting and taxation because "their community system might be interfered with," but commented, "If any good reason exists why 8,000 people

with 905,000 acres of land should live in peace and security and acquire wealth, with every protection of the laws, and pay no taxes to aid in the expense of government it is not apparent; and why the United States should encourage such an idea by keeping an agent to defend them is also not apparent." The Pueblos had their reasons, and stuck to them. See the Rev. H. O. Ladd, *History of New Mexico* (1891), quoted in Thomas Donaldson, Expert Special Agent, *Moqui Pueblo Indians of Arizona and Pueblo Indians of New Mexico*, Extra Census Bulletin, Eleventh Census of the United States (Washington, D.C.: United States Printing Office, 1893), 96.

136. "Statehood Bill in Full," *Cuervo Clipper*, 8 July 1910.

137. "Indians Are Citizens," *New Mexican Review*, 18 July 1912.

Chapter Six

1. Iverson, "The Enduring Hopi," 145; James, *Pages from Hopi History*, 130.

2. James, *Pages from Hopi History*, 78–79. The risk of traveling unaccompanied by military escort was very real. Superintendent of Indian Affairs for Arizona George W. Leihy was killed in December 1866, allegedly by "Tonta [sic] Apaches," while traveling without an escort. See "Annual Report of G. W. Dent, Superintendent," 15 July 1867 (Dent to Hon. N. G. Taylor, Commissioner of Indian Affairs), *Annual Report*, 1867, 154.

3. "Calhoun to Commissioner Brown," 29 March 1850, Abel, *Official Correspondence*, 172–73.

4. "Calhoun to Brown," 12 October 1850, Abel, *Official Correspondence*, 264.

5. Iverson, "The Enduring Hopi," 145–46.

6. Secretary of the Territory of New Mexico William G. Ritch was one such official, who famously stole many documents out of the New Mexico Archives at the Palace of the Governors. They eventually found their way to the Huntington Library in San Marino, California.

7. "Calhoun to Commissioner Lea," 31 August 1851, Abel, *Official Correspondence*, 415.

8. The agency was originally known as the Moqui Pueblo Agency, after the common Spanish term. The name was changed to the Hopi Agency in 1923.

9. Ives, *Report Upon the Colorado River of the West*, 119–20. Ives was an astute observer. After being led to a dwelling where he and his men were to spend the night, he commented on being brought "a tray filled with a singular substance that looked more like sheets of thin blue wrapping paper rolled up into bundles than anything else that I had ever seen. I learned afterwards that it was made from corn meal, ground very fine, made into a gruel, and poured over a heated stone to be baked. When dry it has a surface slightly polished, like paper. The sheets are folded and rolled together, and form the staple article of food with the Moqui Indians" (Ives, 121). This, of course, was the famous Hopi piki bread. Furthermore, while Hopi chiefs wielded some sort of traditional ceremonial club or staff, as had the Rio Grande Pueblo leaders in the precontact period, the term "baton" has a certain connotation, one that lends itself well to the idea of the varas de justicia. Unfortunately, Ives makes no comment on the physical appearance of the "baton." Given his other observations, he likely would have noted tassels and a silver knob if they had been present.

10. Ives, 122, 124, 126–27.

11. Thomas Edwin Farish was an explorer, miner, and politician. He served as Arizona State Historian in the 1910s. Dr. Edward Palmer was born in England in 1821, and after emigrating from England to the United States at the age of eighteen, he became enamored with natural history. He was associated with the American Academy of Sciences and undertook numerous expeditions to locations in both North and South America. After serving as a surgeon in the U. S. Army during the Civil War, Palmer was sent by the Commissioner of Agriculture in 1869 to New Mexico to report on agricultural resources, soil and climate, commercial products, and the general habitability of the territory. He crossed into Arizona during this expedition, and spent time among the Hopis [see Safford, "Edward Palmer," 341, 345].

12. Farish, *History of Arizona, Volume VII,* 148.

13. Dr. Palmer's story is the only source I have come across that refers to Lincoln canes' being presented to Hopi leaders. It presents an intriguing possibility. According to LaCroix Dailey, Steck's accounts only showed receipts for nineteen canes (see LaCroix Dailey, "Symbolism and Significance of the Lincoln Canes," 133). Furthermore, Steck had the canes made in 1864, and Arizona gained territorial status in 1863. Hopis would have been administered through the Arizona Superintendency. In addition, no scholar of the Hopis that I know of has mentioned Lincoln canes. Suffice it to say that the possibility of Hopi Lincoln canes is an intriguing one, and will be quite a discovery if it can be further verified. There is also the possibility that the Hopi "Governor" had a fake cane, purposely copied to legitimate his authority in Anglo-American eyes. A few Hopi scholars I have spoken with were not aware of Lincoln canes among the Hopis.

14. *The Howell Code. Adopted by the First Legislative Assembly of the Territory of Arizona* (Prescott: Office of the Arizona Miner, 1865), 172.

15. "Annual report of Captain A. D. Palmer, United States Army, agent for Moquis Pueblos," 30 September 1870 (Palmer to Commissioner Parker), *Annual Report,* 1870, 134–35.

16. "Report of W. D. Crothers, Moquis Pueblo Agency, Arizona," 20 September 1872 (Crothers to Commissioner Walker), *Annual Report,* 1872, 324.

17. "Report of W. B. Traux, Moquis Pueblos Agent," 31 August 1875 (Traux to Smith), *Annual Report,* 1875, 212, emphasis my own.

18. Thomas Donaldson, *Moqui Pueblo Indians of Arizona and Pueblo Indians of New Mexico,* 40.

19. "Report of W. B. Traux, Moquis Pueblo," 26 September 1876 (Traux to Commissioner), *Annual Report,* 1876, 5–6.

20. "Report of William R. Mateer, Moquis Pueblo Agency," 24 August 1878 (Mateer to Commissioner), *Annual Report,* 1878, 8–9.

21. "Report of J. H. Fleming, Moquis Pueblo Agent," 31 August 1882 (Fleming to Commissioner), *Annual Report,* 1882, 5.

22. James, *Pages from Hopi History,* 100–101, 106–7.

23. James, 108.

24. Brooks, *Mesa of Sorrows,* 93.

25. James, *Pages from Hopi History,* 110.

26. Adams and Zedeño, "BAE Scholars as Documenters of Diversity and Change at Hopi," 313.

27. James, *Pages from Hopi History,* 111–12, 114.

28. Donaldson, *Moqui Pueblo Indians of Arizona,* 42.

29. Commissioner D. N. Browning quoted in James, *Pages from Hopi History*, 114.

30. "Report of Navajo Agency," E. H. Plummer, 17 August 1894 (Plummer to Commissioner), *Annual Report*, 1894, 100.

31. Plummer, 101.

32. The effort to allot Hopis in 1910 mostly failed, as well. See Singletary et al., *People of the Land*, 22. The net result of Hopi allotment was 11 twenty-acre allotments near the village of Moenkopi.

33. "Report of Navajo Agency," Constant Williams, 27 August 1897 (Williams to Commissioner), *Annual Report*, 1897, 107.

34. "Report of Navajo Agency," Constant Williams, 27 August 1898 (Williams to Commissioner), *Annual Report*, 1898, 124. Williams also reported on the Hopi allotments made at Moenkipi Wash, and noted that these allotments had been confirmed by the Department of the Interior, with all white claimants to these lands having been notified of Hopi ownership (Williams, 124).

35. "Report of Navajo Agent," G. W. Hayzlett, 18 August 1899 (Hayzlett to Commissioner), *Annual Report*, 1899, 158–59.

36. "Report of the School Superintendent in Charge of Moqui," Charles E. Burton, 7 August 1902 (Burton to Commissioner), *Annual Report*, 1902, 151–53, emphasis my own.

37. "Report of School Superintendent in Charge of Moqui," Charles E. Burton, 15 July 1904 (Burton to Commissioner), *Annual Report*, 1904, 140.

38. It is impossible to know who Burton's young Hopis were, and whether they had taken up allotments.

39. Charles Burton was involved in a notorious haircutting incident that drew significant national attention to Hopi and its school superintendent. Charles F. Lummis, who had crusaded for Isleta Pueblo rights, also took up the Hopi cause against Burton, and particularly his treatment of the children and others at Oraibi, where Hopis had put up staunch resistance to the civilization program. Lummis referred to Burton's time in charge at Hopi as a "reign of terror," observing that he had done terrible things to the Hopis in the name of "Education." He described Hopis as "the People of Peace; the gentlest, most tractable and most inoffensive of American Indians; the first Quakers in America." Lummis wrote that Burton was a "salaried representative of the United States Government, with absolutely despotic power over 2,600 Indians, who after four years among them can neither talk to them nor understand them; who, in place of having acquired leadership among them, has gained neither their liking, their confidence, nor their respect." Lummis described "screaming children of three or four years old dragged forcibly from their weeping mothers and driven off through the snow down to the schoolhouse." He also referred to Burton's "notorious 'Hair-Cut Order,'" whereby numerous Hopis had their hair brutally and forcefully cut. Overall, Lummis decried Burton's attempts to educate and civilize the Hopis, characterized him as a bully, and lamented the fact that he was the man charged with the work "to fit them for the duties and responsibilities of American citizenship.... Mr. Burton is absolutely unfit for such a position." See "The Sequoya League," 478–81.

40. "Report of Superintendent in Charge of Moqui," Theo. G. Lemmon, 30 June 1905 (Lemmon to Commissioner), *Annual Report*, 1906, 164.

41. "Report of Superintendent of Moqui School," Theo. G. Lemmon, 3 September 1906 (Lemmon to Commissioner), *Annual Report*, 1906, 180.

42. Lemmon, 181.

43. Donaldson, *Moqui Pueblo Indians of Arizona*, 9–10. Donaldson also argued that prohibitions against Indian citizenship because of their "not taxed" status in the Fifteenth Amendment to the U.S. Constitution did not apply to Pueblo Indians and Hopis because of their citizenship status under Mexico (Donaldson, 10). The Eleventh Census also put the population at Hopi at only 1,996, though census takers acknowledged difficulty in getting accurate numbers at some of the more resistant villages (Donaldson, 15).

44. Munk, *Arizona Sketches*, 205. Munk also wrote critically of the school incidents with Superintendent Burton.

45. Saunders, *The Indians of the Terraced Houses*, 238, 270.

46. A handful of individuals registered at Keams Canyon between 1906 and 1911, but none were Hopis. Voters registered at Keams Canyon included Lorenzo Hubbell, the famous trading post owner/operator. See *Great Register, Navajo County, Territory of Arizona, 1906–1911*.

47. Lumholtz, *New Trails in Mexico*, 136–37.

48. Meeks, *Border Citizens*, 11.

49. Hu-DeHart, "Development and Rural Rebellion," 75–76.

50. Hu-DeHart, 76.

51. Hu-DeHart, 74.

52. Cajeme purportedly learned to speak, read, and write English while in California. His parents had been forced to flee to Hermosillo to escape reprisals in the wake of Banderas's uprising. Although he was born in the Sonoran capital, much of his childhood was spent in Bacum. See Hillary, "Cajeme, and the Mexico of His Time," 120, 123, 125, 127–28, 129–31.

53. Hillary, 131.

54. Spicer, *The Yaquis*, 155, 146.

55. Corral, *Obras Historicas*, 155–56, translation my own.

56. Hillary, "Cajeme, and the Mexico of His Time," 133–34.

57. Hu-DeHart, "Development and Rural Rebellion," 78–79.

58. Troncoso, *Las Guerras con las Tribus Yaqui y Mayo*, 232–33. Troncoso includes the text of the Act of Submission.

59. Hu-DeHart, "Development and Rural Rebellion," 79.

60. Spicer, *The Yaquis*, 154–55.

61. Hu-DeHart, "Development and Rural Rebellion," 79.

62. "Chief of Yaqui Falls Fighting," *Los Angeles Herald*, 31 July 1901, 14.

63. Sheridan, "The Yoemem (Yaquis)," 44–45. Interestingly, deportation was not necessarily the only solution considered for the "Yaqui problem." A number of Mexican medical doctors, intellectuals, and others representing the state participated in the discussion, proposing a variety of solutions.

64. Manuel Balbás, *Recuerdos del Yaqui: Principales Episodios Durante la Campaña de 1899 a 1901* (1927), trans. and quoted in Spicer, *The Yaquis*, 141–42.

65. Spicer, 158.

66. McGuire, *Politics and Ethnicity on the Río Yaqui*, 33.

67. Turner, *Barbarous Mexico*, 7–8, 10, 27–28.

68. Hu-DeHart, "Development and Rural Rebellion," 80, 83.

69. The intermixing of these two groups can be readily seen at the Mission San Xavier del Bac, which still serves a local congregation largely composed of Tohono O'odhams and

Yaquis. I attended Easter morning Mass in 2015 and observed both Yaqui and Tohono O'odham parishioners and their interactions.

70. Spicer, *The Yaquis*, 158–59.
71. Trujillo, "The Yaqui of Guadalupe," 73–74.
72. Spicer, *The Yaquis*, 160.
73. Trujillo, "The Yaqui of Guadalupe," 74.
74. Moisés, Kelley, and Holden, *A Yaqui Life*, xxii, 15, 34.
75. Moisés, Kelley, and Holden, 37–38, 39–40, 40–41, 49.
76. Savala, *Autobiography of a Yaqui Poet*, xiii–xiv, 5–7.
77. Sheridan, "The Yoemem (Yaquis)," 46.
78. Spicer, *Pascua*, 4.
79. Spicer, *People of Pascua*, 39.
80. Spicer, 40–41, 43–44.
81. Spicer, 44–45; Arizona Constitution Article 7, Section 2, quoted in McCool et al., *Native Vote*, 15.
82. Spicer, *People of Pascua*, 45.
83. Even if they were not citizens and could not or did not vote, Yaquis still acted like citizens in some ways. According to Spicer, Yaquis in Tucson made use of the justice system as far back as at least 1918 (and perhaps earlier). Cases involving Yaquis brought before Tucson courts or peace officials included adoption of children, bootlegging, assault and battery, adultery, and even witchcraft. He also commented, "Yaquis do and have had for some time a political life involving participation in the various political institutions of the state of Arizona." See Spicer, *People of Pascua*, 43, 50. Spicer's comments refer to growing Yaqui political participation after statehood and into the 1930s and 1940s. Before 1912, Yaquis kept a low profile as much as possible.
84. "Pascua Diary," 25 April 1937, Edward H. and Rosamond B. Spicer Papers, MS 5 (hereafter Spicer Papers), Arizona State Museum, Archives, box 91.
85. Castile, "Yaquis, Edward H. Spicer, and Federal Indian Policy," 389.
86. Willard, "The Comparative History of Two Tribal Governments," 59.
87. Trujillo, "The Yaqui of Guadalupe," 67–68.
88. Trujillo, 74.
89. Glaser, "The Story of Guadalupe, Arizona," 23.
90. Glaser, 20–22, 15.
91. Spicer, "The Yaqui Indians of Arizona," 23.
92. Edward Spicer, "A Brief History of the Yaqui Indians of Tucson" [1967], Spicer Papers, box 13, p. 2.
93. Coolidge, "The Yaqui in Exile," 301.
94. Notes from interview with Lucas Chaves, 31 October 1936, Spicer Papers, box 1, "Additions." Loose note cards.
95. Garcia y Alva, *México y sus Progresos*, no pagination in original. Appears in section titled "Raza Yaqui."
96. Notes from interview with Lucas Chaves, 8 October 1936, Spicer Papers, box 1, "Additions." Loose note cards.
97. While assisting Yaquis with Alien Registration in August of 1940, Spicer noted that one Yaqui by the name of Jose Alipas was in possession of an official document that referred

to the creation of a "Council of Yaqui Indian Affairs," with Henry Sabala "elected" to fill the chieftainship. It seems that such a formal council did not exist in the Arizona Yaqui towns during the first decade of the twentieth century. See "Alien Registration," 30 August 1940, Spicer Papers, box 13. Loose note cards.

98. Spicer, *The Yaquis*, 244. A few abortive attempts were made at at electing officials, such as one in which "judges" were elected at Pascua in 1923. But these attempts failed to take root. However, to the south in Sonora, Yaquis who reoccupied their traditional homelands after 1910 did reconstitute their systems of government. Several works describe these structures in detail, with depictions of councils at the village level, elections, and even a more national Yaqui governors' council. See Alfonso Fabila, *Las Tribus Yaquis de Sonora: Su Cultura y Anhelada Autodeterminacion*, Clásicos de la Antropología Mexicana, Colección Número 5 (México D. F.: Instituto Nacional Indigenista, 1978) and Holden et al., *Studies of the Yaqui Indians of Sonora, Mexico*.

99. A word on Akimel O'odhams is in order: they can be considered the cousins of the Tohono O'odhams. The two groups were, historically, closely related, sharing not only a common language but also economic and social ties. They traded, shared resource zones, and intermarried. See Erickson, *Sharing the Desert*, 13, 16–17. Akimel O'odhams are deserving of their own study as it relates to voting and citizenship.

100. Erickson, 59–60, 62. Erickson undertook this study at the behest of the Tohono O'odham Nation. It combined extensive documentary research with oral histories from numerous Tohono O'odhams (pp. ix–x).

101. Erickson, 64.

102. Erickson, 69–70, 72.

103. A. T. Kilcrease, "Ninety Five Years of History of the Papago Indians," 299. The calendar stick was deciphered by Sevier Juan from Covered Wells and then burned (p. 297). The Tohono O'odham calendar stick that Ruth Underhill wrote about had no record for many "major events" such as the passing of Papaguería from Spain to Mexico and Mexico to the United States, the U.S. Civil War, allotment coming to San Xavier, Arizona statehood, and so forth. See Ruth M. Underhill, "A Papago Calendar Record," 13–14.

104. The same could be said of Pueblos, Hopis, and Yaquis, thus linking these four groups together.

105. Erickson, *Sharing the Desert*, 76.

106. "Report of Governor David Merriwether [sic], superintendent *ex officio*," 30 September 1856 (Meriwether to Manypenny), *Annual Report*, 1856, 183–84.

107. Froebel, *Seven Years' Travel*, 499–500.

108. Andrew B. Gray, "Letter Addressed to Dr. John Torrey, on the Ammobroma SonorÆ," in *Proceedings of the American Association for the Advancement of Science*, 233.

109. Piipaash are Yuman speakers who migrated from the Colorado River to the Gila and took up residence with O'odhams there in the early 1800s. See "History and Culture," on the Official Website of the Salt River Pima-Maricopa Indian Community, http://www.srpmic-nsn.gov/history_culture/, accessed 1 June 2015.

110. "Report of J. L. Collins, superintendent," 30 August 1857 (Mowry to J. W. Denver, Commissioner of Ind. Affairs), *Annual Report*, 1857, 297, 299, 303–304. Superintendent Collins

reproduced Lieutenant Mowry's report, but introduced it by stating, "The Indians acquired by the Gadsden Purchase are mostly Pueblos" (p. 276).

111. Report of Lieutenant A. B. Chapman, First Dragoons, quoted in "Report of G. Bailey, special agent, in regard to the Indians of Arizona," 4 November 1858 (Bailey to Commissioner), *Annual Report*, 1858, 203–5.

112. Emory, *Report on the United States and Mexican Boundary Survey*, 1:96.

113. Underhill, "A Papago Calendar Record," 26.

114. "Report of John Walker, agent for the Indians within the Tucson agency," 28 September 1859 (Walker to Collins), *Annual Report*, 1859, 352.

115. "Report of Sylvester Mowry, upon the condition of the Pimas and Marricopas [sic], of Arizona," 21 November 1859 (Mowry to Greenwood), *Annual Report*, 1859, 353–54, 359–60, 361.

116. Kilcrease, "Ninety Five Years of History of the Papago Indians," 301.

117. Meeks, *Border Citizens*, 137.

118. Irwin, "Sanitary Report—Fort Buchanan," *Statistical Reports on the Sickness and Mortality in the Army of the United States*, 211–12.

119. "Report of John Walker, agent for the Indians within the Tucson agency," 6 September 1860 (Walker to Collins), *Annual Report*, 1860, 167–68. Walker also commented that there were "Pueblos or tame Apaches [living] in the immediate vicinity of Tucson, numbering, perhaps 150 souls. They have no lands, and work in the same manner as, and are upon an equality with the Mexican peons" (p. 169).

120. "Report of Michael Steck, superintendent," 19 September 1863 (Steck to Dole), *Annual Report*, 1863, 109.

121. "Report of Charles D. Poston, suprintendent," 30 September 1864 (Poston to Commissioner Dole), *Annual Report*, 1864, 153–54.

122. Browne, *Adventures in the Apache Country*, 138, 140–42, 276. The largely Tohono O'odham choir at San Xavier still continues to impress listeners today.

123. "Report from M. O. Davidson, relative to character, traditions, habits, &c., of Papagos," 16 June 1865 (Davidson to Dole), *Annual Report*, 1865, 133.

124. Davidson, 133–34.

125. Davidson, 134. Agent Davidson also recounted that the O'odhams and so-called tame Apaches had supplied some 150 soldiers for a campaign against the "barbarous Apaches." Their service had been "really valuable" (p. 134).

126. Van Valkenburgh served as acting commissioner only briefly in 1865 before going on to become U.S. Minister Resident to Japan.

127. "Instructions to Mr. Davidson, relative to his agency," 7 September 1865 (Acting Commissioner R. B. Van Valkenburgh to Davidson), *Annual Report*, 1865, 137–38.

128. Erickson, *Sharing the Desert*, 75.

129. "Annual report of Levi Ruggles, special agent in charge of Pimas and Maricopas," 20 June 1867 (Ruggles to Superintendent Dent), *Annual Report*, 1867, 162, 165.

130. "Report of Lieutenant Colonel R. Jones, U. S. A., relative to Indian tribes in Arizona," 21 July 1869 (Jones to Brevet Major General R. B. Marcy, Inspector General U. S. A., Washington), *Annual Report*, 1869, 215, 220.

131. Jackson, *Descriptive Catalogue of Photographs of North American Indians*, 91.

132. Pima and Maricopa Agent J. H. Stout reported on Cook's activities in 1871 and the various challenges he faced in establishing schools among the Pimas. See "Annual report of J. H. Stout, special agent Pima and Maricopa agency," 18 August 1871 (Stout to Bendell), *Annual Report*, 1871, 355–56.

133. "Annual report R. A. Wilbur, special agent Papago agency," 26 August 1871 (Wilbur to Bendell), *Annual Report*, 1871, 365–66.

134. "R. A. Wilbur, Papago agency, Arizona," 31 August 1872 (Wilbur to Bendell), *Annual Report*, 1872, 321.

135. The 372,000-acre Gila River Pima Reservation was established by act of Congress in 1859, while the 52,600 Salt River Pima-Maricopa Reservation was established by Executive Order in 1879. See Inter Tribal Council of Arizona website, "Gila River Indian Community," http://itcaonline.com/?page_id=1158, and "Salt River Pima-Maricopa Indian Community," http://itcaonline.com/?page_id=1175, accessed 1 June 2015. While there were always issues of competition for irrigating waters, and encroachments by Anglo-American settlers, there was a pronounced neglect of the Tohono O'odhams when it came to a reservation.

136. Jacoby, *Shadows at Dawn*, 37.

137. Jacoby, 41, 186.

138. R. A. Wilbur to Herman Bendell, 17 October 1871, Reuben Augustine Wilbur papers (AZ 565), Special Collections, University of Arizona Libraries (hereafter Wilbur Papers), box 1, folder 2.

139. Wilbur to Bendell, 31 December 1871, Wilbur Papers, box 1, folder 2.

140. Jacoby, *Shadows at Dawn*, 193–94.

141. Cozzens, *Eyewitnesses to the Indian Wars, 1865–1890*, 1:115, 122.

142. "R. A. Wilbur, United States Indian Agent for the Papagoes [sic] to H. Bendell, Esq., Superintendent of Indian Affairs, Prescott, Arizona Territory," 31 August 1872, *Annual Report*, 1872, 321.

143. Erickson, *Sharing the Desert*, 77–78; Joseph, Spicer, and Chesky, *The Desert People*, 22.

144. "Report of John W. Corynyn, Papago Agency," 14 September 1875 (Cornyn to Smith), *Annual Report*, 1875, 213.

145. "Report of Charles Hudson, Pima and Maricopa Agency," 31 August 1876 (Hudson to Commissioner), *Annual Report*, 1876, 8–9.

146. Erickson, *Sharing the Desert*, 77.

147. "Report of Charles Hudson, Pima Agency" [actual report is from J. H. Stout], 31 August 1877 (Stout to Commissioner), *Annual Report*, 1877, 33–34.

148. "Report of Roswell G. Wheeler, Pima Agent," 29 August 1885 (Wheeler to Commissioner), *Annual Report*, 1885, 4.

149. "Report of Roswell G. Wheeler, Pima Agent," 2 August 1886 (Wheeler to Commissioner), *Annual Report*, 1886, 39.

150. "Report of Claude M. Johnson, Pima Agent," 1 July 1889 (Johnson to Commissioner), *Annual Report*, 1889, 120–21.

151. "Report of Cornelius W. Crouse, Pima Agent," 18 August 1890 (Crouse to Commissioner), *Annual Report*, 1890, 7.

152. Erickson, *Sharing the Desert*, 92.

153. Marak and Tuennerman, *At the Border of Empires*, 20.

154. Lumholtz, *New Trails in Mexico*, 6.

155. Blaine as told to Adams, *Papagos and Politics*, 17, 32.

156. Kilcrease, "Ninety Five Years of History of the Papago Indians," 307.

157. Erickson, *Sharing the Desert*, 92–93. Blaine reported on farming: "At San Xavier we ran our own farms. We didn't have nobody telling us how to farm." See Blaine, p. 34. Blaine was describing his own farming a few decades after the 1890 allotments were made, but this still indicates a continuation of traditional Tohono O'odham farming practices, in spite of allotment.

158. Meeks, *Border Citizens*, 46.

159. Biographical information on Berger is somewhat difficult to come by, but much of it has been compiled on the Find a Grave website, including his obituary in *The Arizona Daily Star*. See page for "Maria Policarpia Martinez Berger" (his wife), http://www.findagrave.com/cgi-bin/fg.cgi?page=gr&GRid=115238196, accessed 8 June 2015.

160. "Report of Pima Agency," Cornelius W. Crouse, 1 July 1893 (Crouse to Commissioner), *Annual Report*, 1893, 114. He urged the allotment of the Gila Bend Papago Reservation, which was much smaller: only six square miles (p. 114).

161. "Report of Farmer, Papago Reservation," J. M. Berger, 4 August 1893 (Berger to Crouse), *Annual Report*, 1893, 117–18.

162. "Report of Papago Subagency," J. M. Berger, 28 August 1894 (Berger to Young), *Annual Report*, 1894, 108–10.

163. "Report of Farmer in Charge of Papagoes [sic]," J. M. Berger 3 September 1898 (Berger to E. Hadley, United States Indian Agent), *Annual Report*, 1898, 129.

164. Berger put the population on the San Xavier Reservation in 1894 at 492. See "Report of Papago Subagency," J. M. Berger, 28 August 1894, *Annual Report*, 1894, 108.

165. "Report of Farmer in Charge of San Xavier Papagoes [sic]," J. M. Berger, 15 August 1899 (Berger to Hedley), *Annual Report*, 1899, 165, emphasis my own.

166. "Report of Farmer in Charge of San Xavier Papagoes," J. M. Berger, 18 August 1900 (Berger to Hadley), *Annual Report*, 1900, 199.

167. "Report of Farmer in Charge of San Xavier Papago," J. M. Berger, 17 August 1901 (Berger to Hadley), *Annual Report*, 1901, 190.

168. "Report of Farmer in Charge of San Xavier Papago," J. M. Berger, 28 August 1902 (Berger to Commissioner), *Annual Report*, 1902, 167.

169. Berger, 167–68.

170. "Report of Farmer in Charge of Papago," J. M. Berger, 24 September 1904 (Berger to Commissioner), *Annual Report*, 1904, 149.

171. Pima County voter rolls do show a small number of registered voters from the San Xavier Precinct in 1910, for example. The individual registrants have Spanish names, which would be expected with many O'odhams at that time. But it is very difficult to determine if these individuals were O'odhams. The voter registration makes no mention of race or ethnicity, only "Country of Nativity." The country of nativity for some registered voters from San Xavier is the United States, while for others it is Mexico. For some San Xavier voters, the notation of citizen "By virtue of Gadsden Treaty" is included. See *Great Register of Pima County, Territory of Arizona*. There are a few possibilities. These voters could have been Tohono O'odhams who registered to vote, or they could have been Mexicans who became U.S. citizens. They could also have been Tohono O'odhams from Mexico who became naturalized U.S.

citizens. Given Berger's statements, the most reasonable conclusion is that these were Mexican Americans, not Tohono O'odhams. In 1910, the San Xavier Precinct, which included the San Xavier Indian Reservation, had 1,569 total residents, but only 541 were on the reservation. See Table 1, "Population of Minor and Civil Divisions: 1910, 1900, and 1890," in United States, Bureau of the Census, *Thirteenth Census of the United States Taken in the Year 1910*, 574.

172. Meeks, *Border Citizens*, 49. Allotted Indians declared competent, and granted citizenship, were often celebrated in highly-scripted "Last Arrow Ceremonies." An Indian candidate for citizenship was called out by his "white" name, and then asked to tell his "Indian" name. He was then handed a bow and arrow, and told to shoot the arrow. After doing so, a federal official—in some cases the Secretary of the Interior—would tell the Indians, "calling him by his Indian name: 'You have shot your last arrow. That means that you are no longer to live the life of an Indian. You are from this day forward to live the life of the white man. But you may keep that arrow; it will be to you a symbol of your noble race and of the pride you feel that you come from the first of all Americans.'" The Indian was then called by his white name, and directed to take a plow. He was told, "This act means that you have chosen to love the life of the white man—and the white man lives by work." The Indian was then given a leather purse, a small flag, and a badge inscribed with "A Citizen of the United States." See "A Ritual of Citizenship," *New Outlook*, 24 May 1916, 161–62. In other versions Indians appeared in traditional dress, and were then made to enter a teepee, from which they would emerge in citizen dress and holding the bow and arrow. After shooting the arrow they were told, "You have shot your last arrow." See Hoxie, *A Final Promise*, 180. Certificates of citizenship abound in Record Group 75 for a number of groups, particularly those from allotted tribes. But, I was unable to locate any from Pueblos, Hopis, Yaquis, or Tohono O'odhams.

173. "Notes," *Weekly Arizona Miner*, 3 May 1878.

174. Editorial, *Arizona Citizen*, 10 December 1870.

175. McClintock, *Arizona*, 324.

176. "Local News," *Arizona Weekly Citizen*, 12 December 1896.

177. Alden Jones quoted in Bob Bunker, "Hand Book for Civil Servant," Spicer Papers, box 37, no date, unpaginated.

178. The entry for 1895 recorded the death of a councilman, who was "killed by lightning." See Kilcrease, "Ninety Five Years of History of the Papago Indians," 305.

179. Underhill recorded the title as "kovenal." See Underhill, *Social Organization of the Papago Indians*, 84. Whatever the spelling, the name was an O'odhamized version of the Spanish "gobernador."

180. Jose Lewis, "Papago Government," NAA MS 1744, Vol. 2, National Anthropological Archives, Smithsonian Institution, 1. I assume the selecting body was the village council, which consisted of the adult men of the village.

181. Lewis, 2.

182. Lewis, 3.

183. Joseph, Spicer, and Chesky, *The Desert People*, 104, emphasis my own.

184. Blaine, *Papagos and Politics*, 40; Michael S. Adams quoted on 2–3.

185. *The Thirty-First Annual Report of the Executive Committee of the Indian Rights Association, for the Year Ending December 10, 1913*, 26, 28.

186. Meeks, *Border Citizens*, 135–137; Daniel Bruce Ferguson, "The Escuela Experience: The Tucson Indian School in Perspective" (master's thesis, University of Arizona, 1997), 38,

43–44. The disputes between Presbyterian and Catholic Tohono O'odhams were quite heated at times. Father Bonaventure Oblasser, who served as a Catholic missionary among the Tohono O'odhams for nearly forty years during the first half of the twentieth century, wrote quite frequently as a partisan observer of the Presbyterian-Catholic power struggle. On 21 April 1912, two short months after Arizona statehood, he wrote dejectedly, "Chief Albino from the Quijotoa district has fallen away and joined the two Presbyterian chiefs in their agitation for a Government School to be erected either at Fresnal or Burro Pond." See Father Bonaventure Oblasser to Reverend Juston Deutsch, O.F.M., 21 April 1912. Father Bonaventure Oblasser, O.F.M. Collection (MS 543). Special Collections, University of Arizona Libraries, 2. The two sides grappled for converts, access to land for chapels, and government support for denominational schools. These conflicts played out in the 1910s and after in Tohono O'odham leadership.

187. McCool, Olson, and Robinson, *Native Vote*, 15. Article 7, Section 2. C. now reads: "No person who is adjudicated an incapacitated person shall be qualified to vote at any election...." See Article 7, Section 2. C. of Arizona Constitution, Arizona State Legislature Website.

188. "An Apache Gets Papers as a Citizen," *Bisbee Daily Review*, 16 July 1908. Yavapais were frequently misidentified as Apaches and referred to as Mohave-Apaches or Yuma-Apaches.

189. Letter from Mike Burns to Carlos Montezuma, 16 December 1911, Mike Burns (Hoomothya) Papers, Sharlot Hall Museum Library and Archives, box 1, folder 12.

Conclusion

1. At the time, it was known as the Fort McDowell Mohave Apache Tribe. Outsiders had long mistaken Yavapais for a band of Apaches. Even the famous Progressive Era Yavapai physician Carlos Montezuma frequently referred to himself as an Apache or a Mojave Apache.

2. Frank Harrison, quoted in Anne T. Denogean, "60 Years Ago in Arizona, Indians Won Right to Vote," *Tucson Citizen*, 25 July 2009.

3. McCool et al., *Native Vote*, 15–16; Denogean, "60 Years Ago in Arizona."

4. Indian Voting Commemoration Poster, Monday, 21 July 2014. Poster in possession of the author.

5. Article 7, Section 1, "Message from the President of the United States Transmitting Copy of the Constitution of New Mexico with Formal Approval Thereof, and Recommending the Approval of the Same by Congress," 61st Congress, 3rd Session, Senate Document No. 835, 24 February 1911 (Washington, D.C.; Government Printing Office), 25.

6. Matthew Martinez (Ohkay Owingeh Pueblo), "Pueblo People Win the Right to Vote—1948," from New Mexico Office of the State Historian Website, http://dev.newmexicohistory.org/filedetails.php?fileID=415; Dean Chavers, "A History of Indian Voting Rights and Why It's Important," *Indian Country Today Media Network*, 29 October 2012, http://indiancountrytodaymedianetwork.com/2012/10/29/history-indian-voting-rights-and-why-its-important-vote-140373. Both accessed 29 September 2015.

7. Mikhail Sundust, "GRIC Celebrates Arizona Native Right to Vote," *Gila River Indian News*, 15, no. 8 (August 2012), 1, 6.

8. Sánchez, Spude, and Gómez. *New Mexico*, 307–8, emphasis my own.

9. Simpson, *Mohawk Interruptus*, 2.

10. González, *Refusing the Favor*, 15.

11. See "Government," official website of the Yavapai-Apache Nation, http://yavapai-apache.org/government-issues/1262806, accessed 29 September 2015. Headquartered in Middle Verde, Arizona, the Yavapai-Apache Nation, of which I am a citizen, is a combination of two distinct peoples: Dilzhe'e, or Western Apaches (Athabaskan speakers); and Yavapais (Yuman speakers). The two groups historically inhabited neighboring territory along the Verde River.

12. See Yavapai-Apache Nation Constitution, National Indian Law Library Website.

Bibliography

Archival Collections

ARIZONA

Tucson
    University of Arizona, Arizona State Museum
        Edward H. and Rosamond B. Spicer Papers
    University of Arizona Libraries, Special Collections
        Father Bonaventure Oblasser, O.F.M. Collection
        Reuben Augustine Wilbur Papers

Prescott
    Sharlot Hall Museum, Library and Archives
        Mike Burns (Hoomothya) Papers

CALIFORNIA

San Marino
    Huntington Library
        William G. Ritch Collection, 1539–1901. Microfilm.

MISSOURI

St. Louis
    Knights of Columbus Vatican Film Library
        Pastells Collection, Sevilla. Secretaria de Nueva España, Audencia de Mexico y Guadalajara. Microfilm.

NEW MEXICO

Albuquerque
    University Libraries, University of New Mexico
        American Indian Oral History Collection, 1967–1972
        Documents from the Archivo General de la Nación, Mexico and other Related Archives, 1520–1878
        Eleanor B. Adams Papers
        Indian Affairs Collection
        Santa Fe, New Mexico Records

Santa Fe
  Archives of the Archdiocese of Santa Fe
  Museum of New Mexico, The Palace of the Governors, Fray Angélico Chávez History
    Library
    Bureau of Indian Affairs Collection
  New Mexico State Records Center and Archives
    Arthur Bibo Collection of Acoma and Laguna Pueblo Documents
    Mexican Archives of New Mexico. Microfilm.
    Spanish Archives of New Mexico II. Microfilm.
    Territorial Archives of New Mexico, 1846–1912. Microfilm.
    WPA Translations of Spanish Archives of New Mexico I Documents. Microfilm.

UTAH

Salt Lake City
  J. Willard Marriott Library, University of Utah
    Doris Duke Indian Oral History Project

WASHINGTON, D.C.

  National Archives
    State Department Territorial Papers, New Mexico, 1851–1872. Microfilm.
  Smithsonian Institution
    National Anthropological Archives

Government Documents and Reports

Eleventh Census of the United States, Extra Census Bulletin: Moqui Pueblo Indians of Arizona and Pueblo Indians of New Mexico. Washington, D.C.: United States Census Printing Office, 1893.

Emory, William H. *Report on the United States and Mexican Boundary Survey*, 2 vols. Washington, D.C.: Cornelius Wendell, 1857.

Irwin, Bernard I. D. "Sanitary Report—Fort Buchanan." *Statistical Reports on the Sickness and Mortality in the Army of the United States, Compiled from the Records of the Surgeon General's Office; Embracing a Period of Five Years, from January, 1855, to January, 1860.* Washington, D.C.: George W. Bowman, 1860.

Ives, Joseph C. *Report Upon the Colorado River of the West, Explored in 1857 and 1858 by Lieutenant Joseph C. Ives, Corps of Topographical Engineers, Under the Direction of the Office of Explorations and Surveys, A. A. Humphreys, Captain Topographical Engineers, In Charge. By Order of the Secretary of War.* Washington, D.C.: Government Printing Office, 1861.

Jackson, William H. *Descriptive Catalogue of Photographs of North American Indians.* Miscellaneous Publications, No. 9, Department of the Interior, United States Geological Survey of the Territories. Washington, D.C.: Government Printing Office, 1877.

Kilcrease, A. T. "Ninety Five Years of History of the Papago Indians." *Southwest Monuments Monthly Report.* Washington, D.C.: Government Printing Office, United States Department of the Interior, National Park Service, April 1939.

United States Bureau of the Census. *Thirteenth Census of the United States Taken in the Year 1910: Statistics for Arizona Containing Statistics of Population, Agriculture, Manufactures, and Mining for the State, Counties, Cities, and Other Divisions.* Washington, D.C.: Government Printing Office, 1913.

United States Office of Indian Affairs. *Annual Report of the Commissioner of Indian Affairs, Transmitted with the Message of the President at the Opening of the First Session of the Thirty-Third Congress, 1853.* Washington, D.C.: Robert Armstrong, Printer, 1853.

———. *Annual Report of the Commissioner of Indian Affairs, Transmitted with the Message of the President at the Opening of the Second Session of the Thirty-Third Congress, 1854.* Washington, D.C.: A. O. P. Nicholson, 1855.

———. *Annual Report of the Commissioner of Indian Affairs, Transmitted with the Message of the President at the Opening of the First Session of the Thirty-Fourth Congress, 1855.* Washington, D.C.: A. O. P. Nicholson, 1856.

———. *Report of the Commissioner of Indian Affairs, Accompanying the Annual Report of the Secretary of the Interior, for the Year 1856.* Washington, D.C.: A. O. P. Nicholson, 1857.

———. *Report of the Commissioner of Indian Affairs, Accompanying the Annual Report of the Secretary of the Interior, for the Year 1857.* Washington, D.C.: William A. Harris, Printer, 1858.

———. *Report of the Commissioner of Indian Affairs, Accompanying the Annual Report of the Secretary of the Interior, for the Year 1858.* Washington, D.C.: William A. Harris, Printer, 1858.

———. *Report of the Commissioner of Indian Affairs, Accompanying the Annual Report of the Secretary of the Interior, for the Year 1859.* Washington, D.C.: George W. Bowman, Printer, 1860.

———. *Report of the Commissioner of Indian Affairs, Accompanying the Annual Report of the Secretary of the Interior, for the Year 1860.* Washington, D.C.: George W. Bowman, Printer, 1860.

———. *Report of the Commissioner of Indian Affairs, for the Year 1863.* Washington, D.C.: Government Printing Office, 1864.

———. *Report of the Commissioner of Indian Affairs for the Year 1864.* Washington, D.C.: Government Printing Office, 1865.

———. *Report of the Commissioner of Indian Affairs, for the Year 1865.* Washington, D.C.: Government Printing Office, 1865.

———. *Report of the Commissioner of Indian Affairs, for the Year 1866.* Washington, D.C.: Government Printing Office, 1866.

———. *Report of Indian Affairs, by the Acting Commissioner, for the Year 1867.* Washington, D.C.: Government Printing Office, 1867.

———. *Report of the Commissioner of Indian Affairs, Made to the Secretary of the Interior, for the Year 1869.* Washington, D.C.: Government Printing Office, 1870.

———. *Report of the Commissioner of Indian Affairs to the Secretary of the Interior for the Year 1871.* Washington, D.C.: Government Printing Office, 1872.

———. *Annual Report of the Commissioner of Indian Affairs to the Secretary of the Interior for the Year 1872.* Washington, D.C.: Government Printing Office, 1872.

———. *Annual Report of the Commissioner of Indian Affairs to the Secretary of the Interior for the Year 1873.* Washington, D.C.: Government Printing Office, 1874.

———. *Annual Report of the Commissioner of Indian Affairs to the Secretary of the Interior for the Year 1875.* Washington, D.C.: Government Printing Office, 1875.

———. *Annual Report of the Commissioner of Indian Affairs to the Secretary of the Interior for the Year 1876.* Washington, D.C.: Government Printing Office, 1876.
———. *Annual Report of the Commissioner of Indian Affairs to the Secretary of the Interior for the Year 1877.* Washington, D.C.: Government Printing Office, 1877.
———. *Annual Report of the Commissioner of Indian Affairs to the Secretary of the Interior for the Year 1878.* Washington, D.C.: Government Printing Office, 1878.
———. *Annual Report of the Commissioner of Indian Affairs to the Secretary of the Interior for the Year 1879.* Washington, D.C.: Government Printing Office, 1879.
———. *Annual Report of the Commissioner of Indian Affairs to the Secretary of the Interior for the Year 1880.* Washington, D.C.: Government Printing Office, 1880.
———. *Annual Report of the Commissioner of Indian Affairs to the Secretary of the Interior for the Year 1882.* Washington, D.C.: Government Printing Office, 1882.
———. *Annual Report of the Commissioner of Indian Affairs to the Secretary of the Interior for the Year 1884.* Washington, D.C.: Government Printing Office, 1884.
———. *Annual Report of the Commissioner of Indian Affairs to the Secretary of the Interior for the Year 1885.* Washington, D.C.: Government Printing Office, 1885.
———. *Annual Report of the Commissioner of Indian Affairs to the Secretary of the Interior for the Year 1886.* Washington, D.C.: Government Printing Office, 1886.
———. *Annual Report of the Commissioner of Indian Affairs to the Secretary of the Interior for the Year, 1889.* Washington, D.C.: Government Printing Office, 1889.
———. *Fifty-Ninth Annual Report of the Commissioner of Indian Affairs to the Secretary of the Interior. 1890.* Washington, D.C.: Government Printing Office, 1890.
———. *Sixty-First Annual Report of the Commissioner of Indian Affairs to the Secretary of the Interior. 1892.* Washington, D.C.: Government Printing Office, 1892.
———. *Sixty-Second Annual Report of the Commissioner of Indian Affairs to the Secretary of the Interior, 1893.* Washington, D.C.: Government Printing Office, 1893.
———. *Annual Report of the Commissioner of Indian Affairs, 1894.* Washington, D.C.: Government Printing Office, 1894.
———. *Annual Reports of the Department of the Interior for the Fiscal Year Ended June 30, 1897. Report of the Commissioner of Indian Affairs.* Washington, D.C.: Government Printing Office, 1897.
———. *Annual Reports of the Department of the Interior for the Fiscal Year Ended June 30, 1898. Indian Affairs.* Washington, D.C.: Government Printing Office, 1898.
———. *Annual Reports of the Department of the Interior for the Fiscal Year Ended June 30, 1899. Indian Affairs. Part I.* Washington, D.C.: Government Printing Office, 1899.
———. *Annual Reports of the Department of the Interior for the Fiscal Year Ended June 30, 1900. Indian Affairs, Report of Commissioner and Appendixes.* Washington, D.C.: Government Printing Office, 1900.
———. *Annual Reports of the Department of the Interior for the Fiscal Year Ended June 30, 1901. Indian Affairs, Part I. Report of Commissioner, and Appendixes.* Washington, D.C.: Government Printing Office, 1901.
———. *Annual Reports of the Department of the Interior for the Fiscal Year Ended June 30, 1902. Indian Affairs, Part I. Report of Commissioner, and Appendixes.* Washington, D.C.: Government Printing Office, 1903.

———. *Annual Reports of the Department of the Interior for the Fiscal Year Ended June 30, 1904. Indian Affairs. Part I. Report of the Commissioner, and Appendixes.* Washington, D.C.: Government Printing Office, 1904.

———. *Annual Reports of the Department of the Interior for the Fiscal Year Ended June 30, 1905. Indian Affairs. Part I.* Washington, D.C.: Government Printing Office, 1906.

———. *Annual Reports of the Department of the Interior. 1906. Indian Affairs: Report of the Commissioner and Appendixes.* Washington, D.C.: Government Printing Office, 1906.

U.S. Congress. House. "House Miscellaneous Document No. 15" ("New Mexico Contested Election"), *United States Congressional Serial Set 866.* 34th Cong., 1st sess., 1855.

———. "House Report No. 121." *United States Congressional Serial Set 742.* 33rd Cong., 1st sess., 1854.

U.S. Congress. Senate. "Message from the President of the United States Transmitting Copy of the Constitution of New Mexico with Formal Approval Thereof, and Recommending the Approval of the Same by Congress." Senate Document No. 835. 61st Congress, 3rd Session, 24 February 1911. Washington, D.C.: Government Printing Office, 1911.

Legal Cases

The Cherokee Nation v. The State of Georgia, 30 U.S. 1 (1831).
Territory of New Mexico v. Delinquent Taxpayers, 12 N. M. 139, 76 Pac. 316 (1904).
United States v. Joseph, 94 U.S. 614 (1876).
United States v. Lucero, 1 N.M. 422 (1869).

Books, Articles, Dissertations, and Theses

Abel, Annie Heloise, ed. *The Official Correspondence of James S. Calhoun.* Washington, D.C.: Government Printing Office, 1915.

Aberle, Sophie D. "The Pueblo Indians of New Mexico: Their Land, Economy and Civil Organization," *American Anthropologist* 50, no. 4 pt. 2 (October 1948): 4–93.

Adams, David Wallace. *Education for Extinction: American Indians and the Boarding School Experience, 1875–1928.* Lawrence: University Press of Kansas, 1995.

Adams, E. Charles, and M. Nieves Zedeño. "BAE Scholars as Documenters of Diversity and Change at Hopi, 1870–1895." *Journal of the Southwest* 41, no. 3 (Autumn 1999): 311–34.

Adams, William Y. *Indian Policies in the Americas: From Columbus to Collier and Beyond.* Santa Fe: School for Advanced Research Press, 2014.

Adler, Michael A., and Herbert W. Dick, eds. *Picuris Pueblo through Time: Eight Centuries of Change at a Northern Rio Grande Pueblo.* Dallas: William P. Clements Center for Southwest Studies, Southern Methodist University, 1999.

Alegre, Francisco Javier. *Historia de la Compañia de Jesus en Nueva-España, Vol. 2.* Mexico: Impr. De J. M. Lara, 1841–42.

Anna, Timothy E. "Iguala: The Prototype." In *Forceful Negotiations: The Origins of the Pronunciamiento in Nineteenth-Century Mexico,* edited by Will Fowler, 1–21. Lincoln: University of Nebraska Press, 2010.

Armstrong, William H. *Warrior in Two Camps: Ely S. Parker, Union General and Seneca Chief.* Syracuse, N.Y.: Syracuse University Press, 1978.
Babcock, Matthew M. *Apache Adaptation to Hispanic Rule.* Cambridge: Cambridge University Press, 2016.
Bandelier, Adolph Francis. *Final Report of Investigations Among the Indians of the Southwestern United States, Carried on Mainly in the Years from 1880 to 1895, Vol. 2.* Papers of the Archaeological Institute of America, American series, vols. 3–4. Cambridge, Mass.: Archaeological Institute of America, 1890–1892.
Barr, Juliana. "Geographies of Power: Mapping Indian Borders in the 'Borderlands' of the Early Southwest." *The William and Mary Quarterly* 68, no. 1 (January 2011): 5–46.
Bartlett, John Russell. *Personal Narrative of Explorations and Incidents in Texas, New Mexico, California, Sonora, and Chihuahua, Connected with the United States Boundary Commission, During the Years 1850, '51, '52, and '53.* New York: D. Appleton, 1854.
Bayer, Laura, with Floyd Montoya and the Pueblo of Santa Ana. *Santa Ana, the People, the Pueblo, and the History of Tamaya.* Albuquerque: University of New Mexico Press, 1994.
Benedict, Kirby. *A Journey through New Mexico's First Judicial District in 1864: Letters to the Editor of the Santa Fe Weekly New Mexican,* Great West and Indian Series 4. Los Angeles: Westernlore, 1965.
Bieber, Ralph P., ed. *Letters of William Carr Lane, 1852–1854.* Historical Society of New Mexico Publications in History, vol. 6. Santa Fe: El Palacio Press, 1928.
Blaine, Peter Sr., as told to Michael S. Adams. *Papagos and Politics.* Tucson: The Arizona Historical Society, 1991.
Bloom, Lansing B., ed. and trans. *Antonio Barreiro's Ojeada sobre Nuevo Mexico.* Historical Society of New Mexico Publications in History, vol. 5. Santa Fe: El Palacio Press, 1928.
———. "A Glimpse of New Mexico in 1620." *New Mexico Historical Review* 3, no. 4 (October 1928): 357–89.
———. "New Mexico under Mexican Administration, 1821–1846." *Old Santa Fe,* vols. 1–3. Santa Fe: Old Santa Fe Press, 1913–1915.
Bolton, Herbert Eugene. *Rim of Christendom: A Biography of Eusebio Francisco Kino, Pacific Coast Pioneer.* New York: Russell & Russell, 1960, repr. The Macmillan Company, 1936.
Borah, Woodrow. *Justice by Insurance: The General Indian Court of Colonial Mexico and the Legal Aides of the Half-Real.* Berkeley: University of California Press, 1983.
Bourke, John G. *The Snake-dance of the Moquis of Arizona: Being a Narrative of a Journey from Santa Fe, New Mexico, to the Villages of the Moqui Indians of Arizona.* London: Sampson Low, Marston, Searle, and Rivington, 1884.
Bringas de Manzaneda y Encinas, Father Diego Miguel, O.F.M., with Daniel S. Matson and Bernard L. Fontana, ed. and trans. *Friar Bringas Reports to the King: Methods of Indoctrination on the Frontier of New Spain, 1796–97.* Tucson: University of Arizona Press, 1977.
Brooks, James F. *Captives and Cousins: Slavery, Kinship, and Community in the Southwest Borderlands.* Chapel Hill: University of North Carolina Press, 2002.
———. *Mesa of Sorrows: A History of the Awat'ovi Massacre.* New York: Norton, 2016.
———. "Women, Men, and Cycles of Evangelism in the Southwest Borderlands, A.D. 750 to 1750." *American Historical Review* 118, no. 3 (2013): 738–64.

Brown, Tracy L. *Pueblo Indians and Spanish Colonial Authority in Eighteenth-Century New Mexico.* Tucson, Ariz.: University of Arizona Press, 2013.

Browne, J. Ross. *Adventures in the Apache Country: A Tour through Arizona and Sonora, with Notes on the Silver Regions of Nevada.* New York: Harper & Brothers, 1869.

Burrus, Ernest J., and Félix Zubillaga. *El Noroeste de México: Documentos sobre las Misionoes Jesuíticas, 1600–1769.* México, D.F.: Universidad Nacional Autónoma de México, 1986.

Calabaza, Estefania Lynne. "Through Pueblo Oral Tradition and Personal Narrative: Following the Santo Domingan 'Good Path.'" Master's thesis, University of Arizona, 2011.

Canedo, Lino Gómez, ed. *Sonora hacia fines del siglo XVIII: Un informe del misionero franciscano Fray Francisco Antonio Barbastro, con otros documentos complementarios,* Documentación Histórica Mexicana, Tomo 3. Guadalajara, Jalisco: Librería Font, S. A., 1971.

Caraman, Philip. *The Lost Paradise: The Jesuit Republic in South America.* New York: Seabury Press, 1976.

Carroll, H. Bailey, and J. Villasana Haggard, trans., intro., and notes. *Three New Mexico Chronicles: The Exposición of Don Pedro Bautista Pino 1812; the Ojeada of Lic. Antonio Barreiro 1832; and the additions by Don José Agustín de Escudero, 1849.* Quivira Society Publications, vol. 11. Albuquerque: University of New Mexico Press, 1942.

Castile, George Pierre. "Yaquis, Edward H. Spicer, and Federal Indian Policy: From Immigrants to Native Americans." *Journal of the Southwest* 44, no. 4 (Winter 2002): 383–436.

Chávez, Fray Angélico. "José Gonzalez, Genízaro Governor." *New Mexico Historical Review* 30, no. 3 (July 1955): 190–94.

Classen, Albrecht, ed. *The Letters of the Swiss Jesuit Missionary Philipp Segesser (1689–1762): An Eyewitness to the Settlement of Eighteenth-Century Sonora (Pimería Alta).* Tempe: Arizona Center for Medieval and Renaissance Studies, 2012.

Clemmer, Richard O. *Roads in the Sky: The Hopi Indians in a Century of Change.* Boulder, Colo.: Westview Press, 1995.

Cohen, Felix S. *Cohen's Handbook of Federal Indian Law.* Albuquerque: University of New Mexico Press, 1971.

Coolidge, Dane. "The Yaqui in Exile." *Sunset: The Magazine of the Prairie and of all the Far West* 23 (September 1909): 299–302.

Corral, Ramon. *Obras Historicas,* No. 1. Hermosillo, Sonora: Biblioteca Sonorense de Geografia e Historia, 1959.

Courlander, Harold. *Hopi Voices: Recollections, Traditions, and Narratives of Hopi Indians.* Albuquerque: University of New Mexico Press, 1982.

Cozzens, Peter, ed. *Eyewitnesses to the Indian Wars, 1865–1890,* 5 vols. Mechanicsburg, Pa.: Stackpole Books, 2001.

Crandall, Maurice. "The Early Life of Ned Russell, Yavapai-Apache, 1924–1946." Master's thesis, University of New Mexico, 2007.

Crane, Leo. *Desert Drums: The Pueblo Indians of New Mexico, 1540–1928.* Boston: Little, Brown, and Company, 1928.

Cruz, Gilbert R. *Let There Be Towns: Spanish Municipal Origins in the American Southwest, 1610–1810*. College Station: Texas A&M Press, 1988.

Cutter, Charles. "The Administration of Colonial Law in New Mexico." *Journal of the Early Republic* 18, no. 1 (Spring 1998): 99–115.

———. *The Protector de Indios in Colonial New Mexico, 1659–1821*. Albuquerque: University of New Mexico Press, published in cooperation with the Historical Society of New Mexico, 1986.

Davenport, James J., rev. and arranger. *Revised Statutes of the Territory of New Mexico*. Santa Fe: Santa Fé Weekly Gazette Office, 1856.

Dedrick, John M. "Las Cartas en Yaqui de Juan 'Bandera.'" *Tlalocan: Revista de Fuentes para el Conoscimiento de las Culturas Indígenas de México* 10 (1985): 120–87.

Deeds, Susan M. "Indigenous Rebellions on the Northern Mexican Mission Frontier: From First-Generation to Later Colonial Responses." In *Contested Ground: Comparative Frontiers on the Northern and Southern Edges of the Spanish Empire*, edited by Donna J. Guy and Thomas E. Sheridan, 32–51. The Southwest Center Series. Tucson: University of Arizona Press, 1998.

Deloria, Vine, Jr., and Raymond J. DeMallie, eds. *Documents of American Indian Diplomacy: Treaties, Agreements, and Conventions, 1775–1979*, vol. 2. Norman: University of Oklahoma Press, 1999.

Deloria, Vine, Jr., and Clifford M. Lytle. *American Indians, American Justice*. Austin: University of Texas Press, 1983.

Denogean, Anne T. "60 Years Ago in Arizona, Indians Won Right to Vote." *Tucson Citizen*, 25 July, 2009.

Dippie, Brian. *The Vanishing American: White Attitudes and U.S. Indian Policy*. Lawrence: University Press of Kansas, 1982.

Dobyns, Henry F., ed. *Hepah, California! The Journal of Cave Johnson Couts from Monterrey, Nuevo Leon, Mexico, to Los Angeles, California During the Years 1848–1849*. Tucson: Arizona Pioneers' Historical Society, 1961.

———. "Indian Extinction in the Middle Santa Cruz River Valley, Arizona." *New Mexico Historical Review* 38, no. 2 (April 1963): 163–81.

———. *The Papago People*. Phoenix: Indian Tribal Series, 1972.

———. *Spanish Colonial Tucson: A Demographic History*. Tucson: University of Arizona Press, 1976.

Docher, Rev. Anton. "The Quaint Indian Pueblo of Isleta." *Santa Fe Magazine* 7, no. 7 (June 1913): 29–32.

Dozier, Edward P. *The Pueblo Indians of North America*. Case Studies in Cultural Anthropology series. New York: Holt, Rinehart and Winston, 1970.

Ducey, Michael T. *A Nation of Villages: Riot and Rebellion in the Mexican Huasteca, 1750–1850*. Tucson: University of Arizona Press, 2004.

Dumarest, Father Noël, with a preface by Stewart Culin. *Notes on Cochiti, New Mexico*. Edited and translated by Elsie Clews Parsons. Memoirs of the American Anthropological Association, no. 6. Lancaster, Pa.: New Era Printing Company, 1919.

Dunbar, Laird J. "A Study of the Suffrage of the Arizona and New Mexico Indian." Master's thesis, University of New Mexico, 1948.

Ebright, Malcolm, and Rick Hendricks. *Advocates for the Oppressed: Hispanos, Indians, Genízaros, and Their Land in New Mexico*. Albuquerque: University of New Mexico Press, 2014.

———. *The Witches of Abiquiu: The Governor, the Priest, the Genízaro Indians, and the Devil*. Albuquerque: University of New Mexico Press, 2006.

Ebright, Malcolm, Rick Hendricks, and Richard W. Hughes. *Four Square Leagues: Pueblo Indian Land in New Mexico*. Albuquerque: University of New Mexico Press, 2014.

Eickemeyer, Carl, and Lilian Westcott Eickemeyer. *Among the Pueblo Indians*. New York: The Merriam Company, 1895.

Ellis, Richard. "Hispanic Americans and Indians in New Mexico State Politics." *New Mexico Historical Review* 53, no. 4 (October 1978): 361–64.

Emory, W. H. *Notes of a Military Reconnaissance from Fort Leavenworth, in Missouri, to San Diego, in California, Including Parts of the Arkansas, Del Norte and Gila Rivers*, 30th United States Congress, 1st Session, Senate, Executive, No. 7. Washington, D.C.: Wendell and Van Benthuysen, Printers, 1848.

Erickson, Kristin C. *Yaqui Homeland and Homeplace: The Everyday Production of Ethnic Identity*. Tucson: University of Arizona Press, 2008.

Erickson, Winston P. *Sharing the Desert: The Tohono O'odham in History*. Tucson: University of Arizona Press, 1994.

Espinosa, J. Manuel. *The Pueblo Indian Revolt of 1696 and the Franciscan Missions in New Mexico: Letters of the Missionaries and Related Documents*. Norman: University of Oklahoma Press, 1988.

Evers, Larry, and Felipe S. Molina. "Haikim: The Yaqui Homeland." *Journal of the Southwest* 34, no. 1 (Spring 1992): 1–2.

Ezell, Paul H. "The Hispanic Acculturation of the Gila River Pimas." Memoir 90 of the American Anthropological Association 63, no. 5, part 2, (October 1961).

Fabila, Alfonso. *Las Tribus Yaquis de Sonora: Su Cultura y Anhelada Autodeterminacion*. Clásicos de la Antropología Mexicana, Colección Número 5. México D. F.: Instituto Nacional Indigenista, 1978.

Faulk, Odie B., ed. and trans. *The Constitution of Occidente: The First Constitution of Arizona, Sonora, and Sinaloa (1825–1831)*. Tucson: Arizona Pioneers' Historical Society, 1967.

Fear-Segal, Jacqueline. *White Man's Club: Schools, Race, and the Struggle of Indian Acculturation*. Lincoln: University of Nebraska Press, 2007.

Ferguson, Daniel Bruce. "The Escuela Experience: The Tucson Indian School in Perspective." Master's thesis, University of Arizona, 1997.

Flint, Richard, and Shirley Cushing Flint, ed., trans., annot. *Documents of the Coronado Expedition, 1539–1542: "They Were Not Familiar with His Majesty, nor Did They Wish to Be His Subjects."* Albuquerque: University of New Mexico Press, 2005.

Folsom, Raphael Brewster. *The Yaquis and the Empire: Violence, Spanish Imperial Power, and Native Resilience in Colonial Mexico*. New Haven, Conn.: Yale University Press, 2014.

Font, Friar Pedro, and Dan S. Matson. "Letters of Friar Pedro Font, 1776–1777." *Ethnohistory* 22, no. 3 (Summer 1975): 262–93.

Fontana, Bernard. "The O'odham." In *The Pimería Alta: Missions and More*, edited by James E. Officer, Mardith Schuetz-Miller, and Bernard L. Fontana, 19–28. Tucson: The Southwestern Mission Research Center, 1996.

Fontana, Bernard L. *Of Earth and Little Rain: The Papago Indians.* Flagstaff, Ariz.: Northland Press, 1981.

Forbes, Jack D. *Apache, Navaho and Spaniard.* Norman: University of Oklahoma Press, 1960.

Frank, Ross. "From Settler to Citizen: Economic Development and Cultural Change in Late Colonial New Mexico, 1750–1820." PhD diss., University of California, Berkeley, 1992.

Froebel, Julius. *Seven Years' Travel in Central America, Northern Mexico, and the Far West of the United States.* London: Richard Bentley, 1859.

Frost, Richard H. *The Railroad and the Pueblo Indians: The Impact of the Atchison, Topeka and Santa Fe on the Pueblos of the Rio Grande, 1880–1930.* Salt Lake City: University of Utah Press, 2016.

Galvin, John, ed. *Western America in 1846–1847: The Original Travel Diary of Lieutenant J. W. Abert, Who Mapped New Mexico for the United States Army.* San Francisco: John Howell Books, 1966.

García Icazbalceta, Joaquín. *Colección de Documentos para la Historia de México*, vol. 2. México: Antigua Librería, 1866.

Garcia y Alva, Federico, ed. *México y sus Progresos. Album-Directorio del Estado de Sonora. Obra Hecho con Apoyo del Gobierno del Estado.* Hermosillo: Imprenta Oficial Dirigida por Antonio B. Monteverde, 1905–1907.

Geertz, Armin W. *The Invention of Prophecy: Continuity and Meaning in Hopi Indian Religion.* Berkeley: University of California Press, 1994.

Glaser, Leah S. "The Story of Guadalupe, Arizona: The Survival and Preservation of a Yaqui Community." Master's thesis, Arizona State University, 1996.

González, Deena J. *Refusing the Favor: The Spanish-Mexican Women of Santa Fe, 1820–1880.* New York: Oxford University Press, 1999.

Gram, John R. *Education at the Edge of Empire: Negotiating Pueblo Identity in New Mexico's Indian Boarding Schools.* Seattle: University of Washington Press, 2015.

Gray, Andrew B. "Letter Addressed to Dr. John Torrey, on the Ammobroma SonorÆ." In *Proceedings of the American Association for the Advancement of Science*, vol. 9. Cambridge: Joseph Lovering, 1856.

Gregg, Josiah. *Commerce of the Prairies*, edited by Max L. Moorhead. Norman: University of Oklahoma Press, 1954.

Guedea, Virginia. "The First Popular Elections in Mexico City, 1812–1813." In *The Origins of Mexican National Politics, 1808–1847*, edited by Jaime E. Rodríguez O., 39–64. Wilmington, Del.: Scholarly Resources, 1997.

Gutiérrez, Ramón A. Introduction in Elsie Clews Parsons, *Pueblo Indian Religion*, vol. 2, Bison Books Edition. Lincoln: University of Nebraska Press, 1996.

Hackel, Steven W. *Children of Coyote, Missionaries of Saint Francis: Indian-Spanish Relations in Colonial California, 1769–1850.* Chapel Hill: University of North Carolina Press, 2005.

Hackett, Charles Wilson, ed. *Historical Documents Relating to New Mexico, Nueva Vizcaya, and Approaches Thereto, to 1773*, vol. 1. Washington, D.C.: Carnegie Institution of Washington, 1923.

———. *Historical Documents Relating to New Mexico, Nueva Vizcaya, and Approaches Thereto, to 1773*, vol. 2. Washington, D.C.: Carnegie Institution of Washington, 1926.

———. *Historical Documents Relating to New Mexico, Nueva Vizcaya, and Approaches Thereto, to 1773*, vol. 3. Washington, D.C.: Carnegie Institution of Washington, 1937.

———. *Revolt of the Pueblo Indians of New Mexico and Otermin's Attempted Reconquest, 1680–1682*, vol. 2. Albuquerque: University of New Mexico Press, 1942.

Hall, G. Emlen, and David J. Weber. "Mexican Liberals and the Pueblo Indians, 1821–1829." *New Mexico Historical Review* 59, no. 1 (January 1984): 5–32.

Hamill, Hugh M., Jr. "An 'Absurd Insurrection'? Creole Insecurity, Pro-Spanish Propaganda, and the Hidalgo Revolt." In *The Birth of Modern Mexico, 1780–1824*, by Christon I. Archer, 67–84. Wilmington, Del.: Scholarly Resources, 2003.

———. *The Hidalgo Revolt: Prelude to Mexican Independence*. Gainesville: University of Florida Press, 1966.

Hammond, George P., and Agapito Rey, eds. *Don Juan de Oñate: Colonizer of New Mexico, 1595–1628*, vol. 1. Albuquerque: University of New Mexico Press, 1953.

———. *The Rediscovery of New Mexico, 1580–1594: The Explorations of Chamuscado, Espejo, Castaño de Sosa, Morlete, and Leyva de Bonilla and Humaña*. Albuquerque: University of New Mexico Press, 1966.

Hardy, Lieutenant R. W. H., R.N. *Travels in the Interior of Mexico, in Baja California and Around the Sea of Cortes, 1825, 1826, 1827 and 1828*. 1829; repr., Glorieta, N. Mex.: Rio Grande Press, 1977.

Hart, E. Richard. *Pedro Pino: Governor of Zuni Pueblo, 1830–1878*. Logan: Utah State University Press, 2003.

Haskett, Robert. *Indigenous Rulers: An Ethnohistory of Town Government in Colonial Cuernavaca*. Albuquerque: University of New Mexico Press, 1991.

Hawley, Florence M. "Pueblo Social Organization as a Lead to Pueblo History." *American Anthropologist*, New Series, 39, no. 3, part 1 (July–Sept. 1937): 504–22.

Hendricks, Rick, and W. H. Timmons. *San Elizario: Spanish Presidio to Texas County Seat*. El Paso: Texas Western Press, University of Texas at El Paso, 1998.

Herman, Daniel J. *Rim Country Exodus: A Story of Conquest, Renewal, and Race in the Making*. Tucson: University of Arizona Press, 2012.

Hill, W. W., and Charles H. Lange, ed. and annot. *An Ethnography of Santa Clara Pueblo New Mexico*. Albuquerque: University of New Mexico Press, 1982.

Hillary, Frank M. "Cajeme, and the Mexico of His Time." *The Journal of Arizona History*, 8, no. 2 (Summer 1967): 120–36.

Hodge, Frederick Webb, George P. Hammond, and Agapito Rey, eds. *Fray Alonso de Benavides' Revised Memorial of 1634*. Coronado Cuarto Centennial Publications, 1540–1940, vol. 4. Albuquerque: University of New Mexico Press, 1945.

Holden, W. C., C. C. Seltzer, R. A. Studhalter, C. J. Wagner, and W. G. McMillan. *Studies of the Yaqui Indians of Sonora, Mexico*. Scientific Series no. 2. Lubbock: Texas Tech Press, 1936.

Horvath, Steven. "The social and political organization of the Genízaros of Plaza de Nuestra Senora de los Dolores de Belén, New Mexico, 1740–1812." PhD diss., Brown University, 1979.

The Howell Code. Adopted by the First Legislative Assembly of the Territory of Arizona. Prescott: Office of the Arizona Miner, 1865.

Hoxie, Frederick E. *A Final Promise: The Campaign to Assimilate the Indians, 1880–1920.* Bison ed. Lincoln: University of Nebraska Press, 2001.

———. *This Indian Country: American Indian Activists and the Place They Made.* New York: Penguin Press, 2012.

Hu-DeHart, Evelyn. "Development and Rural Rebellion: Pacification of the Yaquis in the Late Porfiriato," *Hispanic American Historical Review* 54, no. 1 (Feb. 1974): 72–93.

———. *Missionaries, Miners, and Indians: Spanish Contact with the Yaqui Nation of Northwestern New Spain, 1533–1820.* Tucson: University of Arizona Press, 1981.

———. *Yaqui Resistance and Survival: The Struggle for Land and Autonomy, 1821–1910.* Madison: University of Wisconsin Press, 1984.

Hyer, Sally. *One House, One Voice, One Heart: Native American Education at the Santa Fe Indian School.* Santa Fe: Museum of New Mexico Press, 1990.

Indian Rights Association. *The Thirty-First Annual Report of the Executive Committee of the Indian Rights Association, for the Year Ending December 10, 1913.* Philadelphia: Office of the Indian Rights Association, 1914.

Iverson, Peter. "The Enduring Hopi." In *Hopi Nation: Essays on Indigenous Art, Culture, History and Law*, edited by Edna Glenn, John R. Wunder, Willard Hughes Rollings, and C. L. Martin. Lincoln: University of Nebraska-Lincoln Digital Commons, 2008. http://digitalcommons.unl.edu/cgi/viewcontent.cgi?article=1015&context=hopination.

Jackson, Earl. *Tumacacori's Yesterdays*, Southwestern Monuments Association Popular Series, no. 6. Santa Fe: U.S. Department of the Interior, National Park Service, Southwestern National Monuments, 1951.

Jacoby, Karl. *Shadows at Dawn: A Borderlands Massacre and the Violence of History.* New York: Penguin Press, 2008.

James, George Wharton. *A Little Journey to Some Strange Places and Peoples in Our Southwestern Land (New Mexico and Arizona).* Chicago: Flanagan, 1911.

James, Harry C. *Pages from Hopi History.* Tucson: University of Arizona Press, 1974.

James, Thomas. *Three Years Among the Indians and Mexicans*, Keystone Western Americana Series. New York: Lippincott, 1962.

Johnson, George. "Alfonso Ortiz, 57, Anthropologist of the Pueblo, Dies." *New York Times* obituary, 31 January 1997. http://www.nytimes.com/1997/01/31/us/alfonso-ortiz-57-anthropologist-of-the-pueblo-dies.html.

Jones, Rachel. "Inside Deb Haaland's Historic Bid to Become One of the First Native Congresswomen." *National Geographic*, 7 November 2018. https://www.nationalgeographic.com/culture/2018/11/debra-haaland-first-native-american-congresswoman-new-mexico-midterm-election/.

Joseph, Alice, M.D., Rosamond B. Spicer, and Jane Chesky. *The Desert People: A Study of the Papago Indians.* Chicago: University of Chicago Press, 1949.

Joseph, Gilbert M., and Timothy J. Henderson, eds. *The Mexico Reader: History, Culture, Politics.* Durham, N.C.: Duke University Press, 2002.

Keleher, Julia, and Elsie Ruth Chant. *The Padre of Isleta.* Santa Fe: The Rydal Press, 1940.

Kessell, John L. *Friars, Soldiers, and Reformers: Hispanic Arizona and the Sonora Mission Frontier, 1767–1856.* Tucson: University of Arizona Press, 1976.

———. *Kiva, Cross, and Crown: the Pecos Indians and New Mexico, 1540–1840.* Albuquerque: University of New Mexico Press, 1987.

———. *Mission of Sorrows: Jesuit Geuvavi and the Pimas, 1691–1767*. Tucson: University of Arizona Press, 1970.

———. "San José de Tumacácori—1773: A Franciscan Reports from Arizona." *Arizona and the West* 6, no. 4 (Winter 1964): 303–12.

———. "The Ways and Words of the Other: Diego de Vargas and Cultural Brokers in Late Seventeenth-Century New Mexico." In *Between Indian and White Worlds: The Cultural Broker*, edited by Margaret Connell Szasz, 25–43. Norman: University of Oklahoma Press, 1994.

Kessell, John L., and Rick Hendricks, eds. *By Force of Arms: The Journals of Don Diego de Vargas, 1691–1693*. Albuquerque: University of New Mexico Press, 1992.

Kessell, John L., Rick Hendricks, and Meredith Dodge, eds. *Blood on the Boulders: The Journals of Don Diego de Vargas, 1694–97*. Books 1 and 2. Albuquerque: University of New Mexico Press, 1998.

———. *To the Royal Crown Restored: The Journals of Don Diego de Vargas, New Mexico, 1692–1694*. Albuquerque: University of New Mexico Press, 1995.

Kessell, John L., Rick Hendricks, Meredith D. Dodge, and Larry D. Miller, eds. *That Disturbances Cease: The Journals of don Diego de Vargas, New Mexico, 1697–1700*. Albuquerque: University of New Mexico Press, 2000.

King, James F. "The Colored Castes and American Representation in the Cortes of Cadiz." *Hispanic American Historical Review* 33, no. 1 (Feb. 1953): 33–64.

Kino, Eusebio Francisco. *Kino's Biography of Francisco Javier Saeta, S. J.* Edited by Ernest J. Burres, S.J. Translated by Charles W. Polzer, S.J. St. Louis, Mo.: Saint Louis University, Jesuit Historical Society, 1971.

———. *Kino's Historical Memoir of Pimería Alta*. Edited and translated by Herbert Eugene Bolton. Berkeley: University of California Press, 1948.

LaCroix Dailey, Martha. "Symbolism and Significance of the Lincoln Canes for the Pueblos of New Mexico." *New Mexico Historical Review* 69, no. 2 (April 1994): 127–43.

Lange, Charles H. *Cochiti: A New Mexico Pueblo, Past and Present*. Repr. Albuquerque: University of New Mexico Press, 1990.

Lange, Charles H., and Carroll L. Riley, ed. and annot. *The Southwest Journals of Adolph F. Bandelier, 1883–1884*. Albuquerque: University of New Mexico Press, 1970.

Lange, Charles H., Carol L. Riley, and Elizabeth M. Lange, ed. and annot. *The Southwest Journals of Adolph F. Bandelier, 1885–1888*, vol. 3. Albuquerque: University of New Mexico Press, 1975.

Lecompte, Janet. *Rebellion in Río Arriba, 1837*. Albuquerque: University of New Mexico Press, published in cooperation with the Historical Society of New Mexico, 1985.

Lewis, David Rich. *Neither Wolf nor Dog: American Indians, Environment, and Agrarian Change*. New York: Oxford University Press, 1994.

Liebmann, Matthew. *Revolt: An Archaeological History of Pueblo Resistance and Revitalization in 17th Century New Mexico*. Tucson: University of Arizona Press, 2012.

Lockhart, James. *The Nahuas after the Conquest: A Social and Cultural History of the Indians of Central Mexico, Sixteenth through Eighteenth Centuries*. Stanford, Calif.: Stanford University Press, 1992.

Lumholtz, Carl. *New Trails in Mexico: An Account of One Year's Exploration in North-Western Sonora, Mexico, and South-Western Arizona, 1909–1910*. New York: Charles Scribner's Sons, 1912.

Lummis, Charles F. *Mesa, Cañon and Pueblo*. New York: Century, 1925.

———. "The Sequoya League." *Out West: A Magazine of the Old Pacific and the New* 18, no. 4 (April 1903): 477–84.

———. *A Tramp across the Continent*. New York: Charles Scribner's Sons, 1892.

Malotki, Ekkehart, coll., ed., and trans. *Hopi Tales of Destruction*. Lincoln: University of Nebraska Press, 2002.

Mangusso, Mary Childers. "A Study of the Citizenship Provisions of the Treaty of Guadalupe Hidalgo." Master's thesis, University of New Mexico, 1966.

Manje, Captain Juan Mateo, trans. Harry J. Karns. *Unknown Arizona and Sonora, 1693–1721*. Tucson: Arizona Silhouettes, 1954.

Marak, Andrea M., and Laura Tuennerman. *At the Border of Empires: The Tohono O'odham, Gender, and Assimilation, 1880–1934*. Tucson: University of Arizona Press, 2013.

Mathes, Valerie Sherer. "Mary Bonney, Amelia Quinton, and the Formative Years." In *The Women's National Indian Association: A History*, edited by Valerie Sherer Mathes, 25–45. Albuquerque: University of New Mexico Press, 2015.

———. *The Women's National Indian Association: A History*. Albuquerque: University of New Mexico Press, 2015.

Mattison, Ray H. "The Tangled Web: The Controversy over the Tumacácori and Baca Land Grants." *Journal of Arizona History* 8, no. 2 (Summer 1967): 71–90.

McCarty, Kieran, ed. *Desert Documentary: The Spanish Years, 1767–1821*, historical monograph no. 4. Tucson: Arizona Historical Society, 1976.

———. *A Frontier Documentary: Sonora and Tucson, 1821–1848*. Tucson: University of Arizona Press, 1997.

McClintock, James H. *Arizona: Prehistoric, Aboriginal, Pioneer, Modern: The Nation's Youngest Commonwealth within a Land of Ancient Culture, Volume Two*. Chicago: S. J. Clarke, 1916.

McCool, Daniel, Susan M. Olson, and Jennifer L. Robinson. *Native Vote: American Indians, the Voting Rights Act, and the Right to Vote*. New York: Cambridge University Press, 2007.

McDonald, Laughlin. *American Indians and the Fight for Equal Voting Rights*. Norman: University of Oklahoma Press, 2010.

McGuire, Thomas R. *Politics and Ethnicity on the Río Yaqui: Potam Revisited*. Tucson: University of Arizona Press, 1986.

Meeks, Eric V. *Border Citizens: The Making of Indians, Mexicans, and Anglos in Arizona*. Austin: University of Texas Press, 2007.

Meredith, John D. "The Yaqui Rebellion of 1740: A Jesuit Account and its Implications." *Ethnohistory* 22, no. 3 (Summer 1975): 222–61.

Meyer, Michael C., William L. Sherman, and Susan M. Deeds. *The Course of Mexican History, Sixth Edition*. New York: Oxford University Press, 1999.

Minge, Ward Alan. *Ácoma: Pueblo in the Sky, Revised Edition*. Albuquerque: University of New Mexico Press, 1991.

Moisés, Rosalio, Jane Holden Kelley, and William Curry Holden. *A Yaqui Life: A Personal Chronicle of a Yaqui Indian*, Bison Book Edition. Lincoln: University of Nebraska Press, 1977.

Montgomery, Ross Gordon, Watson Smith, and John Otis Brew, *Franciscan Awatovi: The Excavation and Conjectural Reconstruction of a 17th-Century Spanish Mission Establishment at a Hopi Indian Town in Northeastern Arizona*, Papers of the Peabody Museum of American Archaeology and Ethnology, Harvard University 36. Reports of the Awatovi Expedition, Peabody Museum, Harvard University, Report no. 3. Cambridge, Mass.: Peabody Museum of American Archaeology and Ethnology, Harvard University, 1949.

Morrow, Baker H., ed. and trans. *A Harvest of Reluctant Souls: Fray Alonso de Benavides's History of New Mexico, 1630*. Albuquerque: University of New Mexico Press, 1996.

Munk, Joseph A. *Arizona Sketches*. New York: Grafton Press, 1905. Books of the Southwest Series, University of Arizona Library Southwest Electronic Text Center. http://southwest.library.arizona.edu/azsk/.

Nabakov, Peter. *How the World Moves: The Odyssey of an American Indian Family*. New York: Viking, 2015.

Navarro García, Luís. *La Sublevacion Yaqui de 1740*. Sevilla, España: Escuala de Estudios Hispano-Americans, 1966.

Nentvig, Juan, S.J. *Rudo Ensayo: A Description of Sonora and Arizona in 1764*. Translated by Alberto Francisco Pradeau and Robert R. Rasmussen. Tucson: University of Arizona Press, 1980.

Nequatewa, Edmund. "A Mexican Raid on the Hopi Pueblo of Oraibi." *Plateau* 16, no. 3 (January 1944), 45–52.

———. *Truth of a Hopi: Stories Relating to the Origin, Myths and Clan Histories of the Hopi*. 1936; repr., Flagstaff: Northland Publishing in cooperation with the Museum of Northern Arizona, 1993.

Och, Joseph. *Missionary in Sonora: The Travel Reports of Joseph Och, S. J., 1755–1767*. Translated by Theodore E. Treutlein. San Francisco: California Historical Society, 1965.

Officer, James E. "Government, Mining, and Agriculture." In *The Pimería Alta: Missions and More*, edited by James E. Officer, Mardith Schuetz-Miller, and Bernard L. Fontana, 47–54. Tucson, Ariz.: The Southwestern Mission Research Center, 1996.

———. *Hispanic Arizona, 1536–1856*. Tucson: University of Arizona Press, 1987.

Ortega Noriega, Sergio. "El Sistema de Misiones Jesuíticas, 1591–1699." In *Tres Siglos de Historia Sonorense (1530–1830)*, edited by Sergio Ortega Noriega and Ignacio del Río, 41–94. México: Universidad Nacional Autónoma de México, 1993.

Ortiz, Alfonso, ed. *Handbook of North American Indians, Vol. 9, Southwest*. Washington, D.C.: Smithsonian Institution, 1979.

Ortiz, Alfonso. "Po'pay's Leadership: A Pueblo Perspective." In *Po'Pay: Leader of the First American Revolution*, edited by Joe S. Sando and Herman Agoyo, foreword by Governor Bill Richardson, 82–92. Santa Fe: Clear Light Publishing, 2005.

———. *The Pueblo*, Indians of North America series. New York: Chelsea House, 1994.

———. *The Tewa World: Space, Time, Being, and Becoming in a Pueblo Society*. Chicago: University of Chicago Press, 1969.

Ortiz, Fernando. *Cuban Counterpoint: Tobacco and Sugar*. Translated by Harriet de Onís. Durham, N.C.: Duke University Press, 1995.

Parsons, Elsie Clews. *The Pueblo of Isleta*, Indian Classics Series, vol. 1. Albuquerque: University of Albuquerque, in collaboration with Calvin Horn Publisher, 1974.

Pérez de Ribas, Andrés. *History of the Triumphs of Our Holy Faith Amongst the Most Barbarous and Fierce Peoples of the New World*. Translated by Daniel T. Reff, Maureen Ahern, and Richard K. Danford. Tucson: University of Arizona Press, 1999.

Pfefferkorn, Ignaz. *Sonora: A Description of the Province*, Coronado Cuarto Centennial Publications, 1540–1940, vol. 12. Translated by Theodore Treutlein. Albuquerque: University of New Mexico Press, 1949.

Pino, Don Pedro Baptista, ed. and trans. *The Exposition on the Province of New Mexico, 1812*. With a preface by Adrian Bustamante and Marc Simmons. Santa Fe and Albuquerque: El Rancho de las Golondrinas and the University of New Mexico Press, 1995.

Polzer, Charles W. *Rules and Precepts of the Jesuit Missions of Northwestern New Spain*. Tucson: University of Arizona Press, 1976.

Prucha, Francis Paul, ed. *Americanizing the American Indians: Writings by the "Friends of the Indian," 1880–1900*. Cambridge, Mass.: Harvard University Press, 1973.

———. *The Great Father: The United States Government and the American Indians, Abridged Edition*. Lincoln: University of Nebraska Press, 1986.

Radding, Cynthia. "The Colonial Pact and Changing Ethnic Frontiers in Highland Sonora, 1740–1840." In *Contested Ground: Comparative Frontiers on the Northern and Southern Edges of the Spanish Empire*, edited by Donna J. Guy and Thomas E. Sheridan, 52–66. The Southwest Center Series. Tucson: University of Arizona Press, 1998.

———. *Landscapes of Power and Identity: Comparative Histories in the Sonoran Desert and the Forests of Amazonia from Colony to Republic*. Durham, N.C.: Duke University Press, 2005.

Refugio de la Torre Curiel, José. *Twilight of the Mission Frontier: Shifting Interethnic Alliances and Social Organization in Sonora, 1768–1855*. Stanford, Calif.: Stanford University Press, 2012.

Reilly, Katie. "North Dakota's Voter ID Law Disproportionately Affects Native Americans: Here's How They're Mobilizing to Fight It." *Time*, 2 November 2018. http://time.com/5442434/north-dakota-voting-law-native-american-activism/.

Reno, Philip. "Rebellion in New Mexico—1837." *New Mexico Historical Review* 40, no. 3 (1965): 197–213.

Rentería-Valencia, Rodrigo F. "Colonial Tensions in the Governance of Indigenous Authorities and the Pima Uprising of 1751." *Journal of the Southwest* 56, no. 2 (Summer 2014): 345–64.

Reséndez, Andrés. *Changing National Identities at the Frontier: Texas and New Mexico, 1800–1850*. Cambridge: Cambridge University Press, 2004.

Robinson, Jacob, with historical introduction and notes by Carl L. Cannon, from the edition of 1848, *A Journal of the Santa Fe Expedition Under Colonel Doniphan*, Narratives of the Trans-Mississippi Frontier Series. Repr., Princeton: Princeton University Press, 1932.

Rodríguez O., Jaime E. *The Independence of Spanish America*, Cambridge Latin American Studies series. Cambridge: Cambridge University Press, 1996.

Rosen, Deborah A. *American Indians and State Law: Sovereignty, Race, and Citizenship, 1790–1880*. Lincoln: University of Nebraska Press, 2007.

Rosier, Paul C. *Serving Their Country: American Indian Politics and Patriotism in the Twentieth Century*. Cambridge, Mass.: Harvard University Press, 2009.

Safford, William Edwin. "Edward Palmer." *Popular Science Monthly* 78 (April 1911): 341–54.

Salmón, Roberto Mario. "A Marginal Man: Luis of Saric and the Pima Revolt of 1751." *The Americas* 45, no. 1 (July 1988): 61–77.

Sánchez, Joseph P. "It Happened in Old Santa Fe: The Death of Governor Albino Pérez, 1835–1837." In *All Trails Lead to Santa Fe: An Anthology Commemorating the 400th Anniversary of the Founding of Santa Fe, New Mexico in 1610*, 267–78. Santa Fe: Sunstone Press, 2010.

Sánchez, Joseph P., Robert L. Spude, and Art Gómez. *New Mexico: A History*. Norman: University of Oklahoma Press, 2013.

Sánchez, Pedro, trans. Ray John de Aragon. *Recollections of the Life of the Priest Don Antonio José Martínez*. Santa Fe: Lightning Tree, 1978.

Sando, Joe S. *Five Ancient Pueblo Warriors*. Albuquerque: Minuteman, 2009.

———. *Nee Hemish: A History of Jemez Pueblo*. Santa Fe: Clear Light, 2008.

———. *Pueblo Nations: Eight Centuries of Pueblo History*. Santa Fe: Clear Light, 1992.

———. "The Pueblo Revolt." In *Po'Pay: Leader of the First American Revolution*, edited by Joe S. Sando and Herman Agoyo, foreword by Governor Bill Richardson, 5–53. Santa Fe: Clear Light, 2005.

Saunders, Charles Francis. *The Indians of the Terraced Houses*. New York: Knickerbocker Press, 1912. Books of the Southwest Series, University of Arizona Library Southwest Electronic Text Center. http://southwest.library.arizona.edu/inte/.

Savala, Refugio. *Autobiography of a Yaqui Poet*. Tucson: University of Arizona Press, 1980.

Scholes, France V. "Church and State in New Mexico," chapter 3, *New Mexico Historical Review* 11, no. 2 (April 1936).

———. *Church and State in New Mexico, 1610–1650*. Historical Society of New Mexico Publications in History, vol. 7. Albuquerque: University of New Mexico Press, 1937.

Schroeder, Albert H. "Rio Grande Ethnohistory." In *New Perspectives on the Pueblos*, edited by Alfonso Ortiz, 41–70. School of American Research Advanced Seminar Series. Albuquerque: University of New Mexico Press, 1972.

Scott, James C. *Domination and the Arts of Resistance: Hidden Transcripts*. New Haven: Yale University Press, 1990.

Sedelmayr, Jacobo, S.J. *Before the Rebellion: Letters & Reports of Jacobo Sedelmayr, S.J.* Translated by Daniel S. Matson. Tucson: Arizona Historical Society, 1996.

Sheridan, Thomas E. *Landscapes of Fraud: Mission Tumacácori, the Baca Float, and the Betrayal of the O'odham*. Tucson: University of Arizona Press, 2006.

———. "The Yoemem (Yaquis): An Enduring People." In *Paths of Life: American Indians of the Southwest and Northern Mexico*, edited by Thomas E. Sheridan and Nancy J. Parezo, 35–59. Tucson: University of Arizona Press, 1996.

Sheridan, Thomas E., Stewart B. Koyiyumptewa, Anton Daughters, Dale S. Brenneman, T. J. Ferguson, Leigh Kuwanwisiwma, and Lee Wayne Lomayestewa, eds. *Moquis and Kastiilam: Hopis, Spaniards, and the Trauma of History Volume I, 1540–1679*. Tucson: University of Arizona Press, 2015.

Shorter, David Delgado. *We Will Dance Our Truth: Yaqui History in Yoeme Performances.* Lincoln: University of Nebraska Press, 2009.

Sigüenza Y Góngora, Don Carlos de. *The Mercurio Volante of Don Carlos de Sigüenza Y Góngora: An Account of the First Expedition of Don Diego de Vargas into New Mexico in 1692.* Translated by Irving Albert Leonard. Los Angeles: The Quivira Society, 1932.

Simmons, Marc, ed. *Coronado's Land: Essays on Daily Life in Colonial New Mexico.* Albuquerque: University of New Mexico Press, 1991.

Simmons, Marc. *New Mexico: An Interpretive History.* New York: Norton, 1977; repr., Albuquerque: University of New Mexico Press, 1988.

———. *Spanish Government in New Mexico.* Albuquerque: University of New Mexico Press, 1968; repr., Albuquerque: University of New Mexico Press, 1990.

———. *Witchcraft in the Southwest: Spanish and Indian Supernaturalism on the Rio Grande.* Flagstaff, Ariz.: Northland Press, 1974; repr., Norman, Okla.: Bison Books, 1980.

Simpson, Audra. *Mohawk Interruptus: Political Life Across the Borders of Settler States.* Durham, N.C.: Duke University Press, 2014.

Simpson, Lesley Byrd, trans. *The Laws of Burgos of 1512–1513: Royal Ordinances for the Good Government and Treatment of the Indians.* John Howell Books, 1960; repr. Westport, Conn.: Greenwood Press, 1978.

Singletary, Loretta, Staci Emm, Micah Loma'omvaya, Janine Clark, Matthew Livingston, Michael Kotuwa Johnson, and Ron Oden. *People of the Land: Sustaining Agriculture on the Hopi Reservation.* Reno: University of Nevada Cooperative Extension. https://www.unce.unr.edu/publications/files/ag/2014/cm1402.pdf.

Smith, Fay Jackson, John L. Kessell, and Francis J. Fox, eds. *Father Kino in Arizona.* Phoenix: Arizona Historical Foundation, 1966.

Solórzano Pereyra, Juan. *Política Indiana, Tomo I.* Madrid: Biblioteca Castro, 1996.

Spalding, Karen. *Huarochirí: An Andean Society under Inca and Spanish Rule.* Stanford, Calif.: Stanford University Press, 1984.

Spicer, Edward H. *Cycles of Conquest: The Impact of Spain, Mexico, and the United States on the Indians of the Southwest, 1533–1960.* Tucson: University of Arizona Press, 1962; repr., Tucson: University of Arizona Press, 1976.

———. *Pascua: A Yaqui Village in Arizona.* Tucson: University of Arizona Press, 1984.

———. *People of Pascua.* Edited by Kathleen M. Sands and Rosamond B. Spicer. Tucson: University of Arizona Press, 1988.

———. "The Yaqui Indians of Arizona." *Kiva* 5, no. 6 (March 1940): 21–24.

———. *The Yaquis: A Cultural History.* Tucson: University of Arizona Press, 1980.

Stuart, Tessa. "Meet Deb Haaland, Likely to Be the First Native Woman Elected to Congress." *Rolling Stone*, 18 August 2018. https://www.rollingstone.com/politics/politics-news/deb-haaland-first-native-woman-elected-congress-712408/.

Stubben, Jerry D. *Native Americans and Political Participation: A Reference Handbook.* Santa Barbara, Calif.: ABC-CLIO, 2006.

Sundust, Mikhail. "GRIC Celebrates Arizona Native Right to Vote." *Gila River Indian News* 15, no. 8 (August 2012): 1, 6.

Tanck de Estrada, Dorothy. Mapas de Jorge Luis Miranda García y Dorothy Tanck de Estrada, con la colaboración de Tania Lilia Chávez Soto. *Atlas Ilustrado de los Pueblos de Indios: Nueva España, 1800.* México, D.F.: El Colegio de México, A.C.; Comisión

Nacional para el Desarrollo de los Pueblos Indigenas; Fomento Cultural Banamex, 2005.

———. *Pueblos de Indios y Educación en el México Colonial, 1750–1821*. México, D.F.: El Colegio de México, 1999.

Taylor, William B. *Drinking, Homicide, and Rebellion in Colonial Mexican Villages*. Stanford, Calif.: Stanford University Press, 1979.

Thomas, Alfred Barnaby, ed., trans., and annot. *Forgotten Frontiers: A Study of the Spanish Indian Policy of Don Juan Bautista de Anza, Governor of New Mexico, 1777–1787*. Norman: University of Oklahoma Press, 1932.

Troncoso, Francisco P. *Las Guerras con las Tribus Yaqui y Mayo*, Clásicos de la Antropología Mexicana. México, D.F.: Instituto Nacional Indigenista, 1977.

Trujillo, Octaviana Valenzuela. "The Yaqui of Guadalupe, Arizona: A Century of Cultural Survival through Trilingualism." *American Indian Culture and Research Journal* 22, no. 4 (1998): 67–88.

Turner, John Kenneth. *Barbarous Mexico*, The Texas Pan American Series. Austin: University of Texas Press, 1969.

Twitchell, Ralph Emerson. *The Spanish Archives of New Mexico, Volume II*. Cedar Rapids, Iowa: The Torch Press, 1914.

Tyler, Daniel. *Sources for New Mexican History 1821–1848*. Santa Fe: Museum of New Mexico Press, 1984.

Tyler, S. Lyman, ed. *The Indian Cause in the Spanish Laws of the Indies*. Western Civilization and Native Peoples series. Salt Lake City: American West Center, University of Utah, 1980.

Underhill, Ruth M. "A Papago Calendar Record." *University of New Mexico Bulletin*, Anthropological Series 2, no. 23 (1 March 1938): 1–66.

Underhill, Ruth Murray. *Social Organization of the Papago Indians*. New York: Columbia University Press, 1939.

Van Valan, Gary. "In Search of Juan Antonio Ignacio Baca, a Pueblo Participant in the Shifting Politics of Nineteenth-Century New Mexico." In *Transnational Indians in the North American West*, edited by Andrea Marak, Clarissa Confer, and Laura Tuennerman. College Station: Texas A&M Press, 2015.

Venturini, Carol. "The Fight for Indian Voting Rights in New Mexico." Master's thesis, University of New Mexico, 1993.

Victory, John P., comp. *1897, Compiled Laws of New Mexico: in accordance with an act of the legislature, approved March 16th, 1897. Including the Constitution of the United States, the treaty of Guadalupe Hidalgo, the Gadsden treaty, the original act organizing the territory, the organic acts as now in force, the original Kearny code, and a list of laws enacted since compilation in 1884, as well as those in that work*. Santa Fe: New Mexican Print Co., 1897.

Vidargas del Moral, Juan Domingo. "Sonora y Sinaloa Como Provincias Independientes y Como Estado Interno de Occidente: 1821–1830." In *Tres Siglos de Historia Sonorense (1530–1830)*, edited by Sergio Ortega Noriega and Ignacio del Río, 411–54. México: Universidad Nacional Autónoma de México, 1993.

Voth, H. R. *The Traditions of the Hopi*. Anthropological Series, pub. 96, vol. 8, the Stanley McCormick Hopi Expedition. Chicago: Field Columbian Museum, 1905.

Wallace, Susan E. *The Land of the Pueblos*. New York: Provident Book Company, 1888.

Wasserman, Mark. *Capitalists, Caciques, and Revolution: The Native Elite and Foreign Enterprise in Chihuahua, Mexico, 1854–1911*. Chapel Hill: University of North Carolina Press, 1984.

Weber, David J. *Bárbaros: Spaniards and Their Savages in the Age of Enlightenment*, The Lamar Series in Western History. New Haven: Yale University Press, 2005.

———. "Hopi Land and Water Rights under Spain and Mexico." Prepared for the Hopi Tribe for General Adjudication of All Rights to Use Water in the Little Colorado River System and Source, Superior Court of Arizona Case NO. CV-6417, March 2009.

———. *The Mexican Frontier, 1821–1846: The American Southwest Under Mexico*. Albuquerque: University of New Mexico Press, 1982.

———. "An Unforgettable Day: Facundo Melgares on Independence." *New Mexico Historical Review* 48, no. 1 (January 1973): 27–44.

Welsh, Herbert. *Report of a Visit to the Navajo, Pueblo, and Hualapais Indians of New Mexico and Arizona*. Philadelphia: The Indian Rights Association, 1885.

West, Robert C. *Sonora: Its Geographical Personality*. Austin: University of Texas Press, 1993.

White, Leslie A. *The Acoma Indians: People of Sky City*. Repr. Glorieta, N. Mex.: Rio Grande Press, 1973.

———. *The Pueblo of San Felipe*. Memoirs of the American Anthropological Association, no. 38. Menasha, Wis.: American Anthropological Association, 1932.

———. *The Pueblo of Santa Ana, New Mexico*. Memoirs of the American Anthropological Association, no. 60. Menasha, Wis.: American Anthropological Association, 1942.

———. *The Pueblo of Santo Domingo, New Mexico*. Memoirs of the American Anthropological Association, vol. 43. Menasha, Wis.: American Anthropological Association, 1935.

Wilkins, David E. *American Indian Sovereignty and the U.S. Supreme Court: The Masking of Justice*. Austin: University of Texas Press, 1997.

Willard, William. "The Comparative History of Two Tribal Governments." *Wicazo Sa Review* 6, no. 1 (Spring 1990): 56–62.

Wilson, John P., foreword by Patricia M. Spoerl. *Islands in the Desert: A History of the Uplands of Southeastern Arizona*. Albuquerque: University of New Mexico Press, published in cooperation with the Historical Society of New Mexico, 1995.

Wunder, John R. *"Retained by the People": A History of American Indians and the Bill of Rights*. New York: Oxford University Press, 1994.

Yava, Albert, and Harold Courlander, ed. and annot. *Big Falling Snow: A Tewa-Hopi Indian's Life and Times and the History and Traditions of His People*. New York: Crown Publishers, 1978.

Zuñiga, Ignacio. *Rapida Ojeada al Estado de Sonora (1835)*. Hermosillo: Gobierno del Estado de Sonora, 1985.

Online Sources

Arizona Constitution. Arizona State Legislature website. http://www.azleg.gov/FormatDocument.asp?inDoc=/const/7/2.htm.

Arizona-Sonora Documents Online, University of Arizona Libraries Digital Collections. http://www.library.arizona.edu/contentdm/asdo/index.html.

"Ely Parker—Chief, Lawyer, Engineer, and Brigadier General." Appomattox Courthouse website, National Park Service. http://www.nps.gov/apco/parker.htm.

Farish, Thomas Edwin. *History of Arizona, Volume VII*. San Francisco: Filmer Brothers Electrotype Company, 1918. Books of the Southwest Series, University of Arizona Library Southwest Electronic Text Center. http://southwest.library.arizona.edu/hav7/.

"Gen. William H. Emory (b. 1811–d. 1887)." *Archives of Maryland (Biographical Series)*. http://msa.maryland.gov/megafile/msa/speccol/sc3500/sc3520/009400/009485/html/09485bio.html.

Google Maps. https://maps.google.com.

Great Register, Navajo County, Territory of Arizona, 1906–1911. Retrieved through Ancestry.com.

Great Register of Pima County, Territory of Arizona, 1886–1910. Retrieved through Ancestry.com.

Indian Pueblo Cultural Center website. http://indianpueblo.org.

Inter Tribal Council of Arizona website. http://itcaonline.com.

"James S. Calhoun." New Mexico Office of the State Historian website. newmexicohistory.org/people/james-s-calhoun.

"Joseph Henry Suina: Cochiti, N. Mexico." North Dakota Study Group Oral History Project. http://www.ndsg.org/oralhistory/jsuina/index.html.

"Laws of the Territory of New Mexico, Santa Fe, October 7, 1846: The Kearny Code." New Mexico State Library Digital Collections. nmdigital.cdmhost.com/cdm/ref/collection/p267801coll5/id/5292.

Martinez, Matthew (Ohkay Owingeh Pueblo). "Pueblo People Win the Right to Vote—1948." New Mexico Office of the State Historian website. http://dev.newmexicohistory.org/filedetails.php?fileID=415.

Minge, Ward Alan. "A History of the Pueblo Indians." Prepared for the Bureau of Indian Affairs, United States Department of the Interior, n.d. https://sandramathews.files.wordpress.com/2011/04/minge_historyofpi_4.pdf.

Pecos National Historic Park website. http://www.nps.gov/peco/index.htm.

The Political Constitution of the Spanish Monarchy: Promulgated in Cádiz, the nineteenth day of March. Biblioteca Virtual Miguel de Cervantes. http://www.cervantesvirtual.com/obra-visor/the-political-constitution-of-the-spanish-monarchy-promulgated-in-cadiz-the-nineteenth-day-of-march—0/html/ffd04084-82b1-11df-acc7-002185ce6064_1.html#I_1_.

Pueblo de Cochiti website. http://www.pueblodecochiti.org.

Pueblo of Acoma website. http://www.puebloofacoma.org.

Pueblo of Jemez website. http://www.jemezpueblo.org.

Pueblo of Sandia website. http://www.sandiapueblo.nsn.us.

Salt River Pima-Maricopa Indian Community website. http://www.srpmic-nsn.gov.

"Solórzano Pereira, Juan de (1575–1655)." Universidad de Navarra. http://www.unav.es/biblioteca/fondoantiguo/hufaexp20/Deleitando_ensena/4._Autores/Entradas/2009/10/29_Solorzano_Pereira,_Juan_de_(1575-1655).html.

Taos Pueblo website. http://www.taospueblo.com.

Torrez, Robert J. "A Cuarto Centennial History of New Mexico." http://www.nmgs.org/artcuar4.htm.

Town of Clarkdale website. http://www.clarkdale.az.gov.
Wroth, William H. "1837 Rebellion of Rio Arriba." Office of the State Historian of New Mexico. http://newmexicohistory.org/places/1837-rebellion-of-rio-arriba#.
Yavapai-Apache Nation Constitution. National Indian Law Library website: http://www.narf.org/nill/constitutions/yavapai_apache/.
Yavapai-Apache Nation website. http://yavapai-apache.org.

Films

Canes of Power. Santa Fe: Silver Bullet Productions with funds from the San Manuel Band of Mission Indians, 2012.

Unpublished Materials

Aguilar, Joseph "Woody." "Postcolonialism in Borderlands and Pueblo Histories." *Joe Sando Symposium for Pueblo Indian Studies*, Albuquerque, 5 March 2015.
"Coffee and Conversation with Verna Teller, Former Governor of Isleta Pueblo, and Lela Kaskalla, Former Governor of Nambé Pueblo." Public speaking event. Indian Pueblo Cultural Center, Albuquerque, 14 March 2015.
Museo de los Yaquis, Cócorit, Sonora, Mexico.
Notes from conversation with Juan Silverio Jaime León, Director of Indigenous Education for the State of Sonora. Vícam Switch, Sonora, 22 June 2018, in possession of author.

Index

References to images and maps are in italics.

Abbott, A. J., 212
Abeita, Ambrosio, 212
Abeita, Juan, 199
Abeita, Juan Andres, 203
Abeita, Pablo, 212
Abert, J. W., 179–80
abuse: by authorities, 85, 97, 105, 127; by community outsiders, 41, 107, 298; by Franciscans, 61–62, 68, 126–27, 302–3n26, 315n34; by Jesuits, 82, 88–89, 105, 305n96, 307n128, 316–17n58; traditional justice seen as, 44, 197
Acevedo, Pedro Alvarez, 82
Acoma, 22, 24–25, 60, 63, 121, 183
Acoma Pueblos, 21, 24–25, 29–30, 115, 121, 183, 326–27n135; leaders, 45, 210–11, 323n73, 324n95; Spanish violence against, 24, 60
Aguilar, Alfonso Rael de, 30, 43, 45
Aguilar, Joseph "Woody," 6
Akimel O'odham (Gila River Pimas), 90, 257–58, 260–63, 267–68, 271, 273, 280, 332n99
Alcina, Teodoro, 53
Alegre, Francisco Javier, 74
All Indian Pueblo Council (AIPC), 46, 212
Alvarado, Hernando de, 23
Alvarez, Nicolás María, 148–49
Anaya, Robert, 127
Antonio (Zuni Pueblo governor), 47
Antonio, Diego, 44
Antonio, José, 262
Anza, Juan Bautista de, 32, 52
Anza, Juan Bautista de, the Elder, 83
Apaches, 1, 27, 40, 43, 131, 154, 173–74, 333n125; Apaches de Paz, 145, 171, 174, 301n172; Camp Grant massacre of, 269–70; raids by, 9, 11, 44–45, 86, 97, 100–102, 130, 140–41, 144, 158, 170–71, 228, 258, 286, 318n83
Appropriation Act of 1906, 222–23
Aquibuamea, Luis, 84
Archibeque, Josecito, 133
Archuleta, José Ramon, 224
Arellano, Cristóbal, 43
Armenta, Juan Zacaria, 152
Armijo, Juan, 126
Armijo, Manuel, 120, 135–37
Arny, William, 200–201, 204–5
Arthur, Chester A., 233
Atienza, Juan de, 37
Augustín (Pecos Pueblo lieutenant governor), 39
Austin, Harry, 283
Awat'ovi, 57; destruction of, 8, 67–69, 104, 303n38, 303n43; missionization, 59–66
ayuntamientos, 7, 17–18, 108–9, 112–13, 293n30; Hopi; 58, O'odham, 144–45, 170 Pueblo, 8–9, 52–53, 116–29, 131–32, 138, 311n60, 312n69, 312n71; Yaqui, 156–57, 159, 175. *See also* cabildos; Cortes

Baboquivari Peak, 93, 248
Baca, Bartolomé, 118
Baca, Juan Antonio Ignacio, 112, 119
Baca, Marcos, 127
Bácum, 70, 71, 159, 254, 330n52
Balbás, Manuel, 246–47
Baltasar, Juan Antonio, 105
Bandelier, Adolph, 67, 213, 324n95
Banderas, Juan, 139, 149–56, 158–60, 241, 316n43, 316–17n58

Barbastro, Antonio, 101–2
Barr, Juliana, 101
Barreiro, Antonio, 120–22
Bartlett, John Russell, 168
Basoritemea, Bernabé, 83–90, 104, 306n107
Beitia, Agustín, 124
Bélem, 70, 71, 149
Benavides, Alonso de, 5, 60–61
Bendell, Herman, 270
Benedict, Kirby, 199
Berger, John M., 227, 274–77, 335–36n171
Bernabé, 83–90, 104, 306n107
Bernal, Cristóbal Martín, 94
Bibo, Solomon, 210–11, 323n73
Blaine, Peter, Sr., 273, 279–80, 335n157
Bloom, Lansing, 119, 134
Bolsas, Antonio, 35
Bolton, Herbert Eugene, 90
Bonaparte, Joseph, 107
Bonaparte, Napoleon, 107
Bonavía, Bernardo, 47–48
Bourke, John G., 65
Bradshaw, W. H., 278
Brady, Peter R., 278
Bringas, Diego Manuel, 100
Brooks, James, 67, 106
Brown, Orlando, 189
Brown, Tracy, 34
Browne, J. Ross, 264
Browning, Daniel N., 235
Bua, Nicolás, 49
Buimea, Juan Mateo, 86–87
Buitemea, Juan, 148–49
Burns, Mike (Hoomothya), 281–82
Burton, Charles E., 236–37, 329nn38–39
Bustamante, Juan Domingo de, 42

cabildos (town councils), 8–9, 17–18, 20, 37–38, 79, 99, 120–22, 293n30; diminution of, 54, 116–17; mixed municipal government replacement, 112–13
Caborca, La Concepción de Nuestra Señora del, 94–96, 99, 161, 165, 273
Cabredo, Rodrigo de, 80
Cachupín, Tomás Vélez, 42
caciques, 21–22, 28–29, 34, 78, 218–19, 324n95; conflicts with civil leadership, 47–49, 295n73; as negotiators, 74, 228–29; opposition to Spanish control, 67, 70; role in Pueblo elections, 7, 36, 38–39, 119, 213
Cajeme, 243–44, 330n52
Calhoun, James S., 182–93, 216, 228–29, 320n24
Camp Grant Massacre, 269–70
Cañas, Cristóbal de, 81
canes (of power), 20, 297n85; confiscation of, 37, 43, 47, 218; Hopi, 62, 230, 327n9; Lincoln canes, 29, 123h, 199, 218, 230–31, 296n83, 328n13; O'odham, 79, 94–96, 98, 279, 325n125; Pueblo, 14–15, 29–30, 32, 38–39, 42–48, 50, 171, 179, 180, 199, 218, 296n83; religious significance of, 29–30, 81, 220, 297n87; relinquishment of, 85, 87, 218; Yaqui, 79, 81
Canjuebes (Santa Clara Pueblo), 53–54
Cano y Moctezuma, Dionisio, 110
Cantón, 132–33, 135–38, 288
Carros, Francisco, 170, 174
Casados, Antonio, 52
Castañeda, Pedro de, 58
Castellana, Joaquin, 128
Castelo, María Ignacio, 102
Castile, George Pierre, 253
Castro, Pedro de, 89
Catholics: among Hopis, 65–69; among O'odhams, 98, 172, 250, 264, 267–68, 274, 280, 308n148, 337nn43–44; Spanish officials, 14–15, 20, 25, 31–33; among Yaquis, 70, 78–79, 241, 250. *See also* Awat'ovi; Franciscans; Jesuits
Cebrian, Pedro, 89
Chacón, Fernando de, 44
Chapman, A. B., 261
Charles III, 99
Charles IV, 107
Chaves, Lucas, 256–57
Chávez, Angélico, 134–35
Chávez, José, 124
Cherokee Nation v. Georgia, 185

Chimayó Rebellion, 9, 129–37, 313n89
Chistoe, Felipe, 45, 50
Chiuta, Juan, 39
Choice, Cyrus, 189
Clemente, Esteban, 44–45
Clemmer, Richard, 70
Cochiti, 22, 123, 125, 289, 312n73
Cochiti Pueblos, 5, 21, 112, 119, 126, 132–33, 192, 209, 296n80; elections, 27–28, 36, 45, 112, 121–22, 286; land encroachment and, 119, 200–201; leaders, 25, 28, 47–48, 119, 133
Cócorit, 70, 71, 254
Cocóspera, 92, 162–63, 173–74
Coctze, Pedro, 39
Coggeshall, Harold F., 219–20
Cohen, Felix S., 2, 284
Collins, J. L., 197–200, 216
Comadurán, Antonio, 171
Concepción, Cristóbal de la, 59
Conde, Alejo García, 116
Conitzu, Luis, 45
Coolidge, Dane, 255
Cooper, Charles L., 202
Cordova, Diego Fernandez de, 26
Corís, Christóbal, 45
Cornyn, John W., 271
Coronado, Francisco Vásquez de, 56–58
Corral, Ramón, 242–43
Cortes, 47–48, 108–13; creation of town councils, 117; rejection and reestablishment, 117; on status of Indian citizenship, 116, 119
Cossio, Antonio, 45
Cota, José, 118
Council of the Indies, 17
Couts, Cave, 167–68, 314n18
Coxi (O'odham headman), 91
Crandall, C. J., 212, 217
Crane, Leo, 219–20, 325–26n126
Crepúsculo de la Libertad, El, 121
Cristóbal (Keres governor), 38
Cristóbal (Sandia Pueblo accused witch), 44
Crothers, W. D., 232
Crouse, Cornelius W., 272–74

Crumpacker, J. W., 221–22
Cuate, Juan, 171
Cubero, Pedro Rodriguez, 47, 67
Cuervo Clipper, 224
Cuervo y Valdés, Francisco, 40–41, 45
Cuna, Juan, 62–63
Cuntzi, Mathias, 42–43
Curtis, Edward S., 239
Cushing, Frank Hamilton, 36

Dagenett, Charles, 215
Davids, Sharice, 3
Davidson, M. O., 264–66, 267, 333n125
Dawes Act, 127–28, 214, 226, 234–35, 272–74, 277, 281–82, 325n110
Dedrick, John M., 152–53, 315–16n36
Deeds, Susan M., 80
Delgado, Felipe, 207
deportations, Yaqui, 10, 226–27, 242, 244–52, 253, 282, 288, 330n63
Díaz, Francisco Xavier, 102
Díaz, Porfirio, 242, 247
Díaz, Rafael, 162–63, 170
Diego, Juan, 39
Dippie, Brian, 207
Dirucaca, Jerónimo, 37
ditch captains (mayordomos), 7, 292n21, 317n67
Dobyns, Henry F., 173
Docher, Anton, 218–19
Dole, William P., 207, 264
Donaldson, Thomas, 235, 238–39, 330n43
Doniphan, Alexander William, 180
Dozier, Edward, 34
Ducey, Michael, 32
Dudley, L. Edwin, 205
Duranes, Manuel, 126

Eastman, Charles, 215
Ebright, Malcolm, 40
Echos, Miguel, 39
Eight Northern Indian Pueblos Council, 236n134
Elías, Ignacio, 174
Elías, Joaquín Vicente, 174

Elk, John, 214
Elkins, Stephen B., 200
Elk v. Wilkins, 214
Ellis, Richard N., 207
Emory, William H., 174–79, 261–62, 318n5
Enjenoe, Francisco, 45
Erickson, Winston P., 258–59, 332n100
Escalante, Francisco Silvestre Vélez de, 69–70, 140
Escalante y Arvizu, Manuel, 164
Espejo, Antonio de, 23, 58, 65
Espeleta, Francisco de, 67
Espeleta, Jose de, 64–67
Esquibel, Juan José, 132, 137
Eulate, Juan de, 25–26
Eusebio (Bac governor), 95
Executive Order: establishment of Hopi Reservation, 233; establishment of Salt River Pima-Maricopa Reservation, 334n135; establishment of San Xavier (Tohono O'odham) Reservation, 271
Exposition on the Province of New Mexico, 116, 310n35

Farish, Thomas Edwin, 230, 328n11, 328n13
Felipe (Santa Ana Pueblo governor), 45
Felipe V, 107
Ferdinand VII, 107, 111, 117
Figueroa, José, 148–51, 154
Fillmore, Millard, 193
Fitch, A. M., 213
Flores, Manuel Gaspar de, 85
Font, Pedro, 100, 160
Fontana, Bernard, 91
Ford, George E., 202
Fort McDowell Yavapai Nation (FMYN), 283, 337n1
franchise, Indian: Hopi rejection of, 10, 226, 238; O'odham exclusion from, 274; O'odham rejection of, 10–11, 227, 257–58, 276–77, 282; Pueblo exclusion from, 184–88, 195–96, 207, 212, 221–23; Pueblo rejection of, 9–10, 205, 212, 220, 224, 238–39, 288, 326–27n135; under U.S. rule, 2–5, 201–2, 212–14, 231, 266, 280–83, 286

Franciscans: abuse by, 61–63, 68, 126–27, 302–3n26, 315n34; conflict with government, 24, 162–63, 165–66, 395n73; Hopi missionization, 55–56, 59–61, 63–65, 67–70, 104; Indian election involvement, 7–8, 18, 33, 103, 287, 298n103; O'odham missionization, 99–104, 140, 161–64, 317n74; Pueblo missionization, 5–6, 25, 43, 72, 126–27, 218, 295n73, 297n97
Friends of the Indian, 214
Froebel, Julius, 260

Gaceta Imperial, 114
Gadsden Treaty, 231, 258–60, 332–33n110, 335–36n171
Gallaher, James, 234
Gallegos, Hernán, 23
Gallegos, José Manuel, 194, 196
Garcés, Francisco, 100
Garicochea, Juan de, 45, 67
Garley, Eloy, 283–84
General Allotment Act. *See* Dawes Act
genízaros, 16, 51–53, 121, 143–44, 310n37
Gila River Reservation, 271, 280, 284, 334n135
Glaser, Leah S., 255
Glasgow, William, 193
Gocho, Augustín, 39
Gonzales, José Maria, 130, 133–38
González, Deena J., 287
Gonzalez, Diego, 82
González, Elías, 149
González, Faustino, 165
González, José, 130, 133–38
Gonzalvo, Valenciano Francisco, 96
Good Government League (GGL), 280
Grande, Fernando, 163–65
Grant, Ulysses S., 177
Graves, E. A., 195
Gray, Andrew B., 280
Gregg, Josiah, 120, 131–33, 142
Grito de Dolores, 106, 110–11
Guadalupe, 248, 250, 251, 252, 254–55
Guadalupe Hidalgo, Treaty of, 9, 144, 319n15, 323n82; Hopi citizenship and,

238–39; Pueblo citizenship and, 181–82, 184, 197, 201–2, 210, 320n30, 321n51; Tohono O'odham citizenship and, 259, 261
Guerra, Salvador, 62–63
Guevavi, San Gabriel de, 91, 92, 93–94, 96–97, 99, 168
Gurrola, Cristóbal de, 82–83, 85–86
Gutiérrez, Andrés, 59
Gutiérrez, Narcisco, 102–3
Guzmán, Diego de, 72

Haaland, Deb, 3
hair-cutting, forced, 78, 236–37, 329n39
Hall, G. Emlen, 126
Hardy, R. W. H., 151, 155
Harrison, Frank, 283
Harrison v. Laveen, 283
Hart, E. Richard, 36
Hayzlett, G. W., 236
Hendricks, Rick, 40
Hernandez, Juan Bautista, 43
Hernández, Ramón, 75
Herreros, León, 145
Hidalgo y Costilla, Miguel "Father Hidalgo," 106, 110–11
hidden transcript, 6–7, 296n79
Himuiro, Miguel, 39
Ho-Chunk Nation, 3
Hopis, 7–12, 55–70, 104, 139–44, 174–75, 188, 226–57, 277–78, 281–82, 287–89. *See also* Awat'ovi; Mishongnovi; Oraibi; Shungopavi; Walpi
Hopi-Spanish government system, 7–8, 58–59, 62–63; erasure from Hopi oral tradition, 62, 69
Howard, Oliver O., 270–71
Howell Code, 231
Hoxie, Frederick, 215
Hu-DeHart, Evelyn, 242–43, 314–15n25
Hudson, Charles, 271–72
Hughes, Richard W., 40
Huidobro, Manuel Bernal de, 81–83, 85–89, 306n107, 307n128
Huírivis, 70, 71, 83–88, 148–49

Hurdaide, Diego Martínez de, 73–74, 78
Hurtado, Juan Páez, 43

Ignacio, Juan Antonio, 47
Ímuris, 92, 173
Indian Citizenship Act, 2–3, 215, 281, 284–85
Indian Homestead Act, 271–72
Indian Reorganization Act, 279–80, 289
Indian Rights Association, 214–15, 280
Indian Service. *See* Office of Indian Affairs (OIA)
Iriarte, Francisco, 164
Isleta, 22, 63, 121–24, 295–96n77; alleged election, tampering in, 124–25
Isleta Pueblos, 21, 135–36, 203, 217–19, 311n60; Business Council of Twelve, 218, 325n122; leaders, 27, 49, 199, 217–19, 293n18, 296n81, 313n106; self-government, 33, 202–3, 212, 219
Iturbide, Augustín de, 111
Ives, Joseph C., 229–30, 327n9
Izábel, Rafael, 242

Jackson, William H., 268
James, Thomas, 114
Jaravilla, Domingo, 94
Jemez, 21, 22, 33, 39, 63, 121–22, 126
Jemez Pueblos, 21, 30, 32, 37, 50, 296n80, 297n97; leaders, 27, 32, 45, 312n70
Jesuits: abuse by, 82, 88–89, 105, 305n96, 307n128, 316–17n58; O'odham electoral control by, 97–99, 287; O'odham missionization, 8–9, 56, 95–100, 140, 262, 307n132; Spanish political manipulation by, 83–86, 306n107, 307n128; Yaqui electoral control by, 78, 80–82, 87; Yaqui missionization, 8, 70–74, 76–90, 304n70, 305n82; Yaqui resistance to, 82–85, 88–90, 104, 286
Jesús, José de, 152
Jesús, Juan Felipe de, 152
Johnson, Claude M., 272
Jones, Alden, 278
Jones, R., 267–68
Jones, William A., 237

José (Pirigua governor), 171
José (Santa Fe Pueblo governor), 35
José (Tohono O'odham governor), 246
Joseph (Acoma Pueblo governor), 45
Joshevama, Elgean, 68
Juan (Zuni Pueblo cacique), 47
Juan Diego, 111
Jusacamea, Juan Ignacio "Banderas," 139, 149–56, 158–60, 241, 316n43
Jusacamea, Juan María, 158–60
Jusacamea, Ysidro Juan Maria, 153
Juzgado General de Indios, 18

Kearny, Stephen Watts, 177–78
Kearny Code, 178
Keller, Ignacio, 105
Kellogg, Laura Cornelius, 215
Kendrick, Silas F., 216
Kessell, John, 103
Kie, Charles, 212–13, 281, 326–27n135
Kino, Eusebio Francisco, 56, 91–96, 227

Laguna, 22, 31ph, 121–22, 180, 211, 283
Laguna Pueblos, 3, 21, 127, 183, 209; voting, 194, 212, 284, 326–27n135
Lamar, L. Q. C., 221
land encroachment: O'odham, under Mexican rule, 9, 140, 165–69, 172, 176; O'odham, under Spanish rule, 103; O'odham, under U.S. rule, 258–59, 264, 267–72, 274, 286; Pueblo, under Mexican rule, 106, 117–19, 127–28; Pueblo, under Spanish rule, 40–43; Pueblo, under U.S. rule, 181, 183–86, 192, 195–202, 204–7, 216, 286; Yaqui, under Mexican rule, 156, 242
Lane, William Carr, 193–94
Lara, Joseph de, 32
Laveen, Roger, 283
Lea, Luke, 191, 193, 229
League of Papago Chiefs, 280
Lecompte, Janet, 134
Legarra, Juan, 103
Lemmon, Theodore G., 238
León, José de, 145
Lequerica, José Mejía, 108

Leupp, Francis, 212
Lewis, Jose, 278–79
Leyes de Burgos, 16–17
Leyes de Indias, 17, 109
Leyva, José María "Cajeme," 243–44, 330n52
Liberós, Ramón, 162, 163
Liebmann, Matthew, 67–68
Llera, José María Peréz, 164–65
Lonergan, Phillip T., 220
Los Angeles Herald, 245–46
Lucas, Jose Victoriano, 262
Lucero, Juan José, 201
Lucero, Juan Rey, 203
Lucero, Pedro, 218–19
Lumholtz, Carl, 240–41, 273
Lummis, Charles F., 177, 235, 238, 329n39

Made People, 14, 36
Magdalena, 92, 164, 173, 250
Malacate, Antonio, 38
Maldonado, Juan "Tetabiate," 244–46, 249
Manje, Juan Mateo, 93–95
Manypenny, George W., 194
Many Skirts, 266
Marcos, Diego, 39
Marmon, Mrs. Walter K., 127
Marquín, Juan Gerónimo, 153
Marquina, Diego, 85–87
Marshall, John, 185
Martínez, Antonio José, 135
Martinez, Mariano, 125
Mateer, William R., 233
Maynez, Alberto, 47–48
Mayoroqui, Julio, 243
McCormick, Richard, 278
McGee, William John, 279
Medill, William, 182, 184
Meeks, Eric, 241, 274
Melgares, Facundo, 113–14, 124, 126, 129, 149
Mena, Manuel de, 83–84
Menchero, Miguel de, 51
Mendinueta, Pedro Fermín de, 49
Meriwether, David, 194–97, 259–60

Mier, Ramón, 149
Miguel (Hopi governor of Awat'ovi), 65–67, 303n38, 303n43
Minge, Ward, 115, 310n33
Miranda, Antonio, 65
Miranda, Guadalupe, 134
Mishongnovi, 57, 61–62, 65–67, 80
Mix, Charles E., 202–3
Moctezuma, inspiration to Banderas, 153–56, 160, 316–17n58
moieties, Pueblo, 21–23, 36; role in leadership selection, 7, 13–15, 28–29, 46; Summer and Winter, 13–15, 23, 29, 213, 292n22; Turquoise and Pumpkin/Squash, 23, 28
Moisés, Rosalio, 249–50
Montezuma, Carlos (Wassaja), 215, 281
Montoya, Juan, 218–19
Montoya, Pablo, 136
Moore, Perry, 1
Moquis. *See* Hopis
Morfí, Juan Agustín de, 41, 51, 103–4
Mowry, Sylvester, 260–63
Muni, 83–90, 104, 306n107, 315n27
Munk, Joseph A., 239
Munroe, John, 190–91

Nambé, 22, 121, 200, 205
Nambé Pueblos, 21, 50, 121, 183, 192–93, 197, 224, 292n4; elections, 29, 45, 296nn80–81, 312n71
Napoli, Ignacio María, 83–89, 307n128
Naranjo, José, 47–48
Naranjo, José Miguel, 128–29
Naranjo, Santiago, *180*
Narvona, Antonio, 121
National Congress of American Indians, 283
Neblina, Francisco, 165–66
Nentvig, Juan, 8, 97, 99
Nequatewa, Edmund, 69, 142
New Mexican Review, The, 224–25
Nonintercourse Act, 185–92, 200–202, 205–6, 225
Nordstrom, C. E., 208–10
Norton, A. B., 199–200

Oacpicagigua, Luis, 105
Occidente, Constitution of: citizenship, 145–46; land distribution, 146, 156, 316n52; subdistrict, 156; subordination of Indian towns, 148; taxation, 148; voting requirements, 157
Occidente, state of, 145–46, 148–50, 256–57
Och, Joseph, 8, 97–98, 101
Ocheguene (Hopi fiscal), 63
O'Donojú, Juan, 111
Office of Indian Affairs (OIA): "civilizing" project, 10, 196–97, 205, 226, 269, 275–76; graduated citizenship hurdles, 182–84, 203–4, 211, 232–34, 237; Hopi allotment, 234–35; Hopi legal status, 229–34; land encroachment opposition, 197–204; Pueblo legal status, 187, 196–99, 211, 216, 218–20; Tohono O'odham allotment, 273–75. *See also* Canes (of power): Lincoln canes; Schools
Officer, James E., 139, 145
Ohkay Owingeh, 22, 25, 39, 45, 121, 209
Ohkay Owingeh Pueblos, 13, 21, 25, 299n138; governor recall, 219–20; leaders, 27–29, 36–37, 39, 45, 121–22, 183, 224, 292n2, 292n4; Pueblo Revolt, 49–50
Ojeada sobre Nuevo México, 121
Ombire, Juan, 39
Oñate, Juan de, 24–25, 46, 58–59
O'odham-Spanish government system, 8, 11, 93, 97–104; under Mexican rule, 166, 168, 170–72; under U.S. rule, 229, 282
Oquitoa, San Antonio de, 96, 172
Oraibi, 57, 58, 61, 64, 66, 69, 141, 143ph; Awat'ovi destruction and, 67–69; Franciscan abuse, 61–63, 302–3n26; leaders, 62–63, 67, 230–31; Mexican kidnapping incident, 142–44, 314nn10–11, 314n14; school resistance, 232, 235, 239–40, 329n39
Ordoñez, Francisco, 83
Ortiz, Alfonso, 13–15, 25, 27–29, 31, 36–37, 46, 49, 119, 129, 312n82
Ortiz, Benigno, 200
Otermín, Antonio, 49

Otero, Miguel A., 196
Ozuna, Manuel, 153

Pacheco, Juan, 45
Pacheco, Mateo, 27
Padilla, Alejandro, 202
Palmer, A. D., 231
Palmer, Edward, 230–31
Pamplona, Ramón, 163
Papago Reservation, 272–74, 335n160
Papagos. *See* Tohono O'Odhams (Papagos)
Papaguería, 266, 280, 332n103. *See also* Pimería Alta
Parker, Ely S., 203
Parsons, Elsie Clews, 199, 217–18, 296n80
Pascua, 250, 251, 252, 255–57, 332n98
Pascua Yaquis, 248, 256ph
Pawnees, 1
Peace Policy, 177
Peck, George W., 213
Pecos, 22, 29, 114, 121; Spanish outsider ban, 40–41
Pecos, Regis, 5
Pecos Pueblos, 21, 29, 118; officers, 30, 38–39, 45, 49–50, 121, 126–27, 312nn69–70
Pedro (Santa Rosa governor), 171
Peralta, Martín Cayetano Fernández de, 85–86
Perea, Estevan de, 77
Pereyra, Juan Solórzano, 18–19
Pérez, Albino, 130–32, 313n87
Pérez de Ribas, Andrés, 72, 74–80
Perico, Juan Roque, 112
Pfefferkorn, Ignaz, 8, 97–98
Picuris, 22, 40, 121; Spanish outsider ban, 40–41
Picuris Pueblos, 21, 30, 127–28, 297n94; officers, 30, 37, 45, 224
Piipaash (Maricopas), 260–63, 267–68, 270, 332n109
Pima-Maricopa Reservations (Salt River Pima-Maricopa Indian Community and Gila River Indian Community, both O'odham and Piipaash), 268, 272, 332n109, 334n133

Pimería Alta, 8, 11, 259–60; elections, 97–98, 103, 139–40, 145–46; mission decay, 9, 99–102, 105, 160–68, 176, 258–59, 308n198, 317n59, 317n74; missionization, 56, 91, 93, 95–99
Pino, Joaquin, 127
Pino, Pedro, 35–36, 216
Pino, Pedro Bautista, 47–48, 108, 117–18, 120–21, 310n37, 319n18
Plan de Iguala, 111, 118
Plan de Tomé, 135–37
Plummer, E. H., 235
Pojoaque, 22, 121, 137, 200
Pojoaque Pueblos, 21, 121, 183, 224, 292n4
Po'pay, 45, 49, 299n138
Pope, Nathanial, 204
Pope, William H., 224–25
Porras, Francisco de, 59–61
Porter, Peter, 280–81
Porter v. Hall, 280–81
Poston, Charles D., 264, 278
Potám, 70, 71, 75, 156, 245; prison incident, 82–84, 86–87, 98, 244, 306n107
Pratt, Richard Henry, 208, 211, 215
Presbyterians: among the Hopis, 234, 268; among the Tohono O'odhams, 280, 337nn43–44
Priesthood of the Bow, 34
Prucha, Francis Paul, 192
Pueblo Revolt, 6–7, 25, 49–50, 66, 298n101; Hopi participation, 64, 69–70, 302–3n26
Pueblos, 5–12, 13–16, 21–54, 112–40, 171–225, 285–89. *See also specific Pueblos by location*
Pueblo-Spanish government system, 20–29, 33–36, 45, 50, 119, 125, 320n33
Pupo, Pedro, 39

Quesada, Daisy, 1
Quintana, Juan José, 112
Quiroz, Miguel de, 82–83, 89
Quoaes, Antonio, 39

Radding, Cynthia, 146
Rafael (Pecos Pueblo councilman), 126

Ramos, Teodoro, 255
Ráum, 70, 71, 83, 85–88, 149–50, 152, 254, 315n27
Real Audencia de Lima, 18
Recopilación de Leyes de los Reinos de las Indias, 17–18, 42, 305n99, 306n117
Redondo, Santiago, 169–70
Relations de Jésuites de la Nouvelle-France, 76
Reno, Philip, 134
Reno Weekly Gazette and Stockman, 213
Representación del Consulado de México, 109
revolts, Yaqui, 9, 81–90, 104, 244–46, 255, 306n107, 315n27. *See also* Bernabé; Cajeme; Muni; Tetabiate
Rey, Juan, 211
Ribas, Andrés Pérez de, 72, 74–80
Rio Arriba Rebellion, 9, 129–37
Ritch, William G., 327n6
Robertson, John H., 210
Rochester Weekly Republican (Indiana), 214–15
Roldán, José, 83
Roman, Dorothy, 32, 37
Romero, Domingo, 45
Romero, Luis, 45
Romero, Vicente, 127
Roque, Juan, 48
Ross, Edmund G., 221
Roybal, Ygnacio de, 42–43
Ruggles, Levi, 267–68
Ruiz, Joaquín de Jesús, 33
Russell, Bonnie Moore, 1
Russell, Ned, 1–2
Russell, Paul, 283

Saeta, Francisco Javier, 95
Sakiestewa, Robert, 69
Salvatierra, Juan María, 92, 96, 308n136
Sanchez, Ignacio, 30
Sanchez, Pedro, 208
Sandia, 22, 112, 121–22, 192–93
Sandia Pueblos, 21, 44, 121–22, 132, 183
Sando, Joe, 21, 56, 118, 181
Sandoval, Felipe, 224

San Ignacio, 92, *169*, 173
San Ildefonso, 22, 45, 121
San Ildefonso Pueblos, 21, 39, 132, 183, 192–93, 292n4; land encroachment and, 42–43, 200, 205, 326–27n135
San Martín, Juan de, 96
Santa Ana, 22, 121, 179–80
Santa Ana Pueblos, 21, 25, 27, 65, 121, 179–80, 183, 192–93
Santa Anna, Antonio López de, 130–31, 137
Santa Clara, 22, 39, 45, 121–23, 128–29, 183, 192, 209
Santa Clara Pueblos, 21, 34, 42, 183, 188, 213, 223–25, 296n80; petitions by, 42, 48, 53, 128–29, 192–93, 292n4, 326–27n135
Santa Fe Magazine, The, 219
Santo Domingo, 21, 22, 63, 132, 179, 183
Santo Domingo Pueblos, 21, 24–25, 46, 132, 179, 183, 192, 295n61, 300n146; leaders, 36, 39, 45, 209–10
San Xavier del Bac, 91, 92, 93, 102, 161–62, 164, 166, *169*, 170, 173, 260–65, 267, 271–82, 286, 332n103
San Xavier del Bac Tohono O'odhams, 8–10, 173, 227, 258, 260–65, 268–82, 286, 288, 330–31n69
San Xavier Reservation, 157, 164, 270–80, 330–31n69, 333n122, 335–36n171
Saunders, Charles Francis, 239
Savala, Refugio, 250
Scholes, France, 25
schools: alumni, 2, 199, 213, 237, 280, 324n95; boarding schools, 2, 177, 199, 208–9, 211, 213, 232, 234, 268, 280, 322n62, 324n90; establishment of, 102, 158, 165, 204, 226, 269, 280; Hopi, 232–34, 236–37, 239–40, 337nn43–44; O'odham, 102, 165–66, 184, 267–68, 275; Pueblo, 178–79, 198, 204, 207–10, 300n146, 322n60, 324n90; resistance to, 221–22, 233, 236–237, 329n39; Yaqui, 158
Scott, James C., 6
Sección Patriotica, La, 174
Sedelmayr, Jacobo, 8, 97

Segesser, Philipp, 89, 99
Segura, José, 217
Sheridan, Thomas, 173
Sherman, William Tecumseh, 268
Shungopavi, 57, 58, 61–62, 66–67, 69
Simmons, Marc, 117, 191, 320n33, 321n48
Simpson, Audra, 285
slavery, 7, 51; of Apaches, 270; of Hopis, 9, 141, 143–44, 174; peonage or encomienda as, 16, 247, 293n24, 333n119; of Yaquis, 247–48, 288
Sloan, Thomas, 215
Slough, John P., 200–201
Sobaipuris, 90, 100, 161, 257, 273, 275
Soba Nation, 94
Society of American Indians (SAI), 215
Solisair, Pedro, 189
Solorse, José Victoriano, 264
Sosa, Gaspar Castaño de, 24
Spicer, Edward, 76, 155, 160, 243, 252–53, 254, 256, 331n83, 331–32nn97–98
staffs. *See* canes (of power)
Standing Bear, Henry, 215
Stayo, Diego, 39
Steck, Michael, 199, 231, 263–64
suffrage. *See* franchise, Indian; women and elections
Suina, Joseph Henry, 25, 27–29

Tafoya, Antonio, 42
Tafoya, Juan, 42
Tafoya, Marcos, 128–29
Tafuno, Augustín, 39
Talking Tree prophecy, 75–76, 304n73
Taos, 22, 40, 63, 121–22, 125, 128, 130, 134, 195, 209; Spanish outsider ban, 40–41
Taos Pueblos, 21, 132, 134–35, 186–88, 318–19n10; land encroachment and, 205–6; leaders, 30, 32, 45, 136, 192, 224; voting, 194, 320n34
Taos Revolt, 136, 189
Ta'palo (Hopi leader at Awat'ovi), 68, 303n43
taxation: as goal, 16–17, 56, 105, 107, 161; Hopi, 141–42; as implemented, 130–37, 156, 181, 313n87; O'Odham, 99–100; as proxy for citizenship, 117, 126, 141–42, 175, 184, 281; Pueblo, 32, 53–54, 126, 130, 221–25, 286, 297n97, 326–27n135; Yaqui, 81–82, 148–49, 175, 315n34
Taylor, Zachary, 182
Tenakhongva, Clark, 61–62, 64
Territory of New Mexico v. Delinquent Taxpayers, 221, 224
Tesuque, 22, 121, 200
Tesuque Pueblos, 21, 114; leaders, 29, 39, 45, 113, 133, 192, 224, 292n4
Tetabiate, 244–46, 249
Tewa World: Space, Time, Being, and Becoming in a Pueblo Society, The, 13
Thomas (Zuni Pueblo Indian), 43
Thomas, Benjamin H. "B. H.," 37, 208
Thomas, B. M., 207
Tohono O'odham Revolt, 170–71
Tohono O'odhams (Papagos), 5, 9, 90–91, 92, 100–101, 266–67, 332n100, 332n103; leaders, 103–4, 169–72. *See also* Pimería Alta; San Xavier del Bac Tohono O'odhams
Tomas (Indian interpreter), 58
Tónolic (Papago governor of Cubó), 170
Toribio (Cochiti Pueblo official), 48
Tórim, 70, 71, 78, 149
Torres, Lorenzo, 242
Torres, Luis E., 242, 244, 247
Tovar, Pedro de, 56, 58
Treaty of Córdoba, 106
Tres Garantías, 111, 113, 129, 174
Troncoso, Francisco P., 72, 315n28
Truax, W. B., 232–33
Trujillo, Miguel Sr., 283–85
Trujillo, Octaviana Valenzuela, 248–49, 253, 254
Tubac, 145, 162–63, 167, 173
Tucson, 100, 102, 162, 165–67, 314n18; Tohono O'odham, 92, 139, 145, 260–62, 268–69; Yaqui, 248–50, 251, 253
Tumacácori, San Cayetano de, 8, 91, 92, 94–96, 99–103, 161–63, 167, 173
Tundias, Pedro Cristóbal, 39

Tunoque, Salvador, 39
Tuque, Pedro Lucero, 39
Turimea, Juan, 85–87
Turner, John Kenneth, 247
Tyler, David, 120

Ulibarrí, Juan de, 47
Umviro, Diego, 50
United States v. Benigno Ortiz, 200–201, 203–5
United States v. Joseph, 206–7, 225
United States v. Lucero, 201–5, 221
United States v. Sandoval, 224–25
United States v. Santistevan, 205
Urrea, José, 169
Usacamea, Juan Ignacio "Muni," 83–90, 104, 306n107, 315n27
U.S.-Mexico War, 5, 178–80, 261, 310n30, 319n20
Uwaikota (Hopi from Moencopi), 143–44

Valdés, Francisco, 40–41, 45
Valverde, José Narváez, 65
Van Valen, Gary, 112, 113, 119
Van Valkenburgh, Robert B., 266, 333n126
varas de justicia. *See* Canes (of power)
Vargas, Diego de, 35, 38, 50, 64–67
vecinos, 29, 58, 113, 116, 127, 140, 146, 157; as Indian allies in revolt, 81–82, 85, 88–89, 153–54, 174, 307n128; land encroachment by, 52–54, 103, 156–58, 161–66, 169, 172, 175, 306n107; as voters, 113, 161
Vícam, 70, 71, 87
Vicente (Isleta Pueblo governor), 218–19
Victoria, Guadalupe, 151
Vigil, Donaciano, 180–81, 319n11
Vigil, Gil, 29
Vildósola, Agustín de, 89
Villas, Ascención, 270–71
Villaseñor, José María Melquiades, 148
Virgen de Guadalupe, la: as inspiration to Father Hidalgo, 110–11; as inspiration to Juan Banderas, 150, 153–56, 160, 316n43, 316–17n58
Vizarrón, Juan Antonio de, 87
voting. *See* franchise, Indian; women and elections
Voting Rights Act (VRA), 4

Walker, John, 262–63, 333n119
Walker, Joseph, 228
Wallace, Susan E., 204
Walpi, 57, 61, 66–68
Ward, John, 200, 202
wardship, 178, 200–201; O'odhams and, 280–81; Pueblo support for, 10, 205; U.S. officials' support for, 9–10, 185–89, 197, 199, 221–22; Yaquis and, 241, 253
Watts, John, 201
Webb, L. E., 203
Weber, David, 115, 126
Weekly Arizona Miner, 278
Wheeler, Roswell G., 272, 274
White, Leslie, 36
Wíkvaya (Oraibi informant), 69, 142–43
Wilbur, R. A., 268, 270
Wilkins, Charles, 214
Williams, Bill, 228
Williams, Constant, 236
Wingfield, E. H., 191–92
women and elections: candidates, 3, 289, 291n9; gendered disenfranchisement, 110, 207, 325n107; internal community discourse, 45–46, 297n94; non-participation, 14, 287; Ráum electoral majority, 85, 88, 306n110
Women's National Indian Association, 214
Wunder, John R., 2

Ximeno, Bartolomé, 100
Xiveni, Juan, 62

Yaquis, 8–12, 55–56, 70–90, 104–5, 147–60, 173–76, 226–27, 240–57, 285–89. *See also* Bácum; Bélem; Cócorit; Guadalupe; Huírivis; Pascua; Potám; Ráum; Tórim; Vícam

Yaqui-Spanish government system, 70–72, 76–78, 139–40, 158–60, 331–32n97; in Arizona, 252; under Mexican rule, 175, 247, 314–15n25
Yava, Albert, 58, 61, 67–68, 144
Yavapai-Apache Nation, 1, 289
Yavapais, 1, 215, 278, 281, 283, 289, 337n1, 337n188, 338n11
Ybargaray, Antonio de, 62–63
Ye, Lorenzo de, 39, 49
Yost, Samuel, 198

Ystico, Diego, 39
Yupangui, Dionisio Inca, 108

Zapata, Juan Ignacio, 164–65
Zia, 22, 39, 62, 121
Zia Pueblos, 21, 23–24, 39, 183, 192–93; elections, 38–39, 45
Zuni, 22, 43, 66, 121, 123, 183, 248
Zuñiga, Ignacio, 151–52
Zuni Pueblos, 21, 30, 43, 56, 211, 216, 230; leaders, 35–36, 45, 47, 215–16, 310n37, 319n18

www.ingramcontent.com/pod-product-compliance
Lightning Source LLC
Chambersburg PA
CBHW021650271125
36038CB00002B/37